Praise for *The Handbook of Political Economy of Communications*

"Political economy has roared back into town. Terms like 'net neutrality', 'creative labor', 'the precariat', and 'global capital' are in every critic's vocabulary – or should be. The editors of this *Handbook*, all leading figures, have assembled an equally distinguished group of authors to lead the charge."

Toby Miller,
author of Makeover Nation: The United States of Reinvention

"This is an excellent book that moves from heritage sites to new destinations, and from the old standards to innovative research."

James Curran,
Director, Goldsmiths Leverhulme Media Research Centre,
University of London

"The power of the communications media to shape people's cultural, political and social lives is immense. We should never lose sight of the bases to their political and economic potency, and the political economy of communications is a crucial intellectual tradition in both analysing the media, and in giving sound critical foundations to challenge and intervention. In this important collection the editors have brought together an authoritative and diverse collection of original essays that reaffirm the importance of this tradition and make an irreplaceable contribution to it."

Peter Golding,
Northumbria University

"This is not only a welcome package of scholarship but also a timely reminder of the vitality of critical political economy, serving to keep the research tradition straight and wide under pressures of marketization and globalization."

KaarleNordenstreng,
Tampere University

D1573229

Global Handbooks in Media and Communication Research

Series Editor: Annabelle Sreberny (School of Oriental and African Studies, London)

The Global Handbooks in Media and Communication Research series is co-published by Wiley Blackwell and the International Association for Media and Communication Research (IAMCR). The series offers definitive, state-of-the-art handbooks that bring a global perspective to their subjects. These volumes are designed to define an intellectual terrain: its historic emergence; its key theoretical paradigms; its transnational evolution; key empirical research and case study exemplars; and possible future directions.

Already published

The Handbook of Political Economy of Communications edited by Janet Wasko, Graham Murdock, and Helena Sousa

The Handbook of Global Media and Communication Policy edited by Robin Mansell and Marc Raboy

The Handbook of Media Audiences edited by Virginia Nightingale

The Handbook of Development Communication and Social Change, edited by Karin Gwinn Wilkins, Thomas Tufte, and Rafael Obregon

About the IAMCR

The International Association for Media and Communication Research (IAMCR) (http://iamcr.org) was established in Paris in 1957. It is an accredited NGO attached to UNESCO. It is a truly international association, with a membership representing over 80 countries around the world and conferences held in different regions that address the most pressing issues in media and communication research. Its members promote global inclusiveness and excellence within the best traditions of critical research in the field. The current president of the IAMCR is Janet Wasko.

The Handbook of
Political Economy
of Communications

Edited by

Janet Wasko, Graham Murdock, and Helena Sousa

WILEY Blackwell

This paperback edition first published 2014
© 2014 John Wiley & Sons, Ltd

Edition History: Blackwell Publishing Ltd (hardback, 2011)

Registered Office
John Wiley & Sons, Ltd, The Atrium, Southern Gate, Chichester, West Sussex, PO19 8SQ, UK

Editorial Offices
350 Main Street, Malden, MA 02148-5020, USA
9600 Garsington Road, Oxford, OX4 2DQ, UK
The Atrium, Southern Gate, Chichester, West Sussex, PO19 8SQ, UK

For details of our global editorial offices, for customer services, and for information about
how to apply for permission to reuse the copyright material in this book please see our website at
www.wiley.com/wiley-blackwell.

The right of Janet Wasko, Graham Murdock, and Helena Sousa to be identified as the authors of
the editorial material in this work has been asserted in accordance with the UK Copyright,
Designs and Patents Act 1988.

Library of Congress Cataloging-in-Publication Data

The handbook of political economy of communications / edited by Janet Wasko, Graham Murdock,
and Helena Sousa.
    p.   cm. – (Global handbooks in media and communication research)
  Includes bibliographical references and index.
  ISBN 978-1-4051-8880-7 (hardback) – ISBN 978-1-118-79944-4 (paperback)
1. Communication–Economic aspects.   2. Communication–Political aspects.   3. Mass media–Economic
aspects.   4. Mass media–Political aspects.   I. Wasko, Janet.   II. Murdock, Graham.   III. Sousa, Helena.
  P96.E25H355 2011
  384–dc22

                                        2011001902

A catalogue record for this book is available from the British Library.

Cover image: © Images.com/Corbis

Set in 11/13pt Dante by SPi Publisher Services, Pondicherry, India
Printed in Malaysia by Ho Printing (M) Sdn Bhd

1   2014

Contents

Contents   vii

About the Editors

Janet Wasko is Professor and Knight Chair in Communication Research at the University of Oregon, USA. She is the author and editor of 18 books relating to the political economy of communication and democratic media. She was the head of the Political Economy Section of the International Association of Media and Communication Research (IAMCR) when this volume was prepared.

Graham Murdock is Professor of Culture and Economy at Loughborough University, UK. He has been a Visiting Professor at the Universities of Bergen, Stockholm, Helsinki, California, and Brussels. A former head of the Political Economy Section of the IAMCR, his writings have been translated into 19 languages. His recent publications include, as co-editor, *Digital Dynamics: Engagements and Exclusions* (2010) and *The Public Sphere: A Four-Volume Collection of Key Texts* (2010).

Helena Sousa is Professor of Communications Sciences at the University of Minho, Portugal. She has written about Portuguese and EU media policy, and about media structures and content production in Portuguese-speaking countries (Lusophone cultural area).

Notes on Contributors

Sarah Baker is lecturer in cultural sociology at Griffith University, Australia. She has previously held research fellowships at The Open University and University of Leeds, UK, and the University of South Australia. She is the author of *Creative Labour: Media Work in Three Cultural Industries* (with David Hesmondhalgh, 2010).

Martín Becerra is Professor at the Social Sciences Department, Universidad Nacional de Quilmes (UNQ, Argentina). He received his PhD from the Universitat Autònoma of Barcelona, where he studied communication policies. He is Associate Researcher at the CONICET (Argentina), where he teaches courses in Political Economy of Communications and Media History. Dr Becerra also teaches postgraduate courses at the Universidad Nacional de La Plata and the Universidad de Buenos Aires (Argentine) and the Universidad Diego Portales (Chile). He has written books and articles on media policy.

Daniel Bilcereyst is Professor in Film and Cultural Studies at the Department of Communication Science, Ghent University, Belgium, where he leads the Centre for Cinema and Media Studies. His research on film and screen culture as sites of public controversy has been published in many journals, readers, and collections. He is preparing a book on film censorship in Europe and with Richard Maltby and Philippe Meers, he is currently editing two books (*The New Cinema History: Approaches and Case Studies,* Wiley-Blackwell, 2010, and *Cinema, Audiences and Modernity: European Perspectives of Film Cultures and Cinema-going,* forthcoming).

Andrew Calabrese is Professor of Media Studies and Associate Dean, School of Journalism and Mass Communication, University of Colorado. His research and publishing focuses on media and citizenship, and the public policies that govern the media industries. He edits the Rowman & Littlefield and Lexington book series, "Critical Media Studies," and the book series "Global Media Studies" (with Paula Chakravartty) for Paradigm Publishers.

Giovanni Cesareo is a member of the reference commission of the Faculty of Design, Milan Polytechnic. He is a member of Euricom, East-West European Institute of Research, the World Future Society, and the cultural committee of the Courmayeur Noir in Festival. He has acted as a consultant to the Italian Authority of Guarantee in Communication. He published *La contraddizione femminile* in 1979. He was editor of *Ikon*, a monthly review on communication processes and media, from 1978 to 1982; editor of *Sapere*, a science monthly review, from 1976 to 1982; and founded and edited *Se, Scienza Esperienza*, another science monthly, from 1982 to 1988. He was a member of the academic committee of the School of Journalism in Milan from 1985 to 1990. He also writes for the public radio and television networks.

Michael Curtin is the Duncan and Suzanne Mellichamp Professor of Global Media, and Professor of Film and Media Studies at the University of California at Santa Barbara. His books include *Redeeming the Wasteland: Television Documentary and Cold War Politics, Playing to the World's Biggest Audience: The Globalization of Chinese Film and TV, The American Television Industry* (with Jane Shattuc), and *Reorienting Global Communication: Indian and Chinese Media Beyond Borders* (with Hemant Shah). He is coeditor (with Paul McDonald) of the "International Screen Industries" book series for the British Film Institute and coeditor (with Paul S. N. Lee) of the *Chinese Journal of Communication*.

John D. H. Downing is an emeritus faculty at Southern Illinois University Carbondale, where he founded the Global Media Research Center in the College of Mass Communication and Media Arts. His research interests are international communication, alternative media and social movements, and racism, ethnicity, and media. In addition to numerous publications in these areas, he is one of the Vice-Presidents of the International Association for Media and Communication Research.

Jan Ekecrantz was Professor of Media and Communication Studies at Stockholm University from the mid-1970s until his death in July 2007. His work dealt with such diverse areas as journalism's construction of reality and the media situation in contemporary China. In later years, his primary interest was in processes of globalization.

Roque Faraone is a professor of Communication Theory at the University of the Republic of Uruguay and a founding member of the International Association for Media and Communication Research in 1957. He is also a Uruguayan lawyer, who, before going into exile in 1974, wrote the first book on the Uruguayan media. He spent 15 years in Paris as a correspondent for Agency France Press and consultant to UNESCO. He has numerous publications on the media and politics in Latin America.

Joaquim Fidalgo is Assistant Professor at the University of Minho in Braga, Portugal, working in the Social Sciences Department / Social Sciences Institute. He is also a senior researcher at the Centro de Estudos de Comunicação e Sociedade, a research center belonging to the Institute of Social Sciences of the same university. He has published several books, book chapters, and articles in scientific journals, mainly regarding the press and journalism (journalists' professional identity, journalists' ethics, media accountability systems and regulation). He is an active member of the International Association for Media and Communication Research, being presently the Deputy Head of its Journalism Research and Education section. He is also a member of the European Communication Research and Education Association, as well as a founding member of the Portuguese Communication Sciences Association.

Oscar H. Gandy, Jr is Professor Emeritus at the University of Pennsylvania. He was previously the Herbert I. Schiller Term Professor at the Annenberg School for Communication. His research and writing has emphasized privacy, surveillance, race, and discrimination as aspects of the political economy of communication and information. His forthcoming book, *Coming to Terms with Chance*, brings those elements together in a critical assessment of the ways in which statistical analysis and rational discrimination contribute to cumulative disadvantage. His previous works include *The Panoptic Sort, Communication and Race, Beyond Agenda Setting*, and more than 100 articles and chapters. He was a founding member of the Union for Democratic Communications, Board Chairman of the Electronic Privacy Information Center, and is currently working within the local movement for sustainability in Tucson, Arizona.

Nicholas Garnham worked as a TV filmmaker from 1962 to 1972, and then from 1972 to 2002 was Head of Communications Studies and Professor of Media Studies at the University of Westminster, UK, where he also directed the Centre for Communication and Information Studies. He was a founding editor of *Media, Culture and Society*. Garnham is now Emeritus Professor of Media Studies at the University of Westminster. He is the author of *Samuel Fuller, The Structures of Television, Capitalism and Communication*, and *Emancipation, the Media and Modernity*.

David Hesmondhalgh is Professor of Media and Music Industries at the University of Leeds, UK, where he is Head of the Institute of Communications Studies and Director of the Media Industries Research Centre. He is the author of *The Cultural Industries* (2nd edn, 2007) and *Creative Labour: Media Work in Three Cultural Industries* (with Sarah Baker, 2010). He has also edited a number of books including *The*

Media and Social Theory (with Jason Toynbee, 2008), *Media Production* (2005) and *Western Music and its Others: Difference, Appropriation and Representation in Music* (with Georgina Born, 2000).

Wayne Hope is Associate Professor of Communication Studies at the Auckland University of Technology, New Zealand. His areas of research include time and globalization, New Zealand political economy and media history, public sphere analysis and sports–media relationships. He is at present writing a series of linked essays on time, temporality, and global capitalism. The most recent of these publications, for *The International Journal of Communication*, is entitled "Time, Communication and Financial Collapse" (2010). Within New Zealand, Associate Professor Hope is a regular media commentator who has written and spoken against virulent local manifestations of neoliberalism.

Sophia Kaitatzi-Whitlock is Professor in Politics and Communication in the School of Journalism and Mass Communication of Aristotle University of Thessaloniki, Greece. Her research interests include the interfaces between political communication, the political economy of media organizations and of communicative practices, and public policy making in this field. In 2005 she published *Europe's Political Communication Deficit*, focusing on the EU's democracy deficit and its relation to EU-wide political communication deficits. She is the author of the chapter "The Political Economy of the Media at the Root of Europe's Democracy Deficit" (2008), in the edited volume *Media, Democracy and European Culture*. Her latest book *Forms and Means for Political Communication*, was published in 2010 (in Greek), by University Studio Press, Thessaloniki.

Guillermo Mastrini is a professor at the Communication School, National University of Quilmes, where he is also Director of the Master in Cultural Industries. He was president of the Argentine Federation of Social Communication Schools. His publications include: *Globalización y monopolios en la comunicación en América Latina* (Globalization and monopolies in Latin America's media, 1999, with César Bolaño), *Mucho ruido, pocas leyes. Economía y políticas de comunicación en la Argentina* (Much ado about laws: economy and politics of communication in Argentina, 2005), *Periodistas y Magnates*, (Journalists and tycoons, 2006, with Martín Becerra), *Los duenos de la palabra* (The owners of speech, 2009, with Martín Becerra).

Armand Mattelart is Professor Emeritus of Information and Communication Sciences at the University of Paris VIII. His areas of studies include communication theories and history, media studies and international communication. His books include *Mapping World Communication: War, Progress, Culture, The Invention of Communication, Networking the World 1794-2000*, and, with Michèle Mattelart, *Rethinking Media Theory: Signposts and New Directions*. His most recent book is *The Globalization of Surveillance* (2010).

Eileen R. Meehan is a professor in the Department of Radio-Television at Southern Illinois University, Carbondale. She is the author of *Why TV is Not Our Fault*, and coeditor of *Sex and Money: Feminism and Political Economy in Media Studies* (with Ellen Riordan), and *Dazzled by Disney?: The Global Disney Audiences Project* (with Janet Wasko and Mark Phillips). Her research examines the structures of media corporations and markets and their influence over commercial expression.

Philippe Meers is an associate professor in the Department of Communication Studies, Visual Culture Research Group, at the University of Antwerp, Belgium. His publications on popular media culture and film audiences have appeared in *Media, Culture and Society, The Journal of Popular Film and Television, The Bulletin*, and *Iluminace*. He has edited two Dutch language readers with Daniel Biltereyst (*Film/TV/Genre*, 2004, *De Verlichte Stad* (The Enlightened City, 2007) and contributed to several books, including *Big Brother International* (2004), *Hollywood Abroad: Audiences and Cultural Relations* (2004), *The Lord of the Rings: Popular Cinema in Global Culture* (2007), and *Watching The Lord of the Rings* (2007). With Richard Maltby and Daniel Biltereyst, he is currently editing two books (*The New Cinema History: Approaches and Case Studies*, 2010, and *Cinema, Audiences and Modernity: European Perspectives of Film Cultures and Cinema-going*, forthcoming).

Bernard Miège is Emeritus Professor of Communication and Information Science at Stendhal University in Grenoble, where he served as the President from 1989 to 1994. He has a PhD in economics (Paris) and another in humanities (Bordeaux). Miège is the author of numerous publications concerning the cultural industries, information and communication technologies and organizations, and theories of communication.

Colleen Mihal is a doctoral candidate in media studies at the School of Journalism and Mass Communication, University of Colorado. She currently is completing her PhD dissertation on the exceptions to the rule of law governing communication by social activists, introduced during the presidential administration of George W. Bush.

Vincent Mosco is Canada Research Chair in Communication and Society, Queen's University, Kingston, Ontario. Professor Mosco received his PhD in Sociology from Harvard University in 1975. He is the author of numerous books in communication, technology, and society. His most recent books include *The Political Economy of Communication* (2nd edn 2009), *The Laboring of Communication: Will Knowledge Workers of the World Unite* (with Catherine McKercher, 2008), *Knowledge Workers in the Information Society* (with Catherine McKercher, 2007), and *The Digital Sublime: Myth, Power, and Cyberspace* (2004). *The Digital Sublime* won the 2005 Olson Award for outstanding book in the field of rhetoric and cultural studies.

Graham Murdock, Reader in the Sociology of Culture at Loughborough University (UK), has written widely on the social organization of culture and communications and has a particular interest in the transformation of the cultural commons and debates around cultural citizenship. He has been a Visiting Professor at the Free University of Brussels, and the Universities of California at San Diego, Bergen, Stockholm, and Helsinki. His work has been translated into 19 languages. His recent books include, as coauthor, *The GM Debate: Risk, Politics and Public Engagement* (2007), and as coeditor *Digital Dynamics* (2010) and *The Idea of the Public Sphere* (2010).

Giuseppe Richeri is Professor of Communication Studies at the University of Lugano (Switzerland) and PhD candidates supervisor at the Communication University of China (Beijing). His recent books are available in translation in China, Argentina, and the UK.

Dan Schiller received his PhD in Communications in 1978 from the University of Pennsylvania. A historian of information and communication systems, he has been a member of the faculty at Temple University, UCLA, UCSD, and the University of Illinois at Urbana-Champaign, where his main appointment is in the Graduate School of Library & Information Science. His books include: *Objectivity and the News* (1981), *Telematics and Government* (1982), *Theorizing Communication* (1996), *Digital Capitalism* (1999), and *How To Think About Information* (2006). He has authored several prominent articles explicating aspects of the Internet bubble and its aftermath for *Le Monde diplomatique*, and he continues to lecture internationally. He is writing an archivally grounded study, *The Hidden History of U.S. Telecommunications*, and he continues to research the history and theory of information commodification.

John Sinclair is currently researching the role of advertising in the globalization of media in Australia, as an Australian Research Council Professorial Fellow. His published work over the last 25 years covers various aspects of the globalization of the media and communication industries, with a special emphasis on television and advertising in the Latin American and Asian regions. His books include *Latin American Television: A Global View* and the edited work, *Contemporary World Television*.

André Sirois (aka DJ Food Stamp) is a PhD candidate at the University of Oregon and a professional DJ. His current research looks at the relationships between hip hop DJ culture and the recording and DJ technology industries, as well as the antagonisms brought about by intellectual property law. He also likes to collect records and vintage DJ technology.

Helena Sousa is Associate Professor of the Communication Sciences Department, University of Minho, Portugal. She received her PhD in Communications Policy from the City University, London (1996). Presently a member of the Communication and Society Research Centre Scientific Council, Sousa is also Vice-Chair of the Political Economy Section of the International Association for Media and Communication Research, and member of the EuroMedia Research Group. She is the editor of the *European Journal of Communication*. She has published in scientific journals including *Convergence: The International Journal of Research into New Media Technologies, International Communication Gazette, European Journal of Communication, Telecommunications Policy*, and *Intercom*. She is currently leading two research projects: one on media policy and regulation in Portugal and another on the media structures and policies in Portuguese-speaking countries.

Paul J. Torre is an assistant professor in media industries at Southern Illinois University, Carbondale. His research explores entertainment industry structures and practices, media regulations and policies, the interplay between US and global media markets, and how new technologies are shaping the media business models of the future. His previous entertainment industry experience includes positions in film and television production management and global media distribution. He has written about intersections between media policy and global television distribution for *Television and New Media* and has authored chapters on global television formats and the global battle over launching satellite television in Germany.

Nathan Vaughan worked on issues around political economy in the Social Sciences Department at Loughborough University, with particular reference to the expansion of synergies in the Hollywood film industry. His contribution to this volume derives from his doctoral work on this topic.

Janet Wasko is the Knight Chair for Communication Research at the University of Oregon. She is author, editor, or coeditor of 18 books and specializes in the study of the political economy of the media, especially the US media industry.

Yuezhi Zhao is Professor and Canada Research Chair in the Political Economy of Global Communication at the School of Communication, Simon Fraser University. Her work concerns both domestic Chinese communication politics and the role of media and information technologies in the global transformations linking to China's real and imagined rise as a major world political economic power. Her recent publications include *Communication in China: Political Economy, Power, and Conflict* (2008) and *Global Communications: Toward a Transcultural Political Economy* (with Paula Chakravartty, 2008).

Series Editor's Preface

Welcome to the *Global Handbooks in Media and Communication Research* series. This grew out of the idea that the field needed a series of state-of the-art reference works that was truly international. The International Association for Media and Communication Research (IAMCR), with a membership from over 80 countries, is uniquely positioned to offer a series that covers the central concerns of media and communications theory in a global arena.

Each of these substantial books contains newly written essays commissioned from a range of international authors, showcasing the best critical scholarship in the field. Each is pedagogical in the best sense, accessible to students and clear in its approach and presentation. Theoretical chapters map the terrain of an area both historically and conceptually, providing incisive overviews of arguments in the field. The examples of empirical work are drawn from many different countries and regions, so that each volume offers rich material for comparative analysis.

These handbooks are international in scope, authorship, and mindset. They explore a range of approaches and issues across different political and cultural regions, reflecting the global reach of the IAMCR. The aim is to offer scholarship that moves away from simply reproducing Westcentric models and assumptions. The series formulates new models and asks questions that bring communication scholarship into a more comprehensive global conversation.

The IAMCR (http://iamcr.org) was established in Paris in 1957. It is an accredited nongovernmental organization attached to UNESCO. It is a truly international association, with a membership around the world and conferences held in different regions that address the most pressing issues in media and communication research. Its members promote global inclusiveness and excellence within the best traditions of critical research in the field.

This series supports those goals.

Annabelle Sreberny
President of IAMCR and Series Editor
London, December 2010

Acknowledgments

The editors would like to thank the contributors to this volume for their hard work and patience.

Also, thanks to Elizabeth Swayze at Wiley Blackwell and Annabelle Sreberny at the IAMCR, for their work in establishing the Blackwell/IAMCR series, Global Handbooks in Media and Communication Research.

Thanks also to Jenny Roberts for her fine copyediting, as well as to University of Oregon doctoral students, Jacob Dittmer and Jennifer Elliott, for their editorial assistance.

Introduction: The Political Economy of Communications
Core Concerns and Issues

Janet Wasko, Graham Murdock, and Helena Sousa

What is Critical Political Economy?

Running through the revolution in European thought that came to be known as the Enlightenment were three central ambitions. The first was to develop new accounts of the natural and social worlds that were empirically grounded and expressed in rationally informed theoretical systems. The second was to replace the arbitrary power of kings and despots with a system of government in which every adult participated in political debates and decision as a free and equal citizen. And the third was to provide a nonreligious basis for moral action that would balance the pursuit of personal interests against the demands of the common good.

Political economy was, from the outset, caught up in all three projects. For its early practitioners, like Adam Smith, theoretical and empirical questions about how to organize economic life and balance markets against state intervention were inextricably bound up with questions about the constitution of the good society. Marx, who presented his magnum opus, *Capital*, as a critique of political economy, shared this ethical concern, but argued forcefully that it could only be pursued by abolishing capitalism. Other socialists opted for a more gradualist approach in which the negative impacts of capitalist dynamics would be disciplined by strong public regulation and countered by substantial investment in public services.

The Handbook of Political Economy of Communications, First Edition.
Edited by Janet Wasko, Graham Murdock, and Helena Sousa.
© 2014 John Wiley & Sons, Ltd. Published 2014 by John Wiley & Sons, Ltd.

Both positions, however, produced strong conceptual critiques of capitalism's claims about itself and sustained empirical investigations of how its everyday operations perpetuated exploitation and injustice, manufactured inequalities, and undermined mutuality and solidarity. This critical tradition has had a major impact on the political economy of culture and communications precisely because the communications industries play a central double role in modern societies, as industries in their own right and as the major site of the representations and arenas of debate through which the overall system is imagined and argued over.

The approach to these questions developed by critical political economists differs from the analyses of culture and communications produced by most economists in four important respects. Firstly, it is holistic. Rather than treating "the economy" as a specialist and bounded domain, it focuses on the relations between economic practices and social and political organization. Secondly, it is historical. Rather than concentrating solely or primarily on immediate events, it insists that a full understanding of contemporary shifts must be grounded in an analysis of transformations, shifts, and contradictions that unfold over long loops of time. Thirdly, in contrast to economics that severed its historic links with moral philosophy in an effort to present itself as an objective science, critical political economy continues to be centrally concerned with the relations between the organization of culture and communications and the constitution of the good society grounded in social justice and democratic practice. Fourthly, critical analysis places its practitioners under an obligation to follow the logic of their analysis through into practical action for change. Many of the contributors to this volume think of themselves as public intellectuals as well as academics, informed citizens engaged in public political argument.

Why Political Economy? Why Now?

It is clear that the logic of capitalism has massively extended itself, with marketization emerging as the defining force of the last several decades. Capitalism is more global than ever, not only in North America and Europe, but expanding to other parts of the world, including China and other key locations. Indeed, capitalism has become a generalized phenomenon with the globalization of markets now a central theme. Along with these developments, the tension between private interest and public good has been significantly exacerbated. While public policy efforts are strained, privatization moves forward, and the abuse of private power is blatant and commonplace (as discussed by Graham Murdock at the beginning of the first chapter in this volume).

Critical political economy is more important than ever for understanding these developments, as well as for understanding contemporary media and communications. There is a universal belief that the cultural or "creative" industries are no longer peripheral, but occupy a central role in the economy. However, the analysis of this phenomenon is often problematic and inadequate. A few contemporary approaches deserve mention (and critique) here.

Political Economy and Other Approaches

Media economics

Just as critical political economy can be distinguished from neoclassical economics, as we noted above, the critical study of the political economy of media is also different from media economics.

More specific attention to economics has been evident in the field of communication and media studies since the late 1980s, with scholars identifying media economics as a distinct focus of research activity. Early examples included Compaine's *Who Owns the Media?* (1979) and textbooks by Robert Picard (1989), Allison Alexander et al. (1993), Alan Albarron (1996), and more recently, Gillian Doyle (2002). *The Journal of Media Economics* was introduced in 1988, with a goal, as stated in its Contributor Information section, "to broaden understanding and discussion of the impact of economic and financial activities on media operations and managerial decisions." Generally, these media economics texts and the journal echo the concerns of mainstream (neoclassical) economics.

For the most part, the emphasis of media economics is on microeconomic issues rather than macroanalysis, and focuses primarily on producers and consumers in media markets. Typically, the concern is how media industries and companies can succeed, prosper, or move forward. While competition may be assessed, little emphasis is placed on questions of ownership or the implications of concentrated ownership and control. These approaches avoid the kind of moral grounding adopted by political economists, as most studies emphasize description rather than critique. A common approach is the industrial organization model, as described here by Douglas Gomery:

> The industrial organization model of structure, conduct, and performance provides a powerful and useful analytical framework for economic analysis. Using it, the analyst seeks to define the size and scope of the structure of an industry and then go on to examine its economic behavior. Both of these steps require analyzing the status and operations of the industry, not as the analyst wishes it were. Evaluation of its performance is the final step, a careful weighing of "what is" versus "what ought to be."
> (Gomery 1989, 58)

Generally, then, media economics represents the application of neoclassical economics to media. And while there may be some issues and forms of analysis that are shared by political economy and media economics, for the most part the fundamental assumptions and motivations are quite different. In most cases, media economics avoids political and historical analysis, both fundamental components of the critical study of political economy. Importantly, media economics mostly accepts the status quo, whereas political economy represents a critical orientation to the study of the media, challenging unjust and inequitable systems of power.

Creative industries

Living in the United States during World War II as an exile from Nazi Germany, the cultural analyst Theodor Adorno, observing the world's largest and most successful commercial media system, concluded that the industrialization of culture was narrowing the range of expressive activity and popular choice by pouring creativity into the preset molds of the dominant commercial genres. He saw the combination of standardized expression and rationalized distribution through the new mass media creating a new "Culture Industry" that severely limited imaginative horizons (see Adorno 1991). This resonant phrase enjoyed considerable currency and focused critical attention on the ways diversity of expression was compromised by the commercial pursuit of maximum sales and audiences.

This critical perspective has now been almost entirely overtaken by the incorporation of commercial media into the newly designated complex of "creative industries." Governments in the advanced capitalist economies now see the media and information industries as central to the "knowledge economy" that will replace the old reliance on heavy industry. Academic advocates add that with the rise of the Internet, creative production in the service of profit is no longer the exclusive preserve of the major media companies; it has been democratized and flows through the new digital circuits of peer-to-peer exchange, shifting the locus of innovation and control from company boardrooms to teenage bedrooms (Hartley 2009). In this formulation, commerce no longer constrains creativity, but enables and promotes it. As a number of the contributors to this volume point out, this argument ignores the fact that the spread of the Internet has coincided with the rise of marketization, the consequent consolidation of corporate power, and the expansion of strategies for incorporating popular creativity into revenue generation.

New media

Overvaluations of the Internet's impact follow logically from a foreshortened time perspective coupled with an underdeveloped analysis of the resilience of structural inequalities and the persistence of embedded structures of power. The ubiquitous term "new media" is symptomatic. It inevitably draws analysis toward one version or another of technological determinism where change is initiated by the arrival of a new array of communicative machineries. Rather than starting with the technology and asking what is its likely impact, critical analysis starts from the prevailing distribution of power and inequality and asks whose interests will be best served by these new potentialities. From this perspective, digital media appear not as a primary lever of change but as a new field of struggle dominated by long-standing battles and combatants. The sites and terms of engagement may shift, but the stakes remain the same.

Organization of the Handbook

The chapters in this volume include a sample of debates and legacies, as well as representative discussions of issues and themes that have been addressed within the political economy approach to studying communications/media.

Part I – Legacies and Debates

The contributors to this collection address issues and themes common to the critical study of political economy of communications and media. Although their approaches may differ, we find that discussion of these differences is necessary and constructive for the evolution of the approach. The chapters in Part I represent the diversity that has characterized the political economy tradition in the study of media and communications.

Graham Murdock, in "Political Economies as Moral Economies: Commodities, Gifts, and Public Goods," explores the competing moral economies supported by three systems of production and exchange – commodities, gifts, and public goods – and examines how the relations between them are being played out on the contemporary Internet.

In the next chapter, **Nicholas Garnham** revisits the political economy of communication by arguing that the tradition has focused on the same questions for far too long, not taking into account changes in the field and in the world. He sees problems with the political economy critiques of mass culture that emphasize public service models as an idealized alternative, as well as the market–antimarket debates that have dominated much of political economy research. Garnham argues for a political economy of culture as well as an emphasis on the intertwined relations between information services and culture as an important focus for future study.

Eileen Meehan and Paul Torre explore markets, as a fundamental component of capitalism, as they were idealized and theorized by Adam Smith, as well as liberal market theory. The authors focus on the creation of media markets, and in particular television markets. More specifically, the chapter discusses ratings and formats, as well as the legal and regulatory influences on these markets.

Bernard Miège presents the legacy of cultural industries theory as an idea and approach to research within the political economy of communications. Miège traces the lineage of cultural industries analysis, from the Frankfurt School through the North American political economy tradition, and how it has evolved since the 1990s.

To conclude Part I, **Martín Becerra and Guillermo Mastrini** explore a Latin American approach to political economy of media by examining the analysis of Heriberto Muraro from the late 1980s. Muraro emphasized research that went beyond property relationships, including new technology's role in economic activities, mass media's role in decision making in relation to economic policies, and creating a wider model for transmission of information and communication. Incorporating these issues with theories of international communication and globalization, the authors explore the recent developments in the study of the political economy of Latin American (specifically, Iberoamerican) communications, concluding that these culture industries have been shaped by media policies and technological developments, as well as economic development and its impact on culture.

Part II – Modalities of Power: Ownership, Advertising, Government

In Part II, contributors examine mechanisms of power that relate to media and communications. Political economy has traditionally focused on these areas as crucial to understanding the role of media and communications in society. For instance, **Giuseppe Richeri** begins with an exploration of the relationships between media enterprises, the public, and the state, and points to important areas for future research. **John Downing** considers the fundamental question of ownership and control, tracing the lineage of the debate over the significance of this issue. In **Nathan Vaughan**'s chapter, the concept of synergy is thoroughly explored as he considers the various factors contributing to economic as well as cultural synergies and how this development has been studied by political economists of the media.

Chapters by **Roque Farone** and **John Sinclair** discuss the highly important role of advertising, including its ideological significance and the evolution of branding. Farone draws attention to the typical defense of advertising as natural and productive, as well as critiquing numerous examples of this specific ideology. Sinclair provides a historical look at brands, examining the concept within political economy, but arguing for a cultural economy approach.

The remaining chapters in Part II address issues relating to the state. **Andrew Calabrese and Colleen Mihal** focus directly on media relations with government, exploring current debates about public policy and private power. The state also is at the heart of **Dan Schiller's** discussion of the historical evolution and current developments in the militarization of communications in the US. His overview of the political economic roots of militarized communications reveals that it is deep-seated and multifaceted, and in need of further attention. Finally, **Helena Sousa and Joaquim Fidalgo** consider state power in relation to professional journalists, focusing especially on Portugal as a case study.

Part III – Conditions of Creativity: Industries, Production, Labor

The study of the political economy of media requires a thorough understanding of media companies and industries, as well as attention to issues related to labor. Chapters in Part III exemplify this type of research with discussions of recent developments in the US film industry (or Hollywood) and the historical and current status of the recorded music industry. **Janet Wasko** discusses recent arguments that Hollywood is dead, noting that such claims lack historical perspective. In the next chapter, **André Sirois and Janet Wasko** reinforce the importance of history in understanding the recorded music industry, arguing that recorded music has been more about technology and less about art/music from its inception, and that technology has made music into a commodity.

Labor is the focus of the other two chapters in this section. **Vincent Mosco** argues that labor remains a blind spot of western communication studies, including the political economy tradition. Trying to address this gap, Mosco maps the most relevant research on the media labor processes that include diverse theoretical and geographical perspectives. Finally, **David Hesmondhalgh and Sarah Baker** critique the political economy approach as "largely marginal in major critical studies of the Internet and new media," pointing to the entrance of new theoretical competitors in the media sphere. They argue that "political economy ... has had very little to say about the rise of creative industries policies in many parts of the world ... or about the fundamental importance of copyright to media and cultural production and consumption." Echoing Mosco, they also find less attention has been given to issues relating to labor and media, and propose more research on "creative labor" through an analysis that combines understanding of power, institutions, and subjectivity.

Part IV – Dynamics of Consumption: Choice, Mobilization, Control

Despite claims to the contrary, political economy of the media has directed special attention to issues relating to consumption. Part IV features several chapters that focus on this issue, albeit in different ways.

Giovanni Cesareo addresses key questions of how consumers are defined and considers the work of consumption. He also introduces the idea of new types of producer-consumers (dubbed "prosumers") who arise with new media platforms, such as blogs that involve citizen journalists.

Daniel Biltereyst and Philippe Meers observe that political economy perspectives play an important role in understanding various key issues relating to media audiences. They argue that a political economy of audiences helps clarify core questions on media, power, and society. Biltereyst and Meers deconstruct the complex concept of audience, incorporating political economy approaches that are perceived as extremely important for investigating questions on media power, particularly in exploring the conditions and the limits of cultural production, control, and governmentality. They claim that "In its engagement with questions of 'justice, equity and the public good,' critical political economy, as Golding and Murdock … have forcefully argued, is much more than the study of structures and economic dynamics behind (the range of) cultural production and texts, but it also incorporates questions on cultural consumption, access, and cultural competence."

Further discussion of consumption is offered by **Oscar Gandy**, who explores the political economy of personal information. Gandy is concerned with a particular kind of commodity: information about individuals or personal information with its role in the identification, classification, and evaluation of individuals. While personal information is a commodity, it is nevertheless a difficult product that is tricky to value.

And, finally, **Sophia Kaitatzi-Whitlock** focuses attention on the political economy of political ignorance, which is, in her view, increasing even though we ostensibly live in "knowledge societies" and an age of momentous scientific advances. Kaitatzi-Whitlock conceptualizes the notions of knowledge and ignorance and discusses instances of political ignorance and its growth in Europe over the last decades. She claims that the production of political ignorance is inherent in the prevailing political economy, notably that of symbolic goods, and argues that this is a media-induced affliction.

Part V – Emerging Issues and Directions

As noted in Parts I–IV, the study of political economy of media is (or at least, should be) flexible and dynamic, responding to social changes within a historical context. Some of the emerging issues and directions of the approach are considered in the final part of the volume.

In one of the last articles he wrote before his death in 2007, **Jan Ekecrantz** calls for more emphasis on international research that is cross-disciplinary and focuses on global inequalities and social transformation, as well as involving dialogue with nonwestern theories. While the author does not explicitly discuss political economy in this article, his work most often embraced a political economic approach. This is evident in his call for a macrosociology of media to address global and national class systems and collaboration with other disciplines, as well as comparative historical analysis.

In the following chapter, **Armand Mattelart** also addresses international issues, as he outlines the global debates pertaining to culture, information, and communication. The chapter details discussions among various international organizations that have set the agenda for principles such as cultural diversity, audiovisual flows, information society, and intellectual property. Mattelart observes that industry trade associations and lobbies are increasingly exerting pressure to break down public regulations in the name of freedom of trade and self-regulation, although other new forces such as professional coalitions and collectives of citizens have also become involved in this international debate.

Another new theoretical development in the political economy of communication is discussed by **Wayne Hope**, who addresses the concept of temporality and its relationship to global capitalism. He notes that information-communication technologies drive the temporal accelerations of global capitalism and discusses significant examples of this phenomenon, including satellite television and global news.

Michael Curtin offers a spatial analysis focusing on cities as creative and operational centers of the international media economy. Curtin points to the diversity and significance of peripheral media centers that have grown substantially since the 1980s, encouraged in part by the growing transnational flow of media products via satellite, cable, Internet, and home video. The chapter explains key principles that have been driving the commercial development of screen media for more than a century, as well as discussing policy implications of media capital in an era of globalization.

China is the focus of the final chapter in this volume by **Yuezhi Zhao**. Zhao's chapter contributes to a "transcultural" political economy of communication that aims to transcend the Euro-American biases of the field. She presents the Chinese case as a way to explore some of political economy's basic conceptual categories in relation to communication: the nature of the state; the relationships between class, nation, and empire; the problem of history and culture; and finally, agencies and alternatives.

This volume represents the type of work that has been presented in the Political Economy Section of the International Association for Media and Communication Research (IAMCR) since its founding in the late 1970s. The following is a description of the section, prepared by former section head, Vincent Mosco.

IAMCR/Political Economy Section

The Political Economy Section examines the role of power in the production, distribution, and exchange of mediated communication. Drawing from the rich history of political economic theory, section members study social relations in their totality, consider how they have developed historically, evaluate them according to standards of social justice, and intervene to bring about a more just and democratic world.

The research interests of section members include developing a richer theoretical foundation in communication research by incorporating an understanding of how structures of power operate, particularly in the process of transforming messages into commodities. Specifically, this means research on the global political economy which is centrally dependent on communication for its growth and on transnational media companies, which are increasingly in control of communication systems. It also includes research on how this global political economy is constituted out of various national corporate and government institutions as well as class formations that mediate global and local power.

Research interests also include the conflicts that arise over who benefits from control over communication resources. This research documents the interventions of workers, particularly over the consequences of an increasingly sophisticated international division of communication labor, and of women and racial minorities who seek to redress fundamental imbalances in global communication power. Recently, this research has expanded to include social movements in the communication arena, the state of the public sphere in an increasingly privatized audio-visual space, and the status of citizenship in a world that addresses people primarily as consumers.

References

Adorno, T. (1991) Culture industry reconsidered. In: Adorno, T. W., *The Culture Industry: Selected Essays on Mass Culture*. Routledge, London, pp. 85–92.

Albarron, A. (1996) *Media Economics: Understanding Markets, Industries, and Concepts*. Iowa State University, Ames, IA.

Alexander, A., Owers, J., and Carveth, R. M. (eds) (1993) *Media Economics: Theory and Practice*. Lawrence Erlbaum, Hillsdale, NJ.

Compaine, B. (ed.) (1979) *Who Owns the Media?* Harmony Books, New York.

Doyle, G. (2002) *Understanding Media Economics*. Sage Publications, London.

Gomery, D. (1989) Media economics: Terms of analysis. *Critical Studies in Mass Communication*, 6(2), 43–60.

Hartley, J. (2009) *The Uses of Digital Literacy*. University of Queensland Press, Brisbane.

Picard, R. G. (1989) *Media Economics: Concepts and Issues*. Sage Publications, London.

Part I
Legacies and Debates

1
Political Economies as Moral Economies
Commodities, Gifts, and Public Goods

Graham Murdock

Goods and the Good Life

Economics, as it emerged as an academic discipline at the turn of the twentieth century, claimed to offer a scientific basis for the study of economic affairs. Its dominant form presented capitalism as a network of markets, regulated by rational self-interest, whose organization and outcomes could be modeled mathematically. Empirical inquiry was fenced off from questions of value, cutting the links to moral philosophy that had been central to the project of political economy launched in the late eighteenth century as part of a more general search for a secular basis for moral action. The catastrophic financial crash set in motion by the collapse of the Lehman Brothers bank in September 2008 has now forced questions of ethics back into discussions of economic affairs in the most brutal way.

This "moral turn" is particularly marked in Britain where, for over a decade, the City of London has been uncritically celebrated as one of the key hubs of the new capitalism and left to compete in the global marketplace with the minimum of oversight. The social and human costs are now being counted in rising unemployment, decimated retirement savings, and savage cuts in public provision as funding for essential services is diverted to pay for the unprecedented scale of government borrowing required to bail out failing banks. Despite the havoc visited on countless working lives, many bankers have continued to display a callous disregard for public misery and to pay themselves huge bonuses. Faced with this selfishness and self-regard several notable celebrants at the altar of finance have

The Handbook of Political Economy of Communications, First Edition.
Edited by Janet Wasko, Graham Murdock, and Helena Sousa.

been moved to recant, or to voice major doubts about their former faith. Stephen Green, the Group Chairman of HSBC, one of the world's largest banks, has been moved to argue that "capitalism for the 21st century needs a fundamentally renewed morality to underpin it," one that asks again "what progress really is. Is it the accumulation of wealth, or does it relate to a broader, more integrated understanding of well-being and quality of life" (Green 2009, 35). Gordon Brown, who as Chancellor, and then Prime Minister, presided over a radically deregulated financial sector, belatedly concludes that "we have discovered to our cost, without values to guide them, free markets reduce all relationships to transactions [and] unbridled and untrammelled, become the enemy of the good society" (Brown 2010).

This admission would have come as no surprise to Adam Smith, born like Brown, in the town of Kirkaldy in Scotland, and one of the founding figures in developing a political economy of complex societies. From the outset, political economists saw questions about how the production and circulation of goods should be organized as part of a more general philosophical inquiry into the constitution of the good society. Smith's promotion by neoliberals as a militant apostle of free markets conveniently elides the strong moral basis of his thought. His lectures as Professor of Moral Philosophy at Glasgow University were the basis for his first book, *The Theory of Moral Sentiments* (1759), in which he famously argues that although the rich may only be interested in "the gratification of their own vain and insatiable desires ... They are led by an invisible hand," which without them intending it or knowing it leads them to "advance the interest of the society" by dividing "with the poor the produce of all their improvements" (Smith 1969, 264–5). This, as the radical political economist Joan Robinson tartly noted, was the "ideology to end ideologies" (Robinson 2006, 76), an act of intellectual alchemy that turned the base metal of self-interest into the gold of social equity. By assuming that accumulation always produced benign outcomes, it abolished exploitation with the stroke of a pen. But as Smith acknowledged elsewhere in the text, while commercial calculation provided a practical basis for social order, it did not produce the good society. This required generosity and mutuality. Societies, he argued, "may be upheld by a mercenary exchange of good offices according to an agreed valuation," but "not in the most comfortable state" (Smith 1969, 125). For Smith: "All members of society stand in need of each other's assistance [and] where [this] is reciprocally afforded from love, from gratitude, from friendship and esteem, the society flourishes and is happy [and] all the different members of it ... are, as it were, drawn to one common centre of mutual good offices" (p. 124).

In Smith's view, however, since egotism was a stronger motivating force than altruism, the spirit of beneficence and reciprocity could not be relied on to take the weight of a complex society. It was "the ornament which embellishes, not the foundation which supports the building" (p. 125). Order required an effective justice system to punish wrongdoers.

Putting the "Political" into Political Economy

In 1776 Smith published his second major work, *The Wealth of Nations*. Within months of its appearance, the American Declaration of Independence accelerated the struggle for full popular participation in the process of government. The American and French Revolutions announced the death of the subject and the birth of the citizen. People were no longer to be subjected to the unaccountable power of monarchs, emperors, and despots. They were to be autonomous political actors, with full and equal rights to participate in social life and in the political decisions affecting their lives. From that point on, the terms of debate changed irrevocably. Discussion about how best to respond to the expansion of capitalism, and its transition from a mercantile to an industrial base, was bound up with debates on the constitution of citizenship and the state's role in guaranteeing the concrete resources that supported full participation. Analysis of the economic order could not be separated from considerations of extended state intervention, its nature, rationale, and limits. Questions of political economy were more than ever questions about the political.

Smith saw a clear role for the state in addressing market limits, arguing that: "When the institutions or public works which are beneficial to the whole society ... are not maintained by the contribution of such particular members of the society as are most immediately benefitted by them, the deficiency must in most cases be made up by the general contribution of the whole society" (Smith 1999, 406).

Which institutions qualified for public subsidy, however, became a focus for heated argument. Smith himself was cautious. He saw a role for public money in supporting universal basic education, but argued that the state could best support general cultural life, "painting, music ... dramatic representations and exhibitions" by "giving entire liberty to all those who for their own interest" would provide them (1999, 384). As the struggle for full citizenship escalated, however, increasing doubts were raised over the market's ability to guarantee cultural rights.

It was clear that some of the essential resources required for full participation – minimum wages, pensions, unemployment and disability benefits, holiday entitlements, housing, and healthcare – were material and these became the site of bitter struggles over the terms and scope of collective welfare. But it was equally clear that they were not enough in themselves. They had to be matched by essential cultural resources; access to comprehensive and accurate information on contemporary events and to the full range of opinions they have generated; access to knowledge, to the frameworks of analysis and interpretation that place events in context, trace their roots, and evaluate their consequences; the right to have one's life and ambitions represented without stereotyping or denigration; and opportunities to participate in constructing public images and accounts and contribute to public debates (Murdock 1999).

Delivering these resources on an equitable basis shifted the state from a minimalist to a more expansive role. As well as deterring crime and guaranteeing the orderly social and financial environment required for commercial transactions, it was increasingly expected to deliver on the promise of citizenship. As part of this process, the management of cultural provision and mass communication, pursued through varying combinations of regulation and subsidy, became very much part of public policy. Regulation aimed to ensure that the public interest was not entirely subordinated to the private interests of media owners and advertisers. Subsidy addressed the market's perceived failure to deliver the full range of cultural rights by financing cultural institutions organized around the ideal of "public service" rather than profit generation.

These initiatives constructed a dual cultural and communications system. On the one side stood a dominant commercial sector, either selling cultural commodities (books, magazines, cinema tickets, hit records) directly to consumers or selling audience attention to advertisers and offering the product (commercial radio and television programming) free. On the other side stood a less well-resourced public sector providing a range of public cultural goods and services: libraries, museums, galleries, public broadcasting organizations. This was the landscape that the political economy of communications in western capitalism encountered when it emerged as a specialized field of academic study after World War II.

It produced a preoccupation with capital–state relations that spoke to the shifting organization of capitalism at the time. The project of reconstruction in Europe produced varying forms of welfare capitalism in which the state took on an increasing range of responsibilities for cultural and communications provision. Decolonization struggles created a proliferating number of newly independent states, many of which opted for "development" strategies that relied on concerted state intervention in major sectors, including culture and communications. The global ascendancy of American capitalism and the growing power and reach of the media majors raised pressing questions of regulation at home and cultural imperialism abroad. As centrally planned economies with no legal countervailing private sector, the two major communist blocs, controlled by the Soviet Union and China, remained largely outside this debate, however. Consequently, though they were of intense interest to political scientists, they were largely ignored by political economists of communication.

This landscape changed again in the late 1970s, as the balance between capital and state shifted decisively in favor of capital. The collapse of the Soviet Union, Deng's turn to the market in China in the aftermath of the Cultural Revolution, and India's break with Gandhi's ethos of self-sufficiency, reconnected three major economic regions to the circuits of global capitalism after decades of isolation or relative distance. At the same time, concerted neoliberal attacks on the inefficiency and unresponsiveness of the public sector ushered in an aggressive process of marketization in a number of emerging and established economies, including Britain (Murdock and Wasko 2007). Against this background, it is not surprising that critical political economists of communication have given priority to challenging the key tenets of "market fundamentalism" and defending public sector institutions.

This binary mindset abolishes almost entirely any sustained consideration of the economy of gifts and the many ways that mutual assistance and reciprocity have been expressed in a variety of practical forms throughout the history of modern capitalism. Gifting is the central organizing principle of civil society. Whenever people mobilize spontaneously to protect or pursue their shared interests, we see labor given or exchanged voluntarily with no expectation of monetary payment. "Civil society is where we express 'we' rather than just 'me', where we act with others rather than only doing things for them or to them" (Carnegie UK Trust 2010, 148). With the rise of the Internet, and the proliferating range of collaborative activities it supports, this neglected economy has been rediscovered and its "most radical parts ... from the open source movement and creative commons to the activists innovating around social networks" hailed as a new basis for civil society (p. 148). Unfortunately, rather than seeing it as a necessary third term, its most ardent enthusiasts have constructed another binary opposition in which online social sharing is locked in an escalating battle with corporations intent on extending their reach by commandeering unpaid creative labor and developing new revenue streams. This struggle is real enough, but it is not the whole story. It omits the ways that the expansion of the Internet has also revivified public cultural institutions.

Competing Moral Economies

Whenever we engage in transactions involving the consumption or exchange of goods and services, we enter a chain of social relations stretched over time. Looking backward poses questions about the conditions of production and the social and environmental costs incurred, forcing considerations of justice and equity to the forefront of debate. Looking forward raises issues of waste, disposability, sustainability, and shared fate. These concerns are underpinned by fundamental questions about our responsibilities and obligations toward all those people who we will never meet but whose life chances and opportunities for self-realization are affected by the modes of production and forms of exchange we choose to enter into. This is the central moral question facing modern societies, but it immediately bumps up against the militant promotion of the ethos of possessive individualism that underpins capitalism.

If we trace the fate of the demands for liberty, equality, and fraternity announced by the French Revolution, we see the rhetoric of individual freedom annexed by the champions of the minimal state and the "consumer society," equality transmuted into the chance to enter structurally unequal contests for personal

CAPITAL	STATE	CIVIL SOCIETY
Commodities	**Public Goods**	**Gifts**
Prices	Taxes	Reciprocities
Personal Possession	Shared Use	Co-creation
Consumers	Citizens	Communards
Liberty	Equality	Mutuality

Figure 1.1 Contested moral economies

advancement, and mutuality as a sadly diminished third term. As Richard Titmuss reminds us, capitalism constantly prompts us to ask: "Why should men not contract out of the 'social' and act to their own immediate advantage? Why give to strangers? – a question provoking an even more fundamental moral issue: who is my stranger in relatively affluent, acquisitive and divisive societies …? What are the connections if obligations are extended?" (Titmuss 1970, 58). How we answer, or sidestep, this central moral question will vary depending on the nature of the transactions we engage in. Each of the three main ways of organizing exchange relations in contemporary societies – commodities, public goods, and gifts – invites us to assume a particular identity, to balance private interests against the public good in particular ways, and to recognize or deny our responsibilities to strangers. These three political economies are therefore also moral economies. Figure 1.1 sketches out the main differences between them. In the rest of this chapter I want to elaborate on these contrasts, to explore their consequences for the organization of culture and communications, and to examine how the relations between them are shifting in the emerging digital environment.

Commodities: Possessions, and Dispossessions

A commodity is any good or service that is sold for a price in the market. A range of economic systems contain elements of commodity exchange. Command economies have "black" markets in scarce goods. In colonial societies, commodities have coexisted with barter and gift exchange. But only in a fully developed capitalist system is the production and marketing of commodities the central driving force of growth and profit. Writing in 1847, observing the social order being reshaped in the interests of industrial capital, Marx was in no doubt that the process of commodification, which sought to convert everything into an article for sale, was at the heart of this process. He saw the new capitalism ushering in "a time in which even the things which until then had been communicated, but never exchanged, given but never sold, acquired but never bought – virtue, love, conscience – all at last enter into commerce – the time where everything moral or physical having become a saleable commodity is conveyed to the market" (Marx 2008, 86–7).

A number of commentators have seen the onwards march of commodification as a generalized form of enclosure extended to more and more kinds of resources (see Murdock 2001). The first enclosure movement began in Tudor times when agricultural entrepreneurs fenced off land previously held in common for villagers to graze sheep and collect firewood and wild foods, and incorporated it into their private estates. It is a useful metaphor because it highlights the fact that capitalist accumulation always entails dispossession (see Harvey 2005, 137–82).

By stripping villagers of access to many of the resources that had enabled them to be mostly self-sufficient, the original enclosure movement forced them to become agricultural workers for hire, selling their labor for a wage. Then, as they moved to the new industrial cities, their vernacular knowledge and skills in building, self-medication, growing and preserving foods, gradually atrophied as they were beckoned to enter the new consumer system in which the powers of self-determination taken away by the industrial labor process were returned in leisure time as the sovereign right to choose between competing commodities. Against a backdrop where routine industrial and clerical work was repetitive and alienating, and offered little intrinsic satisfaction or opportunity for self-expression, it was essential to promote consumption as the sphere where one was free to be fully oneself. By hailing people as first and foremost consumers, making personal choices in the marketplace, rather than workers making common cause, commodification helped to underwrite social stability while at the same time ensuring that rising levels of production were met by increased levels of demand.

As Marx noted in his famous discussion in the opening chapter of the first volume of *Capital*, commodities conceal the secret of their production, and present themselves as magical objects, endowed, like religious fetishes, with the power to change lives. In common with evangelical preachers who persuaded believers that they could be "born again," commodities held out the perpetual promise of a better, more comfortable, more satisfying life. The transition from generic to branded goods, which took off only after Marx's death, consolidated this appeal. Brands either bore the name of the manufacturer (Colman's Mustard, Lipton's Tea, Gillette Razors) and appeared as the exclusive products of invention and entrepreneurship, or like Kodak, assumed imaginary names that removed them from mundane discourse. The effect was to abolish any talk of labor processes, of exploitative working conditions or environmental degradation, and focus attention solely on the object itself and the projected pleasures and gains of possession. Brands were presented not simply as external markers of quality or distinction, but as badges of personal identity, ways of announcing who one was and wanted to be. Consumers were encouraged to brand themselves, to contract out of the "social" and focus on the transformative power of personal purchases. Commodity transactions carried no social obligations. They supported a moral economy rooted in disengagement and self-regard in which the freedom of individual choice was the sole and sovereign value. They were inhospitable to all mutualities other than communities of brand users.

Cultural and communications goods have a unique triple relationship to commodity culture. Firstly, a number of media products and cultural services are commodities in their own right. This has two consequences that have been major areas of investigation for critical political economy. It cedes enormous potential control over public culture and debate to private ownership and the dynamics of profit maximization, and creates substantial inequalities in capacities to participate by tying access to communication to ability to pay. Secondly, media provide the primary platforms for advertising and promoting general commodities. As the only ideological position that secures continuous access to the heartlands of public culture, through payments to place self-created publicity, this gives consumerism a unique advantage. Thirdly, the dominant genres of popular media extend this naturalization of commodity culture by filling expressive space with images of locations and people that present it as the taken-for-granted backdrop of social action. Their dominant aesthetic is "capitalist realism" showing "life and lives worth emulating" (Schudson 1984, 215). Soviet "socialist realism" displayed heroes of production, steel workers marching into a future bathed in light, smiling tractor drivers bringing home a record harvest from sunlit fields. "Capitalist realism" celebrated heroes of consumption living lives grounded in a plenitude of goods and a heightened awareness of fashion and style, wives caressing the rounded doors of their new refrigerators, husbands admiring the swooping lines of their new saloon cars.

As D. W. Griffith complained in 1923: "Motion pictures have received, and merited, much criticism about the type of rooms they photograph to represent the homes of the rich. … Persons of wealth, family and education flash their jewels in the atmosphere of a furniture shop or an auctioneer's showroom. The rooms are crowded with objects …" (Griffith 1923, 13). A decade later, Max Horkheimer, founder of the influential Frankfurt School of critical cultural analysis, argued that even the background landscapes of popular films had become assimilated into a promotional aesthetic, noting that: "For a long time now, Raphael's blue horizons have been quite properly a part of Disney's landscapes. The sunbeams almost beg to have the name of a soap or a toothpaste emblazoned on them; they have no meaning except as a background for such advertising. Disney and his audiences … unswervingly stand for the purity of the blue horizon" (Horkheimer 1972, 281).

This promotion of commodity culture did not go uncontested, however. It was countered by the long struggle to provide cultural and communicative resources for full citizenship by reclaiming the idea of the commons.

Public Goods: Reclaiming the Commons

The battle to construct a public commons in the new industrial cities was waged on two fronts: for shared public space and for public cultural provision. Both were essential resources for full citizenship. Political expression required public spaces where people could gather to discuss issues and attend rallies and demonstrations. As the *Saturday Review* observed in 1856, however, the helter-skelter expansion of central London was driven by "the simple unchecked competition of rival estates sent into the market to hustle against each" (quoted in Minton 2009, 19). The new developments were controlled by private landlords led by members of the old aristocracy (the Earls of Bedford and Southampton and the Duke of Westminster), who resorted to the tried and trusted practice of enclosure, erecting fences and gates patrolled by ex-servicemen and prison officers. Faced with mounting skirmishes over access and growing opposition to what one contemporary characterized as the "disgraceful" behavior of government "in allowing these squares and places to be closed to the public," control over urban space was progressively transferred to local authorities and public access guaranteed from 1864–5 onwards (Minton 2009, 20). The following year, 1866, saw another turning point, when a crowd protesting the defeat of the Reform Bill to extend the right to vote arrived at Hyde Park intent on holding a rally, and, finding the gates locked, removed part of the railings and entered a space that up until then had been seen and used as a pleasure garden for the well-to-do (Murdock 2001, 444–5).

These reassertions of rights of access to a shared physical commons were accompanied by the rapid expansion of collective cultural resources – museums, galleries, libraries, and adult education facilities – administered by central and local government. These facilities were public goods in three senses. Firstly, in contrast to commodities, which were private possessions, they were available for shared use. Secondly, because they were financed collectively out of taxation, they countered the exclusions generated by the unequal ability to pay the prices demanded by market systems. People might not be able to buy all the books they wanted for their personal pleasure and self-development, but they could borrow them from a public library. Thirdly, they were intended to advance the common good by promoting a commitment to equality of entitlement and encouraging a sense of belonging to a shared imaginative world confronting common problems.

The promise of open and equal access, however, remained bounded by the confines of location and pressure of numbers. To borrow books from a public library, users needed to travel to a building that was only open at certain times. Once there, they might find the book they wanted already on loan to another borrower. Similarly, public art galleries and museums could only display a fraction of their collections in the space they had available, leaving many items in store, and viewing the most popular exhibits often entailed jostling with crowds for a favorable position.

In addition, public cultural institutions were the site of power struggles from the outset. There were insistent pressures from state and government to employ them as instruments of social control. By hailing users as members of national and local communities, they displaced solidarities of class. At the same time, they were administered on an everyday basis by the rapidly expanding ranks of cultural professionals – curators, archivists, librarians, and lecturers – who saw themselves as missionaries bringing the great achievements of human knowledge and expression within the reach of all. Their claim that decisions about what books should be stocked, what art should be shown, and what ideas should be taught, should be governed by professional judgment rather than political considerations, created permanent tensions around the notion of the "relative autonomy" of cultural workers paid out of the public purse. While this insistence on the primacy of intellectual expertise and cultivated taste offered some protection against political encroachment, it also operated to largely exclude lay knowledge and vernacular cultural expression. The culture promoted by public cultural institutions was overwhelmingly spelled with a capital "C" and identified with the works of the thinkers, writers, artists, and musicians who had passed into the pantheon of intellectual and creative heroes selected by cultural elites. It was informed by the entirely honorable motive of wanting to expand people's intellectual and imaginative horizons, to say to people "try this first and then that, then come back and ask us what you ought to read next" (Williams 1989, 25). But for many at the receiving end, it smacked of paternalism.

Audiences, however, were far from being blank sheets waiting to be written on by copperplate messages, penned by cultural professionals. "In the late nineteenth and early twentieth centuries, after the achievement of mass literacy but before radio and television, working-class culture was saturated by the spirit of mutual education … Knowledge was something to be shared around" (Rose 2002, 83–9). Newspapers and novels were read aloud and discussed in a range of social settings from workplaces, pubs, and street corners to classes organized by the Workers' Education Association. This commitment to sharing and cocreation also characterized myriad forms of collective cultural expression, from brass bands and choral societies to "Sunday painters."

The public broadcasting organizations that emerged in a number of countries across Europe and elsewhere in the 1920s, however, largely ignored these initiatives. By releasing public cultural intervention from the constraints of physical space and allowing the same material to be accessed simultaneously by anyone with the appropriate reception equipment, the technology of free-to-air broadcasting reinforced prevailing maps of cultural worth by universalizing them. By valorizing the home as the center of cultural encounters, it also accelerated the domestication of popular culture activity. By that time, however, observers had already begun to look elsewhere for expressions of mutuality.

Gifts: In Search of Generosity

The emergence of public broadcasting coincided with the rise of anthropology as an academic discipline based on extended first-hand observation and interviews with native informants. From the outset gift exchanges emerged as a central focus of concern for two reasons: firstly, because they combined the economic, social, and symbolic domains, they offered a convenient point of entry into understanding the overall organization of native systems. Secondly, in a context where commodity relations and calculations of personal advantage were entering more and more areas of social life, the gift, freely given, appeared "as the last refuge of a solidarity, of an open-handedness" (Godelier 1999, 208) that seemed to be disappearing from capitalist societies. "One of the main functions of the theory of the gift has accordingly been to provide an account of ... non-exploitative reciprocity as a basis of community" (Frow 1997, 104). As the fieldwork evidence accumulated, however, it became clear that far from displaying an absence of calculation, gift exchange was central to the competition for personal advantage.

This conclusion was stated in its most influential form by Marcel Mauss in his 1925 book, *The Gift*, in which he argued that "All in all, gifts are not ... disinterested [but] made with a view to ... maintaining a profitable alliance" (Mauss 1990, 73). The value of the gift lay in its ability to cement social connections and reaffirm prestige. Mauss's most striking evidence for the incursion of calculation came from his reading of Franz Boas's studies of the potlatch (a Chinook word for "give away") practiced by the Kwakiutl people in the area around Vancouver. Boas arrived for his first fieldwork visit in 1886, just as the new law banning the potlatch was coming into force. His respondents were recalling a system that had changed radically during their lifetimes as a result of encounters with capitalist modernity.

Kwakiutl society was headed by nobles who claimed to be reincarnations of the founding ancestor animal spirits. By staging ritual ceremonies centered around the distribution of property, they legitimated both their social status and their claim to the supernatural powers believed to be essential for the regeneration of the natural realm (Masco 1995, 44). The gifts given included animal skins, a tangible link between the material and spiritual worlds. From the 1750s onwards, furs, particularly sea otter pelts, the "soft gold" of the fashion industry, became the basis of a lucrative trade. Although this brought the Kwakiutl into increasing contact with British merchants and their envoys, they remained relatively autonomous culturally, incorporating Hudson Bay blankets, the main form of payment for furs, into potlatch ceremonies but investing them with ritual meaning as proxies for animal skins. Then, in 1849, the British occupied Vancouver Island and embarked on a concerted effort to incorporate indigenous residents into the social and moral order of capitalism. The new commercial opportunities opened up by colonization led to an escalating competition within the native population. For the first time, native notables other than chiefs could amass sufficient resources to stage a potlatch. The resulting competition for status led to bigger, more frequent, pot-latches in which more and more objects were given away, many of them com-modities purchased from the British. The paradoxical result was that "maintaining the cosmology" that supported native identity increasingly depended on "partici-pation in the colonial economy," so that "capitalism came increasingly to lie at its centre" (Saunders 1997, 143).

It is tempting to read this as a classic instance of incorporation, but here, as in other colonial contexts, the entanglements of native moral systems with capitalist trade had more complex outcomes (see Thomas 1991). A prospector, who had arrived in 1862 for the Gold Rush on the Fraser River, initiated a smallpox epidemic and "within three years, two-thirds of the total indigenous population … were obliterated" (Masco 1995, 55). Against this background, the escalation of potlatch-ing can also be seen as "the effort of dying people … to regain control over their lives" (Masco 1995, 57). It was precisely this symbolic resistance to incorporation that led to the Statutes of Canada being amended in 1884 to make potlatching an imprisonable offense.

Mauss does not touch on this alternative explanation but there are strong paral-lels with the situation he himself faced when writing *The Gift*. Observing France in the early 1920s, he saw a society decimated by the terrible slaughter of World War I and becoming increasingly commercialized, with Paris still claiming to be in the vanguard of consumer culture, having pioneered two of the most influential mechanisms of promotion, the department store and the cinema. But he argued strongly that commercial enclosure was not yet complete. As he noted, "fortu-nately, everything is still not wholly categorised in terms of buying and selling … A considerable part of our morality and our lives are still permeated with the same atmosphere of the gift, where obligation and liberty intermingle … We possess more than a tradesman morality" (Mauss 1990, 65). The question was how best to protect and support this ethos of "reciprocating generosity" (Mauss 1990, 83) against the incursion of "icy, utilitarian calculation" (p. 76).

Mauss was a convinced socialist, and although he was a gradualist rather than a revolutionary, he was initially attracted to the social experiment set in motion by the Bolshevik's seizure of power in Russia. However, he soon became disillusioned, publishing a fierce attack in 1925 (Mauss 1992). He was particularly critical of the Soviet centralization of state power, arguing that it taught "nations who want to reform how not to do it" (Mauss 1992, 203). Casting around for an alternative, he drew on his long involvement in the co-operative movement to insist on the urgent need to strengthen civil society by developing a range of "intermediary institu-tions" that would be relatively independent of both the state and the market (1992, 191). At the same time, he assigned a key role to government, "representing the community," in acknowledging that "the worker has given his life and labour to the collective" as well as to the employer and in honoring the social obligation "not discharged by the payment of wages" (Mauss 1990, 67). The guarantees of "secu-rity against unemployment, sickness, old age" (p. 67) that he had in mind were basic building blocks for a new kind of welfare state which he thought Britain, "where municipal and administrative socialism have been in vogue for a long time," was most likely to develop (Mauss 1992, 206).

Mauss's politics have been almost entirely deleted from later anthropological work on gift exchange, which has preferred to search "every act for the degree to which it could be said to mask some hidden selfishness" (Graeber 2010, 5). One notable exception is the Swiss anthropologist Gerald Berthoud, who, together with the French sociologist Alain Caille, launched the Mouvement Anti-Utilitariste dans les Sciences Sociales (MAUSS) in 1981 to oppose the instrumental view of social democracy and the constant exhortations for France to adopt a more market-oriented model of the state. Their core proposal revived the idea, originally proposed by the eighteenth-century revolutionary Tom Paine, for the government to pay every citizen a social wage to underwrite their social participation.

This proposal was not part of the program instituted by the Labour government elected in Britain after World War II, but the new administration pursued the provision of collective resources for citizenship with vigor in a variety of other ways. The social provision offered by an expanded national insurance scheme, an ambitious program of social housing, and a new national health service, was accompanied by a series of cultural initiatives. Compulsory schooling was extended up to the age of 15. The BBC monopoly over broadcasting was confirmed and extended to television. An Arts Council (the idea of the political economist John Maynard Keynes, the principal architect of the new orthodoxy on managing capitalism) was launched to fund creative activity. Observing this flurry of activity in 1951, the young social policy analyst Richard Titmuss saw it driven by "the war-warmed impulse for a more generous society" (Titmuss 1950, 508). Two decades later, his vision was altogether darker. Watching neoliberal economic ideas steadily gaining ground throughout the 1960s, he imagined the bastions of the welfare state – "hospitals, schools, universities" – steadily exposed to "the forces of economic calculation and to the laws of the marketplace" (Titmuss 1970, 213). With Margaret Thatcher's arrival as prime minister, Titmuss's prophecies were confirmed, as government embarked on a concerted push to roll back the state and expand the scope of market relations, selling public assets to private investors, opening up restricted markets and protected areas of activity, shifting regulation to a more business-friendly mode, and urging public institutions to think and behave like commercial corporations and "monetize" their assets.

Titmuss did not live to see the ascendancy of marketization, but in his last book, *The Gift Relationship* (Titmuss 1970), he mounted a strong counterargument in defense of generosity as the foundation of the good society. Taking voluntary blood donation as a limit case of giving with no prospect of return or advantage, he demonstrates with great elegance and force that compared to selling blood, donation is both more efficient and morally superior. Not only does it cut wastage by reducing the chances of contamination, it confirms, in the most intimate way, the essential role of generosity in sustaining a democratic society anchored in mutuality.

This concern with gifts that circulate with no assurance of anything in return was taken up by the critic Lewis Hyde in his analysis of relations between the "inner" gift of creativity and the "outer" cultural forms through which it is expressed and circulated. For Hyde, "the spirit of the gift is kept alive by its constant donation" and "where commerce is exclusively a trade in merchandise, the gifted cannot enter into the give-and-take that ensures the livelihood of their spirit" (Hyde 1979, xvi). For many cultural workers trying to support themselves from the returns on their work, however, economic livelihood takes precedence. Mauss was sympathetic to the case for authors' rights, arguing that although everyone wishes artistic and literary works "to fall into the public domain ... as quickly as possible," laws defending creators' rights to benefit financially from the continuing uses of their labor are entirely justified (Mauss 1990, 67). With the rise of the Internet and the unprecedented ease with which works can be copied and circulated, this clash between the defenders of extended intellectual property rights and advocates of unrestricted sharing has become a central fault line running through current debates. Although it has generated a substantial specialist literature, it is more usefully seen as one element in the escalating conflict between the competing moral economies of gifts, commodities, and public goods, now rippling out across the range of digital technologies, but concentrated particularly on the Internet.

The Internet's power to disrupt established structures and institutional divisions lies in its simultaneous promotion of top-down and bottom-up systems of exchange. On the one hand, it offers established commercial and public cultural organizations more efficient and flexible ways of distributing their output and tracking audience reactions and responses. On the other, it supports multiple networks of peer-to-peer sharing and collaboration. The battle now in progress is over the way relations between these vertical and horizontal dimensions should be organized.

Kevin Kelly, the founding executive editor of *Wired* magazine, speaks for many digital utopians when he claims that the new collaborative social technology is forging a "socialism uniquely tuned for a networked world" in which "masses of people who own the means of production work toward a common goal and share their products in common [and] free of charge" (Kelly 2009, 122–3). His argument, that this new "third way ... renders irrelevant the old ... zero-sum trade off between free market individualism and centralized authority" (p. 124), ignores both the concerted corporate push to enclose digital gifting and the central role of government in guaranteeing access to cultural resources for social participation. As we argued earlier, "A social democratic vision of the good society entails from the outset a greater role for the state and the public sector" (Judt 2010, 2) in building and defending a genuinely open and diverse cultural commons. Despite the recent assaults on public cultural institutions generated by the onward march of marketization, the Internet offers an unprecedented opportunity to revivify this project.

Digital gifting: net returns

Digital gifting outside the price system operates at three basic levels. Firstly, there is sharing where individuals circulate self-produced or found material using their own website or web space. This can range from posting photos on a personal social network page or video clips on YouTube, to exchanging downloaded music files. At the next stage up, there is co-operation, where individuals contribute to making a shared domain more useful, for example, by labeling the photos they post on Flickr with key words to make the archive more easily searchable. Finally, there is collaborative activity designed to create a new cultural product or resource that can be freely shared. The freely downloadable add-on "Home Front," produced by dedicated fans of the successful action-adventure video game, *Battle Field 1942*, based on events in World War II, offers one example (Postigo 2007). Another, more ambitious instance is *Born of Hope*, the 70-minute prequel to the highly successful *Lord of The Rings* trilogy, made by the independent film-maker Kate Madison. The budget was raised by donations. Actors gave their time free and technical support drew on a global network. "Costume designs were sent from the Netherlands. The hero's sword was designed in Ontario ... footage of trees sent from Germany, and lightning added by an effects wizard in Greece" (Lamont 2010). Released free on three video streaming sites, the film attracted almost a million viewers.

As these examples make clear, in the domain of genuine origination, to talk about the Internet as a site of expanding "amateur" activity is to use the term "not in the sense of inexperienced but in the sense of not paid" (Lessig 2004, 44). Even where projects are open to a wider constituency, the majority of active contributors remains concentrated among a small group of dedicated enthusiasts. Fewer than 2 percent of users of the online encyclopedia Wikipedia ever contribute (Shirky 2008, 125). Similarly, "By far the highest number and quality of innovative ideas" to the website Niketalk, dedicated to suggesting modifications to the shoes used by basketball players, are proposed by 20 or so contributor "designers" out of a total membership of 34,000 (Fuller et al. 2007, 66).

Observing the time and commitment devoted to these interventions, it is tempting "to assume that for most peer producers, voluntary peer production [is] central to the identity and meaning-making aspects of their lives, as the place in which passion, community and creativity can be applied in a way almost impossible to achieve with the corporate context" (Bauwens 2009, 131). "Socially recognized self-realization," extending one's skills, and developing an elegant solution to a problem that earns respect and status within one's community of peers, are certainly major sources of motivation (Arvidsson 2008, 332). But voluntary participation can just as easily be a precursor to work within a "corporate context" as a compensation or counter to it. The "designers" on the Niketalk site "dream of becoming professional basketball footwear designers for one of the major brands," and some, like "Alphaproject," who was taken on by Nike, succeed (Fuller et al.

2007, 66–7). Similarly, the most active games "modders" studied by Hector Postigo, saw creating add-ons as "a good way of exhibiting/increasing skills and adding content" to their résumés (Postigo 2007, 310).

In a situation where labor in the creative industries is becoming increasingly casualized and more and more functions are outsourced, "network sociality" and the maintenance of networks and connections, Mauss's "profitable alliances," becomes a central resource (Wittel 2001, 51). "In the digital economy of ideas that the web is creating, you are … who you are linked with, who you network with" (Leadbeater 2008, 6).

In the linked and very visible arenas of action created by the Internet, participants hoping for employment, or simply wanting to express themselves and earn the respect of their peers, are actively solicited by corporations bent on commandeering their skills and engagement.

Digital Enclosures

Although the rapid expansion of personal credit over the last decade has intensified consumerism, creating a "turbo-consumer society" (Lawson 2009, 2), mobilizing the Internet to sell cultural commodities has so far proved difficult. Users, particularly younger users who have grown up with the web, expect free access and resent having to pay. This is particularly marked in the field of recorded music where the International Federation of the Phonographic Industry claims that 95 percent of downloads are illegal (Singing a different tune 2009, 79). In response, the music and audiovisual industries have lobbied hard and successfully for the extension of copyright with the average term in the United States tripling from 32.2 years to 95 years since 1973 (Lessig 2004, 135). As with the first enclosure movement, this erection of new fences has been accompanied by penalties for trespass though the original strategy of suing users for illegal downloads has been replaced by a graduated response of warnings followed by disconnection. The argument that free downloads always and everywhere represent a loss of potential income is, however, contestable. The most avid downloaders are often the most avid music fans. When the band Boxer Rebellion had one of their tracks selected as the "Free Single of the Week" on the Apple iTunes paid-for download system, the 560,000 downloads it attracted in the first week helped to make their album the first by an unsigned band to enter the Billboard top 100 list (Topping 2009, 13).

Illegal downloads may operate as a loss leader but because the link is problematic, companies have opted for the more secure revenue stream provided by systems that bundle free access to music in with other services. Internet service providers, such as Virgin in Britain, sell access alongside broadband subscriptions. Mobile phone companies include download systems as part of the price of the handset. Newspapers that, from an early point in the development of the Internet, offered free access to web-based content alongside subscriptions and purchases of the paper version, are pursuing a different strategy. Led by Rupert Murdoch, a number are drastically reducing the amount of free online access and moving content behind newly erected electronic fences, available only to subscribers. This is a version of the "freemium" strategy where "a few paying customers subsidize many unpaying ones" (Anderson 2009, 165). How willing people will be to pay for material that was previously free is, however, an open question. The uncertainties surrounding these business models have increased reliance on the other main option: advertising support. Spotify, which was installed on six million computers across Europe by the end of 2009, and offers users a free music streaming service interrupted by ads, is prototypical. Users who want an advertising-free service are required to pay a monthly fee.

In his path-breaking analysis of commercial free-to-air television, Dallas Smythe famously compared programming to the "potato chips and peanuts given to customers of the pub bar, or cocktail lounge," free incentives to keep them relaxed and ready to buy more drinks (Smythe 1981, 37–8). Commercial television is an attention economy. The price of placing a 30-second slot is determined primarily by the number of viewers watching (the rating). In addition, programming is required to provide a "positive selling environment" by privileging genres that employ the same capitalist realist aesthetic as the advertising that surrounds them. For Smythe, the pleasures of viewing and the activity of audiences are incorporated into the continuous labor of "marketing consumer goods and services to themselves" (1981, 34), and reaffirming consumption as the primary source of self-chosen identity. The massive new field of operations opened up by the Internet and the greater ease of tracking consumer preferences and choices has generalized this "ad-driven business model to an unlimited range of other industries" (Anderson 2009, 143–4). It has also extended the process of commodification. In Smythe's analysis, audience attention is the commodity traded between advertisers and television companies. On the Internet there is an emerging trade in social relations and everyday interactions exemplified by the invitation to young people issued by the British marketing company Dubit:

> Dubit believes that you are the best people to promote brands, products and services ... Dubit Insider lets young people aged 7–24 do exactly this ... you will work with some of the UK's top brands. You can use this experience to enhance your CV and even earn yourself a little cash, as well as a few freebies along the way. All you have to do is tell your friends about the brands YOU love! (Dubit Informer 2010)

This is one of a growing number of marketing initiatives that commodify personal talk about brands in everyday encounters or on social networking sites, and capitalize on the trust embedded in friendship. It points to a more general incorporation of gift relations into the economy of commodities.

In 1980, the futurologist Alvin Toffler coined the term "prosumption" to describe the combination of production and consumption entailed in the "unpaid work done directly by people for themselves or their community," arguing that it had been virtually excluded from economic analysis because it did not contribute to production for exchange (Toffler 1980, 277). The Internet allows this neglected economy to be comprehensively incorporated, leading recent writers on the digital economy to develop "a new model of prosumption, where customers participate in the production of products in an active and ongoing way" (Tapscott and Williams 2008, 127). Not only does this model smooth over the intensification of exploitation, but its disinterest in corporate control over cultural production supports an analysis of the "creative industries" that presents critical political economy as outmoded and conservative.

Creativity, Convergence, and Exploitation

There is now an emerging consensus that the productive core of the advanced capitalist economies is shifting from a base in "heavy" industries to a new center in the "weightless" realms of information and cultural goods with many commentators assigning a pivotal role to the "creative industries," defined as all those sectors "where value is primarily dependent upon the play of symbolic meaning" (Bilton and Leary 2002, 50). For Melvin Bragg, the crowds thronging Britain's free museums and galleries are "helping to transform [the] country from one based on the toil and wealth of heavy industry to one enriched by the pleasure and equal promise of wealth that comes from the creative industries" (Bragg 2010, 51). For others, cultural engagement is not simply "helping" transformation, it is its primary engine.

In 2006, *Time* magazine nominated "YOU," the "ordinary" woman and man in the street, as "Person of the Year," arguing that the arrival of a faster, more capacious, Internet, Web 2.0, is: "about community and collaboration on a scale never seen before ... about the many wresting power from the few and helping one another for nothing ...We're looking at an explosion of productivity and innovation ... as millions of minds that would otherwise have drowned in obscurity get backhauled into the global intellectual economy" (quoted in Siegel 2008, 129). In the space of this brief passage, the world turned upside down by the power of the "many" is immediately turned right way up again as we move seamlessly from gifting to commodity production, from "helping one another for nothing" to being dragged, "backhauled," into the "new" capitalism.

For John Hartley, one of the leading advocates of the "creative industries" perspective, this sector is not simply central, it is *the* "empirical form taken by *innovation* in advanced knowledge-based economies" (Hartley 2009, 204). This is a very large claim indeed. Firstly, innovation in two other key emerging areas, biotechnology and nanotechnology, remains highly centralized and capital-intensive.

Secondly, "a great deal of the economy," food production, energy supply, transport infrastructures, financial services, "is not susceptible to this collaborative, open ethos" (Leadbeater 2008, 24), at least not yet. Ignoring these obvious caveats and focusing attention exclusively on "creative" production, however, allows Hartley to argue that understanding innovation in the "new economy" requires us to shift our focus "from closed expert process (professional production in vertically inte-grated firms) and structural analysis to an open innovation system and complex adaptive networks" (Hartley 2009, 217). He castigates "ideologically motivated political-economy approaches" for devoting too much attention to analyzing the operations of media industries and "too little to consumers and markets" (p. 39) and for failing to take seriously their agency "within an overall system in which major enterprises are *also* at work" (p. 49, my italics). Within this new horizontal landscape he sees the social networks supported by the "growing ubiquity of dig-ital media becoming a more dynamic source of productivity than industrial inno-vation" (p. 216). In which case, "critical analysis need not take sides" since opposing "new-media developments and their marketisation" not only misses the extent and radicalism of the change now in motion, but for economies hoping to compete effectively in the future, it is "industrial suicide" (p. 41).

Avoiding this outcome has been a major concern for Henry Jenkins, who, like Hartley, has been a long-standing celebrant of audience activity. He sees a new convergence emerging between the "top-down decisions made in corporate board-rooms by companies wishing to tap their cross-media ownership and bottom-up decisions made in teen's [sic] bedrooms" (Jenkins 2006b, 1). Faced with the "new participatory folk culture" created by "giving average people" the digital tools "to annotate, appropriate and recirculate content," he argues that companies need to "tap this culture to foster consumer loyalty and generate low-cost content" (Jenkins 2001). To aid them in this task, while at MIT he set up the Convergence Culture Consortium, to provide "insights into new ways to relate to consumers, manage brands, and develop engaging experiences to cut through the increasingly clut-tered media environment and benefit from emerging cultural and technological trends" (Convergence Culture Consortium 2009, 1).

There are two major problems with these attempts to replace the critical politi-cal economy of culture and communications with an analysis of "creative indus-tries" or "convergence culture." Ethically, they reproduce corporate ideology by presenting the public interest as synonymous with business interests and privileg-ing consumer activity over citizen involvement. From this perspective, a critical analysis of capitalism appears as a barrier rather than a resource for change. As John Hartley argues: "to maintain a *structural* model (of inequality, struggle and antagonism) in the face of *dynamic* disequilibrium (change and growth) is ... to deny an open future" (Hartley 2009, 202). Empirically, they fail to confront the full cultural consequences of increased corporate power. The enlarged scope for com-modification opened up by marketization has not only accelerated the formation of multimedia conglomerates of unprecedented scale and scope (including

Time-Warner, the champion of "YOU"), it has fostered concentration rather than dispersal on the Internet, with dominant firms emerging in each major sector of use and new conglomerates forming. Google has used the profits from selling advertising on its main search site to expand into a variety of other areas, creating new de facto monopolies and new enclosures. Its project of digitalizing the holdings of some of the world's leading libraries is a case in point. Of the seven million books processed by the end of 2008, one million were in the public domain and available for anyone to use free of charge. The rest were still covered by copyright and accessible only as extracts. Anyone wishing to read the full text is obliged to buy it or borrow a physical copy from a public library. Added to which, the rights agreements that Google have signed give it "what can only be called a monopoly … since no new entrepreneurs will be able to digitize books within that fenced-off territory, even if they could afford it" (Darnton 2009, 6). The result is not simply the loss of any chance of creating a comparable public digital collection, but the transfer of control over an essential cultural resource to a private company.

Unlike Hartley, who presents consumers as equal participants in value creation, Jenkins, who puts his analysis at the service of the media majors, is well aware of the continuing structural skew in the balance of power, acknowledging that "Not all participants are created equal. Corporations – and even individuals within corporate media – still exert greater power than any individual consumer or even the aggregate of consumers. And some consumers have greater abilities to participate than others" (Jenkins 2006a, 3). Or as Jimmy Wales, the cofounder of Wikipedia, put it without a trace of irony, "In part Wikipedia is anarchy [but] there is also an element of aristocracy: people who have acquired a reputation have a higher standing in the community. And then there is monarchy – that's me" (quoted in Leadbeater 2008, 16). In a comment that he fails to pursue Hartley acknowledges the continuing power of ownership, noting that even in "a complex open system in which everyone is an active agent … Individuals originate ideas; networks adopt them; [but] enterprises *retain* them" (Hartley 2009, 63, my emphasis). The easy rhetoric of coproduction and cocreation conceals a reality of exploitation.

This applies even where the basic raw materials for self-generated production are provided by the corporation as they are in the virtual world, *Second Life*. The site's owners, Linden Lab, actively encourage participants to use the basic digital building blocks they provide to "create anything you can imagine" (Second Life, 2007) by granting them intellectual property rights over anything they produce. This has created a thriving internal economy as the site's residents trade the objects and buildings they have made with each other for a virtual currency convertible into US dollars. It is this creative labor that builds the environments that constitute the site's attraction. Without it there would literally be nothing there. The company benefits in two ways. Participants pay a monthly subscription for the privilege of doing most of the work and their labor saves the owners an estimated $410 million a year in programming and development costs (Hof 2006).

This case is prototypical. As one influential business commentator candidly admits "through co-production, consumers relieve manufacturers and retailers from performing various activities along the value creation chain," and absorb the costs not only of the time and effort involved, but also of the knowledge and skills deployed, which may often require years of personal and public investment to acquire (Etgar 2009, 1–2). Fans' work on the smaller add-ons to the computer games studied by Hector Postigo, for example, saved the companies an average of $2.5 million in labor costs (Postigo 2007, 305). By offering new features and providing free marketing through fan websites, they also help sustain interest in the original commodity and allow companies to identify and track consumption patterns that "are increasingly disjointed, heterogeneous, and less amenable to corporate categorization and control" (Bonsu and Darmody 2008, 357). And, crucially for products aimed at the youth market, they help bolster a brand's image as fun and in touch. The result is that working consumers are opened to double exploitation. Firstly, they are "not generally paid for the know-how, enthusiasm and social cooperation they contribute" to commodity production. Secondly, as customers they may pay a "price premium" for the "fruits of their labor" as the use-value of cocreated products is often higher than those generated by standardized production systems (Cova and Dalli 2009, 327).

The added value of vernacular production is also evident in the sphere of marketing. In 2007, the corn chip manufacturer, Doritos, launched their "Smash the Superbowl" competition, inviting consumers to submit self-made advertisements for the product, the best of which would be screened during the Superbowl, the climax of the American football year and the premier television advertising slot. The winning entry was made using a standard camcorder and computer software. As one of the executives of the agency that helped launch the competition noted, "We saw how technology is helping consumers create things to the point where you don't know what's consumer-generated and what's not" (Jones 2009). At the same time, amateur productions still seem "rawer, less polished, and somehow more 'real' or true than ads prepared by a professional agency" (Keen 2008, 61). This appearance of authenticity is central to retaining the trust and loyalty of youthful consumers.

Don Tapscott and Anthony Williams, leading advocates of cocreation, argue that critics who suggest that they are promoting an economy "where unpaid volunteers are exploited by corporations" have failed to notice that "the majority of people who participate in peer production communities are profiting, sometimes monetarily and other times by using their experience to further their careers or expand their networks" (Tapscott and Williams 2008, xi). It is true that some labor is paid for, albeit almost always at a lower rate than would be paid to professionals. The T-shirt manufacturer, Threadless, for example, pays $2,000 for any design submitted to their website and chosen for production on the basis of votes from the site's members (Threadless 2010). It is also true, as we noted earlier, that a number of the most active peer producers harbor ambitions of becoming full-time cultural workers. Volunteer labor online is no different from the unpaid internships that are now a standard part of many media companies' employment practices and which recent British research condemned as "the outright exploitation of emerging workers" (Arts Group 2010, 2). In both cases, the balance of power lies overwhelmingly with the companies.

The high-end fashion shoe manufacturer John Fluevog, for example, has adapted the title of the most celebrated instance of collaborative production, the Open Source Software movement, and launched the Open Source Footwear initiative, which invites anyone to submit ideas for new lines. The terms of trade are clearly set out in the organizer's answer to the obvious question about rewards. "Will I be rich? Are you insane? Nobody gets paid for designs because nobody owns them. ... once you send us your design, it becomes public domain, freely available to all." However, since designs are submitted to the firm rather than being posted directly on a public domain site, it gets first sight of them, giving it a clear competitive advantage. As they explain: "We might use the whole thing or just part of it," and appropriate the whole of any resulting profit. The rewards to the designers are purely symbolic: "if you're chosen, we'll send you a free pair!" and "name the shoe after you" (Fluevog's Open Source Footwear 2010).

In this pastiche of reciprocity, the company gets cost-free research and development and first sight of innovative ideas, the participants get the recognition that comes from having "ideas become actual shoes," and their photo on the website (Fluevog's Open Source Footwear 2010).

Available evidence suggests that opportunities to gain even an unpaid foot in the door of professional cultural production go disproportionately to those who have high stocks of cultural and social capital. The Internet confirms this unequal access by mostly rewarding those "who are already well connected, by allowing them to network together, reinforcing their privilege" (Leadbeater 2008, 2).

The Internet does offer opportunities to equalize opportunities for creative expression and deploy expertise in the service of the public good rather than corporate interests, but realizing them requires a rethink of the moral economy of public goods. If the extension of commercial enclosure confirms Mauss's pessimistic view that gifts are always tainted by the pursuit of personal advantage, the revivification of public cultural institutions holds out the prospect of a resurgence of gifting informed by altruism.

Digitalizing the Commons

The neoliberal project of maximizing the freedom of action of commercial corporations has had two major impacts on the public cultural commons. Firstly, public assets, both material and intellectual, have been privatized and enclosed. For example, an estimated fifth of the genes identified by research, mostly funded out of the public purse, have already been patented, allowing the companies holding the rights to monopolize the market for tests for diseases generated by future discoveries, selling them back to the public at "prohibitive prices" (Sulston 2009, 38). Secondly, faced with cuts and squeezes on public subsidy, cultural institutions have been both encouraged and compelled to turn to commercial sources to make up the shortfall. It is now impossible to mount a major public art exhibition without commercial sponsorship. Leading public libraries have ceded the task of digitalizing their collection to Google because they have been unable to find the necessary funds themselves, raising major questions about future control over access. Public service broadcasters have adopted the strategies developed by multimedia conglomerates and set out to maximize the commercial value of their symbolic assets. The BBC has been particularly active. Its brand has been stretched over a portfolio of magazines linked to programs. Successful program franchises such as *Teletubbies* and *Doctor Who* provide platforms for a proliferating range of merchandise in the valuable child and teenage markets. These commercial activities are justified by the argument that the profits generated are returned to program budgets and boost "public value" rather than shareholder value. By introducing calculations around the potential for commodification into institutional strategies, however, they compromise the moral economy of public goods.

Commercial initiatives in the public cultural sector have been enthusiastically pursued by a new class of entrepreneurial managers who regard public institutions mainly as businesses whose success is measured primarily by levels of income generation. This view of public enterprise has been strongly opposed by employees in public institutions who follow Susan Hockfield, the President of the Massachusetts Institute of Technology (MIT), in seeing their work "as a public good for the benefit of all" (MIT OpenCourseWare 2010), and insisting that, since it has largely been paid for out of taxation, the public should not have to pay again to have access to it. In 2000 the faculty of MIT put this principle into practice, voting to forgo the substantial profits made from commercial distance learning and to post all their teaching materials online for anyone to access. This decision is the symbolic equivalent of voluntary blood donation in the physical realm. Both acknowledge the needs and rights of strangers and both offer central sources of the self with no expectation of tangible reward.

This movement to democratize expertise is gathering momentum across the range of public cultural institutions as digital storage and Internet delivery abolish the constraints on access imposed by fixed locations with limited space. The Art Collection held by the Arts Council of England, for example, was launched in 1946, as part of the drive to widen access to cultural resources mentioned earlier, but in 2009 only 18 percent of its total holdings were on public display. Now, in collaboration with the BBC, a free digital archive of the entire collection is being created (Doward and Flyn 2010, 18–19). The role played by the BBC is not accidental. There are a variety of reasons why public service broadcasters are best placed to operate as key nodes in a network that links public cultural institutions together and provides the essential search and navigation tools that allow users to maximize the use value of the resources available (see Murdock 2005).

If, however, the Internet is employed only as a distribution system, making the materials created or selected by professional cultural workers more readily available, it will do little or nothing to advance the essential cultural rights of representation and participation. Its radical potential lies in its ability to forge a new relationship between expertise and lay knowledge, amateur and professional creativity, grounded in the convergence of the economies of gifting and public goods.

The outlines are already discernible. Early in 2010, to celebrate the 250th anniversary of the opening of the British Museum, one of the first publicly accessible collections, the BBC launched a series recounting world history through the stories behind 100 objects selected from the museum's holdings. At the same time, it invited audience members to donate their own object to the digital archive. As the invitation to contribute stressed, the project "is all about participation ... Adding your object to the site, and telling its story, will ensure that these stories of how we and our ancestors have become part of history will be remembered" (BBC 2010). These vernacular stories of high hopes and hard times are told through mundane objects: ration books, immigration cards, a university degree certificate. This and similar initiatives and the continuing dialogues across professional and cultural boundaries they set in train, hold out the prospect of moving from a "convergence culture" in which decisions taken in company board rooms write the rules of engagement, to a genuinely common culture rooted in an ethos of citizenship and energized by grassroots participation, operating outside and counter to the commodity economy and the culture of consumerism.

This alters the role of expertise but it does not abolish it. Underpinning many celebrations of the new opportunities for participation opened up by the Internet is the figure of the "noble amateur ... a digitalized version of Rousseau's noble savage" (Keen 2008, 36). This romantic image operates as both a source of spontaneity and authenticity and a guarantor that choices are democratically arrived at. This has two consequences: it identifies value with popularity and it elevates information and experience over knowledge.

Google's advertising profits are generated by its Page Ranking system (modestly named after the company's cofounder, Larry Page), which ranks web pages by the number and density of links they attract. The sites "most frequently visited by users" are jumped "to the top of the search results" generated by user inquiries (Auletta 2010, 38). It is a measure of popularity, not of value. Expertise, grounded in mastery of bodies of knowledge and the arguments surrounding them, is an essential resource both for sifting "through what's important and what's not, what's credible from what is unreliable" (Keen 2008, 45) and for transforming information into knowledge. Information comprises discrete packages of facts, observations, and experience. User-generated information on the Internet is dominated by "random photos, private blatherings ... homemade video diaries," and personal blogs and Twitterings (quoted in Siegel 2008, 52). It is the fulfillment of Jeremy Rifkin's vision of a capitalism "whose product is access to time and mind," where every user's "life experience will be commodified" (Rifkin 2000, 29). Knowledge is an essential guarantee of autonomy, but it requires contextualization, a grasp of causes and consequences, conceptual frameworks. This is why constructing a public digital commons requires the democratization of expertise as well as the expansion of popular participation.

Arguing the case for a public cultural commons for the digital age, examining the institutional arrangements that might anchor it and the forces ranged against it, and engaging in the struggle to realize its full potential, is one of the major tasks now facing a critical political economy of culture and communications.

References

Anderson, C. (2009) *Free: The Future of a Radical Price*. Random House Business Books, London.

Arts Group (2010) *Emerging Workers: A Fair Future for Entering the Creative Industries*. The Arts Group, London.

Arvidsson, A. (2008) The ethical economy of customer coproduction. *Journal of Macromarketing*, 28(4), 326–38.

Auletta, K. (2010) *Googled: The End of the World As We Know It*. Virgin Books, London.

Bauwens, M. (2009) Class and capital in peer production. *Capital & Class*, 33, 121–41.

BBC (2010) A History of the World: Join the Project. Online at http://www.bbc.co.uk/ahistoryoftheworld/get-involved/join-the-project/ (accessed April 22, 2010).

Bilton, C. and Leary, R. (2002) What can managers do for creativity? Brokering creativity in the creative industries. *International Journal of Cultural Policy*, 8(1), 49–64.

Bonsu, S. K. and Darmody, A. (2008) Co-creating Second Life: Market consumer cooperation in contemporary economy. *Journal of Macromarketing*, 28(4), 355–68.

Bragg, M. (2010) Cultural revelation. *New Statesman*, April 26, pp. 50–1.

Brown, G. (2010) Unbridled and untrammelled, free markets become the enemy of the good society. *Saturday Guardian*, February 27, p. 2.

Carnegie UK Trust (2010) *Making Good Society: Final Report of the Commission of Inquiry into the Future of Civil Society in the UK and Ireland*. Carnegie UK Trust, London.

Convergence Culture Consortium (2009) Welcome to the MIT convergence culture consortium. Online at http://www.convergenceculture.org/ (accessed July 20, 2009).

Cova, B. and Dalli, D. (2009) Working consumers: the next step in marketing theory? *Marketing Theory*, 9(3), 315–39.

Darnton, R. (2009) Google & the future of books. *The New York Review of Books*, 56(2), February 20. Online at http://www.nybooks.com/articles/22281 (accessed September 11, 2009).

Doward, J. and Flyn, C. (2010) Online gallery will open forgotten art to the public. *The Observer*, April 18, pp 18–19.

Dubit Informer (2010) Dubit Informer-S-cool:S-zone. Online at http://www.s-cool.co.uk/s-zone/page/dubit-informer (accessed September 16, 2010).

Etgar, M. (2009) Ways of engaging consumers in co-production. *Open Source Business Resource*, December. Online at http://www.osbr.ca/ojs/index.php/osbr/article.viewArticle/1011/972 (accessed February 11, 2010).

Fluevog Open Source Footwear (2010) Online at http://www.fluevog.com/files_2/os-1.html (accessed February 1, 2010).

Frow, J. (1997) *Time and Commodity Culture: Essays in Cultural Theory and Postmodernity*. Clarendon Press, Oxford.

Fuller, J., Jawecki, G., and Muhlbacher, H. (2007) Innovation creation by online basketball communities. *Journal of Business Research*, 20, 60–71.

Godelier, M. (1999) *The Enigma of the Gift*. Polity Press, Cambridge, UK.

Graeber, D. (2010) Give it away. *Freewords*. Online at www.freewords.org/graeber.html (accessed February 11, 2010).

Green, S. (2009) Seeking salvation. *New Statesman*, July 6, 34–5.

Griffith, D. W. (1923) Are motion pictures destructive of good taste? *Arts and Decoration*, September, 12–13, 79.

Hartley, J. (2009) *The Uses of Digital Literacy*. University of Queensland Press, Brisbane.

Harvey, D. (2005) *The New Imperialism*. Oxford University Press, Oxford.

Hof, D. B. (2006) My virtual life. *Business Week,* May 1. Online at http:www.businessweek.com/magazine/content/06_18/b3982001.htm (accessed March 20, 2010).

Horkheimer, M. (1972) Art and mass culture. In: Horkheimer, M., *Critical Theory: Selected Essays*. Continuum, New York, pp. 273–90.

Hyde, L. (1979) *The Gift: How the Creative Spirit Transforms the World*. Canongate, Edinburgh.

Jenkins, H. (2001) Convergence? I diverge. *Technology Review*, June, 93.

Jenkins, H. (2006a) *Convergence Culture: Where Old and New Media Collide*. New York University Press, New York.

Jenkins, H. (2006b) On convergence culture. *bigshinything*, August 14. Online at http://www.bigshinything.com/henry-jenkins-on-convergence-culture (accessed September 16, 2009).

Jones, C. (2009) Winning Doritos ad was made for less than $2,000. *USA Today*. Online at http://www.usatoday.com/money/advertising/admeter/2009-02-02-doritos-admeter-winner_N.htm (accessed February 2, 2010).

Judt, T. (2010) What is to be done? *Guardian Saturday Review*, March 20, pp. 2–3.

Keen, A. (2008) *The Cult of the Amateur*. Nicholas Brealey Publishing, London.

Kelly, K. (2009) The new socialism. *Wired*, July, 120–5.

Lamont, T. (2010) Film. *The Observer New Review,* March 7, pp. 16–17.

Lawson, N. (2009) *All Consuming*. Penguin Books, London.

Leadbeater, C. (2008) *We-Think*. Profile Books, London.

Lessig, L. (2004) *Free Culture: How Big Media Uses Technology and the Law to Lock Down Culture and Control Creativity*. Penguin Books, New York.

Masco, J. (1995) "It is the strict law that bids us dance": Cosmologies, colonialism, death, and ritual authority in the Kwakwaka'wakw potlatch, 1849-1992. *Comparative Studies in Society and History*, 37, 41–75.

Mauss, M. (1990/1925) *The Gift: The Form and Reason for Exchange in Archaic Societies*. Routledge, London.

Mauss, M. (1992/1925) A sociological assessment of Bolshevism (1924-5). In: Gane, M. (ed.), *The Radical Sociology of Durkheim and Mauss*. Routledge, London, pp. 165–208.

Marx, K. (2008/1847) *The Poverty of Philosophy*. Cosimo Inc., New York.

Minton, A. (2009) *Ground Control: Fear and Happiness in the Twenty-First Century*. Penguin Books, London.

MIT OpenCourseWare (2010) President's message. Online at http://ocw.mit.edu/about/presidents-message/ (accessed September 17, 2010).

Murdock, G. (1999) Rights and representations: Public discourse and cultural citizenship. In: Gripsrud, J. (ed.), *Television and Common Knowledge*. Routledge, London, pp. 7–17.

Murdock, G. (2001) Against enclosure: Rethinking the cultural commons. In: Morley, D. and Robins, K. (eds), *British Cultural Studies: Geography, Nationality, and Identity*. Oxford University Press, Oxford, pp. 443–60.

Murdock, G. (2005) Building the digital commons: Public broadcasting in the age of the Internet. In: Lowe, G. F. and Jauert, P. (eds), *Cultural Dilemmas in Public Service Broadcasting*. Nordicom, Göteborg University, pp. 213–30.

Murdock, G. and Wasko, J. (2007) *Media in the Age of Marketization*. Hampton Press, Cresskill, NJ.

Postigo, H. (2007) Of mods and modders: Chasing down the value of fan-based digital game modifications. *Games and Culture*, 2(4), 300–13.

Rifkin, J. (2000) *The Age of Access: How the Shift from Ownership to Access is Transforming Modern Life*. Penguin Books, London.

Robinson, J. (2006) *Economic Philosophy*. Aldine Publishing Co., Chicago.

Rose, J. (2002) *The Intellectual Life of the British Working Class*. Yale University Press, New Haven, CN.

Saunders, B. (1997) From a colonized consciousness to autonomous identity: Shifting relations between Kwakwaka'wakw and Canadian nations. *Dialectical Anthropology*, 22, 137–58.

Schudson, M. (1984) *Advertising: The Uneasy Persuasion*. Basic Books, New York.

Second Life (2007) Create anything. Online at http://secondlife.com/whatis/create/ (accessed September 17, 2010).

Shirky, C. (2008) *Here Comes Everybody: The Power of Organizing Without Organizations*. The Penguin Press, New York.

Siegel, L. (2008) *Against the Machine: Being Human in the Age of the Electronic Mob*. Spiegel and Grau, New York.

Singing a different tune (2009) *The Economist*, November 14, pp. 79–80.

Smith, A. (1969/1759) *The Theory of Moral Sentiments*. Arlington House, New York.

Smith, A. (1999/1776) *The Wealth of Nations, Books IV-V*. Penguin Books, London.

Smythe, D. (1981) *Dependency Road: Communications, Capitalism, Consciousness and Canada*. Ablex, Norwood, NJ.

Sulston, J. (2009) Science in shackles. *The Guardian*, November 26, p. 38.

Tapscott, D. and Williams, A. D. (2008) *Wikinomics: How Mass Collaboration Changes Everything*. Atlantic Books, London.

Thomas, N. (1991) *Entangled Objects: Exchange, Material Culture and Colonialism in the Pacific*. Harvard University Press, Cambridge, MA.

Titmuss, R. (1950) *Problems of Social Policy*. HMSO, London.

Titmuss, R. (1970) *The Gift Relationship: From Human Blood to Social Policy*. Allen and Unwin, London.

Threadless (2010) Submit. Online at http://www.threadless.com/submit (accessed April 21, 2010).

Toffler, A. (1980) *The Third Wave*. Pan Books, London.

Topping, A. (2009) Net-savvy bands reshaping music business, say experts. *The Guardian*, May 19, p. 13.

Williams, R. (1989) Communications and community. In: Williams, R., *Resources of Hope: Culture, Democracy, Socialism*. Verso, London, pp. 19–31.

Wittel, A. (2001) Toward a network sociality. *Theory, Culture and Society*, 18(6), 51–76.

2

The Political Economy of Communication Revisited

Nicholas Garnham

It is now 40 years since I started work in the broad field of research and policy debate and advocacy to which the name "political economy of communication" or "of the media" has been applied. I personally am unhappy with this title because it indicates a narrowing of the field's focus upon either channels and processes of communication modeled on those of interpersonal communication, or upon the mass media, especially the press and broadcasting, in ways which block understanding of many of the crucial relationships and dynamics involved. I prefer to think of this research tradition as a historical materialist analysis of the cultural sphere – the production, circulation, and consumption of symbolic forms in all their variety – of which the study of communication channels and processes and of the mass media are subfields. This research tradition I will call "the political economy of culture" (PEC).

However, for reasons I hope the following analysis will make clear, this title is also now misleading. It has tended to focus analysis only on culture as goods and services consumed by people in their leisure time and paid for out of disposable household income. There is still a lingering tendency to see culture in this sense as separate from the rest of the economy rather than as a special case within a wider set of developments and problems. This has led to a disabling neglect of the dynamic effects of the immaterial producer goods and services market and of the wider analysis of immaterial labor and the immaterial commodity which are better captured by the terms information, information economy, and information society. In short, I am arguing here that, despite all the problems with the term "information," we now need to think of the field as the "political economy of information." As I hope to demonstrate in what follows, one of the major problems with work in the field of the political economy of communication is that

The Handbook of Political Economy of Communications, First Edition.
Edited by Janet Wasko, Graham Murdock, and Helena Sousa.
© 2014 John Wiley & Sons, Ltd. Published 2014 by John Wiley & Sons, Ltd.

it has remained stuck with a set of problems and terms of analysis that history has simply passed by.

My motivation for revisiting the PEC tradition at this moment is a strong sense that the field has become associated, by both its practitioners and defenders and by its critics, with a tired and narrow orthodoxy. The term "political economy" (PE) has become a euphemism for a vague, crude, and unself-questioning form of Marxism, linked to a gestural and self-satisfied, if often paranoid, radicalism. The story it tells has become drearily familiar. The capitalist mass media are increasingly concentrated on a global scale under the control of corporations and media moguls leading to a decline in cultural diversity, the suppression of progressive political views, and the destruction of local cultures. The proposed cure for this situation is some form of regulation and/or state-supported public service media and cultural production sometimes linked to appeals to grass roots activism and "democratization." In my judgment, this general position is both empirically questionable and theoretically and politically dubious. It will be my purpose in the remainder of this chapter to explain why I think this is the case and why I think it does a disservice to the tradition it claims to represent.

In so doing, I will briefly outline the history of the development of the PEC. What research and policy questions did it pose? What problems were revealed in the attempts to answer those questions? And importantly, therefore, what did it learn? The major problem with much current work in PEC is that, like the Bourbons, it has forgotten nothing and learnt nothing. It is important in my view to stress that PE is an open field of inquiry. Its theoretical presuppositions must be open to change in the face of empirical evidence – its assessment of research and policy priorities and its explanations changing as the world around it changes. Much current work in PEC is locked in the position with which the tradition started in the late 1960s, as though since then neither the material and social world nor the analytical tools of PE had changed. In particular, much current PE is underpinned by a crude and unexamined romantic Marxist rejection of the market per se, which has blocked analysis of how actual markets work and with what effects. This has meant that, like its supposed opponents in cultural studies, it has not taken the economics in PE with the seriousness it deserves and requires.

The tradition of PE derived from the work of Adam Smith was what we would now think of as a historical sociology, an attempt to understand the structure and dynamics of a new social form – what has come to be known more generally as modernity. Central to that form was the development of greater scale and internal specialization of function requiring ever more complex and mediated networks of social co-ordination and control linking anonymous others. Chief among these networks were expanded monetary-based markets within the sphere of material production, what became known as the capitalist mode of production. Within this general development, the very concepts of art and culture in their modern senses came into existence. It is important to stress that for Smith and other political economists, including Marx, the capitalist form of modernity was an open-ended historical process. Its success was by no means guaranteed. In particular, political struggles between major interest groups or classes over the distribution of the surplus were endemic. The capitalist mode of production was thus not seen as automatically equilibrating. Thus the great split between even liberal political economists and the neoclassicists was not over the market per se, but between a static equilibrium account and a dynamic disequilibrating account of how markets worked. It was in this important sense that political economics was political. For Smith markets were specific social institutions that required a supporting framework of laws, institutions, and cultural practices that were always objects of political struggle, not just between capital and labor, but between capitals, in Smith's time in particular between the owners of land and of industrial and mercantile capitalists.

Thus from its origins PE has been closely related to policy debate. This close relationship has two results. First, PE tends to shift both its focus of concern and its theoretical approach in response to general shifts within economy and society and the problems for all participants that these shifts highlight. Second, it is influenced by the specific policy problems exercising governing institutions and by the strategic problems facing corporate management at different times. But this does not, as some would claim, make these responses mere ideology. Of course, different PE analyses will be taken up and propagated by interested parties, usually in highly simplified versions, within public debate and political negotiation in an effort to advocate and propagate their position in what they see as their own interest. But to see this as mere ideology is to assume that the various interest groups either know what is happening or have a very clear idea as to what their interest might be. As the current conjunctural crisis eloquently demonstrates, this is clearly in most cases far from the truth.

So PE is not a functionalism. From the start, this raised the problem of legitimation – the response to the Hobbesian political challenge of modernity. It should be remembered that for Smith, markets were institutions which disciplined socially destructive, private, and predatory acquisitive instincts for the general public good by making the interactions public and transparent. Thus for Smith, markets were not an example of the private winning out over the public, but on the contrary of the public and the public interest winning out over all forms of private, secretive, and therefore inherently corrupt forms of power, including economic power. It was here that the development of a diverse and specialized cultural sphere became a problem. The rise of a critical intelligentsia, the spread of secularism, the growth of literacy and a reading public, and the associated circulation of printed material represented, in the eyes of the established ruling elite, subversion and potential anarchy. Important for my subsequent argument is the fact that this produced a reaction, on what became known as both the right and left of the political and intellectual spectrum, that shared a remarkably similar romantic rejection of modernity, of the market and of the products of an increasingly commercialized cultural sphere in the name of a supposedly "purer" ideal of community and human essence.

The Development of the Political Economy of Culture

The research school that I am calling the political economy of culture initially developed as a return to this old set of questions and problems. But it did so in a specific context that marks it to this day. In the 1960s in the developed capitalist democracies, the long postwar economic boom came to an end. As rates of productivity growth and market expansion slowed, the compact between organized labor and capital that had produced in the US and Western Europe the broad political consensus dubbed "the end of ideology," came under increasing strain. Labor militancy rose, and within Europe, within the context of the social democratic welfare state, there were growing tensions between the aspirations fueled by the long boom and tightening public budgets. These broad social struggles were then further fueled by the rise, in the context of a more heated Cold War, of the antinuclear and anti-imperialist movements. Indeed, it is no accident that early US work in PEC by Herbert Schiller, Dallas Smythe, and Thomas Guback focused on US imperialism and the broad struggle over the free flow of information in and around UNESCO, echoes of which now reverberate within the debates and struggles around globalization.

In Europe, against the background of a general revival of western Marxism, scholars studying the media and culture returned to the central questions of political economy. In particular, this was a reaction against (1) a sociology of communication focused on "effects," (2) a liberal/pluralist political science based upon the interplay of political positions within a free press model, and (3) a mass culture tradition within which the industrialization and mass circulation of cultural products was seen by conservatives as a destructive process of vulgarization and by supposed progressives as an ideological process of circuses and opiates.

Ownership, control, regulation, and ideology in the mass media

Early work in PEC developed as a critique of the liberal free press position and against a background of dominant ideology theory. It focused on the press and broadcasting and analyzed the vertical and horizontal processes of integration and the resulting concentrations of corporate ownership, both within the media sector, between media and other industrial and commercial sectors, and both nationally and transnationally. It analyzed the competition and shifting boundaries between the commercial and public sectors – particularly in broadcasting – and the role of regulation in this process. The underlying assumption was that capitalist corporate control contributed to a dominant ideology. It led, in particular via advertising, to the production of broadly capitalist-friendly content and to a more general reduction in cultural and informational diversity, which broadly under-pinned the political status quo.

The problems with this general analysis were various. First, it soon became apparent that the relatively stable reproduction of capitalism did not require a dominant ideology; that while life within a capitalist society, as with modernity more generally, might favor certain common patterns of social behavior and related structures of feeling and thought, the capitalist economic system was com-patible with a wide range of political and social systems. Second, there was little evidence that the controllers of the capitalist economy and their supposed political representatives themselves shared a common ideological position. Third, even in noncultural sectors the notion of control in the sense of being able to produce planned outcomes through the employment of subordinate economic agents was very tenuous. Fourth, in the cultural sector itself, while one could turn up occa-sional cases where advertisers censored copy or where proprietors placed stories in their own economic or political interest, there was no evidence that this was sys-temic. Rather to the contrary, the problem seemed to be the exact inverse. In fact, increasingly the owners of cultural enterprises would produce anything that could be sold at a profit – the problem was to find out what those were. It became increas-ingly clear that a more likely thesis was that the industrialization of cultural pro-duction and circulation had produced just that breakdown of ideological control that the original feudal and religious opponents of modernity and capitalism feared. The concentration/loss of diversity thesis also in my judgment failed to recognize one of the defining features of modern mass media and a central feature of Marx's mature analysis of capitalism. The development of modern mass media, their wide distribution and the resulting relative democratization of cultural con-sumption, linked as they were to the spread of literacy and schooling, were the result of the exploitation of economies of scale and associated low prices, which were themselves inevitably linked to market concentration. However, as capitalist economies have grown, the associated lowering of the costs of material goods linked to the release of higher proportions of household expenditure for the satis-faction of immaterial wants, including cultural products and services, and the expansion of the commercial cultural sector to meet the resulting demand, has clearly widened cultural diversity on both a national and international scale, even if it continues to be unevenly spread.

Thus the theses of Schiller and Guback, focused on the free flow of informa-tion, and on the film and advertising industries in particular, as the tools of a "soft" US imperialism, have turned out to be largely unfounded and based too narrowly on a temporary historical moment within a longer development. So far as film is concerned, while it is true, to take the case of Europe, that in spite of EU and especially French state intervention, US films retain a dominant share of European box office, this has been accompanied by the development of TV with a reduced share of US-originated programming and by the development of a global film market in which the US industry is increasingly dependent on non-US sales. Thus the thesis central to the original argument against free flow and US cultural imperialism, that it can dominate those markets on the basis of a dumping strategy founded upon control of its large domestic market, no longer holds. At the same time, indigenous centers of competitive media production have arisen. The evidence is that as countries get richer they want and can afford to support more indigenous national or regional production and that while global diversity overall may decline, at the same time, owing to the operations of economies of scale and scope, national diversity may rise. I should make it clear that at one time, I too supported and propagated this thesis of general ownership concentration, control, suppression of diversity, and dominant ideology. But as Keynes responded to a critic "If the facts change I change my mind. What do you do?" Thus in my view the evidence supports not a dominant ideology/US cultural imperialism thesis, but rather Marx's thesis as to the dialectical nature of capitalist development – it produces the very culturally enriched and educated workers and citizens necessary for its own supersession.

The political economy of culture and regulation

The second major weakness of the thesis was its treatment of regulation and the relation of the public and private sectors. Within the dominant ideology thesis, there was a general assumption that the public sector represented a barrier or bulwark – depending on your point of view – against the spread of profit-based competition and so-called commercialization. It was argued that capitalist societies produced, and could only tolerate, regulation that furthered and supported corporate interests. Thus the political economists drew up their battle lines to defend the public sector, especially public service broadcasting, against the assaults of the new barbarians represented by the so-called "neoliberal" deregulators. This resulted in an extreme simplification of the debate, the neglect of a proper analysis of both the operation of the public sector and of regulatory regimes. This involved in its turn a neglect of the diverse and conflicting interests of different corporate actors and sectors vis-à-vis regulation, and to the rich analytical tradition on the political economy of regulation from a variety of perspectives and thus to a neglect of the specific and different regulatory problems of different market sectors. All these lacunae effectively disarmed many of the defenders of public interest regulation and public service, as it now does many antiglobalization activists, reducing them to a mere knee-jerk opposition that is both theoretically and politically weak.

The Culture Industries, Cultural Labor, and the Cultural Commodity

The inadequacies of the simple ownership and control thesis were made more apparent by the PE analysis of cultural production in general. This development in PEC was part of the wider cultural turn in sociology and a response to what was seen as the idealist elitism of the mass culture critics. The culturalists quite rightly argued that the focus on the press and broadcasting and on more overt forms of political information, debate, and ideology neglected the greater portion of people's cultural consumption – music, films, and entertainment generally in print, audio, and audiovisual forms – and thus the role those cultural forms might play within hegemony. Those within PE who turned to the analysis of the industrialization of culture in this sense in general took as their starting point a return to the Frankfurt School thesis of the "Culture Industry." The broad Culture Industry thesis will be familiar. The potentially oppositional and utopian function of art was being destroyed by an industrialization of culture that involved, on the side of production, the destruction of artistic autonomy as artists became industrialized cultural wage labor, and on the side of consumption, the narrowing of interpretative possibilities, whereby as a result of planned marketing, cultural products became advertisements for themselves. This led, it was argued, despite apparent cultural diversity and freedom of choice, to a homogenization of cultural products. The Culture Industry was likened to the US motor car industry where repeat consumption of an essentially unchanging basic product was assured by the built-in obsolescence of ever-changing superficial features. The problem with this thesis rapidly became apparent.

Cultural labor

First, as the pioneering work of Miège and Flichy showed (Flichy 1978, Miège 1989), culture industries demonstrated very different levels of industrialization and wage labor. Essentially it was confined to what they called flow industries – the press and broadcasting – which required constant, rapidly repeated, and thus carefully planned and co-ordinated cycles of production. The majority of cultural workers, even in the flow industries, certainly the key producers of cultural content, operated in a craft, contractual mode. Importantly, unlike the wage labor in material production, their remuneration could not be tied to a relationship between measurable labor input and output. Thus the related concepts of productivity and efficiency, so central to the political economy of capitalism, could not be applied. Given the inherently uncertain relationship between labor inputs and outputs, there was what economists have variously called a principal/agent or labor discipline problem. While capitalist owners and managers might want to control production, they had few tools for so doing. In particular, this has meant that one of the major means of increasing labor productivity and disciplining labor, a process central to industrial capitalism, the substitution of capital for labor through mechanization (a process captured in the classic debate over deskilling that deeply influenced radical political economy in the 1970s) was unavailable. The unveiling of these problems within cultural labor led in two directions which have taken on ever greater salience as PEC has turned to the analysis of the wider so-called information economy/information society. First, it led to the discovery of Baumol's Disease (Baumol and Bowen 1976). Baumol argued that the impossibility of labor productivity growth in cultural production meant the inevitable increase in the relative costs of cultural production and thus a rise in the relative price of cultural products and service. This, through a relative price effect, would produce either a rise in the proportion of consumer expenditure on cultural consumption or a decline in cultural consumption. Importantly, this led Baumol himself to defend an increase in public subsidies to cultural production. Second, it led to a stress on the use of technology in distribution to obtain, through market expansion, the economies of scale and scope unattainable in production per se. This then led into the political economic debate over the impact of technological change, first on the cultural sector and then, as the wider information sector expanded, on the economy as a whole. These insights gained from the analysis of cultural labor were then reinforced by insights gained from an analysis of the cultural commodity and cultural demand.

Culture and commoditization

The second major problem with the Culture Industry thesis was an assumption concerning a general process of commodification. For the Marxist tradition, an alternative to the dominant ideology thesis had long been commodity fetishism. The argument was that central to capitalist development and domination was a process of ever-widening commodity exchange, whereby human social relations were increasingly mediated by the exchange of commodities on monetized markets, and that this disguised from the participants the power relationships involved. In particular, commodities were fetishes because, although created by humans for their own use, they came to rule over them as an apparently autonomous force – a process also referred to as alienation. Now I would want to reject on sociological and philosophical grounds this whole theory of alienation that has been so influential upon Marxist and other "radical" traditions of opposition to capitalism and modernity. Any historical materialism worthy of the name has to accept, it seems to me, the mediated and therefore alienated nature of all human relations both with their material environment and with other human beings. This alienation long predates capitalism and modernity. Indeed it is, I would argue, an aspect of our species-being. We are all now, and must be in effect, symbolic interactionists. There is no "true" humanity or human essence to which we can return if only the system can be removed. The question, therefore, is to study as clear-sightedly as possible the actual structures and practices of mediated social interaction and their dynamics of development. But for the purpose of my argument here, I will now focus solely on the economic process of commodification.

The Cultural Commodity and Cultural Demand

It was soon found in studying the culture industries that far from the process of commodification remorselessly expanding in the cultural sector, it was highly problematic. Capital in the culture industries faced real and fundamental problems of realization and reproduction. The history of the culture industries' development, up to and including the present, can in large part be read in terms of the varying strategies adopted by corporate managers and investors to deal with this problem. In analyzing culture industry development from this perspective, political economy has needed to draw on industrial and business economics. Rather than attempting to deploy a very generalized theory of industrialization and commodification, it has needed to look at both specific markets and specific industry structures and dynamics as highly differentiated.

Reproduction and distribution

Study of the culture industries soon showed that not only did cultural labor not follow the classic capitalist development path to wage labor under a regime of machinofacture, but the cultural products and services could not be either easily or fully commoditized. Indeed, broadly liberal political economic concepts of public goods and market failure provided a better understanding of the economics of cultural production and consumption, and of the resulting and unavoidable need for forms of regulation, than Marxist commodification theory. The analysis of this problem is by now well known. Because the value of cultural products and services is largely immaterial, they are not worn out by use. There is thus no scarcity and no inherent incentive to repeat purchase; in information and culture, economic reproduction and growth depends on the constant production of novelty. Thus what in a normal industry is referred to as production is, in the cultural sector, closer to R and D. It is therefore better understood from the perspective of the political economy of innovation than from a classic industrial development model. This means that culture industries are systems not of production but of reproduction. Once the prototype has been produced, the marginal cost of extra copies is close to zero. When allied to the nature of cultural labor, this means that productivity gains found in economies of scale can only be found in distribution. Hence, the centrality of distribution networks, and of the technologies upon which they are based, to the political economy of culture.

Cultural demand

Linked to the above characteristics of cultural goods and services are problems on the demand side. Because there is no inherent scarcity, and because faced with new products consumers cannot judge in advance the value of what they will receive, there is a great resistance to paying for cultural commodities. This is reinforced by their public good characteristics – the marginal cost of serving extra consumers is zero, one person's consumption does not detract from anyone else's consumption, and in some cases the costs of preventing freeloading are high compared with the potential returns from any single user. While highlighted by the development of the web, this problem of freeloading has always been endemic to cultural and information markets. Thus there is a constant problem of realization, partially solved historically by various forms of indirect payment – advertising, subscription, and public subsidy. At the same time, contrary to the Frankfurt School assumption of the planned control and manipulation of consumer taste, the nature of demand is very uncertain. There is a famous maxim in the industry about market demand: "Nobody knows." Thus there is no alternative to a scattergun approach and survival depends upon economies of scope, the spreading of risk across a range of products, to ensure the 10 percent or so chance of the hit that will provide a viable average return. Sustainably viable industries are impossible without the level of concentration that enables these economies of scope. At the same time, this economic model positively requires diversity. Indeed, for this reason there is a constant tendency to overproduction. See, for example, the ever-increasing number of book titles published every year. Indeed, the capitalist cultural sector is characterized by overproduction and underconsumption – not a good basis for either stability or growth.

The problem for the political economy of culture was that any public sector – for instance, public sector broadcasting – is faced by the same problem. The uncertainty and unknowability of demand leads too easily either to producer capture and justifiable charges of elitism, inefficiency, and featherbedding, or to charges of "dumbing down" and doing what the commercial sector can and does do perfectly well. While it may in certain contexts be the case that a secure stream of public subsidy enables a higher degree of inherently risky creative innovation, it is by no means, as history shows, necessarily the case. It is also the case that the instability of culture industry business models has meant and continues to mean that there is no simple dichotomy between regulated public interest cultural institutions, on the one hand, and an unregulated private commercial sector, on the other. Corporate interests in the cultural sector have long sought various forms of regulatory support, the most obvious at the present moment being in the field of intellectual property.

Cultural consumption time

Finally, it was realized that the differential distribution of cultural consumption was determined both by available disposable income and by available consumption time. This very importantly leads to an analysis of the link between the size and growth of the cultural sector and the ways in which socioeconomic changes differentially effect the availability of consumption time. The growth of the cultural sector has been associated historically with a long-term decline in working hours. For reasons that are not entirely clear, this process appears recently to have gone into reverse, a reverse associated both with the absorption of women into the paid labor force and by the decline in productivity growth linked to the expansion of information labor.

From the Political Economy of Culture to the Political Economy of Information

The political economy of culture now reached a crucial turning point. Up to this point, PEC had focused on the effects of the capitalist mode of production of culture on patterns of cultural consumption, on the nature and quality of the cultural goods and services produced, and on their possible ideological effect. The focus now shifted to the relationship between the cultural sector, thus narrowly defined, and the wider economy. The cultural industries supplying final cultural demand were now seen as a subsector of a much larger information sector supplying a range of informational goods and services, a sector whose structure and dynamics was largely shaped and driven from within production in general. The problem of immaterial labor and the immaterial commodity were seen as increasingly central across the capitalist mode of production in general.

This shift in focus also involved a crucial shift in perspective. A major weakness of PEC had been, drawing on a partial reading of its Marxist heritage, a one-sided focus on the distributional conflict between labor and capital as mediated through consumer markets and the state. This neglected competitive conflicts between capitals, which in its turn led to a tendency to regard the system of production as a black box, the only barrier to the relatively smooth reproduction and expansion of which was labor and state intervention on its behalf. This had important analytical consequences. First, by focusing on the distributional effects of capitalism it neglected its productivity/efficiency-enhancing effects. This is important for any PEC because it remains the case that it is the huge, and to date self-sustaining, process of material productivity growth that has produced the time and resources necessary for the vastly expanded production and consumption of culture we associate historically with capitalist modernity. Second, by working within a simple market–nonmarket dichotomy it was ill-equipped to analyze the complex ways in which different market structures, systems of regulation, and institutional structures worked together in responding to the unavoidable problems posed by co-ordination.

With this general shift in focus and perspective, PEC merged with other streams of political economy studying capitalist development and policy debates within what has become known as the information economy/information society perspective. The terms information, information economy, and information society are certainly as unsatisfactory as the terms culture, communication, or media. I use them here as a convenient shorthand description of this important and, in my judgment, necessary shift in perspective. Recognizing the need for and importance of this shift does not, however, involve accepting any of the specific analyses that have come under the heading of the political economy of the information society (PEIS), far less the correctness of any policies based upon them.

This shift involved three major changes in focus. First, the increasing recognition of the modern mode of cultural production as a technology-based system of reproduction and distribution based on specific economies of scale and scope led to a focus on technological development and, in particular, on the economics and regulation of networks. Second, the recognition of the specificities of immaterial, cultural labor led to the wider study of what became known as information or knowledge workers and the more general problem of productivity within the growing service sector. Third, the recognition of the specificities and instabilities in the markets for symbolic goods and services led into the wider political economy of information. The effect of all three developments was to decisively shift the focus from the study of culture as final demand toward the study of information goods, services, and communication networks as primarily producer goods and services, the development of which was driven not by the cultural demands of households, but by dynamics within production in general.

The Political Economy of the Information Society (PEIS)

The PEIS is a complex field which I have analyzed elsewhere in greater depth than I have space for here (Garnham 2005b). But I think one can identify two major axes around which PEC merged with PEIS. The first concerned technology – an analysis of the development of information and communication technologies (ICTs) and their impact. The second concerned information – an analysis of the general growth of information production and distribution in its various forms across the economy as a whole, and its implications.

ICTs

It is clear that the major meeting point between PEC and PEIS was around ICTs and their regulation. As a result of the analysis outlined above, PEC had been forced to recognize that the culture industries were the way they were because they had developed historically as different ways of harnessing technologies of reproduction, and above all, distribution. The central debate over private commercial versus public service broadcasting was in essence a debate over regulation and the public powers derived from the control and allocation of the radio spectrum. The main drive behind the growth of and economic interest in ICTs stemmed from the needs of production in general. The cultural industries became involved via the development and regulation of telecommunication networks in the 1980s.

Telecommunications, networks, and their regulation

Within the broad privatization and deregulatory current that characterized the 1980s, the center of focus was telecommunications, their ownership and regulation. It is in my view too simple to characterize this as a general neoliberal, market fundamentalist thrust. Opposing it in the name of an antimarket fundamentalism was and is disabling, because it involved a lack of serious attention to the relevant political economy. Political economy, even in its liberal guises, has recognized since Adam Smith, the special case of communication networks. As public goods with natural monopoly characteristics, they require, and have always required, either direct state provision or close state regulation. It is important to stress here that the primary regulatory argument is not about ordinary consumer access, but about ways in which controllers of such networks can extract rents from their monopoly control from other sectors of production and distribution. This is why the debate about universal service and its successor debate about the so-called digital divide are largely beside the point. Telecommunication networks and services were developed for and largely funded by business use, itself the result of the spatial expansion of markets and the increased scale and complexity of industrial production and supply chains, and the problems of co-ordination that resulted. Domestic use expanded because economies of scale in switched network provision meant that it could be cross-subsidized from business use. Until the 1970s, it was in the mutual interest of all parties – network owners, business and household consumers – to keep this system in place. But, as Eli Noam has argued (Noam 1994), this coalition broke down under two pressures. On the one hand, as productivity growth faltered and the information overhead rose as a proportion of corporate costs, the corporate sector sought cost reductions. On the other hand, in response, the major ICT firms, such as IBM, had both the technical capability and the incentive to serve this market by providing their own information and value-added services over telecommunication networks. The resulting economic and regulatory playing field became ever more complex. The interplay between technological development, intercorporate and intersectoral competition, and different public interests is one of a constantly shifting dynamic within which there can never be, in my judgment, more than a temporarily sustainable compromise. There is certainly not a simple dichotomy between corporate interest and public interest. There may at any one time be a range of possible cost–benefit trade-offs and politically defensible regulatory compromises.

Telecommunications and the Culture Industries

From this perspective, I would like to illustrate how development dynamics originating in production in general were mediated, via telecommunication network developments, into the cultural sector and how this in turn reflects upon earlier debates within the political economy of culture and current debates over the information society and the so-called creative industries. I would stress that I propose this as only one possible, partial, and historically conjunctural explanation.

The dynamics leading to the growth of the information and communication overhead in production in general and the productivity/efficiency problems it raised for corporate management produced ever greater switched network capacity, ever more competition between providers of such capacity, and ever more sophisticated and low-cost peripherals with which to use that capacity. This growth was primarily directed at business users. This had two consequences.

Driven by regulatory induced competition and technological uncertainty, network operators, both incumbents and new entrants, overbuilt networks and so went in search of the increased traffic necessary to cover their high and growing fixed investment costs. At the same time, as pure carriage became commoditized and its price driven down by both competition and tariff regulation, the operators of networks wished to move up the value chain and capture a proportion of enhanced revenues accruing to value-added services – thus, for instance, the continual search for a viable video-on-demand service (video is a great consumer of bandwidth). On the other side, the media industry bought into the convergence argument, that digitalization enabled the exploitation of a range of content across competing delivery platforms and that to ensure economies of scale and scope, it was necessary to be present on all platforms. The death of Vivendi/Universal and the decay of AOL/Time Warner serve as only the most obvious signs of the fallacies of this strategy. It is this double dynamic that explains the continuous and tense regulatory battle over the price and conditions for network access and the relationship between network control and ownership, on the one hand, and the market for information services, on the other.

This general development made large extra distribution capacity available to existing cultural industry firms as well as providing space for new entrants. It did not, however, provide significant new revenue to fund content, and so the increased competition has not been for an expanded market. At the same time, the inherent leakiness of this new capacity, especially the Internet, has undermined the business models of existing firms and sectors, both by making copyright avoidance easy and by shifting the advertising revenue base from established media, especially newspapers, to the Internet and especially Google. Thus this whole process does indeed have cultural effects, but they are not in any sense planned or controlled and they cannot be understood from within an analysis confined to the cultural industry sector in a narrow sense. In addition, it does not show the evidence of dynamic market growth in the cultural sector that lies behind the claims now made for the creative industries as the new focus of economic development policies.

Information Economics

I have argued that the dynamics of network growth were driven by the expansion of information production and use within business in general. Thus the primary political economic question was what was the reason for this growth and what were its economic implications.

A major strand of information society (IS) thinking about this problem has been information economics and the analysis of the firm that has stemmed from it. Starting with the work of Arrow (1979) and Machlup (1980–4), this school began by arguing against the neoclassical market model, which assumed market actors were rational and that the knowledge upon which such rationality was necessarily based, was costless. Arrow argued on the contrary that market interactions were characterized by information asymmetry because information was not a free good, but, quite the reverse: information searching cost both time and money. This had two important consequences. First, that markets were games in which the cost of investment in information search had to be taken into account, and second, that market actors could skew the market in their favor through higher investments in, or more efficient searching for, information and its transformation into useful knowledge. It is, of course, also the case that such competitive information management may involve the withholding of information. A competitive process then led to both higher investments in information-related activities, including marketing and advertising, and thus to a rise in those employed in these activities, now called information labor or knowledge workers. But note that these are essentially overhead costs.

When applied to dynamic as opposed to static market interactions, this analysis also linked up with a more general analysis of uncertainty in economic decision making. Because economic decisions under dynamic conditions are necessarily time-dependent, it had long been argued by political economists, including importantly Keynes, that economic actions must necessarily be irrational in the sense that the outcomes could never be fully known and all economic decisions involved risk based upon calculations of probability of outcomes in interactions best understood as a game. It also, and this is important for the regulatory theory that has accompanied IS thinking, undercuts all theories of efficient markets and rational choice, as well as the basic premise of most policy that we can match planned interventions to future outcomes.

Theories of the firm

This school of information economics was then linked to theories of the firm. This is important because much of IS thinking focuses on changes in corporate structure and performance and is propagated by management consultants and gurus. We see this both in Castells' (1996) stress on the network firm and on a more general management discourse of corporate re-engineering, knowledge management, and so forth. Coase (1952) famously argued that the reason the firm existed was as a haven from market forces. It was because there were always costs (what became known as transaction costs – e.g., the cost of lawyers to draw up contracts) and risks involved in market transactions, that it was more efficient for firms to be set up as a series of bureaucratic relations between the necessary inputs to a production process. This was particularly true when the exchange involved factors the quality of which it was inherently difficult to assess and to price, for instance, white-collar labor time. Thus for Coase, the firm in general, and the large modern industrial corporation in particular, was explained not primarily, as by Chandler (1977), in terms of efficiencies in the search for economies of scale, but in terms of savings in transaction costs. The result for Coase was that the firm as an economic institution was not explained by the superior efficiency of market outcomes but precisely its opposite. While investment in directly productive labor and plant, because there was a relationship between directly measurable inputs and outputs, was subject to the least cost disciplines of the market, the transaction costs school argued that not only the absolute proportion but also the relative cost of the corporate bureaucracy – broadly, white-collar employment – rose, and that this overhead cost was increasing the inefficiency of large corporations. This was a version of the general low service productivity problem which we have already seen in the cultural sector as Baumol's Disease and a response, within the then contemporary environment of new managerialist thinking, to the crisis of profitability in the US economy. This then led in its turn to a detailed analysis of these growing corporate bureaucracies – now retitled information workers – with a view to seeing which information labor could be made subject to market disciplines by "outsourcing," or replaced by ICTs. The classic marker of this moment in PEIS is Porat's (1977) *The Information Economy*.

Digitalization and the "frictionless" economy

It is here we find the roots of that version of IS thinking that went by the name of the "New Economy" and that focused on information and information work within the corporate sector and on the possible efficiency benefits to be gained from investment in ICTs. In particular, the vision that placed the Internet and e-business at its center argued that the main impact of what was referred to as digitalization came from what they called disintermediation and thus the stripping out of transactions and transaction costs both in the supply chain through e-business and in distribution through e-commerce. Here the empirical test of the IS vision is the extent to which disintermediation has in fact taken place: the returns both financial and in terms of enhanced productivity from ICT investment, corporate re-engineering, knowledge management, and all the other fads associated with this approach. I think it fair to say that current research would confirm that, in spite of huge investments in ICTs, the information overhead cost in both the private corporate and public sectors has continued its remorseless rise. So far as the cultural sector is concerned, the issue is whether web-based distribution and transaction systems have or have not radically shifted the relationship between symbol production and consumption and thus the basic economics of the industry. In particular, has it broken the power of the distribution-based conglomerates? The music industry is clearly at present the focus of this debate, but it is rapidly spreading across the traditional media. I think at present we must be honest and say that, while it is clear that the old structure is undergoing dynamic restructuring, we do not know what the outcome of this process will be.

Technologies of Freedom and the "Third Wave"

A central component of the information society vision is that the economic, social, and cultural developments that go to make up the transition to an information society are technologically determined by the rapid development and widespread adoption of ICTs. Within the Schumpeterian long wave school, the developments described as the information society are seen as the next long wave of capitalist growth based on a new technosocial paradigm founded on ICTs. Within this general argument, ICT developments have little if anything to do with the cultural sector. They are rather the deployment of microprocessors and digital networks to produce a new generation of products and services and a new generation of process innovations in the production and delivery of other goods and services. The main beneficiaries of this new wave of growth have in fact been the ICT-producing sector itself, the financial service sector, and the telecommunications industry. There is, however, a version of this technologically determinist argument that places the media and communication sector center stage.

This school argued that the mass culture that accompanied Fordism, and the rising relative real prices of cultural goods and services identified by Baumol, were due to the high costs of both production and distribution, both of which the ICT revolution would radically reduce. According to this argument, the domination of cultural sectors by large oligopolistic organizations, whether in the private or public sector, was due to the high, capital-intensive costs of production and the scarcity, and therefore high cost, of distribution channels. It was then argued that new cheap recording and editing technologies in print, audio, and audiovisual media, and cheap and abundant multifunctional digital network capacity via cables, satellites, and later fiber optics and wireless, was radically altering what economists call the production function in the cultural sector, undermining the oligopolies and their high cost structures, and thus at the same time the arguments for regulating them. ICTs were ushering in, it was argued, an era of cultural abundance and choice in which the original creator rather than the mediating middle men would be king. It is this version of postindustrialism, dubbed the Third Wave by Alvin Toffler (1981), that underpins the revolutionary hopes still held out for the Internet and the incantatory reference to the digital in much cultural discourse.

The result of this vision was to turn cultural policy into industrial policy, based on the renaming of culture industries as creative industries (Howkins 2001; Garnham 2005a; Department for Media, Culture and Sport 2008, 2009). The culture and communications sector was now seen as the new leading growth sector of the economy, driven – as historically such growth sectors have been – by radical improvements in function and reductions in costs. The problem, however, was that while distribution costs had in fact been radically reduced, the costs of producing the cultural goods and services carried over these new high capacity networks had not. This then led to the argument, which is a central component of creative industry thinking in the UK and other EU countries, that "Content is King," that the economic growth problem was not technological innovation, but shortage of product to fill the networks and meet what was assumed to be an unsatisfied demand. In this vision, it is cultural innovation that is the key, and "creative" workers narrowly defined (those in the arts and media) who are the key information workers. While it was network operators and equipment manufacturers who had made money in the first stage of this new growth wave, it would increasingly be content producers, it was now argued, who would reap the rewards. In terms of competition between national economies on a global market, it would be those who fostered their content-producing industries rather than those who controlled the technology who would capture market share and the resulting export earnings.

The Information/Copyright/Creative Industries as the New Growth Sector

This version of information society theory has been particularly attractive, both to those who study the culture industries and to those who work in them, for obvious reasons. In my view, this approach has tended to take the propaganda (or wish fulfillment) of the cultural sector itself at face value, and also failed to distinguish the economics of content production from the economics of distribution. There has been a seamless move from the general, postindustrial, Third Wave argument to seeing the cultural sector as the major economic beneficiary of this development. The policy imperative is well captured in the title of an OECD report, *Content as a New Growth Industry* (OECD 1998). In examining the reality of this argument, we need first to be extremely wary of the slippery term "creative" and thus the slide in the policy discourse from media or information industries to creative industries. No one, of course, can be against creativity. Its recent high valuation within information society discourse stems from (1) the high value placed upon innovation, (2) the stress in developed economies on the returns to human capital and its relation to a high skill/high value-added strategy in the face of competition from cheap labor economies, and (3) the centrality in service-dominated economies of human-to-human relations rather than human-to-machine. It has little to do with creativity in the artistic or cultural sense, although the cultural industries and some sectors of education have adopted the creative industries nomenclature in an attempt to capture the concept of creativity exclusively for themselves.

So what has been the impact of these developments on the cultural sector? In order to understand the structure and dynamics of the cultural sector in relation to the larger economic context, whether of an information economy or not, we need to make a crucial distinction that is too often ignored. The culture industries serve two distinct markets, that for intermediate goods and services, as well as that for final consumer demand or, as Marxists used to say, Dept. 1 and Dept. 2. This is important because central to classic political economy has always been the problem, in relation to the analysis of reproduction, the business cycle, and crisis, of the co-ordination between Dept. 1 and Dept. 2. It is also important because information industry growth in recent years has been largely in business services, not in final consumer demand. But it is the culture industries as suppliers of goods and services to consumers in their leisure time that has dominated attention and analysis. The problem is further complicated in the media sector by advertising. Advertising is a business service. Its cyclical growth dynamic is determined by corporate profitability and the intensity of competition between firms. But it is an essential ingredient in the financing of consumer media. Thus the cultural sector marches to two tunes which are often out of sync. The growing crisis in the traditional press and broadcasting sectors caused by the shift of advertising to the web, and in particular to Google, are just the latest manifestation of a deep-seated problem.

So far as final demand is concerned, we can observe for the US, supposedly the most advanced information society, over the last two decades, a modest growth above the growth rate of GDP. A large component of this growth has been a cyclical boom in advertising (now followed by an equally severe slump), a large fraction of which was internal to the information sector itself (financial service advertising, etc). But this growth has been largely a relative price effect since consumption itself has not risen proportionally. Indeed, it is better to understand recent developments in the culture industries as intensified competition for stagnant demand than as driven by explosive demand growth. The result of this has been the rise in the price to consumers of each unit of media consumption time, in economic theory not a good recipe for dynamic sectoral growth. Of course, the information society theorists were arguing that prices would fall because the cost of distribution was falling. This was central to the whole Third Wave deregulation argument that saw the Internet as the provider of nil cost information abundance. Unfortunately, they overlooked both the rising relative costs of production (including importantly rising marketing costs) and the demand side. In fact, rising disposable income has not been mainly channeled toward cultural demand growth. Rather it has gone to higher cost, but now affordable, ways of enhancing leisure, such as tourism, restaurants, interior decoration, fitness, and health and beauty. The big cultural sector story of the last decades has not been growth in demand, but a struggle for market share, which has taken the form of a struggle over distribution. If we look at US figures, we see that the result has been declining margins, declining rates of return on capital, and declining rates of profit, especially in the high growth sectors of cable and satellite. Beneath the froth, we see a classic over-investment boom driven by a search for market share during a period of technological uncertainty in distribution.

Conclusion

I have tried to argue that we can only understand the main drivers of cultural industry development if we look at the system of production in general against the background of the problems raised for capitalist reproduction and growth by the rise of immaterial labor and products and services. This requires us to take the problems of productivity and efficiency seriously. I have argued that concepts of ownership, control, and ideological domination are not useful in understanding the processes and stakes involved, and nor is a simple market–antimarket dichotomy. We have to accept, I think, that the processes of development of capitalist modernity are complex and their outcomes always uncertain. As the current conjuncture shows, no one is in control. It therefore befits political economists to be equally open and to accept that there is no totalizing explanation of where we have come from or where we are going. All approaches may have something to offer and all must be subject to the tests of evidence and history. Neither the questions nor the answers are eternal, but are those thrown up by an always temporary conjuncture.

References

Arrow, K. (1979) The economics of information. In: Dertouzos, M. and Moses, J. (eds), *The Computer Age: A Twenty-Year View*. MIT Press, Cambridge, MA, pp. 306–17.

Baumol, W. and Bowen, W. (1976) On the performing arts: The anatomy of their economic problems. In: Blaug, M. (ed.), *The Economics of the Arts*. Martin Robertson, London, pp. 218–26.

Castells, M. (1996) *The Rise of Network Society*. Blackwell, Oxford.

Chandler, A. (1977) *The Visible Hand: The Managerial Revolution in American Business*. Harvard University Press, Cambridge, MA.

Coase, R. (1952) The nature of the firm. *Economica* 4, 386–405. Reprinted in Stigler, G. and Boulding, K. (eds), *Readings in Price Theory*. Irwin, Homewood, IL, pp. 331–51.

Department for Culture, Media and Sport (2008) *Creative Britain - New Talents for a New Economy*. DCMS, London.

Department for Culture, Media and Sport (2009) *Digital Britain*. DCMS, London.

Flichy, P. (1978) *Contribution à une Etude des Industries de l'Audiovisuel*. Institut National de l'Audiovisuel, Paris.

Garnham, N. (2005a) From cultural to creative industries: An analysis of the implications of the creative industries approach to arts and media policy making in the United Kingdom. *International Journal of Cultural Policy*, 11, 15–29.

Garnham, N. (2005b) The information society debate revisited. In: Curran, J. and Gurevitch, M. (eds), *Mass Media and Society*, 4th edn. Hodder Arnold, London, pp. 287–302.

Howkins, J. (2001) *The Creative Economy*. Penguin, Harmondsworth, UK.

Machlup, F. (1980–4) *Knowledge: Its Creation, Distribution, and Economic Significance* (3 vols). Princeton University Press, Princeton, NJ.

Miège, B. (1989) *The Capitalization of Cultural Production*. International General, New York.

Noam, E. (1994) Beyond liberalization II: The impending doom of common carriage. *Telecommunications Policy*, 18(6), 435–52.

OECD (1998) *Content as a New Growth Industry*. Paris, OECD.

Porat, M. U. (1977) *The Information Economy*. Office of Telecommunications, US Department of Commerce, Washington, D.C.

Toffler, A. (1981) *The Third Wave*. Bantam Books, New York.

3

Markets in Theory and Markets in Television

Eileen R. Meehan and Paul J. Torre

Contemporary discourse finds many uses for the word "market." Perhaps the most specific uses are these three: a place where people go to sell or buy goods and services; an actual assemblage of such persons; and the abstract assemblage of such persons whose transactions involve a single commodity. These standard uses of the term "market" highlight the economic nature of markets and the autonomy of those who enter markets. More imaginative uses are also available in contemporary discourse. Bear or bull markets have nothing to do with selling animals. Instead, the terms describe the pace of trading by contrasting supposedly cautious bears to bold bulls. Markets are anthropomorphized when described as ailing, depressed, skittish, sluggish, or exuberant. The political slogan "let the market decide" regarding matters of public policy suggests that markets transcend mere humans and their democratic institutions. These imaginative uses of "market" imbue markets with a life force that has its own innate characteristics, rhythms, and intelligence. This is problematic because it shifts our attention from the economic and political relationships, structures, and supports that actually constitute markets.

In this chapter, we describe those relationships, structures, and supports in both abstract and concrete terms. We begin with Adam Smith's liberal market model, the first political economic model of a capitalist economy. This model idealizes a fully free and competitive market, which is often lauded in contemporary discourse but rarely seen in reality. Using Smith and referencing his critics, we then provide an abstract definition of "market" that can be used to study markets in theory as well as markets in television. We then analyze two television markets to understand how that definition may be deployed to illuminate a particular market's origins, operations, and outcomes. Our case studies are

The Handbook of Political Economy of Communications, First Edition.
Edited by Janet Wasko, Graham Murdock, and Helena Sousa.
© 2014 John Wiley & Sons, Ltd. Published 2014 by John Wiley & Sons, Ltd.

the national market for television ratings in the United States and the global market for television formats.

Markets and the Liberal Market Model

In *The Wealth of Nations* (2009/1776), Smith presented a model of how markets should work. He argued that fully free and competitive markets guaranteed economic growth and political stability for all nations in the global economy. Thus governments should pass laws and provide services to support such markets. Smith knew other kinds of markets existed, including monopolies and oligopolies, but believed them inefficient. Given the significance of Smith's ideals in contemporary discourse, we will briefly present key elements in Smith's liberal market model.

First, the market needed to have large numbers of buyers and sellers. Sellers competed for buyers' money and buyers competed to purchase desired commodities at low prices. Buyers expressed their demands for certain commodities and bargained with sellers who had those commodities. Sellers tried to spot trends and anticipate changes in demand so that they could profit by serving buyers' demands. For buyers, sellers, and governments, Smith argued that non-economic concerns – like religious or ethical convictions – should not influence the expression and satisfaction of demand. An economic system that could not consistently satisfy buyers' demands might foster dissatisfaction with the political status quo. An important side effect of the free market, then, would be political stability.

To get buyers and sellers into the market, governments needed to provide easy entry to and exit from the market. That meant providing roads and ensuring travelers' safety as they went to markets. Further, governments should eliminate licensing fees, sales tax, or other schemes to earn revenues from market transactions as well as regulations, laws, or limitations that might hinder the market's working.

Because demand drove supply, advertising would be limited to information regarding time, place, and asking price. That information would be augmented by the buyer's examination of all relevant commodities in terms of asking price and quality. Of course, sellers would have gathered this information themselves and set prices accordingly in preparation to bargain. This access to complete information made competitive markets efficient because it allowed participants to calculate their self-interest in a transaction. Sellers wanted to get high prices for commodities that cost little to make; buyers wanted to pay low prices for the highest quality product. Through bargaining, they determined the degree to which their individual greed would be satisfied. If bargaining brought the calculations together, a sale resulted. If no compromise could be reached, the buyer might engage a different seller or exit the market. Through bargaining, sellers could learn how much buyers would really pay and to what degree quality mattered. By tracking that information, smart sellers might determine if demand was waning or if decreasing product quality would be reasonable given the strength of demand. Bargaining gave smart sellers some information about trends in demand.

In a market driven by demand, sellers had to be both innovative and imitative. Although innovation was risky, a successful innovation could attract buyers willing to pay top price for the new product. The innovator would briefly enjoy a monopoly position and profits. However, other sellers would quickly move into the new, profitable area, bringing nearly identical products into the market. As buyers had more choices of where to buy the innovation, they would bargain harder and decrease prices. With still more sellers trying to profit through imitation, prices would eventually fall below the break-even point. Foolish sellers would go bankrupt; patient buyers would reap a windfall. Smith saw the relationship between innovation and imitation as a sure guarantee that prices always fell. That also meant profits would be rare and require risk-taking innovation.

What kept sellers from changing their behaviors to assure profits, control demand, and limit competition? These goals could be achieved if sellers co-operated. This was a problem for Smith's model. He could have solved it by suggesting that governments regulate markets through antitrust laws or similar procompetition measures. But while he thought governments should support markets, Smith did not want governments intervening in markets. To solve the problem, Smith claimed that the very structure of the free market guaranteed its competitiveness. He argued that because sellers were greedy and quick to take advantage, co-operating sellers would always see a way to betray their fellows for a quick profit. In modern terms, we would say that sellers' socialization as rugged individuals and sharp competitors would work to restore competition. In the poetic style of the time, Smith argued that "the invisible hand" of self-interest would right anticompetitive wrongs.

Smith's liberal market model has been variously interpreted and critiqued by different schools of political economists. Starting in the 1800s and continuing today, the school of radical political economy does research on work processes, labor relations, corporate control, and power structures at a macroeconomic level, demonstrating how market forces lead to concentration of ownership, worker exploitation, and economic instability (e.g., Marx 1977/1887; Baran and Sweezy 1966). Some of this critique was shared by John Maynard Keynes (1936), whose theories on how to decrease instability and exploitation undergirded progressive policies addressing the 1930s global economic collapse. The Austrian and Chicago Schools countered by arguing that changes in the supply of money (monetarism), deregulation of markets, and privatization of governmental services would generate more economic growth than Keynesian policies (Hayek 1948; Friedman and Schwartz 1963).

This last position, generally known as neoliberalism but called neoconservativism in the United States, achieved global prominence in 1980 and guided the restructuring and integration of national economies and global markets for over two decades. Despite frequent homage to Smith's notion of free markets, neoliberal policies did not restructure markets according to Smith's model. Instead, policy makers deregulated markets in ways that fostered concentration of ownership (fewer sellers), conglomeration across related industries (less innovation), and fewer consumer protections (incomplete information, price fixing), among other things. Critiques of the Austrian and Chicago Schools from both the radical and Keynesian schools were vigorous (respectively, Seabrook 1991; Reich 1991) and, with the meltdown of the finance sector of the global economy in 2008, rather prescient.

Defining Markets: Legal Basis

Given our discussion of the liberal model and our brief indication of disparate views regarding that model, we are ready to define the term "market." Our definition is abstract because it has a lot of ground to cover: a market is an economic construct that emerges from a combination of legal strictures, economic relationships between entities capable of engaging in transactions, and the structures resulting from those elements that may become institutionalized within an economy over time.

This degree of abstraction allows the definition to cover a market in which transactions involve individual persons buying and selling as well as markets inhabited by such entities as small companies, big corporations, transnational conglomerates, nonprofit organizations, nongovernmental organizations, governmental agencies, nation-states, and international organizations. The definition highlights the fact that markets are constructed through human action in both the economic and political spheres. It does not limit the market to a specific place or to an actual assemblage of people, implicitly recognizing that electronic communications have played key roles in national and international markets. By noting the importance of legal strictures à la Smith, Marx, and Keynes, the definition recognizes that laws, regulations, constitutions, treaties, and so forth, may support, shape, or criminalize particular forms of trade and certain trade practices. The move from buyers and sellers bargaining over goods, which suggests individual persons in an equal relationship, to entities in economic relationships, incorporates the radical political economists' understanding that production, distribution, and consumption involve relations of power and control that are often unequal. The generic nature of transaction opens our analysis to markets involving outright purchase, leasing, licensing, downloading, and so forth. Finally, the definition references the historical processes through which markets develop and become institutionalized as structures. Although participants may come and go, the structure of a particular market may persist, thereby setting the parameters of participants' entry, actions, and exit.

This abstract definition, then, allows us to identify features common to markets despite the fact that any particular market will also have distinctive features. Every market has a legal basis, which begins with the degree to which the commodity being traded is licit or illicit. National and local markets for pornographic films, for example, vary from country to country depending on the degree to which it is legal to produce, trade, possess, or gain access to such movies. Where that trade is legal, governments may still impose restrictions regarding, for example, who can legally purchase pornography, who is licensed to sell it, and whether the films can be cablecast. Such variations in legality and trade restrictions across countries shape the global market for pornographic films.

Assuming that a media market trades licit goods, a crucial legal protection required to facilitate trade is intellectual property law. Each country articulates its own theories, laws, and regulations regarding intellectual property, that is, the ownership of ideas, specific expressions, technologies, and practices. Within intellectual property law, copyright law addresses ownership of specific expressions, like the television series *Dog the Bounty Hunter* or the songs on the program's soundtrack (Bettig 1996). Copyright law plays a key role in markets for television formats in which the concept for a specific series and its production guidelines are sold. Trademark law covers the use of logos or other symbols used to identify a company, its operations, or products, like the British Broadcasting Corporation's use of BBC to identify itself. Patent law addresses ownership of inventions, including technologies like DVD recorders and chemical products like film emulsion. Also covered under intellectual property law is the practical knowledge not available from the patent that is necessary to successfully use the patent (know-how) as well as information regarding corporate policies, practices, and secrets (proprietorial knowledge). For media markets, proprietorial knowledge plays a significant role in studios' accounting practices (Kunz 2007) and in measurements of television audiences (Meehan 2005). Companies with operations in both media production and technologies, like Sony, have considerable investments in technologies and systems that increase their ability to control consumers' access to and use of media products (Burkart and McCourt 2006).

Different countries have different approaches to intellectual property law. Some, like the United States, consider copyright in economic terms only: authors can hold or sell their copyrights but, if they work for hire, authors have no rights in the resulting creations. Companies that own copyrighted works can do whatever they wish to the work including suppressing it. Other countries, like France, grant authors moral rights in their creations, even if the authors worked for hire. Moral rights generally include the author being identified as such and the integrity of the work being protected regardless of ownership. Through international accords like the Berne Convention and organizations like the World Intellectual Property Organization, countries try to co-ordinate their practices in order to facilitate global trade in intellectual properties.

A market's legal basis sets in place the legal strictures that function as ground rules for relations between buyers and sellers. Law and regulation may encourage some activities and discourage or ban others. Buyers and sellers may try to change the ground rules in order to get more favorable laws and regulations. For example, News Corporation used its political influence with Prime Minister Margaret Thatcher (UK) to encourage President Ronald Reagan (US) to support changes in the laws governing ownership of US television stations so that News Corporation could operate the seven stations that it had acquired illegally in 1986.

Defining Markets: Economic Relationships and Capable Entities

The second element in our abstract definition focuses on economic relationships between entities capable of engaging in transactions. The most obvious relationship is demand and supply. Some entities exert demand, that is, they know what they want, they can communicate that to potential sellers, and they have the money necessary to purchase the desired commodity. An entity must command all three elements to be a bona fide buyer. When a market is driven by demand, as Smith argued, sellers compete with each other to identify the precise dimensions of demand and to satisfy demand. In such markets, advertising that appeals to emotion is unproductive: sellers do not need to persuade buyers to want what they have already demanded. The relevant entities in a demand-driven market can vary. In farmers' markets, individual people may engage in transactions; in the world market for food, Walmart buys its wares from smaller companies that compete for Walmart's business. Due to the volume of goods demanded, Walmart can force prices down. Similarly, in countries with national health services, the nation-state's monopoly on demand can keep costs low. When examining a demand-driven market, we need to identify the relevant entity or entities exerting demand and analyze the structure of that demand to discover the degree to which it is inflexible or negotiable. We also need to look for evidence of suppliers' strategies for dealing with strong demand and thereby avoiding becoming slaves to demand. Finally, we need to uncover the supports for the particular market's relationships within its legal basis.

Markets can also be supply–driven, especially if a few companies control the markets, thereby oligopolizing them. (A monopoly is by definition a supply-driven market.) In supply-driven markets, firms can make long-term plans regarding what products will be offered, when, at what price, and when they will obsolesce. Planning allows firms to develop product lines that may persist for decades. Companies use image-based advertising to create needs that the pre-existing product satisfies as well as to create demand. In an oligopolized market, sellers typically offer products that are functionally identical (fungible) but differentiated through advertising and branding. These practices discourage buyers from calculating their self-interest and encourage them to become consumers who purchase brand-name products loyally and impulsively. This apparent contradiction undergirds consumerism as a sociocultural worldview. As both the radical political economists and the Keynesians noted, most national and global markets in which ordinary people buy goods are oligopolized markets driven by supply and image-based advertising. When examining these consumerist markets, we need to identify the relevant suppliers and analyze the structure of their companies, product lines, and advertising strategies. We also need to examine the fit between supply and people's needs as well as the persistence or emergence of nonconsumerist or anticonsumerist practices. Complementing these analyses is a further examination of the markets' legal basis to determine what laws and regulations protect suppliers or consumers.

In some markets, human beings are neither buyers nor sellers. In these markets, organizational entities take on those roles, as when corporations transact business with other corporations, governmental agencies, or nation-states. Entry into such markets is often highly controlled either through governmental action or corporate preference. In such established and closed markets, demand tends to be strong because buyers are powerful entities in their own rights. Often, buyers serve as gatekeepers, letting some potential suppliers in and blocking others. The relevant corporations act in ways designed to advance their self-interest and perhaps to damage or limit the self-interest of other corporations. These markets tend to be oligopolized and stratified, with the proverbial "big boys" exerting the most influence over the market's shape and workings. When examining markets where organizations are the relevant entities, we need to first determine if the market is emerging or established. Emerging markets tend to be more dynamic, while established markets tend to be more stable. For an emerging market, we trace interactions between relevant entities, analyze products and corporate alliances to track the market's trajectory, and map ongoing negotiations with political entities over the market's legal basis. With established markets, we trace the market's origin, track its current trajectory, and map the particularities of its legal basis. In both types of markets, we look for tensions, rivalries, alliances, and parallel self-interests among and between entities.

Defining Markets: Institutional Structures

The final element in our definition recognizes that, over time, elements of the market may become institutionalized as relatively stable structures. One path to institutionalization is the expansion of a market's legal basis to include governmental entities charged with oversight. Oversight signals a governmental commitment to the particular market, its entities, and their relationships. For media and telecommunications that use natural resources like the electromagnetic spectrum, governments initiate regulation to set technical standards to ensure that ongoing operations do not interfere with each other, that new operations do not interfere with older operations, that content conforms to legal standards, and so forth. As bureaucratic entities, oversight agencies have an interest in perpetuating themselves, which may foster support for perpetuating the conditions that have brought the agency into existence, for example, the market's status quo (Weber 1957/1925). While such agencies have a manifest function of oversight, they take on a latent function of protecting the market. For the US's Federal Communications Commission (FCC), protecting the oligopoly in network television was a preoccupation from the 1950s to the 1970s, as the FCC blocked potential rivals like the Hollywood studios from owning networks (Hilmes 1990) and attempted to stifle the emerging cable television industry through onerous regulation (Mullen 2008).

Because the electromagnetic spectrum is a global resource, international accords are necessary to divide that resource among nation-states and co-ordinate their use of spectrum space. Historically, geopolitical hierarchies allowed highly developed regions like Western Europe and North America to take a greater share of spectrum space than less developed regions. For example, in 1865, 20 European states founded the International Telegraph Union (ITU) to set technical standards for telegraphy. The advent of radio-telegraphy (1890s) and then radio broadcasting (1920s) positioned the Europe-based ITU as the international forum in which nation-states, corporations, and noncorporate organizations discussed spectrum use. Now called the International Telecommunications Union, the ITU continues in that function as an agency of the United Nations. In its 1989 Plenipotentiary Conference, the ITU reorganized to deal with the impact of neoliberal policies on national and global markets. It also has recognized the persistence of a telecommunications gap between developed and developing nations. Deinstitutionalizing that gap may require highly developed nations to cede some of their spectrum space.

The intermeshing of national and international regulation, then, expands the legal basis for a market and institutionalizes that market. However, these are not the only forces that foster institutionalization. Markets become institutionalized when the process of demand and supply becomes a matter of routine. When demand is predictable, responses to demand become generic, encouraging suppliers to respond with fungible products differentiated mainly through claims about style. Dynamism and innovation decrease as stability increases. Institutionalized markets tend to have a few sellers (oligopoly) or one seller (monopoly). When buyers are individual people, sellers use branding and advertising to make stylistic differentiations between fungible products offered by different suppliers (e.g., all cola-flavored sodas vs. Coca Cola) as well as nearly identical products within one company's product line (Coca Cola, Classic Coke, Diet Coke, Diet Coke without caffeine, Cherry Coke, Cherry Coke without caffeine, Coca Cola Zero, Coca Cola with lime, lemon, or raspberry flavoring, etc.). In markets where buyers and sellers are companies, promotional campaigns differentiating the products of rival sellers are common. In those markets, institutionalization offers companies stability: a steady supply of interchangeable products that perform adequately at acceptable prices. Corporate buyers need not conduct expensive searches to find the right product at the right price for every single purchase; corporate sellers are not confronted by ever-changing demand. Institutionalization makes long-term planning feasible. Although certain participants may enter or leave the particular market, the overall structure persists, thereby setting the parameters of each participants' entry, actions, and exit. We turn now to an example of an institutionalized market in television, first describing its origin and legal basis, and then noting key developments.

Measuring Audiences for National Networks: The US Market for Ratings

Historically, the key relationships in national networking of radio and television have centered on the flow of money from advertisers owning name brands to agencies contracted to promote the brands, and networks (or now networks and cable channels) assembling audiences targeted by advertisers in order to expose those audiences to commercials promoting advertisers' brands. Advertisers' inflexible demands for consumers drive the market in which ad agencies compete for exclusive contracts and the market in which audience assemblers compete for advertising dollars. For agencies and networks, the problem is how to demonstrate their effectiveness in reaching people with the disposable income, access to retail outlets, and desire to buy name brands whose prices are inflated by branding and advertising. For advertisers, the problem is how to evaluate agencies' and networks' necessarily biased accounts of their success. For advertisers and networks, this is complicated by their conflicting interests about how advertisers' access to audiences should be priced. In order to examine how problems in pricing and measuring effectiveness were worked out, we turn to a brief account of how the market for ratings originated.

In the United States, the first national market for ratings was organized between 1927 and 1930 by the Association of National Advertisers (ANA) and the American Association of Advertising Agencies (AAAA). Both associations were reluctant to accept audience estimates published by the Columbia Broadcasting System (CBS), which owned one network, and the Radio Corporation of America (RCA), which owned two. In their reports on radio listening, CBS and RCA claimed that their networks reached vast audiences composed of eager consumers. The implication was that advertisers should pay networks considerable amounts of money to get access to such audiences. As program sponsors, advertisers had effectively communicated an inflexible demand for large audiences of eager consumers and the networks, as sellers, responded with a blitz of apparent information. But as buyers of network time, advertisers had a vested interest in lower prices. This pricing relationship necessarily made advertisers suspicious of networks' claims about their audiences. Advertisers began searching for a way to counter CBS's and RCA's reports.

In 1927, the ANA and AAAA addressed that problem by hiring the market researcher Archibald Crossley to devise a method for audience measurement. The subtext here was a demand for ratings that would give advertisers an advantage over CBS and RCA in negotiating prices for audiences. Crossley proposed a measurement system that relied on telephone interviews. Using a random sample drawn from telephone directories, Crossley's interviewers contacted respondents (classified as either the head of household or lady of the house) and asked if the person had listened to radio during the prior day. If the person had, the respondent was then asked to name every program heard during the entire day. With programs running 15 minutes and schedules spanning early morning to late evening, naming every program was a daunting task.

Methodologically, Crossley's approach had three serious problems. First, the sheer number of programs broadcast made it probable that respondents would forget to mention some programs, name others that they usually heard but had missed, and confuse names of some programs with other similarly named programs. Second, telephone service was concentrated in cities and towns that the American Telephone & Telegraph Company (AT&T) deemed profitable. AT&T focused on serving businesses and considered residential service as a way to link heads of households to the businesses that they owned or managed (Danielian 1939). Third, more households had radios than telephones and residential telephony was not widely spread across the population. Indeed, having a residential phone and a telephone listing were marks of status. From a social science perspective, Crossley's interview and sample could neither provide a reasonably accurate description of the general population's use of radio nor a reasonably accurate description of radio listening in telephone households.

However, Crossley's sample targeted people who could afford telephony during a depression, indicating that they might afford name brands, want to buy name brands, and have access to appropriate retailers. That satisfied advertisers' demand for bona fide consumers as opposed to merely anybody who listened to radio. Crossley's interview made it easy for people to underreport and misreport their listening. Further, the period's notion of polite society could also decrease estimates of numbers of listeners. When faced with the onerous task of recounting a day's listening, respondents could avoid the task without giving offense by suddenly remembering that they hadn't listened yesterday.

In 1929, the ANA and AAAA announced that Crossley's approach was the only acceptable form of audience measurement. They enshrined it in an organization, the Cooperative Analysis of Broadcasting (CAB), which they jointly owned, and hired Crossley to run. Members of the ANA and AAAA could subscribe to CAB's ratings reports. CAB subscribers were warned not to let nonsubscribers or outsiders see the reports, and CBS and RCA were banned from subscribing. Thus the ANA and AAAA created a closed market for national ratings in which ratings reports targeted upscale consumers and underestimated the number of listeners. This market was heavily skewed in the advertisers' favor. The agencies' support suggests the degree to which they depended on advertisers. But by banning networks, ANA and AAAA ensured the ratings market's instability. But before we address that, let us turn to the legal basis for the market in ratings.

The market's legal basis rested on laws governing copyright, proprietary information, contracts, and ownership. Under US law, copyright applied to a specific expression of an idea, and expressions created for hire belonged not to their creator but to the employer. Thus ANA and AAAA owned the specific interview that Crossley created and neither CBS nor RCA could appropriate Crossley's interview to generate their own ratings. However, because protection was limited to specific expression, ANA and AAAA could not claim ownership of all interviews regarding radio use. Under the laws regarding proprietary information, the associations could restrict the circulation and use of CAB's ratings. Hence, ANA and AAAA could legally deny networks access to or use of CAB's ratings. However, the ratings were bound to leak through casual conversation, business negotiation, industry gossip, and trade press coverage of successful and failing programs. That leakage encouraged some ANA and AAAA members not to subscribe, which put pressure on CAB's operating funds. Because it was owned by ANA and AAAA, CAB could not take the logical step and sell its rating to CBS and RCA.

That left room for another entity to enter the market for ratings and at least target CBS and RCA. Presumably ratings that responded only to networks' demand would differ from ratings that responded to the shared demand of advertisers and agencies. But having one set of ratings for networks and another for advertisers could complicate the process of networks selling time to advertisers. Conflicting reports would have to be negotiated before networks and advertisers could complete transactions. That would increase both parties' costs of doing business. Avoiding that meant compromising on a single set of ratings, which served the shared interests of advertisers and networks regarding business costs, while balancing their conflicting interests in pricing strategies for ratings. Their conflicting interests in the market for access to audiences worked against either side solving their joint problem in the market for ratings.

The solution was proposed by the C. E. Hooper Company (CEH) and its Hooperatings. First, like CAB, CEH used telephone interviews but only in big cities. Second, CEH's interview required little effort from respondents who were asked if they were currently listening to radio (and if so, name the program) and if they had listened to the program directly before the current show (and if so, name that program). Third, CEH offered its product to any buyer (i.e., ratings syndication). Finally, C. E. Hooper relentlessly promoted himself, contrasting his flamboyant personality with CAB's drab organizational identity, and hyped Hooperatings as a scientific breakthrough. CEH offered a ratings product that met the shared demand for measurements of upscale households and that met the networks' demand for increasing the number of reported listeners. But CEH's approach to increasing estimates of listeners also increased ratings' accuracy and narrowed focus to urban consumers, which benefited networks and advertisers. For advertisers, CEH had another benefit: syndication increased the volume of report sales, therefore decreasing the per unit costs for a report. Finally, CEH used style to differentiate its numbers from CAB's numbers while essentially measuring the same thing. With CEH's solution, the conflict between advertisers and networks over ratings was settled. Demand became predictable and CEH became the ratings monopolist.

Here we see the bare bones of the ratings market. The legal basis for the ratings market rested on laws regarding the manufacture of intellectual property, the ability of the manufacturer to sell information products and control proprietary information, and contracts between and among the relevant corporations. Ratings buyers shared demand in three areas: preference for upscale households, for low per unit prices for ratings reports, and for a single set of ratings in order to simplify transactions in the market where networks sold commercial space to advertisers. Demand for ratings focused on the number of audience members described according to a set array of demographic characteristics. Demand regarding estimates of audience size was bifurcated: advertisers preferred underestimates to deflate costs while networks preferred overestimates to inflate prices. Buyers' interest in a single set of ratings meant a preference for a single seller. That monopolist needed to satisfy shared demand and balance bifurcated demand. The balancing process gave a seller the possibility of strategic action while shared demand kept the monopolist focused on the limited number of measurements required. To challenge the monopolist, a new firm needed to address shared demand, rebalance bifurcated demand, and differentiate itself and its fungible product from that of the old monopolist. The new ratings would still report audience size and demographics but get the information in a different manner.

Much has changed in the United States from 1942 to the present day. In the market for ratings, advertisers, agencies, and network owners have been acquired, merged, dissolved, expanded into nonbroadcast media, and so forth. In that market, advertisers, agencies, and networks have been joined by cable channels – some owned by the firms that own the six commercial networks – as the source of demand. Yet the institutional structure of the ratings market has remained. Demand is still shared and bifurcated. The ratings monopolist still serves at the pleasure of its buyers. Challenges are still based on new ways to produce fungible ratings and are promoted as scientific breakthroughs. Since 1950, when its metered ratings won out over telephone interviews, the A. C. Nielsen Company (ACN) has monopolized ratings. Subsequent challenges by Sindlinger & Co., Arbitron, AGB, and Percy have focused on building different meters to produce the same kinds of measurements. ACN has beaten back those challenges by reinventing its meters, through fierce promotional campaigns, and by building alliances across its buyers' vested interests. In a manner emblematic of nearly 50 years of political and economic change domestically, ACN has gone from a family enterprise to a side operation of Dunn & Bradstreet, a Wall Street firm, to a central operation of VNU, a Dutch information company that renamed itself the Nielsen Company in 2007. Nielsen currently experiments with devices that track co-operators' television use at home, Internet use, and exposure to "intelligent" ads outside the home. Recognizing that all such changes are significant, we still note that they have occurred within a market where demand is routinized, relations among buyers and seller are institutionalized, and monopoly persists.

The Right to Reproduction: The Global Market for Television Formats

A television format is a collection of elements that constitute a television series. Format sellers package these elements for sale to television producers or networks. For a scripted series like *Ugly Betty*, a package may include detailed descriptions of the premise, the characters, and the storylines. For game shows like *Who Wants to be a Millionaire?* and reality contests like *Survivor*, packages may contain contest details, set design plans, catchphrases, lighting and music cues, and other production details. Format buyers utilize this combination of elements to produce their own versions of a series (Moran and Malbon 2006). The global market for television formats has expanded rapidly, particularly in the last decade. In order to define the global market for television formats, we first discuss the legal basis for the distribution of television formats and the legal complexities surrounding this specific market for media programming. We then turn to the economic relationships between capable entities, the buyers and sellers of television formats. Finally, we examine whether institutionalization has occurred within the global market for television formats.

The legal basis for this market is intellectual property law. At the national level, media products are protected by copyright law and, to a lesser extent, trademark law, which are articulated and amended by a legislative system and interpreted by a judicial system. At the global level, matters are much more complex with frequent incompatibilities between national intellectual property laws and enforcement regimes. In order for the global market to develop, television formats must be recognized as intellectual properties similar to television programs. We turn our attention to treaties governing international intellectual property and to national intellectual property lawsuits that have influenced global activity.

To facilitate international trade, countries have signed trade agreements extending beyond manufacturing and agricultural products to include intellectual property. For instance, since 1886, the Berne Convention covering literary, artistic, and "cinematographic" works has played an important role in global markets for intellectual properties. Revised many times, the 1971 version (amended in 1979) has drawn support from more than 160 nations. The Convention protects "works expressed by a process analogous to cinematography," which includes television programs. However, the Berne Convention stipulates that "works shall not be protected unless they have been fixed in some material form" (Berne Convention, Article 2). This would suggest that television formats currently fall outside the Berne Convention.

The World Intellectual Property Organization (WIPO), a specialized agency of the United Nations, administers the current Berne Convention. WIPO drew up a separate copyright treaty that was ratified in Geneva in 1996 to update the Berne Convention by "recognizing the profound impact of the development and convergence of information and communication technologies on the creation and use of literary and artistic works" (WIPO Copyright Treaty, Preamble). Here, again, intellectual property protections were limited to fixed works, "to expressions and not to ideas, procedures, methods of operation or mathematical concepts as such" (Article 2). This language is repeated in the World Trade Organization's agreement on Trade-Related Aspects of Intellectual Property Rights (TRIPS), which binds the WTO's 153 member nations to the Berne Convention regardless of their signatory status (Part II Article 9, 2).

These principles from the Berne Convention and the WIPO/TRIPS agreements are especially important to the legal basis for global trade in television formats. The Berne Convention requires that intellectual property be "fixed in some material form" in order to be protected by copyright law. A television format, as a collection of elements waiting to be expressed in a particular version of a program, is clearly not fixed. A format is a prescription for a program, not a completed work in and of itself. The WIPO copyright treaty underscores the difference between literal expressions and prescriptions for expression. Procedures and methods – which are often important elements in a game show format – are not protected by the intellectual property agreements. WIPO has addressed this directly on its website: "television formats, however, have not been discussed at WIPO as subject of a separate international protection" (WIPO FAQs).

With the legal status of television formats left indeterminate, plagiarism or "cloning" has been widespread and persistent, destabilizing the global market. Various intellectual property cases have tested the extent of the gap in statutory protection, yielding precedents at the national level that may eventually shape a consistent legal basis for global trade in television formats. One foundational case concerns Hughie Green, the television producer and host of the talent contest *Opportunity Knocks* that ran in England from 1956 to 1978. Green brought a series of unsuccessful copyright infringement cases against the Broadcasting Corporation of New Zealand (BCNZ), first to the High Court and Court of Appeal in New Zealand and subsequently to the Privy Council in the United Kingdom. In the 1989 *Green v. Broadcasting Corporation of New Zealand* case, the Council drew upon the New Zealand rulings to rule against Green. The Council noted that "the copyright alleged to have been infringed was claimed to subsist in the scripts and dramatic format," yet "no script was ever produced in evidence." Without evidence of appropriation of Green's specific expression, the Council noted that BCNZ's *Opportunity Knocks* used the same "clapometer" to measure audience reaction to a competitor's performance as well as three catchphrases from Green's original program: "for [name of competitor] opportunity knocks," "this is your show folks, and I do mean you," and "make up your mind time." Recognizing this replication of distinctive elements from Green's *Opportunity Knocks* by the BCNZ's version, the Council deemed these mere "accessories." Further, the Council held that "the protection which copyright gives creates a monopoly and there must be certainty in the subject-matter of such monopoly in order to avoid injustice to the rest of the world" (*Green v. Broadcasting Corporation of New Zealand*). This 1989 ruling affirms the distinction between general ideas and specific expressions.

In a case more supportive of format protection, the Netherlands' Endemol sued Brazil's TV SBT for copying Endemol's *Big Brother*. The two companies had entered negotiations over the format rights but TV SBT declined a format license for *Big Brother*. Subsequently, TV SBT produced a strikingly similar show. The Brazilian court ruled in favor of Endemol, charging TV SBT with copyright infringement. The court noted that a television program format, "is a much wider concept that does not only include the central idea of the program but also encompasses an extensive group of technical, artistic, economical, and business information" (*Endemol & TV Globo v. TV SBT*). The Brazilian court awarded more than $2 million to the plaintiffs. However, this ruling has been accepted as precedent only in Brazil.

Suits over television formats are not always decided solely on the basis of intellectual property law and may have complex histories. In the United Kingdom, Castaway Productions filed a 2002 suit claiming that its version of *Survivor*, based on the format of the Swedish program *Expedition: Robinson*, had been plagiarized by Granada PLC's *I'm a Celebrity … Get Me Out of Here*. Both shows placed contestants in a hostile outdoor environment, required survival skills, and had contestants voted off the show until a winner was declared. Castaway dropped its suit in 2003. In the United States, the CBS network sued the ABC network, charging that ABC's *I'm a Celebrity … Get Me Out of Here!* plagiarized CBS's *Survivor*. While CBS's *Survivor* used ordinary people, *Celebrity* used such persons as the ex-husband of Jennifer Lopez and the daughter of comic Joan Rivers. A US District Court in New York refused to grant an injunction, ruling that the two series were substantially different "in total concept and feel." The Court decided that *Survivor* had a serious tone and high production values, while *Celebrity* was comedic and looked like a home video. Despite any basic similarities, the judge ruled that "providing protection to a combination of elements without consideration of the *presentation or expression* of those elements would stifle innovation and would stifle the creative process that spawned the two shows at issue here." More broadly, television programming was "a continual evolutionary process involving borrowing frequently from what has gone before." Beyond these considerations, the judge claimed that removing *Celebrity* from its February advertising sweeps time slot, "would bring to a screeching halt the progress ABC has made in regaining its ratings" (*CBS Broadcasting Inc. v. ABC, Inc.* 2003). While ABC's performance in the national market for ratings was irrelevant to the legal issues at hand, it was one factor in the American court's ruling.

As these cases suggest, the distinction between an underdeveloped *idea* and an actual and fixed *expression* is fundamental to the legal basis for intellectual property protections. That distinction is also the primary obstacle to global television formats being protected by intellectual property law. However, other legal bases might be found in international regulations on unfair competition, protection of trademarks, and violations of confidentiality or contracts. Differences in national laws regarding these matters keep companies improvising as they attempt to protect or change distinctions between ideas and expressions. Events in the UK suggest some of the complexities. In 2003, Parliament adjusted program ownership regulations, reassigning intellectual property rights for programs once held by networks to production companies. This gave British format producers an added incentive to develop programming concepts for worldwide franchising. In recent years, the television industry in the UK has earned 40 percent of its export revenue from format sales, though piracy continues. Yet, in 2006, the BBC responded to a government review of intellectual property policies by recommending against any formal legal remedies to prevent cloning of television formats. The BBC contended that "current laws provide adequate protection" and that "a more prescriptive approach will create difficulties" (Her Majesty's Treasury 2006).

Clearly, the legal basis for a global market in television formats is problematic. Whether at the national or global levels, governmental structures and intellectual property law offer little basis on which to build a global market for formats. In response, the Format Recognition and Protection Association (FRAPA) was founded in 2000 (Keane and Moran 2008). Comprising only 100 companies in 30 countries, FRAPA recognizes that "only exclusive rights can create a scarcity value in the market" but notes that "exclusivity is a hollow promise if one is not in a position to block unlicensed copying by competitors" (FRAPA 2010). FRAPA promotes the extension of copyright to formats and encourages its members to register their original ideas with it. Like most efforts at self-regulation, FRAPA has been ineffective, and cloning remains rampant. If law and self-regulation cannot protect sellers from cloning by potential buyers, then sellers have two choices: exit the market or sweeten the deal to the point of undercutting the cost-effectiveness of cloning. Perhaps the latter is one impetus for sellers to meet with buyers and individually negotiate the terms of each transaction.

Sellers and buyers gather at literal markets hosted by the National Association of Television Producers Exhibition (NATPE) in Las Vegas, the Marché International des Programmes de Télévision (MIP-TV) in Cannes, and the Asia Media Festival (AMF) in Singapore (Havens 2006). In these venues, transactions vary in nature, forming a continuum of potential formatting arrangements that are negotiated for each individual transaction. Thus the individuality of buyer–seller relationships mitigates against routinization of transactions. Some format buyers require only quick delivery of the relevant documents, much like buyers purchasing the license for an existing television series. Other buyers require occasional consultations or troubleshooting sessions. Some buyers, however, prefer relationships that mimic traditional television coproductions in which sellers provide key personnel and resources. Sellers like Sony Pictures Television International and FremantleMedia Productions have supplied a "flying producer" to work with the buyer's writing team, oversee the initial shoot, and assist with postproduction for buyers in Asia, Europe, and South America. While remaining in the seller's employ, these producers have the know-how to fully exploit the format's prescription while achieving efficiencies in costs and operations. One of the reasons that sellers offer extensive production assistance is to dissuade buyers from the temptations of cloning. To the degree that sellers can make it cost-efficient for buyers not to do the work of recognition, appropriation, and generalization, sellers can protect their know-how while catering to buyers' needs. One by-product of intensive formatting relationships, however, is that over the course of the transaction buyers often do recognize, appropriate, and generalize know-how of the broader business of formatting itself. As a result, buyers learn new business practices, management techniques, and efficiencies (Keane, Fung, and Moran 2007).

We can trace this potential outcome through a brief sketch of one particular formatting production process. Throughout the 1990s, Sony sold six seasons of the television series *The Nanny* to more than 90 countries around the world. In addition, Sony worked with a dozen producers and broadcasters to launch formatted versions, among them TVN in Poland, Indosiar in Indonesia, and STS in Russia. In Argentina, Sony partnered with Telefe to produce *La Niñera*, launching the series in the Argentinean market in 2004. Interestingly, Telefe also worked with Sony to format the US series *Married with Children, Who's the Boss, Bewitched*, and *Charlie's Angels*.

These formatting experiences with Sony equipped Telefe to expand its own formatting productions. Notable was Telefe's formatting of the telenovela *Montecristo* (2006). As with Sony and *The Nanny*, Telefe sold *Montecristo* to 40 countries in its original form, and then sold the format to Television Azteca in Mexico, Caracol in Colombia, Mega in Chile, SIC in Portugal, and Amedia Russia. In these instances, Telefe employed the production techniques that it had garnered from its previous experiences with Sony in deals with broadcasters around the world. Given that buyers are more likely to enter into formatting partnerships with companies that have a track record, Telefe's previous projects with Sony aided in its own format sales efforts.

Barriers to entry do exist, as format producers are typically producer/broadcasters. Broadcasters control access and having an outlet for local distribution is often a precondition to attracting regional buyers. The global success of television formats depends upon domestic and regional success, which can generate the track record/

critical mass necessary for global distribution. Nonetheless, the market for television formats is expanding to include additional capable entities. In addition to Argentina's Telefe, producer-broadcaster-distributors are proliferating rapidly, including Israel's Dori Media Group, Columbia's RCN Television, Brazil's TV Globo, Venezuela's Venevision, Mexico's Televisa, Japan's TBS, and China's Beijing Television.

Monopolies may exist in the broader business of global television distribution, where the Hollywood studios still exert considerable power in markets for completed series. Companies that produce and distribute global television formats are part of a dynamic and unstable market. Stabilizing that market may require a legal basis that extends intellectual property protections from specific expressions to prescriptions for possible expressions. The ramifications of that are considerable: companies could have separate property rights in a specific television series and the idea upon which the series was based. Individuals, organizations, and companies that used similar ideas could be sued for copyright violation. If that had been the state of affairs in 1998, the similarities between Dreamworks SKG's *Antz* and Disney/Pixar's *A Bug's Life* probably would have generated significant litigation. Extending copyright to formats might stabilize the format market but destabilize trade in other markets where intellectual properties are traded while further encroaching on freedom of expression and the cultural commons.

Given the lack of copyright protection for formats, piracy remains a problem. Attempts at self-regulation have fallen short of the critical mass necessary to stem piracy. To make piracy less attractive, some sellers offer extensive assistance in development, production, and marketing in the hope that tailored, individualized buyer–seller relationships will make piracy less attractive. However, buyers may use these relationships to "learn the ropes" and subsequently re-enter the format market as sellers. This proliferation of buyers keeps the format market dynamic and militates against institutionalization.

Conclusion

As we have sketched these markets, the national market for ratings in the US contrasts sharply with the global market for television formats. We suggest that this has less to do with the distinction between the national and the global than with the differences between these markets in terms of legal basis, economic relationships among capable entities, and degrees of institutionalization. While the market for ratings has a firm legal basis in intellectual property laws dealing with the specific forms of audience measurement and proprietary information, the market for formats has no protection as long as copyright excludes prescriptions for how to produce versions of a specific, fixed expression. These differing legal bases foster different relationships between capable entities, which we will review in turn.

To maximize efficiency in the ratings market, buyers prefer to deal with a single seller, which fosters routinization of demand and supply. Routinization is further supported by buyers' unified demand for measurements of audience quality. Given bifurcation of demand regarding audience size, the ratings monopolist balances conflicting interests in prices paid for audiences to achieve an acceptable compromise among advertisers, networks, and channels. This again fosters routinization of demand and institutionalization of the market for ratings.

In sharp contrast, format sellers respond to an array of demands made by potential buyers. Demand ranges from one-stop purchases to quasi-coproduction relationships in which format sellers may essentially train buyers to become format sellers. This transformation of buyers into sellers allows new competitors to enter the market. The market for formats includes a variety of buyers, each desiring different transactions. These exchanges are joined by the possibility of each buyer subsequently becoming a seller, also offering an array of products and transactions. Both of these factors contribute to a market that is anything but routinized.

Despite the differences between the American market for ratings and the global market for formats, trade in both markets is shaped by their legal basis in intellectual property law. In the market for ratings, legal protections for specific expressions of audience measurements and proprietary information have been used historically by the ratings monopolist to consolidate its position. Since the 1930s, intellectual property law and bifurcated demand have combined to clearly separate buyer from seller. Such clarity is lacking in the global market for formats. The ownership of programming prescriptions generally lacks copyright protection, allowing some potential buyers to clone formats while others demand quasi-coproduction deals that may train buyers to become sellers. As economic entities position themselves using their market's legal basis, we see how the political and the economic intertwine. The particular articulation of that interdependence varies from market to market, from continent to continent. But the recognition of that intertwining undergirds all of political economy.

References

Baran, P. A. and Sweezy, P. M. (1966) *Monopoly Capital*. Monthly Review Press, New York.

Berne Convention for the Protection of Literary and Artistic Works, Paris Act of July 24, 1971, as amended on September 28, 1979. Online at at http://www.wipo.int/treaties/en/ip/berne/trtdocs_wo001.html (accessed September 21, 2010).

Bettig, R. V. (1996) *Copyrighting Culture: The Political Economy of Intellectual Property*. Westview, Boulder, CO.

Burkart, P. and McCourt, T. (2006) *Digital Music Wars: Ownership and Control of the Celestial Jukebox*. Rowman & Littlefield, Lanham, MD.

CBS Broadcasting Inc. v. ABC Inc. (2003) US Dist. LEXIS 20258 (SDNY January 14, 2003).

Danielian, N. R. (1939) *AT&T: The Story of Industrial Conquest.* Arno Press, New York.

Endemol v. TV SBT (2004) Brazil.

Format Recognition and Protection Association (2010), About FRAPA. Online at http://www.frapa.org/about-frapa.html (accessed September 21, 2010).

Friedman, M. and Schwartz, A. J. (1963) *A Monetary History of the United States.* Princeton University Press, Princeton, NJ.

Green v. Broadcasting Corporation of New Zealand (1989) RPC 700.

Havens, T. (2006) *Global Television Marketplace.* British Film Institute, London.

Hayek, F. (1948) *Individualism and Economic Order.* University of Chicago Press, Chicago.

Her Majesty's Treasury. (2006) Response to Gowers Review from BBC and BBC Worldwide. Online at http://webarchive.nationalarchives.gov.uk/+/http://www.hm-treasury.gov.uk/media/192/37/bbc_and_bbc_worldwide_ltd_142_83kb.pdf (accessed September 21, 2010).

Hilmes, M. (1990) *Hollywood and Broadcasting: From Radio to Cable.* University of Illinois Press, Urbana.

Keane, M., Fung, A.Y. H., and Moran, A. (2007) *New Television, Globalisation, and the East Asian Cultural Imagination.* Hong Kong University Press, Hong Kong.

Keane, M. and Moran, A. (2008) Television's new engines. *Television and New Media,* 9 (2), 155–69.

Keynes, J. M. (1936) *The General Theory of Employment, Interest, and Money.* Harcourt, Brace, New York.

Kunz, W. M. (2007) *Culture Conglomerates: Consolidation in the Motion Picture and Television Industries.* Rowman & Littlefield, Lanham, MD.

Marx, K. (1887/1977) *Capital,* vol. 1. Fowkes, B. (trans.). Vintage Books, New York.

Meehan, E. R. (2005) *Why TV Is Not Our Fault.* Rowman & Littlefield, Lanham, MD.

Moran, A. and Malbon, J. (2006) *Understanding the Global TV Format.* Intellect, Portland, OR.

Mullen, M. (2008) *Television in the Multichannel Age.* Blackwell, Malden, MA.

Reich, R. (1991) *The Work of Nations.* A.A. Knopf, New York.

Seabrook, J. (1991) *The Myth of the Market: Promises and Illusions.* Black Rose Books, Montreal.

Smith, A. (1776/2009) *The Wealth of Nations.* Classic House Books, New York.

Weber, M. (1925/1958) Bureaucracy. In: Gerth, H. H. and Mills, C. W. (eds), *From Max Weber* Oxford University Press, New York, pp. 196–262.

World Intellectual Property Organization Copyright Treaty. Adopted in Geneva, December 20, 1996. Online at http://www.wipo.int/treaties/en/ip/wct/trtdocs_wo033.html (accessed September 21, 1910).

World Intellectual Property Organization FAQs. Online at http: www.wipo.int/copyright/en/faq/faqs.htm (accessed September 21, 2010).

Suggestions for Further Reading

Curtin, M. (2007) *Playing to the World's Biggest Audience: The Globalization of Chinese Film and TV.* University of California Press, Berkeley.

Flew, T. (2007) *Understanding Global Media.* Palgrave Macmillan, New York.

Fung, A. (2008) *Global Capital, Local Culture: Transnational Media Corporations in China*. Peter Lang, New York.

Galbraith, J. (2009) *The Predator State: How Conservatives Abandoned the Free Market and Why Liberals Should Too*. Free Press, New York.

Moran, A. (2008) Makeover on the move: Global television and programme formats. *Continuum*, 22(4), 459–69.

Mosco, V. (1996) *The Political Economy of Communication*. Sage Publications, London.

Straubhaar, J. D. (2007) *World Television: From Global to Local*. Sage Publications, Thousand Oaks, CA.

Thussu, D. K. (ed.) (2007) *Media on the Move: Global Flow and Contra-flow*. Routledge, London.

4

Theorizing the Cultural Industries

Persistent Specificities and Reconsiderations

Bernard Miège (translation by Chloé Salles)

Arguments around the cultural industries, neglected by some but regarded as fundamental by others, have taken on a new importance in recent years as governments in the capitalist west have come to see them as central to an economy moving from a base in traditional industrial sectors to one organized around the production and manipulation of information and symbolic forms. This chapter traces the development of the cultural industries as an idea and area of research within the political economy of communication and explores some of the challenges to established conceptions posed by contemporary developments.

The Origins of "Cultural Industries" Theory

Theoretical approaches to the cultural industries have two main points of origin. The first can be traced back to the Frankfurt School of thought, and particularly to the analysis of "the administration of art" elaborated by Theodor Adorno and Max Horkheimer as part of their project of developing a "Critical Theory" of contemporary capitalism. Within this theoretical framework, the industrial production of cultural goods is seen as a decisive factor in the *Entkunstung* (literally, de-arting) of art. Degrading itself and losing its aura once it is put on the market, the cultural commodity invites consumers to look not for enlightenment or transcendence,

The Handbook of Political Economy of Communications, First Edition.
Edited by Janet Wasko, Graham Murdock, and Helena Sousa.
© 2014 John Wiley & Sons, Ltd. Published 2014 by John Wiley & Sons, Ltd.

but for a utility that will be a source of happiness, and from which would emerge an appropriation, providing them with prestige or satisfying some sort of desired pleasure. This critical conception of the cultural industry exerted a strong pull on participants in the social and cultural movements around 1968, and is still influential today, most notably among artists and dissenting environments, particularly in the performing and plastic arts. It must be added that Adorno, who showed himself to be very critical toward the mass culture of the 1940s and 1950s, saw technical progress and the industrial means of production as the main sources of domination in the cultural industry, leading him to distance himself from the emerging arts such as cinema and jazz. This general denunciation was not, however, shared by all of his contemporaries, some of whom, like Walter Benjamin (himself a member of the Frankfurt School), offered a more nuanced and positive interpretation of art in the era of technical reproducibility.

The second source of work on the cultural industry comes from the North American pioneers of the political economy of communication, and more particularly from Herbert Schiller and Dallas Smythe, both of whom strove, from the late 1960s onwards (and even earlier in the case of Smythe), to analyze the growing hold of the most dynamic sectors of financial and industrial capital on the communication industries. Their analyses covered a wide field, looking at the expansion and intersections between telecommunications, mass media, mass market, and professional news / general information, and the cultural industries. They paid particular attention to the consequences of corporate concentration, to transnationalization and multimedia coverage, and, last but not least, to the control of information and culture.

Although these two starting points had radically different preoccupations, one centered on the fate of art and aesthetic creativity, the other on the domination of the economy and its consequences for democratic culture, both became influential because the changing conditions of the 1970s invited new questions under new terms. How can that period be characterized? Its main traits are directly linked to the primary object of our reflections here since the strategic reorientation of industrial production then taking place saw the emergence of information processing and cultural production as leading sectors in the new capitalism. This shift was accompanied by decisive cultural changes and the extension of what, from then on, was called "mass culture," together with the changing political management of cultures and representations of identity. At the same time, terms of trade and exchange between nations were also changing and were marked by the confrontation between antagonistic political and economic systems resulting in the Unesco report on global communications put together by the McBride Commission, and in animated debates and open oppositions to Unesco over the new global order for information and communication. In this context, it is hardly surprising to see new questions raised about the nature and future of the cultural industries, not in an attempt to link irreconcilable theoretical currents – that would have been in vain – but to take into account new observations, whether within national frames or in wider contexts.

The designation that came to be called the "Theory of Cultural Industries" was employed by a diverse group of writers from the 1990s onwards, including Ahmed Silem (1991), Alain Herscovici (1994, 26) and Paul Beaud (Beaud et al. 1997, 33). One could add to this list, while still not being exhaustive, a number of earlier writers working mostly within the political economy of communications, including a group of French authors who started their work in 1973: Huet et al. (1984/1978), Graham Murdock and Peter Golding (1977), Patrice Flichy (1991/1980), Nicholas Garnham (1979, 1990), Bernard Miège (1979, 1987, 1989, 2000, Miège et al. 1986), Jean-Guy Lacroix and Gaëtan Tremblay (Lacroix and Levesque 1986, Tremblay 1986, Lacroix 1990, Tremblay 1990, Tremblay et al. 1991, Lacroix and Tremblay 1997), Enrique Bustamante and Ramon Zallo (Bustamante and Zallo 1988, Zallo 1988), and Pierre Moeglin (1998), the first to extend the paradigm to the educational industry. One should also take into account the reflections and work conducted within the framework of international organizations, particularly Unesco (Unesco 1980, 1982).

Defining the "Cultural Industries":
Five Propositions

Within this diverse body of writing, we can identify a series of core elements that underpin "Cultural Industries" theory. These can usefully be presented in the form of five propositions.

First proposition: the diversity of cultural merchandise is grounded in differential relations to industrial production

It is one thing to notice that cultural (and informational) products lead to the consumption of various forms of commodities (devices allowing access to cultural resources, goods like books and disks, tickets to performances, art purchases). It is another to specify what differentiates the various fields (book editing, general public or professional information, phonographic editing, cinematographic and audiovisual industries, the sale of paintings and plastic art in galleries, the production of games) that have appeared during different historical periods. It is yet another to illuminate the relation that they do or do not maintain with the system of industrial production, which is more central than ever in contemporary capitalism. The key question is whether cultural commodities that are produced according to artisanal and small production modalities fall within the orbit of the cultural industries. This issue is correlated with the often-made opposition between mass markets and segmented markets. To address it, typologies were elaborated combining criteria of a technical order (such as the possibility or not to reproduce goods in industrially produced series), an economic order (the serialization allowing a closer relation between market prices and value), and social and cultural orders (do artists and intellectuals participate in the design of products?). This last criterion generated the following distinctions:

Type 1: reproducible products not requiring the involvement of informational workers in their production. We are dealing here essentially with technical devices allowing access to cultural and informational resources whose consumption we know has grown rapidly over the past 30 years;

Type 2: reproducible products which involve cultural (and informational) workers in their production, such as books, disks, films, and television programs. We are here at the heart of industrialized cultural merchandise;

Type 3: semireproducible products requiring the intervention of artists, but whose reproduction is limited by technical or socially distinctive processes: lithographs and limited reproductions of fine art, for example;

Type 4: commodities that fall outside the orbit of the cultural industry such as unique pieces of art.

This typology assigns a central position to the notion of reproducibility and presents it as the cultural industry's defining feature.

Second proposition: the unpredictable (or uncertain) character of cultural (or informational) use values generated by industrialized cultural products is another one of its defining features

For cultural products, but also for informational products that are distributed under the form of merchandise or through media, there is one persistent difficulty: that of turning use value (often strongly symbolically charged, as with popular music or entertainment) into an exchange value that can be realized in the market. This operation needs to be renewed regularly because it isn't guaranteed. More than in other categories of industrialized products in daily use, a considerable number of cultural or informational goods are unsuccessful and remain unsold, or are distributed only in very small quantities. In an effort to minimize, or even just control, the uncertain character of product value, industrial corporations implement a series of strategies. These include: calculating costs per series or catalogue rather than per product; price fixing with wide margins, beyond usual norms; not paying wages to the creative / design staff (a point we will return to later); "outsourcing" economic risks to smaller subcontractor firms who are called upon to bear the initial artistic risks of innovation; detailed stock management (sometimes charged by the distributors); regular resorting to public state funding justified by the specificity of the products; confinement in protected linguistic or national spaces; and refinement of the target market with the help of various audience studies. These features can be regarded as structural and have justified the separate treatment of cultural and informational industries among other industrial fields, not as a historical sector (as it may have been assumed in the past), but as one irreducible, at least until now, to the traditional forms of industrialization. Recently, however, the emergence of new information and communication technologies which are subject to capitalist production norms has raised the important question of whether historically specific practices will be abandoned or relegated to marginal or minor branches of production.

Third proposition: artistic and intellectual workers think of their products mostly according to artisan modalities that are supposed to guarantee autonomy in creation

It's important here to note the recurring particularities of the payment modalities for most of those taking part in the creation of cultural products: artists (authors and interpreters), freelance and occasional journalists, and the editorial and design professionals working on books prior to publication. Payment for the majority of these workers escapes the wage system, forcing them to accept other systems of reward such as copyright and freelance payments. There are some permanent workers in newsrooms, as well as in publishing houses and the audio-visual sector, but in most companies half or more of the workforce is made up of precarious and intermittent workers without any secure status. This trait is not a hangover from the past, but a settled characteristic that allows companies to manage a fluid artistic and intellectual workforce and adapt quickly to multiple new demands, genres, forms, and standards, and cope with the risks of failure. This system creates permanent insecurity, and generates a reservoir of workers whose maintenance is only partially at the expense of industrial corporations, and who are always ready to work for minimum pay and conditions. But why do cultural workers agree to work in conditions that have long been rejected in other industries?

Part of the explanation is structural and arises from the increasing generalization of arrangements originally developed to handle relations between writers and book editors under which authors handed in their manuscripts to editors who then dealt with all later operations (such as the manufacturing, marketing, and distribution). Under contemporary conditions, managing rights in the audio-visual industries has become an increasingly complex operation leading to a marked increase in more specialized forms of labor grounded in various branches of law. That the initial simplicity of the system has now given way to increasing complexity and opacity is evidenced by the tendency to replace author rights by copyright that doesn't recognize the patrimonial rights to the work and by the growing interest taken in intellectual property law (as used in computing companies).

As David Hesmondhalgh and others have pointed out, however, innovations in the management of cultural work is not a sufficient explanation. There is also the persistence of professional ideologies of authorship and creativity as a result of which cultural workers are willing to

> trade in financial reward and security for creative autonomy. But a model of power as coercion is insufficient to explain this. There is rarely an authority figure present to tell symbol creators to work so hard for so little reward. In fact, all creative workers … seem to accept poor working conditions (for example, long, difficult hours) for the benefits of being involved in creative projects and the glamour surrounding these worlds. (Hesmondhalgh 2007, 207)

Fourth proposition: the exploitation of industrialized cultural merchandise (from creation to consumption) is based on two fundamental generic models, the editorial model and the flow model

Because the universe of cultural and informational products is extremely diverse, it isn't surprising that relations between artistic and intellectual workers, on the one hand, and readers, listeners, viewers, and Internet users, on the other, display considerable variations. The development of radio broadcasting after World War I introduced a new relationship, based not on purchasing access to a particular cultural production or service, but on accessing a schedule of news and entertainment programming presented, if not continuously, then over long periods of time, and according to a regular schedule. Henceforth, consumers, who still needed to pay to access a book, newspaper, vinyl record, or movie theater ticket, had access to the entire output of commercial broadcasting in the United States (where the model first appeared) free at the point of use, since the costs were covered by earnings from the sale of advertising.

These considerations and others led scholars (initially in France with Patrice Flichy's work in the 1980s) to suggest a fundamental distinction between an *editorial model* (that applied to purchasable cultural goods such as books and disks, and a *flow model* (for mass radio and television). In the first model the locus of creative decision making lies with the editor (e.g., of a newspaper or publishing house). In the second, it lies with the programmer, who assembles and orchestrates the schedule. Yet there are still at least three essential details to add in order to move beyond a superficial approach:

1   Since the model applies throughout the chain of production, distribution, and consumption, and since the same product can be consumed in a variety of forms (as with the possibility of watching the same movie in a movie theater, on a TV channel, or on a DVD), the main agents may differ in different situations. The editor or producer may make way for a programmer, for example. Thus the characterization of the way cultural and media industries function inside this model's frame cannot be narrowly considered, as it is just as much socioeconomical as it is sociosymbolical.

2   The distinction between the two models is based neither on their material nature (the fact that they are distributed using a material base), nor on their immaterial nature, as often thought. The exploitation of cinema in movie theaters that has continued for over a hundred years, for example, is to be considered within the editorial model. At the level of consumption a number of criteria have to be taken into account, the main one being whether individual consumers pay for the right to own an object or good or to take a service *or* become part of a mass audience who choose such and such programs and enjoy free access, either because the media in question have a public service mission and are subsidized out of taxation or because they are financed by advertising resources.

3   Because particular instances often cannot be considered as belonging solely to one model or the other, editorial and flow models should be considered as ideal types. This is particularly important now since arguably the distinction may be getting less and less obvious. Consequently, it is preferable to consider that such and such product borrows aspects from one model or the other, or stands closer to one or the other. Print news, for example, now integrates an almost complete range of situations involving both editorial and flow models (from political weeklies that receive very little revenue from advertising, to the free daily press). Online documentary products may now combine subscriptions and piece rates, as well as advertising. A club package allows subscribers (such as those to the French channel, Canal Plus, or Videotron in Canada) to access a certain number of services during the length of the subscription. We also see the rise of brokerage, where an intermediary or some kind of a representative negotiates with the distributors as to what products may be of interest to the consumer. Added to which, the online generalist with specialized portals that are currently in development, though they don't have stabilized payment methods, may yet generate different formulas.

As these examples show, employing these models and their various permutations not only aids the advance of knowledge, but it also helps in interpreting changes.

Fifth proposition: conceptions of internationalization need to take into account both national cultures and regional configurations

At the beginning of the 1970s, we were able to observe two major trends: a growing concentration and internationalization of appliances and objects (Type 1 products), and the significant presence of small and medium companies owned by national capital for semireproducible products (Type 3). As for edited products (Type 2), they showed themselves to be sites of lively competition between national and transnational capitals, more so for recorded music, audiovisual media, and games than for book editing or mass public-oriented news. The challenges were as much industrial as they were political, cultural, or linguistic, yet the transnationalization that was mainly the initiative of major American companies and Japanese conglomerates (although spreading) was encountering strong resistance because of the space left for national and regional companies to develop. This growth was encouraged by the standardization of technical bases, the emergence of communication networks, and the strategic importance of distribution rights.

However, in contrast to the simplistic views that have ignored diversity and complexity, the entry of cultural industries into global markets did not follow a simple course or a peaceful progression, as later confirmed by the negotiations that subsequently took place within regional bodies (like the European Union) and international authorities (such as GATT and the WTO on cultural merchandise, and Unesco on cultural diversity).

To sum up, the five propositions outlined here have shaped the development of Cultural Industries Theory over three decades. As indicated, changes and mutations in the organization of these industries have been continuous to the point that the end of their specificities (or their originality) is regularly announced. The reconsideration of protective regulations, the development of networks, and the erosion of national cultures by transnational standards are all cited as factors incorporating the cultural industries into the ranks of industries in general. If this argument is correct, then their life cycle would be coming to an end, a cycle that would have lasted for approximately a century, if we leave out book and newspaper editing with their roots in the eighteenth century. This conclusion deserves to be looked at more closely, however, before we rush to endorse first impressions or general announcements.

Mutations and Reconsiderations

There are good reasons why the cultural industries have been experiencing important developments since the end of the twentieth century, not least the fact that they are now seen to be particularly representative and emblematic of the general transformations of contemporary capitalism and globalization. The terms employed to describe the major shifts pinpoint the main changes that have attracted attention: financialization, concentration, internationalization, multimediation, medialization, digitization, convergence, new media, deregulation and reregulation, industrialization (of content creation), commodification, rationalization, standardization (of technical norms and uses), individualization of practices. All these define the major forces at work, as well as the fact that we are in the presence of some major issues.

What follows is an attempt to characterize the mutations now taking place in the cultural industries by grouping them into four series.

First series of mutations: those that reveal the economic and financial strategies of capital holders

Concentration   The issue of increasing *concentration* in the media and cultural industries and the rise of more and more powerful communication groups (themselves often controlled by financial centers and industrial conglomerates), has recently emerged as a central preoccupation. But as Vincent Mosco has argued, despite its growing importance, it remains a mistake to make concentration the sole focus of attention. As he notes:

> rethinking political economy includes recognizing that, though important, corporate size and concentration are just starting points for understanding the transformation of the communication business. Global restructuring offers numerous opportunities to expand control from the conglomerate form to the range of flexible alternatives. The chief requirements include controlling central points in the production, distribution and exchange process (outright ownership is one among numerous alternatives) and remaining flexible to respond to changing markets and technologies. (Mosco 1996, 198)

Various authors have tried to analyze the concentration phenomenon using empirical and historical data to trace the strategies adopted by the large communication groups. They include (chronologically): Armand Mattelart (1976), Enrique Bustamante and Ramon Zallo (1988), Ramon Zallo (1992), Gaëtan Tremblay (1990), Edward Herman and Robert McChesney (1997), Bustamante (2002, 2003, Bustamante and Miguel de Bustos 2005), Guillermo Mastrini and Martin Beccera (2003), as well as the research on 19 French communication groups directed by Bernard Miège (see also 2005 *Réseaux* articles by Philippe Bouquillion and Christian Pradié). This list, though incomplete, illustrates the desire by those working in the field to develop validated knowledge concerning the evolution of major groups and their strategies. Research in this area, however, remains primarily national, and more recently regional, with authors having trouble proposing a worldwide approach.

There is, however, a widespread consensus that concentration is accelerating and that this movement will further intensify. Herman and McChesney, for example, argue that:

> The global media market is dominated by ten or so vertically integrated media conglomerates, most of which are based in the United States. Another thirty or forty significant supporting firms round out the meaningful position in the system. These firms operate in oligopolistic markets with substantial barriers to entry. They compete vigorously on a non-price basis, but their competition is softened not only by common interest as oligopolies, but also by a vast array of joint ventures, strategic alliances, and cross-ownership among the leading firms ... The market is still in the process of rapid change, and more mergers, acquisitions, and joint ventures can be expected before the dust clears. (Herman and McChesney 1997, 104)

Bustamante and Miguel de Bustos conclude their analysis of the situation in Latin America by arguing that: "the concentration seems in every case, and in nearly every country of Latin America, to be an essential characteristic in cultural industries, television and press markets being extremely concentrated, unlike the radio market that sees far more competition" (Bustamante and de Bustos 2005, 61).

Werner Meier, commenting on the Europe situation, notes that:

> Concentration in media means the concentration of economical and societal power used by dominating communication firms against their competitors ... [it] operates through internal and external growths of communication companies ... concentration of property does not only constitute an economic drift, it is also a fundamental problem for democracy because economic power can be turned into political power as well as into power of opinion, therefore being a menace for democracy. The concentration and power of media are phenomena that fundamentally characterize the modern media system based on competition. (Meier 2005, 21, 22, 42)

Philippe Bouquillion, Bernard Miège, and Claire Moriset, observing the recent moves towards further concentration in the French cultural and media industries in 2004 and 2005 argue that "Concentration of financial operations are accelerating ... leading to important multi media integration ... accentuating in the print industries" (Bouquillion et al. 2006, 151–2).

All of these authors deplore the lack of significant available data. Furthermore, they underline the complexity of the global tendency toward concentration, pointing out that it is constituted by multiple movements (e.g., a rapid concentration in the print press field, but with multimedia synergies yet to come), and embraces phenomena that aren't as easy to explain as it may first appear.

But beyond the general insistence that concentration of ownership leads to a strengthening of domination and control as well as a weakening of pluralism and quality (in a growing international frame), its specific impacts in particular circumstances often remain difficult to trace. Werner Meier, for example, lists no less than 28 possible consequences of media concentration on media organization and journalism, the media market, and the political power of culture (Meier 2005, 39–40). They certainly cannot be mechanically deduced from control takeovers for a variety of reasons. First, they manifest themselves mostly over long periods of time, rather than immediately as direct consequences to changes made to the composition of corporate capital. Second, capital centralization in financial centers controlling communication groups does not automatically produce changes in firms or synergy attempts between them (they could, for example, be of a multimedia nature). Third, increased pressure on independent production and on national and regional productions, and moves toward their extinction, is not always the case. Fourth, the extension of the market doesn't necessarily lead to the industrialization of content. Finally, the growing resort to information and communication techniques does not inevitably mean that content becomes more and more serialized.

On the other hand, we need to keep Philippe Bouquillion's central conclusion in mind: "concentration allows dominant oligopoly actors to develop market power at the expense of consumers as well as economic agents that don't belong to the oligopoly, particularly small agents that are frequently related to production" (Bouquillion 2008, 278). It has been clear for some time that cultural industry fields (or branches) are generally marked by the coexistence of oligopoly with a competitive fringe (or anthill). In this structural formation, a small number of dominant groups mostly control distribution while a multitude of small independent producers, who have no option but to take artistic risks, are responsible for the majority of creative innovations. Over the last 25 years, although the anthill hasn't reduced (it has even grown in some branches, sometimes in increasingly precarious conditions), oligopoly has tended to become duopoly, not to say monopoly, as well as internationalizing. This is an essential characteristic which deeply marks the contemporary cultural and media industries. The dominant groups in a monopolistic position do not, however, usually have stakes across the entire chain of production. They prefer to control distribution and dispose of program bases while taking advantage of their privileged position to buy up distribution rights. At the same time, this tendency hides other decisive changes, although they aren't yet completed, in the sphere of finance.

Financialization   During recent years we have witnessed important shifts in patterns of investment in communication, particularly in the content industries with the growing centrality of financial institutions. In order to analyze these movements, however, we need to distinguish between several different trends:

1 Investments in media and cultural corporations coming from, for example, pension funds with financial efficiency objectives on a scale from 12 to 15 percent (*financialization*, strictly speaking);

2   The *financial operations* of financial groups. Philippe Bouquillion insists perti-
    nently on the autonomy of these financial operations, pointing among other
    cases to the link-ups between AOL and Time Warner, or Disney and ABC, and
    arguing that speculative financial operations are at the root of some strategies
    in the information, culture, and communication spheres (Bouquillion 2008,
    25–40);
3   The *capital operations* that are part of an industrial strategy that, in the media
    and cultural industries, aren't yet fully analyzed.

Only operations of this third type have direct implications for cultural creation and
the quality of information. The other two, however, have the power to rigorously
question the value of various activities or editorial projects.

It isn't easy to find one's way around the maze of multiple operations and financial coups, and we need to be careful not to mistake *firms* (such as Canal Plus
International), with *groups* (like Canal Plus), *financial conglomerates* (like Vivendi
Universal), and *financial centers* (such as the banks or insurance companies that
control the conglomerates).

These technical and conceptual difficulties, however, have not prevented new
detailed analyses being done. We can cite Scott Fitzgerald's conclusions (Fitzgerald
2008, 284), that financialization, associated with reregulation and vertical integration movements, has "reinforced the inherently anti-competitive context in which
the majority of global media operate." This clearly appears in the agreements that
the seven main media groups operating in Australia have recently concluded, establishing a 50 percent joint venture with a big financial group. This trend needs to be
emphasized because it seems to be strengthening in all regions of the world. Even
if they are in a situation of strong competition for a share of audiences or the
distribution of products, major groups (most often in oligopolistic situation in their
respective areas of distribution) agree to establish anticompetition measures, likely
to curb the ambitions of new entrants. Nuria Almiron, however, argues that simply
studying the relations between the financial sphere and new informational
industries is insufficient (Almiron 2008a, 2008b, 287). She attempts to measure the
financialization of the six big American media conglomerate groups using six
criteria: the corporation's property holdings, its stock shares, its debts, financial
tools, the board of directors, and corporate goals. She is right to insist that to understand the growth of financialization and to evaluate the dominant position of finance
at the center of corporate media, one cannot be satisfied with an approach concentrated on property control only, and that other criteria have to be taken into account.

Widening and refinement of advertising strategies   The next major
shift to be taken into account is the widening and refinement of *advertising strategies*. Advertising and media have been inextricably bound together for a long
time, generating a "double market" produced by two related and successive
operations:

- the constitution of a regular audience (the first clients), whose loyalty is to be secured and authenticated with measures as precise as possible.
- the evaluation of these audiences by advertisers (the second clients), who are then invited to buy advertising space priced according to audience size, social composition, and attention potential.

This second market puts into motion a logistic, generally hidden from consumers, that was perfected during the second half of the twentieth century with the diversification of media forms and the related intensification of competition for audience time and attention.

Although the links between media and advertising funding are often hidden, or presented as accidental or even contingent, their constant interrelation is suspected by a large number of users. But outside of public service media endowed with sufficient and regular resources, there hasn't been until now any alternative means of financial support others than those provided by either advertisers or consumers.

This being said, established media (particularly the press and commercial broadcasting) are becoming less and less significant for advertising. In the 1990s, a largely unnoticed transfer of resources occurred in which nonmedia outlets (principally direct marketing) overtook media outlets (such as press, radio, cinema, outside posters, and television). In France nowadays (according to professional estimations), advertising spending on nonmedia promotion is double that spent on media. In financial terms, the total resources going to media are stationary, and growth is mainly happening in areas (such as flyers and coupons) that aim to establish and maintain a personalized relation with consumers. The same is true of the Internet over the past 10 years. Of course, the evolution we have just described should not be overestimated because advertising campaigns know very well how to operate across different bases and combine different platforms, and sociosymbolic impact cannot be equated with the distribution of total spending. From the point of view of the advertiser's interests, however, dominant media are currently proving relatively inadequate. At the same time, although the formation of new media on the Internet is now well advanced and their growth rapid, their relative importance should not be exaggerated.

It should also be added that the advertising industry is encountering, as John Sinclair noted during an investigation in four Latin America countries, "complex dynamics of the global/local dialectic" generating "an intricate and shifting set of institutional relations between advertising agencies, their clients ... and the media," that "binds the leading nations ... into both economic and cultural globalisation" (Sinclair 2008, 284).

Alongside advertising we need to add to our analysis other tools for promoting markets and stimulating expectations and requests. These marketing techniques assume multiple forms and are mainly mobilized in conjunction with product commercialization, but are still only rarely used to stimulate artistic creation. On the other hand, a lot of work is now done on the consumption environment, where corporate promotional discourses are now omnipresent and largely uncontested due to the decline and marginalization of critical rhetorics. The colonization by brand magazines of the spaces usually occupied by specialized journals and critical columns is a prime example.

The rationalization of editorial strategies   Although financialization and the concentration of ownership in media and cultural industrial groups tend not to have immediate and mechanical effects on given content, they are at the center of analysts' preoccupations for an obvious reason. Acquired economic power easily transforms itself into market power that encourages action on social practices and even on public opinions. The acquisition and control over media and cultural firms may also have connections with the winning or conservation of political power as shown by such cases as Silvio Berlusconi in Italy, Rafic Hariri in Lebanon, and the obvious complicities between groups such as Lagardère or Bolloré and the most senior French leaders. The fact is, however, that we shouldn't assume that linkages between company aims and political objectives operate as a matter of course, firstly because games of power are often very complex, secondly because we also need to develop an "analysis of changing media policy" that sees it as the site of continual conflicts of interest whose outcome cannot always be easily predicted in advance (IAMCR, 2008, 276), and thirdly because focusing solely on the political deployment of corporate power ignores the central role played by profit-maximization strategies in exerting pressure on editors, series editors (in book and music editing), as well as program directors and producers (in cinema and audiovisual media) and authors.

At the same time, recent research on book editing in France offers another perspective. The author Christian Robin, examining long-term developments and drawing on a very complete list of criteria, concludes that:

> To the question of whether management tools got in the way of ambitious production projects and limited creativity, the answer is clearly negative. Important studies are still published today, including some on large groups. Creativity has not disappeared – on the contrary. The effect of management tools on content, if it still exists, has more to do with the representations that actors have of it than what they are used for … However, the use of management tools tends to put pressure on the coherence of the project's internal choices. On these concerns, pushed too far in the framework of bad quality or unproductive relations between managers and editorial directors, these managing methods risk restraining creativity. Indeed, systematically rationalizing can reach irrational and counterproductive decisions, especially in literature. (Robin, 2003)

The author also emphasizes the essential role played by new technical tools in the conception and making of books during the period he considers. The perspective suggested here is very promising, as it shows how an approach focusing solely on cases considered as exemplary risks giving a truncated vision. Added to which, this perspective bases reflections on a long-term period, whereas the social discourses coming from professionals or users are essentially working with a short, or very short, time scale. Of course, we cannot neglect emerging tendencies or what the present turbulent circumstances might portend, but before anything else, we must continue to place current changes and movements in the context of longer term processes or else locate (with methodological precaution) "threshold effects." We need to remain continuously questioning when coming face to face with emerging logistics, that may not be continued or reinforced or whose effects take time to gather momentum. The digitalization of press news, for example, prompted some initial work in the 1990s, but it is only since 2006 that its full implications have begun to become clear.

Faced with the technical and practical difficulties in following the major developments in different fields in a detailed way, one way forward is to employ a series of indicators that seem to have a strong potential to fill in the most obvious gaps in the analysis of the mutations being experienced by informational and communicational industries. The term "indicator" is used here to designate a synthetic tool of analysis for charting a movement in progress. The most relevant indicators are the following (Miège 2007, pp. 235–238):

- Independent production: maintained, done away with, or in difficulty?
- The "tube and catalogue" dialectic: does the calculation of profitability depend on reliance on the catalogue or series, or title by title?
- The internationalization of norms and standards, resulting in the formatting of products: is this happening?
- The socialization and technical medialization of the products' conception: is it accelerating?
- The accelerated distribution of art works through various bases and media: is this happening?
- The uniqueness of the art work: is it maintained or inserted into a larger group of products, including derived ones, and with the partial payment of production costs by promotional resources?

Second series of mutations: legal and political shifts

Under this heading, two fundamental movements can be identified: the readjustment of regulatory regimes, and shifts in the copyright system.

Regulatory adjustments   The constant adjustment of the regulations governing radio broadcasting, telecommunications, and content industries, according to a position combining economic liberalization and reregulation, began a quarter of a century ago and is still in process. It has proceeded by way of leaps crossing successive thresholds, and although it isn't specific to information and communication fields, and has provoked strong critiques and resistance from consumers and professionals, it has introduced into Europe a radically new economic environment. Although results and perceptions differ from one country to another (notably between Britain on the one hand, and the Northern countries and France on the other), similar consequences can be found, as for example, the strong commodification of telecommunications, the multiplication of private television channels, and wider openings in worldwide markets for cultural and informational products. Two essential questions remain, however: first, are we moving toward the definitive weakening of public broadcasting, and more particularly of established political and normative criteria defining what constitutes a public service? And second, in the matter of cultural and artistic content, will government organizations continue to take primary responsibility for making policy (thus promoting cultural and linguistic identities), or will they give way to the private sector?

Both questions need be asked with greater urgency now as it is becoming harder and harder to find the necessary resources for the production of diverse programming and content, whether from private foundations (the 2008 crash didn't help), or from the consumers' side with people less inclined to pay for content and more interested in apparently "free" access. The strong rhetorical resistances to culture's commodification, and its widened transnationalization, hide a continuing, and arguably deepening, problem of resource availability.

Shifts in copyright   The second major movement concerns shifts in the copyright system, and authors' rights in the whole production–consumption chain. The conclusions arrived at by Vincent Bullich in his study of the evolution of recorded music regulations in the United States from 1877 to 2007, can easily be generalized to the rest of the cultural industries:

> Far from being autoregulated, the phonographic market is thus fundamentally the result of a political construction that creates and guarantees an "authority resource" (the exclusive right to use and broadcast a piece of work) and partly organizes the transmutation into "allocation resources" (the definition of economic transaction modalities, related to the users' license) ... This relation results in an organization of political, economic, and legal perspectives, that renew with every media-related innovation; it mobilizes different agents in the music recording world (and namely the biggest pressure groups that exist) who push their interests forward and express their capacity to intervene in the processes of law elaborations and applications. (Bullich 2008, pp. 455–6)

This legal and regulatory framework is no longer limited to the United States, nor to recorded music, and it is likely that its reach will be accentuated, although contested (as it has always been) by consumers, by new agents in the cultural and informational industries (in particular computing companies), and by emerging countries.

More generally, it has to be expected that with globalization, a more or less global regime will emerge, constructed around the interests of the most powerful firms in controlling the cost of artistic and intellectual production and maximizing returns. This process has already been engaged during the various commercial negotiations inside the World Trade Organization aiming to position cultural merchandise on the same level as other goods and services.

Third series of mutations: the individualization, differentiation, and mediatization of practices

Several developments in the organization of consumption practices need to be taken into account here. They are each distinct, although they are interrelated and mutually supportive.

Individualization and differentiation   The plural individualization of cultural and informational practices is confirmed by the available data as well as the convergence of widely observable tendencies around the world, including those in the leading countries. Key features include:

- the growing use and access to personalized cultural goods, tools, and devices, all massively produced (for the past 30 years)
- the underlying connection, that is much more recent, between these tools, communication networks, and contents
- a double polarization: the persistence of inequalities and social distinction effects and the reinforcement of individual strategies of action
- the significant impact of generational and genre effects, on growth of differentiations
- the emphasis placed on the interpenetration and shift in spheres of action, notably between professional and private lives.

But rather than follow the majority of authors, in particular cultural sociologists, who conclude, with only a cursory look at the data, that we are currently witnessing the growing individualization of social practices, we prefer to note the simultaneous pluralization and differentiation of these same practices. The individualization argument makes too many concessions to technodeterminism and underestimates the historical grounding of practices. Information and communication technologies (ICTs), as well as other emerging media technologies, may encourage and support more individualized practices, but they didn't invent them. Peer-to-peer sharing, for example, belongs to a long tradition of archiving, collecting, exchanging, and copying recorded music, legally allowed or not. It is amplified by, but does not originate in, the use of powerful online systems.

Mediatization   It was observed a long time ago that mediated communication has progressively entered into every aspect of social life and relations. This trend is seen to have accelerated with the growth of ICTs and digital devices. Despite the negative estimations of some intellectuals, what we are witnessing is coexistence and even complementarity, rather than displacement. The time spent in front of computer screens for private activities hasn't been to the detriment of interindividual exchanges, for example, nor has the rise of home schooling – a possibility that was originally seen as occupying a growing proportion of curriculum time – enjoyed the success that was predicted for it.

Supporters of the mediatization of communication as a liberating force, however, ignore the fact that it is supported by a series of organizational modalities that are part of programs conceived by specialists, and implemented by industrial groups who have rapidly acquired a worldwide reach and a quasi-monopolist position. Take, for example, the "Googlization" of information processing, archiving, and formatting that has become a central phenomenon in culture and information industrialization in the last few years. This new communication form is presented by its enthusiasts as open, and favoring personal initiatives, reinterpretations, and diversion by final users. At the same time, it conceals within itself everything that was conceived and preconstructed by the makers, and controlled by the firms, in order to adapt the products to expectations, and thus ensure their commercial distribution.

The process of digitalization, that is now on the way to becoming relatively generalized, isn't driven by an imperial technological trend but has to be considered as a socioeconomic construction to which powerful actors contribute. In this respect, the issue of "free" access to cultural practices must be raised again. While user-consumers, or at least, a certain number of them, are willing to pay the connection costs and purchase the required tools and appliances and computing services, they show considerable reluctance to pay for cultural and informational services, and try to escape charges by using (or abusing?) various open technological possibilities. This raises a very important quasi-global issue, that will be discussed later.

Fourth series of mutations, the ones specifically affecting cultural and media industries in their functioning modalities

Four issues need to be considered here: convergence, homogenization, the future of editorial and flow models, and relations between the "creative industries" and the cultural industries

Convergence   Under this heading we need to consider the bringing together of the cultural industries with media, and the partial integration of performing arts into the industrial sphere.

The industrialization process, defined earlier on, should not be confused with the marketing movement nor understood in a metaphorical sense (as is often the case in artistic professions), or seen only as the resort to new technical means, such as with ICTs. At the base of its formation is the centrality of reproduction. An original copy can either be inscribed on a material base (paper, vinyl, plastic) or it can assume a virtual or immaterial character (a possibility first introduced by the projection of films in movie theaters). That is why, together with other commentators, we have excluded public cultural institutions (such as museums and historical monuments) from our definition of the cultural industry, together with private organizations responsible for the production and distribution of performance arts, and independent or alternative media. It has always been difficult in the cultural and informational fields to trace a clear border between what belongs to the industrial world and what is to be distinguished from it, because numerous small and medium-sized companies that work in an artisan way are in reality sometimes very profitable subcontractors, and are either industrial companies in their own right or aiming at industrial development. However, the neglect of the core criterion of reproducibility by professionals and experts has led to a series of damaging confusions that arise from the fact that the dominant conception of cultural work is still, as we noted earlier, very much organized according to artisan modalities. The performing arts (essentially theater, dance, and music concerts) present a particular case since, although many remain organized by private entrepreneurs and operate with a degree of durability over time, it is difficult for them to attain a high-scale economy since every evening the artists replay their act in front of various different audiences. This can't really be considered an industrial activity.

The paradox raised by this theoretical perspective is that if it keeps its relevance by tracing clear lines of separation, its crude application leads to oddities, as for example when the production of small publishers is considered to be industrial although they are hardly economically profitable. At the same time, the relations between the two worlds are steadily becoming stronger. Live concerts have long been a promotional base for recorded music, but now a reversal is happening, due to the technical and promotional means employed, as the economic profitability of international stars and their shows outstrips the returns from record sales. In the sphere of mass market-oriented audiovisual media, the generalized resort to subcontracting for production has led, as noted earlier, to oligopolistic groups that are partially in competition. Although their major resources don't come from final consumption, they cannot be classified outside of the industrial world. On the other hand, a whole series of artistic expressions are excluded from this category (such as dramatic arts, choreography, poetry), as well as public initiatives or associative organizations (such as public museums, although they use derived products).

Hence, although the reproducibility criterion retains its relevance when it comes to identifying the industrial sphere of culture, and what differentiates it from industry in general, we need to add that this same sphere is not only enlarged, but now also includes organizations and actors that have created stable and complementary relations with actors at the heart of it, or from other industries, such as network industries.

Homogenization   The development of digital ICTs is considered by some authors and observers to be the origin of decisive transformations that have disrupted the established modalities of cultural and media industries, rendering their promotion unpredictable and random, by allowing amateur or independent productions to offer durable competition to major productions.

The available research, however (see Bouquillion and Combès 2007, Bouquillion 2008), doesn't confirm this conclusion. As we argued earlier, we are also seeing the strengthening of concentration around strongly implanted oligopolies in different fields, as well as the rationalization of editorial choices, both tendencies being facilitated by the constant weakening of public politics. At the same time, we are also seeing polarization in each branch of production between a small number of blockbusters conceived to provide the majority of the sales in terms of profitability (in order to become bestsellers), and a proliferation, a profusion even, of accessible products that work on the margins of economic profit. In brief, we may be witnessing the twilight of the "catalogue and tube dialectic." The consequence will not be a lack of plurality (on the contrary, there has never been so much accessible cultural merchandise), but rather a reduction in cultural diversity, as precarious economic conditions continue to discourage risk taking among the major players, unless a multitude of very segmented "niches" were likely to form mass markets.

However, the shifts in different cultural and media industries (books, recorded music, cinema, mass public and specialized information, and now video games, online or not), doesn't seem to be leading to the homogenization of the cultural and media industries, or the horizontal integration that was announced some time ago. Rather, they work according to common or similar logistics, but they keep their own ways of working, and even accentuate them while presenting their products on various common bases (in a multibase frame).

The future of editorial and flow models   The question of the evolution or future of the models described here cannot be separated from the wider analysis of the cultural industries in contemporary capitalism. We either see these industries as forming the heart of future capitalistic development, which leads us to deny all their originalities and specificities, or else we consider them as remnants or archaisms that are about to disappear. Yet it has to be stressed again that the models that we have defined here are ideal types, and are not restricted to the level of the financing of cultural merchandise. They embrace the whole of the conception-production-consumption chain, and put their stamp on the practices of user-consumers. The present situation is all the more difficult to interpret as it is shaped by the intersection of different disruptive or emerging phenomena. These consist in: (1) the increase or the widening of the industrialized information and cultural products on offer in the different fields, and the development of video games as a new field; (2) the extension of the media field to new media; (3) the increasing competition between artists, designers, producers, and distributors, for the distribution of the resources set aside by consumers for this category of products (against a background of stationary and even falling public funding); (4) the difficulty of raising the prices charged; (5) the continuing diversification of modes of access to products, from the personal acquisition of a concrete product (e.g., a book) to the direct use of content online (watching a commercial television channel talk show), and passing through a whole series of intermediate modes, the most significant being payment per piece, or pay per view, an example of the new rerun of the economy of urban services; and finally (6) the demand by consumers, particularly younger ones, or emerging countries, for free access to content, facilitated by the technical possibilities offered by the tools they have at hand, and reinforced by the means of payment for intellectual production in the computing industries.

We have a complex transitional situation then, characterized by divergent and multiple interests, including major new agents for whom the principal logistics at work can't yet be specified with any certainty. Being generic, the editorial and flow models are still in a strong position. But a very diversified neoclub model interposes itself between them, as much a result of the rise of subscription television as of new platforms (more or less in relation with Internet access). But it must be added that the editorial model, as with the flow and the club, have hybrid variants, with a rising presence of advertising and sponsoring. This evolution currently leaves very little space for brokerage.

The "Creative Industries" and the Cultural Industries

When approaching the question of the creative industries, and their very recent emergence in cultural politics and in the struggle against deindustrialization in European countries, three aspects need to be distinguished.

Firstly, New Labour's pioneering, and influential deployment of the idea of the "creative industries" in the UK, confirms, as Philip Schlesinger has pointed out, that this discourse can provide the basis for an industrial political doctrine, and even an ideology:

> In the UK, the discourse of creativity has been developed by the government for the past decade, and is currently being bound into a "creative economy" conception. Official thinking is discursive in the sense that it is a self-sustaining outlook increasingly driven towards consistency. It has become a doctrine by virtue of being an object of unceasing advocacy by its proponents. It is now an inevitable starting point for those who wish to enter into dialogue with policymakers. (Schlesinger 2007, 378)

In this way, the author goes on to say: "the doctrine of creativity is now an animating ideology for a so-called digital age … [and] may be seen as the latest attempt to rationalize interdepartmental cooperation, to make the flow of business intelligence effective, to encourage networking, to bring together dispersed creative clusters and to foster talent" (Schlesinger 2007, 387). Although the success of this politics has not yet been demonstrated, the European Union is preparing a Green Book, and other countries are ready to head in the same direction.

Secondly, it is important to ask oneself what the economic foundations of this doctrine are, and to examine the work of liberal economists of culture, like David Throsby, who have acted as its spokespeople. According to them, although creative workers are to be found in all industrial sectors, the creative industries are distinguished by the fact that they are made up of organizations where creativity management is considered central, and that offer strongly symbolically charged products that are capitalized by way of intellectual property rights. That is why they may potentially be considered strong job creators. The fields in which they are to be most obviously operational are: fashion, design, advertising, gastronomy, digital platforms, architecture, arts and crafts (partly), cultural heritage (partly also), fields that have been for the most part included in the industrial politics of culture for the past two decades at least (e.g., in France), but that we didn't consider until now as decisive for the production of resources.

Thirdly, we need to ask whether the creative industries include the cultural industries (in the way we have defined them here) or whether they are separate, with some overlap on the margins. For most specialists, one cannot confuse creativity, thought of as the capacity to generate original ideas and new practices, with cultural creation. They are often conflated by political leaders who tend to lump them together, which is a very approximate way of seeing things, theoretically and practically. On the one hand, creativity management techniques are incompletely used in cultural and informational industries. On the other hand creative industries conform hardly or not at all to the core criteria that we employed earlier to define the cultural industries: reproducibility; the uncertain character of use values; organization around editorial, flow, and club models; and moderated internationalization. The conception of creative autonomy may be common to both industries, but the organizational modalities differ, related in one case to author rights or to copyright, and in the other to intellectual property rights. As such, their integration into one another is still an issue to be figured out.

Conclusion

The future, even in the short term of the cultural industries, is not easily predictable. We are witnessing the intersection of various mutations, all as decisive as one another. Against this background, it is obvious that current approaches that consider the future as dependent primarily on either technological changes or financial capital strategies are hasty and false. As we have tried to show, many other elements need to be taken into account. The future is thus neither undetermined nor random. Rather it depends on the shifting balance between structural elements forged over the long development of these industries and current potential vectors for innovation. Within this space, it is the conflicting relation between the strategies of the different agents (the "majors" in communication toward user-consumers) that will get to define, probably with strong variations in different regions of the world, what comes to constitute the old industries and the emerging and dominated ones (both of which show a reluctance to accept models that were formed and perfected among the first wave industries).

Furthermore, as Dal Yong Jin observes, if in the last two decades

> some developing countries, including Mexico, Singapore and Korea, have increased their role in the cross-deal market, the inequality and imbalance in the communication industry between developed countries and developing countries still exist in the midst of neoliberal transformation. Although the US has lightly lost its power in the global Mergers and Acquisitions market, the gap between a few Western countries and developing countries remains significant. (Yong Jin 2008, 370)

The Old World groups' capacity to resist change is particularly observable in the media and cultural industrial field where they have battled hard to hang on to their historic competitive advantages.

Finally, we must not forget to add that all these mutations are supported, promoted even, by actions aiming to impose their own preferred social representations of modernity. This project involves everything that goes into the technical medialization and marketing processes (and thus the organization of payment by consumers) and confirms once more that the development of capitalism is accelerated by modifications of an ideological order.

References

Almiron, N. (2008a) Conglomerats de comunicacio al segle XXI: financiaritzacio i deficit democratic. *L'Espill* 28, 60–74. Online at http://www.almiron.org/L'espill28.pdf (accessed September 22, 2010).

Almiron, N. (2008b) Media conglomerates and the financial system in the USA: Links and dependencies. Paper presented at IAMCR conference, Media and Global Divides, Stockholm, Sweden, July 20–25.

Beaud, P., Flichy, P., and Sauvage, M. (1984) La télévision comme industrie culturell. *Réseaux*, 9, 5–21.

Bouquillion, P. (2005) La constitution des pôles des industries de la culture et de la communication. Entre "coups financiers" et intégration de filières industrielles. *Réseaux*, 23(131), 111–42.

Bouquillon, P. (2008) *Les industries de la culture et de la communication, les stratégies du capital-isme*. Presses Universitaires de Grenoble, Grenoble.

Bouquillon, P. and Combès, Y. (eds) (2007) *Les industries de la culture et de la communication*. L'Harmattan, Paris.

Bouquillon, P., Miège, B., and Moriset, C. (2006) A propos des mouvements récents de concentration capitalistique dans les industries culturelles et médiatiques. *Le Temps des Médias*, 6, 151–64.

Bullich, V. (2008) La régulation de la médiatisation de la musique par le dispositif du copyright. Doctoral thesis, Université Stendhal Grenoble.

Bustamante, E. (1999) *La television economica: financiation, estrategias y mercados*. Gedisa éditorial, Barcelona.

Bustamante, E. (ed.) (2002) *Comunicacion y cultura en la era digital (Industrias, mercados y diversidad en Espana)*. Gedisa editorial, Barcelona.

Bustamante, E. (ed.) (2003) *Hacia un nuevo sistema mondial de comunicacion – Las industrias culturales en la era digital*. Gedisa editorial, Barcelona.

Bustamante, E. and Miguel de Bustos, J. C. (2005) Les groupes de communication ibéro-américains à l'heure de la convergence. *Réseaux*, 23(131), 53–83.

Bustamante, E. and Zallo, R. (1988) *Las industrias culturales en Espana- Grupos multimedia y transnacionales*. Akal/Comunicacion, Madrid.

Fitzgerald, S. (2008) The media in Australia: Contre-marché. Paper presented at the IAMCR conference, Media and Global Divides, Stockholm, Sweden, July 20–25.

Flichy, P. (1980, 1991) Les industries de l'imaginaire. Pour une analyse économique des médias. Presses Universitaires de Grenoble and Institut National de l'Audiovisuel, Paris.

Garnham, N. (1979) Contribution to a political economy of mass communication. *Media, Culture and Society* 1(1), 123–46.

Garnham, N. (1990) *Capitalism and Communication: Global Culture and the Economics of Information*. Sage Publications, London.

Herman, E. S. and McChesney, R. W. (1997) *The Global Media: The New Missionaries of Corporate Capitalism*. Cassell, London.

Herscovici, A. (1994) *Économie de la culture et de la communication*. L'Harmattan, Paris.

Hesmondhalgh, D. (2007) *The Cultural Industries*, 2nd edn. Sage Publications, London.

Horkheimer, M. and Adorno, T. W. (1974) *La dialectique de la raison* (revised edn). Gallimard, Paris.

Huet, A., Ion, J., Lefèbvre, A., Miège, B., and Péron, R. (1984/1978) *Capitalisme et industries culturelles*. PUG, Grenoble.

IAMCR (2008) *Media and Global Divides*. (IAMCR Conference Papers.) Stockholm University, Stockholm, Sweden.

Lacroix, J. G. (1990) *La condition d'artiste: une injustice*. VLB éditeur, Outremont, Québec.

Lacroix, J. G., and Levesque, B. (1986) Les industries culturelles au Quebec un enjeu vital. *Les Cahiers de recherche sociologique*, Département de sociologie de l'UQAM, 4(2), 39–62.

Lacroix, J. G. and Tremblay, G. (1997) The "information society" and cultural industries theory. *Current Sociology* 45(4), 1–153.

Mastrini, G., and Becerra, M. (2003) *Diagnostico para el studio de la concentracion de la propriedad,* Instituto Prensa y sociedad. Online at http://www.ipys.org/index.php (accessed November 1, 2010).

Mattelart, A. (1976) Multinationales et systèmes de communication: Les appareils idéologiques de l'impérialisme. Anthropos, Paris.

Meier, W. (2005) Media concentration governance: Une nouvelle plate-forme pour débattre des risques? *Réseaux,* 23(131), 17–52.

Miège, B. (1979) The cultural commodity. *Media, Culture and Society* 1, 297–311.

Miège, B. (1987) The logics at work in the new cultural industries. *Media, Culture and Society* 9, 273–89.

Miège, B. (1989) *The Capitalization of Cultural Production.* International, New York/ Bagnolet.

Miège, B. (2000) *Les industries du contenu face à l'ordre informationnel.* PUG, Grenoble.

Miège, B. (ed.) (2005) La concentration dans les industries de contenu. *Réseaux,* 23(131).

Miège, B. (2007) Nouvelles considérations et propositions méthodologiques sur les mutations en cours dans les industries culturelles et informationnelles In: Bouquillion, P. and Combès, Y. (eds) *Les industries de la culture et de la communication.* L'Harmattan, Paris, pp. 228–50.

Miège, B., Pajon, P. and Salaün, J. M. (1986) *L'industrialisation de l'audiovisuel: des programmes pour les nouveaux médias.* Aubier-Montaigne, Paris.

Moeglin, P. (ed.) (1998) *L'industrialisation de la formation: état de la question.* Centre National de Documentation Pédagogique, Paris.

Mosco, V. (1996) *The Political Economy of Communication.* Sage, London.

Murdock, G. and Golding, P. (1977) Capitalism, communication, and class relations. In: Curran, J. et al. (eds) *Mass Communication and Society.* The Open University Press, Milton Keynes, UK, pp. 12–43.

Pradié, C. (2005) Capitalisme et financiarisation des industries culturelles. *Réseaux,* 23(131), 83–109.

Robin, C. (2003) La gestion et le contenu des livres In: *Les enjeux de l'information et de la communication.* Gresec, Université Stendhal. Online at http://w3.u-grenoble3.fr/les_enjeux/2003/Robin/index.php (accessed September 22, 2010).

Schiller, H. I. (1976) *Communication and Cultural Domination.* International Arts and Sciences Press, White Plains, NY.

Silem, A. (1991) *Encyclopédie de l'économie et de la gestion.* Hachette, Paris.

Sinclair, J. (2008) The advertising industry in Latin America: A comparative study. Paper presented at IAMCR conference, Media and Global Divides, Stockholm, July 20–25.

Tremblay, G. (1986) Développement des industries culturelles et transformation de la radiodiffusion canadienne. *Les Cahiers de recherche sociologique,* Département de sociologie de l'UQAM, 4(2), 128–68.

Tremblay, G. (ed.) (1990) Les industries de la culture et de la communication au Québec et au Canada. Presses de l'Université du Québec, Télé-université, Sillery/Ste Foy, Québec.

Tremblay, G. and Lacroix, J. G., with Ménard, M. and Régnier, M. J. (1991) *Télévision deuxième dynastie.* Presses de l'Université du Québec, Sillery, Québec.

Unesco (1982) *Cultural Industries: A Challenge for the Future of Culture.* Unesco, Paris.

Unesco (1980) *Les Industries culturelles/The Cultural Industries.* Unesco, Paris.

Yong Jin, D. (2008) Neoliberal restructuring of the global communication system: Mergers and acquisitions. *Media, Culture and Society* 30(3) 357–73.

Zallo, R. (1988) *Economia de la comunicacion y la cultura.* Akal/Comunicacion, Madrid.

Zallo, R. (1992) El mercado de la cultura: Estructura economica y politica de la comunicacion. Tercera Prensa, Donostia, Spain.

See also the following online sites: *Omic (MSH Paris- Nord)*, http:// www.observatoire-omic. org/ , and *Eptic, Latin America*, http:// www2.eptic.com.br/ eptic_es/

5

Communication Economy Paths
A Latin American Approach

Martín Becerra and Guillermo Mastrini

Introduction

During the last five years, there has been a revitalization of the study of political economy of communication and culture in the Latin American region. This process has been accompanied by the need to produce information, knowledge, and reflections, in addition to encouraging debate over the structure and movements of the dynamic sectors of information, communication and culture. This revitalization of political economy studies of communication deserves to be analyzed from its main tendencies and its most outstanding contributions, as well as its "erroneous zones." This chapter presents such an analysis by focusing on Heriberto Muraro's text, "Economía y comunicación: convergencia histórica e inventario de ideas. Con especial referencia a América latina" (Economy and communication: historical convergence and inventory of ideas. with special reference to Latin America) (in Muraro 1987), which proposed an agenda for the field of communication and culture economy in 1984.

Even though it may seem paradoxical to use a reference that is two decades old to analyze the current validity of the study of political economy of communication, Muraro's text (like most of the author's works) presented an original outlook on the convergence and the multiple conditioning factors between communication and the economy in Latin America and elsewhere, in the years following the debate on the New World Information and Communication Order (Nuevo Orden Mundial de la Información y la Comunicación, NOMIC). Though current communication policies represent an antithesis or negation of the NOMIC agenda,

The Handbook of Political Economy of Communications, First Edition.
Edited by Janet Wasko, Graham Murdock, and Helena Sousa.
© 2014 John Wiley & Sons, Ltd. Published 2014 by John Wiley & Sons, Ltd.

this approach argues that this agenda is still appropriate to understand the current path of communication studies.

In his 1984 article, Muraro was specially interested in defining the areas in need of production of knowledge, especially in light of the evolution of industrialized sectors of culture, information, and communication over the two decades following Muraro's text. In this sense, the aim of this chapter is to explore both Muraro's agenda and his definition of necessary research, contrasting them with the contributions developed by studies of political economy of communication since the 1990s up to the present in the same Latin American region that shaped Muraro's text, although for reasons that will be later explained, extending it to "Iberoamerica."

Muraro's Memorandum

Muraro (1987) identified the following agenda:

1   The analysis of cultural industries as complexes technically integrated by economic rules, specific to this productive sector. In this respect, it is important to emphasize the need for studies on cultural production that go beyond the usual analysis of property relationships.
2   The examination of correlations and mutual determinations that exist between the macroeconomic and communication processes, especially everything that relates to the socialization of economic agents.
3   The influence of new technologies on the technical, financial, or administrative organization of economic activities.
4   In more general terms, the role of information transmission and other communicative activities in the everyday organization of economic activities, such as the decision to establish short-term prices, the evolution of the Stock Exchange, or how labor markets work.
5   The role of the mass media, or restricted circulation media, in decision making over economic agents faced with governmental policies of development promotion or economic control of the current situation.
6   Finally, the making of a wider model of rational action within which there is room for the transmission processes of information and communication.

The author then presented, in greater analytical depth, the main streams of thought about economic and social communication development. He assumes the centrality of mass communication research, as well as its corresponding historical explanations, some of which were generated in Latin America (dependence theory, underdevelopment interpretations, etc.). Likewise, his text includes criticism of dependence theory in the communication field and the challenges in the "communicational and economic" revolution implied by the convergent jump of new technologies, concluding with the (re)configuration of "transnational" information flows. It is important to remember that, very early on, Muraro (1974) criticized some interpretations of dependence theory as unsuitable for studying the economic structures of cultural industries.

Overview of theories

The theory of economic and social communication development from mass communication research   The "cultural factor" as the cause of backwardness in the modernization of Latin American societies was one of the aspects included in mass communication research with reference to Latin America. These studies promoted the implementation of the "communication system" notion, considering variables that included social communication processes (oral, written, audiovisual) to attitudinal issues of different social subjects in the process.

Meanwhile, for this theoretical current, measuring communication structure, as well as the influence of mass media messages in development policies, were of cardinal importance, as was the socializing function of the economic agents' communication.

Dependency theory and underdevelopment interpretation   The formula from mass communication research with reference to the obstacles that developing economies must overcome to attain the methods and practices of mature development assumed that the lack of development of those economies was due to internal reasons. But in the 1960s, this thesis was questioned, and true obstacles, such as the international division of labor and structural differences between central and peripheral countries, were identified. To put it in the words of the authors making this argument, the cause of the backwardness was the result of the dependence bonds between central and peripheral countries. In this way, the high rate of production and consumption of the central countries depended on the conditions generated by the dependence and backwardness of the peripheral countries. This division of labor gives rise to a new phase in the internationalization of capital.

The diffusion of the capitalist economy and the transnational venture   In the process of the internationalization of capital, a powerful actor emerges: the transnational venture (or conglomerate), capable of dissociating the routine tasks of a business to simultaneously manage in the industrial, commercial, and financial sector, and at the same time go beyond the classical establishment of subsidiaries in remote countries, which was typical of multinational businesses of the 1930s.

This is a new phase of the world economy, succeeding the competitive phase and then the national monopolist one. In this case, the transnational monopolist phase is characterized by the appearance of regulated spaces of economic activity which overflows the capacity of management and the state to efficiently intervene in the interior of a country. The transnational ventures (and conglomerates) are the protagonists of the productive internationalization which means a new level of integration of the world economy with its corresponding flow, internationalized financial and commercial capitals, productive delocalization, and centralization of control of production functions.

The economic interpretations of cultural dependence   The unprecedented degree of horizontal concentration and vertical integration of cultural industries in the process of the transnationalization of the economy gave rise to studies of the dependence theory focused on the dynamics of property and broadcasting carried out by the mass media.

The "cultural dependence theory" studied the dynamics of the cultural industries and provoked an analysis of the history and organization of transnational ventures in the culture sector and its articulations with other ventures of the sector as well as other fields of economy (mainly with the arms industry). The relationship with the world of advertising then led to a complex landscape of cultural industries, including its relationship of property and financing, as well as its integration.

Review of dependency theory in the communication field   For Muraro, "many of the contributions of the 'dependence supporters' have been widely propped up by irrefutable empirical materials" (1987, 83). One of the main contributions is that the monopolized media contribute to the preservation of the international status quo instead of encouraging a well-balanced development, uniting the relationship between the transnational phase of capitalism and the highly developed communication system of the masses. This debate has effectively precipitated the formulation of the thesis of NOMIC as a correlate to the New International Economic Order, and the approval of the MacBride report by UNESCO in 1980, paradoxically, at the time that UNESCO abandoned the democratizing postulates of the above mentioned report (Reyes Mata 1984, Schmucler 1984, Carlsson 2003, Mastrini and De Charras 2004, Becerra 2005).

But Muraro agrees with the researcher Diego Portales when he suggests that the dependence theory's contribution is a step forward as it exposes the relationship between property and information flow with the aim to illustrate the asymmetry between central and peripheral countries. But, according to Muraro, the dynamic aspect of the complex of communications (for instance, "strictly economic phenomena like the determination of advertising prices, impact of the relative cost of equipment and programming," 1987, 91), has not been covered by research.

For Muraro, the dependency approach generically accepted the model of manipulation theory. He suggests that the inquiry over the diffusion conditions of advertising messages, as well as the need to incorporate some of the contributions of the theory of rewards, are central themes that would enrich the contributions of dependency theorists.

The new technologies: communication and economic revolution   The convergent technological jump between the information and communication industries, and the digitalization that accompanies the emergence of the "new technologies," form an increasingly intersecting area between the economic and the communicational. In a narrow sense, the "new technologies" deeply affect the production method, treatment, and distribution of information. But, precisely because of that, they also have an impact on the productive processes as a whole, placing themselves, as Muraro (1987, 101) said, "in the very center of a renovation process of the industrial methods, which will affect both the advanced and peripheral countries, and may end up in a drastic redesign of the political and economic map of the period."

Muraro was well aware that the development of the convergent technologies of infocommunication, thanks to the intervention of information technology (first macroinformation technology and then microinformation technology), were provided by the governments of the central countries, "specially through military contracts" (1987, 103). However, their dissemination expresses the possibility of reformulating the productive circuit entirely and also generating new products and services which, in the case of cultural industries, can be seen in the appearance of new technologies since the 1980s, such as the PC, the VCR, the compact disc, mobile or cellular telephones, and finally the Internet.

At the same time, a decidedly innovative dimension of the convergent jump in infocommunication at the time Muraro wrote his article was the possibility of avoiding frontiers with information and communication flows, both through audiovisual technology (such as satellite television) and information technology (the Internet). This quality of new technologies, which today makes up the everyday information universe of thousands of millions of people, meant that since the 1980s the absolute power of states to establish regulations began to become blurred (though not eliminated) and parameters for the circulation of information began to fade, although was not eliminated.

Economic power and transnational information flows   Muraro observed that "All the productive activities – and this is so obvious that sometimes it passes unnoticed – require processes related to information transmission" (1987, 109). For Muraro, the effective acquisition and transmission of information is the *only task* incumbent on business directions. But, as Castells (1995) notes, because of the infocommunicational convergent technological jump, the very organization of the productive processes has radically transformed itself in the last three decades as a correlate to the introduction of control technologies, and the processing and implementation of such processes.

This assumes, apart from the costs reduction, a rebalance of the productive functions and their corresponding impact on costs and benefits. In fact, "Toyotism" (i.e., lean manufacturing and production principles originating in Japan and concentrating on the elimination of wasteful practices) would be unthinkable as a form of productive development without the use of infocommunicational technologies in the routine of production, treatment, storage, and commercialization of goods and services.

The so-called information or knowledge economy, which is based on Fritz Machlup and Marc Porat's studies of the American economic structure, corresponds to the information centrality in the design, planning, and execution of all the processes of mature capitalist production. Logically, the effects of this centrality are far from neutral. The social, political, economic, and cultural consequences constitute, in this way, the great challenge for the social scientist: to clarify the current significant changes of contemporary societies.

Debating the Memorandum

Taking as a starting point the descriptive landscape of the contributions and debates of the main trends related to the economic and political aspects of communication, Muraro presented a memorandum of six points that are appropriate in current debates. However, the current situation has developed because of processes and movements that Muraro could not have predicted in the early 1980s. Moreover, if Muraro were writing today, he would need to broaden his statements beyond Latin American to Iberoamerica.

Consequently, because of the structural changes that have taken place during the last two decades and the contributions increasingly made by the political economy studies of communication, it is possible to propose a redevelopment of Muraro's six points in the following terms:

1   Correlations and mutual determinations existing between the macroeconomic and communication processes. The media (mass media or "niche"), socialization, and behavior of economic agents. Information and its influence in the economic-financial structure.
2   Impact of the new technologies on the technical, productive, financial, or administrative organization of economic activities (especially considering the labor issue).
3   The incorporation of socioeconomic dynamics into the cultural, as well as the economic, sociocultural conditioning factors.

4   The cultural industries (as integrated economic and technological complexes) beyond the analysis of property relationships.
5   Policy and legislation over cultural industries in the context of technological convergence and economic concentration.

This agenda is proposed as a necessary update of Muraro's work, based on the transformations which have taken place in the cultural industries sector, at the same time retaining the aim of examining and questioning the basic works of the political economy of communication. It's important to point out that this job is occasionally done asymmetrically in a field (the communication field) which is hesitant to take into consideration economic and historical-political processes and ultimately reluctant to clarify the complexity with which the cultural industries devise a structure of power relationships.

The following sections present a guide to some of the most relevant Iberoamerican references which deal with the five points of the reformulated agenda inspired by Muraro's article.

Point 1

The first point is concerned with correlations and mutual determinations existing between the macroeconomic and communication processes; the media (mass media or "niche"), socialization, and behavior of economic agents; information and its influence in the economic-financial structure.

One of the big transformations of the world economy in the last decades has undoubtedly been the increasing economic weight of cultural industries in all economic indicators. This phenomenon allows us to assert that the cultural sector has reached economic maturity and full commercial exploitation. It is clear that there are still production areas not related to the cultural industry, but these are marginal in terms of popular consumption.

In general terms, the globalization process is a constituent part of the new dynamics of cultural industries, beside the fact that the process would not have been possible without the effective participation of the new information and communication technologies. Alain Herscovici (1994) has studied the links between the effects of economic "deterritorialization" and cultural production, while an excellent collection edited by José Vidal Beneyto (2002) reports the main challenges that globalization has triggered in the definition of a new concept of the public sphere and regulation of the media system. Although not all authors share an approach based on political economy, the works of Armand Mattelart, Miquel de Moragas, and Enrique Bustamante are also relevant.

One of the deficiencies in the political economy approach is the lack of analysis of the impact of so-called "communication global government." Given the fact that cultural production is considered beneficial for many governments and international organizations (such as the World Trade Organization), the regulation of its production and exchange is already part of the international agendas pertaining to the subject. Despite the fact that several studies have addressed this issue, so far few have presented empirical studies that analyze any consequences.

The processes of regional integration and its impact on the audiovisual and telecommunications sector have been more noticeable. The most outstanding work has been done by the Monarch Project (Proyecto Monarca), which analyzed the impact of the North American Free Trade Agreement in the northern countries of the continent (Crovi Druetta 1995). This kind of work is also represented in a collection edited by Guillermo Mastrini and César Bolaño (1999), with outstanding contributions by Gaëtan Tremblay and Delia Crovi. Enrique Sánchez Ruiz has made important contributions focused on the audiovisual sector, especially the cinema. In all these examples, there is an emphasis on the huge challenges that economic liberalization implies for the preservation of cultural policies aimed at encouraging local production.

Probably due to the lower degree of agreement and development of Mercosur (a trade agreement between Argentina, Brazil, Paraguay, and Uruguay), work on integration and culture in the region still have not received significant attention. However, the contributions made by the edited volumes co-ordinated by Sergio Cappareli (1999) and Luis Albornoz (2000) stand out. These collections include a series of comparative studies which consider the impact of the neoliberal period on the structure of the cultural industries of the bloc. Othon Jambeiro (2000) has also presented comparative analysis of the existing regulations for television in Mercosur, while Octavio Getino (2000) examined the economic structure of the cultural industries in this regional bloc.

Although they start from a perspective which is not directly connected with political economy, the work of Néstor García Canclini and Carlos Moneta (2004) complement the studies mentioned above. Germán Rey and Rafael Roncagliolo, in particular, present important contributions that contribute to a better understanding of the socialization processes from the cultural industries.

Most of the studies mentioned in this section acknowledge the influence of Ramón Zallo (1988), who established the foundations for the study of cultural industries from the perspective of the political economy of the region. In Latin America, César Bolaño's work (2000) is especially interesting as he presents the main postulates of political economy and makes an original contribution. Other interesting work is by Alain Herscovici, who represents the French school of culture economy.

Point 2

The second point focuses on the impact of the new technologies on the technical, productive, financial, or administrative organization of economic activities (especially considering labor issues).

The economic centrality of cultural, communication, and information processes and activities increasingly prompt Iberoamerican researchers to analyze their
logic both from the conceptual level and by producing empirical studies. Researchers
such as Ramón Zallo (1988, 1992, 1995, 2000), César Bolaño (2000, Mastrini and
Bolaño 1999, Bolaño and Herscovici 2004), Heriberto Muraro (1987), Claudio Katz
(1997, 1998, 2001), Guillermo Sunkel (1999, Sunkel and Geoffroy 2001), Delia
Crovi Druetta (2001, 2004), and Manuel Castells (1995, Castells and Hall 1995)
stress change in the development mode (which some refer to as the action mode),
the process which (regardless of the terminology) features information and communication activities as its main actors. The direct involvement of these activities
in the productive processes as a whole (whether communicational or not) is of
interest to many of these authors.

The transformation of the productive processes and circuits, and the labor routines affected by the dissemination of convergent technologies which allow the
processing and communicating of volumes of information unimaginable 40 years
ago (see Postolski et al. 2004), is therefore one of the main themes pointed out in
Sociedad de la Información (Becerra 2003). The intangible nature of many of the
economic exchanges (basically the financial ones), which affect the productive
structure and performance of countries and entire regions of the world that receive
feedback from the globalizing tendencies of the capital, are also dealt with as a
critical object of analysis by some of the authors associated with this approach to
the political economy of communication.

The double aspect of communication, which as a resource is infinite but increasingly linked to a logic of economic interventions (a logic which, paradoxically,
usually expands under the claim of scarce goods), is beginning to look like an ideal
instrument to approach the analysis of current social changes.

Point 3

The third point deals with the incorporation of socioeconomic dynamics into the
cultural, as well as the economic, sociocultural conditioning factors.

Néstor García Canclini writes: "cultural and artistic theories have largely proved
that cultural creation is also shaped in the circulation and reception of symbolic
products. Therefore, it is necessary to attach importance, in cultural policies, to
the moments following the generation of goods and messages, that is, to the consumption and appropriation of the arts and mass media" (2004, 65).

The concepts of hybridization and equalization as typical functions of the culture industries' intervention in the configuration of heterogeneous and contradictory societies (frequently mentioned when referring to García Canclini's work as
well as to George Yúdice's contributions, 2002, 2003), account for this third
approach, which moves away from the objects and methodologies of study, and
represents prototypes of communication political economy. However, the above

mentioned authors, as well as Omar Rincón or Germán Rey, offer invaluable contributions when it comes to understanding the (markedly political) tensions that are instituted between economic structure and sociocultural dynamics.

It is possible that this line of exploration allows the building of alliances between contributions from cultural studies and those from political economy, especially in a world where globalization influences are unavoidable in analyzing the cultural routines of different social groups in different latitudes. As Yúdice says, "the notion of culture as a resource implies its management, an approach which was not characteristic of high culture or everyday culture, in an anthropological sense. And to make things even more complex, culture as a resource circulates globally, at an increasing speed" (2002,16).

According to this approach, citizenship with relative autonomy in relation to the established powers cannot support itself unless we understand its constituent bonds with consumption and economic interaction practices in the context of "oligopolization" and aggregation of cultural value of the exchanges in economy. The notion of citizenship cannot elude its doubly significant design: cultural and economic. Authors such as Renato Ortiz, Octavio Ianni, Rosana Reguillo, Aníbal Ford, and José Carlos Lozano Rendón have made substantial contributions to the analysis of cultural production and its collaborative characteristics.

Fourth point

The fourth point is concerned with the cultural industries (as integrated economic and technological complexes) beyond the analysis of property relationships.

The study of cultural industries in Latin America, which began with the unique work of Antonio Pasquali in the 1960s, has an extensive tradition. As Muraro appropriately pointed out, during most of the 1970s there was a strong tendency to study the economy of cultural industries emphasizing the ideological matrix of television messages through a property analysis. However, from the 1990s, studies appeared that aimed at understanding the economic dynamics involved in cultural production. It goes without saying that this does not mean abandoning the study of the power relationships related to cultural production, but it is no longer subordinated as merely a factor of ideological reproduction.

At this point, it is possible to distinguish studies of an empirical kind and/or "case studies," which illustrate the main co-ordinates of the cultural industries, not only taking into account their property structure and scale during the last 15 years since the processes of privatization (transference of state assets to private capital), but also the productive routines of these industries, their programming policies, and their consolidation strategies in markets with restricted access.

As has been pointed out, Ramón Zallo's work (1988) constitutes an obvious starting point for the revitalization of studies of the political economy of communication in the Latin area. His book presents a clear way to understand the macroeconomic dynamics of the cultural industries by rebuilding the main branches of production.

Another important theoretical contribution was made by Enrique Bustamante (1999) when he analyzed the economic structure of television since the transformations characteristic of the neoliberal period. Even though it is difficult to avoid the European context of transition toward competitive television, Bustamante's work constitutes a reference point for the study of television in Latin America. More recently, Bustamante (2003) directed a detailed study of the influence of the digitalization processes on the cultural industries, including the phenomena of convergence, concentration, cultural policies, and intellectual property rights.

The problem of media concentration also has a long tradition in the region. However, it wasn't until the beginning of the 1990s that a study systematized the macroeconomic and mesoeconomic analysis of economic groups, as well as their strategies (Miguel 1993). At the beginning of the twenty-first century, Juan Carlos Miguel completed this study with an analysis of the bond between property concentration and the convergence of the audiovisual and telecommunications sectors (Miguel 2003).

With the aim of presenting an empirical survey of concentration levels, the authors of this chapter have directed an investigation of the structure and concentration levels of the cultural industries in Latin America. In this case, the idea is to consolidate basic information to be able to link the property structure to the informative pluralism problem in the future (Mastrini and Becerra 2006). The first comparative report has confirmed the extremely high level of concentration of cultural industries in Latin America.

Studies on cultural industries, discussing the value chain within the frame of convergent transformations, enable us, at the same time, to understand how key sectors work in full transformation. Examples include research by Juan Calvi, Gustavo Buquet, and Luis Albornoz, among others.

Lately, there have been more and more contributions based on the study of the communicational structure in several countries. For instance, there has been important work by the research teams led by José Carlos Lozano Rendón (Instituto Tecnológico de Monterrey) and Enrique Sánchez Ruiz (Universidad de Guadalajara) in Mexico, as well as case studies by Jenny Ampuero and Rosmery Machicado in Bolivia.

In Chile, Guillermo Sunkel looked at the phenomenon of media concentration from a political economy of communication perspective (Sunkel and Geoffroy 2001). Meanwhile, in Venezuela, Carlos Guzmán Cárdenas (2003, 2005) has done research on the economic dimension of the cultural industries in that country. There is also a renewed look at the relationship between the economy and cultural industries in the work of Luis Stolovich (2001, 2002) on the audiovisual policies and the economic structure of culture in Uruguay.

In Argentina, besides the contributions made by Octavio Getino on the economic dimension of cultural industries (1995), important contributions have been made by other colleagues. Finally, in Brazil, special mention must be made of the research of Valerio Cruz Brittos and César Bolaño (2005) on the Globo group, and Othon Jambeiro, especially for studies of television.

Fifth point

The final point centers on policy and legislation over cultural industries: pluralism and diversity challenges in the context of technological convergence and economic concentration.

Another area in which studies of political economy of communication have recovered an important role of intervention is the field of communication policies. It could not be any different, owing to the fact that the changes in cultural industries legislation have accompanied their vertiginous economic transformation. These new studies have avoided some of the determinisms characteristic of some works of the 1970s, developing the problem in a more complex way and more connected with other problematic questions.

In Spain, the most outstanding works are by the Instituto de la Comunicación de la Universidad Autónoma de Barcelona. The team led by Miquel de Moragas (including María Isabel Fernández and Merce Díez) has done original analysis on the structure, dynamics, and financing of audiovisual activities and the press, together with Emili Prado and Rosa Franquet. Other important work is by the Observatorio de políticas de comunicación of InCom, as well as the monograph produced for the 25th anniversary of the MacBride report, jointly carried out with Consejo Audiovisual de Cataluña (Quaderns del CAC 2005). The contribution of Carles Llorens and his thesis on pluralism – even if it is separated from some of the classical postulates of political economy – stands out in the work of the group led by Alfonso Sánchez Tabernero. An example of research on communication policies related to international structure is represented by Marcial Murciano's book (1992).

In addition, the work of Fernando Quirós Fernández and Ana Segovia, based at Universidad Complutense de Madrid, has contributed to our understanding of the policies that failed during the democratizing stage prior to neoliberalism. Segovia's work has contributed to the North American Critical School in Spanish. In the Basque country, the latest works by Zallo and Patxi Azpillaga have shown a continuous concern for the development of cultural policies in the region. Other researchers who presented an early concern for policies in the audiovisual sector are Eduardo Giordano and Carlos Zeller (1999). The same is true of the contributions made by Universidad de Sevilla, directed by Francisco Sierra Caballero.

If there was a determined impulse for the formalization of the concept of national policies of communication in the 1970s in Latin America, this subject cannot be consigned to oblivion nowadays. In Brazil, Murilo César Ramos at Universidad de Brasilia leads a research team that has produced important contributions on new regulation methods in the audiovisual and telecommunications fields. Other important works are those of Anita Simis, for the film industry, and Valeria Brittos, for television. José Marques de Melo has compiled a volume (Marques de Melo and Sathler 2005) in which the debates over the MacBride report are discussed in light of the information society.

In Argentina, we have contributed to rebuilding the history of communication policies, a task that is long overdue (Mastrini 2005). In addition, collaborative research has been produced on the communication policies in Mercosur (Capparelli 1999) and concentration of media in Latin America (Becerra and Mastrini 2009).

Other interesting contributions with more global outlooks include research by John Sinclair (1999) on Latin American television, and work by Elizabeth Fox and Silvio Waisbord (2002), which presents comparative analysis of communication policies in the main Latin American countries. In most cases, the authors mention the lack of democratic mechanisms in the initiatives in the area.

Though not related directly to the political economy of communication, Valerio Fuenzalida's (2000) and Omar Rincón's (2001) work updates the analysis of public television in the continent. Besides its traditional lack of independence from governmental power, the eruption of neoliberalism seems to have left the state radio and television stations with low rates of legitimacy which lead the authors to question their reform.

Generally speaking, all these works agree on the profound impact that neoliberalism has had on the structure of cultural industries and the policies related to them. In this sense, it is emphasized that technological convergence and economic concentration constitute a renewed challenge for the indispensable democratization of communication.

Final Words

From this general review of the research on the political economy of communication in Iberoamerica based on the revision of the agenda presented over two decades ago by Heriberto Muraro, we can conclude that there has been an important advance in knowledge production of the relationship between economics and communication. We understand that, first, the instrumental approximation by communication studies to the economic structure of cultural industries with the aim of deducing the purpose of the messages has been superseded. On the other hand, studies of the political economy of communication present an increasing range which covers the traditional study of the structure of cultural industries and transformations in the productive system and media policies, but which also aims to investigate the incidence of technological developments and how the general tendencies in the economy have a specific impact on the area of culture.

With regard to the points presented by Muraro, it is necessary to point out that there is still a scarcity of research related to the most specific problems of communication economy, above all, with reference to the socialization of economic agents; the changing modalities of production, dissemination, and appropriation of convergent technologies; the incidence of such changes in government agendas and the strategic behavior of cultural industries; and the production of knowledge which arises from studies of an empirical and comparative type.

References

Albornoz, L. (2000) *Al fin solos: la nueva televisión del Mercosur [Alone at last]*. Ediciones Ciccus-La crujía, Buenos Aires.

Becerra, M. (2003) *Sociedad de la información: proyecto, convergencia, divergencia [Information society: project, convergence, divergence]*. Editorial Norma, Buenos Aires.

Becerra, M. (2005) Las políticas de infocomunicación ante la Cumbre Mundial de la Sociedad de la Información [Infocommunication policies in the presence of the World Summit of Information Society]. *Quaderns del CAC*, 21, 73–4.

Becerra, M. and Mastrini, G. (2009) *Los dueños de la palabra [The word owners]*. Prometeo, Buenos Aires.

Bolaño, C. (2000) *Industria cultural: informação e capitalismo [Cultural industry: information and capitalism]*. Hucitec y Polis, São Paulo.

Bolaño, C. and Herscovici, A. (2004) Economia da informação e conhecimento: Uma abordagem em termos de economia política [Information economy and knowledge: An approach in terms of political economy]. In: *Anais do VII Colóquio Brasil-França de Ciências da Comunicação e da Informção*, mimeo, Porto Alegre, Brazil.

Bustamante, E. (1999) *La televisión económica: Financiación, estrategias y mercados [The economics of television: Financing, strategies, and markets]*. Gedisa, Barcelona.

Bustamante, E. (2003) *Hacia un nuevo sistema mundial de comunicación: Las industrias culturales en la era digital [Toward a new communication world system: The cultural industries in the digital era]*. Gedisa, Barcelona.

Capparelli, S. (1999) *Enfim, sos: A nova televisao no cone sul [Alone, at last: The new television in the Southern Cone]*. L&PM, Porto Alegre, Brazil.

Carlsson, U. (2003) The rise and fall of NWICO – and then?: From a vision of international regulation to a reality of multilevel governance. Paper presented at the EURICOM colloquium, *Information Society: Visions and Governance*. Venice, May 5–7.

Castells, M. (1995) *La ciudad informacional: Tecnologías de la información, reestructuración económica y el proceso urbano-regional [The informational city: Information technologies, economic restructuring, and the urban-regional process]*. Alianza Editorial, Madrid.

Castells, M. and Hall, P. (1994) *Las tecnópolis del mundo: La formación de los complejos industriales del siglo XXI [The world technopolis: The formation of the 21st-century industrial complexes]*. Alianza Editorial, Madrid.

Crovi Druetta, D. (1995) *Desarrollo de las industrias audiovisuales en México y Canadá [Development of the audiovisual industries in Mexico and Canada]*. Facultad de Ciencias Políticas y Sociales, Mexico.

Crovi Druetta, D. (2004) *Sociedad de la información y el conocimiento: Entre lo falaz y lo posible* [*Information and knowledge society: Between what is fallacious and what is possible*]. La Crujía, Buenos Aires.

Crovi Druetta, D. and Girardo, C. (2001) *La convergencia tecnológica en los escenarios laborales de la juventud* [*Technological convergence in youth work scenarios*]. UNAM, México.

Cruz Brittos, V. and Bolaño, C. (2005) *Rede Globo: 40 anos de poder e hegemonia* [*Rede Globo: 40 years of power and hegemony*]. Paulus, São Paulo.

Fox, E. and Waisbord, S. (eds) (2002) *Latin Politics, Global Media*. University of Texas Press, Austin.

Fuenzalida, V. (2000) *La televisión pública en América Latina: Reforma o privatización* [*Public television in Latin America: Reform or privatization*]. Economic Culture Fund, Santiago.

García Canclini, N. (2004) *Diferentes, desiguales y desconectados: mapas de la interculturalidad* [*Different, unequal and disconnected: interculturality maps*]. Gedisa, Barcelona.

García Canclini, N. and Moneta, C. (2004) *Las industrias culturales en la integración latinoa-mericana* [*The cultural industries in Latin American integration*]. Eudeba, Buenos Aires.

Getino, O. (1995) *Las industrias culturales en la Argentina: dimensión económica y políticas públi-cas* [*The cultural industries in Argentina: economic dimensions and public policies*]. Colihue, Buenos Aires.

Getino, O. (2000) *Las industrias culturales en el Mercosur: incidencia económica y sociocultural, intercambios y políticas de integración regional* [*The cultural industries in Mercosur: economic and sociocultural impact, regional integration exchanges, and policies*]. Organización de Estados Americanos, Buenos Aires.

Giordano, E. and Zeller, C. (1999) *Políticas de televisión: la configuración del mercado audio-visual* [*Television policies: the configuration of the audiovisual market*]. Icaria, Barcelona.

Guzmán Cárdenas, C. (2003) *Políticas y economía de la cultura en Venezuela* [*Culture policies and economy in Venezuela*]. Ininco, Caracas.

Guzmán Cárdenas, C. (2005) *La dinámica de la cultura en Venezuela y su contribución al PIB* [*The dynamics of culture in Venezuela and their contribution to the GDP agreement*]. Andrés Bello, Caracas.

Herscovici, A. (1994) *Économie de la culture et de la communication* [*Culture and communication economy*]. L'Harmattan, Paris.

Jambeiro, O. (2000) *Regulando a TV: uma visao comparativa no Mercosur* [*Regulating television: a comparative view at the Mercosur*]. Edufba, Salvador.

Jambeiro, O. (2001) *A TV no Brasil do seculo XX* [*Brazilian television in the 20th century*]. Edufba, Salvador.

Katz, C. (1997) El culturalismo en los estudios de tecnología [Culturalism in technology studies]. *Causas y Azares*, 6, 107–20.

Katz, C. (1998) El enredo de las redes [The entanglement of the networks]. *Voces y Culturas*, 14, 123–40.

Katz, C. (2001) *Mito y realidad de la revolución informática* [*Myth and reality of the information technology revolution*], mimeo, en Portal EPTIC, Textos para Discussao II. Online at http://www.eptic.com.br/arquivos/Publicacoes/textos%20para%20discussao/textdisc2.pdf (accessed September 24, 2010).

Marques de Melo, J. and Sathler, L. (2005) *Direitos a cominicaça na sociedade da informaçao* [*Communication rights in the information society*]. Universidade Metodista de São Paulo, São Paulo.

Mastrini, G. (ed.) (2005) *Mucho ruido, pocas leyes: economía y políticas de comunicación en la Argentina* [*Much noise and few laws: communication economy and policies in Argentina*]. La crujía, Buenos Aires.

Mastrini, G. and Becerra, M. (2006) *Periodistas y magnates: estructura y concentración de las industrias culturales en América Latina* [*Journalists and tycoons: structure and concentration of the cultural industries in Latin America*]. Prometeo, Buenos Aires.

Mastrini, G. and Bolaño, C. (eds.) (1999) *Globalización y monopolios en la comunicación en América Latina: hacia una economía política de la comunicación* [*Globalization and communication monopolies in Latin America: toward a political economy of communication*]. Biblos, Buenos Aires.

Mastrini, G. and De Charras, D. (2004) Veinte años no es nada: del NOMIC a la CMSI [Twenty years means nothing: from the NOMIC (NWICO) to the CMSI (WSIS)]. Paper presented at Congreso IAMCR, Porto Alegre, Brazil, July 25–30.

Miguel, J. C. (1993) *Los grupos multimedia: estructura y estrategias en los medios europeos* [*The multimedia groups: structure and strategies in the European media*]. Bosch, Barcelona.

Miguel, J. C. (2003) Les groupes de communication occidentaux a l'heure de la convergene. In: Miège, B. and Tremblay, G. (eds), *Bogues: Globalisme et pluralisme*. Les Presses de l'Úniversité Laval, Québec.

Muraro, H. (1987) *Invasión cultural, economía y comunicación* [*Cultural invasion, economy, and communication*]. Legasa, Buenos Aires.

Muraro, H. (1974) *Neocapitalismo y comunicación de masa* [*Neocapitalism and mass communication*]. Eudeba, Buenos Aires.

Murciano, M. (1992) *Estructura y dinámica de la comunicación internacional* [*Structure and dynamics of international communication*]. Bosch, Barcelona.

Postolski, G., Santucho, A., and Rodríguez, D. (2004) Las alambradas mediáticas: Concentración de la propiedad y sus consecuencias sobre el empleo en la prensa [Media fencing: Property concentration and its consequences on press employment], mimeo, Observatorio Político, Social y Cultural de los Medios de la UTPBA, Buenos Aires.

Quaderns del CAC (2005) *XXV* Aniversario del Informe MacBride: Comunicación internacional y políticas de comunicación [25th anniversary of the MacBride Report: International communication and communication policies]. Quaderns del CAC, 21.

Reyes Matta, F. (1984) El nuevo orden informativo reubicado: de la UNESCO a la UIT [The new information order relocated: from UNESCO to ITU]. *Comunicación y Cultura*, 11, 9–16.

Rincón, O. (2001) *Televisión pública: Del consumidor al ciudadano* [*Public television: From the consumer to the citizen*]. Andrés Bello, Bogotá.

Schmucler, H. (1984) Año mundial de la comunicación: Con penas y sin gloria [World year of communication: Sorrows and no glory]. *Comunicación y Cultura*, 11, 3–8.

Sinclair, J. (1999) *Latin American Television: A Global View*. Oxford University Press, New York.

Stolovich, L. (2002) *La cultura es capital* [*Culture is capital*]. Fin de siglo, Montevideo.

Sunkel, G. (1999) *El consumo cultural en América Latina: Construcción teórica y líneas de investigación* [*Cultural consumption in Latin America: Theoretical construction and lines of investigation*]. Andrés Bello, Bogotá.

Sunkel, G. and Geoffroy, E. (2001) *La concentración económica de los medios de comunicación* [*The economic concentration of the mass media*]. LOM, Santiago de Chile.

Vidal Beneyto, J. (2002) *La ventana global* [*The global window*]. Taurus, Madrid.

Yúdice, G. (2002) *El recurso de la cultura: Usos de la cultura en la era global* [*Culture as a resource: Uses of culture in the global era*]. Gedisa, Barcelona.

Yúdice, G. (2003) *The Expediency of Culture: Uses of Culture in the Global Era*. Duke University Press, Durham, NC.

Zallo, R. (1988) *Economía de la comunicación y la cultura* [*Economy of communication and culture*]. Akal, Madrid.

Zallo, R. (1992) *El mercado de la cultura: estructura económica y política de la comunicación* [*The culture market: economic and political structure of communication*]. Tercera Prensa, Donostia, Spain.

Zallo, R. et al. (1995) *Industrias y políticas culturales en España y país Vasco* [*Cultural industries and policies in Spain and the Basque Country*]. Servicio Editorial Universidad del País Vasco, Bilbao.

Zallo, R. (2000) La crisis general de paradigmas: El caso de la economía y política de la comunicación y de la cultura [The general crisis of paradigms: The case of communication and culture economy and policy], mimeo, Bilbao.

Suggestions for Further Reading

Bolaño, C. (1988) *Mercado Brasileiro de televisao* [*Brazilian television market*]. Editorial de la UFS, Aracaju, Brazil.

Bolaño, C., Mastrini, G., and Sierra, F. (eds) (2005) *Economía política, comunicación y conocimiento: Una perspectiva crítica latinoamericana* [*Political economy, communication and knowledge: A Latin American critical perspective*]. La crujía, Buenos Aires.

Capparelli, S. and de Lima, V. (2004) *Televisao: Desafios da pos-globalizaçao* [*Television: Postglobalization challenges*]. Hacker editores, São Paulo.

Del Valle Rojas, C. (2004) *Metainvestigación de la comunicación en Chile* [*Communication research in Chile*]. Universidad de la Frontera, Temuco, Chile.

Herscovici, A. (2004) Economia da informação, redes eletrônicas e regulação: Elementos de análise [Information economy, electronic networks, and regulation: Elements of analysis]. *Revista de Economia Política*, 24(1), 95–114.

Quirós, F. and Sierra, F. (2001) *Crítica de la economía política de la comunicación y la cultura* [*Criticism of the political economy of communication and culture*]. Comunicación Social ediciones, Seville.

Stolovich, L. (2001) *La lógica económica del empleo cultural* [*The economic logic of cultural employment*]. Inédito, Montevideo.

Stolovich, L., Lescano, G., and Mourelle, L. (1997) *La cultura da trabajo* [*Culture generates employment*]. Fin de Siglo, Montevideo.

Part II
Modalities of Power
Ownership, Advertising, Government

6

The Media Amid Enterprises, the Public, and the State
New Challenges for Research

Giuseppe Richeri

The media are complex to study because they are composed of diverse elements which constitute both their content and their vehicle, that is, the information and the means of transmitting it. Their character and functioning are an important field of study because the media are becoming increasingly important in the structure and evolution of society. They have an impact on the functioning of democracy and public institutions, on individuals' work and living conditions, on the construction of identity, on the inclusion and the social participation of every citizen in his or her own community of reference, and on the inequalities and the imbalances of its components.

The study of the relations between media and society has a long tradition and has provided social forces, their political expressions, and states with keys for the interpretation and direction of regulatory activities and the promotion of reform. Research in this field, however, is constantly being confronted with a spiral as the media system changes continually due to directions and rhythms that are principally determined by the evolution of social relations (political, economic, or cultural). The media in turn exercise a growing influence on the evolution of social relations and on the social ties of many individuals, to the point of becoming, in many cases, a fundamental element of this evolution. An approach to studying some important aspects of this spiral is by analyzing the interactions between the media industry and society, the access to and consumption of its products and services, and the guidelines and regulatory interventions of the state and public institutions.

The Handbook of Political Economy of Communications, First Edition.
Edited by Janet Wasko, Graham Murdock, and Helena Sousa.
© 2014 John Wiley & Sons, Ltd. Published 2014 by John Wiley & Sons, Ltd.

The Media and Society

The term "media" refers to a sector of activity made up of two distinct components, which can be managed by different subjects but are functionally integrated. On one hand, these activities are designed to create information content; on the other, their purpose is the transfer of content in time and space. Central to the first component is an abstract activity: the creation of content which varies by type of expression, by intellectual and creative complexity, or by function (information, education, entertainment, etc.). The life of these products is determined by two types of incorporated values: the economic and the cultural. At the center of the second component lies a typically concrete activity: the creation of supports and networks for transmission and distribution. This is significantly influenced by technological development. In many cases the supports and networks also have other economic functions that can be distinguished from the media (the telephone, video, telesurveys, etc.). The two components, both the content and the vehicle, have distinct financial-productive characteristics and functions, which are in constant evolution and which also influence each other, but have to be presented in an integrated manner, so as to constitute a single product/service at the point of consumer use.

The relationships between the media and society, and all attempts to analyze them, are rendered more complex by a series of phenomena which have acquired considerable importance over the two last decades. The internationalization of the economy, of politics, and of culture is changing the traditional set-up of governments in many countries (Grandinetto and Rullani 1996, Hirsch 1995). The growing mobility of people, products, and capital is revolutionizing the traditional areas of consumption, culture, and territory. Moreover, mass migration has altered the traditional instruments for social sharing, cohesion, and participation, along with the identity factors of whole communities (Urry 2000). The shift in economic balance toward the east and the growing role of countries such as China and India in the global economy are displacing traditional international patterns for the consumption of raw materials and energy, for industrial production and mass consumption (Rampini 2006, Weber 2004). A new scenario characterized by new opportunities and risks (new markets, new competitors), but equally by new functions (multiculturalism, sharing, identity, citizenship, the public sphere) and new restrictions (censorship, dependency, and control) is opening to the media, implying further mutations. These evolutions directly influence not only the dynamics within the field of the media, such as accelerated processes of concentration, growth, multimedia diversification, and internationalization (Croteau and Hoynes 2001, Herman and McChesney 1998), but also the normative activity of regulation and steering. This, both at the level of single states and of international organizations, from the European Union to the International Telecommunication Union, from the World Trade Organization to Unesco, has acquired unprecedented importance for both vehicles and content in recent years (Zhenzhi 2003, Siochru and Girard 2002).

This outline is sufficient to show the renewed relevance of research into the evolution of the relationships between the media system and the social system, and in particular, the relationships between processes of production, distribution, and consumption of media, the processes of reproduction and transformation of social relationships, and the role of the state. A significant contribution to the analysis and the criticism of these relationships is offered by the field of studies called political economy of communication which has, since the 1970s, occupied a place of prime importance on the international scene (Garnham 1979, Graham 2006, Mosco 1996, Murdock and Golding 1991), to which I have been able to contribute on various occasions (e.g., Richeri 1980, 1985, 1986a, 1986b, 1987, 1988, 1990, 2004, 2006). Attention is concentrated on three major issues; these interact constantly with each other and should therefore not be considered just as single elements but, as far as possible, as mutual influences.

The first issue is the behavior of enterprises. Here interest lies especially in studying the evolution of the structure of media ownership, the characteristics of the markets in which the media operate, and how these relate to their production and distribution choices. It is, in fact, important to highlight how financial organization acts on the creation and circulation of content and its meaning and on audience composition. The second issue concerns the conditions of media access and the processes of media consumption to show which power relations condition them, how these factors change according to differences and social inequalities, and how these conditions determine the public's "work of consuming" content (Cesareo 1978). The third concerns the state and the institutions that regulate and support both media enterprises (vehicles and content) and the public, in order to understand how collective interests can be guaranteed in line with the principles of democracy.

Media Enterprises

At the turn of the millennium, four great, often interconnected, tendencies in the media industry have become incontrovertibly evident. These are changing the general overview of the field, shifting the traditional reference points of research toward a larger, more complex domain.

The first tendency concerns company size. The constant growth of the media market corresponds to a constant growth in the size of enterprises through an intense flurry of acquisition and mergers, leading to the formation of some large groups capable of exercising great influence on domestic and international markets. This phenomenon, present in all developed countries, has assumed emblematic dimensions in the United States since the 1990s, starting from the merger of Time Inc. and Warner Communication for 14 billion US dollars, and ending in 2000 with the merger of AOL and Time Warner, for 166 billion dollars. During that decade, all major North American, European, and Japanese groups were engaged in acquisition and merger operations, from Bertelsmann (Germany) to News Corporation (UK-USA), from Sony (Japan) to Time Warner (USA), Reed Elsevier to Reed International (UK), from Viacom (USA) to Vivendi (France), and from Walt Disney (USA) to Hachette (France), to quote the best-known names, to which dozens of other companies could be added (Gershon 2007, Musso 2000).

The growth was the result of various forms of integration into the same enterprise of a series of activities once carried out by suppliers or clients (upstream or downstream vertical integration), by competitors (horizontal integration), and of activities in other media sectors (transverse integration). This has led to the formation of companies which, on the one hand, are able to control the whole production and distribution channel of a single sector of activity and, on the other, simultaneously operate in various sectors of the media, from press publishing to radio, from television to cinema, from music to the Internet, with considerable advantages in terms of economies of scale, goals, and synergies (Doyle 2002a, Hoskins et al. 1997, Kunz 2007). The integration of content production by enterprises operating in the field of media vehicles also pertains to this phenomenon. The most common case is that of telecommunication companies, such as Telefonica (Spain), British Telecom, Telecom Italia, AT&T (USA), which have integrated activities in the radio and television field.

The growth and multimedia integration of activities reinforce the tendency toward international markets, already significantly present in some sectors of the media like the music and audiovisual industries (Aris and Bughin 2005, Miller et al. 2001). The tendency toward globalization is enhanced by the contextual process, which more generally concerns the economy and finance, but especially by content production where investment is concentrated in fixed costs (prototype) rather than variable costs (transmission and distribution), a phenomenon which puts distribution activities under notable pressure (Comor 1994, Albarran and Mierzejewska 2004).

The fourth tendency concerns the progressive concentration of the media markets on local, national, and international levels. This tendency is present in nearly all media sectors and has been noticed in successive phases, in various national contexts (Doyle 2002b, Compaine and Gomery 2000, Perrucci and Richeri 2004). On an international scale, the two sectors in which concentration has attained the most noticeable levels are the music industry, where nearly 70 percent of the global market is controlled by four large enterprises (the American Warner and Universal, the British EMI, and the Japanese-German Sony-BMG), and the movie industry, where nearly 65 percent of the world market is controlled by a small group of enterprises concentrated in Hollywood (Burkart and McCourt 2006, Miller et al. 2001, Wasko 2003).

In this situation of great evolution of the media industry, it is necessary to understand how the forms of production control, formatting, and diffusion of information, knowledge, and culture change. It is necessary to understand how the formation of large global groups transforms international relations between populations, places, cultures, and media consumption.

Media Access and Consumption

The social importance of the media can be attributed to various elements. Among the most evident is the fact that, at mass level, selection of and access to information, knowledge, and entertainment depends on the media. The second element is that the media are instruments that are increasingly important in the organization of social relations and work. The third element concerns the role the media play in the relationship between the citizen and public institutions, and between the consumer and the market. In order to access the media, some prerequisites are nonetheless needed. These prerequisites are not distributed among people uniformly, even in more advanced societies. In at least three cases, this can easily be observed:

1   To use a country's radio or television, it is necessary to know the national language; to read a newspaper, it is not only necessary to know the language but also to be literate, and in order to use the Internet as an access channel to the media, it is necessary to know the language, be literate, and have technical skills.
2   In order to use some media, one needs a connection to the content distribution network or the hardware necessary to extract it from its support. If the coaxial cable or the optical fibers are not available, or if one lives somewhere not covered by the Hertzian network, access to content transmitted or on demand through the network is excluded. The same applies in the case of music and home video if one does not have the appropriate hardware.
3   The third prerequisite concerns the financial resources necessary for connection to the network, for purchase of the hardware (satellite dish, TV, video recorder, etc.) and of the content (pay-TV, media on demand, newspapers, books, records, etc.).

These are problems which penalize the great majority of the population in disadvantaged countries, and which have not been satisfactorily solved in advanced countries. A smaller but nonetheless consistent part of the population of these countries, from "new illiterates" to migrants, from low-income groups to the inhabitants of poor or marginal urban and rural areas, experiences difficulty accessing a range of media.

The "information poor" also constitute an important problem in advanced countries if one considers the fact that in many countries the number of "new illiterates" is not decreasing while the following are increasing:

- the number of migrants
- the social group considered poor
- the percentage of medium- and high-level programs which are changing from free to fee-paying (pay TV, media on demand, etc.)
- the number of platforms, of channels and supports (from digital TV to mobile TV, to IPTV, I-pod, etc.) and opportunities to access content for those who have the necessary requisites and the skills, excluding the others.

One example is the number of people who risk marginalization or exclusion from access to informative, cultural, and entertainment Internet content, in other words the "digital divide," in one of the most developed areas of the world. According to Eurostat data, referring to 2009:

- 35 percent of the inhabitants of the 27 countries of the European Union, aged between 16 and 74 years, do not use the Internet
- 44 percent of the inhabitants of the 27 countries of the European Union, aged between 16 and 74 years, don't have a broadband connection
- 32 percent of people aged between 25 and 54 rarely use the Internet
- 38 percent of people with a low level of educational attainment rarely use the Internet

The exponential growth in media offerings amplifies another factor of social disruption that derives from the way the media are used to access information, knowledge, and culture. Media consumption is socially conditioned because it comprises an activity or "work," based, among other things, on the attitudes and skills of an individual (Bourdieu 1979), which are, to a large extent, socially determined. It is moreover directed by stimuli and opportunities for "investing" the information and cultural capital acquired through the media, which depends on one's professional field.

The Media and the State

In all democratic countries, the state, recognizing the social relevance of the media, intervenes in various ways. The intention is to ensure that the media industry may grow, compete, and distribute its products; that entrepreneurial activities take place in the public's interest and with respect for pluralism and independence of information; and that access to media and freedom of information are guaranteed.

These objectives should constantly be compared against entrepreneurial and social evolution. The transformations taking place demand constant modification of public interventions concerning ownership and market concentration, the origin and variety of content, forms of access, and the protection and support of the industry.

Considering the ongoing concentration processes, the state should update its regulation instruments in two areas in particular. The first one concerns the ownership of media and its influence on content, since the concentration of ownership can lead to abuses in the financial and political fields. The other is market concentration, which can limit pluralism of information, of viewpoints, of cultural types and expressions. In the transformation of the media landscape, there is also a third area of public intervention to consider, namely the forms of direct and indirect support for the media industry (audiovisual, daily newspapers, periodicals, book publishing, etc.), which in many, mainly European, countries help and guide the development of national enterprises. One example is the activity of the European Union as regards both regulation and support of the development of the European media industry. From 1989–90 on, both the directive "Television Without Borders" and "Program Media" have had to be updated on various occasions in order to respond to changes taking place in individual member states as well as on an international scale. A fourth type of public intervention aims at improving conditions of media access, which, in several countries, particularly concern the periodic press and book publishing, audiovisual media and, most of all, distribution networks and reception equipment.

The intervention of the state, with its constant modifications, is nonetheless an important field of analysis in that steering it demands continuous revision of viewpoints and data, and the quality of the initiatives and the efficiency of the results obtained are not always guaranteed. Among the various aspects most frequently mentioned by critical research is that a great number of the legislative interventions concentrate on financial aspects, in particular on the objective of guaranteeing competition between enterprises. This often leads to unsatisfactory results if one considers the data on the levels of national and local concentration reached in many countries in terms of the print press and radio/television and, internationally, as already mentioned, in terms of recorded music and the cinema.

The measures designed to control concentration, based upon the right to competition and the right of the media, are often revealed as complicated, insufficient, and inefficient (Meier 2005). The media's internationalization process complicates the situation, as only large national companies in each country are able to protect the domestic market from large international groups and to compete with them on the international market.

In the European tradition in particular, the state also enters the media field directly, by means of its own activity in the field of radio and television. This is to reduce market distortions in a sector that is considered important for public interest in many countries, not only in Europe. Pluralism, variety, and quality of content that public television has to guarantee institutionally, together with "universal service," are objectives that appear ever more difficult to reach in the face of increasing infrastructural and content costs, the multiplication of technological and broadcasting platforms, the fragmentation of the public, and the creation of powerful private television channels that compete in the quest for audience.

From the European point of view, the crisis of state radio and television enterprises is increasingly obvious. It is a complex crisis concerning at least three of the aspects under discussion: the legitimacy of public intervention in this sector, the distinctive identity of state radio and television broadcasters, and the ways their activities are financed.

The proposal to privatize public broadcasting companies re-emerges periodically in various countries. Indeed, their programs in many countries are accused of copying those of the private sector too often, guided exclusively by commercial interests, and their costs are constantly rising, whereas their sources of financing, be they from advertising or taxes, are often an object of controversy. In any case, their image has deteriorated to such a degree that they are sometimes represented as old wrecks, subject to political power and incapable of renewing themselves, or even useless. Even though they are still at the center of the information and entertainment system in many cases, they absorb important financial resources, taking them from private enterprises which are sometimes more dynamic, efficient, and independent from political influences.

The importance of reflecting on the role of the state in the field of television does not only derive from the public sector's present state of crisis. The path toward total digitalization, which European countries have taken in a more or less rapid and linear manner, leads to a substantial transformation of the field of television. The multiplication of channels means, on one hand, an increase in the overall quantity of programs broadcast in each country and, on the other, a progressive fragmentation of the audience between a considerably higher number of channels than the five or six traditional, national, and "general" channels. One can think of "multichannel" homes where the state television audience has noticeably diminished in favor of a multiplicity of national and international channels, more or less specialized, each of them gathering much smaller fractions of the public (Richeri 2004).

The perspective that public broadcasters have to face is summarized in a British Broadcasting Corporation document: "The explosion of media choice is causing audience viewing and listening to fragment. People are consuming a wider range of services across a greater range of devices. As a result, we are now in a multi-track media society, in which no two people's media behaviour is the same" (BBC 2004, p. 49). This has significant consequences on the functions of television in general, and, in particular, on some principles which are traditionally behind public television, such as universality of service, collective interest, and mandatory financing by all television viewing families.

Conclusion

The field in question is large and marked, as we have seen, by profound evolution, on the local, national, and international levels. In order to comprehend the phenomenon, its roots and perspectives in all their complexity, it appears ever more urgent to adopt a multifocal approach capable of combining economic, sociological, and political insights. The ambitious objective, besides the constant updating of research in each of the fields mentioned above, is to integrate the specific results into a coherent and unitary vision, for better knowledge of the relationships between the media industry, society, the state, and the laws which govern them.

Research on this level is able to provide the knowledge necessary for identifying emerging problems, directing the interventions of the state and of international organisms in favour of pre-eminent collective interests, and to check the validity of the instruments adopted and the results obtained.

References

Albarran, A. B. and Mierzejewska, B. I. (2004) Media concentration in the U.S. and European Union: A comparative analysis. Paper presented at the 6th World Media Economics Conference, Montreal, Canada, May 12–15.

Aris, A. and Bughin, J. (2005) *Managing Media Companies*. John Wiley & Sons, Chichester, UK.

BBC (2004) *Building Public Value*, British Broadcasting Corporation, London.

Bourdieu, P. (1979) *La distinction: Critique sociale du jugement*. Le Seuil, Paris.

Burkart, P. and McCourt, T. (2006) *Ownership and Control of the Celestial Jukebox*. Rowman & Littlefield, Lanham, MD.

Cesareo, G. (1978) La nuova serie di Ikon. *Ikon*, 1(2), 7–16.

Compaine, B. M. and Gomery, D. (2000) *Who Owns the Media?* Lawrence Erlbaum, Mahwah, NJ.

Comor, E. A. (ed.) (1994) *The Global Political Economy of Communication: Hegemony, Telecommunication, and the Information Economy*. St Martin's Press, New York.

Croteau, D. and Hoynes, W. (2001) *The Business of Media*. Pine Forge Press, Thousand Oaks, CA.

Doyle, G. (2002a) *Understanding Media Economics*. Sage Publications, London.

Doyle, G. (2002b) *Media Ownership*. Sage Publications, London.

Garnham, N. (1979) Contribution to a political economy of mass communication. *Media Culture & Society*, 1(2), 123–46.

Gershon, R. (2007) The transnational media corporation and the economics of global competition. In: Kamalipour, Y. R. (ed.), *Global Communication*, 2nd edn. Wadsworth, Belmont, CA, pp. 55–78.

Graham, P. (2006) Issues in political economy. In: Albarran, B. A., Chan-Olmsted, S., and Wirth, M. (eds), *Handbook of Media Management and Economics*. Lawrence Erlbaum, Mahwah, NJ, pp. 493–522.

Grandinetto, R. and Rullani, E. (1996) *Impresa transnazionale ed economia globale*. La Nuova Italia Scientifica, Rome.

Herman, E. S. and McChesney, R. W. (1998) *The Global Media*. Madhyam Books, Delhi.

Hirsch, J. (1995) Nation-state, international relations and the question of democracy. *Review of International Political Economy*, 2(2), 267–84.

Hoskins, C., McFadyen, S., and Finn, A. (1997) *Global Television and Film*. Oxford University Press, New York.

Kunz, W. M. (2007) *Culture Conglomerates: Consolidation in the Motion Picture and Television Industries*. Rowman & Littlefield, Lanham, MD.

Meier, W.A. (2005) Media concentration governance: Un nouvelle plate-forme pour débattre des risques? *Réseaux*, 21(131), 17–52.

Miller, T., Govil, N., McMurria, J., and Maxwell, R. (2001) *Global Hollywood*. BFI Publishing, London.

Mosco, V. (1996) *The Political Economy of Communication*. Sage Publications, London.

Murdock, G. and Golding, P. (1991) Culture, communication and political economy. In: Curran, J. and Gurevich, M. (eds), *Mass Media and Society*. Arnold, London, pp. 15–32.

Musso, P. (2000) Stratégies des groupes multimédias. *Dossier de l'audiovisuel* 94, Institut National de l'Audiovisuel.

Perrucci, A. and Richeri, G. (2004) *Il mercato televisivo italiano nel contesto europeo*. Il Mulino, Bologna.

Rampini, F. (2006) *L'impero di Cindia*. Mondadori, Milan.

Richeri, G. (1980) Italian broadcasting and fascism 1924–1937. *Media Culture & Society*, 2(2), 49–56.

Richeri, G. (1985) The difficulties involved in the control and organization of telecommunication in Italy. *Media Culture & Society*, 7(3), 49–70.

Richeri, G. (1986a) Television from service to business. In: Drummond, P. and Paterson, R. (eds), *Television in Transition*. British Film Institute, London, pp. 21–36.

Richeri, G. (1986b) Public authorities, cultural industry and telecommunications in Western Europe. In: Miller, J. (ed.), *Telecommunications and Equity: Policy Research Issues*. North Holland, Amsterdam, pp. 285–97.

Richeri, G. (1987) Impact of new communication technologies on the media industry in Italy. In: de Bens, E. and Knoche, M. (eds) *Electronic Mass Media in Europe: Prospects and Developments*. Reidel Publishing Company, Dordrecht, pp. 441–67.

Richeri, G. (1988) Mass communications research in Italy: Crisis and new ferment. *Studies of Broadcasting*, 24, 101–24.

Richeri, G. (1990) Hard times for public service broadcasting: The RAI in the age of commercial competition. In: Baranski, Z. and Lumley, R. (eds), *Culture and Conflict in Postwar Italy*. MacMillan Press, London, pp. 256–69.

Richeri, G. (2004) Broadcasting and the market: The case of public television. In: Calabrese, A. and Spark, C. (eds), *Toward a Political Economy of Culture: Capitalism and Communication in the Twenty-First Century*. Rowman & Littlefield, Lanham, MD, pp. 178–93.

Richeri, G. (2006) State intervention in the new broadcasting landscape: less is best. In: Raboy, M. and Sauvageau, F. (eds) *The Role of State in Broadcasting Governance*. Canadian Media Research Consortium, Vancouver, pp. 111–27.

Siochru, S. and Girard, B. (2002) *Global Media Governance*. Rowman & Littlefield, Lanham, MD.

Urry, J. (2000) *Sociology Beyond Societies: Mobilities for the Twenty-First Century*. Routledge, London.

Wasko, J. (2003) *How Hollywood Works*. Sage Publications, London.

Weber, M. (2004) Cina: locomotive dell'economia mondiale. *L'industria* 1, 33–62.

Zhenzhi, G. (2003) *Television regulation and China's entry into the WTO*. Working Paper no. 168. Institute for Broadcasting Economics, University of Cologne.

7

Media Ownership, Concentration, and Control
The Evolution of Debate

John D. H. Downing

Introduction

The ownership and control debate in media research concerns very different issues from the classic microeconomics debate about corporate ownership and control (Mastrini and Becerra 2008, Sussman 2008). The thesis originally put forward by Berle and Means (1932) was that over the previous 50 years, the control of firms had come to lie with their executives rather than with their legally defined owners, namely their shareholders. However, their seemingly overwhelming data, from no less than 200 firms, turned out to be considerably flimsier than a first glance suggested, not least because of their failure to engage with the actual ascendancy of power blocs among shareholders, rather than aggregated figures. This particular question has considerable implications for assessing control over media, as we shall see.

One crucial issue in any such controversies is the definition of terms. In an essay published nearly three decades ago, Murdock (1982) strove to establish some clarity on this matter. He separated "economic" from "legal" ownership, that is, the power differential between being a member of an effective power bloc of share owners, as opposed to being one of a mass of petty shareholders. He further distinguished "allocative" from "operational" control, namely control over a corporation's policy as distinct from control of its day-to-day implementation.

Media sociologists have mostly been interested in operational control, viewed from the perspectives of the sociology of organizations, and the sociology of

The Handbook of Political Economy of Communications, First Edition.
Edited by Janet Wasko, Graham Murdock, and Helena Sousa.

occupations and professions (e.g., Berkowitz 1997, Part II). They have sometimes had the same straw man implicitly in their sights, namely a traditional leftist stick-figure who denounced the bosses' media for conspiring to poison the workers' minds, parroting the bosses' diktats. It was fairly easy to show how far from subjective professional reality in the newsroom this picture lay, and how important were organizational routines and other social dynamics in the media production process. Studies of readers, listeners, and viewers complicated this picture still further.

Some writers, however, such as journalist Mark Hertsgaard in his study of the US press during the 1981–9 Reagan administration (Hertsgaard 1988), have produced a much more nuanced and systematically evidenced leftist account, far distanced from slogan-Marxism. Another contributor to the debate who sought to fuse Gramsci's notion of hegemony with media organization routines was sociologist Todd Gitlin in his study of news media and the 1960s US student antiwar movement (Gitlin 2003/1981). Below we will review Herman and Chomsky's distinctive propaganda model, which to some degree may be grouped under this heading.

In political economy and conventional economics media research, as corporate mergers have grown ever larger and ever more global, debate has focused particularly on the cultural and political implications of concentrated media ownership. It has polarized around three issues:

1   Is there sufficient evidence for there being concentrated media ownership?
2   Does a high concentration of media ownership risk, or even entail, a dangerous constriction of the interplay of perspectives and information on issues directly relevant to citizens of a democratic polity? This may be termed the "democracy-strangulation" hypothesis.
3   Does a high degree of concentrated media ownership risk, or even entail, a serious shrinkage of media product options available at competitive prices to media consumers? This may be termed the "consumer-frustration" hypothesis.

Conventional economics opinion, focusing strictly on price issues and reflecting the Chicago School's traditional antitrust framework, disputes that there is media ownership concentration, and indeed points to the Internet as a newly liberating force in this regard. The deduction is that there is neither a threat to functioning democracy nor to consumer choice. Political economy opinion sounding the alarm on the danger to democracy, however, sometimes also sounds the alarm on the constriction of consumer choice as well.

Indeed, Entman and Wildman (1992) argued that these concerns were at least potentially compatible. Nonetheless, advocates of one position have quite frequently entered the lists against proponents of the other. Adding zest to the jousting, they have sometimes also attacked each other's methodology. The tournament has been running for decades now, even longer than an English cricket match, so had the maiden princess's hand been the prize, her funeral would surely have anticipated its conclusion.

Interest in this issue has recently been steadily growing around the world, as will be noted toward the close of this chapter, though given the current prominence of the USA in media research and also communication policy making, US debates have often taken center stage.[1] The debates in the USA and Britain will mostly occupy us here.

There are many shoals and reefs to navigate in this debate. Let us illustrate from four brief examples, before plunging into the evolution of the debate.

1   A fascinating quirk in one US research strand has been how arguments emanating from the political Right have sought to snitch the Left's clothes, arguing that established news media are a thought monopoly in the clutches of "East Coast liberals" (for sources and a critique, see Alterman 2003). Some high ranking US military officials and other rightist commentators put this curiously hypergeographical and subsociological designation forward in the aftermath of the Vietnam War, blaming the news media for losing to the Vietnamese. Its ultimate pedigree went back to conservative traditionalist denunciations of East Coast "Rockefeller Republicans," though more recently it resurfaced as the right-wing populist mantra of News Corp's "fair and balanced" Fox Cable News. (Some conservative European commentators subsequently adapted it for local use.)

2   A case indicating the extreme and long-term risks of concentrated media ownership comes from Chile during the years of the People's Unity coalition government (1970–3), led by elected president Salvador Allende. An early study by distinguished French media researcher Armand Mattelart showed how a highly concentrated mainstream press, radio, and television overwhelmingly denounced the socialist coalition, especially after its popular vote increased in the 1972 elections. Aided by a flood of CIA and corporate US money, which also sponsored a new rash of children's comics and other media, and intervening ceaselessly to inflame hostile public opinion among Chile's then-large class of small business owners, the media establishment energetically prepared the ground for the US-planned military coup that ushered in aerial bombing of the presidential palace, the killing of the president, and 16 years of military dictatorship, including tortures, assassinations, and thousands of "disappeared" citizens at the hands of the regime (Mattelart 1980/1973).

3   When the 2000 merger between America Online (AOL) and Time Warner was announced, many shuddered at the prospect of this behemoth, bringing print media, movies, television, Internet, and more together. Yet within two years, the company was in dire straits and soon changed its name from AOL TimeWarner back to TimeWarner. The corporate cultures involved were like oil and water. Furthermore, AOL's 55 percent share of the company and its naming ahead of its partner had reflected the so-called "dotcom bubble" valuation that soon popped and wrecked AOL's stock, and for a while, TimeWarner's with it. High drama with

little substance, it seemed, and all ultimately corrected by free market processes, the miraculous "invisible hand."

4   Murdock (1982) also examines ownership as a function of corporate strategies in a market already deeply structured by imperfect competition. He argues vigorously that analyses of corporate performance which restrict themselves to interpreting the mindsets and priorities of top executives are deeply impoverished, absurdly dismissing the very dynamics to which these actors are responding and endeavoring to manage. It is not that their mindsets and priorities should in turn be dismissed, simply that focusing only on them represents a profound myopia. Since the 1970s, moreover, this market has dramatically globalized, thereby intensely complicating the parameters of analysis.

The issues have also become internationalized along a further alignment as a result of the current weight of US policy making on the world stage. Once the Reagan era shift toward deregulation and privatization gathered momentum with the break-up of AT&T, neoliberal forces in many countries proved eager advocates of the US government's drive within the International Telecommunications Union conferences and the GATT/WTO trade negotiations. Oligopolistic media ownership grew apace, and quite often state telecommunications agencies privatized themselves as commercial monopolies. These telecommunications giants would in turn rapidly become crucial players in the Internet, wireless broadband, and other leading information and communication technologies (ICT) fields.

With these several contradictory cases in mind, let us now proceed to an account of the evolution of prominent contributions to debate, focusing principally on the evolution of debate on this topic within the USA, and to a lesser extent within Britain. The interconnections, or sometimes lack of them, between research and policy making will be an ongoing element in the discussion. This analysis will take up the bulk of this chapter.

Subsequently, there will be a shorter review of evidence and questions based in some other national media systems, thereby hopefully moving away from the assumption that *real* communication policy issues – and solutions – only surface in the USA and one of its global allies, and offering some comparative insight. Finally, there will be an attempt to sort through multiple empirical levels and foci and the discrete conceptual paradigms that we shall see surfacing as we proceed through the debate's stages. This will be in order to establish some of the key vectors that demand fresh research on media ownership and control.

The prominent contributions to US and British debate selected for comment here will begin with the 1947 Hutchins Commission Report *A Free and Responsible Press* (Commission on Freedom of the Press 1947), a foundational statement within the USA concerning media concentration issues. From here we will turn to three researchers from the political Left, namely the late Herbert Schiller, whose research from 1969 onwards on international and US media issues carved out new and controversial dimensions (Schiller 1969, 1973, 1981, 1986, 1989, 1996), and British sociologists Graham Murdock and Peter Golding, whose essay on the political economy of British media had an enduring impact on the field (Murdock and Golding 1973). From there, we shall move to the late Ithiel de Sola Pool, whose book *Technologies of Freedom* set out an interpretation of newer ICTs that was highly influential in US communication policy formulation concerning media concentration (de Sola Pool 1983). Subsequently, we shall move back to two researchers from the political Left, Edward Herman and Noam Chomsky, whose book *Manufacturing Consent* set out a "propaganda" model of media firms that has attracted both multiple translations and routine critiques (Herman and Chomsky 1988). From there, we shall switch to Benjamin Compaine and Douglas Gomery's 2000 edition of *Who Owns The Media?* (Compaine and Gomery 2000), a landmark volume by one neoclassical and one institutional economist. Thereafter, we shall examine the work of Scottish media economist Gillian Doyle, working within a neoclassical microeconomics and industrial sector economics paradigm on media concentration issues in Britain and some European countries (Doyle 2002). Finally, we will address the work of Ben Bagdikian, the doyen of serious journalistic research on media concentration in the USA (Bagdikian 2004), and the recent contribution of legal scholar C. Edwin Baker to debate on both the democracy-strangulation and the consumer-frustration issues (Baker 2007).

There have been many more contributions to the debate than these, and inclusion is bound to have some arbitrariness (and irritation for those not included). But as already indicated, this analysis of the evolution of debate seeks to be more politically comprehensive than many accounts succeed in providing (from across the political spectrum), but also seeks to acknowledge the several paradigms and variety of empirical foci and research methods that have characterized the arguments to date.

The Hutchins Commission Report (1947)

The full title of the report is important to note: *A Free and Responsible Press: A General Report on Mass Communication: Newspapers, Radio, Motion Pictures, Magazines, and Books*. While television was only then entering the "mass" communication firmament, and telephones were 50 years away from today's 3G information packages, the intent was clearly to examine all media, not just print journalism. (Only the recording industry is omitted.) Having said that, however, the leitmotiv addresses news and newspapers, with the film industry primarily cited as an instance of a self-regulatory model, and commercial radio as an object lesson in the abdication of social responsibility.

The report was prepared over the years 1943–6, in other words, while the World War began to turn against the Axis powers, and then while labor's pent-up postwar demand for better wages exploded in the strike wave of 1945–6, but while the Cold

War was in its infancy. In terms of major legal cases affecting US media, its publication date was framed by the antitrust verdicts in the 1945 Associated Press vs. USA and the 1948 Paramount Pictures vs. USA cases, and in the separation of NBC's Blue and Red networks into NBC and ABC. Within the USA, distrust of media concentration had a longer history than this, as Horwitz (2005, 181–2) correctly argues, but here it coincided with labor's self-confidence and the widespread sense of starting a new era. The furious and unrelenting opposition to Roosevelt's New Deal policies led by two press magnates of the time, Robert McCormick through his *Chicago Tribune*, and Randolph Hearst through his media empire, were also much in the minds of those who worked with Hutchins on the report, as its text makes plain at points.

Robert Hutchins penned the report himself, and after summarizing the oligopolistic tendency in US media and their deteriorating performance as viewed by his commission members (Commission on Freedom of the Press 1947, 30–68), he crisply identified the source of the problem: "The major part of the nation's press is large-scale enterprise, closely interlocked with the system of finance and industry; it will not without effort escape the natural bias of what it is" (1947, 129–30). He continued shortly thereafter, much in the vein of A. J. Liebling's aphorism that the freedom of the press belongs to someone who owns one: "Concentration of power substitutes one controlling policy for many independent policies, lessens the number of major competitors, and renders less operative the claims of potential issuers [of opinion] who have no press" (1947, 130).

These formulations adumbrated a continuing theme in US debate concerning media ownership concentration: the threat to democracy from a purely commercially driven media system, and the threat to effective market competition. In this version, the former is given more weight than the latter.

The Commission's principal answer to the threat posed by media oligopoly was self-regulation by the news business, along the lines of the film industry's Hays Committee at that time, which "set standards of acceptability, not of responsibility; and the standards are minima, not goals of adequate or ideal performance" (Commission on Freedom of the Press 1947, 71).

Indeed, the report repeatedly warned (e.g., p. 80) – on the basis of what imminent risk is unclear – that media trusts were liable to be broken up as had other US corporations in the past, and should therefore move immediately toward a form of self-regulation. Journalists were also urged to professionalize, along the lines of medicine and law. The analytical implications of both these unsolicited forms of advice are voluntaristic, namely that acts of will are plausible within the industries to circumscribe media business practice in the directions urged by the Commission. Over 60 years later, we may legitimately wonder.

The influence of the Hutchins Report is hard to determine. Its "social responsibility" argument resurfaced in the *Four Theories of the Press* comparative study of national media systems (Siebert et al. 1956) as the updated US modification of the old free-market philosophy of nineteenth-century competitive capitalism. That book was widely read in succeeding decades, and may have influenced the Federal Communications Commission's retention of limits on broadcast station ownership until the 1981–9 Reagan administration.

Nonetheless, it stands as an early landmark in the ownership concentration debate within the USA. Its methodology consisted, however, of what has become a familiar pattern since. First, the oligopolistic structure of media ownership is established (ch. 3). Then, a series of failures by commercial media to serve the public properly are listed and skewered (ch. 4). These failures mostly fall under two headings: poverty of information, and shallowness and triteness of entertainment. But they are coupled together. One of the standard critiques of this approach is its argument via accumulation of negative cases, on the ground that these have been purposively rather than randomly selected and therefore we have no means of assessing their representativeness.

Herbert Schiller: Worldwide US Media Monopoly? (1969–2000)

Schiller's contribution to US and international media research was remarkable. Much more deeply appreciated by media scholars outside the USA, especially in the global south, than in his own country, his enlargement of the imaginable paradigms of media research within the USA itself stands as a significant achievement in the development of the field.

In his first book, *Mass Communications and American Empire* (Schiller 1992/1969), Schiller set out the basic vision that would inform all his later writings: the integration of all forms of communication technology with domestic corporate monopoly and the USA's global imperial ambition. For media researchers happy with a more benign vision of the USA, this approach generated ire and denunciation among some, and dismissive contempt among others, defining it as "conspiratorial," crude, and, of course, Marxist (i.e., economic reductionist). Even "elitist" in one critique, that claimed his denunciation of cultural imperialism implied "Third World" audiences for US cultural products had no minds of their own but were gullibly absorbing everything that Uncle Sam sent their way (e.g., Tomlinson 1991).

Schiller's basic postulates regarding media concentration in the 1969 book read as follows:

A clutch of corporations (common carriers, manufacturers of electrical equipment, and a few network broadcasting companies) interlock and attempt to arbitrate among themselves, not always with complete success, the domestic communications scene … Mass communications are now a pillar of the emergent imperial society … The facilities and hardware of international information control are being grasped by a highly centralized communications complex, resident in the United States and largely unaccountable to its own population. (Schiller 1992/1969, 147–8)

His inclusion in a single framework of communications hardware for both broadcasting and information networks, corporate concentration, the state, the military's overseas roles and US global strategy, vaulted clean over the conventional walls of US media scholarship at that time, which to this day is often content to luxuriate in its multiple miniscule foxholes.

For Hutchins, the global dimension had lain in the urgent need of the US public for accurate information about events and trends in the rest of the planet, a need he saw as very poorly met by leading media firms in the 1940s which had the resources to do so but did not (Commission on Freedom of the Press 1947: 99, 124, 129). Schiller's vision by contrast pinpointed concentrated media ownership as enabling distorted, consumerist, and proimperial perspectives to hold sway at home and, increasingly, abroad, while developing ever more sophisticated point-to-point information applications to enable military control of trouble spots around the planet.

In his next book, *The Mind Managers* (Schiller 1973), written during the last years of the Nixon Administration, Schiller pursued these themes further:

> most Americans are basically, though unconsciously, trapped in what amounts to a no-choice information bind. Variety of opinion on foreign or domestic news or, for that matter, local community business, hardly exists in the media. This results essentially from the inherent identity of interests, material and ideological, of property-holders (in this case, the private owners of the communications media), and from the monopolistic character of the communications industry in general. (Schiller 1973, 19)

Schiller continues on the next page to argue that even where competition existed among the then three US TV networks, it resulted in mutual imitation rather than true diversity: *"there is no significant qualitative difference"* (Schiller 1973, 20, emphasis in original).

Schiller's work in the later 1970s moved increasingly toward the critical analysis of new forms of information technology application (Schiller 1981, 1986, 1996), and away from mass media. In this, he was both following the comprehensive paradigm he had espoused from the start, but also striking out in directions most US media scholars had yet to pursue. He focused on corporate and imperial features of the computer era, probing the impact of concentrated ownership in this rapidly burgeoning sector. Today, of course, it is clear that ownership and control issues cannot possibly be effectively researched without engaging with the entire communication sector, even though, as we shall see, there are some knotty problems in doing so.

In *Culture Inc.: The Corporate Takeover of Public Expression* (Schiller 1989), Schiller returned to public culture, education, and other realms dominated by concentrated corporate power. In chapter 7, he addressed one of the most common critiques of his work, namely his seemingly elitist dismissal of the public's capacity to resist corporate media messages and assumptions. The argument is a crucial one: in the end, unless concentrated ownership of media and ICT firms has constraining and/or persuasive effects of a negative kind, why would that ownership pattern matter?

Schiller directed his critique primarily at the then-popular "active audience" school of analysis that had emerged out of work in Cultural Studies. He identified it as a mere resurgence of the "limited-effects" paradigm associated with Katz and Lazarsfeld's influential 1955 study *Personal Influence*, in which media effects were argued always to be filtered through primary and secondary group face-to-face communication. He expressed particular irritation with researchers who drew upon Roland Barthes's emphasis in his later work on the pleasurable dimensions of media entertainment, with the effect – in Schiller's view – of displacing concern with its politically desensitizing impact.

However, his counterattack, despite legitimately noting how in extreme versions the "active audience" approach simply evacuated all power from media content and transferred it to audiences, still fell short of a full-scale rebuttal. His enduring mastery of witty formulations in disputing those with whom he disagreed was in full evidence, but belonged rather to the cheap shot than to convincing refutation: "The wide acceptance and the strength of the active-audience thesis reside partly in the theory's capacity to give pleasure to its formulators and believers; much more pleasure, perhaps, than they insist television programs give their viewers" (Schiller 1989, 152).

He went on to list the "very elaborate, expensive, and sophisticated technology – polling and surveying" (153) that media industries deploy to respond, in a fast-changing and conflictual environment, to the public's various moods and aspirations. But there his argument suddenly halts, as though, having demonstrated that large sums of money are spent on trying to make programming attractive, it follows that (1) the money must be intelligently spent, and (2) if intelligently spent, it automatically lassoes audiences back into the corporate corral.

In final support of his overall contention, Schiller cites: "the shadowy but many-tentacled disinformation industry – actually an integral part of the cultural industries, orchestrated by the political elite and the intelligence agencies since the end of World War II" (Schiller 1989, 154). If audience resistance were truly the norm, then, Schiller triumphantly demanded, where was the opposition to the Cold War anticommunism produced by this industry over two generations?

This was a remarkably weak reduction of multifaceted issues to a single binary: the disinformation industry and the US public. Is it really the case that the persistence of Cold War justifications for US aggression overseas can only be laid at this industry's door, and not at the remarkable opportunities presented it by such events as the violent suppression of worker unrest in East Germany in 1953, in Poland in 1956 and 1970, in Hungary in 1956, in former Czechoslovakia in 1968, and not least in China's Great Leap Forward years (1958–61) and the 1966–75 Cultural Revolution? To say nothing of the gulags, psychoprisons, and stifling of media and education freedom in the former USSR? These were never issues Schiller chose to critique, yet they hardly required a sophisticated US propaganda apparatus to make hay with them. On top of this, there are multiple other facets of the Cold War scenario he glided past in this argument, though there is no space to address them here.

Arguably, Schiller's strength lay in his readiness to yoke together the numerous facets of communication that researchers too frequently insulate from each other, his acute sense of global dimensions of media, his readiness to confront power and exploitation issues at home and abroad, whereas many scholars prefer a quiet and uncontroversial life, and the extent to which he blew fresh air into an overly cozy set of academic paradigms in communication research. But his inability to make his argument stick without successfully engaging with reception issues is a serious weakness.

Murdock and Golding, "For a Political Economy of Mass Communications" (1973)

Not long after Schiller's first book, Graham Murdock and Peter Golding, two British sociologists at Leicester University's Centre for Mass Communication Research, published a major article in *The Socialist Register*, a yearbook of nondoctrinaire Marxist scholarship without party affiliation (Murdock and Golding 1973). The essay was very widely read and reprinted, blazing a new trail as well as setting a standard for ensuing media research within that broad paradigm. Their article not only addressed ownership and concentration issues, but also engaged with a range of market dynamics. The authors cautiously emphasized that their study was "a part of a work in progress ... to suggest some directions [for future research]" (Murdock and Golding 1973, 205).

They began by insisting on the necessity of analyzing the media sector as a whole, not just by individual industry, and of linking media research to an understanding of macroeconomic processes, not least the roles of advertising. They also stressed the importance of both "the information and leisure facilities" that media produce (Murdock and Golding 1973, 207), avoiding the frequent segregation of news and entertainment in media research. Finally, their discussion contained careful analysis of a variety of empirical data and sources.

They approached concentrated media ownership historically, moving from early competitive capitalist media in the nineteenth century, through consolidation of ownership, to ownership concentration (or, in Marx's *Capital*, from "concentration" to "centralization"). They produced detailed commentary on both horizontal and vertical integration indices in the UK, as well as on reciprocal shareholdings and interlocking directorships. They also took time to produce an overview of British media export patterns, and of foreign ownership of British media (which they argued was at that point often overstated). For those who assume Marxist scholarship consists merely of the repetition of a few credos, reading the essay would be a helpful education.

Their prime targets as consequences of the oligopolistic media ownership structure were both restriction of consumer choice in leisure and entertainment, and the consolidation of what they termed "the consensus" via information control. By "the consensus", they meant the normal framework of news that (1) ignored, condemned, or politically trivialized strikes and other challenges from below; (2) defined the limits of debate as "those of the existing predominant political spectrum" (Murdock and Golding 1973, 229); (3) emphasized the adequacy of existing channels for grievance negotiation; (4) covered international news mostly within the confines of the former Empire; (5) promulgated the notion of Britain as a healthy meritocracy; and (6) projected as a given that the public's and media firms' values and priorities were one and the same (1973, 228–30).

They were, however, careful to insist that "the relationship between the material interests controlling the media and the cultural products they provide is a complex one, not explicable in terms of conspiracy or conscious intent. The part played by the media in cementing the consensus in capitalist society is only occasionally characterized by overt suppression or deliberate distortion" (Murdock and Golding 1973, 228).

But why, they demanded, do the social classes who are far from rich tolerate the sharp inequalities endemic in British society? Media research, they insist, has an important task to perform in uncovering why; but it is the *routines* of media production and distribution that consistently generate "the consensus," not a series of diktats or interventions from above: "Most generally news must be entertainment; it is, like all media output, a commodity, and to survive in the market-place must be vociferously inoffensive in the desperate search for large audiences attractive to advertisers" (Murdock and Golding 1973, 230).

Thus their discussion of media ownership concentration combined its depiction with full acknowledgment of the intersecting role of market forces, of professional organization routines, and of the growing internationalization of media business. Their analysis of its impact on consumer choice and democracy's vigor solely rests, however, upon a selection of empirical cases – a feature of many critical discussions of media oligopoly that has been a frequent target of more optimistic media researchers.

Implicit at times in their argument is an ambivalence regarding the public's roles in absorbing media products rather than challenging them. We noted above how Schiller emphasized media firms' "very elaborate, expensive, and sophisticated technology – polling and surveying" in his argument for media power. When

Murdock and Golding wrote, similarly, of "the desperate search for large audiences attractive to advertisers," the implication is that media firms, desperate or not, were being largely successful in doing so. But how so? Only further research into "the role of media in legitimating [the] system" (Murdock and Golding 1973, 228) is held likely to explain. Meanwhile, the "vociferous inoffensiveness" of the British media was likely to carry the day. Neither Schiller, nor Murdock and Golding in this essay, really get beyond the media structure to explaining how that structure interacts with other vectors to develop forms of impact. Murdock's 1982 essay, already cited, similarly engages more successfully with dismissing clumsy attempts to characterize the processes than with actually dissecting them.

In the end, we are confronted with a continuing contradiction that reflects in its own way the contrasting paradigms of Marxist political economy and neoclassical economics, the former focusing on the relations of production and dismissing exchange processes as epiphenomenal, and the latter insisting that effective consumer demand, and that only, is the motor of production. We shall return to this theme below.

Ithiel de Sola Pool: Technologies of Freedom (1983)

In terms of marking the evolution of this debate, we should note here the initial 1979 edition of Benjamin Compaine's *Who Owns The Media?* and its second 1982 edition, as well as the first edition of Ben Bagdikian's *The Media Monopoly* (1983). However, since there is a third edition of the Compaine book (Compaine and Gomery 2000), and there were five further updates of the Bagdikian book, culminating in *The New Media Monopoly* (Bagdikian 2004), we will address the latest versions below.

In the meantime, however, de Sola Pool's study sharply changed the very terms of policy debate on concentrated ownership, even though his focus on then-new electronic communication technologies was effectively contemporaneous with Schiller's. But Schiller never had (nor sought) the access to the machinery of national policy making enjoyed by de Sola Pool from his base in MIT's elite political science department, which he founded. The support for writing *Technologies of Freedom* also came from the universities of Cambridge, Keio, and Tokyo, which helped further amplify his voice.

Although the book is crammed with historical, legal, and technological detail, it rests upon one extremely basic proposition which is also easy to grasp. This is that the profusion of communication channels opened up by newer technologies (cable, satellite, phone, and computer networks) meant that restrictions on concentrated press, broadcast, and film ownership were now pointless, in the USA or elsewhere. The restrictions had been put in place to secure a diversity of content and opinion via a reasonable multiplicity of ownership, but that had been on the assumption that market entry to major media was prohibitively costly. Freedom of mediated communication was now in the realm of the present.

De Sola Pool's book was published after the US cable industry had been protesting for some years against restrictions favored by the broadcasters' lobby, and three years after CNN had commercially pioneered the linkage of satellite and cable technologies. It also arrived on the stands one year after the Modified Final Judgment was announced, which led to the breakup of the AT&T/Western Electric/Bell Labs complex and ultimately to the 1996 Telecommunications Act that removed many media ownership restrictions (despite being envisaged by its leading congressional sponsors as freeing up communication access for the public). It fell between the second and third Computer Inquiries that dominated US policy in the network realm (Lentz 2008). Across-the-board deregulation was the order of the day in the Reagan Administration's two terms. In 1986 Robert McChesney published his first essay, "Off-limits: an inquiry into the lack of debate over the ownership, structure, and control of the media in U.S. political life" (McChesney 2008, ch.15), a plaintive reflection of the reigning deregulatory consensus at that time.

Whatever the policy consequences and the opinion that may be held of them, de Sola Pool's establishment of this wider range of communication technologies as vital components of the picture was a very important push – along with Schiller's, though they would likely have jointly shuddered at being bracketed together – toward expanding the terms of debate in media studies and on the issues involved in media ownership. Issues of denial of access, of network neutrality, of "copyleft," and of internet governance have reconfigured the media landscape, and today A. J. Liebling would have to make his point in sharply updated terms.

Herman and Chomsky, *Manufacturing Consent* (1988/2002)

This book is best known for what today has become known as "the" propaganda model of media, but which its authors more modestly termed "a" propaganda model. In particular, their metaphor of the five "filters" that cleanse US media of potentially toxic content regarding US imperial operations has become a well-known, albeit sometimes ferociously derided, position in media research.

The five filters they identify are (1) size, ownership, and profit orientation of the media; (2) advertising as media's financial base; (3) dominant news sources; (4) "flak"; (5) anticommunism (and antileftism across the board). The "filter" metaphor is interesting, suggesting an almost passive structure, without agency or at least initiative, an established complex of routinized interactions, whose tightly woven mesh blocks out most of the ideological pollutants that would otherwise poison the conservative US public sphere. To that extent, the metaphor shuns any conspiratorialism, although that accusation has been the chief rebuke leveled at the model over the years.

In fact, the model's critics have sometimes turned it into a straw man, suggesting that Herman and Chomsky deny the very possibility of dissenting views surfacing in corporate media: five watertight seals rather than five filters, in other words. However, this betrays a failure to read their text: their conceptualization is akin to a statistical regression line of least squares, easily able to accommodate a pattern-less scatter of variances to the main drift of data.

The distinctive aspects of the propaganda model are first, its proposition that all five filters interrelate, and second, its inclusion of ideological vectors (filters 4 and 5), as well as political economic and structural dimensions (filters 1–3).

Indeed, the only "filter" that does not quite fit the image of a routinized system is "flak," the process whose name is derived from the antiaircraft shells launched against incoming enemy aircraft in World War II, and which denotes the highly organized choruses of denunciation emanating from talk radio, letters to corporate media executives and advertisers, and lawsuits, whenever there is need to "contain deviations from the established line" in mainstream media (Herman and Chomsky 2002/1988, 28). The authors argue that this latter operation has greatly stepped up its intensity since the 1970s. It is, therefore, a form of discipline of media exercised from outside the internal workings of media firms themselves.

Overall, the propaganda model's chorus of critics may be argued to be expending too much energy. The model is fundamentally focused on the world news available to US citizens through major US media. Consider what it is not: it is not a model claimed to apply to all national media systems, (though Winter 1998 has attempted to apply it to Canada); it is not a model claimed to apply to entertainment media, in hours spent far the largest element in media provision, (though Alford 2009 makes a case for extending it to Hollywood movies); and it is not a model that fits a considerable number of domestic political issues, outside of direct cover-ups of environmental or similar scandals. It is, then, a theory of the middle range, focused on foreign news reporting in the USA over the last 100 years, especially the last 50.

As such, it does not purport to be a global account. Its focus often seems similar to Schiller's, namely to attempt to explain why the US public is normally so prepared to be told that it needs to go to war, to back colossal military budgets rather than universal health care, and to retain hundreds of military bases all over the planet.[2] But while Schiller tended to point in general to secrecy and deliberate obfuscation, Herman and Chomsky endeavor to take the argument to the next step, dissecting the systemic imperatives they consider to be in place to noiselessly exclude challenging information.

However, providing an explanation for the inadequacies of US foreign news reporting is not, and cannot be, a substitute for a theory of media ownership and control across the board. If the propaganda model is to develop further, it will have to interlock plausibly with additional concepts and arguments that carry traction regarding the whole gamut of domestic US politics and news, and entertainment media. In order to retain validity, however, there is no need for it to carry traction regarding other national media systems.

Benjamin Compaine and Douglas Gomery, *Who Owns The Media?* (2000)

Benjamin Compaine, editor and then coeditor of this twice-updated study, comes at the issues from a substantially different perspective, that of the Chicago School's long-established antitrust policy specialists. His coeditorship of the third edition with Douglas Gomery, film history professor and institutional economist, was clearly an attempt to offer readers alternating perspectives.

The authors provide a mass of empirical information on the US cultural industries, categorized by technology: newspapers, books, magazines, television, radio, recorded music, cinema, and (for the first time) online information industries.[3] The three final chapters (chs 8–9) are devoted to the authors' respective interpretations of media ownership issues, and a final chapter evaluating competition and concentration. They do not stretch as far as Murdock and Golding's emphasis on the leisure industry at large, so theme parks, tourism, and videogames all fall outside their purview.

Compaine raises a number of worthwhile methodological issues not explicitly addressed in the earlier discussions reviewed here. He notes that a media firm or its divisions will be defined as "large" variously, depending upon the sphere of operation. For newspapers, it will be aggregate circulation; for magazines, circulation or revenue; for broadcasting, audience size; for cable TV, subscriber households; for books, films, and recorded music, industry revenue share; and for online services, percentage of monthly access and ad revenue (Compaine and Gomery 2000, 484).

Compaine also takes care to distinguish differing forms of ownership. He notes that many firms nominally owned by shareholders are in fact controlled by families or a small clutch of investors, often via the issue of different share categories (Compaine and Gomery 2000, 490). He also notes the considerable importance of institutional investors (e.g., giant pension funds) in the US media structure (2000, 498ff.). His conclusion regarding the implication of institutional investor media involvement, however, is distinctly upbeat: "so much of the media is owned, indirectly perhaps, but in the interest of tens of millions of working people" (494). "Interest," however, is a term he fails to define. He does expatiate on the motivations of institutional investor owners, proposing that such agencies are concerned with long-term growth prospects of the stocks they buy, not with short-run controversies. Their likely response if averse to a type of media content would be, he insists, to sell off or not invest in the first place, "rather than try to influence the directions of management" (503).

It appears from this that Compaine's sense of the term "control" restricts it to direct and detailed interventions over a sustained period, a fusion of the allocative and operational between which Murdock (1982) carefully distinguished. This also greatly simplifies the forms that influence may take. Those who know the market most certainly have to be keenly aware of its major and medium players, their trajectories and expectations. Feeding that knowledge into market tactics and strategy is a sine qua non of potential market success. Failure to do so could be catastrophic. Anticipation that an institutional investor might sell off its holding, or might be inclined to purchase significant holdings, is arguably a far more powerful discipline than individual interventions in day-to-day decisions.

What is lurking behind the discussion at this point is the question of the multiple meshes between the various cultural industries and the wider political economy, including the ideological climate at any one juncture. It is an issue we shall return to later, and we will suggest that Gramsci's concept of hegemony may be the most helpful portal through which to enter upon an analysis of these meshes.

Compaine's prime analytical tool for measuring media concentration is the Herfindahl–Hirschman Index (HHI), an index developed in the Chicago School to measure industry concentration in general (Compaine and Gomery 2000, 558ff.). It proceeds by squaring the market share of each player in the industry, an approach which assumes that an expanding level of concentration will have increasingly noticeable exponential effects. A score of 1,800 or above is taken to indicate high concentration. Compaine argues that applying this index produces a more level-headed estimate of the degree of concentration than do dramatic news stories of "titanic" mergers. He further proposes that economic indices of media concentration, however subject to discussion and critique, nonetheless provide firmer estimates than public interest or First Amendment criteria, and can stand as a "reasonable surrogate measure" of those (2000, 558). Indeed, it is at the core of his argument that the degree and danger of concentrated media ownership in the USA has been greatly oversold and, as his coauthor suggests, left-wing critics see the mass media as evincing "an all-encompassing conspiracy by monopolists" (507).

Compaine's arguments based on the HHI have been vigorously contested by Baker (see below). However, let us focus in conclusion on some of his other observations. He offers a brisk attack on the oft-proclaimed goal of media content diversity, noting that "greater diversity means … more low-brow shows, trash journalism, pandering politics … Diversity cuts all ways" (Compaine and Gomery 2000, 578).

This comment picks up on a theme in the background of the arguments by Schiller and Murdock and Golding, where quite often the critique is leveled that alternative viewpoints rarely surface into mainstream news media, and where more diversity is called for. What that diversity is never really gets defined, but readers may be left with the suspicion that there is a particular viewpoint they feel is missing, namely a prosocial justice, anti-imperial perspective, which this writer shares, but which is only one of many possible perspectives (including the views of radical rightists or religious zealots). The term often goes blissfully undefined, but Compaine's polemic helps force the issue of definition.

Finally, Compaine voices a common position on media concentration in a globalizing era, namely that concentration should not only be evaluated in domestic terms: "US information providers are facing stiff competition in world markets ... Artificially scaled down institutions will not be able to win their share of the world market" (Compaine and Gomery 2000, 577). This formulation suggests a trump card for media merger advocates: US economic survival in a mean and scary world, a vision of the planet often highly plausible to US Congressional legislators, less than a third of whom are said to own passports. The success of this argument would certainly establish the victory of simple economics over concern for robustly democratic politics – but Gomery for one would disagree: "We need ... not reduce the criterion of what is valued as simply what is most efficient" (2000, 508).

Gillian Doyle, *Media Ownership* (2002)

Doyle's contribution is definitely at the empirical end of the spectrum, focusing especially on evidence from a detailed set of interviews she carried out with broadcasting and press executives in nine major UK media groups (the actual number of interviews is not given in the book). She does not deploy the Herfindahl-Hirschman Index as a measure of media concentration, nor indeed does she discuss it. In the latter part of the book, she moves to consider regulation trends in the UK and Europe, which need not concern us here. Entirely absent from her narrative is the challenging assertiveness of the *Hutchins Commission Report* or the six editions of Ben Bagdikian's *The Media Monopoly*.

Nonetheless, she concludes from British and other European evidence that the media "industry is particularly vulnerable to concentrations of monomedia ownership ... and to concentrations of cross-media ownership" (Doyle 2002, 175). (She uses the term "monomedia ownership" synonymously with "horizontal integration.") She diagnoses the corporate objective in these mergers as the opportunity to create economies of both scale and scope, together with what she terms the "critical mass effect," namely, the opportunity to attract disproportionate shares of advertising revenues, to dominate suppliers, and a number of other advantages. She suggests that the UK experience indicates that vertical integration and diagonal integration (i.e., moving into entirely fresh media sectors) are often pursued for other objectives than pure economic efficiency, and indeed that as of her book's publication date, UK cross-ownership of broadcast and print media had not demonstrated any clear economic advantages: "benefits tend to be of a corporate nature, primarily favouring the private interests of shareholders in specific media firms or, in some cases, managers of these firms" (176).

Despite Doyle's caution in offering generalizations, which makes her conclusions sound almost whispered by contrast with some of our other contributors to the debate, her evidence arguably shores up a number of their contentions. While accepting as legitimate media firms' motivations to improve their market performance, Doyle stands aloof from any automatic assumption that an unregulated market increases the welfare of media users. At the same time, there is a strain of hopefulness in her analysis – some of our contributors might say naïveté – that tends to contradict her main argument: "Although diverse ownership ... will not necessarily guarantee diversity of media output, the existence of a diversity of media owners *should* contribute positively to pluralism ... their rivalry *will* promote a culture of dissent which is healthy for democracy" and "society's interest in achieving the most efficient possible usage of resources ... is, or *ought* to be, the main concern for public policy" (28, 176, my emphases). The first case is a testable but dubious hypothesis, as Baker argues (see below). As to the second, one would indeed love it to be so. But Doyle's analysis provides no carefully crafted reasons for accepting either proposition.

Ben Bagdikian's *The Media Monopoly* (1983–2004)

Bagdikian's long concern with the shrinkage of independent journalistic voices in the USA, first as a journalist and later as dean of the Journalism School at the University of California, Berkeley, achieved a certain monumentalization in this work, culminating in *The New Media Monopoly* in 2004. For many who have never even read the book, his depiction in edition after edition of the gathering slide into monopoly concentration of media ownership in the USA – from 50 major owners in 1984 to five in 2004, by his reckoning – became pretty well taken for granted, and the stuff of Media Studies 101 on many campuses. It is impossible to know, but it is quite plausible that the level of US public concern over media concentration that surfaced most notably at the time of the 2003 Prometheus decision of the Third Court of Appeals, and in the string of large media reform conferences subsequently organized by Free Press (Klinenberg 2007, 221–44, 270–95), was cumulatively fed by reading Bagdikian's successive editions, hearing about his analysis in courses, and by that progressively aggravated statistic.

Bagdikian was careful to dispel the conspiracist charge: "The narrow choices the dominant firms offer the country are not the result of a conspiracy. Dominant media members do not sit around a table parceling out market shares, prices, and products ... [They] don't need to. They share too many of the same methods and goals" (Bagdikian 2004, 7).

On the other hand, his rhetoric sometimes got away with him, as when he characterized the business press as simply corporate propaganda (2004, 159–61), a judgment which despite their broad agreement on media issues would have vitiated Herbert Schiller's research methodology more or less entirely, relying as it did on reading the media trade and business press against the grain.

Bagdikian's approach to analyzing media concentration, as befitted a professional journalist, was to plough through evidence from a variety of sources. He does not once mention the Herfindahl-Hirschman Index, nor does he take up Doyle's microeconomics and industry sector economics approach. Rather, he culls from a lifetime's experience of following Wall Street trends and practices of the on-the-ground realities of, for example, boards of directors. This is a key issue for Bagdikian, who cites a 2003 *Columbia Journalism Review* study that found News Corp., Disney, Viacom, and Time Warner had 45 interlocking directors (Bagdikian 2004, 9). It would have been impossible in Bagdikian's frame to subscribe to Compaine's assumption that institutional investors represent the concerns of tens of millions of hard-working Americans, and equally implausible for him to echo Doyle's more hopeful visions noted above.

In Bagdikian's experience as journalist-observer, the critique of Berle and Means voiced above was unfounded:

> It is not unusual for strong executives to select the directors who are supposed to monitor them ... directors ... are themselves top executives of other large firms ... Some are ... from the largest banks ... who can facilitate credit and money for benefit of both their borrowing firm and their lending bank ... Though the Big Five are multinational ... family members of each firm's president sit on the board. Or the directors are friends who are also corporate executives ... It became clear during the boom, bust, and thievery by high officers during the 1990s and early twenty-first century that boards of directors of some of the largest corporations in the United States had little knowledge of or influence over their top executives. (Bagdikian 2004, 51, 53)

Bagdikian also moves away from strictly intracorporate analysis and directly relates the growing concentration of power in media to the steady rightward shift of the US political spectrum since the Reagan presidency of 1981–9 (2004, 11–17). For him the heroes are the two Roosevelts, who in his view both stood up to conglomerates, but whose legacy has been junked over the past 30 years. Even if his characterization of this shift is conceded, however, it is still the case that to pin prime responsibility on media is to beg a very large number of sociological, cultural, economic, and political questions.

In the clash of rhetorics – for muted social science discourse is also a rhetoric – it may sometimes be hard for readers to feel they are getting closer to the facts of the matter. It can even be refreshing to switch from one such rhetoric to the other, from the sauna to the ice-cold shower and back again, for we are dealing with crucial and also immensely intricate processes and institutions, and the busy play of argument is the only way we are likely to make progress.

Much of Bagdikian's argument consists of sobering, sometimes unnerving, cases. It is a method often attacked by his critics, who argue that selective cases to support a particular position cannot constitute a representative sample of the ordinary flow of media output, and that only a form of random sampling of content can capture the effects, benign or malign, of concentrated media ownership. We would need to add though that the formulation of content categories is far from a random or bloodless procedure, so that this technical solution to the issue is unfortunately still caught up in the miseries of the flesh in an imperfect world. At the same time, there is no reason in principle why both forms of evidence and inquiry should not proceed apace so long as they are prepared to interact constructively.

C. Edwin Baker, *Media Concentration and Democracy: Why Ownership Matters* (2007)

This is the third in a series of texts published by legal scholar Edwin Baker on the First Amendment, media, the market, and related issues. His argument is very thorough and detailed, and only its most salient features can be addressed here. Baker directly engages with Compaine's arguments (Baker 2007, 54–87) and with other positivist sources such as *Journalism Quarterly*[4] (23–6), that claim the extent and impact of media ownership concentration are routinely overhyped. For Baker the essence of the matter is the caliber of democracy we want, not consumer sovereignty: "any minor gains to media consumers would not diminish, would not affect, the central and arguably overriding reasons to oppose concentration: a more democratic distribution of communicative power within the public sphere and safeguards to the democratic system" (2007, 52–3).

Baker's critique of the HHI, or more specifically Compaine's use of it, targets Compaine's methodological decision to apply the measure to the media industry as a whole rather than its component parts: "Any reflection shows that the media business as a whole is an incoherent characterization" (Baker 2007, 60). This is an interesting step in an ongoing argument, given Murdock and Golding's early insistence that focus on the total media picture is crucial. As we have seen along the way, some who write on this subject address a single segment of the cultural industries, very often news to the exclusion of entertainment. We shall have reason to come back to this issue below.

Baker argues that Compaine's own categories of media activity – content, delivery, and format – already signal that the types of economic activity involved in one category are not and cannot be equivalent to the types involved in one of the others. "Competition in one," Baker underscores, "does not show that another is competitive" (Baker 2007, 60). The long dominance of the US distribution companies in film, broadcasting, and videogames, as contrasted with the content creators and exhibitors, is a case in point. Baker cites, too, local monopoly issues, where the same firm operates a small town's only newspaper and only TV station – this scenario would barely register on Compaine's industry-wide application of the HHI. Furthermore, the Chicago School's antitrust framework on which Compaine draws so heavily, with its obsession concerning the power to set uncompetitive prices, would not register a situation in which one distribution firm had close to monopoly control over that circuit, or where there were multiple distribution companies but only one content creation company. (The latter case is rather implausible in the USA at the present time, but nonetheless illuminates the wooden character of Compaine's HHI methodology.)

Compaine's work, like de Sola Pool's, has not remained enclosed in academia. The Federal Communications Commission's construction of a media Diversity Index (DI) was founded upon his arguments and analyses. Yet, Baker argues (2007, 81–6), the empirical problems in applying the HHI and the DI are so evident that the most plausible explanation for the FCC's choice is cynical, namely that an FCC with three presidentially appointed and ideologically committed conservative commissioners out of five simply wanted the legitimacy of positivist social science "findings" to underpin their prior commitment to lifting the barriers to further media concentration.

Baker's discussion of the Internet is a marked advance over Compaine's and Bagdikian's, but of course he had the advantage of some extra crucial years in the middle of the first decade of the 2000s to observe the Internet as its formats and applications began to jell. He particularly takes aim at the rosy scenario that issues of pluralism and democracy, choice, and media concentration, are fast becoming moot as the plethora of opportunities opens up via the Internet. Certain key points of his follow.

1   The Internet principally distributes but does not automatically create as well, even though many individuals and civil society groups create content for distribution on it, albeit overshadowed by the huge media concerns that use it intensively for their commercial products and purposes. The blogosphere has attracted very widespread attention in this regard, but Baker is able to show how figures to date show the blogosphere audience to be even more concentrated than the newspaper audience (Baker 2007, 107–9). Put differently, the US public appears to be receiving ever more of its news information from ever fewer sources.

2   Lower advertising revenues in online journalism are already reducing employment levels for journalists and thereby leading to diminished news content creation. A few news services (Associated Press, *The New York Times*, *The Wall Street Journal*, etc.) will become all the more dominant. Many US commercial news services have extremely inflated profit-margin expectations, often around 25 percent or higher, as contrasted with many other industrial sectors where the figure is usually below 10 percent, a factor which will interact negatively with the others mentioned.

3   While the Internet has dramatically altered barriers of geography, time, and cost to rapid access to information and to networking with others, "these

distributive gains are limited. They hardly eliminate extreme audience concentration of audience attention on information provided by a few corporate entities …
the Internet does not eliminate the force of the democratic distributive objection
to media ownership concentration" (Baker 2007, 122).

International Dimensions and a Provisional Conclusion

To date we have focused on the evolution of debate and research in the USA and
Britain. There is no space to engage in the same detail regarding developments in
other nations, but inevitably they raise questions concerning our understanding of
the issues.

Perhaps the most signal instance is that of Silvio Berlusconi, owner of Mediaset
(Italy's dominant commercial TV operator, with three national channels), and in
his three stints to date as elected premier, ultimately in control of the three public
TV channels as well, not to mention the rest of his extensive media holdings. Given
his global reputation for corruption and reactionary political views, it has been all
too tempting for many inside and outside Italy to define his repeated stints in
power as the product of media monopoly, even as heralding a new "mediacracy"
model for jaded democracies. Yet there is a plausible argument (Shin and Agnew
2008) that his and his cohorts' successful reading and manipulation of regional
discontents and economic insecurities were at least equally responsible, along with
their enthusiastic borrowing of US attack-style political campaigning. Not to mention, as in so many other cases, the pathetic disarray of his opposition.

One might equally cite the long reign of Televisa in Mexico, which until the
mid-1990s had been overwhelmingly the dominant TV channel, and which was
often known as the Culture Ministry of the PRI governing party, in power from
1920 until the year 2000 (Fernández and Paxman 2000). The governing party had a
number of other media control cards it played as well as its intimate relation with
Televisa (Benavides 2000). Yet the slowly developing disruption of the old political
carapace, reflected not only in the election of the first non-PRI president in 2000,
but also in the rising influence of the leftist PRD party, arguably had much to do
with the growth of what Hughes (2006) terms "civic journalism" in Mexico's
newsrooms over a considerable period of years.

The Russian Federation, after an initial period of chaotic media freedom in the
aftermath of the USSR's collapse, experienced a severe reversion (Downing 1996,
ch. 6), especially beginning with the Putin years. There has been a quite extraordinary degree of centralized control over television, one which gives the governing
elite virtually the same effective power on any issue that matters to it as had the old
Soviet control system (Koltsova 2009). Assassinations of journalists such as Anna
Politkovskaya – sadly neither the first nor the last – also served as an object lesson

for cautious behavior. The press was under less scrutiny from the top, though that did not mean it was more responsible. Nonetheless, there were tentative signs at the time of writing that journalists working in magazines and online were flexing some independent muscles (Federman 2010).

There is every reason to think that some careful comparative studies of the Italian, Mexican, and Russian cases, reviewing their evolving trends over the past 10–20 years, would shed useful light on the media concentration issue. An excellent study of media concentration in nine Latin American countries has become available (Mastrini and Becerra 2006).

Studies are certainly emerging, from a variety of perspectives, evidently, in a number of locations, focused on individual countries (e.g., Iglesias González 2004, Sousa and Costa e Silva 2009, Fung 2007, Rolland 2008, House of Lords 2008), or more broadly on the European Union (e.g., Just 2009), where issues of media concentration policy have been intensively reviewed for a couple of decades now (e.g., Palzer and Hilger 2001). In Australia, Botswana, Canada, Croatia, France, Germany, Ireland, Kenya, Poland, to name only a scattering, public debate over concentrated media ownership is active – not surprisingly, especially in Canada, where levels of media concentration have been very high for well over a decade at the time of writing.

The most salient feature of the evolution of the debate to date has been the considerable mixture of foci, concepts, and methodologies brought to bear on media ownership and its implications. Indeed, it has partly been a dialogue of the deaf for, as we have seen, only some of the participants have engaged with others, and when they have done so, it has sometimes been as much a joust as an ideal speech situation.

As just noted, with the exception of Mastrini and Becerra (2008), most sources have focused on a single country, so that the benefits of rigorous comparative analysis are yet to be seen. Some studies focus on a single industry, or even a single aspect of a single technology such as the daily press. Some focus on news across the board. Some entirely exclude entertainment media. Some insist that cultural industries, variously defined, must be viewed as an interrelated complex grounded in the political economy at large, including globally; but there are also arguments about appropriate methods in empirical analysis of media concentration on this model. Only in recent years have the changes opened up by Internet applications come to be included in analysis.

Some studies embrace the global dimensions of media concentration in certain countries (notably the USA), others prefer to skate safely past. Some engage with the state, though it is perceived variously as a more or less neutral arbitrator, a multisite of political struggle, or some version of "the executive committee of the bourgeoisie" (Marx). Some conceptualizations work from a purely or mostly consumer welfare model, others from the yardstick of which information and entertainment needs must be met to feed a vigorously democratic polity. Questions of impact on the public or audiences are very variously addressed, or sometimes not at all. These contributors' disciplinary backgrounds are in law, journalism, neoclassical economics, institutional economics, political economy, sociology, and political science. Contributors are grouped fairly much across the political spectrum, from energetically neoliberal through different forms of political centrism through to the far left. There is advantage in these multiple perspectives, but if the debate is to take real shape as a direct series of exchanges, then models for more systematic future debate may be found in two recent articles by Winseck and Sparks.

Winseck (2008) engages with comparative data from the USA, Canada, and Mexico, and also data on the largest global media firms, and with both news and entertainment issues. His fundamental argument is (1) while channel diversity is clearly expanding, content source diversity is shrinking; (2) profit-level requirements by media firm owners are constantly rising, reducing budgets for creative projects and investigative journalism; and (3) litigation over digital property rights is rapidly enclosing access to new media opportunities. Winseck's overview bypasses a number of the restricted focus and single national media system problems of some existing research. It is a fraction the length of Compaine and Gomery's detailed study, but it sets out a series of helpful parameters on which much more detailed research can be built.

Sparks (2007) offers an ice-cold shower to those who assert without further ado that major media firms are globalizing and to that degree are well on the way to becoming planetarily dominant. He very rigorously analyzes available data, contrasts them with data concerning transnational corporate giants in other economic sectors, and urges strong skepticism in the face of sweeping claims about international media monoliths.

These two authors offer the kind of tough-minded critical approach that is now needed more than ever. As it happens, their identification is with the political Left – and yet it is also possible that they might disagree with some premises of each other's argument. But while a standard critique from neoliberal academics is that only carefully selected scare stories are the stuff of critical research on media ownership and concentration, these two contributions are only indicative of many others from those quarters that clearly give the lie to that caricature.

The leitmotif of this debate's evolution, even more than the consumer choice issue, has been the cultural and political implications of commercial, and especially oligopolistic, media ownership. Earlier I hinted that some of the issues might, at least for those who do not dismiss out of hand fears of an ever-shrinking democracy and the narrowing of debate, be usefully addressed through a Gramscian prism. Admittedly, Gramsci's contribution to a narrowly defined political economy analysis was rather meager, and his rosy vision of the future role of communist parties in national development was framed in enforced isolation from the terrifying turn taken in Stalin's USSR in December 1928. Nonetheless, there are elements in his key concept of *egemonia* (generally translated "hegemony") which suggest a stronger resolution of an issue that has surfaced throughout this discussion.

A persistent issue in this debate has been the problematic linkage between media content and media control. Too often this has been framed in terms of specific immediate issues, very often of war or US forays overseas, and the task has been defined as explaining why large sections of the US public not only tolerate these but at times and for a period, passionately support them. Enter, for example, Herman and Chomsky's five filters.

It is widely understood that Gramsci used his concept of *egemonia* to denote the taken-for-granted cultural frameworks that leave generally unchallenged the ruling circles' authority to lead – allocative and operational control, to reprise terms used above. While members of the general public may and do retain skeptical perspectives regarding the system, only in crises do they cast aside their habitual acceptance of its inevitability, and *egemonia* fractures, for a shorter or longer period of time.

However, in practice, the temporal construction of *egemonia* has been loosely conceptualized, or not at all. Properly understood, however, *egemonia* denotes emergent and long-term processes. Capitalism, even in its modern, let alone its contemporary forms, emerged as dominant over two centuries, and the clusters of national and other cultural accretions that have grown up symbiotically with it – some elements rising to prominence, others sinking to the margins – have a similarly long and checkered history. Thus explaining how publics consent to and even enthusiastically endorse, at least for considerable periods, the policies and strategies of their governing circles, certainly requires explanations that account for media roles in the process. But those media are – to state the banal – elements within a larger inherited political economy and national cultures (plural). While the corporate dimension of this reality has been front and center of this chapter and this collection, it is the partly intentional but substantially intuitive meshing of long-standing cultural themes and tropes with the specifics of the immediate war, the immediate challenge, the immediate controversy, the immediate crisis, which arguably allow corporate media the traction they often enjoy.

Dieter Prokop once proposed the notion of "integrated spontaneity" to characterize the degree to which in cultural industries workers and agents develop new and flexible responses to fresh situations, but within preset frameworks. Their spontaneity is very real – but so are the given channels within which they express it (Prokop 1974).

By pulling these perspectives together, we may avoid a common logjam, created by trying to explain immediate realities only through other immediate realities. If the focus is strictly on current wars in South East Asia, or in Central America, or in the "Middle East," or if the focus is on the empirical social networks, business, and leisure, of corporate media owners, then yes, these are all indubitably part of the picture. Nonetheless, the *egemonia* process, deeply rooted but constantly refreshed and adapting cultural frameworks over the long term, simultaneously provides the media *mise-en-scène* and exonerates media analysts from dutifully trying to pinpoint all the current information supposedly needed to validate the control–content linkage claim.

Elsewhere, for instance, I have argued that the familiar trope of encirclement in popular US art, the Hollywood Western, and many war movies, not only has its roots in English colonialist ideology transferred to North America and in wars against Native Americans, but also is a key element in explaining the US public's ongoing readiness to tolerate, even endorse, foreign wars (Downing 2007). The issues of contemporary media control, culture, and power need to be set within this larger historical epic of power and control, not confined to the straitjacket of the contemporary.

Notes

1   See Robert McChesney's and Benjamin Compaine's articles on the *Open Democracy* website at http://www.opendemocracy.net (accessed September 29, 2010): McChesney, "Policing the thinkable," 10/24/2001; Compaine, "The myths of encroaching media ownership," 11/8/2001; McChesney, "Media corporations versus democracy: a response to Benjamin Compaine," 11/14/2001; Compaine, "The work-able real versus the absolutist ideal," 11/22/2001; McChesney, "It's a wrap? Why media matters to democracy," 5/8/2002; Compaine, "A world without absolutes," 5/8/2002.
2   An unacknowledged weakness among some of Herman and Chomsky's critics, espe-cially among media scholars, is that their rudimentary level of detailed information concerning global realities vitiates their capacity to grasp the nature of the problems in US foreign policy reporting that Herman and Chomsky attempt to unravel.
3   The velocity of change in this latter sphere is shown by the fact that neither Google nor cell phones figure in this discussion.
4   Now the *Journalism and Mass Communication Quarterly*.

References

Alford, M. (2009) A propaganda model for Hollywood. *Westminster Papers in Communication and Culture*, 6(2), 144–56. Online at http://www.wmin.ac.uk/mad/pdf/WPCC-Vol6-No2-Matthew_Alford.pdf (accessed September 29, 2010).

Alterman, E. (2003) *What Liberal Media? The Truth about Bias and the News*. Basic Books, New York.

Bagdikian, B. (2004) *The New Media Monopoly*, 6th edn. Beacon Press, Boston.

Baker, C. E. (2007) *Media Concentration and Democracy: Why Ownership Matters*. Cambridge University Press, New York.

Benavides, J. (2000) *Gacetilla*: A keyword for a revisionist approach to the political economy of Mexico's print news media. *Media, Culture & Society*, 22(1), 85–104.

Berkowitz, D. (ed.) (1997) *The Social Meanings of News: A Text-Reader*. Sage Publications, Thousand Oaks, CA.

Berle, A. A. and Means, G.C. (1932) *The Modern Corporation and Private Property*. Macmillan, New York.

Commission on Freedom of the Press (1947) *A Free And Responsible Press: A General Report on Mass Communication: Newspapers, Radio, Motion Pictures, Magazines, and Books* (The Hutchins Report). University of Chicago Press, Chicago.

Compaine, B. and Gomery, D. (eds) (2000) *Who Owns The Media? Competition and Concentration in the Mass Media Industry*, 3rd edn. Lawrence Erlbaum Publishers, Mahwah, NJ.

de Sola Pool, I. (1983) *Technologies of Freedom: On Free Speech in an Electronic Age*. The Belknap Press of Harvard University Press, Cambridge, MA.

Downing, J. D. H. (1996) *Internationalizing Media Theory: Reflections on Media in Russia, Poland and Hungary, 1980-1995*. Sage Publications, London.

Downing, J. D. H. (2007) The imperiled "American": Visual culture, nationality and U.S. foreign policy. *International Journal of Communication*, 1, 318–41 Online at http://ijoc.org/ojs/index.php/ijoc/article/view/111/74 (accessed September 29, 2010).

Doyle, G. (2002) *Media Ownership*. Sage, London.

Entman, R. and Wildman, S. (1992) Reconciling economic and non-economic perspectives on media policy: Transcending the "marketplace of ideas." *Journal of Communication*, 42, 5–19.

Federman, A. (2010) Moscow's new rules: Islands of press freedom in a country of control. *Columbia Journalism Review* (Jan.-Feb.). Online at http://www.cjr.org/feature/moscows_new_rules.php (accessed September 29, 2010).

Fernández, C. and Paxman, A. (2000) *El Tigre: Emilio Azcárraga y su Imperio Televisa*. Grijalbo Mondadori Sa, Mexico City.

Fung, A. Y. H. (2007) Political economy of Hong Kong media: Producing a hegemonic voice. *Asian Journal of Communication*, 17(2), 159–71.

Gitlin, T. (1981/2003) *The Whole World Is Watching: Mass Media in the Making and Unmaking of the New Left*. University of California Press, Berkeley.

Herman, E. S. and Chomsky, N. (2002/1988) *Manufacturing Consent: The Political Economy of the Mass Media*, 2nd edn. Pantheon, New York.

Hertsgaard, M. (1988) *On Bended Knee: The Press and the Reagan Presidency*. Farrar, Straus, Giroux, New York.

Horwitz, R. (2005) On media concentration and the diversity question. *The Information Society*, 21, 181–204.

House of Lords (2008)? Communications – First Report. Online at http://www.publications.parliament.uk/pa/ld200708/ldselect/ldcomuni/122/12202.htm (accessed September 29, 2010).

Hughes, S. (2006) *Newsrooms in Conflict: Journalism and the Democratization of Mexico*. University of Pittsburgh Press, Pittsburgh, PA.

Iglesias González, F. (2004) Concentración radiofónica en España. *Comunicación y Sociedad*, 17(1), 77–113.

Just, N. (2009) Measuring media concentration and diversity: New approaches and instruments in Europe and the US. *Media, Culture & Society*, 31(1), 97–117.

Klinenberg, E. (2007) *Fighting For Air: The Battle to Control America's Media*. Metropolitan Books, New York.

Koltsova, O. (2009) *News Media and Power in Russia*. New York, Routledge.

Lentz, R. G. (2008) "Linguistic engineering" and the FCC Computer Inquiries, 1966-1989. Unpublished dissertation, University of Texas at Austin.

Mastrini, G. and Becerra, M. (eds) (2006) *Periodistas y Magnates: Estructura y Concentración de las Industrias Culturales en América Latina*. Prometeo Libros, Buenos Aires.

Mastrini, G. and Becerra, M. (2008) Concentration in media. In: Donsbach, W. (ed.), *The International Encyclopedia of Communication*, vol. III. Wiley-Blackwell, Malden, MA, pp. 904–10.

Mattelart, A. (1980/1973) *Mass Media, Ideologies and the Revolutionary Movement*. Humanities, Atlantic Highlands, NJ.

McChesney, R.W. (2008) *The Political Economy of Media: Enduring Issues, Emerging Dilemmas*. Monthly Review Press, New York.

Murdock, G. (1982) Large corporations and the control of the communications industries. In: Gurevitch, M., Bennett, T., Curran, J. and Woollacott, J. (eds), *Culture, Society and the Media*. Methuen, London, pp. 118–50.

Murdock, G. and Golding, P. (1973) For a political economy of mass communications. In: R. Miliband and Saville, J. (eds), *The Socialist Register 1973*. The Merlin Press, London, pp. 205–34.

Palzer, C. and Hilger, C. (2001) Media supervision on the threshold of the 21st century – structure and powers of regulatory authorities in the era of convergence. In: *Iris Plus Legal Observations of the European Audiovisual Observatory*. European Audiovisual Observatory, Strasbourg.

Prokop, D. (1974) Versuch über massenkultur und spontaneität. In: D. Prokop, *Massenkultur und Spontaneität: Zur veränderten Warenform der Massenkommunikation im Spätkapitalismus*. Suhrkamp Verlag, Frankfurt, pp. 44–101.

Rolland, A. (2008) The Norwegian media ownership act and the freedom of expression. *International Journal of Media and Cultural Politics*, 4(3), 313–30.

Schiller, H. I. (1973) *The Mind Managers*. Beacon Press, Boston.

Schiller, H. I. (1981) *Who Knows: Information in the Age of the Fortune 500*. Ablex, Norwood, NJ.

Schiller, H. I. (1986) *Information and the Crisis Economy*. Ablex, Norwood, NJ.

Schiller, H. I. (1989) *Culture Inc.: The Corporate Takeover of Public Expression*. Oxford University Press, New York.

Schiller, H. I. (1992/1969) *Mass Communications and American Empire*. Augustus M. Kelley/Boulder, CO/Westview Press, New York.

Schiller, H. I. (1996) *Information Inequality: The Deepening Social Crisis in America*. Routledge, New York.

Shin, M. E. and Agnew, J. A. (2008) *Berlusconi's Italy: Mapping Contemporary Italian Politics*. Temple University Press, Philadelphia, PA.

Siebert, F. S., Peterson, T., and Schramm, W. (1956) *Four Theories of the Press: The Authoritarian, Libertarian, Social Responsibility and Soviet Communist Concepts of What the Press Should Be and Do*. University of Illinois Press, Urbana.

Sousa, H. and Costa e Silva, E. (2009) Keeping up appearances: Regulating media diversity in Portugal. *International Communication Gazette*, 71(1–2), 89–100.

Sparks, C. (2007) What's wrong with globalization? *Global Media & Communication*, 3(2), 133–55.

Sussman, G. (2008) Ownership in the media. In: Donsbach, W. (ed.), *The International Encyclopedia of Communication*, vol. III. Wiley-Blackwell, Malden, MA, pp. 3480–5.

Tomlinson, J. (1991) *Cultural Imperialism*. The Johns Hopkins University Press, Baltimore, MD.

Winseck, D. (2008) The state of media ownership and media markets: Competition or concentration and why should we care? *Sociology Compass*, 2(1), 34–47.

Winter, J. (1998) *Democracy's Oxygen: How Corporations Control The News*. Black Rose Books, Montreal.

8

Maximizing Value
Economic and Cultural Synergies

Nathan Vaughan

This chapter presents an analysis of synergistic processes within Hollywood production and circulation. Drawing on Janet Wasko's (1994) distinction between economic and cultural synergy, the chapter proposes an argument concerning the homology and interaction of these modes and how they have developed from an intensive to an extensive form.

The analysis combines theoretical perspectives from the political economy of culture and cultural analysis with film studies. It also notes how the study of the synergistic process has been somewhat neglected within management theory as well as in media studies more generally.

A typology is proposed that conceptualizes how synergy is organized and deployed variously within cultural production and circulation. Economic synergy, it is argued, operates both at the level of the firm and at the level of the industry. In addition to synergy at the level of the firm via flexible business networks and interfirm networking, Hollywood functions holistically as an industry and increasingly in co-ordination with cultural industries in general. In effect, such economic synergy is both intensive – that is, at the level of the firm – and extensive – that is, at the level of the industry and interindustry relations.

Additionally, there is a discernible homology between economic synergy and cultural synergy insofar as the meanings of cultural properties are exploited intensively and extensively. Intertextuality is produced at the level of the firm across various platforms and also much more diffusely across the cultural field in general at the level of the industry.

The Handbook of Political Economy of Communications, First Edition.
Edited by Janet Wasko, Graham Murdock, and Helena Sousa.
© 2014 John Wiley & Sons, Ltd. Published 2014 by John Wiley & Sons, Ltd.

Conceptualizing Synergy

Because of the unpredictable nature of producing cultural properties, Hollywood (along with other sectors of the cultural industries) has devised new organizational and business strategies to help overcome the risky, and often costly, process of making money from creative labor. Through these strategies, Hollywood has increasingly pursued diversification of production by turning properties into products. The creation of these additional markets in order to produce merchandising or other means of maximizing revenue has contributed to Hollywood's current dominance within world markets.

This process of diversification and corporate co-ordination has a name: "synergy." While many introductory film and media textbooks make a passing mention of this process, such as David Hesmondhalgh's (2007) *The Cultural Industries*, these texts all contain a common feature in failing to provide a detailed and critical understanding of how it actually operates. Given that the synergistic process has become the foundation upon which today's large media conglomerates are built, it is timely that a deeper examination is provided into how this process affects the mechanics of the Hollywood culture industry. Such an understanding will provide clearer insights into how film texts, genres, and audiences are used in the development of business strategies from a more "economic, political, and social context" (Wasko 2003, 1).

Janet Wasko, in her 1994 book, *Hollywood in the Information Age*, is perhaps the only person to offer any satisfactory critical insight into the synergistic process. Here she argues that the process of synergy can be considered to have two main parts: economic and cultural. However, the central argument in this chapter departs in one significant respect from Wasko's original analysis, and that is in the extended development of synergistic strategies. This idea proposes that the process of synergy has evolved from an *intensive* to a more *extensive* mode of exploitation.

At its most basic level, Wasko's economic synergy means the integration and co-ordination of various functions *within* a company. Such a definition concretizes the idea that synergy is a process that operates at the level of the firm. However, within the organizational dynamics of how Hollywood operates today, compared with its more historical forms of Fordist production, there clearly exists a co-ordination of various functions and strategies *outside* the co-ordinating firm.

The construction of these flexible networks spreads both the economic risk inherent in producing cultural properties across other companies, as well as sharing talent, marketing, and the costs of research and development. It is through considering the multiple logics that exist within Hollywood business that the process of synergy can be argued to work at the level of the *industry* and not just at the level of the firm.

Wasko's point concerning "cultural" synergy describes the process as the multiple exploitation of an intellectual (textual) property to enhance profitability. While Wasko accounts for the various ways in which this can be achieved, most of these (such as theme parks, television, and so forth) can be argued to operate at the level

Table 8.1 Typology of synergy

	Economic synergy	*Cultural synergy*
Property	Firm	Intensive
Commodity / Text	Industry	Extensive

of the firm once again. In her discussion of Hollywood business, Wasko talks of cultural synergy as "overlapping cultural images and ideas" (1994, 217). Such a definition seems to indicate that cultural synergy is not confined to the property itself. The argument would appear symmetrical with the earlier point that there is a level of economic synergy that exists beyond the discrete corporation.

While Wasko does not develop this idea in her definition of cultural synergy, such a proposal would seem to suggest that there may also be a level of cultural synergy that operates beyond the property (at the level of the industry). This moves the concept into issues of diffuse intertextuality. Such an extended notion of cultural synergy is consistent with the way Hollywood properties are produced and marketed. For example, extensive forms of cultural synergy can be seen to operate through the appropriation of myth structures (e.g., *Star Wars* and *Lord of the Rings*), diverse marketing strategies (such as tourism), and the recreation of nostalgia through retrobranding (e.g., prequels and special editions).

The typology in Table 8.1 identifies two axes on which the arguments and definitions proposed in this chapter can be summarized. This provides a clearer conceptualization of synergy that seeks to concretize and clarify the broader and more complex theorization of the process which this chapter discusses.

The process of synergy uses Wasko's original definition as comprising two separate, but nonetheless interconnecting, parts: "economic" and "cultural." Set against this is the intellectual property that is to be produced and marketed. This proposes that the property is both a commodity and a text. The reason for this is twofold. First, intellectual properties that are produced in the market for consumption are commodities. However, as cultural products these commodities also have "textual" meanings or "signification." By interrelating them in this manner, the suggestion is made that the study of production also has an effect on the study of texts.

When crosshatched, the four cells within the typology produce four general forms for how the synergistic process operates. Clearly, the need to produce such a typology as this lies in the desire to create a general framework for both exploring and understanding the highly complex way in which synergy operates.

The typology shows that economic synergy operating at the level of the co-ordinating firm (or corporation) acts *intensively* on the exploitative marketing of commodities when devising cultural synergistic strategies. These can include spin-offs (television, music), theme parks, and so forth. On the other hand, economic synergy operating at the level of the industry acts *intensively* on the commodity text. Such strategies contain a range of different firms and businesses "downstream" producing further examples of merchandising (toys, computer games, etc.) under license from the co-ordinating firm and through product placement. In addition, it also creates extensive meaning through forms of diffuse intertextuality whereby different texts may be combined (or at least their themes and styles) to create something (apparently) new and original. While this latter example sustains constant forms of recycling that Wasko (1994) fears may lead to an unoriginal culture, it does help to sustain the interests of Hollywood as a whole, and perpetuate the extensive nature of the American film industry. It is through such a process that when issues of film are discussed, people generally think of Hollywood rather than other countries such as France or even Britain.

Let us now turn to discussing this conceptualization of the synergistic process in more detail.

Economic Synergy: At the Level of the Firm and the Industry

Understanding the concept of synergy is not as straightforward as it may seem. The term is often used freely within discussions of cultural production and business media, usually at the level of the firm, without examining in sufficient detail how the process actually operates (e.g., Olson 1999, Wolf 1999, Croteau and Hoynes 2001, Branston and Stafford 2003, Hesmondhalgh 2007).

Such discussions are mostly to be found in introductory film and media/business texts for students. Here, commentators and market analysts tend to use a very basic definition of synergy as a "process that brings together the various divisions/departments of a corporation to maximize profits." An example of Disney's approach to this is briefly examined later in this section.

As previously outlined, economic synergy from Wasko's perspective takes place at the level of the firm through the co-ordination and integration of functions/departments *within* a corporation. However, this chapter has already proposed that it also operates at the level of the industry in an "extended" form. Arguably, this can take place in two ways. The first is through the formation of networks and partnerships with companies *outside* the co-ordinating corporation. The second level will be discussed in the next section. This achieves diversification of production for the purposes of cost-cutting and enhanced profitability. This form of economic synergy at the level of the industry witnesses a new form of organization that is suitably adapted to the flexible production system of post-Fordism. Companies that come together to form production networks for the duration of a film project operate under the control of a co-ordinating corporation that remains at the center of the production network.

Interestingly, it could be argued that this is still a form of synergy operating at the level of the firm. However, post-Fordism is not about ownership, but rather a flexible approach to production and circulation by sharing risk with other companies. Economic synergy at the level of the firm is, to return to Wasko's definition, the integration of functions *within* a corporation. Clearly, what is important in distinguishing between economic synergy at the level of the firm or the industry in this respect is the way that production is shared and circulated along a network of different companies that represent the totality of the American film industry as a whole. Furthermore, in the creation of cultural synergistic strategies (discussed below), some of these companies may even be from different industries altogether. These companies may be co-ordinated by the controlling corporation, but they are *not* owned by them. This form of production replaces the vertical integration and co-ordination of departments *within* the same corporation that comprises Wasko's definition of economic synergy working at the level of the firm.

However, it is also much more than this. In isolation, the argument of economic synergy taking place solely through the co-operation of different companies misses the totality of "Hollywood" as a field of practices that has always been promoted by the American government. The argument that this can be seen as economic synergy operating at the level of the industry helps us to a better understanding of issues behind Hollywood's global strength. It accounts for, and provides an examination of, the relationship that exists between Hollywood and Los Angeles, unions, banks, and the organization of labor more generally.

Economic synergy at the level of Hollywood is achieved by the industry's lobbying activities and the support it receives from the US government. The latter can be seen in the way the government has supported Hollywood exports in global markets. Furthermore, it tries to protect the industry via the Motion Picture Association of America (MPAA) from international treaty negotiations (NAFTA, GATT, WTO) that seek to reduce its export quotas, or concerns over runaway production. The government also provides "the clout to back up threats by the industry when countries don't cooperate by opening up their markets" (Wasko 2003, 181).

The way Hollywood uses the MPAA to encourage the American government to protect its interests not only shows the central part the American film industry plays in today's global media marketplace, but the way in which it can impose its standards (technical, aesthetic, etc.) on the industry. Additionally, both this and the way in which Hollywood and its studios have forged new (synergistic) relations among various national police forces and local governments in order to control the distribution of pirated material over the Internet (Goldstein 1994, 197), is a further example of how synergy can work at the level of the industry.

At the level of the firm then, economic synergy is played out through various strategies so that the corporation determines the "general ways it deploys its productive resources" (Murdock 1982, 122) across all the departments, or divisions that comprise it. Such a process is consistent with Murdock's "allocative" form of control. Here, economic synergistic strategies are further mobilized in the decisions of whether the firm should expand or merge, and the best way to achieve this. Economic synergy at the level of the firm includes "the formulation of overall policy and strategy" (Murdock 1982, 118) that determines how that firm operates. Such policies would also contain a range of measures from allocating share interests, through to determining how profits earned from the various divisions of the firm are to be distributed.

One such example of how economic synergy at the level of the firm works can be seen when Disney decided to acquire the animated film production company, Pixar, for $7 billion (Chaffin and Politi 2006). Such a strategy was decided by a board of directors at Disney, and resulted in Pixar becoming part of the Disney Company. The acquisition reinvigorated Disney's flagging animation department through an infusion of new, specialized talent, while providing the company with characters that it could intensively exploit via cultural synergistic strategies (see next section) across its numerous divisions of consumer products, theme parks, and other ancillary businesses.

However, at the level of the industry, economic synergy is achieved by the closer association that Disney now has with Apple Computers. Steve Jobs is both Pixar's and Apple's chief executive. A merger between Pixar and Disney placed Jobs on the Disney board in 2006. Such an appointment helped in creating potential networks between the two companies that, for example, could allow Disney to navigate new digital consumer technologies.

Such economic synergistic strategies at the level of the industry are necessary in today's marketplace, in which media companies are increasingly co-ordinating to make their content available on a number of new devices such as cell phones and the iPod, which is made by Apple.

Such economic strategies were tested when Disney's ABC network agreed to sell its television programs *Desperate Housewives* and *Lost* for download through Apple's iTunes service (Chaffin and Politi 2006). Clearly, there is much potential for companies in forming such synergistic networks at the level of the industry. In the case of Disney and Apple, one of the world's premier content companies "comes together" synergistically with one of the world's most innovative technology companies.

The ability to form synergistic networks between "linked" firms at the level of the industry makes economic sense. The cost of producing and marketing cultural products today has increased exponentially; meaning that the decision for firms to pool their resources not only to share costs, but also to spread their risks over a range of different firms – instead of just one taking all the responsibility – becomes a key business strategy. Such a strategy, then, sees the process of economic synergy working at the level of the industry by linking firms together in a network.

As Rifkin (2000) argues, sharing the losses in a failed venture provides a type of collective insurance. Network relationships are much more flexible than those based around hierarchical organizations. He considers this flexibility to be much better suited to the unpredictable nature of the cultural industries, as co-operation and team work allow for companies to respond more quickly to changes in audience tastes and desires. Of all the different sectors of production, Rifkin considers the Hollywood culture industries to have had the most experience in networked-based business approaches. For this reason, he sees Hollywood as the prototype for the reorganization of other types of production based upon networking principles.

Flexible specialization has the ability to offset risk across a range of companies, while allowing cultural workers a level of autonomy that they had not experienced under Fordist conditions. The flip side though to obtaining this freedom is that companies increasingly create competition for cheaper services. This allows studios to move production to those countries where significant savings can be made in order to exploit the talent of poorer countries via what Toby Miller and his colleagues (Miller et al. 2005, Miller and Yudice 2002) have referred to as the "New International Division of Cultural Labor" (NICL). This has resulted in making employment more fragmented. Cultural workers are now increasingly employed on a freelance, ad hoc, basis, where they find themselves competing for a decreasing number of positions. This means that many people now find themselves unemployed for longer periods of time. The use of flexible networks has arguably fragmented the American film workforce.

Hollywood's exploitation of the NICL has had a significant impact on local American economies and labor markets that depend on Hollywood production for their livelihoods, not to mention those local economies and labor markets that are now being used as sources of cheap labor for film production. Such arguments further illustrate the process of economic synergy working at the level of Hollywood as a whole.

Other geographical implications of developing synergistic networks with independent producers at the level of the industry has led to the re-agglomeration of production in and around Los Angeles. Such a point is consistent with Christopherson and Storper's (1986) examination of Hollywood. Arguably, it was the constant pursuit of economic synergistic strategies that were responsible for this. As Janet Harbord notes:

> the re-assembly of the entertainment industry necessitated a spatial proximity of companies trading among each other, leading once again to a centralised core of production, and a powerful nexus of economic, cultural and social interaction. What appears on the surface as an unraveling spool, on closer inspection is revealed as a tight-knit fabric of integrated working relationships, practices and technologies [that comprise "Hollywood" as an industry]. (Harbord 2002, 98)

It is clear that the pursuit of such networking strategies at the level of the industry has had significant geographic implications for restructuring key sites around Los Angeles and the world. It must be emphasized though that the independents are *not* in any position to challenge the major studios owing to the significant levels of control the majors still have of the overall production and distribution process. In

addition to this, the characterization of the high-concept film (see below) elimi-
nates "the possibility of smaller production units competing in the same market"
(Harbord 2002, 101), illustrating another way in which the major studios can retain
their power over independents. Christopherson and Storper underplay these issues
in their analysis of flexible specialization and organizational change within
Hollywood.

Cultural Synergy

From intensive to extensive

Christopherson and Storper's account of the developments within Hollywood,
and the flexible specialization thesis in general, offer insights into how organizational change has redeveloped film production in the US. Yet many commentators,
particularly Wasko (1994), have questioned their claims of vertical disintegration
within Hollywood. For Wasko, "rather than disintegration, the US film industry
has experienced a process of reintegration in the late eighties" (1994, 16).

The real issue that is at stake here is whether vertical reintegration should be
addressed at the level of the industry as well as the firm. This is important also for
the concept of synergy which also poses the same question, as the reintegration of
Hollywood is related to synergy.

Hollywood at the level of the firm is vertically integrated across a group of
companies that operate at different levels within the production and circulation
network. These exist either as contractors supplying direct labor for the production of the film, or to provide various services such as special effects, catering,
transportation, and so forth. However, at the level of the industry as a whole there
exists a collective body of corporations who co-ordinate production and distribution – such as theatrical, home video, DVD, cable, and television releases as well as
merchandising tie-ins – to achieve diversification of product and expand sales.

The potential profit that exists in turning properties into products through cultural synergistic strategies has led to a period of mergers, with film studios becoming incorporated within larger media conglomerates. Known as "horizontal
integration," this sees new media giants such as Disney and Viacom owning multiple forms of distribution that range from film and publishing to radio and television. Horizontal integration is central to the development and exploitation of
cultural synergy.

From this, it would appear that there is a strong argument for studying the process of cultural synergy as working at the level of the industry, and not just exclusively at the level of the firm/corporation. Without the co-operation of other
industries, principally advertising, Hollywood would not exist in anywhere near
the form it does today. It is clear that the vast majority of Hollywood products are

dependent on other industries for their existence and eventual success. As McGuigan (1996, 94) points out, "production is dependent not only upon advertising finance and effective marketing but also upon the representational discourses and audiovisual formats of commercial speech." Other types of industry, not just those connected solely within Hollywood, are brought together in a synergistic manner throughout the cultural circuit.

Many forms of industry are used to promote films, including newspapers, cinema chains (trailers), the Internet, food manufacturers, soft drink companies, airlines, and so forth. While none of these companies are involved directly in the production of the film, they are essential as a channel of distribution to promote the film to as wide an audience as possible. It sees different types of industry, from transport to food, to clothing and entertainment outlets, coming together in a synergistic way in order to promote a film in anticipation of some of the spin-off interest that the film will hopefully generate being rubbed off onto them. This can be mainly achieved by product placement techniques (Wasko et al. 1993) which allow manufacturers to connect mass market goods to certain films by paying to "place" their products within the film's narrative. Films that lend themselves to this global marketing strategy have been termed "high-concept" (Wyatt 1994, see below).

For Wasko, this saturation and repetition of images from media properties across a wide range of distribution and marketing channels is of great concern. For her, the way in which the persistent stream of images, themes, and characters based on movie franchises (such as *Star Wars* and *Lord of the Rings*) penetrate into all facets of daily life, limits the expression of society's ideas, values, and general original creativity, or what Eileen Meehan (1986) has termed "the cultural fund." Wasko has taken this concept slightly further. For her, the principle of economic synergy can also be extended into popular culture. It is here that Wasko proposes her other dimension to the process of synergy, the *cultural* dimension.

Miller et al. (2005, 264) point out how Justin Wyatt in his 1994 book, *High Concept*, outlines all the various ways that "marketable film content flows from film texts to marketing texts." Arguably, these occur through a range of intensive cultural synergistic strategies. However, as these strategies become more widely spread through domestic and global marketing, they form what Gary Hoppenstand (1998: 232) calls a "film environment" outside the film. It is the externalization of these "extracted" features of a film property that form the basis of cultural synergistic strategies. However, they also "serve more than just economic functions, for when these [marketable elements] penetrate public space they also affect the aesthetic experience of film-going" (Miller et al. 2005, 264). By borrowing and recombining these elements in different ways and means, then the process of exploiting cultural synergy extensively creates an accompanying intertextuality that exists beyond the original property.

The financial logic behind the concept of cultural synergy makes economic sense. Once the idea for a textual property is developed, there obviously exist numerous advantages to using it for a range of products. However, Wasko fears the erosion of diversity and originality as a result of deploying such extensive strategies. Clearly, it can be seen within contemporary Hollywood production and marketing the disadvantage in deploying such cultural synergistic strategies extensively. While characters, stories, themes, and so forth are exploited across a range of products, more often than not we witness a cluster of similar products but across different types of media. The worry is that although the number of media platforms and distribution systems has increased, the content has in fact stayed the same. Wasko's primary concern "that our culture may not be actually evolving, but merely recycling" (1994, 252) is perhaps more prevalent today than at any other time.

Deploying extensive strategies

Wasko's worries are rooted in the extensive deployment of cultural synergistic strategies that exist at the level of the industry. However, Wasko does not develop this extended notion of synergy within her own examination of the process. Here, intertextuality is created through the existence of a recombinant culture, whereby "anything can be juxtaposed with anything else" (Gitlin 1989, 350). Attempts to "(re) construct" seemingly new properties from the recombination of old ones provide not only a safer way of producing cultural properties (i.e., if it worked before, it will work again), but it also creates strong feelings of nostalgia in older audiences/consumers that may then be capitalized upon through various marketing strategies.

George Lucas's *Star Wars* special editions cleverly positioned the first trilogy so that it introduced new audiences to the saga while luring them into the franchise. They skillfully demonstrated the use of retro branding within the intertextual use of connected products that characterizes today's entertainment economy. These intertextual "connections" are then extensively exploited through cultural synergistic strategies at the level of the industry. The concept of intertextuality can be argued to work on several different levels. First, the relationship that exists between texts, either separately or connected within a franchise; second, the relationship between text and marketing strategies; and finally the relationship between the text and the systems of production in which it was created (political, social, and cultural).

The intertextual style of exploiting cultural synergy extensively is very similar to Fredric Jameson's idea of the cultural style of late capitalism. For Jameson this is characterized, among other things, by the desire for nostalgia, whereby history is the object not of representations but of stylistic connotation. This is exemplified by both the Disney theme parks, and how the special editions of the original *Star Wars* trilogy were used as a nostalgic "lure" for the new prequels. What this recycling of cultural symbols, themes, and styles achieves is a sense of the "already said." The extensive exploitation of cultural synergistic strategies at the level of the industry constructs a sense that one cannot invent anything new, but merely play with the already existent. Such observations uphold Wasko's fears of a static and recycled culture.

With regard to extensive cultural synergistic strategies, one particularly salient area concerns tourism. This can be seen in the way the *Lord of the Rings* films were marketed when tourism companies within New Zealand quickly began to develop various marketing strategies in order to take advantage of the publicity created by the films. Such an example provides a further way to illustrate the process of cultural synergy not only working, extensively, at the level of the industry, but also *between* industries. However, the benefits of such extensive synergistic networks are not confined solely to *Lord of the Rings*, but are increasingly becoming characteristic of blockbuster properties more generally. Such examples include *The Da Vinci Code* (2006), *Pirates of the Caribbean: Dead Man's Chest* (2006), and *The Chronicles of Narnia* (2006) – the last of which was also, interestingly, filmed in New Zealand.

Meehan's (2004) argument of "redeployment" is also relevant in the extensive development of cultural synergistic strategies. Here products take the form of merchandise that can either be linked directly to the original property or to a number of associated products that are connected to it. This type of strategy can be seen in the array of *Star Wars* novels and computer games that have been produced to provide an "expanded universe" to the narratives contained in the original films.

However, George Lucas was not the first to exploit cultural synergy extensively. Walt Disney was already developing extensive strategies in relation to his 1937 animated film *Snow White and the Seven Dwarfs*. Apart from creating a range of associated products by granting licenses to other companies "downstream" to produce merchandise, Disney strengthened his brand awareness for both the animated film and his company's range of characters through intertextual recycling. Here an "expanded universe" was created by featuring the characters in *Snow White and the Seven Dwarfs* in a variety of books and magazines that appeared after the film had finished. Often these products also contained other Disney characters and, through this cross-pollinating of the company's best-known characters, readers would not only be familiar with Disney's repertoire, but these "expanded" properties would have a ready-made audience.

However, today the most significant types of film that sustain this form of cultural synergy are arguably the "high-concept" movie, described as a film that has a straightforward, easily pitched and comprehensible story. Many directors of such films (e.g., *Jaws, Top Gun*) often highlight the uniqueness of the film's central idea. However, Wyatt (1994) argues that the concept can be explained as "the look, the hook, and the book." More often than not, these films rely on the same combination and replication of themes, genres, and images, which is an inherent characteristic of extensively exploiting cultural synergy at the level of the industry. For Wyatt, this form of "postgeneric" filmmaking is highly dependent on a simplification of character and narrative that, coupled with an intense interaction between the film and its soundtrack, results in sequences that are ideally reconfigured for a range of different products (i.e., soundtrack, computer games, comics, etc.).

What is essential to make Wyatt's high concept work is that while marketing strategies will try to make any film stand out as a "differentiated product," audiences must understand the role that marketing plays in connecting a film's likeness to other films in order to reduce the uncertainty of its appeal at the box office. Such a process of borrowing and recycling themes and stylistic conventions is central to how the extended notion of cultural synergy operates. The genre system, for example, is of importance in creating a culturally defined referencing system that provides core characteristics that can be used as shorthand in marketing strategies (Miller et al. 2005).

As previously discussed, the role of marketing creates a range of intertextual influences that "spill over" into an area of competing interpretations that exist outside, or beyond, a film's narrative. Through the intertextual recombination of genres, styles, and themes, the notion of an extended form of cultural synergy beyond a single property can be seen. For example, the 2003 Disney film *Pirates of the Caribbean* can be seen as *The Buccaneer* meets *Mutiny on the Bounty*, while the 2004 release of *Alien vs. Predator* saw these past two science-fiction franchises literally coming together. They serve as an effective way of repackaging previously successful ingredients into a new film, making marketing that much easier (Hoskins et al. 1997).

Olson provides a further example of this intertextual recombination in his examination of the 1996 film *Independence Day*:

> its plot line, characters, and sets are a veritable catalogue of science fiction films, including gooey antagonists (from *Alien*, 1979), surprise side effects of alien surgery (from *The Thing*, 1982), a gung-ho kamikaze American (from *Dr. Strangelove*, 1963), space-age aerial dogfights (from *Star Wars*, 1977), friendly and trouble-making computer software (from *2001: A Space Odyssey*, 1968) and human victory thanks to unforeseen infection [albeit a computer virus] (from *War of the Worlds,* 1953), with characters from non-genre films, such as *An American President* (1995), thrown in for those with shorter memories or other generic tastes. (Olson 1999, 78)

These observations closely follow Bernard Miège (1987, 276–7). While Miège was concerned specifically with the "flow" production of broadcasting to fill in large areas of new content schedules, this seems to contain certain parallels to the concept of cultural synergy. The properties of a flow culture tend to be characterized largely as uninterrupted, which the constant recycling of images also allows. Hollywood's properties today are offered as a constant stream of releases, most of which are nothing more than a combination of previous themes, mainly to fill schedules. In fact, Miège's flow culture today is a highly commodified one as properties are available for a succession of realizations, achieved through the process of synergy. In this sense, "flow" is a much industrialized concept which mirrors that of Fordist, or rather *neo*-Fordist production. So it perhaps also makes sense to talk about cultural synergy as an extension to Miège's flow logic of broadcasting.

For Miège (1989) however, this still does not overcome the uncertainty of cultural use values, no matter how much Hollywood relies on market research and pretesting. For him, the spreading of risk is much more effective by offering a list of films, as the cultural producer always has great difficulty determining the conditions of valorization for its properties. Such arguments can be used to explain the constant release of Hollywood films, the shortening of the film distribution period in general, and the fact that many films are only in cinemas for a short period. Such observations have significant parallels with Wyatt's "high concept," whose underlying strategy is that by throwing as many different films at the consumer as possible, a few may find appeal, with one or two appealing in a very large way.

Developing extensive cultural synergistic strategies at the level of the industry can also be viewed as being *hyperreal*. Jean Baudrillard's (1983) position on this has been well documented. For him, media culture in general has created an environment that is saturated with signification. In truth, all this creates is a sensation that meaning has imploded in on itself so that signs only signify other signs. There exists no way of ever being able to connect to the real or the original. For Baudrillard, the hyperreal has become more real than reality. It was, of course, Italian philosopher Umberto Eco (1987) who, along with Baudrillard, popularized the term "hyperreality," and further provided us with the analysis of "faith in fakes."

For Eco, Disneyland is the most prevalent example of hyperreality. For him, Disney's theme parks exude a sense of reality that makes us believe absolutely that what is being seen is actual "reality," rather than simply a representation. They are a form of *environmental simulacra*, what Olson (1999) argues to be environments that are hyperreal, enabling fantasy to take on a physical form and surround the consumer. Eco's "faith in fakes" is most commonly seen in the audioanimatronics of attractions such as "Pirates of the Caribbean" or "the Haunted Mansion," which Eco interprets as producing "iconic reassurance," a factor which Wasko is too quick to dismiss in her analysis of Disney.

Synergy as a Transindustrial Process

Based on the previous arguments and examination, it is also possible to illustrate how the deployment of synergistic strategies can not only work at the level of the industry, but also *between* industries.

For example, what sets the *Lord of the Rings* films apart from those such as *Star Wars* in terms of its development of cultural synergistic strategies is not just the way in which the Internet played a more dynamic role, but also the relationship that existed between the films and the New Zealand tourist industry. Clearly, this is evidence of the way synergy can also operate between industries.

The New Zealand Government was quick to recognize the potential that the films would give to the country in terms of increasing the profile and awareness of New Zealand as a destination. *Lord of the Rings* has a distinct advantage over *Star Wars* in the sense that its locations are generally more "real." For *Star Wars*, most of the action takes place either in space, studio sets, or in a computer-generated scene. While this also is the case for *Lord of the Rings*, many areas that were used for filming outdoor scenes can be visited and enjoyed.

Tourism plays a central part in the New Zealand economy (Jones and Smith 2005, 936). In various ways it contributes almost 10 percent of New Zealand's GDP, while supporting one in ten jobs (Jones and Smith 2005). Owing to the way in which cultural synergistic strategies generally keep recycling cultural properties, and commodifying key aspects of the narrative in particular, repeat viewing is strongly encouraged. Apart from trying to persuade audiences to "buy" into the franchise brand, it further serves to help "reinforce connections between a film and its location as a tourist destination" (Tooke and Baker 1996, cited in Jones and Smith 2005, 936). Such arguments further concretize the observation that synergy can also work at the level of the economy.

For *Lord of the Rings*, the development of cultural synergistic strategies by the US film studio New Line has been extremely useful for Tourism New Zealand (TNZ) and the national tourist promotion board. In addition, further economic networks between New Line, the media, and individual enterprises have been forged to exploit these potential cultural synergistic benefits further. As Jones and Smith (2005, 936) add, "the linkages are obvious from the outset of a visit to TNZ's website which directs the visitor to *The Home of Middle Earth* website and into an interactive discovery of the "country behind *Lord of the Rings.*"

Further examples of synergy working at the level of the industry can be seen in the role that the 2002 Academy Awards played. Following the ceremony, print campaigns in the US advertised New Zealand as "best supporting country in a motion picture" (Jones and Smith 2005). Such strategies develop the notion that identifiable "icons" within films attract viewers to a given location as visitors (Riley et al. 1998, 924). These can be "linked to the film's symbolic content, a single event, a favorite performer, a location's physical features, or a storyline theme; icons, abstract or tangible, become the focal point for visitation and the associated location is tangible evidence of the icon" (Riley et al. 1998, 924). Clearly the use of wide panoramic shots of New Zealand in the *Fellowship of the Ring* (for example), provides iconic status to the New Zealand landscape, while additionally reinforcing the connection that exists between the fictional Middle-earth and New Zealand. By exploiting these connections through cultural synergistic strategies that exist between various industries, not only is New Zealand promoted as "the" tourist destination for fans of *Lord of the Rings*, but it also adds to the legitimacy of the films as being an authentic New Zealand project (Jones and Smith 2005).

Tourism companies within New Zealand have quickly developed various other marketing strategies in response to the opportunities created by the films. A range of themed packages and attractions based around *Lord of the Rings* have been devised. Such strategies further feed into the official promotional rhetoric of New Line that visitors to New Zealand will receive a "genuine," "real," and "authentic" experience of *Lord of the Rings* (Timothy and Boyd 2003, cited in Smith and Jones 2005, 938–9). Such "experiences" are further strengthened by tour operators through the "status of their guides as 'fans', whose claims to authenticity are further enhanced by their personal involvement in the filming process, as extras or as suppliers, for example transporting the cases and daily rushes" (Smith and Jones 2005, 939).

New Line, in their official promotional strategies of the films, showed members of the casts and crew enjoying various parts of New Zealand. While this strengthened the idea that New Zealand was "fun" and "enjoyable," Air New Zealand themed two of its airplanes for *Lord of the Rings* as the centerpiece of its global promotional campaign. While this took the connection between the films and New Zealand around the world, it was also used to promote Air New Zealand as the company that could take you to "Middle-earth" (Jones and Smith, 2005). Such examples are once again an excellent way to see the process of synergy working both at the level of the industry; and also between industries – in the same ways as corporate sponsorship and licensing agreements operate (Wasko et al. 1993) from downstream businesses.

Conclusion

In conclusion, there is a need to emphasize once again the enormous complexity of the synergistic process. To this end, two distinct dimensions, or types, of synergy have been explored: "economic" and "cultural." These provide different lenses for analyzing and evaluating the development and effect of synergy within cultural production. Economic synergy has been identified as a process that can either operate at the level of the firm or the industry. At its most basic, economic synergy means the *integration and coordination of various functions within a firm*. However, what is especially significant today is determining production from the point of consumption. As stressed earlier, this is concerned with making what audiences are said to want. The role of marketing, along with issues of consumer "sovereignty," has grown in importance. It is through exploiting factors such as these by forging "networks" that the first form of economic synergy can be argued to work at the level of the industry. Such arguments can be extended into considering how synergistic strategies are mobilized at the level of Hollywood through US government protection. This is another way in which economic synergistic strategies can be seen to function at the level of the American film industry as a whole.

Economic synergy has a homologous relation to "cultural" synergy. This suggests that "characters, stories and ideas are made into products for different outlets" (Wasko 1994, 252). Cultural synergy originates from economic synergy, and as a result both terms are interrelated. The concept can be succinctly defined as: *the multiple exploitation of (an) intellectual property*. Synergistic strategies of this type that occur at the level of the firm are intensively exploited across the co-ordinating corporation's diverse division of companies. This can take many forms, and includes spin-off merchandising, theme parks, and other forms of media (e.g., television, cable, DVD).

At the level of the industry, such cultural synergistic strategies are deployed extensively across a broad range of different companies that come together in order to promote the film in a number of different ways. Such a conceptualization is consistent with Wasko (1994, 6), who argues that "Hollywood does not merely represent the film industry, but crosses over traditional boundaries and engages in transindustrial activities."

It has also been proposed that because of the extensive way in which cultural synergistic strategies are exploited, an accompanying extensive intertextuality is also created, suggesting that a form of cultural synergy exists *beyond* a single property. Such an idea is symmetrical with the argument that there is a level of economic synergy beyond the discrete corporation. What makes this possible is the "recombinant culture" of postmodernism that typically characterizes contemporary cultural production. Such a feature is a distinct characteristic of cultural synergy, particularly in Hollywood, which is marked by the constant recycling of successful formulae coupled with the remaking of older ones. In addition, the desire to further reduce risk by combining successful properties strengthens the argument of intertextual "borrowing" that largely characterizes Hollywood today.

Synergy as an overall process is a product of changing organizational structures that combine the power to control resources and the flexibility to respond quickly to changing markets and consumer taste. This chapter has attempted to unravel the complexities of synergy as a means of helping to illuminate the intricacies of cultural production within Hollywood. It must be remembered that there exist particular logics at work within the cultural industries that must be accounted for. What has been provided here is a typology that seeks to address such issues.

Note

I would like to express my thanks to the Economic and Social Research Council (ESRC) for providing the funding for my doctoral research. Additionally, I would also like to thank Jim McGuigan and Alan Bryman for helping me to clarify my thoughts on the synergistic process.

References

Baudrillard, J. (1983) *Simulations*. Semiotext(e), New York.

Branston, G. and Stafford, R. (2003) *The Media Student's Handbook*, 3rd edn. Routledge, London.

Chaffin, J. and Politi, J. (2006) Disney board contemplates buying Pixar. *The Financial Times*, January 24.

Christopherson, S. and Storper, M. (1986) The city as studio; the world as back lot: The impact of vertical disintegration on the location of the motion picture industry. *Environment and Planning D: Society and Space*, 4(3), 305–20.

Croteau, D. and Hoynes, W. (2001) *The Business of Media: Corporate Media and the Public Interest*. Pine Forge Press, Thousand Oaks, CA.

Eco, U. (1987) *Travels in Hyperreality*. Picador, London.

Gitlin, T. (1989) Postmodernism – roots and politics. In: Angus, I. and Jhally, S. (eds), *Cultural Politics in Contemporary America*. Routledge, New York, pp. 347–60.

Goldstein, P. (1994) *Copyright's Highway: The Law and Lore of Copyright from Gutenberg to the Celestial Jukebox*. Hill and Wang, New York.

Harbord, J. (2002) *Film Cultures*. Sage, London.

Hesmondhalgh, D. (2007) *The Cultural Industries*, 2nd edn. Sage, London.

Hoppenstand, G. (1998) Hollywood and the business of making movies: The relationship between film content and economic factors. In: Litman, B. R. (ed.), *The Motion Picture Mega-Industry*. Allyn and Bacon, Boston, pp. 222–42.

Hoskins, C., McFadyen, S., and Finn, A. (1997) *Global Television and Film*. Oxford University Press, New York.

Jones, D. and Smith, K. (2005) Middle-Earth meets New Zealand: Authenticity and location in the making of *The Lord of the Rings*. *Journal of Management Studies*, 42(5), 923–45.

McGuigan, J. (1996) *Culture and the Public Sphere*. Routledge, New York.

Meehan, E. (1986) Conceptualizing culture as commodity: The problem of television. *Critical Studies in Mass Communication*, 3, 448–57.

Meehan, E. (2004) Marketization and corporate synergy. Paper presented at the International Association for Media and Communication Research Conference on Communication and Democracy, Porto Alegre, Brazil, July 25–30.

Miège, B. (1987) The logics at work in the new cultural industries. *Media, Culture & Society*, 9(3), 273–89.

Miège, B. (1989) *The Capitalization of Cultural Production*. International General, New York.

Miller, T., Govil, N., McMurria, J., Maxwell, R., and Wang, T. (2005) *Global Hollywood 2*. British Film Institute, London.

Miller, T. and Yudice, G. (2002) *Cultural Policy*. Sage, London.

Murdock, G. (1982) Large corporations and the control of the communications industries. In: Gurevitch, M. et al. (eds), *Culture, Society and the Media*. Methuen, London, pp. 1–15.

Olson, S. R. (1999) *Hollywood Planet: Global Media and the Competitive Advantage of Narrative Transparency*. Lawrence Erlbaum, Mahwah, NJ.

Rifkin, J. (2000) *The Age of Access: How the Shift from Ownership to Access is Transforming Capitalism*. Penguin, London.

Riley, R., Baker, D., and Van Doren, C. S. (1998) Movie-induced tourism. *Annals of Tourism Research*, 25(4), 919–35.

Timothy, D. J. and Boyd, S. W. (2003) *Heritage Tourism*. Pearson Education, Harlow, UK.

Tooke, N. and Baker, M. (1996) Seeing is believing: The effect of film on visitor numbers to screened locations. *Tourism Management*, 17(2), 87–94.

Wasko, J. (1994) *Hollywood in the Information Age*. Polity Press, Cambridge, UK.

Wasko, J. (2003) *How Hollywood Works*. Sage, London.

Wasko, J., Phillips, M., and Purdie, C. (1993) Hollywood meets Madison Avenue: The commercialization of US films. *Media, Culture & Society*, 15, 271–93.

Wyatt, J. (1994) *High Concept: Movies and Marketing in Hollywood*. University of Texas Press, Austin.

Wolf, M. J. (1999) *The Entertainment Economy: The Mega-Media Forces That are Reshaping Our Lives*. Penguin Putnam, New York.

9

Economy, Ideology, and Advertising

Roque Faraone

Jean-Paul Sartre said that in each historical moment, there are only two valid conceptions: one that defends the current productive system, and the other that suggests an alternative. This chapter follows the method suggested by this premise.

Economy

The study of "political economy," sometimes "economy," or "economic sciences," is generally understood to be that branch of inquiry that covers the aspects of social life related to the production and distribution of goods and services, but what exactly we mean by "production" and other key terms, and hence how we approach their study, is open to dispute.

In contrast to the natural sciences, in which taxonomies have a certain character of permanency,[1] in the science of economics, just as in all of the social sciences, the language employed is the site of continual struggle and contention. Take a very basic concept such as "capital." For an economist with tendencies to accept the current productive system as a natural fact (not a social or historical one), or even one who accepts its historicity but views it as inevitable, "capital" could be "an accumulation of wealth" or "an important means of payment available for investment," or other variants inspired by the same perspective. In contrast, for an economist critical of current social reality, "capital" will probably be described as "accumulated work" or another expression that reveals a divergent approach. Let's take another example: a frequently used expression in everyday, and sometimes in scientific, language: "market economy." This term is often preferred to "capitalist

The Handbook of Political Economy of Communications, First Edition.
Edited by Janet Wasko, Graham Murdock, and Helena Sousa.
© 2014 John Wiley & Sons, Ltd. Published 2014 by John Wiley & Sons, Ltd.

economy" because it seems more neutral, but it is inherently ambiguous. Sweden and the United States, as well as Japan, are all "market economies," but they each organize the relations between markets and the state in very different ways. If we look at entitlements to annual vacations, for example, we find that the differences are vast (they range from five weeks to three days). If we then add other variations in social protection plans (health, retirement, etc.), we can identify a cluster of differences that substantially influence production costs and therefore modify the terms of competition in the market.

"Market economies" are far from equal or equivalent, then. However, these differences are obscured by the standard language of government institutions and much of academia with talk about a "natural rate of unemployment" or "a perfect competition market." These expressions would acquire a certain scientific legitimacy if they were reformulated as "a normal rate of unemployment in advanced capitalist societies" or "perfect competition market in an abstract mathematical model."

The goal here is not to invalidate all of the contributions of predominant economic thought, but rather to relativize the taken-for-granted certainties of writers like Alain Minc, who declared in 1997, that: "There's no other economy than the market economy," adding that "In the history of humanity, since it's humanity, the market is a natural state of society" (Minc cited in Brune 1997).

These sorts of statements appear plausible and "scientific" because they ground their claims in complex statistical models and cloak themselves in the borrowed prestige of mathematics. One problem arises from the fact that most of the time the data used to calculate key social statistics come from state sources that created the definitional criteria on which information was collected and which are inevitably conditioned by the relationships of power that exist in every society. The frequent changes to the definition of "unemployed," aimed at reducing records of the real number of those seeking jobs in order to present government action in the best possible light, is a well-known example.

Mathematical models do work up to a point when they are applied to goods or people, but even here the definitions employed serve to obscure key dimensions of economic organization. When we calculate the gross domestic product (GDP) for a specific country, that quantitative information has a value. Subject to the validity of the applied methods and the quality of the basic data sources, we can calibrate changes in the wealth of that country or compare it with another one. But when we speak about GDP *per capita*, we ignore inequalities in the distribution of wealth, which can vary from 20 to 80 between the top and bottom of the scale. When confronted with the *relations* between human beings or the crucial *symbolic* dimension of exchange, however, mathematical models break down.

Nevertheless, in that sector of economic science that is now called "macroeconomics," mathematical models applied to the evolution of national economies and the international economy continue to be well received.[2] However, these models also continue to work with limited variables chosen from the available information (information conditioned by social stratification and ideology) and to produce unverifiable hypotheses.[3] Some of these models, established orthodoxies, and certainties have been badly shaken by the 2008 financial crisis, which many commentators see as serious or more severe than the one in 1929. Others claim that the crisis is systemic rather than conjunctive and heralds the "end of capitalism," at least in its neoliberal form (Stiglitz 2008).

Communication economy

When we turn to the economy of communication, a new set of problems arises. For the economic schools of thought that are less critical of the capitalist system, the economy of communication is the "production and distribution of communication goods and services." That is, it covers one sector of economic activities. For those critical of the current economic system, however, the economy of communication is understood as the pivotal linking mechanism that simultaneously engineers consumption to match production and reproduces the ideological system that supports the prevailing status quo. Consequently, it must be studied from two different angles: as a sector of the total economy, and for its linking function in the production, circulation, and consumption of goods and services and its strategic symbolic role in maintaining and perpetuating political and economic control.

It is also necessary to distinguish at least two categories within the communication economy: first, mass communication grounded in the mass media of dissemination, that is, press, radio, television, film, recorded music; second, social tools for interpersonal communication, including telephony, land and mobile, as well as the mail (public and private) and email. The Internet offers a potential third sector, which combines both mass and interpersonal communication.

No doubt, all of this is "communication." However, while mass communication manufactures messages in centralized sites of production that are received by individuals who do not participate in their composition, the tools for interpersonal communication, although supported by the centralized structures and technical developments typical of capitalism, make possible forms of communication in which individuals are the originators and transmitters of messages. In both types of communicative activities, we see the same expansive logic at work, with specific modalities. Let's take two examples, one from each group: television and the personal computer (PC).

Television, a medium that is little more than half a century old, has expanded geographically to the point where it could now be said that the whole planet receives or is able to receive televised messages. The possibility of universal coverage is limited only by the human prediction of isolation, higher reception costs, and broadcasting politics that regulate access. Nevertheless, the expansive logic imposed by the productive system constantly pushes towards saturation. The possibilities of reception offered by the range of television programs exceeds the capacity of the most extraordinary consumption imaginable. This expanding plenitude aims to fill consumers' unproductive idle time, a goal that shouldn't deserve disapproval if the contents broadcast were culturally enriching, but is increasingly achieved by expanding the number of channels while diminishing the quality of the content.

The PC, which can now claim to be the key instrument for interpersonal communication, is even newer in human history. Its prodigious development is often showcased as the product of successive innovations in "science and technology" presented in the abstract. Buyers are constantly encouraged to acquire the latest machines and software, which are presented in the market in a succession carefully programmed by the companies. While promotional publicity presents innovations and "breakthroughs" exclusively as products of scientific-technological development, they are in fact determined by the corporate drive for present and future economic benefits.

The distinction between mass communication and interpersonal communication is fundamental in any attempt to develop a critical scientific perspective, but it is entirely ignored by the prevailing economic orthodoxy, which, as we noted earlier, tends to remove economic phenomena from their cultural and symbolic contexts, and to ignore the current relations of power, in society as well as in the "market." As a consequence, all "communication" is considered as "investment" and as "services." The expansion of mobile and fixed line telephony when it is privately operated is tied to the mechanisms of rentability, of access to spectrum space or land lines, and in some cases, of the handset itself. In contrast, commercially organized mass communication, even though it also responds in its expansion to the purposes and mechanisms of rentability, is also integrated with other economic activities that condition it. By its nature, mass-produced messages are meant to be received by a great number of readers, listeners, or viewers. This is what differentiates the business of mass communication from other communication businesses, and, from its inception, the expansion of these messages has been associated and developed in tandem with the growth of the advertising market.

The logic of expansion

Since the Industrial Revolution, the expansion of the communications system has been determined by transformations in the productive regime. Let's take a look at some of the evidence from the structural and synthetic history of the press, starting with the everyday press. *The Times*, in London, was the first to apply a steam machine to its flat press in 1812, enabling it to print 10,000 copies a day. Later, the telegraph provided the essential infrastructure that allowed the press to draw on the news agencies' ability to collect and manage the wealth of information required by the global commercial expansion of capital. In the second half of the nineteenth century, and at least in the industrialized west, the press continued to respond to the changing socioeconomic conditions by taking advantage of the introduction of linotype, the rotary press, and photoengraving. This new industrialized press kept on increasing print runs because urban concentration continued, railway communication facilitated distribution, the percentage of the population able to read and write increased, and the buying power of some sectors of the society improved. The afternoon newspaper was born to cater to wage-earners when they came home from work and could purchase an occasional copy, provided that it was not sold solely by subscription. It was a quality change in the "news" concept, which was no longer tied to the 24-hour cycle.

While social changes were certainly important as a motivation for this decision to print an afternoon paper, it was also underpinned by a solid economic logic. The entrepreneur owners of publishing companies decided to benefit from idle presses, as well as composition and pictures that were already made, and almost nonexistent administration expenses for this new paper. The decision to produce a by-product of the main business was designed to secure the profitability of the funds invested, so the company was better placed to face the strong competition amongst the different morning papers. The earnings from the afternoon edition could then be reinvested in improving the morning paper.

This innovation, therefore, was primarily propelled by the expansionist logic of capitalism. Competitors that did not do this disappeared or were taken over, resulting in a concentration process which, in the 1900s in the United States, with very rare exceptions, led to only one regular paper in cities of more than half a million inhabitants.

To sum up: it was the productive regime which primarily determined the transformations of the press, both directly by altering the terms of competition in the newspaper market, and indirectly, by producing social and economic conditions that changed the conditions of readership. The birth of the afternoon paper was one outcome. Another was the effort to acquire more readers with lower reading skills by increasing the fleetingness of the news, the number of photographs, and the size of the headlines. The relative reduction in the labor of "composing" pages, as well as the diversification and growing banality of content, must also be assigned to the underlying economic logic of profit maximization. Traditionally, however, it has been more common to highlight intellectual factors over economic forces.

The majority of analysts argue that these changes were produced when attempting to interpret the public's needs, an idea that is sustained today in attempts to legitimize the most degrading excesses of media output (unnecessary violence, sexism, racism) that are rejected by critical analysts from an ethical point of view. Again, others attribute these changes to "transformations of society" as interpreted by entrepreneurs, an idealist conception that ignores economic influences.

The complex expansion of radio broadcasting

Radio broadcasting began in Europe after World War I and television – despite earlier attempts – developed as a genuinely mass medium after World War II. Unlike the United States, where radio and television broadcasting was organized around private initiatives and the federal and state governments opted for relaxed regulation, in Western Europe, the notion of public service was adopted and institutionalized, especially in Great Britain (with the BBC) and France (with RTF, later ORTF). A combination of material and cultural factors explain the alternatives chosen on different sides of the Atlantic. The factors contributing to the commercial solution to the organization of radio broadcasting in the US included the great geographical expanse of North America and the limited reach of radio waves, the relative continental isolation that reduced the need to defend the national tongue, and the tradition of a less interventionist state power. Conversely, the European approach is explained by a strong tradition of defending national languages, the much smaller territorial expanses, and the experience of public services in other sectors.

There was also a third model born after the Russian Revolution, according to which electromagnetic communication (as well as print) are tools for advancing a revolutionary process, and therefore privileged sites of social and cultural action in countries struggling to institute socialism. This third model has been associated with Marxist thought, but there are reasons to disagree with this interpretation. Marxism claims to be based on a scientific methodology, grounded in contestability and verification – principles that run counter to attempts to secure a monopoly over the production of information.[4] It is one thing for governments to protect information, it is quite another for them to claim a monopoly over its production.

Latin America followed the North American model for both radio and television almost without exception (though Chile could be mentioned as a partial exception); this model also prevailed in African and Asian countries. Asia has public service television in China, Israel, Japan, Pakistan, and Bangladesh.

When we look for the structural underpinnings of these choices we immediately encounter the importance of modes of financing broadcast expansion. It's obvious that the open broadcasting of radio or television only produces minimal resources for the reproduction and sale of some programs or by-products. This is the reason why some European governments decided to set a rate or a yearly tax on each radio receiver, so that the users of the service funded the production cost of programs and maintenance and expansion of the service. In the US commercial system, broadcasters turned to advertising as the principal source of income. And in the "socialist" countries, there was no tax or advertising.[5] When television was introduced in the mid-twentieth century, each European country opted to extend the system already in use for radio broadcasting to the new medium, developing it as either a public service or a commercial enterprise.

This structural history of the press and television in capitalist countries highlights two key points: the determining role of the productive regime, usually and incorrectly called the market, and the key mediating role played by the action or inaction of national governments. Two decades of marketization across the world have tied contemporary "mass communication" even more securely to the logic of capital, confirming Dallas Smythe's argument that its main purpose is cultivating an ethos of possessive individualism and supporting and elaborating on the ideology of consumerism:

> To summarize: the mass media institutions in monopoly capitalism developed the equipment, workers and organization to produce audiences for the purpose of the system between about 1875 and 1950. The prime purpose of the mass media complex is to produce people in audiences who work at learning the theory and practice of consumership for civilian goods and who support (with taxes and votes) the military demand managements system. The second principal purpose is to produce audiences whose theory and practice confirm the ideology of monopoly capitalism (possessive individualism in an authoritarian political system). (Smythe 1977, 20)

The predominant vision tends to analyze these same phenomena in another way: arguing that media executives offer information and entertainment services for free (radio broadcasting), or for a payment that's lower than the cost of production (press), selling advertising time or space to finance all or part of the service offered without necessarily conditioning it, because there are multiple advertisers.

The mirage of progress

We have witnessed amazing transformations in the technological capabilities of communication. In the opulent west and in some other regions of the planet (generally urban areas), the range of communication products is expanding at an increasing rate. All of this, together with the advertising of new products, helps develop and sustain the idea of progress. There is no space here to elaborate on the full meaning of this idea, so we will limit ourselves to analyzing the progress of communications.

The term "progress" carries a variety of connotations. If we talk about the technological breakthroughs that have made possible new forms of communication, both mass and interpersonal, which were nonexistent and unimagined just a few years ago, there would be widespread agreement. But if we went on to argue that these innovations were due to "scientific" breakthroughs and not to lines of technological application decided by industrial capitals, we would disagree. Today, we're offered, at least in lots of cities, the possibility of viewing, via cable or satellite connections, hundreds of television channels broadcasting 24 hours a day, most of which won't be seen by the average person in his or her lifetime. We're offered cellular phones or computers which offer ever-expanding possibilities for use, much higher than average needs. It's no secret that the industry programs such products with the intention of attracting the maximum number of users possible, and it's also no secret that the constant renewal of systems designed to render older devices obsolete and make buyers continually purchase "upgrades," sets the tone for the market. That's not progress. It's a waste of material resources with no ecological consideration whatsoever, but it's especially a manipulation of consumers, who are progressively compelled to buy, most of the time irrationally and superfluously, in the belief that they're being offered new possibilities.

Ideology

Defining "ideology" presents a major difficulty, for the term is loosely used and carries diverse meanings. Even in definitional efforts, amazing differences arise, which sometimes seem to derive from the term's divergent usage in different languages. For example, there are several substantial variations among the three articles about "ideology" in the Spanish, French, and English versions of Wikipedia. The English version defines ideology as "an organized group of ideas," and then adds, "An ideology could be thought out as a global vision, as a way of conceiving things (compare with Weltanschauung), ... or a group of ideas proposed by the dominant class of a society to all the rest of the members of that society."

The first meaning includes the possibility of an undefined number of "ideologies" in very different fields of knowledge. The second limits itself to an "ideology" that is dominant in every society and in each historical moment. The Lalande *Vocabulary* at the beginning of the twentieth century was already using this primary classification of "ideology" (Lalande 1910). As mentioned at the outset of this chapter, Sartre, in his *Critique de la raison dialectique* (1985), argues that just as there can only be one dominant ideology in each historical moment, there can only be one valid "emerging" ideology that opposes it.

Space does not allow us to elaborate on the debates around ideology here, so I want to make it clear that from here on, we'll use "ideology A" to refer to "an organized group of ideas" and "ideology B" to refer to "false or mistaken image of reality."

A simple example from the past

When Guillermo de Nogent, a medieval monk, stated in *Summa de arte praedicandi* that "God made things like this: one prays, others fight, the rest work," he was interpreting social stratification (clergy, nobility, and commoners) according to the dominant theological perspective of the time. To him, the social order was divinely ordained, and therefore, permanent and definite.

His vision of the world, his interpretation of the reality, now seems naïve, but there's no doubt that it was a generalized interpretation then. And we also understand that this formulation served the social function of consolidating the existing order by proposing that it should be accepted not because of the threat of earthly punishment for dissenters, but because it was part of a divine plan.

This is an example of ideology in the sense established by Marx, of a "false idea of the reality." It's not, however, a Machiavellian and conscious creation by the dominant class, invented to perpetuate their control, but a spontaneous vision – a reflection – of the reality that, of course, was favorable to those who could formulate it and had the capability to spread and impose it. The acts of dispersion and reception consecrated it as a dominant ideology in the sense of a worldview that, in the absence of forceful alternatives, dominated people's mental horizons.

A present-day example

"We hold these truths to be self-evident, that all men are created equal," says the Declaration of Independence of the United States of 1774; "Men are born and remain free and equal in rights," says the Declaration of the Rights of Man and the Citizen of 1789; "All human beings are born free and equal in dignity and rights," says the Universal Declaration of Human Rights of 1948.

The original eighteenth-century formulation of fundamental human rights, which contributed to the fall of monarchist absolutism and the disappearance of the nobility, continues to provide the theoretical underpinnings of liberal regimes of government today. However, the Declaration of 1948 constitutes ideology B because it presupposes a nonexistent human equality. People can vote, they can choose, and their votes carry equal weight in politically liberal societies, but they cannot intervene in the same way, in the same conditions, in any of the social systems in which the fundamental decisions affecting their life chances are taken. Not in political, not in economic, not in cultural arenas. They're not even the same by birth because it's known that maternal nutrition, the sanitary conditions and educational attainment of the parents, and the provision of adequate medical preventative care, are all conditioning factors. Science today tells us that malnutrition in early childhood diminishes intellectual development. Pedagogical knowledge shows us that the social, economic, and cultural conditions of families are very influential factors in the development of students. Then in adult life, the great majority of people have no chance to contribute to the messages that dominate public forums.

The idea of equality, then, is not a reality but an aspiration, an ideal that has inspired many movements of solidarity throughout history, particularly in the last two centuries, but now operates more as a conformist ideology regarding the social structure and the government's political machine than as an engine propelling change. The equality instituted in counting votes seems to be enough in those societies with political liberalism. The absence of privileges by birth, consecrated in laws, is enough to obscure the rest of the inequalities.

More difficulties

Let's now take a look at how different economic schools have contributed to the creation of contemporary concepts that legitimize the social and economic order we live by. When we think about the fundamental ideas of the mercantalist school of the eighteenth century, we understand that the immediate reality of the colonial system of that time formed the basis for their intellectual constructions. But there's no doubt that the emphasis on the prestige of wealth accumulation, through the hoarding of currency, now fiduciary, as an expression of power, as a factor for social promotion and a symbol of excellence, has persisted as an active emphasis in subsequent forms of capitalism.

The physiocrats, who were responsible for the collapse of mercantilism, built another myth: naturalism. The evidence (correct) that agriculture is the source of wealth, and the concept (wrong) that circulation does not add value, allowed the construction of the idea that "natural laws" were being discovered. This idea was taken up by the classical school and transferred to the industrial society that was then coming into being. With the observation of the "law" of supply and demand, Adam Smith thought he had discovered an eternal principle, not a contingent and historical reality. Today we have that double inheritance incorporated into common language and, as noted earlier, renowned economists can talk about the "unemployment natural rate," or confuse "market" with "society." Many members of current societies – and not only in the undeveloped world – don't have access to any market or just attend to markets for their immediate needs, which are insufficiently satisfied. Human societies are realities; "markets" are built concepts.

What these examples show is that, while in the Middle Ages there was one overriding principle supporting ideology B, in advanced capitalism the complexity of lived reality leads us to admit the existence of multiple independent principles that intersect and whose effects vary with different subjects, according to their social formation, profession, environment, and practices.

We could continue with the search for examples of intersections. Current Chinese society presents a particularly interesting case with its combination of nationalism, doctrinaire and schematic Marxism-Leninism, and capitalist principles, mobilized in the service of legitimating the social model now emerging. However, unlike the west, the huge and growing contradictions generated by the current process of transformation can be presented as temporary impediments to the achievement of the harmonious society celebrated in the deeply rooted traditions of Chinese thought. There is certainly no way that authoritarianism by itself is enough to maintain social cohesion.

Recognizing the variegated nature of conformist visions under contemporary conditions brings us to Jean Baudrillard's key insight: "If culture, consumption, and signs must be analyzed as ideology, this is not achieved by banishing them, or expelling them to an outer field, but, on the contrary, by integrating them into the very structures of political economy" (Baudrillard 1981, 114).

Advertising

By "advertising," we understand an action that aims, through messages, at advancing the acquisition of goods or services for the purposes of profit. This practice can have diverse objectives, ranging from promoting a brand or company, to combating resistance from the eventual buyers and stimulating behaviors and attitudes that support consumption. (A paradigmatic case is represented by tobacco companies forging scientific knowledge that shows the harmful and lethal effects of tobacco.) It also needs to be differentiated from "propaganda," which in general is perceived as being designed to promote conduct or attitudes favorable to political, religious, and other objectives.

Many studies of advertising trace its origins back to ancient times, citing examples of public messages announcing items for sale. This has the effect of legitimating it as a normal or natural activity, that is, typical of the human species in every historical period. In contrast, a properly constituted historical perspective would emphasize that it is only since the industrial revolution, which made possible the existence of mass means of communication, that advertising started to develop in the way we know it today.

Economic duties of advertising

The primary economic duty of advertising in contemporary capitalist societies is to act like a water pump accelerating the circulation of goods. It's a necessary extension of the productive system, as Galbraith points out:

> This management performs yet another service. For, along with bringing demand under substantial control, it provides, in the aggregate, a relentless propaganda in favour of goods in general. From early morning until late at night, people are informed of the services rendered by goods – of their profound indispensability. Every feature and facet of every product having been studied for selling points, these are then described with talent, gravity and an aspect of profound concern as the source of health, happiness, social achievement or improved community standing. (Galbraith 2007/1967, 259–60)

The consequence is that if the products are more abundant, their importance seems to diminish. On the contrary, it's necessary to make an effort to imagine that here's something else that presents an equivalent importance. Morally, we admit that the abundance of goods is not synonymous with human success; in reality, we don't doubt it's considered as such.

If the first economic function advertising plays is accelerating circulation, then the second is to increase consumption: "Use it and toss it." The first function is accomplished by getting people to *buy* the products. The second, regardless of whether the purchased products have been used or not, develops an appetite for new products, or additions to ones already purchased.

This applies especially to communication products or services that need to sell additional services or functions, over and above the basic ones (such as voice telephony, or basic cable packages), in order to expand profits.

Advertising and technological advances

A "naturalist" interpretation could argue that each technological advance is accompanied by a new expansion of advertising. And in part this is true. For example, the Internet is born and, at the same time, Internet advertising is born. Newspapers introduce Internet editions and those editions are progressively occupied by advertising spaces. And so on. According to this perspective, advertising follows technological "progress."

But before we accept this argument, let's review the origins of capitalism. Technological advances did not trigger the first industrial revolution. They were encouraged and stimulated by the accumulation of capital and the search for maximum profitability. In textile production, new energy sources and transportation systems were financed by capitalists intent on strengthening their competitive position. Since then, scientific knowledge has made possible changes of great magnitude, while helping to conceal the underlying mechanisms of investment. The current computing and communication revolution has certainly required significant advances in scientific knowledge, but its major social applications have been fundamentally driven by the search for new horizons for profitability. Advertising has long been incorporated into this expansionist dynamic generating an *advertising strategy* that predates each new innovation in economic activity.

There is, of course, an alternative view of this development. As we mentioned before in connection with the idea of progress, the transformations of advanced capitalism are considered by the majority of analysts as an almost natural evolution.

Advertising and legitimation

This "naturalist" conception of society, logically, also involves advertising, and many analysts tend to accept it without major questioning, based on the tradition of political liberalism that includes the fundamental principles of freedom of speech and thought. Without a second thought, these commentators apply this principle to the transmission of advertising messages.

A critical analysis of the principle of freedom of speech and thought, however, needs to distinguish sharply between the messages that each person, as an individual, wants to transmit, propelled by his or her need to communicate with others, and the messages which only certain people, because of their economic disposition and motivated by profitability, want to disseminate as widely as possible. This distinction has been made by the Supreme Court of the United States when they concluded that the first type of message deserves maximum protection, while the second should be regulated by law (Chamberlin and Brown 1982, Gartner 1989). These rulings are very important if we keep in mind that the American constitutional system states in its first amendment that there can be no legislation that inhibits "press freedom." In addition to the US example, we could mention numerous national legislations, especially in European countries, in which some aspects of the advertising message are prohibited, limited, or subject to conditions, for instance, messages advertising tobacco, alcohol, or narcotics, messages addressed to children or using degrading images of women.

These legal-political decisions point to a certain critical coincidence in different societies about the harmful effects of certain types of advertisement. In turn, they tap into a generalized popular unease, a discomfort in the face of constantly growing, repetitive, invasive advertising messages. Advertising agents have taken note of that discomfort, and tend to refer to it in the messages they transmit, which aim to recover the trust of the audience.[6]

The apology for advertising

Advertising informs, it allows the consumer to choose. … It brings him or her close to new elements that arise from the progress of science and technology applied to each new product, without which he or she would be defenseless to make the best purchasing decisions. … Advertising develops imagination, it sometimes uses humor, it's creative, it makes life beautiful, it's a (utilitarian) art, but it is a form of art.

Advertising has some reasons to see its future through rose-colored glasses. While the total volume of advertising investments are constantly rising, it's still invading new spaces: state television, conference talks, art and sport events, movies, articles of every kind, from T-shirts to sailboat sails, names of brands are everywhere in our day-to-day universe. … Socially legitimized communication has access to artistic endeavors: advertising is shown in museums, poster retrospective expositions are organized, awards for excellence are presented. … Advertising has contributed to disqualify the saving habit in favor of spending and immediate pleasure: paradoxically, through the spreading hedonist culture, advertising could be seen as an agent of people's individualism, an agent which accelerates the search for personality and autonomy of individuals. (Lipovetzky 1987, 126)

This speech, while undoubtedly marked by brilliant rhetoric, is totally inconsistent with scientific thought. It is reproduced here as an instance of ideology B.

Two significant examples

On March 6, 1990, a full-page advertisement for *Fortune* magazine in the *New York Times* included this eye-catching caption: "We made an issue for people who can't read." The accompanying copy indicated that 700,000 secondary school graduates were unable to read their own diplomas, and went on to ask: "How many of them would you hire?" It ended by urging readers to buy advertising in the forthcoming edition of *Fortune,* which it promised would carry advice and solutions from business people who had successfully addressed the problem of relative illiteracy.

In this example, we find the intersection of: (1) the *Fortune* magazine *economy* (to attract more advertising by carrying eye-catching ads); (2) the legitimizing *ideology* of the productive system (what's important is the efficient functioning of the companies, not achieving better efficiency in the education system); and (3) the general promotion of the magazine (by making it more attractive to the public).

A second example is the full-page advertisement from the Philip Morris Tobacco Company carried in several European newspapers and designed to fight a European board that had established prohibitions on smoking and other regulations for smokers' protection. The ad (in *El País*, April 7, 1995) said the following:

El Teorema de Pitágoras contiene 24 palabras. [The Pythagorean Theorem has 24 words]
El Principio de Arquímedes, 67. [Archimedes'axiom, 67]
Los Diez Mandamientos, 179. [The Ten Commandments, 179]
La Declaración de Independencia de los Estados Unidos de América, 300. [The Declaration of Independence of the USA, 300]
Y la legislación en Europa para regular dónde y cuándo se puede
fumar, 24.942. [And the European law about where and when you can smoke, 24,942]

Here, several well-known examples of communication with no connection are bundled together, suggesting that because of its verbosity, the proposed legislation could not possibly be clearly thought out and was therefore invalid and inappropriate. It does not matter that biblical precepts have nothing to do with mathematics, physics, or political liberalism, and especially not with tobacco use. Nor does it matter that the claim that the Declaration of Independence of the United States has only 300 words is false, when in fact it contains more than 1,800. Neither health, nor truth, nor logic matter. What matters is the overall impression made on the reader.

In summary, what we see here is the intersection between the *economy* of the tobacco company (and the imperative to discredit health protection regulation in order to maintain sales), *ideology* (achieved through the arbitrary juxtaposition of popular cultural symbols), and *advertising* of the brand.

General Interaction

Economics, ideology, and advertising are just analytical, intellectual *constructions*. Social reality is always more complex. Consequently, when we say that there is an "interaction" between economics, ideology, and advertising, we are adding a second level to this construction.

The rationality and irrationality of the economy

One quarter of humanity lives in misery. At the other extreme, a group of about 500 multimillionaires have accumulated as much wealth as the 1.5 million poorest. This irrational situation is not new in history. What's new is that the food and clothes that are now produced would be sufficient to cover the needs of all of the planet's inhabitants, and that the potential resources available would allow universal access to shelter, water, and adequate sanitary conditions, at least in the short term.

Investments in weaponry are an additional irrationality. How is this phenomenon commonly interpreted? Again, there are divergent explanations. The drive to build up armaments in the modern period has traditionally been interpreted as a consequence of the rise of nation states and their real and potential conflicts of interest. For the last two decades, however, recognition that the military capacity of the United States exceeds that of all other powers put together has prompted a new rationale that claims that war is necessary to "preserve peace" and "defend against terrorism." Whatever the historical origins of war, the maintenance and growth of the military in advanced capitalism has been more of a response to the dynamics of the competitive system and the prestige of power than any alleged strategic balance. In their 1981 program, the French Socialist Party intended to reduce the arms industry. Ten years later, France had increased their war-related exports, with the intention of not laying off some 300,000 workers in that industry and avoiding the costs of converting it to alternative forms of production and finding new markets.

Let's apply the same methodology we have just used for the arms industry to television. As we noted earlier, the most widely accepted interpretation of its origin assigns it, in the abstract, to "technology" – as if this was casual or almost "natural," as if there were no planned investments (like the manufacturing of stations and receptors), and no push from advertisers wanting to extend their choice of arenas for display. The alternative interpretation highlights the fact that its initial expansion occurred first in urban centers where the first signals arrived and among the social sectors with the greatest discretionary income.

In the case of commercial services, expansion was from the outset inextricably bound up with the economics of profit maximization. When the market for black and white television sets was saturated, color was introduced, allowing the industry to renew itself.[7] Cable, satellite broadcasting, and now digital terrestrial television have all served primarily as devices for promoting expansion in the service of capital placement rather than the human need for more (and better) communication. The privatization of public television services in Europe makes perfect sense as part of this general dynamic, even though the output of public service organizations was arguably more diverse and addressed needs that the market could not or would not meet.

As Maurice Godelier (1985) has argued, however, these social and cultural contradictions and irrationalities are overridden by an underlying economic rationality which continually propels the system toward nonstop expansion and the constant search for new niches in which profitability can be generated for capitals that each time become more concentrated.

The critical study of the political economy of communication in advanced capitalism aims to illuminate this logic. The nonstop expansion and conquest of new markets, the production of new goods and services, the saturation of users through the creation of new communication needs, and at the same time, the impoverishment of content, are all inherent in the basic dynamics of the productive system. Consequently, to pretend that the study of "communication," and more specifically, the means of communication, could lead to greater rationality or lesser irrationality without changing the productive system is foolish.

Mass ideological reproduction

In order to comply with its function, advertising must keep abreast of the stereotypes, commonplaces, and common vocabulary current among the audiences or audience segments it targets. In the process, it reproduces ideology B. There are rare exceptions, such as Toscani's campaigns for Benetton, that employ news photos to question received ideas, but even these instances are more often provocative than subversive.

Liberal theories of the media place great stress on the preservation of informative independence, and attribute silence, misinformation, and other departures from this ideal primarily to pressure from political powers. When we speak of ideological reproduction in the media, however, we're not talking about highly notable instances of intervention, but about the range of more subtle constraints that operate through the selection of topics, in the analytical perspective given prominence, in modes of storytelling, in vocabularies of description, and in the selection of graphics or filmed inserts. This routine is, to a great extent, accomplished by subordinated agents, through complex mechanisms marked by dependency and competitive dynamics.

All companies have hierarchical organizational structures that control, as a last resort, the production of content, but it would be naïve to assume that this verticality is the only or prime cause of the resulting array of public communication. An army of message writers contribute to ideological reproduction. When the economic crisis that started in September 2008 was recounted, analyzed, and explained, the media initially described it as a financial (or stock market) crisis. After a few days, when the full dimension of the financial and stock market disturbances had been noted, and it was clear that they were going to strongly affect everyday life, it was redescribed as an economic crisis. Attention began to focus on its impact on the "real economy," meaning the concrete production of goods and services as opposed to the manipulation of money, as if, in the capitalist system, the instruments that link people to production and to goods are not equally real. This obfuscation was accompanied by a concerted effort to *naturalize* events, to uncouple them from systemic failure. There were constant references to "earthquakes," "hurricanes," "tsunamis," "shipwrecks," and "heavy seas." And when responses from the governments were announced, their actions were characterized as "salvaging," "rescuing," "helping" – the same vocabulary routinely employed in the coverage of natural disasters. This is ideological reproduction.

It is also valuable research material for a critical political economy of communication aimed at challenging standardized practices. We need to ask whether and how the publications produced by journalism schools, professional unions, parties, and Left political groups report the mechanisms for ideological reproduction. Are they efficient when doing it? Is there any known electoral campaign in which this theme is explicit?

As critical analysts committed to planning for better results, we have to try to understand the direction in which the whole society is moving, foregrounding the primary role played by economic strategies in driving the direction and pattern of change. By better results, we mean peace, solidarity, and real equality in class, gender, and race relations, as well as respect for the environment. I advance this argument as a basis for common ground and concerted action, and invite you to join me in contributing to its development.

Conclusions

For a handbook, it is useful to present different and controversial perspectives. Those presented here do not belong to prevailing tendencies.

1   Prevailing economic thought (accepted by governments, international bodies, etc.)[8] underestimates its own value.

2   Quite commonly ideology B is ignored or underestimated.

3   Academics always have difficulties with advertising because students must be trained to *produce* advertising in the way market conditions demand. Most of them simply adapt to prevailing thought.

4   Theoretically, only deep changes in the system of production will lead to new perspectives about the future. At the same time, only new ideas followed by actions, can produce changes.

This unsolved contradiction suggests a permanent conflict in intellectual matters, the political economy of communication included.

Notes

1   So far, the effect of that taxonomy seems to fit Kuhn's paradox, that is, that convergent research produces convergent results.

2   For example, dynamic stochastic general equilibrium, computable general equilibrium, or agent-based computational economics.

3   For example, adaptive expectations, representative agents, representative firms, rational choice, etc.

4   The term "Marxism-Leninism" was adopted by the USSR around 1927 and made evident the purpose of political use that had the rigid canonization of Marxist thought.

5   A question arises in the case of China, where television advertising has existed for several decades: did advertising (of course, of government companies) predict today's forms of capitalism in that country or just produce prestige?

6   Among others, the Bureau pour la Vérification de la Publicité of France has done this.

7   In 1974, in Tampere, Finland, the company executives of the state television station explained the start of color broadcasting to visiting academics. When asked about having to take into account that during the previous year an economic crisis had started and that the audience would have to finance a new receiver, they answered that the decision was a consequence of the fact that the manufacturers weren't producing any more parts for black and white transmission.

8   Even the so-called Nobel Prize in Economics, awarded since 1967, is financed by bankers, not by the Nobel Foundation.

References

Baudrillard, J. (1981) *For a Critique of the Political Economy of the Sign*, C. Levin (trans.). Telos Press, St. Louis, MO.

Brune, F. (1997) Un marché à l'état de nature. *Le Monde Diplomatique, Mai*. Online at http://www.monde-diplomatique.fr/1997/05/ (accessed October 16, 2010).

Chamberlin, B. E. and Brown, C. J. (1982) *The First Amendment Reconsidered*. Longman, New York and London.

Gabszewicz, J. and Sonnac, N. (eds) (2006) *L'industrie des medias* [*The Media Industry*]. La Decouverte, Paris.

Galbraith, J. K. (2007/1967) *The New Industrial State*. Princeton University Press, Princeton, NJ.

Gartner, M. (1989) *Advertising and the First Amendment*. Priority Press Publications, New York.

Godelier, M. (1985) *Rationnalité et irrationnalité en économie*. [*Rationality and Irrationality in Economics*]. Gallimard, Paris.

Lalande, A. (1910) *Vocabulaire critique de la philosophie*. PUF, Paris.

Sartre, J. P. (1985) *Critique de la raison dialectique* [*Critique of Dialectic Reason*]. PUF, Paris.

Smythe, D. (1977) Communications: Blindspot of western Marxism. *Canadian Journal of Political and Social Theory*, 1(3): 1–28.

Stiglitz, J. (2008) El "blues" del rescate de Wall Street. *El País*, October 1.

Suggestions for Further Reading

Biolay, J. (1995) *Le droit de la publicité* [*The Right of Advertising*]. PUF, Paris.

Boudon, R. (1986) *L'idéologie* [*Ideology*]. Points, Paris.

Brune, F. (2003) *De l'idéologie, aujourd'hui* [*Ideology Today*]. Parangon, Paris.

Eagleton, T. (1997) *Ideology: An Introduction*. Verso, London.

Fontanel, J. (1976) *L'antipublicité* [*Against Advertising*]. Université de Grenoble, Grenoble.

Haug, W. F. (1989) *Publicidad y consumo* [*Advertising and Consumerism*]. FCE, Mexico.

Jhally S. (1987) *The Codes of Advertising*. Frances Printer, London.

Leiss, W., Kline, S., and Jhally, S. (1990) *Social Communication in Advertising*. Nelson Canada, Ontario.

Mattelart, A. (1989) *L'Internationale publicitaire* [*International Advertising*]. La Découverte, Paris.

Ziegler, J. (2005) *L'empire de la honte* [*The Empire of Shame*]. Fayard, Paris.

10

Branding and Culture

John Sinclair

Introduction

As early as Roman times, sword blades and wine containers were marked to identify the producer, suggesting that branding has always had basic functions which we have easily lost sight of in the brand-saturated culture of global capitalism today. Again, in the medieval era, craft workers identified their products with trademarks, the forerunner of the distinctively packaged and widely distributed branded goods which came to characterize the industrial era. Thus the elementary purposes of the trademark, and hence, the brand, are to "uniquely identify" the maker of a given product, to differentiate that product from its competitors (and imitators), and to provide a warrant of quality and consistency to the purchaser (Aaker 1991, 7).

By the nineteenth century, rather than buying bulk, generic goods like oats, weighed out by the grocer, shoppers were learning to identify their preference amongst the packets on the shelf – would it be Quaker or Scott's Porage Oats? And around the same time, householders were coming to appreciate the convenience of branded products, like Ivory, Pear's, or Lifebuoy soap in packets, rather than having to make their own lye soap at home. In this way, manufacturers were using the distinctiveness of brands, along with their display and packaging, to establish a direct relationship with consumers, so that the traditional intermediary role of the retailer was bypassed by the brand itself serving to sell the product, a shift ultimately resulting in the "self-service" supermarket (Lury 2004, 19). Before long, even the retailers found that they had to adopt some of the characteristics of a brand if they were to prosper in a shifting and competitive market – Sears, Roebuck in the United States, Selfridge's in Britain, David Jones in Australia, to name a few.

The Handbook of Political Economy of Communications, First Edition.
Edited by Janet Wasko, Graham Murdock, and Helena Sousa.
© 2014 John Wiley & Sons, Ltd. Published 2014 by John Wiley & Sons, Ltd.

With the rise of the press, then radio and television coming to dominate social communication in the twentieth century, branding found its supreme vehicle in the advertising which impelled the commercial growth of these media. More than uniquely identifying a product or its manufacturer, advertising enabled brands to acquire cultural meanings, such as hierarchies of status (Nieman Marcus versus Wal-Mart); associations with certain kinds of people ("The Pepsi Generation"); and even something like their own personalities (stylish Lexus versus reliable Toyota). This capacity of goods to evoke and claim cultural meanings for themselves is called "brand equity," or "brand image," to which we shall return shortly. The point here is to show how the brand has become much more than the trademark from which it began, involving "the transfer of value through images" achieved especially, but not only, by advertising and other forms of marketing (Lash and Urry 1994, 138).

Branding is thus deeply implicated in the emergence of "consumerism" and the "consumer society." This prominent moral and ideological aspect of capitalist society has been subject to sustained critique from both conservatives and Marxists, the former concerned with the materialism attributed to consumer society and its values, the latter with the functions such values are seen to serve in perpetuating capitalism. Among the latter, for example, Andrew Wernick (1991) offers a critique of "promotional culture" in which both individuals and institutions take on the character of brands, familiar to us respectively from the world of celebrities, and the way universities, for example, once aloof from the world of commerce, now position themselves with slogans and logos in an internationally competitive "marketplace."

Naomi Klein (2001) demands "No Logo," as her protest against "the new branded world," and refers particularly to the rise of rapidly globalized "lifestyle" brands of the 1990s, like Nike. Her book on branding shows how brands conceal a worldwide struggle between capital and labor, and has become a founding text of the antiglobalization movement. She exposes the manner in which the actual manufacturing of sportswear and other such products has been outsourced, usually to low-wage, developing countries, leaving the company free to concentrate on marketing, which mainly means building up the brand. In this new paradigm, she says, "the product always takes a back seat to the real product, the brand" (2001, 21).

This insight takes Klein close to Celia Lury's more abstract view that the brand is an "object," that is, a thing, but not so much a single thing as a set of relations which mediate between producer and consumer, or supply and demand. More concretely, the brand is the management of the relations between what the traditional marketing textbooks call the "five Ps": product, price, place, packaging, and promotion. Like Wernick, Lury also draws attention to the pervasiveness of branding, how it turns people into celebrities, and stretches across institutional spheres which have not seen the need to brand themselves in the past, like political parties and charities. She also notes the rise in the branding of places, even whole nations (2004, 5–16).

The pervasive branding of institutions, places, and spaces is a theme also found in the work of Liz Moor (2007), but whereas most writers on branding focus on advertising and promotion generally as the main means of establishing and building a brand, Moor draws attention to the role of design, both in the product itself and its packaging: think of the distinctive shape of the Coke bottle which has been maintained now over several decades. She points out that it is only since the mid-1990s that the concept of branding has come into everyday public discourse, a symptom of what she calls "a more reflexive capitalism" (2007, 5), that is, in the sense of it being more self-aware.

Perhaps the most recent and influential analysis of branding to emerge is from Adam Arvidsson, whose contribution is to show how consumers, rather than being the passive dupes of the marketers, actually participate in the making of a brand, albeit unequally. His insight is that brands capitalize upon "people's ability to create trust, affect and shared meanings: their ability to create something in common. … it is the meaning-making activity of consumers that forms the basis of brand value" (2005, 236–7). Common meanings created collectively by people (whether a nation or a subculture) is one of the main things we mean when we talk about "culture," so in other words, Arvidsson's view is that although it is people who create cultural meanings, what brand marketers do is to pick up on these meanings and exploit them by associating them with particular products and services. This is a capitalism which is more reflexive in the sense that it recognizes the rise of an independent popular culture, but seeks to bring it under control to serve commercial interests.

Branding and Value

Influential writers such as those just discussed are pointing toward the significance of branding as a cultural phenomenon, yet they also recognize that it is an economic instrument of capitalism – indeed, some go further in arguing that the economic asset of a brand is not just based on, but actually is the equivalent to, the cultural meaning which exists for it. The capacity to endow a certain good or service with cultural value, that is, to transform a product into a brand, and sustain it as such, is called brand equity in the business management literature. According to Aaker, for example (1991), brand equity is composed of:

- brand loyalty, or the ability to retain satisfied customers
- familiarity and recognition of a brand name and/or symbols
- perceived quality of products offered under the brand name
- associations, including positioning of a brand relative to competitors
- other proprietary brand assets, such as control of distribution outlets.

In other words, brand equity mainly consists in the relation of a brand with its actual or potential consumers, at the level of culture. As early as the 1950s, the advertising industry was referring to this quality of a brand – to evoke loyalty, familiarity, and positive associations – as "brand image," which is the character or personality which branding bestows upon a product to make it a "public object" (Gardner and Levy 1955, 35).

In this perspective, we see that the brand is not so much a mere image in the form of a logo or symbol, but a form of intellectual property, and as such, "an important immaterial asset in contemporary capitalism" (Arvidsson 2005, 238). As early as the 1980s, the value of established brands was apparent in high-profile, large-scale takeovers, such as when the US cigarette manufacturer Philip Morris took over General Foods in 1985, and then Kraft in 1988, as it became clear that tobacco had little future (Sandler and Shani 1992, 28). The 1990s and 2000s have seen sometimes long-standing brands being acquired in a process of continued global corporate expansion and consolidation of brand portfolios, such as Procter & Gamble's acquisition of Gillette in 2005.

What is being bought in such transactions is brand equity – that is, brand image is given a financial value so that it can change hands. Since there are high costs and often also long years involved in building up brand equity, corporations that want to take over an existing brand via acquisition or merger have to compensate the seller, not just for the investment embedded in the brand, but for the meaning it commands as a public object. The elusive, intangible quality of a brand image is thus given a concrete value, or specific, calculated quantity. Since the 1980s formal accounting methods of putting a figure on both the present and future value of brands have become standardized to facilitate such takeovers and mergers, which in effect are methodologies for transforming quality into quantity (Lury 2004). Certain marketing communications companies also measure brand performance. Notably, in recent years the UK-based marketing research company Millward Brown Optimor has captured the attention of the business world when it publishes annually, from its BrandZ survey, its calculations and ranking of brands on a world-regional and global basis, using their metric of dollar value to identify "the world's most powerful brands" (Millward Brown Optimor 2008).

As with mergers and takeovers, when global companies like Coca-Cola enter licensing arrangements with local bottling and distribution companies, or McDonald's sell franchises to the "Mom and Pop" operators of particular outlets, the principal part of what is being licensed or franchised is brand equity. Indeed, the extensive growth of brand licensing and retail franchising arrangements, seen for example in the same range of shops being found from one main street or shopping mall to another, is a potent, though understudied, form in which brands now pervade our environment as "capitalism in kit form" (Perry 1998, 51). As for licensing, some corporations reach the point where they find it is more profitable to sell the rights to their brand, rather than keep producing it themselves: for example, the Australian-based global brewing company Foster's closed down its breweries in Europe and Asia, and sold the rights to brew the brand to its former distributors.

Thus, whether it is stock market evaluations, takeovers and mergers, or licensing and franchising contracts, capitalism requires that a calculable value can be put on a brand. This value allows the brand to be traded, or financially negotiated in some way, and because it has financial value, the brand owner needs to protect it. It is in this sense that a brand is a form of intellectual property. Once again, the trademark can be seen as the ancestor and paradigm of the legal protection with which brands are now surrounded, but patents, copyright, and design rights may also apply. All these rights prevent competitors from imitating or otherwise encroaching upon the brand's equity, thus protecting the company's investment in developing or acquiring the brand. Consumers are protected also, to the extent that the brand owner has an incentive to maintain the brand's quality, and in the sense that they are assured of what it is that they are buying. However, in the era of corporate globalization, intellectual property law has become something of a weapon to eliminate local competitors, especially in new markets (Moor 2007).

For instance, the UK-based global confectionery company Cadbury pursued, and lost, a lawsuit against an Australian firm, which, like Cadbury, also used the color purple as part of its brand image. The issue was not so much whether Cadbury could "own" the color purple, but whether consumers would be "confused" by both companies using it. This ostensible protection of the consumer is a key concept in trademark law, but clearly can benefit more the market power of producers, even if not in this particular case (Lury 2004).

Indeed, just as an older generation of political economists identified advertising in general as a "barrier to entry," so can this criticism be more precisely leveled at branding. To say branding is a barrier to entry means that prospective competitors are discouraged from entering a market because of the high costs which those new entrants would have to invest in branding so as to match the levels which the incumbents already have put into developing and/or acquiring existing brands. Branding is thus a bulwark of market power, and so favors oligopolistic market structures; that is, where there are just two or three corporations which share a market for a given kind of good or service, such as the global dominance of Procter & Gamble and Unilever in so many "fast moving consumer goods" (FMCG) brands.

Marxist Political Economy and Branding

"The treatment of the commodity in the first hundred or so pages of *Capital* is arguably one of the most difficult, contradictory, and ambiguous parts of Marx's corpus" (Appadurai 1986, 7). The question with which Marx began his major work was how it was that goods, or "commodities," which he defined as any object that satisfied wants, were able to conceal the real relations between capital and labor under which they were produced. For Marx, labor was the true source of value, but the mystique of the commodity made it seem that it was valuable in itself. To be under this illusion was what Marx famously called "commodity fetishism." Intrinsic to his analysis of the commodity was the distinction between use value and exchange value, which actually derives from the classical political economy of Adam Smith. Use value was just that – what an object was useful for, its utility – but exchange value was what someone would give for it in exchange. For Marx, it was in exchange that the commodity became fetishized, that is, when its mystique overshadowed the labor that produced it, and particularly when it was being exchanged for money. In practical terms today, we are talking about the difference between what a certain "good" is good *for*, and the price we are prepared to pay for it.

In Marxist critical discourse, "commodification" has become a key concept, applied to situations where what was once free now comes with a price attached; where what was once publicly available has become privately held; and where what was once natural and authentic has been contaminated, diluted, dumbed down, or otherwise corrupted, and then usually packaged for mass, or perhaps niche-market, consumption. "Commodification," in fact, has come to serve as a critical metonym used to denounce all cultural forms in which commerce is seen to encroach upon spheres of life where it ought not belong. As such, it is more of a rhetorical than an analytical and heuristic concept, though one authoritative contemporary political economist gives it this formal definition: "Commodification is the process of transforming use values into exchange values" (Mosco 1996, 141).

However, from the perspective of branding, it would be more true to say, "*Branding* is the process of transforming use values into exchange values," in the sense that while one commodity will perform the same function as any other, branding differentiates commodities and provides exchange value for the consumer who seeks out one in preference to others. In that light, it is actually brands, not commodities, which are fetishized, though modern-day Marxists would agree that branding certainly contributes to the mystique that conceals the value of the labor which made the product; it is part of what they mean by commodification.

Yet for those not schooled in Marxist discourse, the concept of commodity itself can be confusing. While Marxists do commonly refer to branded products as commodities, such usage completely inverts the hierarchical relation between brands and commodities now understood in contemporary "bourgeois" economics. In the current business literature, for instance, commodities are seen as fungible and undifferentiated, merely the raw materials from which products, whether as goods or services, are made for exchange (Pine and Gilmore 1999, 6). Indeed, Marx himself specifically had in mind commodities like corn, iron, or silk, which, although there may be variations in quality, are generic: one load of corn is much like any other. By contrast, branding creates differentiation – even in Marx's own time, to hark back to an example given in the introduction, soap (in the UK) became Pear's. And as also noted above, differentiation can involve one or more of the "five Ps": product, price, place, packaging, and promotion. Differences can be actual, such as in quality, origin, or design; or rather based more on the brand image – what distinguishes Coke from Pepsi, for example. Indeed, when brand owners talk about "commodification," what they mean is their fear that their brand will lose its distinctive image, and the product become readily substitutable for any other of its kind, an MP3 player rather than an iPod.

More than for their use value, or mere competitive display in what Thorstein Veblen famously called "conspicuous consumption," there is an anthropological argument that all societies need goods "for making visible and stable the categories of culture" (Douglas and Isherwood 1979, 59). Similarly, Appadurai, following Georg Simmel, argues that "It is exchange that sets the parameters of utility and scarcity, rather than the other way around, and exchange that is the source of value" (1986, 4). For Appadurai, the meaningful criteria of exchange are governed by "regimes of value," which enable exchange to take place not only within cultures, but between them (1986, 14–15). More broadly, Douglas and Isherwood take the view that "the very idea of consumption itself needs to be set back into the social process ... Goods, work and consumption have been artificially abstracted out of the whole social scheme" (1979, 4).

This anthropological idea, that goods do not so much derive their meaning from culture, but on the contrary, provide culture with meaning, perhaps surprisingly finds some resonance with modern Marxists. Jean Baudrillard is notorious among them for his rejection of use value in his analysis of consumption, in favor of a semiotic hierarchy of symbolic exchange value, although he largely restricts the meaning of such value to its role in making and keeping class distinctions (1981). That is, for Baudrillard, the cultural significance of goods forms a kind of pecking order that reflects and reinforces the social system. More recently, there is the contribution of Arvidsson, who draws on the current strain of "autonomist" Marxism to argue that the "productivity of consumers," that is, the cultural capital which they collectively produce and which marketers exploit in branding, is a kind of "immaterial labour" which forms the context of consumption, "within which goods can acquire use-value" (2005, 242). By "use-value" here, he means the social identity and cultural belonging bestowed by the consumption of goods; for Arvidsson, use value is the good's cultural meaning, not its utility. Yet since Baudrillard's exchange value seems to equate to Arvidsson's use value, it is difficult to see how the classic distinction can have either utility or meaning in the contemporary analysis of branding and consumption.

However, setting aside this considerable conceptual problem in Arvidsson's approach, there is his insight, already quoted more fully in the introduction, that brands capitalize upon "people's ability to create trust, affect and shared meanings" (2005, 236–7). Once again, this can be matched to the anthropological argument which implicitly fits this sharing to brand-names, the view that "Goods are endowed with value by the agreement of fellow consumers. ... Enjoyment of physical consumption is only a part of the service yielded by goods; the other part is the enjoyment of sharing names. ... by far the greater part of utility is yielded ... in sharing names that have been learned and graded. This is culture" (Douglas and Isherwood 1979, 75–6).

From Political Economy to Cultural Economy

Since the conceptual language of traditional Marxist political economy lacks analytical edge when confronted with the phenomenon of branding, and seems especially unsuited to explaining how the economic functions of a given brand depend upon its cultural significance, we need to find a conceptual framework that can comprehend both the economic and cultural dimensions of branding. Although we abstract concepts from the reality we observe around us so that we can understand it, sometimes we then forget that these concepts are abstractions of our own making, and they become reified or hypostasized. That is, we come to think of the concepts as being real, not the actual world from which they have been abstracted.

We are especially prone to mislead ourselves with this fallacious way of thinking when the concepts form a mutually dependent pair, or structured opposition. For example, although consumption is not conceivable without production, and vice versa, or in Marxist theory, the superstructure without a substructure or base, and vice versa, there is an inclination to argue for the significance of one at the expense of the other. Furthermore, the way in which theoretical understanding is organized into disciplines and fields encourages this tendency. To take the most pertinent case, Marxist political economy puts its primacy on the substructure of production, leaving the superstructure of consumption to fields such as cultural studies. This has meant that in studies of marketing, advertising, and branding, political economy is prone to concentrate upon the institutional relations between the consumer goods and services companies, their marketing agencies, and the media; while the content of their marketing and advertising campaigns is left to cultural studies. So on these grounds too there needs to be a more integrated theoretical understanding of the economic and the cultural dimensions of branding.

One of the most useful and influential formulations to attempt this in recent decades has come from Mike Featherstone, who has argued in favor of the concept of "consumer culture" to characterize contemporary capitalist societies, not as a form of moral condemnation, but analytically:

> this involves a dual focus: firstly on the cultural dimension of the economy, the symbolization and use of material goods as "communicators" not just utilities; and secondly, on the economy of cultural goods, the market principles of supply, demand, capital accumulation, competition and monopolization, which operate within the sphere of lifestyles, cultural goods and commodities. (Featherstone 1987, 57)

This two-way understanding of the relationship between economic processes and cultural meanings opens up fertile ground for the study of branding. In the 1990s, another fruitful contribution came from Scott Lash and John Urry, who argued that the economy and culture were becoming ever more integrated: "the economy is increasingly culturally inflected and … culture is more and more economically inflected" (1994, 64). They particularly see an "aestheticization" of economic production, meaning that goods have come to be designed to attract certain kinds of consumers and to fit with their lifestyles; indeed, the concept of lifestyle is very much a buzzword of the 1990s. Prior to the "cultural turn" in that decade, it was sufficient to have a life, but the discourse of marketing promoted the idea that we each needed a lifestyle, a way of defining ourselves in terms of a certain constellation of brands.

However, the notion that there was something new and epoch-making in this alleged "culturalization" of the economy has been criticized by a group of theorists forming the emergent "cultural economy" school. Instead, they argue that culture and economy are not hitherto mutually distinct, stable, and coherent macrostructures in society, but rather, they both have always been embedded in observable, analyzable institutions and practices which can not be disentangled into the cultural and the economic – that is, they constitute each other. Their refusal to accept a theoretical distinction between culture and economy leads the cultural economy school into a predominantly empirical approach which seeks to observe and understand how the economy is "performed" culturally. It follows that if the cultural and the economic can only be observed in actual empirical situations, neither culture nor the economy can overshadow the other. Liz McFall explains this standpoint in relation to advertising (though not branding as such): "The cultural is not something that intervenes in economic processes; rather it is constitutive of them. … the approach advocated here is to focus on the performance of advertising as a *constituent material practice*. … In as far as they exist at all, 'culture' and 'economy' exist in concrete instances of material practice" (2004, 86, emphasis in original).

A further contribution from the cultural economy school is its introduction of "actor-network theory." Derived from science and technology studies, actor-network theory gives explicit recognition to the role of objects in bringing about social change. Although often controversial, this "agency of nonhumans" notion is quite comprehensible if we consider how certain objects have facilitated the mass transition from being served by the grocer to serving oneself by selecting brands in the supermarket: the shopping cart or trolley most obviously, but also packaging, display shelving, and refrigerator installations. More abstractly, Lury (2004) asserts that the brand is an "object," actively mediating between supply and demand as a kind of interface or platform which uses information to frame exchange across time and space.

Like Lury, McFall also explicitly draws upon actor-network theory, specifically the work of Michel Callon on markets, and identifies the role of information in the "reflexive attachment" with which consumers perceive and grade differences between products, a process in which the brand is central as a "complex socio-technical device" (McFall 2004, 83). Similarly, Callon is also cited by Arvidsson in his account of how markets are brought into being, and once again, information is seen to provide an interface. For Arvidsson, ultimately, branding is a set of relations "between things, people, images, texts and physical and informational environments" (2006, 126). He stresses that the brand is more than the goods or services which are offered under its sign; the brand transcends the product to become its "context of consumption" (Arvidsson 2005, 244).

In brief, with the cultural economy school, we arrive at a more complex and relational conception of branding which goes beyond the sterile dualism, however conceived, of economy / culture, culture / economy, and directs our attention to the actual interaction between brand owners and their prospective consumers in the marketplace. Furthermore, particular attention is given to the active role of information, which includes not just the marketing campaigns of the brand owners, but the knowledge, emotional associations, and perceptions of a brand which consumers bring to the market. The cultural economy approach thus offers a significant advance over traditional Marxist analysis in two related ways: it escapes both the trap of economic determinism, and also the "cultural authority model" derived from it; that is, the belief that the brand-owning corporations have omnipotent control over "how people think and feel through branded commercial products" (Holt 2002, 71).

Branding and National Cultures

Thus, rather than the "cultural dopes" of past theory, consumers are now seen to "use goods productively; they use them to construct social relations, shared emotions, personal identity or forms of community" (Arvidsson 2006, 18). Nevertheless, this does not amount to the all-out victory of the sovereign consumer. There is a hegemonic struggle going on in which marketers constantly seek to engage and mobilize the "meaning-making activity" of consumers with their branding (Arvidsson 2005, 237). A whole range of marketing practices, such as the current vogue for "experiential marketing" (Pine and Gilmore 1999), are deployed by corporations in order to build brand image and hence equity, but such "brand management" has its limits. It should not be thought that a certain kind of image can be arbitrarily imposed upon a brand by manipulative brand managers, for they must work with what is already in the culture. Arvidsson goes so far as to suggest that consumers collectively have "a high degree of autonomy" in this regard, or at least that consumer perceptions are "beyond the direct control of capital" (2005, 242). For example, the universally positive associations enjoyed by Rolls-Royce is not something which has been implanted by years of active marketing, but rests upon popular cultural notions of quality, design, and engineering.

The images and narratives of branding can be powerful vehicles of myth, in the ideological sense used by Roland Barthes in his classic analysis of the new Citroën, "consumed in image ... by a whole population" (1973, 88). Douglas Holt argues that the most important of such myths, as in this case, "concern how citizens are linked to the nation-building project," especially when these myths motivate and are performed in acts of everyday consumption of particular brands that encourage the consumer to identify with the "populist world" of the nation (Holt 2004, 57–8). In this sense, national identity can be taken to refer to things as well as persons. Drawing on actor-network theory, Tim Edensor asserts that "things are partly understood as belonging to nations," and observes that "mass manufactured commodities are associated with particular nations, also often carrying mythic associations that connote particular qualities and forms of expertise" (Edensor 2002, 103–5). More than a kind of broad "reputational capital" (O'Shaughnessy and O'Shaughnessy 2000, 59) which nations have for their goods – Italian style, Germanic quality – or national comparative advantage in a generic sense – the Scots make whisky, the French make wine – this insight can be applied to particular brands. To take Edensor's own examples, the Swedes have their Volvo, while the British have, on the one hand, the Aston Martin, yet on the other, the Mini (2002, 118–37). These associations are symbolic, not actual – it is beside the point that Volvo is now owned by Ford, and Mini by BMW, and given that automotive production has become highly globalized, there is no knowing exactly where in the world any of these "national" brands are actually produced.

When we talk about national identity, we not only mean the identity of the nation in relation to other nations, but also the identity of those persons who see themselves as belonging to the nation, and for whom that is a dimension of their personal identity. In this second sense, and in line with the view that consumers make meaningful choices for themselves, it can be argued that they choose national belonging rather than have it imposed on them, an allegiance which they express in making purchases of certain brands which are represented to them as embedded in an everyday, popular national culture that they identify with as their own; "it is in consumerism that we most express our sense of social belonging. ... Culture is the society we build with our brands" (Davidson 1992, 124).

While it is difficult to generalize across all product types and all segments in any given national market, suffice it to say that while there are certain international brands which are bought as such and valued for their own sake, such as Rolex, Louis Vuitton, and other prestigious designer labels, other brands have their equity grounded in an established association with the nation. Tim Edensor goes so far as to suggest that the demonstrable demand for "certain exemplary national products" (2002, 113) may be motivated by a desire to stabilize identity in a turbulent world: "In the face of globalization commonly shared things anchor people to place. ... The ability of things to connote shared histories is potent" (116). In the United States, the kind of person who flies the stars and stripes on their lawn will have a Chevrolet rather than a Toyota in the driveway; some

Britons traveling abroad might feel more secure when flying British Airways; while Australian backpackers find their comfort in a jar of Vegemite. Thus, in addition to whatever utility branded goods may have, and however much they may mark our social distinction as individuals, they also can express our belonging to a nation.

Modern nation-states have their own interests to pursue in promoting images of national unity and belonging, and in cultivating support for their policies at home and abroad. They do so increasingly as a form of branding – Cool Britannia (McLaughlin 2002), India Shining (Bijoor 2004), and Australian Made/True Blue (Australian Made 2003) are recent examples. That is, the nation itself now presents itself as a brand, both internally and externally. Internally, in the interests of governance and as the custodian of the national culture with which it legitimizes its authority, the nation-state addresses its citizens as members of the "imagined community" of the nation, and hence as participants in its supposed "deep horizontal comradeship" (Anderson 1983, 6). However fraught and tenuous national cultures have become in the era of global flows, cultural belonging continues to be associated with place and nationhood (Morley 2000). Externally, many nations now cultivate a brand identity, each seeking to position itself vis-à-vis other nations in the global marketplace, competing for trade, tourism, and investment, or protecting the unique "nation of origin" status of their exports (Anholt 2000, Moor 2007).

Tourism is an instructive case. As O'Shaughnessy and O'Shaughnessy point out, the nation is "awkward" as a brand because "there is a general level of ignorance of countries other than one's own" (2000, 57). While on one hand, this ignorance allows national tourism authorities and promoters a certain latitude in how they selectively shape the brand image of their nation, they are also constrained by the stereotypes which are already established in their target markets: the United States as the country we see in Hollywood films; Britain as a nation of historical and cultural heritage; Australia as a frontier land of desert, bush, and beaches. Yet from a branding point of view, the images that people have of other nations are more than just stereotypes of this or that country. Brands acquire their meaning from their position relative to their competitors, so rather than being condemned for the ignorance which they no doubt represent, stereotypes need to be understood in relation to each other, collectively forming a system in which each nation is assigned a position. This position can change, but any change may thus require a repositioning of the others, so in practice it is difficult to move position. The broader point is that national identities, like personal identities, are relational; their meaning derives from where they stand in comparison with others.

For example, an expensive international campaign launched in 2004 which sought to cast Australia in "a different light" with an aesthetic, reflective, and personalized approach, was soon terminated when tourist agencies overseas objected that they could not convince prospects to make the trip with such an unfamiliar, abstracted image of Australia- they all wanted the beaches – that was what Australia was about. A country can claim a new position for itself within the total system of national identities, yet like love or social status, position is something which cannot be demanded, only given by others.

To the extent that "the market rather than the state has become the key reference point for national identity" (Foster 1999, cited in Edensor 2002, 111), the "official nationalism" of the nation-state is now infused with what has been called the "commercial nationalism" of the market (James 1983, 79), which also addresses people in their capacity as members of the nation, not as citizens but as consumers, calling upon the same "trust, affect and shared meanings" involved in national belonging (Arvidsson 2005, 236). This ascendance of the values of the market over those of the nation-state also entails a shift from the formal, official markers of nationhood toward those that are more grounded in popular culture and its commercialization by the media. Indeed, more than "print capitalism," it has been commercial television, in its dual role of nation-building and the forming of national markets for advertisers, which has led so many contemporary developed nations to become "imagined communities of consumption" (Foster 1991, 250). Thus, in addition to diffuse popular traditions and narratives of national belonging, and the "shared meanings" of nationhood expressed in televisual and media culture in general, branded goods, "as advertised on television" and elsewhere, also become mediators of membership of the nation.

As Robert Foster observes, "Nations, and national cultures are artifacts – continually imagined, invented, contested and transformed by the agency of individual persons, the state, and global flows of commodities" (1991, 252). We should also be aware that the global flows of persons in the form of migration, displacement, tourism, and other forms of "deterritorialization" mean that contemporary nation-states and markets alike are confronted as never before with culturally diverse and fluid populations. In these circumstances, myths of national belonging and their expression in communities of consumption also exclude at the same time as they include – the mainstream, dominant culture is affirmed, while minority cultures and subcultures are "othered." In terms of marketing and branding, minorities within a given national market mostly lack the critical mass necessary to attract the attention of marketers, although members of the same minority living in different countries, as in the case of diasporas, can form transnational markets for certain branded goods and services, Western Union for example, literally transnational in the sense of cutting across national boundaries.

Branding and Global Culture

In the "metaculture" of the "global ecumene" today (Hannerz 1996), many, perhaps most, of the brand-names that we know in our national markets are in fact those of global corporations. Interestingly, Lury points out that most of the major global brands are 50–100 years old, that is, older than most of their consumers (Lury 2004, 101). From that perspective we see that, at least in the main consumer capitalist societies, people experience certain brands just as they do their national language: brand-names and associations are an integral aspect of the complex cultural world in which each of us must learn how to function. Major brands like Coca-Cola can truly say "Always Coca-Cola" after having been part of a given culture for generations, just as McDonald's, with its happy meals and birthday parties, has secured a place in the childhood memories of those who do not remember a time when there was no McDonald's.

Importantly, however, brands extend themselves over space as well as time. These older brands have not always been household names throughout the world, and even now, they are not literally "global." Rather, such brands point proudly to a constructed, anecdotal heritage of entrepreneurism, which has taken them from modest, unlikely local origins to global scale, and even critical accounts recognize how companies like Coca-Cola have been able to extend their markets over time from, in that case, the city of Atlanta to the state of Georgia, then to the south as a region, and from that to the United States as a nation, and then to particular foreign markets, before claiming global status (McQueen 2001). On the other hand, while it may be true that many global brands have had this extended period of development, contemporary marketing structures have allowed many others to achieve global reach in a matter of decades (Frith and Mueller 2003, 1). What is striking in recent times has been the sudden rise of communication and information technology corporations, including mobile telephony companies. In the BrandZ survey of 2008, 28 of the world's top 100 brands were in this category, and with a faster growth rate than any other. Just to take the top 10, Coca-Cola and McDonald's are still there, along with General Electric and Marlboro, but Google is in first place (again), and Microsoft, China Mobile, IBM, Apple, and Nokia fill out the list. Other brands much further down in the top 100, which also have achieved global presence within a fairly short time, have more to do with contemporary leisure activities and lifestyles, such as Ikea and Starbuck's (Millward Brown Optimor 2008).

While the technology corporations can be said to be the most truly global, in the sense that information and communication technologies are both cause and effect of the global era, branding is a major means by which all global corporations maximize the advantages that accrue to them via globalization, particularly the opening up of huge new markets and licensing opportunities, and the rationalization of distribution systems (Arvidsson 2006, Holt 2002). In the case of the technology corporations, what the orthodox economists call "first mover advantage" seems to be significant, first in achieving market power in the home market, and then by pressing that advantage when entering foreign markets. In such cases, first mover advantage is about technical innovation, and the protection of that innovation against competition and imitation at home and abroad – for example, Microsoft's dominance in operating systems and Google's pre-eminence in commercializing Internet search. In such cases, branding is less important than other forms of intellectual property, namely technology patents, but corporations have found it difficult to wield these against competitors in particular foreign markets. Thus Microsoft battles rampant piracy of its software in China, to take the most significant case, while China's Baidu completely overwhelms Google in the search market. There are many factors involved here, including regulatory ones, but some may be cultural, given that there are other major culturally distant markets where Google also lags behind national corporations, for instance, Japan, Korea, and Russia (Waters 2008).

The strategic use of branding and the handling of cultural differences is more clear-cut and established in the case of traditional corporations like Coca-Cola and McDonald's, and the FMCG giants like Procter & Gamble and Unilever. As noted, many of these expanded beyond their North American or European domestic markets several decades ago, and have become most experienced in managing their brands in culturally alien markets. Even so, they made some of the same cultural gaffes with brand-names which later became common with the high tide of international corporate expansion in the 1960s. While many of the stories about these are inaccurate, one which does seem to be true is that when "Coca-Cola" was first transliterated into Chinese characters in the 1920s by its distributors (not the corporation itself, they insist), it meant "bite the wax tadpole" when sounded out. A more contemporary one which can be confirmed is that the Mitsubishi Pajero is called a Montero in Spanish-speaking countries, where a *pajero* is a "wanker" or a "jerk." Even within the same linguistic world, problems can arise: XXXX ("Fourex") is a brand of beer in Australia, but of condoms in the United States (Ricks 1999). Clearly, if not even the meaning of a brand-name can be carried intact across national borders, then its brand image has no chance of going along with it.

This and other kinds of experience with cultural and linguistic barriers undermined the enthusiasm for "standardization," which had been built up during the 1980s in certain quarters among marketers and their agencies. Standardization was an attractive ideal to corporations, because it seemed to offer a consistent global image for a brand, as well as economies of scale in having just "one sight, one sound, one sell" around the world (Mattelart 1991, 55). However, while this might have worked for the Marlboro cowboy, there were some spectacular failures – not necessarily to do with branding and culture as such, but also complications due to national regulations and problems with distribution systems in the target markets. Product type emerged as a factor as well – airlines could standardize their campaigns, but coffee manufacturers like Nestlé knew better than to even try.

By the 1990s, the buzzword became "glocalization," or global localization, meaning an adaptive strategy in which the marketer seeks a practical balance between the organizational and economic advantages of standardization, and the necessities of responding to cultural and other differences between markets

(Herbig 1998), a notion which takes account of the consumer's cultural realities. The degree to which marketers are prepared to glocalize varies enormously, once again, depending on the product, but also upon the target market and its distribution. While there are cases of tailoring brand advertising for different cities in the same national market, more often if the same campaign will serve for "country clusters" and even a whole world region, then marketers will not glocalize any more specifically than they consider necessary: this is "strategic regionalism" (Sinclair and Wilken 2009).

The penetration of global brands, both in the national markets themselves and the media that carry their advertising, has generated a considerable critical academic literature and even debate in world forums over the last several decades. While the "cultural imperialism" critique of the late 1960s has morphed into fears of cultural homogenization in the global era, other theorists have drawn attention to the multiple "local" adaptations which global cultural forms undergo, thus counterposing homogenization to heterogenization (Sinclair 2007). Interestingly, the academic debate between theorists of homogenization and heterogenization runs parallel to that just noted in marketing, between the advocates of standardization and those who favor adaptive "multidomestic" strategies. And just as the latter debate has found a consensus in the middle ground of glocalization, the theorists are coming to recognize a process of "hybridization" in which consumer markets and media audiences consciously negotiate between the global and the local (McMillin 2007), once again conceding much more agency to consumers than was ever allowed for in the "cultural authority" model of traditional Marxism (Holt 2002).

However, it is the marketers who are engaged upon this complex and contradictory middle ground in practical terms. For example, Watson's (1997) study of McDonald's in Asia is instructive in showing not only how the corporation has glocalized the menu items in accordance with the tastes of the various nations of the region, but also how the outlets have to manage the tension which exists between their need to discipline customers to the ways of eating fast food, Western style, and the customers' desire to spend time in the stores for a whole range of social purposes. This question of "consumer discipline" is a major issue, even when the corporations are seeking actively to bridge cultural differences. Indeed, there is a sense in which brand management takes on a kind of teaching function, which is most certainly ideologically loaded, a form of induction into modern consumer capitalism. Even in the West, McDonald's has redefined "restaurant" to mean a place where you serve your own table, eat with your hands, and clean up after yourself. This kind of discipline is about the acquisition of the cultural competencies associated with consumption, which could mean how to use a supermarket, or just learning how to interpret unfamiliar visual language in television commercials (Wang 2003, 252).

When what were then called the "multinational" corporations entered the "underdeveloped nations" of the "Third World" in the 1960s, those markets typically were divided between a small wealthy elite who could easily afford branded goods, and the great mass of people who could not. In a process dubbed as "the internationalization of the internal market," the multinationals set up subsidiaries to manufacture their brands for both the "primary" (elite) and "secondary" (mass) markets. For the latter, cheap branded products in small packages were made and widely distributed, and backed with advertising, for example, Maggi soup cubes made by Nestlé in African and Latin American countries were considered a marketing success of this kind (Sinclair 1987). As one contemporary advocate enthused, "In what is called its pioneering phase, advertising's function is not to rob sales from competitors, or gull the unsophisticated, but to teach new consumption behaviour. Western European/North American-style advertising has demonstrated itself as an enormously effective teacher of new ways of living" (Stridsberg 1974, 77). In more recent decades, there has developed a discourse about the expanding "middle class" in countries such as China and India. However, the bulk of the populations of such countries live outside the main urban areas which have been incorporated into global modernity, so that while the residents of Shanghai or Mumbai might grow up in brand-aware environments, their rural and provincial counterparts do not. Nor do they have the same purchasing power. Consequently, they tend to exhibit a stubbornly premodern inclination to buy goods on the basis of their price and reliability, rather than the kind of brand image cultivated by advertising. That is, they do not necessarily see products in terms of brands, and because their purchasing power is limited, they have very little experience of brands. One strategic corporate response to this form of consumer resistance is the "downward brand extension"; that is, offering more cheaply formulated versions of their premium brands (Doctoroff 2005). This strategy enables the advertiser to give prospective consumers an affordable product with which they may experience the brand, and perhaps thus to extend consumer discipline over them as they learn to respond to the aura of the brand name.

However, it is worth mentioning that although global FMCG conglomerates like Procter & Gamble and Unilever appear listed among the biggest advertisers in China and India in *Advertising Age's* Global Marketers Report for 2008, there continues to be also a strong presence of Chinese and Indian brands, notably for traditional herbal and ayurvedic medicines, reflecting their respective cultures. Furthermore, although dominance of such lists by FMCG marketers tends to be typical of less developed national markets, there are significant advertisers in more sophisticated categories. As noted above, one of China's biggest advertisers, China Mobile, made it into the BrandZ top 10 for 2008, while one of the biggest marketers in India, Tata Group, acquired the prestigious Jaguar and Land Rover brands from Ford that same year. On such indications, global brands are no longer the exclusive properties of the usual suspects, the major corporations based in North America and Europe.

Note

This chapter is an output from a program of research under ARC Discovery - Project, DP0556419, "Globalisation and the Media in Australia," funded 2005–9. The author gratefully acknowledges the ARC's financial support, and research assistance provided to the program by Dr Rowan Wilken.

References

Aaker, D. A. (1991) *Managing Brand Equity: Capitalizing on the Value of a Brand Name.* The Free Press, New York.

Anderson, B. (1983) *Imagined Communities: Reflections on the Origin and Spread of Nationalism.* Verso, London.

Anholt, S. (2000) *Another One Bites the Grass: Making Sense of International Advertising.* John Wiley, New York.

Appadurai, A. (ed.) (1986) *The Social Life of Things: Commodities in Cultural Perspective.* Cambridge University Press, Cambridge, UK.

Arvidsson, A. (2005) Brands: A critical perspective. *Journal of Consumer Culture,* 5(2), 235–58.

Arvidsson, A. (2006) *Brands: Meaning and Value in Media Culture.* Routledge, London.

Australian Made. (2003) Together again – Australian Made and True Blue celebrate 21 years. August 26. Online at www.australianmade.com.au/news/6944.asp (accessed May 22, 2007).

Barthes, R. (1973) *Mythologies.* Paladin, St Albans, UK.

Baudrillard, J. (1981) *For a Critique of the Political Economy of the Sign.* Telos Press, St Louis, MO.

Bijoor, H. (2004) Branding the govt of India. *The Hindu Business Line,* Internet edition, February 19. Online at www.thehindubusinessline.com/catalyst/2004/02/19/stories/2004021900180400.htm (accessed May 22, 2007).

Davidson, M.P. (1992) *The Consumerist Manifesto: Advertising in Postmodern Times.* Routledge, London.

Doctoroff, T. (2005) *Billions: Selling to the New Chinese Consumer.* Palgrave Macmillan, New York.

Douglas, M. and Isherwood, B. (1979) *The World of Goods: Towards an Anthropology of Consumption.* Allen Lane, London.

Edensor, T. (2002) *National Identity, Popular Culture and Everyday Life.* Berg, Oxford.

Featherstone, M. (1987) Lifestyle and consumer culture. *Theory, Culture & Society,* 4, 55–70.

Foster, R. J. (1991) Making national cultures in the global ecumene. *Annual Review of Anthropology,* 20, 235–60.

Foster, R. (1999) The commercial construction of new nations. *Journal of Material Culture,* 4(3), 263–82.

Frith, K. T. and Mueller, B. (2003) *Advertising and Societies: Global Issues.* Peter Lang, New York.

Gardner, B. B. and Levy, S. J. (1955) The product and the brand. *Harvard Business Review, 33* (March-April), 33–9.

Hannerz, U. (1996) *Transnational Connections: Culture, People, Places.* Routledge, London.

Herbig, P. A. (1998) *Handbook of Cross-Cultural Marketing.* The Haworth Press, New York.

Holt, D. B. (2002) Why do brands cause trouble? A dialectical theory of consumer culture and branding. *Journal of Consumer Research,* 29 (June), 70–90.

Holt, D. B. (2004) *How Brands Become Icons: The Principles of Cultural Branding.* Harvard Business School Publishing Corporation, Boston, MA.

James, P. (1983) Australia in the corporate image: A new nationalism. *Arena,* 63, 65–106.

Klein, N. (2001) *No Logo.* Flamingo, London.

Lash, S. and Urry, J. (1994) *Economies of Signs and Space.* Sage, London.

Lury, C. (2004) *Brands: The Logos of the Global Economy.* Routledge, London.

Mattelart, A. (1991) *Advertising International: The Privatisation of Public Space.* Routledge, London.

McFall, L. (2004) *Advertising: A Cultural Economy.* Sage, London.

McLaughlin, E. (2002) Re-branding Britain. *Open2.net.* Online at http://www.open2.net/society/socialchange/new_brit_coolbritainnia.html (accessed October 4, 2010).

McMillin, D. C. (2007) *International Media Studies.* Blackwell, Malden, MA.

McQueen, H. (2001) *The Essence of Capitalism.* Hodder, Sydney.

Millward Brown Optimor (2008) Press Release. Online at http://www.millwardbrown.com/Sites/mbOptimor/Ideas/BrandZTop100/BrandZTop100.aspx (accessed October 11, 2010).

Moor, L. (2007) *The Rise of Brands.* Berg, Oxford.

Morley, D. (2000) *Home Territories: Media, Mobility and Identity.* Routledge, London.

Mosco, V. (1996) *The Political Economy of Communication.* Sage, London.

O'Shaughnessy, J. and O'Shaughnessy, N. J. (2000) Treating the nation as a brand: Some neglected issues. *Journal of Macromarketing,* 20 (1), 56–64.

Perry, N. (1998) *Hyperreality and Global Culture.* London: Routledge.

Pine, B. J. and Gilmore, J. H. (1999) *The Experience Economy: Work is Theatre and Every Business a Stage.* Harvard Business School Press, Boston, MA.

Ricks, D. A. (1999) *Blunders in International Business.* Blackwell, Oxford.

Sandler, D. M. and Shani, D. (1992) Brand globally but advertise locally?: An empirical investigation. *International Marketing Review,* 9 (4), 18–31.

Sinclair, J. G. (1987) *Images Incorporated: Advertising as Industry and Ideology.* Croom Helm, London.

Sinclair, J. G. (2007) Cultural globalization and American empire. In: Murdock, G. and Wasko, J. (eds), *Media in the Age of Marketization.* Hampton Press, Cresskill, NJ, pp. 131–50.

Sinclair, J. G. and Wilken, R. (2009) Strategic regionalization in marketing campaigns: Beyond the standardization/glocalization debate. *Continuum: Journal of Media and Cultural Studies,* 23(2), 147–57.

Stridsberg, A. (1974) Can advertising benefit developing countries? *Business and Society Review,* 11, 76–7.

Wang, J. (2003) Framing Chinese advertising: Some industry perspectives on the production of culture. *Continuum: Journal of Media and Cultural Studies,* 17(3), 247–60.

Waters, R. (2008) Google still struggling to conquer outposts. *Financial Times,* September 16.

Watson, J. L. (ed.) (1997) *Golden Arches East: McDonald's in East Asia*. Stanford University Press, Palo Alto, CA.
Wernick, A. (1991) *Promotional Culture*. Sage, London.

Suggestions for Further Reading

du Gay, P. and Pryke, M. (eds) (2002) *Cultural Economy*. Sage, London.
Howes, D. (ed.) (1996) *Cross-Cultural Consumption: Global Markets, Local Realities*. Routledge, London.
Wang, J. (2008) The power and limits of branding in national image communication in global society. *Journal of International Communication*, 14(2), 9–24.

11

Liberal Fictions
The Public–Private Dichotomy in Media Policy

Andrew Calabrese and Colleen Mihal

Introduction

Following the administrations of British Prime Minister Margaret Thatcher (1979–90) and US President Ronald Reagan (1981–9), the belief that there is no alternative to neoliberal political-economic theory and practice became widespread (Harvey 2005). The collapse of the Soviet Union somehow lent credence to that belief, which was reinforced by triumphalist proclamations about the inevitability of a liberal-democratic global order (Fukuyama 1989). Since then, a number of globally significant events have called into question the merits of these beliefs, not least of which have been the uprisings against neoliberal economic policies through mass mobilizations in many parts of the world. Then al Qaeda attacks in 2001 against human and architectural symbols of the global domination of US financial and military interests, as well as the more recent crisis of the US-led global financial industry, have heightened distrust of the values of neoliberalism that have been forcefully championed by US leaders worldwide. These events also have contributed to efforts in many countries to renew social policy principles and priorities that were discredited and discarded through assaults on welfare state policies and the imposition of structural adjustment policies on countries of the global south by the World Bank and the International Monetary Fund. Today there is widespread intellectual and political skepticism about the ability of the market to self-regulate and to respond effectively to the full range of basic human needs, including food, shelter, health care and education.

The current global financial crisis, from which even optimistic forecasts predict it will take several years to recover, has dramatically illustrated liberalism's failure

The Handbook of Political Economy of Communications, First Edition.
Edited by Janet Wasko, Graham Murdock, and Helena Sousa.

to deliver on its promise that markets can effectively self-regulate, let alone be constituted by and reflect moral consciousness. But there is irony in this, because while economic (neo)liberalism has disastrously displayed its limitations, it is less clear that some of the core values of political liberalism can or should be so easily discarded. This, of course, raises the question of which liberalism has presumably triumphed and, more recently, failed. *The Palgrave Dictionary of Economics* cites certain core values that define liberalism, namely, the rule of law, due process, the inviolability of the person, and the rights of free expression (Dahrendorf 1987). As to what priority should be given to ordering these values, this seems a matter for disagreement and debate, and *Palgrave* notes that "A certain tension between liberal thought and the notion of natural rights is unmistakable" (Dahrendorf 1987, 173). In 1690, a time when liberalism was first being shaped as a political and economic project, John Locke argued that, first and foremost, the role of civil government is the protection of property rights: "The great and chief end, therefore, of men uniting into commonwealths, and putting themselves under government, is the preservation of their property; to which in the state of Nature there are many things wanting" (Locke 1924, 180). As others have observed since the time Locke wrote, there are ways in which giving property rights primacy above other rights results in the denial of fundamental rights that historically have been associated with liberal democracy. In Robert Dahl's *A Preface to Economic Democracy*, he defines "economic liberty" as subordinating the right to self-government to the right to private property, whereas under "political liberty" the right to property is subordinated to the right to self-government (Dahl 1985, 162–3).

The dichotomy of "public" and "private" lies at the foundation of liberal political thought. Immanuel Kant invoked it when he argued that human enlightenment depends on the "public use of reason." For Kant, an enlightened society depends on the use of publicity, by which he meant the opportunity for a flow of ideas that is unencumbered by domination and fear. Kant, in 1784, emphasized the importance of disagreement and debate in public, which he acknowledged sometimes requires courage as the alternative to cowering in private, or simply tending to one's private interests (Kant 1991). For Kant, the public sphere is the place in which private interests can be reconciled with a moral view of the world that insists upon treating individuals and relationships as ends in themselves, and not simply as means to other ends (Kant 1991, 45). Such a view imposes a public-mindedness that is missing when we justify our actions strictly according to material self-interest. For Kant, the principle of publicity was the proper foundation of a legal order. And for Kant, the ends we seek should not be determined by moral dogma but rather they should be justified through and judged by *public reason*. Jürgen Habermas embraced this ideal in his historical reconstruction of the idea of "the public sphere" (Habermas 1989). In between and since, many writers have defended the value of "public reason" and "the principle of publicity" as necessary for enabling democratic life to flourish (Rawls 1996, Splichal 2002a, 2002b).

Unfortunately, Kant did not concern himself with the requirements that would make effective participation in the public sphere equally possible for all. His theory of a liberal public sphere fails to adequately account for the role of power, privilege, and competence (which also is largely a function of privilege) in differentiating among those members of society who are more and less likely to be effective in exercising their formal right to reason in public. Unlike Kant, who neglected how material interests might present barriers to effective participation in the public sphere, Karl Marx demonstrated the historical limits of this liberal ideal. In 1843, Marx lamented the failure of the French Revolution to deliver the "rights of man and citizen" to everyone. Instead, Marx noted, the rights of citizenship were in fact conditional upon one's membership in the bourgeoisie. That is, one had to be a property owner, according to the law, in order to enjoy the rights of political participation. Being a human being with basic human needs was not a sufficient precondition to justify political inclusion (Marx 1978b). It took the rise of the postwar modern welfare state to formally justify the provision for basic human requirements as a matter of social right, thus enabling the full exercise of formally guaranteed, but practically inaccessible, political rights (Marshall 1950). Were he alive, Marx no doubt would have viewed the capitalist welfare state as a social advancement beyond the cruel conditions of the industrial capitalism of his day, just as he viewed the social conditions he witnessed as an advancement beyond those of feudal society (Jameson 1996). To be sure, Marx's critique of the French declaration was not a dismissal of liberal rights. Rather, he was lamenting the gap between political liberalism's promise and the limitations placed upon it through its subordination to capitalism. In Marx's early writings, he was concerned explicitly with the rights of the individual in relation to the political community, and with how capitalism thwarts the fulfillment of the promise of liberal citizenship. But what Marx valued, and what he found to be denied when the rights of private property, market exchange, and capital accumulation are given primacy over all other rights, is that the right to participate in the political community is stunted and distorted (Bernstein 1991, Marx 1978a). Similarly, C. B. MacPherson's critique of liberalism, sustained over his life's work, was an attempt to uphold certain core liberal values about political freedom that get lost when economic interests and private property rights serve as the primary means for defining political rights (MacPherson 1973, 1962). But as we have seen with the rise of neoliberal theory and practice, the social rights that were secured by modern welfare states – the rights of social citizenship – have been shown to be reversible (Turner 1992).

Today, claims that neoliberalism has lost its grip on the global economic order are commonplace, the implications of which are that the moral groundwork now exists to again secure social rights (Wallerstein 2008). Again, however, such confidence may be premature, as there is no clear evidence that the many problems related to the outsourcing of vital state functions to the voluntary associations of "civil society" – or the move from a social contract between states and citizens to a dependence on voluntarism, charity, and philanthropy to answer to basic human needs – will be altered or rectified, despite disillusionment with neoliberalism's failures (Fraser and Gordon 1992, Wood 1990). This is not simply a problem for the United States, the bellwether and testing ground for so many of neoliberalism's most radical ideas. Neoliberalism's failures, particularly the *harm* it has brought to so many people throughout the world (Frank 2000, Giroux 2004), illustrate the distortion that unrestrained economic power brings to the fulfillment of the promise of political liberalism. The unwarranted triumphalist proclamation of Fukuyama – that liberal values have prevailed – neglects many things, not least of which is one of liberalism's core values: the belief that individual freedom should know no restraint unless its expression brings *harm to others*. This value, often referred to as "the harm principle," is famously articulated in one of the most famous defenses of liberalism, J.S. Mill's essay "On Liberty":

> The object of this essay is to assert one very simple principle, as entitled to govern absolutely the dealings of society with the individual in the way of compulsion and control ... That principle is that the sole end for which mankind are warranted, individually or collectively, in interfering with the liberty of action of any of their number is self-protection. That the only purpose for which power can be rightfully exercised over any member of a civilized community, against his will, is to prevent harm to others. His own good, either physical or moral, is not a sufficient warrant. (Mill 1974, 68–9; see also Feinberg 1984, Smolla 1992)

There is no mistaking that structural decision making that rests in the hands of, or is significantly influenced by, ostensibly "private" interests, can and often does produce widespread harms, as the effects of the recent global financial crisis demonstrates. Likewise, inegalitarian and corrupt controls over the infrastructures of communication are significant means through which the prospects for democracy are threatened.

Knowing well that control of publicity about important and even potentially harmful information can be vital to maintaining social order, Margaret Thatcher declared in 1985 that airplane hijackers who had taken hostages ought to be deprived of the "oxygen of publicity," as publicity was what they sought through their actions.[1] The analogy here is not that average citizens are potential terrorists, against whom governments and complicit media are waging or should wage deliberate informational warfare. Rather, the "oxygen of publicity" of which average citizens are deprived on a daily basis is the basic information and knowledge needed to make effective use of the political institutions that are their right to understand, question, and transform. More mundane than restrictive measures to thwart political violence, government and a complicit media have demonstrated the capacity and the will to contribute to narrowing and shrinking the public's political imagination and effective engagement (Calabrese 2004, 2005). That is the profound social harm that concerns us in this chapter. Our underlying assumption below is that, in the service of the healthiest possible public sphere of a free and democratic society, the promotion of the oxygen of publicity of the widest sort is the highest, and necessary, calling of media and telecommunication services that have been granted the opportunity to serve the public interest.

In this chapter, we examine how a core feature of liberal theory – the distinction between "public" and "private" – actually functions in practice, specifically within the media and telecommunications industries. As the discussion below of specific media policies and practices illustrate, the unraveling of ideological distinctions between public and private – what Norberto Bobbio refers to as "the publicization of the private" and "the privatization of the public" (Bobbio 1989a, 15) – did not happen suddenly, and it is unlikely that the legal (and extralegal) maneuvering that led to this condition will be easily undone or brought under democratic control. What follows is a discussion of some of the lingering causes for concern about this condition.

Privatization of Media

In the late twentieth century, media privatization accelerated worldwide. The term "privatization" refers to the transfer of property and/or operations from state or public ownership and control into private hands. Among the principal reasons given to justify privatization is that private ownership and operation will make a company perform more efficiently because its managers will be financially obligated to make the company accountable to shareholders. By contrast, government operations are often criticized for being inefficient, corrupt, and insufficiently responsive to the interests of the taxpayers who fund them. Advocates of privatization argue that the competitive environment of private industry fosters greater innovation, and that it pressures companies to maintain lower costs of doing business.

Privatizations of vital public services have become a lightning-rod topic in recent decades, most notably in countries where economic and political institutions have undergone radical structural transformations, for example in Central and Eastern Europe, and in Latin America. Following the collapse of the Soviet Union, gas and oil industries were privatized and then became the focus of corruption scandals and civic unrest as former government officials and Communist Party leaders became wealthy "oligarchs" through massive stock acquisitions. Elsewhere, recent attempts to privatize water services have led to public outrage and riots, most notably in Bolivia in 2000. Government efforts to privatize universal health care services, education, and other social services have also led to significant debate and protest in several countries throughout the world. In many poor countries, privatizations have taken place as a form of "structural adjustment" in response to pressures from the International Monetary Fund and the World Bank in exchange for loans.

The government of the United States has been in the global vanguard in promoting a political-economic ideology that favors the privatization of state and public services. In its foreign policy initiatives, in bilateral and multilateral agreements, and as an influential model for other governments, the US government premises its global policy agenda on firm beliefs in the value of market self-regulation, liberalization, and privatization, beliefs which been reproduced, sometimes with disastrous effects, in many countries. In ways that are seen as extreme both within the country and throughout the rest of the world, the US government subcontracts with private companies for the performance of sensitive government functions. Hundreds of prisons, particularly in the southern and western parts of the country, are run by large for-profit corporations, and the US military is supported by many private enterprises, from defense contractors who design and build high-technology weapon systems, to "private military companies" who provide such support services as security forces, interrogation of prisoners, and training. Many of the basic infrastructures and vital services in the United States are built and/or owned by private corporations, including telecommunications. United States domestic policy historically has favored private ownership of media and telecommunications companies, and has tended to subordinate "public interest" regulation to the imperatives of profitable private ownership and control. The global market power of US media and telecommunications companies, combined with the high-level participation of official US representatives at global trade, investment, and policy summits, have made the United States and its media industries a formidable presence, which has been an ongoing cause of tension and controversy.

The nature and extent to which private enterprise can be made to supplant state and public services seems to be unlimited, and the rationales and processes of privatization are especially relevant for understanding the economic and political history of the telecommunications and mass media industries. Of particular significance is the fact that media institutions, technologies, and policies are widely considered vital to sustaining public life. In the case of the United States, the media or, at an earlier period in US history, "the press," have been given the privileged position of being the only industry with explicit constitutional protection (through the First Amendment). On a global basis, there is strong and widespread opposition to treating media and cultural industries as any other industry, such as steel, coffee, or coal. Instead, the governments of most countries in the world view media and culture as exceptional because of the role they play in sustaining public life and culture. The argument in favor of such a "cultural exception" is in part a response to the threats posed by global media giants who dwarf most nationally based media industries, threatening them with extinction in the absence of governmental intervention. Although media privatization is on the rise worldwide, most governments tend to enable such arrangements while also attempting to sustain the viability of their media industries through import quotas and subsidies.

Media industries have been privatized in many countries throughout the world for the past several decades, but the pace has accelerated significantly over the past 20 or so years, particularly in postsocialist Central and Eastern Europe, following the end of military dictatorships in Latin America, and after apartheid in South Africa. Liberal-democratic welfare states in Western Europe and other parts of the world have also embraced media privatization. In the United States, the radio and television broadcasting system as a whole is overwhelmingly commercial, and the US system of public broadcasting, especially television, historically has been small, economically weak, and buffeted by the changing media marketplace and shifts in the political agendas of the legislative and executive branches of the government. Consequently, public broadcasting in the United States generally lacks influence and importance as a vital stage for American culture and politics. Historic resistance to socialism in the United States has provided an ideological framework for denying government support to noncommercial media.

By comparison, in many other countries, public service broadcasting has been articulated through government interventions, with reference to liberal democratic ideals, affirming a role for public leaders to develop and sustain political and cultural discourse through the media. Such systems have been well-funded and insulated from political pressure (for example, through license fees rather than direct government appropriations), and have been much more central to national public life. The United Kingdom's BBC, Germany's ARD, Japan's NHK, Canada's CBC, and Australia's ABC are among the systems that serve as public service models, particularly because of their commitments to innovative quality programming, and to the insulation of programming from direct government and market influence. However, due to pressures from global competition and the rapid increase in the availability of new media sources, even where they are well established and relatively successful, public service broadcasters (PSBs) have found themselves having to compete for audiences in an unfamiliar commercial and multichannel media landscape. One result has been that PSBs have had to adapt at a faster pace to technological change, and they have had to develop business models that enable them to compete with commercial networks. Such changes have led to concerns about the demise of the distinct identity and mission of public service broadcasting. Although not technically privatized, numerous PSBs have taken on more characteristics of private, commercial broadcasters, including paid advertising.

Perhaps even more dramatic than the changes to broadcasting have been the trends in privatizations of telecommunications infrastructures and the convergence of mass media and telecommunications infrastructure ownership. In the past 20 years, many governments around the world have privatized their PTTs (postal, telegraph, and telephone companies), resulting in numerous subsequent mergers with and acquisitions by larger foreign companies. As well, foreign telecommunications firms, particularly from the United States, entered new markets in which privatizations and market liberalization occurred. For example, US cable and telephone companies invested heavily to set up new landline and wireless infrastructures in postsocialist Central and Eastern Europe, in partnership with PTTs and newly privatized companies, and as separate competitors.

In the United States, the telegraph and telephone industries historically have been privately owned, with little exception of note, whereas PTTs throughout most of the world have functioned as government-owned and operated agencies. Despite the fact of private ownership, under heavy government regulation to control prices and ensure quality of service, the US telephone industry functioned in many ways like a PTT. Prior to the break-up of AT&T, the national monopoly controlled all aspects of telephone service, functioning as a single company that provided local and long-distance service, and that designed and manufactured all equipment used throughout the network. Through a nationwide system of cost-averaging, AT&T's revenues from profitable subsidiaries could be used to subsidize its more costly operations.

When a federal court decided in 1982 that the AT&T monopoly should come to an end, the results were very much like a privatization. The subsequent break-up was intended to promote a more competitive, innovative, and open network environment. In 1984, AT&T was divested of its local telephone companies, leaving the parent company in possession of its profitable long distance and manufacturing businesses, and also leaving it less restricted from entering into new lines of business. The break-up contributed to the destabilization of familiar distinctions between telecommunications and the mass media, and US telecommunications policy has moved progressively in the direction of encouraging the "convergence" of previously separate industries and technologies through the promotion of cross-industry "synergies." Also since that time, the US telephone industry has undergone a process of reconsolidation, and there are now fewer regional companies, some of which have also become vertically integrated firms through mergers with and acquisitions of "content" providers such as cable television systems.

As in the case of cable television systems, US telephone companies now have a conflict of interest in that their own content providers compete with other content providers needing access to the same infrastructure. Today, public interest advocates worry about the possibility that the telephone/telecommunications industry in the United States is losing its historic neutrality as a "common carrier" by having a vested interest in the success of its own content subsidiaries, which are in competition with other content providers on the same system, potentially resulting in discriminatory pricing and lower quality of service provided to competitors needing access to the same infrastructure. Whereas an original goal of the break-up of AT&T was to promote a more "open network," subsequent vertical integration of content and infrastructure has introduced a disincentive for telecommunications carriers to keep their networks open and accessible to all content providers.

The break-up of AT&T contributed to the opening up of market opportunities within the United States, both for domestic and foreign competitors, and these developments have stimulated trends in the deregulation, privatization, and liberalization of "media" industries in many other countries. As a watershed both for symbolic and for practical reasons, it signaled a concerted political and economic willingness to break with a relatively stable and arguably less innovative past in favor of transforming property relations and ownership structures in the media industries, theoretically to make them more dynamic, competitive, and of greater value to the public. It would be an exaggeration to attribute to the break-up of AT&T all of the global trends in telecommunications liberalization and privatization, but that moment was a defining one as concerns the approach that was subsequently taken by the US government to pressure foreign governments to open up their telecommunications markets. This was clearly evident in the shift toward privatization, coupled with an emphasis on "open networks," in telecommunications policies in numerous countries in Europe, Asia, and Latin America.

Beyond the question of whether media are privately or publicly owned is the matter of what is the relationship between privately owned media and the state. As telecommunications firms develop increasingly sophisticated capacities for audience surveillance and data mining, they are able to use that information not only to place their content services at a competitive advantage compared with content provided by other firms on their networks. Again in the vanguard, US telecommunications firms now provide surveillance services to the federal government through the use of data gathered about the communication patterns and information-seeking behavior of average citizens. These developments illustrate that media privatization does not necessarily signal an absence of government control or abuse of powers, nor does it ensure greater public accountability.

The Public–Private Dichotomy: A Western Fantasy?

The public–private dichotomy is deeply embedded in European intellectual history and political theory, but it is not as clear how well these concepts are reflected in political theory and practice elsewhere in the world. European views on the proper relationship between government and industry are more uniquely situated when contrasted with other traditions. The case of China, for example, makes for an especially interesting comparison. China's post-Communist modernization process, which began in the 1980s after Mao Zedong's death, was marked by a rapid transition from a state-centered, planned economy to a socialist market economy. The sweeping economic, political, and social changes entailed shifting dynamics between public and private spheres (Lu and Weber 2007). For example, China's media system changed from a state-run party media system, which was heavily censored, to a more plural and privatized system. In general, the changes have included greater formal independence for media workers. For example, in the lead-up to the 2008 Beijing Olympics, the Chinese government passed a series of media reform measures. One of the measures eased travel restrictions and freed journalists from the need to seek authorization from provincial official authorities before conducting interviews (Earp 2009).

However, the more permeable boundaries between public and private spheres allow the government to exert subtler forms of control through regulation than through open censorship or propaganda (Earp 2009). For example, the government allows news outlets to repackage government propaganda so as to increase its commercial value and appeal (Esarey 2005). Another problem is that most Chinese media firms are large conglomerates, which the government promoted in the 1990s (Tong and Sparks 2009). These large conglomerates engage in self-censorship and are not likely to pursue stories critical of the government or political elites (Tong 2007). Government regulation also censors media content through bans on issues perceived to threaten national security, such as the Tiananmen Square protests, Falun Gong, and various independence movements (Tong 2007). China has the highest number of journalists in prison, most serving long prison terms (Reporters Without Borders 2009a).

Iran represents another interesting contrast in practice to western conceptions of the public–private dichotomy. Since the 1990s, liberalization and privatization have increasingly come to define the political and economic policies of the Iranian state, with parliamentary measures revising restrictions on private media ownership (Khiabany 2007, 2006). The Iranian media market is divided between dominating, large state-owned companies and smaller, private companies.

The state-run Islamic Republic of Iran Broadcasting (IRIB) is the largest media organization in Iran. In news, broadcast, and film production, the IRIB has contracted with private and international production companies to produce content for the domestic Iranian market. With the growth of the middle class in Iran, the IRIB and other state-run organizations have expanded their media activities, including an increase in sports and entertainment content. State-run media is a significant profit center for the country (Khiabany 2007, 2006).

Despite increasing ownership diversity and privatization, Iran has the lowest diversity of media ownership of all Muslim countries in the world. The Islamic state exerts ideological control and strictly censors the majority of media content in Iran, including content on the Internet, through a number of official regulating bodies (World Information Access 2008). Since 2005, when President Mahmoud Ahmadinejad came to power, there has been an increase in violence against media workers. Iran consistently ranks at the bottom of the Reporters Without Borders press freedom index (Reporters Without Borders 2009b).

Although much less restrictive than Iran's media system, South Korea's is tightly controlled through a combination of public and private mechanisms. In South Korea, the government exerted control over broadcasting regulations, ownership, and programming from 1963, when Major General Park Chung-hee became South Korea's president, until the 1990s (Kwak 2009). After the 1987 democratization effort, the Korean government began making strides toward media reform, beginning with cable. Korea's government owns three of the top four broadcast television networks, the Yonhap news agency, and a 24-cable news channel (Nam 2008). Three private companies account for 70 percent of readership and dominate the newspaper industry (Ramstad 2009).

Korea's National Assembly passed three bills in 2009 that allow cross-ownership of broadcast and print properties (Simon 2009). The legislation is controversial because the only companies wealthy enough to benefit are ideologically conservative (South Korea's media is openly partisan). Another concern is that the government will sell its broadcast holdings to the large conglomerates that provide little public service programming, focusing instead on economic profit (Simon 2009).

Government pressure on news content is also a concern in South Korea. In 2009, Munhwa Broadcasting Corporation (MBC), the second largest national broadcaster, which was previously government-owned, replaced its prime-time news anchor Shin Kyung-min (Ji-Sook 2009). While MBC cited economic concerns and a desire for more objective reporting as the reasons for replacing Shin, many believe that he was replaced due to his criticism of the government and its policies (Simon 2009). MBC's actions led to a boycott by over 130 media workers associated with MBC (Ji-Sook 2009).

In sum, the nature and normative understanding of the public–private dichotomy varies significantly across national contexts. However, as the title of this chapter suggests, it is not so clear that the self-understanding of what takes place "on the ground" in the application of this dichotomy is what its liberal defenders say it is, even in Western contexts. Lobbying in the European Union reveals that blurred relationships between private wealth and public power is a growing concern that is not easily brought under democratic control, nor is it one that truthfully supports faith in the liberal fiction of a clean separation of the private and the public (Gathmann 2009, Brussels Sunshine 2009). It is a fiction that is even more severely challenged in the United States.

Media–Government Symbiosis in the United States

Ben Bagdikian's book, *The Media Monopoly*, originally published in 1983, examines abuses of power characteristic of a highly concentrated, advertiser-supported, corporate mass media system (Bagdikian 2004). He addresses the power nexuses between government and media in a case study analyzing the 1970 passage of the Newspaper Preservation Act (NPA). According to Bagdikian, the passage of the NPA rested on the ability of Richard Berlin, CEO and President of Hearst Corporation, to exert pressure on the Nixon administration. While the NPA only directly impacted one of the newspapers owned by Hearst, when Berlin pressured the Nixon administration, he did so with the full power of his entire media empire. The events surrounding the passage of the NPA reveal how the mutual dependence of government and media can contribute to unethical and undemocratic behavior.

In 1969, the Supreme Court found 44 newspapers in violation of antitrust law for price rigging, profit pooling, and market control. The Court's decision led to the NPA, which sought to legitimize joint operating agreements and to exempt failing newspapers from the antitrust violations cited in the 1969 case. Initially, the Nixon administration testified against the NPA, but weeks later they reversed their position and supported the bill. The administration's reversal can be traced, according to Bagdikian, to two letters sent by Berlin, one to President Nixon and one to Nixon's assistant attorney general, who was in charge of antitrust issues. Berlin's letters outlined his concern over the failure of the Nixon Administration to support the NPA. Berlin wrote:

> Those of us who strongly supported the present administration in the last election are the ones most seriously concerned and endangered by failure to adopt the Newspaper Preservation Act … the fact remains that there was almost unanimous support of the Administration by the newspapers who are proponents of the Newspaper Preservation Act. It therefore seems to me that those newspapers should, at the very least, receive a most friendly consideration. (Bagdikian 2004, 212)

In this excerpt, Berlin implied that if the administration failed to endorse proindustry regulation, the administration might no longer enjoy unanimous support from the press.

In Bagdikian's case study, he reveals how the symbiotic relationship between elected officials and the media industry can lead to a situation in which government officials deliver proindustry legislation in return for positive, or at least uncritical, press coverage. While the exchange of political pressure between government and media industry is rarely as direct or well documented as the events in Bagdikian's case study, the continuous exchange of money, in the form of various types of campaign donations, and bonuses, such as travel provisions and expensive speaker fees, between the media industries, media lobbying firms, special interest groups, and politicians creates a climate in which potential conflicts of interest abound (Calabrese 2005).

Government pressure

As the media industries and their lobbying arms pressure politicians for proindustry regulation, the government tries to pressure the media industries for favorable coverage. For example, following the September 11 attacks in New York, Condoleezza Rice, Bush's national security advisor, asked CBS, NBC, FOX, CNN, and other broadcast and cable networks to "exercise caution" in replaying video and audio from Osama Bin Laden or the al-Qaeda network

(MacDonald 2001). The stated purpose of the censorship, coming from Rice and the Bush Administration, was to prevent Bin Laden from sending secret messages to his followers. In the following days, the networks issued statements agreeing to Rice's request, claiming they would screen materials first and rely on editorial judgment before airing (MacDonald 2001). After the first release of an al-Qaeda tape following the agreement, CNN, Fox, MSNBC, and CBS waited longer and aired significantly less material than they previously had (Smith 2001).

In 2004, CBS aired a report on *60 Minutes* that criticized the legitimacy of George W. Bush's Air National Guard service by relying on documents whose authenticity was later disputed. A White House correspondent, Jeff Gannon of Talon News, was one of the first journalists who raised questions about the legitimacy of the documents used in the *60 Minutes* story (Gannon 2004). The mainstream media quickly followed suit in questioning their authenticity. In response to the controversy, CBS dismissed four executives and relieved Dan Rather from his duties as evening news anchor (Murphy 2005). Just weeks after the controversial *60 Minutes* story, the CEO and chairman of Viacom, CBS's parent organization, who was previously a major contributor to Democratic candidates, publicly endorsed George W. Bush for president in 2004, stating, "I vote for Viacom. Viacom is my life" (Redstone 2004). Media Matters later revealed Talon News, the source that spearheaded investigation of the National Guard memos, to be identical to GOPUSA. com, a Republican activist website (Media Matters for America 2005). Media Matters also noted questions raised by journalists about Gannon's links to the Bush Administration, including the matter of how Gannon was able to obtain a White House press pass.

The revolving door

The "revolving door" is another practice that contributes to the power nexus between government and the private media industry and raises ethical concerns. The revolving door practice describes the career rotation of individuals through a variety of government, industry, advocacy, lobbyist, and consultant jobs. This practice creates a situation in which former government employees are able to use their public sector experience and contacts to influence public policy from private sector positions. Such private sector jobs might include positions as lobbyists, consultants, industry executives, think tank members, public affairs strategists, or influential members of organizations (Center for Responsive Politics 2010c). The result is a network of individuals, influence, power, and money that bears on matters of public policy.

The Federal Communication Commission (FCC) was created by the Federal Communications Act of 1934 and is charged with regulating communications and the communications industry. According to John Dunbar, Director of the

Center for Public Integrity's telecommunication project, "While every government agency suffers from the 'revolving door' syndrome, the traffic of top FCC officials working in the industry is extraordinary" (Dunbar 2005, 127). The FCC, according to the Center for Responsive Politics, ranks as the third top revolving door agency, with a total of 127 employees who were either lobbyists or industry workers, and who now work within the FCC, or who were FCC employees who now work for lobbying firms or special interest groups (Center for Responsive Politics 2010c).

A good example of revolving door personnel is Michael K. Powell, who served as a FCC commissioner from 1997 to 2001 and as FCC chairman, appointed by George W. Bush, from 2001 to 2005 (FCC 2005). Before entering the FCC, Powell worked from 1994 to 1996 for the Washington, DC branch of O'Melveny & Myers LLP law firm (Forbes 2002). One of the top clients for the firm is Verizon Communications, formed out of 2000 merger between GTE Corp. and Bell Atlantic (O'Melveny and Meyers 2010). Powell's personal financial disclosures confirm that GTE Corp., a former telephone phone company with international and national interests, was one of his major clients while employed by the firm (Heller 2008).

Within 11 months of serving as an attorney for GTE Corp., Powell accepted the nomination as an FCC commissioner in 1997 (Heller 2008). Then, on June 17, 2000, during Powell's tenure as chairman, the FCC approved the merger of GTE Corp. and Bell Atlantic, creating the nation's largest telephone company, Verizon (Labaton 2000). In 2007, CNN's Fortune 500 listed Verizon Communications as the 13th largest corporation in America, with over $93 billion in revenues and $6 billion in profits (CNN Money 2007). Powell failed to recuse himself or to seek guidance from an ethics officer on potential conflicts of interest in policy matters related to Powell's former clients, such as the GTE–Bell Atlantic merger (Heller 2008).

In January of 2005, Powell announced that he was resigning from the FCC. Two years later, Powell took a position on Cisco Systems, Incorporated's Board of Directors (Forbes 2002). Cisco provides communication hardware, software, and services worldwide, specializing in network routing and switching technologies (Cisco 2009). Cisco Systems is opposed to regulations protecting network neutrality, a principle that holds that all content, platforms, and hardware should be treated equally (Cisco 2006). During his term as FCC Chairman, Powell shared Cisco's opposition to regulation enforcing network neutrality (Powell 2004).[2] From 1998 to 2004, Cisco has spent over $3.7 million on lobbying efforts related to communications policy, with $1.38 million spent in 2004 alone. While Powell's position with Cisco does not violate the minimal restrictions set by the United States Office of Government Ethics, the fact that a former FCC chairman occupies a top position in a corporation that invests heavily in lobbying the government and regulatory agencies on issues directly related to his former responsibility raises significant ethical concerns.[3]

Lobbyists

Telecommunications lobbies refer to groups and organizations that form in order to pressure government on issues and polices related to the telecommunications and media. As mentioned above, a job as an industry lobbyist is one of the career positions within the revolving door practice. Frequently, government officials are offered high-paying positions with lobbying firms when they leave office. Telecommunications lobbyists work for industry, industry organizations, and special interest groups to pressure or "lobby" politicians and elected government officials, such as those holding positions in key committees, and members of regulatory bodies, like the FCC, to support legislation and regulation favorable to their clients. The telecommunications industry's heavy investment in lobbying campaigns increases their power and tips the scale in favor of industry-friendly legislation. In 2008, total lobbying spending reached an all-time high of $3.27 billion, with the lobbying industry employing close to 15,000 employees (Center for Responsive Politics 2010b). In that same year, General Electric, a company with extensive media holdings, Verizon Communications, AT&T Inc., and the National Cable & Telecommunications Association (NCTA) were among the top 20 companies in all industries in terms of money spent on lobbying efforts (Center for Responsive Politics 2010b).

Questions about ethical governance arise not only from the power these lobbying firms and their clients exert on elected officials, but also from the rotation of lobbyists through the revolving door. The close relationships and career rotation between legislators and lobbyists can pose additional problems. Take for example, the ties of John McCain, former presidential candidate and a current US Senator, to telecom lobbies and political action committees (PACs). From 1997 to 2001 and from 2003 to 2005, John McCain served as chairman of the US Senate Committee on Commerce, Science, & Transportation (Commerce Committee), a position with considerable power over the fate of telecommunications policies as the committee is in charge of all proposed legislation related to communication issues and policies. As such, he was in frequent contact and relationship with representatives of telecom lobbies and PACs. Political action committees, or PACs, are political committees, many of the most powerful of which represent the interests of business, industry, or labor, formed in order to raise money to elect or defeat particular candidates (Center for Responsive Politics 2010d). For the 2000 election cycle, McCain, as a presidential candidate running for the Republican Party nomination, raised $32,000 from major telecom PACs, over three times what George W. Bush, the other major Republican presidential candidate, raised from these same sources (Hirschman 2000).

During John McCain's 2008 presidential campaign, in which he received the Republican Party nomination, 23 of the campaign's 66 lobbyists had lobbied on behalf of the telecom industry within the previous 10 years (Kelly 2008). Key positions occupied by the previous telecom lobbyists included the campaign manager, deputy campaign manager, unpaid chief adviser, Senate chief of staff, campaign cochairman, and campaign finance manager. Previous clients of the McCain lobbyists include telecom moguls such as AT&T, SBC Communications, Verizon, Qwest, BellSouth, Qualcomm, Sprint Nextel, and MCI (Kelly 2008). Of course, conflicts of interest arise when a candidate, such as McCain, hires lobbyists who previously lobbied the candidate on behalf of industry or business interests, to raise money for his campaign.

Soft money and PACs

Telecommunications firms also use political campaign contributions to influence policy decisions and gain access to key politicians. These funds are funneled primarily through PACs and soft money donations. A common practice is for an organization to commonly manage both a regulated PAC and a relatively unregulated soft money organization (Weissman and Sazawai 2009).

PACs, described above, contribute to political campaigns through what are considered "hard money" donations, meaning their contributions are limited to $5,000 per candidate per election and are monitored by the Federal Elections Commission (Center for Responsive Politics 2010d). Alternatively, soft money refers to contributions without a financial limit. Soft money can be given to political parties for activities unrelated to supporting or attacking specific candidates for federal office and to host committees for party conventions. Soft money also describes finances spent by organizations on issue advocacy, which entails advertising or publicity campaigns that use an issue or event in attempt to persuade voters to vote a particular way without openly endorsing a particular candidate. While the Bipartisan Campaign Act Reform Act of 2002 (BCRA) placed greater restrictions on soft money contributions, soft money continues to be a source of relatively unregulated and unreported political funding (Center for Responsive Politics 2010e).[4]

Telecommunications and media firms funnel large sums to support political candidates, political parties, and national party conventions through hard and soft money donations. For example, the telephone utility PACs, representing companies such as AT&T and Verizon Communications, spent close to $5.9 million dollars on federal candidates in 2008, contributing roughly the same percentage to both parties (Center for Responsive Politics 2010a). Television and movie PACs, representing companies like Comcast, Walt Disney, Clear Channel, and Time Warner, spent close to $6.7 million on federal candidates (Center for Responsive Politics 2010a). Despite the 2002 BCRA reforms, soft money contributions continue to flow into party conventions through 527s (tax-exempt organizations), with 2008 contributions totaling around $118 million for both parties (Center for Responsive Politics 2010e). During the 2008 election cycle, Cisco, a communications firm, was the top contributor to the Democratic convention with $1.7 million in donations, and Qwest was the second top contributor to the Republican convention with $2.9 million (Campaign Finance Institute 2008).

PACs and soft money contributions help enable telecommunications firms to have access to federal candidates and politicians. Additionally, campaign contributions frequently correlate with industry-friendly legislation. For example, in 2008 the House of Representatives voted on two bills that dealt with providing retroactive immunity to telecommunications firms that participated in an illegal government wiretapping program. Retroactive immunity would protect telecommunications firms from around 40 lawsuits seeking billions in potential liability payments. Ninety-four members of the House Democrats who had initially rejected retroactive immunity changed their vote to support immunity on the second bill (MapLight.org 2008). Of those House Democrats who changed their vote, 88 percent of those had received PAC contributions from Verizon, AT&T, and Sprint, averaging $9,659 per representative, over the previous three years (MapLight.org 2008).

Case Study: The Rights of the Corporate Person

The blurring of the liberal distinction between public and private is insidious in the United States. It is evident in many forms of "corporate welfare," through which ostensibly private corporations are financially supported by government largesse, either directly through subsidies, or indirectly, for example, through tax breaks. In the case of monopoly regulation (or deregulation), the US government historically has played a very big part in protecting large telecommunication service providers from competition and made it possible for them to have undue control over pricing and quality of service, and to engage in predatory practices against competitors. The case study that follows illustrates the distortion of the liberal ideal of the rights-bearing individual as it examines how such rights are conferred upon corporate monopolies. This distortion exists because a quasi-public (but ostensibly private) monopoly is given the ability (the right) to censor as a private entity, but with the full backing of the state.

Participants in today's "net neutrality" debates over telecommunications system development in the United States can learn much from the evolution of the industry over the past 30 years. The history of cable and telephone regulation, although quite distinct in many ways during that period of time, is instructive insofar as being able to explain why the two industries have been treated differently, why some of the differences are only superficial (both have enjoyed monopoly positions through high barriers to entry that were government-induced), and how attempts are being made by both industries to eliminate their more significant differences, to the detriment of citizens and consumers. This case illustrates the value in grounding discussions about access to digital broadband infrastructures in knowledge of key concerns that emerged in the period immediately preceding and following the breakup of AT&T. Chief among the persistently relevant questions is under what conditions, if any, would it be appropriate to permit a rate-regulated common carrier to enter into the business of electronic publishing (of text, voice, data, and video). Although the train of completely blurred boundaries between infrastructure "carrier" and content provider has already left the station, the dubious rationale and conditions for indulging this scenario is a subject about which the public unfortunately knows very little. At the same time that regulators and the courts were puzzling over this question, newly emerging cable television services were finding their feet in a regulatory context that favored a different model than what had been used to govern telephony. Instead of being treated as a "common carrier," like the telephone industry, cable system operators managed to establish their closer affinity to broadcasters. That historical difference between the regulation of two industries, cable and telephony, is in part what explains the recent Supreme Court victory of the cable companies in being able to refuse to carry any Internet Service Provider (ISP) besides their own. But the telephone industry is also not interested in being a common carrier for all ISPs who wish to connect to their infrastructure. Instead, like the cable companies, the telephone companies are lobbying for an exclusive form of control over their infrastructure that many fear will not only make independent ISPs who don't own their own wires a thing of the past. Another fear is that broadband access to the telephone system by independent information providers – ones in which phone companies have no financial interest – will become prohibitively expensive. Commercial information providers like Amazon.com, MapQuest, Google, and Yahoo have been strange bedfellows with public interest advocates, the latter of whom fear that independent and community media will find no place in a new telecommunications marketplace in which access to bandwidth will be based on the principle of "pay to play." Resisting the move by telephone companies to develop costlier pricing models for high-bandwidth information providers to have access to their infrastructure, this coalition's arguments may buy some delays. But it seems likely that in the end, the big users among information providers are going to part company with small-scale public service organizations needing to reach clientele for purposes of social, political, and cultural association and exchange, but whose enterprises are not designed to draw a profit.

In considering the prospects for renewal and future success for "public service media" in a digital broadband environment, it seems that the providers who fall under this (admittedly nebulous) category face a presumption against communication policy as a means of ensuring social welfare. The argument against "positive rights" or "positive liberty" has been a powerful one in recent decades, as evidenced by the progressive and successful assault on the theory and practice of welfare states (Berlin 1969). That being the case, the advocates for such rights should more closely examine what it means to enjoy positive rights. The large telecommunications monopolists – the national cable and telephone companies – are among the greatest beneficiaries of positive rights in the twenty-first century.

The sanctity of private property

Classical liberal political economy historically supported the treatment of infra-structures (roads, harbors, canals, etc.) as "public goods," designed to "facilitate commerce" (Gaus 1983, 192–3). Today, that sentiment seems, well, sentimental, especially in terms of telecommunications infrastructures. The sanctity of private property has been the pre-eminent value underlying broadcast and telecommunication policy in the United States since its inception. Although significant public interest standards have been applied along the way, such accommodations have been implemented through a pattern that does not significantly impede the central and defining feature of US media policy.[5] Notwithstanding brief periods of exception, the US telephone industry grew up as a system nurtured by the core belief that the system would run better – more efficiently and effectively – if it were privately owned and operated. Likewise, despite resistance, radio and television broadcasting emerged in the United States as a system designed to serve the public interest in such a way as to impose minimal interference upon the editorial control of the private owner/publisher/broadcaster.

Arguably, from the start, broadcasting and telephony in the United States had the relationship to government that would aptly illustrate the principles of the twentieth-century welfare state within the means of communication. As two prominent theorists of the welfare state have observed, the primary historical role of the state in such regimes has not been to impede capital accumulation, but rather to facilitate its smooth flow, while at the same time lending legitimacy to the process by extracting a modicum of concessions in the name (if not the fulfillment) of the public interest. According to Jürgen Habermas, one of the key imperatives for legitimating advanced capitalist institutions is through their depoliticization, which is accomplished by attempting to establish their "natural-ness" (Habermas 1989, 37). Likewise, Claus Offe notes the necessity for the state to intervene on behalf of capital, while simultaneously needing to conceal and deny the fact that it is doing so (Offe 1975, 144). As Offe has observed, the welfare state historically has not only played a vital role in sustaining capital accumulation, but it depends for its legitimacy on the success of that function (Offe 1975, 144, 1984). More recently, Habermas has noted the degree to which states have been migrating away from the "welfare state constellation" and toward a "postnational constellation," in which states play markedly different roles in the fulfillment of accumulation imperatives.

The financial strength and global dominance of the US media industries would not have been possible without the historic largesse of the American taxpayer, consumer, and cable and telephone ratepayer who has involuntarily bankrolled the US media and telecommunications industries. To attribute the vast wealth of the US media industries to a historical process that did not involve myriad forms of government intervention at public expense would be absurd. The only "natural" feature of markets is that they are products of *human construction*. US media markets did not emerge spontaneously, but rather they generally have arisen through the heavy hand of a federal government that has made particular arrangements of property rights (intellectual and infrastructural) its foremost concern. There are many individuals and organizations who have forcefully asserted the primacy of property rights in digital media policy, among them the visionaries who crafted a "Magna Carta for the Knowledge Age," which states:

> Defining property rights in cyberspace is perhaps the single most urgent and important task for government information policy. Doing so will be a complex task, and each key area – the electromagnetic spectrum, intellectual property, cyberspace itself (including the right to privacy) – involves unique challenges. The important points here are:
>
> - First, this is a "central" task of government. A Third Wave government will understand the importance and urgency of this undertaking and begin seriously to address it; to fail to do so is to perpetuate the politics and policy of the Second Wave.
> - Secondly, the key principle of ownership by the people – private ownership – should govern every deliberation. Government does not own cyberspace, the people do.
> - Thirdly, clarity is essential. Ambiguous property rights are an invitation to litigation, channeling energy into courtrooms that serve no customers and create no wealth. From patent and copyright systems for software, to challenges over the ownership and use of spectrum, the present system is failing in this simple regard. (Dyson et al. 1994)

This "Magna Carta," with its emphasis on the private property of "the people," is featured prominently among the "Classic Publications" of the Progress and Freedom Foundation (PFF), a Washington, DC-based "market-oriented think tank that studies the digital revolution and its implications for public policy" (Progress and Freedom Foundation 2010). The PFF counts among its powerful "supporters" the leading media and entertainment conglomerates, telephone companies, digital equipment manufacturers, Internet Service Providers, and industry lobbies of the United States, including Apple, Disney, AT&T, Clear Channel, Comcast, the National Cable and Telecommunications Association, Time Warner, Sprint, T-Mobile, Verizon, EMI Group, Sony Music Entertainment, NBC Universal, and News Corp. The PFF regularly supplies testimony to receptive Congressional committees and the Federal Communications Commission. Its understanding of who "the people" are is, not surprisingly, large corporations. By the force of its principles and the vast wealth of its clients, the rights-bearer who matters to the Progress and Freedom Foundation is the *corporate person* who, by some lights, is a legal fiction who only enjoys provisional status, but who, by a much wider consensus, is the only citizen who consistently matters in the world of US communication policy.

Tom Streeter aptly characterizes the history of the regulation of commercial broadcasting in the United States as a ritual through which market behavior is made to seem as though it were devoid of the artifices of government regulation that in fact make it possible: "The problem with the claim that commercial broadcasting in the United States operates according to the dictates of the natural marketplace, then, is not that there is no marketplace but that the marketplaces that do exist are neither natural nor apolitical" (Streeter 1996, 203). In essence, Streeter's analysis demonstrates how the property relations that define the profitable realities of commercial broadcasting in the United States are themselves the products of government intervention, not spontaneous and uncontrolled markets. Consistent with Offe's observations about the need for states to conceal and deny playing the role of being preoccupied with the health of capital, the federal government and the media must work closely together as coauthors of the fiction of media markets and property relations as constitutive elements of a natural environment. A more accurate term for the "invisible hand" that governs media markets in the United States would perhaps be the "well-hidden hand."

Two paths in US public interest reasoning

Prior to the advent and wide diffusion of wireless telecommunications, the "landline" telephone system and cable television were the two primary infrastructures serving US residences. However, historically they were viewed quite distinctly according to the law. The telephone system was defined by the Federal Communications Act of 1934 as a "common carrier":

> The term "common carrier" or "carrier" means any person engaged as a common carrier for hire, in interstate or foreign communication by wire or radio or interstate or foreign radio transmission of energy, except where reference is made to common carriers not subject to this chapter; but a person engaged in radio broadcasting shall not, insofar as such person is so engaged, be deemed a common carrier.

Among the principal defining characteristics that defined a telephone common carrier for many decades was that there was only one company operating in a given geographic area, and thus it held a monopoly for that area. Consumers had no option to decide among competing service providers. Secondly, in the era when AT&T was the dominant carrier nationwide, it controlled service from end to end. AT&T not only controlled transmission services, it also controlled equipment, so that not long before the breakup of the company (in 1982), AT&T could prevent any other equipment manufacturer from attaching its products to

AT&T lines, and it long succeeded in preventing interconnection from companies wanting to sell long-distance services to its customers.[6] Thirdly, as a monopoly that controlled most of the business and residential service in the country, AT&T was able to average its high and low costs of providing service (between business and residential customers, urban and rural customers, and local and long-distance service users). In other words, through a complex system of cross-subsidization, costs were averaged, and therefore rates were not necessarily accurate reflections of the cost of providing service to particular individuals or groups. Such were the advantages and disadvantages of doing business with a national monopoly.

Based on the Congressional definition of a common carrier, telephone companies were obligated to do business with any company or individual who was willing to pay for service. In principle, the phone company could not discriminate between customers on the basis of price or quality of service. As a monopoly, the primary protections for price and quality that were afforded consumers were provided through regulation. But over a period of many years, starting with the antitrust case filed against AT&T's equipment manufacturing subsidiary, Western Electric, the problem of distinguishing "data processing" and regulated telephone service became a central issue. In the case of US v. Western Electric, AT&T was required to restrict its business operations to the regulated telephone business and prohibited from engaging in "data processing."

Predictably, over time, the 1956 distinction between data processing and telecommunications service became less sustainable, despite the FCC's 1972 attempt to clarify and reinforce it in a "computer inquiry." As data processing became increasingly integral to the provision of even basic telecommunications services, the FCC was forced to reconsider its rules, and in 1980 it launched a second inquiry, this time in response to AT&T's attempt to market computer communications equipment and service. Opponents argued that AT&T should sell a data communications terminal through a separate, unregulated subsidiary, rather than through its regulated services. The chief concern was that AT&T had an unfair advantage over other competitors in computer communications, because AT&T would be able to use the guaranteed stream of its rate-regulated telephone service revenues to cross-subsidize the computer communication venture. As a result, the FCC drew a distinction between "basic" and "enhanced" services, the former being defined as rate-regulated (tariffed) monopoly services that were the historical bread-and-butter of the telephone system, and the latter being unregulated, competitive services. To the extent that data processing services were essential for providing its "basic" transmission services under monopoly conditions, AT&T could use them. But "enhanced" services had to be "unbundled," and marketed separately, the idea being that these services would be in competition with other companies who should not be unfairly disadvantaged by not having access to the "deep pockets" of a monopolist parent company. The hard-line divisions between basic and enhanced services were referred to as "structural safeguards," aimed at ensuring that no illegal cross-subsidization would occur between monopoly services and competitive services.

In the meantime, another major antitrust case against AT&T had been mounted, this time resulting in the divestiture of all of the regional Bell Operating Companies (BOCs), of which there were seven at the time; AT&T kept its long-distance, manufacturing, and R&D companies. Among the key restrictions of the decision (referred to as the "Modified Final Judgment," or MFJ) that were applied to the BOCs was that they initially were prohibited from entering a variety of lines of business. Essentially, the federal district court that decided the case applied the "basic" and "enhanced" distinction from the second computer inquiry, thereby requiring that the regional companies establish separate, unsubsidized subsidiaries if they wished to enter into competitive (unregulated) enhanced service markets. Under the terms of the MFJ, both AT&T and the BOCs were prohibited from engaging in "electronic publishing," which it defined as "the provision of any information which a provider or publisher has, or has caused to be originated, authored, compiled, collected, or edited, or in which he has a direct or indirect financial or proprietary interest, and which is disseminated to an unaffiliated person through some electronic means." Although this definition does not refer to specific types of services, elsewhere the court indicated its intention to keep the phone companies from providing cable television service as well. Not surprisingly, newspaper lobbyists at the time were fearful that their local advertising revenues would be siphoned by online directories ("electronic yellow pages") that could incorporate advertising. Anticipating the possible movement by phone companies into broadband markets, the cable industry lobbied against this as well.

While the breakup of AT&T was underway, the FCC continued to struggle with how to distinguish between regulated common carrier ("basic") services and unregulated competitive ("enhanced") services, and in 1986 announced its third computer inquiry. This inquiry, like the MFJ, addressed many important issues, perhaps the most important of which were the claims made by AT&T and the BOCs that they could not effectively compete in enhanced service businesses because of the hard-line distinction ("structural safeguards") they were forced to observe between basic and enhanced services. Sympathetic toward this complaint, the FCC decided to take a new approach by eliminating the separate subsidiary requirement and replacing it with "nonstructural safeguards," which meant that AT&T and the BOCs had to maintain public accounting records that made it clear that no cross-subsidization was taking place between basic and enhanced services. Along with this provision, the FCC also stated its support of "open network architecture," designed to enable and facilitate an "à la carte" concept of national telecommunications system development. The FCC also imposed on the common carriers that they offer "comparably efficient interconnection" to any competitor who wanted to offer enhanced services on the system, regardless of whether such services were in direct competition with enhanced service offerings from the phone company. A clear concern raised by this decision was that, in the absence of structural separations, ratepayers of regulated services would involuntarily be subsidizing BOC entry into competitive, enhanced service business ventures. Another concern was that, despite the language and expectations of "comparably efficient interconnection," the BOCs would discriminate against enhanced service competitors on their systems, providing them with a quality of service that would be inferior to what they would provide in delivering their own enhanced services. Not long afterwards, in 1991, Harold Greene, the District Court judge who presided over the breakup of AT&T, lifted the ban prohibiting BOCs from offering electronic information services. Soon after, a federal appeals court granted BOCs permission to offer information services, a decision that was later upheld by the Supreme Court. Since that time, BOCs have entered into new ventures involving partnerships with other information providers, including cable television service.

When Congress passed the Telecommunications Act of 1996, much of the patchwork of FCC and court decision making was streamlined and consolidated, with the aim of promoting competition in the provision of basic telephone service as well as a variety of "enhanced" information services, including cable television. Unlike basic telephone service, cable television service has not been regulated as a common carrier. From its humble origins as a means for retransmitting broadcast signals, cable service has moved in a much different direction than telephony in regulatory terms. In a sense, cable became an unlikely stepchild of broadcasting, which was established when the Supreme Court declared that the FCC's jurisdiction over cable was justified as an extension of cable's relationship to broadcasting. In the 1968 case of US vs. Southwestern Cable, the Court reasoned that, because cable companies carry broadcast signals, the FCC's authority over cable was "reasonably ancillary" to its authority over broadcasting. Although it would be inaccurate to say that cable has been regulated as a broadcaster, the relationship between the two industries helps explain why the cable industry has succeeded in avoiding being regulated as a common carrier. To begin, it is helpful to note how "broadcasting" has been defined by statute. According to the Federal Communications Act of 1934, as amended, "broadcasting" is defined as follows: "The term 'broadcasting' means the dissemination of radio communications intended to be received by the public, directly or by the intermediary of relay stations." And the term "radio communication" is defined in the 1934 Act as follows: "The term 'radio communication' or 'communication by radio' means the transmission by radio of writing, signs, signals, pictures, and sounds of all kinds, including all instrumentalities, facilities, apparatus, and services (among other things, the receipt, forwarding, and delivery of communications) incidental to such transmission." Although the television industry came later, this definition has been applied not only to radio, but also to television broadcasting.

Importantly, despite efforts in the early days of radio to make broadcasting a common carrier service "for hire," this did not happen. Instead, the broadcaster was treated as a publisher, and not just a carrier. In comparing the two models – common carriers and commercial broadcasters – the former historically has had no control over the content it delivers, whereas the latter has had nearly complete control, notwithstanding some minor public service obligations. The last truly significant attempt to extract common carrier obligations from a broadcaster came in 1973, when the Supreme Court stated unequivocally (in the case of Columbia Broadcasting System, Inc. v. Democratic National Committee) that no group has the right to demand access to airtime. By most accounts, the high-water mark of public service obligations receded at the time in which the Reagan FCC reviewed its "Fairness Doctrine" rules and determined that they were not only unnecessary (because of the emergence of new means of communication, e.g., cable and direct broadcast satellites), but that they had a "chilling effect" on the speech of broadcasters.[7]

As these decisions have illustrated, the model of broadcasting in the United States has treated station operators not simply as carriers of the messages of others, but as publisher/author/speakers in their own right. Curiously, cable system operators have managed to enjoy a similar sort of treatment. In US cable history, attempts were also made to impose public service obligations that tested where cable stood with respect to the boundaries between broadcasters and common carriers. In 1972, a case decided by the Supreme Court (United States vs. Midwest Video Corp) expanded FCC jurisdiction over cable by enabling it to require cable system operators to originate local programming, consistent with local programming obligations imposed on broadcasters. Then, in 1979, the FCC pushed further toward common carriage by creating rules requiring cable companies to carry channels for public, educational, governmental (PEG) and leased commercial access. With respect to this requirement, the Supreme Court determined that the FCC was now trying to regulate cable as a common carrier, and that it was violating the statutory distinction between broadcasters (to which cable was seen as somehow joined) and common carriers. Although the Court did not allow the FCC to impose these access requirements, in 1984 Congress passed legislation (the Cable Communications Act) that, while not imposing such requirements, did authorize cities to extract such obligations of cable companies in fulfillment of their municipal franchise agreements.

This obligation remains a matter of agreement between cable companies and municipalities. But a new twist has come about in recent years, as the cable industry has moved into the business of providing Internet service. Once again, the waters have been tested to see if cable companies should be required to act as a common carrier and provide access to their wires by third-party Internet Service Providers (ISPs). In the case of National Cable & Telecommunications Association v. Brand X, the Supreme Court upheld the FCC determination that it is the right of a cable company to *not* provide broadband cable modem connections for third parties. The reasoning of the Court was that ISPs are offering "information service," which is not subject to common carrier regulations, unlike "telecommunications services."[8]

Since Brand X did not own its own infrastructure ("telecommunications service"), and since cable companies had already established their free speech rights to determine what content is purveyed on their systems, Brand X was not seen as having any justified claim to access on the cable operator's infrastructure. Cable's history of being "reasonably ancillary" to broadcasting came in handy once again, as the industry has established that cable operators can be the exclusive providers of Internet service on their own wires. This case followed on the heels of a 2002 declaratory ruling by the FCC, stating that cable modem service is an "information service," not a "telecommunications service." To be a provider of the former, one acts in essence as a broadcaster does, the role of content provider being of the foremost significance, whereas to be a provider simply of the latter, one acts in essence as a common carrier. Never wanting to be cast as the latter, despite being the operator of an infrastructure bearing some resemblance to a telephone system (wires to residences, relying on the use of a city's "rights of way," etc.), the cable industry association successfully tipped the emphasis on the importance of "information" in its cable modem service.

The case was a watershed, and one that has been seen as having dealt a serious blow to public interest groups wanting to secure Internet access to the nation's telecommunications infrastructure. Writing an amicus brief when the case was before the Appeals Court, the American Civil Liberties Union argued:

> Without regulations treating cable modem service as a common carrier telecommunications service, cable companies can leverage ownership of the physical infrastructure into control of citizens' access to and use of the Internet. … This threatens free speech and privacy. A cable company that has complete control over its customers' access to the Internet could censor their ability to speak, block their access to disfavored information services, monitor their online activity, and subtly manipulate the information services they rely on. Customers may have no choice but to submit to this surveillance. (Brief Amicus Curiae 2005)

This is the essence of concern today about what role the local telecommunications monopolies – cable and telephone – are able to play with respect to citizens and the conditions under which the latter are able to participate in the public sphere. Because cable companies are private entities, their ability to censor is not a matter of First Amendment concern. And if telephone companies manage to secure a comparable degree of control over the use of the Internet over their wires, they would appear poised to enjoy similar powers of "market censorship." Furthermore, given their concentrated power, telecommunications companies can serve as convenient "one-stop-shopping" outlets for the National Security Agency's fishing expeditions in surveillance of US citizens (Cauley and Diamond 2006). While these two problems – market censorship and surveillance – are not directly connected, both stem from the concentration of market power that telecommunications companies have been granted by the federal government. The illusion that both the government and the telecommunications companies aim to perpetuate is that this concentration of power is somehow the result of the vicissitudes of a healthy marketplace, rather than one of corporate welfare.

Corporate welfare and the corporate legal person

At the federal level, little momentum has ever been sustained around the idea of government ownership, or even of substantial direct government financing, of the means of electronic communication. That is not to deny the substantial indirect forms of government financing, which exist to this day, and which today are properly understood as "corporate welfare." Most notable in recent years was the spectrum giveaway to broadcasters that resulted from the Telecommunications Act of 1996, which had an estimated value of $70 billion (Nader 2000, Aufderheide 1999, 63–4). Ironically, the idea and reality of the welfare state has been anathema to the postdepression values of government that prevailed in the United States since the era of the Johnson administration's "Great Society" programs. Perhaps more accurately, it would be Richard Nixon, a Republican who called himself a Keynesian in 1971 when he introduced wage and price controls and a budget of deficit spending aimed at "full employment," who presided over "the last liberal administration" (Yergin and Stanislaw 2002, 42–6). But it was William Jefferson Clinton who presided over the first fully fledged neoliberal administration, and it was Clinton who most effectively led the charge to "end welfare as we know it," demonstrating just how reversible welfare rights were (Turner 1992)[9] by introducing the Personal Responsibility and Work Opportunity Reconciliation Act of 1996, a moralistic policy that made good on the rhetorical assault Ronald Reagan launched on "welfare queens," the mythical black urban women on welfare driving around town in pink Cadillacs. The Welfare Reform Act of 1996, as it is more commonly known, had as its highest profile symbolic target the dismantling of a program called "Aid to Families with Dependent Children" (AFDC). AFDC's undoing was a moral victory for those who adhere to the "welfare-as-semen theory," as Barbara Ehrenreich refers to the belief that making public money available for single mothers encourages unmarried women to have children. But more significantly, Ehrenreich detailed how the efforts to end "welfare as we know it" produced a new clientele on the dole: corporate welfare scam artists who became the targets of federal spending for privatized social services (Ehrenreich 1997, Brodkin 1995). The era of Clinton's assault on welfare was a significant one, as it was a phase in the "creative destruction" of an old economy – the welfare state – which was followed by initiatives to foster a new one: the information society (Calabrese 1997).

For a brief time after Clinton's welfare legislation was passed, corporate welfare became the focus of public outrage, and even dominant media outlets found the topic difficult to ignore. In 1998, *Time* magazine did a cover story on the topic, following an 18-month investigation that revealed "how hundreds of companies get on the dole – and why it costs every working American the equivalent of two weeks' pay every year" (Barlett and Steele 1998). The Cato Institute, the Washington, DC-based libertarian think tank, is a harsh critic of federal corporate welfare programs. According to the 2005 edition of the *Cato Handbook for Congress*, in 2002, "the federal government spent about $93 billion on programs that subsidize businesses" (Crane and Boaz 2005, 337). The *Cato Handbook* defines "corporate welfare" as: "government programs that provide unique benefits or advantages to specific companies or industries" (Crane and Boaz 2005, 338). In Ralph Nader's treatment of the subject, corporate welfare comes in many forms, including giveaways, as in the case of the 1996 spectrum bonanza for broadcasters, research and development, bailouts, tax expenditures ("special exclusions, exemptions, deductions, credits, deferrals, or tax rates"), government-sponsored enterprises, and export and overseas marketing assistance (Nader 2000). Cato adds to these:

> Many corporate welfare programs provide useful services to private industry, such as insurance, statistics, research, loans, and marketing support. Those are all functions that many industries in the private sector do for themselves. If the commercial activities of government are useful and efficient, then private markets should be able to support them without subsidies.
>
> In addition to spending programs, corporate welfare includes barriers to trade that attempt to protect U.S. industries from foreign competition at the expense of U.S. consumers and U.S. companies that use foreign products. Corporate welfare also includes domestic legal barriers that favor particular companies with monopoly power over free-market competitors. Corporate welfare sometimes supports companies that are already highly profitable. Such companies clearly do not need any extra help from taxpayers. In other situations, corporate welfare programs prop up businesses that are failing in the marketplace. Such companies should be allowed to fail because they weigh down the economy and reduce overall U.S. income levels. (Crane & Boaz 2005, 337)

In the case of the US telecommunications industry, the means through which corporate welfare has been enjoyed have been myriad, not least of which has been through the historical cultivation of the status of "natural monopoly." Telephone and cable companies have had a strong incentive to appeal to governments to grant them "natural monopoly" franchises, as success in gaining such status provides legitimacy in the face of what would otherwise be considered anticompetitive behavior. Thomas DiLorenzo cites a study that "found no significant differences in prices and profits of utilities with and without regulatory commissions from 1917 to 1932," and notes how in that case, "rate regulators did *not* benefit the consumer, but were rather 'captured' by the industry, as happened in so many other industries, from trucking to airlines to cable television" (DiLorenzo 1996, 50). DiLorenzo also notes that when AT&T's initial patents expired in 1893, many new independent phone companies sprouted up. In 1894, independents had 5 percent of market share, but by 1907, "AT&T's competitors had captured 51 percent of the telephone market." The competition helped to significantly drive down prices. "Moreover, there was no evidence of economies of scale, and entry barriers were obviously almost nonexistent, contrary to the standard account of the theory of natural monopoly as applied to the telephone industry" (DiLorenzo 1996, 50). In looking more specifically at the cable industry, Thomas Hazlett has argued that the federally authorized local franchising process is not justified on the basis of cable service being a "natural monopoly." Instead, potential competitive entrants have been disadvantaged by cozy relationships established by incumbents who pay monopoly rents to municipal officials in exchange for what in essence is protection from competition, creating market conditions that "prove hostile to competition and to consumer interests" (Hazlett 1990, 66).

The benefits of corporate welfare have been the foundation of the market power of the corporate persons/cable monopolies. The legal convention of the corporate person was invented in order to reinterpret and extend to private corporations the rights that previously had been available only to individuals. The paradox of this entity is, on the one hand, the great importance that is attached to the enjoyment of citizenship rights by corporations, while on the other hand, the degree to which powerful corporations are adamant and effective in resisting the elaboration of formal codes of civic obligation. In other words, and not surprisingly, corporations have been effective in claiming the rights of citizenship, while avoiding the responsibilities – not at all in keeping with the spirit of civic republicanism that today's communitarians are so quick to ask of the weakest citizens of society. As legal scholar Samuel Walker notes of communitarians, "Even to mention some restrictions on big business would expose them to attacks as 'radicals' and frighten off much of their present membership" (Walker 1998, 168). Moreover, he notes, "Communitarian spokespersons have a bad tendency to avoid any direct challenge to powerful economic interests and instead attack the far less powerful groups" (Walker 1998, 178).

As we can see in the case of global trade and investment policy, although efforts have been underway for decades to establish a dialogue about, if not the realization of, corporate obligations, these have been effectively avoided. But the vigor, speed, precision, and effectiveness with which transnational corporate rights have been formally articulated and legally enforced has been uncanny. Adding further complexity and contradiction to this situation are the substantial and ongoing government expenditures that go not only into the processes of articulating and enforcing corporate rights of property and contract, but also into direct and indirect financial subsidies of corporate activity. More commonly known as "corporate welfare," such subsidies are where neoliberal and communitarian forces show similarly conspicuous blindness. While, for different sets of reasons – mainly economic and moral – neoliberals and communitarians argue that citizenship should not be a pork barrel project, both groups tend to be silent when corporate citizens belly up to the public trough. This is no novelty in American telecommunications policy.

The corporate person has individual rights of free expression. But as Holmes and Sunstein (1999) demonstrate, no rights are free, and it is at citizens' expense that corporate free speech is protected. If government largesse provides the economic basis upon which a corporation speaks, is not the resulting expression a form of state action? This view accurately punctures a vital foundation upon which liberal speech rights rest. Given the amount of taxpayer expense that is dedicated to keeping corporate free speech rights afloat, it makes perfect sense to place obligations upon those corporations. A familiar view among communitarians is that rights must be accompanied by responsibilities (e.g., Etzioni, 1995). The implications of formalizing corporate free speech rights especially are that there are associated corporate responsibilities. It was not always the case that the rights of the corporate person prevailed in American jurisprudence. Rather, it was an invention whose origins date back to the late nineteenth century, when the Supreme Court determined (in an 1886 judgment in Santa Clara v. Southern Pacific Railway) that, under the Fourteenth Amendment, corporate property could not be taxed differently than the property of individuals. Today, as one legal theorist has noted, "The protests of modern legists notwithstanding, the business corporation has become the quintessential economic man" (Mark 1987, 483). That being the case, and having assigned "economic man" the role of "person" and, indeed, of "citizen," it stands to reason that the standards of good citizenship must be defined and sustained. As another writes, "Corporate persons, like natural persons who fail to live up to society's expectations, might be coerced into doing the right thing" (Millon 2001, 51).

"Convergence" ends the need for the liberal policy fiction of public and private

In 1923, in a moment of frustration about being pushed out of radio broadcasting, an AT&T executive made the following prescient statement:

> We have been very careful, up to the present time [1923], not to state to the public in any way, through the press or in any of our talks, the idea that the Bell System desires to monopolize broadcasting; but the fact remains that it is a telephone job, that we are telephone people, that we can do it better than anybody else, and it seems to me that the clear, logical conclusion that must be reached is that, sooner or later, in one form or another, we have got to do the job. (Danielian 1939, 123–4)

Out of the ashes, the phoenix of AT&T, and the entire telephone industry, stands poised to alter the terrain of mass communication in the United States in unprecedented ways, and perhaps, by its model and by its market power, in much of the rest of the world. It is commonplace to celebrate or lament the dislodging of corporations from the moorings of the nation state, especially in discourses about global communication (Calabrese 1999). But lest they stand nakedly accused of escaping the accountability to the states and citizens from whom they profit, global corporations have taken on the mantle of the "global corporate citizen" (Sklair 2001, 149–97). In the case of telecommunications, transnational operations date back to the late nineteenth century telegraph cables that connected countries across borders and oceans. In the 1990s, following the breakup of AT&T, there was rapid acceleration of foreign direct investments by US telecommunications companies, particularly in wireless telephony and cable television service (Calabrese 1995). Today, with more relaxed ownership policies than ever, privatized national firms have joined forces with US companies to create behemoths of global telecommunications infrastructures.

The US model of telecommunications policy is one of powerful corporations that accumulated their massive wealth not through competition but through cozy deals as "protected" (read "regulated") monopolies, whose profits were assured and whose exposure to competition was kept to a minimum. Protection of an industry is not an intrinsic evil, especially in exchange for public service obligations. But now the deep pockets of ostensibly private telephone and cable monopolies are being deployed increasingly to control the flow of news and entertainment, working as they are to define their rights to purvey content on infrastructures that were unwittingly financed by the public. Cable and telephone monopolies gained their wealth the old-fashioned way: through deals that had more to do with seeking protection from competition than with embracing it. Although the history of telecommunications infrastructure development is indelibly marked by corporate welfare, the sleight-of-hand rhetoric about bootstrap entrepreneurship that has gotten the telephone and cable companies to their present positions of market dominance has been accompanied by policy neglect toward their public service obligations, including shouldering the financial burdens of sustaining a healthy public service communication environment.

It is too soon to tell in what direction the winds will blow in the United States with respect to the future relationship between telecommunications services and information services, as we are in the midst of a major re-examination and redefinition of this arena. However, among the basic principles that should be most dear to sustaining the spirit of public service obligation are that networks not be permitted to prevent access to any legal content, that they not be permitted to favor their own services over those of competitors (either in terms of price or quality of service offered), and that they share significantly in bearing the cost of the reinvention of public service media for the digital age, whether it be through universal service funding, cofinancing of municipal broadband services, or other means as yet unforeseen (Boucher 2006).[10] The bottom line should be a sustained resolve by policy makers to not forget that the success and concentrated market power of the US telecommunications industry was extracted from the hide of the American public, courtesy of the US government, and that the public is owed much in return.

Conclusions

It is premature, and perhaps much too optimistic, to predict that the crisis of neo-liberal economics will generate new strength and resolve to bring the state back into a more visible and active role in raising the moral standard applied to the regulation of markets, or that states will make a long-term commitment to social provision as a bulwark against the reality and potential for profound market corruption and failure in the future. And it is equally premature to assume that the many problems associated with the lack of accountability measures in transnational trade and investment will be resolved because of recently renewed interest by the United States government in participating in multilateral governance agreements and enforcement procedures. But there is at least reason to be hopeful that such measures will become more commonplace, and more effectively enforced, as leaders of powerful states slowly recognize the degree to which "enlightened self-interest" is at stake. The public–private dichotomy has considerable value as a heuristic for guiding policy making that is designed to prevent private wealth from controlling public communication. That policy practice fails in so many ways to live up to the promise of liberal theory is commonplace. That it is so frequently allowed to do so in the absence of adequate oversight or safeguards to prevent it is criminal. In the case of telecommunications policy, the stakes include systemic harm to the quality of public communication, the public sphere, and the public itself.

Notes

Portions of this chapter were previously published as: Andrew Calabrese (2007) The letter of the law: Telecommunications and the corporate person. *Info: The Journal of Policy, Regulation, and Strategy for Telecommunications, Information, and Media*, 9(2/3), 122–35; and Andrew Calabrese (2008) Privatization of media. In: Donsbach, W. (ed.), *The International Encyclopedia of Communication*. Wiley-Blackwell, Malden, MA.

1 The full statement made by Thatcher in a London speech at a 1985 meeting of the American Bar Association was "[Democratic nations] must try to find ways to starve the terrorist and the hijacker of the oxygen of publicity on which they depend" (Thatcher 1985).
2 Both Powell and Cisco also agree that while regulation is unnecessary, network providers should work towards supporting network neutrality practices.
3 Specifically related to former executive branch employees, such as FCC employees, who seek industry and lobbying positions after they leave their government post, the OGE states, "If the matter was under the employee's official responsibility ... then the employee is barred for two years after leaving Government service from representing anyone back to the Government in the same manner." United States Office of Government Ethics, Common Ethics Issues: Post-Employment, 18 U.S.C. § 207; 5 C.F.R. parts 2637 and 2641, available at http://www.usoge.gov/common_ethics_issues/post_employment.aspx

4   For information on the Bipartisan Campaign Reform Act of 2002, see Federal Election Commission, "Bipartisan Campaign Reform Act of 2002," http://www.fec.gov/pages/bcra/bcra_update.shtml.

5   For the sake of convenience, we use the term "media" in this paper to refer to all technological forms of mediated communication, both in terms of "content" and "structure." We are referring to the print media of newspapers and magazines, radio and television broadcasting, cable television, satellite communication, telephony, and Internet communication. We realize that the term media does not always get used in this expansive way, so we beg the reader's forbearance regarding our choice of a convenient umbrella term.

6   The policies for loosening end-to-end control began decades earlier, beginning with a 1956 federal court decision to allow there to be "foreign attachments" (hardware not manufactured by AT&T) to the Bell system. Also, in 1971, the FCC decided to allow "specialized common carriers" to market telecommunication services requiring interconnection to the AT&T system. Nevertheless, it was not until the 1982 breakup of AT&T that such piecemeal decisions were consolidated into a more coherent policy.

7   Meredith Corp. v. FCC (D.C. Cir, 1987): re: Syracuse Peace Council, Memorandum Opinion and Order (2 FCC Rcd. 5042, August 6, 1987): The circuit court mandated that the Commission consider the constitutionality of the Fairness Doctrine. The court found that the FCC, based on the evidence in the case, properly recognized that the television station, WTVH-Syracuse, had failed to meet its fairness requirement. However, the court sent the case back to the FCC (remanded it) because it wanted the FCC to consider the constitutionality of the Fairness Doctrine. The FCC drew the conclusion that the Fairness Doctrine unduly restrained the free speech rights of broadcasters.

8   According to the United States Code, "The term 'telecommunications service' means the offering of telecommunications for a fee directly to the public, or to such classes of users as to be effectively available directly to the public, regardless of the facilities used" (47 U.S.C. Sec. 153(46)). Also, according to the US Code, "The term 'information service' means the offering of a capability for generating, acquiring, storing, transforming, processing, retrieving, utilizing, or making available information via telecommunications, and includes electronic publishing, but does not include any use of any such capability for the management, control, or operation of a telecommunications system or the management of a telecommunications service"(U.S.C. Sec. 153(20)).

9   As Bryan Turner aptly notes, "welfare-state rights are clearly reversible and [should] not be taken for granted" (1992, 37).

10   Some of this thinking is inspired in part by Virginia Democratic Congessman Rick Boucher.

References

Aufderheide, P. (1999) *Communications Policy and the Public Interest: The Telecommunications Act of 1996*. Guilford Press, New York.

Bagdikian, B. (2004) *Media Monopoly*. Beacon Press, Boston.

Barlett, D. L. and Steele, J. B. (1998) What corporate welfare costs you. *Time*, November 9.

Berlin, I. (1969) Two concepts of liberty. In: *Four Essays on Liberty*. Oxford University Press, New York, pp. 118–72.

Bernstein, J. (1991) Right, revolution and the community: Marx's "On the Jewish Question." In: Peter Osborne (ed.), *Socialism and the Limits of Liberalism*. Verso, London, pp. 91–119.

Bobbio, N. (1989a) The great dichotomy: public/private. In: *Democracy and Dictatorship: The Nature and Limits of State Power*. University of Minnesota Press, Minneapolis.

Bobbio, N. (1989b) Liberalism old and new In: *Democracy and Dictatorship: The Nature and Limits of State Power*. University of Minnesota Press, Minneapolis.

Boucher, R. (2006) Beware of a two-lane Internet. *Business Week*, March 7.

Brief Amicus Curiae of the American Civil Liberties Union and the Brennan Center for Justice at NYU School of Law in Support of Respondents in the case of National Cable & Telecommunications Association, et al., v. Brand X Internet Services, et al. (2005). On Writ of Certiorari to the United States Court of Appeals for the Ninth Circuit, p. 4.

Brodkin, E. Z. (1995) The war against welfare. *Dissent*, Spring, 211–20.

Brussels Sunshine (2009) Ex-Commissioners lobbying at 500 Euro per hour. *Brussels Sunshine*. October 2. Online at http://blog.brusselssunshine.eu/.

Calabrese, A. (1995) Local versus global in the modernisation of Central and Eastern European telecommunications: A case study of US corporate investments. In: Preston, P. and Corcoran, F. (eds), *Re-Regulating European Communications*. Hampton Press, Cresskill, NJ, pp. 233–56.

Calabrese, A. (1997) Creative destruction? From the welfare state to the global information society. *Javnost/The Public*, 4(4), 7–24.

Calabrese, A. (1999) Communication and the end of sovereignty? *Info: The Journal of Policy, Regulation, and Strategy for Telecommunications, Information, and Media*, 1(4), 313–26.

Calabrese, A. (2004) Stealth regulation: Moral meltdown and political radicalism at the Federal Communications Commission. *New Media and Society*, 6(1), 18–25.

Calabrese, A. (2005) Casus belli: U.S. media and the justification of the Iraq war. *Television and New Media*, 6(2), 53–175.

Campaign Finance Institute (2008) New analysis of FEC October 15th Reports of the Host Committees for the 2008 Presidential Nominating Conventions, December 10. Online at http://www.cfinst.org/pr/prRelease.aspx?ReleaseID=218 (accessed October 6, 2010).

Cauley, L. and Diamond, J. (2006) Telecoms let NSA spy on calls. *USA Today*, February 6.

Center for Responsive Politics (2010a) Communications/Electronics. *OpenSecrets.org*. Online at http://www.opensecrets.org/pacs/sector.php?txt=B08&cycle=2008 (accessed October 15, 2010).

Center for Responsive Politics (2010b) Lobbying database. Online at http://www.opensecrets.org/lobbyists/ (accessed October 5, 2010).

Center for Responsive Politics (2010c) Revolving door: Former members. *OpenSecrets.org*. Online at http://www.opensecrets.org/revolving/top.php?display=Z (accessed October 5, 2010).

Center for Responsive Politics (2010d) What is a PAC? *OpenSecrets.org*. Online at http://www.opensecrets.org/pacs/pacfaq.php (accessed October 15, 2010).

Center for Responsive Politics (2010e) 527s Organizations. *OpenSecrets.org*. Online at http://www.opensecrets.org/527s/index.php#tots (accessed October 15, 2010).

Cisco (2006) Statement on network neutrality [press release]. Online at http://newsroom. cisco.com/dlls/2006/corp_031506b.html (accessed October 5, 2010).

Cisco (2009) Corporate information. Online at http://newsroom.cisco.com/dlls/corpinfo/ corporate_overview.html (accessed October 5, 2010).

CNN Money (2007) Fortune 500 2007. *CNN Money*. Online at http://money.cnn.com/ magazines/fortune/fortune500/2007/full_list/index.html (accessed October 6, 2010).

Crane, E., and Boaz, D. (eds) (2005) *Cato Handbook for Congress: Policy Recommendations for the 108th Congress*. Cato Institute, Washington, DC.

Dahl, R. (1985) *A Preface to Economic Democracy*. University of California Press, Berkley.

Dahrendorf, R. (1987) Liberalism. In: J. Eatwell, M. Milgate, and P. Newman (eds), *The New Palgrave Dictionary of Economics*, vol. 3, pp. 173–5.

Danielian, R. (1939) *A.T.&T.: The Story of Industrial Conquest*. The Vanguard Press, New York.

DiLorenzo, T. J. (1996) The myth of the natural monopoly. *The Review of Austrian Economics*, 9(2), 50, 56–7.

Dunbar, J. (2005) Who is watching the watchdog? In: McChesney, R., Newman, R., and Scott, B. (eds) *The Future of Media: Resistance and Reform in the 21st Century*, Seven Stories Press, New York, pp. 127–40.

Dyson, E., Gilder, G., Keyworth, G., and Toffler, A. (1994) Cyberspace and the American dream: Magna Carta for the knowledge age. August. Online at http://www.pff.org/ issues-pubs/futureinsights/fi1.2magnacarta.html (accessed October 5, 2010).

Earp, M. (2009) China's media and information controls: The impact in China and the United States [testimony before the U.S.-China Economic and Security Review Commission]. September 10. Online at http://cpj.org/blog/2009/09/cpj-testifies-on-chinas-media-controls.php (accessed October 6, 2010).

Ehrenreich, B. (1997) Spinning the poor into gold: How corporations seek to profit from welfare reform. *Harper's*, August.

Esarey, A. (2005) Cornering the market: State strategies for controlling China's commercial media. *Asian Perspective*, 29(4), 37–83.

Etzioni, A. (ed.) (1995) *Rights and the Common Good: The Communitarian Perspective*. St. Martin's Press, New York.

Federal Communications Commission (2005) Former Chairman Michael K. Powell. Online at http://www.fcc.gov/commissioners/previous/powell/biography.html (accessed October 5, 2010).

Feinberg, J. (1984) *Harm to Others: The Moral Limits of the Criminal Law*, vol. 1. Oxford University Press, New York.

Forbes (2002) People: Michael K. Powell. *Forbes*. April 10. Online at http://www.forbes. com/2002/04/10/mpowell.html (accessed October 6, 2010).

Frank, T. (2000) *One Market Under God: Extreme Capitalism, Market Populism, and the End of Economic Democracy*. Random House, New York.

Fraser N. and Gordon L (1992) Contract versus charity: Why is there no social citizenship in the United States? *Socialist Review*, 22(3), 45–67.

Fukuyama, F. (1989) The end of history? *The National Interest*, 16 (Summer), 3–18.

Gannon, J. (2004) Rathergate: Jeff Gannon and Talon news. *SourceWatch*. Online at http:// www.sourcewatch.org/index.php?title=Rathergate:_Jeff_Gannon_and_Talon_ News (accessed October 5, 2010).

Gathmann, F. (2009) German Ministry outsources legislation. *Spiegel Online*. August 12. Online at http://www.spiegel.de/international/germany/0,1518,642083,00.html (accessed October 6, 2010).

Gaus, G. (1983) Public and private interests in liberal political economy, old and new. In: Benn, S. I. and Gaus, G. F. (eds), *Public and Private in Social Life*. Croom Helm, London, pp.183–222.

Giroux, H. (2004) *The Terror of Neoliberalism: Authoritarianism and the Eclipse of Democracy*. Paradigm, Boulder, CO.

Habermas, J. (1989). *The Structural Transformation of the Public Sphere*. MIT Press, Cambridge, MA.

Harvey, D. (2005) *A Brief History of Neoliberalism*. Oxford University Press, New York.

Hazlett, T. W. (1990) Duopolistic competition in cable television: Implications for public policy. *Yale Journal on Regulation*, 7, 65–120.

Heller, N. (2008) New FCC Chairman had big telephone player as major client. *Center for Public Integrity*. Online at http://projects.publicintegrity.org/telecomm/report.aspx?aid=311(accessed October 5, 2010).

Hirschman, C. (2000) Buying influence: Telecom companies, exec invest in candidates, push interests. *Telephony Online*, February 14. Online at http://telephonyonline.com/mag/telecomm_buying_influence_telecomm/ (accessed October 6, 2010).

Holmes, S. and Sunstein, C. (1999) *The Cost of Rights: Why Liberty Depends on Taxes*. Norton, New York.

Jameson, F. (1996) Five theses on actually existing Marxism. *Monthly Review*, 47(11), 1–10.

Ji-sook, B. (2009) MBC reporters balk at anchor replacement. *Korea Times*. April 9. Online at http://www.koreatimes.co.kr/www/news/include/print.asp?newsIdx=42909 (accessed October 5, 2010).

Kant, I. (1991) An answer to the question "What is Enlightenment?" In: Reiss, H. (ed.) *Political Writings*. Cambridge University Press, Cambridge, UK, pp. 54–60.

Kelly, M. (2008) Telecom lobbyists tied to McCain. *USA Today*, March 23.

Khiabany, G. (2006) Religion and media in Iran: The imperative of the market and the straightjacket of Islamism. *Westminster Papers in Communication and Culture*, 3(3), 3–21.

Khiabany, G. (2007) Iranian media: The paradox of modernity. *Social Semiotics*, 17(4), 479–501.

Kwak, K. (2009) Broadcasting Deregulation in South Korea. *Korea Economic Institute Academic Paper Series*, 4(6).

Labaton, S. (2000) F.C.C. approves Bell Atlantic-GTE merger, creating no.1 phone company. *New York Times*, June 17.

Locke, J. (1924) *Of Civil Government, Second Treatise*. J. M. Dent & Sons, London.

Lu, J. and Weber, I. (2007) State, power and mobile communication: A case study of China. *New Media & Society*, 9, 925–44.

MacDonald, G. (2001) Media fear censorship as Bush requests caution. *Toronto Globe & Mail*, October 11. Online at http://www.commondreams.org/headlines01/1011-02.htm (accessed October 6, 2010).

MacPherson, C.B. (1962) *The Political Theory of Possessive Individualism*. Clarendon Press, Oxford.

MacPherson, C. B. (1973) *Democratic Theory: Essays in Retrieval*. Clarendon, Oxford.

MapLight.org (2008) House Dems who changed their vote to support FISA bill [press release], June 24. Online at http://maplight.org/FISA_June08 (accessed October 6, 2010).

Mark, G. (1987) The personification of the business corporation in American law. *University of Chicago Law Review* 54, 1441–84.

Marshall, T. H. (1950) *Citizenship and Social Class and Other Essays*. Cambridge University Press, Cambridge, UK.

Marx, K. (1978a) Economic and philosophic manuscripts of 1844. In: Tucker, R. C. (ed.) *The Marx-Engels Reader*. W. W. Norton, New York, pp. 66–105.

Marx, K. (1978b) On the Jewish question. In: Tucker, R. C. (ed.). *The Marx-Engels Reader*. W. W. Norton, New York, pp. 26–52.

Media Matters for America (2005) Jeff Gannon reverses course, quits as Talon News 'reporter'. *Media Matters for America*. Online at http://mediamatters.org/items/200502090010 (accessed October 5, 2010).

Mill, J. S. (1974) *On Liberty*. Penguin Books, London.

Millon, D. (2001) The ambiguous significance of corporate personhood. *Stanford Agora: An Online Journal of Legal Perspectives* 2(1). Online at http://agora.stanford.edu/agora/libArticles2/agora2v1.pdf (accessed October 5, 2010).

Murphy, J. (2005) CBS ousts 4 for Bush guard story. *CBS News*. January 10. Online at http://www.cbsnews.com/stories/2005/01/10/national/main665727.shtml (accessed October 6, 2010).

Nader, R. (2000) *Cutting Corporate Welfare*. Seven Stories Press, New York.

Nam, S. (2008) The politics of compressed development in new media: A history of Korean cable television, 1992-2005. *Media, Culture & Society*, 30, 641–61.

Offe, C. (1975). The theory of the capitalist state and the problem of policy formation. In: Lindberg, L., Alford, R. R., Crouch, C., and Offe, C. (eds) *Stress and Contradiction in Modern Capitalism*. Lexington Books, Lexington, MA, pp. 125–44.

Offe, C. (1984). *Contradictions of the Welfare State*. MIT Press, Cambridge, MA.

O'Melveny and Meyers LLP (2010) Offices: Washington, DC. Online at http://www.omm.com/offices/office.aspx?office=26 (accessed October 5, 2010).

Powell, M. (2004) Preserving Internet freedom: Guiding principles for the industry. Remarks at the Silicon Flatirons Symposium, Boulder, CO, February 8. Online at http://net.educause.edu/ir/library/pdf/CSD5428.pdf (accessed October 6, 2010).

Progress and Freedom Foundation (2010) Who we are. Online at http://www.pff.org/about/whoweare.html (accessed October 5, 2010).

Ramstad, E. (2009) South Korea passes media-overhauled bills. *Wall Street Journal*, July 23.

Rawls, J. (1996) *Political Liberalism*. Columbia University Press, New York.

Redstone, S. (2004) 10 questions for Sumner Redstone. *Time*, September 27.

Reporters Without Borders (2009a) Annual Reports: China 2009. Online at http://en.rsf.org/report-china,57.html?annee=2009 (accessed October 15, 2010).

Reporters Without Borders (2009b) Annual Reports: Iran 2009. Online at http://en.rsf.org/report-iran,153.html (accessed October 15, 2010).

Simon, J. (2009) CPJ concerned by South Korean pressure on media [letter], *Committee to Protect Journalists*. May 7. Online at http://cpj.org/2009/05/cpj-concerned-by-south-korean-pressure-on-media.php (accessed October 6, 2010).

Sklair, L. (2001) *The Transnational Capitalist Class*. Blackwell, Oxford.

Smith, T. (2001) Censoring the enemy. *PBS Online NewsHour*. October 15. Online at http://www.pbs.org/newshour/bb/media/july-dec01/cens_10-15.html (accessed October 6, 2010).

Smolla, R. A. (1992) *Free Speech in an Open Society*. Knopf, New York.

Splichal, S. (2002a) The principle of publicity, public use of reason and social control. *Media, Culture & Society*, 24(1), 5–26.

Splichal, S. (2002b) *Principles of Publicity and Press Freedom*. Rowman & Littlefield, Lanham, MD.

Streeter, T. (1996) *Selling the Air: A Critique of the Policy of Commercial Broadcasting in the United States*. University of Chicago Press, Chicago.

Thatcher, M. (1985) Speech to the American Bar Association, July 15. Margaret Thatcher Foundation. Online at http://www.margaretthatcher.org/document/106096 (accessed October 15, 2010).

Tong, J. (2007) Guerilla tactics of investigative journalists in China. *Journalism*, 8(5), 530–5.

Tong, J. and Sparks, C. (2009) Investigative journalism in China today. *Journalism Studies*, 10 (3), 337–52.

Turner, B. (1992) Outline of a theory of citizenship. In: Mouffe, C. (ed.), *Dimensions of Radical Democracy*. Verso, London, pp. 33–62.

Walker, S. (1998) *The Rights Revolution: Rights and Community in Modern America*. Oxford University Press, New York.

Wallerstein, I. (2008) 2008: The demise of neoliberal globalization. *YaleGlobal Online*, 4 February. Online at http://yaleglobal.yale.edu/content/2008-demise-neoliberal-globalization (accessed October 6, 2010).

Weissman, S. and Sazawai, S. (2009) Soft money political spending by 501(c) Nonprofits tripled in 2008 election. *The Campaign Finance Institute*, February 25. Online at http://www.cfinst.org/pr/prRelease.aspx?ReleaseID=221 (accessed October 6, 2010).

Wood, E. M. (1990) The uses and abuses of civil society. In: Miliband, R. and Panitch, L. (eds), *The Socialist Register 1990*. Merlin Press, London, pp. 60–84.

World Information Access (2008) Ownership diversity in Muslim media systems. June 10. Online at http://www.wiareport.org/index.php/68/ownership-diveristy-in-muslim-media-systems (accessed October 6, 2010).

Yergin, D. and Stanislaw, J. (2002) *The Commanding Heights: The Battle for the World Economy*. Simon & Schuster, New York.

12

The Militarization of US Communications

Dan Schiller

Introduction

Cavernous knowledge gaps disfigure communications study. Owing to persistent efforts by resolute scholars, the long-neglected but foundational role of labor in communications now claims at least some visibility. For all the noise about globalization, on the other hand, the field continues mostly to neglect the ways in which the "space of flows" is actually organized, so that communications may be incorporated – previously around private line circuits, now also around virtual private networks – as an enabling infrastructure for the transnationalization of capitalist production. And what of the vast and continuing process of commodification, that is, the takeover of other forms of cultural-informational production and distribution by for-profit employers of waged labor? A central vector of communications history, commodification is apprehended by mainstream study as, at most, a sideshow. Taken together, these marginalized subjects would go far to constitute an alternative basis for the entire discipline. As it happens, however, still another knowledge gap is even more urgent.

At the height of the US war on Vietnam, Herbert I. Schiller (1969) pointed to the formative linkages between electronic communications and the US military; yet, nearly two decades later, Mosco (1986, 76) observed that "With few exceptions, communications research has ignored the role of the military in media and information systems." Another 20 years have passed, and yet this verdict remains valid. Although some attention has been paid to war-inflected processes of ideological construction (Herman and Chomsky 2002, Andersen 2006), and – a

The Handbook of Political Economy of Communications, First Edition.
Edited by Janet Wasko, Graham Murdock, and Helena Sousa.
© 2014 John Wiley & Sons, Ltd. Published 2014 by John Wiley & Sons, Ltd.

welcome portent – a scholarly journal has been established to engage the theme of "media, war and conflict," the militarization of communications as a dynamic political economic project continues to be lost in obscurity: how militarization calls forth innovations in information and communications technology (ICT), structures the institutions of communications system development, and helps set communications policy priorities. What are the historical origins and shaping forces behind the militarization of communications? What are its principal features today? In what follows, I offer an initial assessment.

From Continental Conquest to Global Power

Communications and military purpose have been entangled throughout all of US history. Their relationship has been basic and enduring rather than haphazard: a major facet of what the great historian William Appleman Williams (1980) called "empire as a way of life." Throughout the nation's first century, military force constituted an essential basis for continental occupation – and a process into which US communications system resources were deeply integrated. Initially enlisted was the Post Office. Six of the twelve US postmasters general who served between 1789 and 1845 had been high-ranking army officers; and, according to Richard John (1995, 133–4), the early Post Office was organized on a "military model." The first US mail to be carried overland from the Pacific to the Atlantic coast was borne by Kit Carson in 1848, as an explicit military operation. In 1855, looking to populate the newly bicoastal country with newcomers, California Senator Weller underlined the close identity between Post Office and Army: "by the establishment of a mail route with little posts every ten miles you will have in fact military posts all along that road. In this way you will give protection to your emigrants" (Hafen 1969/1926, 86). Through the era of Manifest Destiny and on to the 1870s, such interlocks sustained the takeover of a continent, at the expense both of its prior inhabitants and designing European rivals. During the late nineteenth century, however, the militarization process shot beyond continental boundaries even as it also incorporated new communications technologies.

Disparate historical actors and structural forces contributed to the rise of the US as an international power. Christian missionaries and admirals, Boy Scouts and Wall Street financiers, leaders of corporations and executive branch agencies, and Hollywood moguls: all made distinctive contributions. Yet, in addition to the contributions made by its burgeoning export–import trade, the US ascendancy was vitally reliant on rapidly expanding foreign direct investment. United States capital's bid for a larger share of the international market beginning in the late nineteenth century called forth a concurrent demand to safeguard the economic fruits of that enterprise. Efforts to protect US foreign investments in factories, mines, plantations, and infrastructures became as expansive as the desires of the hard-eyed men whose profits were at stake, as far-ranging and open-ended as their fears. As foreign direct investment and in some cases a full-blown imperialism stimulated recourse to force of arms, a politically connected industry of war supply grew prominent. The secular build-up of US hard power targeted both indigenous radical movements and rival great powers.

By the 1880s, Congress was authorizing construction of the first US battleships, the globally mobile assault force of that day. United States international communications likewise began to project into the Pacific and the Caribbean. In a message to Congress in 1899, President McKinley underlined the strategic significance of international communications in the context of territories the US had recently wrested, some as spoils from the interimperialist conflict known as the Spanish–American War:

> The United States will come into possession of the Philippine Islands on the farther shore of the Pacific. The Hawaiian Islands and Guam becoming US territory, and forming convenient landing places on the way across the sea, the necessity for cable communication between the United States and all these Pacific Islands has become imperative. Such communication should be established in such a way as to be wholly under the control of the United States whether in time of peace or in war. (McKinley 1899, 1712)

From McKinley forward, US leaders struggled to establish an independent and comprehensive American system of extraterritorial communications. Jostling with one another as they pursued competing extraterritorial visions, corporate executives, civilian political leaders, and military officers undertook expansionary system development initiatives. "Among naval and military authorities," wrote communications expert Walter S. Rogers in 1922 (146), "there is a growing appreciation of the communications factor." Military demand and strategic potential weighed heavily in the innovation of new communications technologies, from naval radio to radar and beyond. "Chosen instrument" organizations attempting to join corporate capital to military requirements comprised exemplars of a multifaceted attempt to project US power. This model, forged around RCA in radio (1919), carried forward – despite reverses and contingencies – to Comsat in satellite communications (1962).

A watershed was reached during the aftermath of World War II, when the nation's political economy was rebuilt as an armamentarium with communications at its center. This was not a smooth, one-way process, but its basic contour lines may be simply traced. Initiated as a countermovement against the welfare-state reforms of the New Deal, a big-business-led mobilization created some of the crucial domestic and international institutions for the global Pax Americana that was crafted after World War II. From the late 1940s forward, US leaders worked to reorganize the domestic political economy to prepare for permanent war. The principal strategic goal was to combat socialism, although this was often euphemistically called "containment." The Soviet Union comprised the primary target.

However, the US strategy was worldwide in scope. Neither European states nor Japan was in a position to prevent scores of countries throughout Asia, Africa, and Latin America – a collectivity that began to be called the "Third World" – from embracing a political project of national self-determination. Under this rubric, leading Third World countries, such as India and Brazil, initiated import-substitution and related policies aimed at achieving a greater measure of economic self-reliance as well as growth. Others, such as China in 1949 and Cuba a decade later, undertook revolutionary withdrawals from the capitalist world market. In this environment, the US-led Cold War quickly became a contest for the dispensation of the world's peoples, states, and resources.

To place its strategic net (often called an umbrella) over Western Europe, the US helped partition Germany, anchored troops there, and erected the North Atlantic Treaty Organization; in Japan and the Republic of Korea, camping out on the eastern flanks of the Soviet Union and China, the US garrisoned tens of thousands of additional soldiers. Throughout the poor world, in Asia, Africa, and Latin America, US authorities repeatedly supported kleptocratic dictators, and unseated popular, sometimes democratically elected, leaders. From Iran to Guatemala, from Chile to Indonesia, and from the Congo to Vietnam, the United States relied on military intervention, either covert or overt, small or large scale, directly or by proxy. United States government propaganda campaigns directed against the American people presented these campaigns as the defense of democracy (Osgood 2006, Wilford 2008). Corporate media complicity aimed to ensure that, whether led by Democrats or Republicans, the war party might prevail.

United States efforts to dominate a restored world market system were predicated on the establishment of a perilously encompassing institutional circuitry at home. During the late 1940s, the Defense Department was set up to unify control over previously separate military services. The National Security Council was created, as a superexecutive department that would foreground strategic issues. The CIA and other intelligence agencies were brought to life. For the first time in US history, the military establishment was turned into a permanent force, hugely overrunning its earlier, more limited, channels. Under the aegis of little-known agencies – the Inter-Department Radio Advisory Committee and the National Security Agency – what had been civilian functions, including spectrum allocation for government users and management of the government's own communication system, became subject to substantial military/intelligence agency control. In tandem with the reorganization of the state came a radical reorganization of corporate America. From the 1940s onward, its strategic priorities combined unremitting high-tech military innovation and procurement with the supply of consumer goods and services. Companies developing every conceivable kind of communications and information hardware and software were showered with military contracts.

War industry constituted an enormous, multifaceted, and highly profitable endeavor – with communications at its center. At the peak of US involvement in World War I, as AT&T CEO Walter Gifford (1937) recalled in a speech to the Army

Industrial College, "over 90 per cent of the activity of the research and development departments of the Bell System was on war work"; Bell employees sufficient to staff 14 Signal Corps battalions built a European telephone network during the war consisting of 100,000 miles of wire, around 100 switchboards, and 3,000 local stations (Sterling 2008, 21). Only during and after World War II, however, did the military hook permanently into the nation's science infrastructure, focusing it on weapons systems incorporating advanced communications and on upgraded and modernized communications to enhance the traditional military functions of command, control, and intelligence. This prodigious military research effort spun out microelectronics, digital computing, software advances, and foundational network technologies growing out of the Distant Early Warning line and IBM's Semi-Automated Ground Environment. Throughout the new information and communications technology's formative decades, "the armed forces of the United States were the single most important driver of digital computer development" (Edwards 1996, 43). During the 1960s, as the US war on Vietnam was escalated by Defense Secretary Robert McNamara for Presidents Kennedy and Johnson, communications gained additional prominence via emerging concepts of an "electronic battlefield" (Klare 1972); fantasies of automating the killing function circulated as a deadly serious strategy among military leaders (Edwards 1996).

The reorganization of the political economy was not free of conflict and contingency; and it engendered some disparate outcomes, for example, in regard to AT&T – the corporate manager of the nation's telecommunications infrastructure. On one hand, the Department of Defense (DoD) in 1949 initiated a special contract with AT&T to manage the Sandia Laboratory, perhaps the nation's pre-eminent nuclear weapons facility. The relationship burgeoned and blossomed: AT&T ranked as the nation's eighth largest recipient of prime military contracts between 1960 and 1967, garnering a total of $4 billion (Leslie 1993, 293). Following a seven-year antitrust prosecution by the Justice Department, on the other hand, in 1956 AT&T was compelled to open up its unrivaled trove of patents to other corporate military contractors and to limit its own operations to regulated telecommunications (Schiller 2007). Not for the first time and, as we shall see, not for the last, state intervention resulted in a rearrangement of the monopoly carrier's accumulation strategy and, ultimately, in a more encompassing system of military-industrial profit making. But this result was a complex eventuality, rather than a mechanical reflex of corporate aspiration.

System Stress and Elite Response

Beginning during the late 1960s, destabilizing stress factors started to loom large. Because of Vietnam War spending, a fiscal crisis encumbered the state; owing to intensifying international market rivalries, during the 1970s US capital faced a protracted profit squeeze. Policy makers responded with alacrity to craft measures aimed at restoring profitable capital accumulation. First, they began to cut the limited social welfare programs, which had been established by the New Deal and further expanded by President Johnson's "Great Society." Second, they targeted information and communications as a prospective new pole of rejuvenating – that is, profitable – market growth, among other means through the Reagan Administration's huge boosts to military spending. These two trends have persisted. Even though with the defeat of the Third World's bid for national self-determination (Prashad 2007) and the collapse of Soviet socialism, US military spending momentarily declined and major military contractors were encouraged to consolidate, no real change was wrought in the nation's social direction or in its production system. The "peace dividend," such as it was, did nothing to disestablish either the war economy or the national security state at its helm. During the 1980s, therefore, Mosco (2005) aptly conceived of the United States as a "militarized information society." This conception is, if anything, still more apt today. Within the context of this overarching historical continuity, however, significant changes continued to emerge, and so we may ask: how has the militarization of communications evolved throughout its most recent phase?

Several trends merit discussion. First, the policy decision to liberalize telecommunications markets destabilized existing arrangements for joint military-corporate co-ordination of network infrastructures; new mechanisms pivoted not around a single monopoly network operator, but around an enlarged and increasingly transnational set of corporate actors. Second, as capital investment and government subsidy continued to flow into information and communications, the beltway of military-industrial innovation provided a widening array of networked weapons – to which civil society was rendered increasingly vulnerable. Third, while net-centric weaponry became the central component of military contracting, combat and intelligence functions that had previously been performed directly by government became centers of profit-making private business. Fourth, while the theater of US military operations remained global, as new adversaries swam into view the orientation of forces underwent strategic shifts. Last but hardly least, processes of ideological construction continued to be closed to meaningful discussion of the basics of US foreign policy: war continued to be presented as a needful defensive measure. The remainder of the discussion considers these axes of development.

Co-ordination of Network Infrastructure

Historically, the US telecommunications infrastructure has created a problem of control for the military in that planning and mobilization require co-ordination with private carriers. A workable accommodation has long since been reached.

But the issue acquired fresh urgency as policy makers liberalized access to and use of telecommunications.

Throughout the 1970s, the US Department of Defense adamantly opposed decisions taken by the Federal Communications Commission (FCC) (notably, the Second Computer Inquiry) to open US telecommunications markets to competition (Temin with Galambos 1987, 223–9). To be sure, this ascending policy of liberalization succeeded in engendering a host of new ICT suppliers, and these companies in turn contracted with military agencies to produce dazzling new weapons, intelligence, and command and control systems. But the same liberalization process also rendered problematic the intimate relationship that DoD had contrived to enjoy with AT&T – the vertically integrated company that acted as the de facto network manager of the nation's telecommunications infrastructure. A telling limit on military policy-making power appeared when, despite its best efforts, DoD failed to avert the break-up of AT&T as a result of a new Justice Department antitrust suit. This signified that, once again, the accumulation strategies of the capitalist class overall held higher priority than those of any single corporation – even the largest one in the world.

The 1982 divestiture "poses a special problem for the Department of Defense," declared Lieutenant General Richard D. Lawrence, because the military "has relied for decades on AT&T's integrated management and unified network." Lawrence, President of the National Defense University, spelled out the decisive issue: the sudden "lack of end-to-end control by a single organization jeopardizes effectiveness" (1983, xi). This fragmentation of the national network infrastructure, and the authorization of competing carriers and opening up markets for network equipment, as Colonel George H. Bolling observed, made it necessary to create alternative means by which "to reintegrate the separated components into an instantaneously responsive, reliable whole" (1983, 2). How might such a new co-ordinating mechanism be established?

The Reagan Administration engaged this issue from the moment when AT&T was ordered to break itself up (in 1982), initially by creating a National Security Telecommunications Advisory Committee to advise the president on telecommunication issues relating to emergency preparedness. NSTAC, which continues to function, affords high-level interchange between the military and intelligence agencies and a changing matrix of executives representing the nation's principal telecommunications, computing, and information-processing companies. "Establishment of the NSTAC," explained a military analyst (Bolling 1983, 12), "gave the industrial captains" of an enlarged sector "a share of the responsibility for preserving capabilities." Top-down planning for crisis management in a newly liberalized market environment also occasioned changes on the government side.

Military dominance in overseeing nationwide network security had been formalized in the National Communications System, established by President Kennedy. This system was broadened by President Reagan in 1984, and then relocated in 2003 to the Information Analysis and Infrastructure Protection Directorate of the new Department of Homeland Security (DHS). Meanwhile, co-ordination and oversight were additionally strengthened during the 1990s, when President Clinton issued Executive Order 13010 and Presidential Decision Directive 63, mandating policy for "Critical Infrastructure Protection." Under President George W. Bush, similarly, the Homeland Security Act of 2002 and related federal policy made the DHS, according to the U.S. Government Accountability Office (2005, 19, 22), "the focal point" for coordinating activities to protect the computer systems that support the country's "critical infrastructures." The mission of DHS itself was likewise to help institute "an effective relationship between the public and private sectors" (Auerswald et al. 2006, xv). Behind these bland formulations lay a more directed and pervasive coupling of the repressive apparatus of the state with the corporate economy, as we will see momentarily.

The effect of the post-9/11 mobilization was to expedite and enlarge the trend to top-down coordination within the seemingly disparate, decentralized context of an Internet-based infrastructure. A group of 160 CEOs representing the top echelons of corporate America (Business Roundtable 2006) called on government to "fortify the Internet and the infrastructure that supports Internet health." The vulnerability of US companies was a function not only of terrorists, but also of any number of other threats, from outages and hackers to disgruntled employees. In February 2006, the Department of Homeland Security, joined by seven other cabinet level departments alongside Intel, Microsoft, Symantec, Verisign, and other companies, as well as representatives of the governments of the UK, Australia, New Zealand, and Canada, staged the first "full-scale cyber security exercise" – "Cyber Storm" – to test response mechanisms to a simulated cyber attack; a second such effort followed (U.S. Government Accountability Office 2008). The military aspect of such measures is presented as purely defensive in nature. This impression is profoundly misleading.

Networks: Society as Target

During the Reagan military build-up, an analyst influenced by the thinking of economist John Kenneth Galbraith called the US Department of Defense "an immense planning system that is larger than any other single economic entity in the noncommunist world" (Tirman 1984, 4). DoD's effectiveness as a planning agency is debatable, but the demise of the Soviet Union did not alter its crucial economic function: to boost demand by shoring up profits, output, and employment – in that order. Since 9/11, the scale of US military expenditure has massively increased; in 2005, the US spent as much on its military as the next 14 countries combined. Put differently, as Ian Roxborough observes, "Each of America's four military services is more powerful than the armed forces of any other country" (Roxborough 2007, 123). Weapons spending has risen even faster than total Pentagon outlays.

The George W. Bush administrations formalized US reliance on a military doctrine, foregrounding what is called "force transformation," so that – in theory – weapons systems and intelligence sensors are reorganized and melded into a single system built around the emerging precepts of network-centric warfare. "Boiled down to its essentials," explains Shorrock (2008, 162), "network centric warfare means two things: harnessing information technology to maximize the power and accuracy of weapons; and using computer networks to instantly link ships, planes, satellites, and ground forces into a single, integrated unit connecting every player in the military chain of command, from the highest-ranking general to the lowliest war-fighter on the ground." To preside over this process, putatively on behalf of the commonweal, there is an Assistant Secretary of Defense for Networks and Information Integration and the Defense Information Systems Agency. Responsibility for combat using US network capabilities is vested in a descendant of the Strategic Air Command known as STRATCOM – which, in a significant expression of the continuing US weaponization of space (Moltz 2008, Moore 2008), was merged in 2002 with the Space Command. STRATCOM (as distinct from the now-defunct Strategic Communications Command, which was confusingly also known as STRATCOM) pursues four key tasks: global strike; missile defense integration; information operations; and global command, control, communications, computers, intelligence, surveillance, and reconnaissance (U.S. House of Representatives Armed Services Committee 2007a). General James E. Cartwright, director of STRATCOM, testified forthrightly before Congress about these functions, expressing what had been at least a decade-long gestation process:

> Cyberspace has emerged as a war-fighting domain not unlike land, sea, and air ... The National Strategy to Secure Cyberspace describes cyberspace as the nervous system of our country and as such, essential to our economy and national security. It describes a role for all federal departments and agencies, state and local government, private companies and organizations, and individual Americans in improving cyber-security ... Fundamental to this approach is the integration of cyberspace capabilities across the full range of military operations ... Strategic Command is charged with planning and directing cyber defense within DoD and conducting cyber attack in support of assigned missions ... History teaches us that a purely defensive posture poses significant risks; the "Maginot Line" model of terminal defense will ultimately fail without a more aggressive offshore strategy ... If we apply the principles of warfare to the cyber domain, as we do to sea, air, and land, we realize the defense of the nation is better served by capabilities enabling us to take the fight to our adversaries, when necessary to deter actions detrimental to our interests. (U.S. House of Representatives Armed Services Committee 2007b, 11–12)

An offensive arsenal is being fashioned around and through networks. A *New York Times* account, after emphasizing that "both China and Russia have offensive information warfare programs," concedes seemingly as an afterthought that "The United States is also said to have begun a cyberwarfare effort" (Landler and Markoff 2007, A1, C7). A scholarly study is more straightforward: "The military vision is that by the application of millions of dollars and hundreds of people ... viruses, suitable as weapons in military conflicts, can be developed" (Diffie and Landau 2007, 114). Other exotic cyber-weapons are also being fashioned. The BBC (Brookes 2006) publicized a declassified, heavily redacted 2003 Defense Department document – a so-called "Information Operations Roadmap" – which, it related, revealed that "The US military seeks the capability to knock out every telephone, every networked computer, every radar system on the planet." Of course, such a capability remains easier to imagine than to actualize.

The development of these new US weapons has been only guardedly acknowledged in public, and considerable effort has been taken to vest them with a defensive function. Recurrent linkages in the news to incursions on US military computer networks by China (Mallet 2008, 9) and North Korea (Gorman and Ramstad 2009, A1, A4) are one shielding measure. Bland reassurances suggesting that their devastating potential will be handled with prudence and due caution are another: "U.S. Weighs Risks of Civilian Harm in Cyberwarfare" ran one headline (Markoff and Shanker 2009, A1). General Cartwright (U.S. House of Representatives Armed Services Committee 2007b, 11) acknowledges, moreover, that the US role in cyberwar is already extraterritorial: "we are engaged in a less visible, but none-the-less critical battle against sophisticated cyberspace attacks. We are engaging these cyberspace attacks offshore, as they seek to probe military, civil, and commercial systems, and consistent with principles of self defense, defend the DoD portion of the Global Information Grid (GIG) at home." (The GIG will be discussed further below.)

Not surprisingly, the prospect of netwar looks considerably different when approached from the target side. As network infrastructures are hardwired into social and political life, society as a whole is rendered vulnerable. Banks, schools, traffic flows, power plants, municipal offices, libraries, supermarkets, hospitals: the operations of each and every network-enabled organization and activity stand to be lethally undermined. Well-informed observers have long comprehended that – as Anthony G. Oettinger (1980, 197) once put it – "The line between the civilian and the military seems to have grown thin." Less well-acknowledged is that, by systematically blurring the distinction between civilian and military domains, netwar promises again to extend this horrific trend line in modern warfare. A foretaste of what may be in store came via the closely watched denial-of-service attacks staged against Estonia for a period of weeks during 2007, which disrupted government agencies, banks, and media – but which offered valuable real-world object lessons to US cyber-warriors (Marsan 2007).

Contracting for Net-Centric War

The symbiotic relationship that existed between corporate contractors and top military and intelligence officials engendered not only the new strategy of force transformation for net-centric war, but also a corresponding reshaping and reorientation of the industry of war supply. Activities that had long been seen as inherent government functions, including both intelligence collection and analysis and offensive combat operations, were opened widely to corporate contractors. Capital's accentuated need for new sources of accumulation in an age of overproduction and escalating competition was, of course, a major motivation. Other countries, from Britain and Australia to France and Russia, shared this concern and participated in the trend, but the US was its undoubted leader.

One resulting market segment gained at least some notoriety. In early modern Europe, mercenary forces were gradually supplanted by citizen recruits motivated – or beguiled – by state-sanctioned patriotism rather than by the expectation of profit. During the late twentieth century, this trend reversed, but on a dramatically altered institutional basis. What its leading chronicler (Singer 2003) has called "corporate warriors," depending on huge contracts from the military and intelligence agencies of government, transformed net-centric war-making operations into a profitable endeavor. Military recruitment uncertainties that stemmed from the absence of a draft and the unwillingness of many families to send their children to die for the state were certainly one inducement for this privatization process. At the point of the US spear were shadowy, unaccountable corporations like Blackwater (renamed Xe) and CACI (some of whose operatives were parties to the Abu Ghraib prison scandal in Iraq), which employed ex-military personnel to take over war-making functions on a cost-plus basis. As late as mid-2009, 32 corporate contractors – 11 based in the United States – employed 132,000 foreign nationals and 36,000 Iraqis to perform military and military-related services in Iraq (Hastings 2009). This was merely the tip of a much larger iceberg.

Net-centric war supply proffered many new and tempting market segments. Overall, however, its development comprised an extension of 60 years of fraternal ties between the military and the members of the Armed Forces Communications and Electronics Association; thus it drew in different ways not only on specialized newcomers, but also on the corporate titans of military contracting: Lockheed Martin (ranked number one on a tally of 2008's top 100 government information technology contractors), Boeing (2), Northrup Grumman (3), Raytheon (4), General Dynamics (6), and the like. Long-standing computer and telecommunications suppliers were also well-represented: Dell (15), IBM (16), Verizon (18), Sprint Nextel (25), AT&T (38), and Qwest (51). However, an array of companies not hitherto much associated with military markets, or simply less familiar, also assumed major roles in the business of net-war: Science Applications International Corporation (5), L-3 Communications (8), Computer Sciences Corporation (9), EDS (10), Booz Allen Hamilton (11) (Top 100 Government IT Contractors 2008; Shinjoung Yeo in an unpublished manuscript on the cyber-warfare industry).

Emergent US strategy and the industry of war supply established a new congruence through a specialized organization, formed by some of the chief purveyors to the new market: the Network Centric Operations Industry Consortium. The 28 founding members of this group included not only some of the companies just listed, but also Microsoft, Hewlett-Packard, and Cisco – and a scattering of corporations based in the United Kingdom, Israel, Sweden, and Germany (Shorrock 2008, 164–5).

The involvement of foreign corporate suppliers points to an especially delicate feature of the altering political economy of war-making. Military contractors continue to claim a unique national strategic importance (and are much given to flights of nationalistic rhetoric); yet, akin to other industries and for the same sorts of reasons, they are also transnationalizing their markets and their supply chains. How was the much-vaunted need to retain national control of strategic war industries to be reconciled with the exigencies of cross-border corporates? How were foreign-based and US military companies to undertake mergers and acquisitions; to engage in joint-ventures aimed at new markets; to contract and subcontract with one another in order to serve specific program goals? These became especially sensitive issues as the balance of global political-economic power continued to veer away from the United States and a more multipolar world economy began to take form (Wallerstein 2006, National Intelligence Council 2008, xi).

US military procurement indeed was undergoing a transnationalization process, but this process was extensively channeled through the executive branch. On one hand, it occurred within, or at least in light of, the dense matrix of military treaties binding allied nations to US strategy. Danish and Australian contractors participated on a team to develop the F-35 Lightning II fighter, for example, in a trend that helped sustain international sales of major US military companies such as Lockheed Martin and Boeing (Cole 2008). Especially notable were the unusually tight and extensive linkages developing between US and UK-based companies, no doubt an expression of the decades-long alliance between the two countries and their long-time sharing of strategic planning and intelligence operations. In 2008, UK-based BAE (the erstwhile British Aerospace) was the 12th largest supplier of information technology to the US Government; 24th on the list was QinetiQ, a British military and intelligence research company formed through the privatization of Britain's Defense Evaluation Research Agency and controlled between 2003 and 2007 by the US Carlyle Group private equity fund before being spun off (Shorrock 2008, 128, Top 100 Government IT Contractors 2008). On the other hand, the US began to make wider use of its secretive Committee on Foreign Investment in the United States in order to vet international corporate transactions possessing ostensive impact on national security and, where deemed desirable, to place limits and conditions on foreign purchases of sensitive US assets.

Moves to privatize, or outsource, intelligence gathering and infowar made discernible contributions to the overall trend toward net-centric war-making. Procurement by the nation's 16 major federal intelligence agencies amounted to a $40 billion annual inflow to business – having undergone sharp acceleration during the Clinton and George W. Bush Administrations. By 2006, almost three-quarters of the US intelligence budget was spent on contracts (Shorrock 2008, 13, 368). Long narrowing, the distinction between inherently governmental functions and corporate supply chains was virtually erased, as executives shuffled back and forth between corporate and governmental offices and companies assumed responsibilities that brought them into the chain of command but simultaneously removed them from public oversight or accountability (Shorrock 2008).

Strategic International Communications

The theater of US military operations has long been extraterritorial, but its strategic objectives and the geopolitical orientation they express are undergoing a dramatic shift. Forty years ago, the United States already maintained hundreds of major military bases in dozens of countries; and this, according to DoD (U.S. Department of Defense 2007), remains true today. With the collapse of the Soviet Union, and the rise of threats associated with Mid-East oil, China, and Russia, however, bases have begun to be relocated from Western Europe (and perhaps elsewhere) to Eastern Europe, the Middle East, and Central Asia (Johnson 2006, 171–206). The Bush Administration (U.S. Office of Management and Budget 2007) assured that "This new basing strategy will provide the United States with rapid access to areas where we are likely to be engaged, but where a large permanent presence is not needed." Military supremacy continued to play a crucial role in enabling the US to monitor and shape the ever-changing world market, but this imperative vied with another: the need to combat challenges to US system dominance by would-be rival powers.

To unify its dispersed operations, the US has built and rebuilt globe-straddling communications systems for command, control, communications, and intelligence. In addition to STRATCOM, these are managed and co-ordinated by the different services – Army, Navy, Air Force; by intelligence agencies; and by DISA, the Defense Information Systems Agency. DISA, created in 1991, is the successor to the Defense Communications Agency (established 1960); DISA has 7,000–8,000 employees spread across 27 offices worldwide, compared with the 1,850 employees of the Federal Communications Commission (Mayer 2007). Within DISA are nested layers of subagencies: the mission of the Strategic Planning Office, housed within DISA's Defense Spectrum Organization (U.S. Defense Information Systems Agency 2008) "is to maximize global spectrum access for US forces both now and for the future." This innocuous-sounding goal is actually a paramount strategic necessity. The US military long has been the largest spectrum user on the planet; and DoD acknowledges that its ability to operate large weapons systems and satellites "depends on international agreements with other countries that allow DOD to use certain frequencies within other countries' borders." Moreover, military spectrum usage "has grown exponentially since Desert Storm in 1991" and, "since September 11th, DoD's spectrum needs have further increased" (U.S. Government Accountability Office 2003, 30). Presumably, the Strategic Planning Office works with European allies via the little-known NATO Frequency Authority (successor to the even more obscure Allied Radio Frequency Association), which organizes spectrum access in that region within the context of the NATO Communications and Information Systems Agency (Johnson 2008).

Building on a Distributed Common Ground System of internetworking designed for the Air Force by Raytheon, the so-called Global Information Grid (GIG) is slated to be a 20-year endeavor; investment commenced in 1999. Organizationally, the effort encompasses DISA, STRATCOM, and other DoD offices, as well as the military and intelligence services. The goals to be served by the GIG encapsulate the evolving information technology-based framework for war: it "is intended to integrate virtually all of DoD's information systems, services, and applications into one seamless, reliable, and secure network," and thereby "to facilitate DoD's effort to transform to a more network-based, or 'netcentric,' way of fighting wars and achieving information superiority over adversaries" (U.S. Government Accountability Office 2004). Many weapons systems and sensors under contract in turn are "critically dependent" on this still-unrealized and perhaps unrealistic program for development, which seeks to unify the full range of intelligence data into combat operations in real time.

To succeed, the GIG not only will have to overcome organizational rivalries, but also bind together several next-generation communications technologies, each of which presents considerable technical and operational problems: extremely high frequency communications satellites, software-defined radios, an enhanced ground-based optical network using upgraded routers and switches, improved cryptography. In 2004, the Government Accountability Office underscored that the effort to build the GIG poses "enormous challenges and risks" and, two years later, it produced an even more critical assessment (U.S. Government Accountability Office 2006). However, the GIG's spectacular price tag – which has risen from a 2004 estimate of $21 billion (through fiscal 2010), to a 2006 estimate of $34 billion (through 2011) – ensures that whether or not it accomplishes its military objectives, it will help generate a new wave of ICT innovation based on Internet technology. Once again, accumulation is being tightly linked to repression. The DoD boasted in 2006 that just one component of the GIG, its Navy Marine Corps Intranet, constitutes "the largest corporate intranet in the world" serving 550 locations and hundreds of thousands of users. The experience gained by building and managing this multibillion dollar intranet affords Electronic Data Systems, its prime contractor, lessons it can apply in nontax-subsidized customer contexts. In an interlocking initiative, commencing in 2008, the US Defense Advanced Research Projects Agency announced plans for a multibillion dollar National Cyber [warfare] Range, where experiments with newly created forms of electronic combat can be undertaken and assessed (U.S. Defense Advanced Research Projects Agency 2008).

Vast though they may be, the GIG and the National Cyber Range do not exhaust the role of information and communications in today's transnational US military and intelligence complex. Satellite-based, the Global Positioning System continues to be integrated into US weapons systems and electronic warfare strategies. An additional fleet of perhaps as many as 100 specialized satellites, anchored by down-link listening posts in Europe, Japan, Australia, Cyprus, Ascension, and the United States, delivers streams of data drawn from every corner of the globe; over the last 40 years, the US has spent an estimated $200 billion on spy satellites (Keefe 2006, 72, Graham and Hansen 2007, Bamford 2008). The Armed Forces Network, run by the American Forces Radio and Television Service out of Alexandria, Virginia, maintains nine television channels, and broadcasts to all overseas military installa-tions – located in 177 countries – as well as to Navy ships (Phillips 2007). Such is the dependence on satellites of the US force structure, both operational and prospec-tive, that any hint of threat to these assets itself engenders additional rounds of US space militarization (Moltz 2008).

Empire as American Ideology

Although its killing power is overwhelming, the US military is paradoxically far from omnipotent. Major wars in Vietnam and Iraq have underscored that it is poorly matched strategically against some foes. The military's capacity to produce what US leaders regard as politically favorable outcomes therefore is variable. It may become powerfully constrained not only abroad, moreover, but also at home – above all, when US casualties escalate. This vulnerability prompts efforts to shape and maintain a supportive public opinion. War-related processes of ideological construction have helped sustain policies hurtful not only to their immediate tar-gets, but also to the interests of the great majority of the US population. During the 2000s, efforts to spin news coverage in support of the "War on Terror" testified to a pervasive institutional corruption of the commercial media system, bearing witness in about equal proportion to corporate contractors' accumulation strate-gies and official manipulation (Barstow 2008, Kumar 2006).

To their credit, leading academic journals of communication have accorded some attention to the mechanics of war-related ideological construction. Most of the work of documenting and explicating propaganda has been performed by radical scholars writing not for specialized academic fields, but for the overall citizenry; in this connection, the tireless Edward Herman merits special mention. Understandably, and perhaps deservedly, analysts have granted the press pride of place; yet not only the corporate press, but also television drama, Hollywood film, and new media such as video games also have been recruited for active duty as promoters of militarism and "citizen-soldiers." Indeed, in the post 9/11 United States, as David L. Altheide (2006, 2) recounts – not for the first time in US his-tory – "fear as entertainment informs the production of popular culture and news, generates profits, and enables political decision makers to control audi-ences through propaganda."

This repressive ideological formation is not simply a function of representational strategies in a narrow sense, but of more comprehensive political-economic control. The opaquely named Communications Assistance for Law Enforcement Act of 1994 (CALEA), for example, makes a discernible contribution. CALEA, as interpreted by the Federal Communications Commission, ensures that surveillance capabilities may be built lawfully into all US network infrastructures including the Internet. Monitoring of international communications has occurred since World War II, while warrantless eavesdropping on domestic US calls by the National Security Agency has also been documented – though only after the *New York Times*'s management sat on the story for a year, allowing its release only well after the 2004 election.

Long noted by critics, the military's hooks into the nation's schools and colleges morphed into a permanent fixture. On one side, to ensure that strategy, language training, logistics, procurement, and every other requirement of the modern major-generals are continually refreshed, the Pentagon "has an entire system of education and training institutions of its own ... totaling approximately 150 military-educational institutions" (Turse 2008, 33). On the other side, the war-making function also pervades the nation's civilian educational institutions. In 2002, nearly 350 US colleges and universities conducted research for the Pentagon, and the military accounted for 60 percent of all federal funding for electrical engineering and 55 percent for the computer sciences (Turse 2008, 35). Novel academic specializations, such as "terrorism informatics," attained an immediate legitimacy.

The most basic and enduring element in attempts to channel and color public opinion was an unquestioning support for US global dominance. More than a quarter of a century ago, William Appleman Williams wrote that "The State used its extensive control of information, and its ability to make major decisions in the name of security, to create an ideology ever more defined in content as well as rhetoric as an imperial way of life" (1980, 197). Absolutely off-limits for discussion, now as then, was the supposed necessity – indeed, the essential rectitude – of deploying US military power to reshape other economies and cultures.

The militarization of US communications, we have seen, is both deep-seated and multifaceted. Notwithstanding that the arc of American power continues to trend downward (Wallerstein, 2006), unless and until the people of the United States decide to engage politically with this imperial legacy, the road to democratic reconstruction will remain closed. Research into the political economic roots of militarized communications makes a modest contribution to that objective.

References

Altheide, D. L. (2002) *Terrorism and the Politics of Fear*. AltaMira Press, Lanham, MD.

Andersen, R. (2006) *A Century of Media, A Century of War*. Peter Lang, New York.

Auerswald, P. E., Branscomb, L. M., La Porte, T. M., and Michel-Kerjan, E. O. (eds) (2006) *Seeds of Disaster, Roots of Response: How Private Action Can Reduce Public Vulnerability*. Cambridge University Press, New York.

Bamford, J. (2008) *The Shadow Factory: The Ultra-Secret NSA from 9/11 to the Eavesdropping on America*. Doubleday, New York.

Barstow, D. (2008) One man's military-industrial-media complex. *New York Times*, 30 November, 1, 26.

Bolling, G. H. (1983) *AT&T Aftermath of Antitrust: Preserving Positive Command and Control*. National Defense University Press, Washington, DC.

Brookes, A. (2006) US plans to 'fight the net' revealed. *BBC News*, 27 January. Online at http://news.bbc.co.uk/2/hi/americas/4655196.stm (accessed February 1, 2006).

Business Roundtable (2006) Essential steps to strengthen America's cyber terrorism preparedness. Online at http://www.businessroundtable.org/sites/default/files/200606220 02CyberReconFinal6106.pdf (accessed October 6, 2010).

Cole, A. (2008) Boeing looks to foreign buyers to boost its military sales. *Wall Street Journal*, July 17, B5.

Diffie, W. and Landau, S. (2007) *Privacy on the Line: The Politics of Wiretapping and Encryption*, updated and expanded edn. MIT Press, Cambridge, MA.

Edwards, P. N. (1996) *The Closed World: Computers and the Politics of Discourse in Cold War America*. MIT Press, Cambridge, MA.

Gifford, W. S. (1937) Address before the Army War College. Washington DC. In: *Addresses, Papers and Interviews by Walter S. Gifford*, vol. 2, October 13, 1928 – December 2, 1937. Compiled by the Information Department of the American Telephone and Telegraph Company, December, 203.

Gorman, S. and Ramstad, E. (2009) Cyber blitz hits U.S., Korea. *Wall Street Journal*, July 9, A1, A4.

Graham, Jr., T., and Hansen, K.A. (2007) *Spy Satellites and Other Intelligence Technologies That Changed History*. University of Washington Press, Seattle.

Hafen, Leroy R. (1969/1926) *The Overland Mail 1849-1869: Promoter of Settlement, Precursor of Railroads*. AMS Press, New York.

Hastings, M. (2009) Soldiers of fortune cannot remain outside the law. *Financial Times*, August 14, 7.

Herman, E. S. and Chomsky, N. (2002) *Manufacturing Consent: The Political Economy of the Mass Media*. Pantheon, New York.

John, R. (1995) *Spreading The News: The American Postal System From Franklin To Morse*. Harvard University Press, Cambridge, MA.

Johnson, C. (2006) *Nemesis: The Last Days of the American Republic*. Metropolitan Books, New York.

Johnson, D. (2008) North Atlantic Treaty Organization (NATO) Communications and Information Systems Agency. In: Sterling, C. H. (ed.), *Military Communications: From Ancient Times to 21st Century*. ABC-CLIO, Santa Barbara, CA, pp. 338–9.

Keefe, P. R. (2006) *Chatter: Uncovering the Echelon Surveillance Network and the Secret World of Global Eavesdropping*. Random House, New York.

Klare, M. T. (1972) *War Without End: American Planning for the Next Vietnam*. Vintage, New York.

Kumar, D. (2006) Media, war, and propaganda: Strategies of information management during the 2003 Iraq War. *Communication and Critical/Cultural Studies*, 3(1, March), 48–69.

Landler, M. and Markoff, J. (2007) After computer siege in Estonia, war fears turn to cyber-space. *New York Times*, May 29, 1.

Lawrence, R. D. (1983) Preface. In: Bolling, G. H., *AT&T Aftermath of Antitrust: Preserving Positive Command and Control*. National Defense University Press, Washington, DC.

Leslie, S. W. (1993) *The Cold War and American Science*. Columbia University Press, New York.

Mallet, V. (2008) Mutually assured destruction in cyberspace. *Financial Times*, August 21, 9.

Markoff, J. and Shanker, T. (2009) U.S. weighs risks of civilian harm in cyberwarfare. *New York Times*, August 2, A1, A9.

Marsan, C. D. (2007) How close is World War 3.0? *Network World*, 24(33), August 27, 1, 22–5.

Mayer, L. R. (2007) Wired. *CapitalEye*, January 7. Online at http://www.capitaleye.org/inside.asp?ID=242 (Accessed April 21, 2007).

McKinley, President W. (1899) Islands. *Congressional Record*, U.S. Congress, House, 5th Cong, 3rd Sess. February 10. GPO, Washington, DC.

Moltz, J. C. (2008) *The Politics of Space Security*. Stanford University, Palo Alto, CA.

Moore, M. (2008) *Twilight War: The Folly of U.S. Space Dominance*. Independent Institute, Oakland.

Mosco, V. (1986) New technology and space warfare. In: Becker, J., Hedebro, G., and Paldan, L. (eds), *Communication and Domination: Essays to Honor Herbert I. Schiller*. Ablex, Norwood, NJ, pp. 76–83.

Mosco, V. (2005) *The Pay-Per Society*. MIT Press, Cambridge, MA.

National Intelligence Council (2008) *Global Trends 2025: A Transformed World*. GPO, Washington, DC. Online at www.dni.gov/nic/NIC_2025_project.html (accessed December 1, 2008).

Oettinger, A. G. (1980) Information resources: Knowledge and power in the 21st century. *Science*, New Series, 209, 191–8.

Osgood, K. (2006) *Total Cold War: Eisenhower's Secret Propaganda Battle at Home and Abroad*. University Press of Kansas, Lawrence.

Phillips, M. M. (2007) Soldiers, beware: Going to the mall might be risky. *Wall Street Journal*, April 3, A1, A12.

Prashad, V. (2007) *The Darker Nations: A People's History of the Third World*. New Press, New York.

Rogers, W. S. (1922) International electrical communications. *Foreign Affairs*, 1(2), December.

Roxborough, I. (2007) Weary titan, assertive hegemon: Military strategy, globalization, and U.S. preponderance. In: Mazlish, B., Chanda, N., and Weisbode, K. (eds), *The Paradox of a Global USA*. Stanford University Press, Palo Alto, CA, pp. 122–47.

Schiller, D. (2007) The hidden history of U.S. public service telecommunications, 1919–1956. *Info* 2/3, 17–28.

Schiller, H. (1969) *Mass Communications and American Empire*. Augustus M. Kelley, New York.

Shorrock, T. (2008) *Spies For Hire: The Secret World of Intelligence Outsourcing*. Simon & Schuster, New York.

Singer, P. W. (2003) *Corporate Warriors: The Rise of the Privatized Military Industry*. Cornell University Press, Ithaca, NY.

Sterling, C.H. (2008) *Military Communications: From Ancient Times to the 21st Century*. ABC-CLIO, Santa Barbara, CA.

Temin, P. with Galambos, L. (1987) *The Fall of the Bell System*. Cambridge University Press, New York.

Tirman, J. (1984) The defense-economy debate. In: Tirman, J. (ed.), *The Militarization of High Technology*. Ballinger, Cambridge. MA, pp. 1–32.

Top 100 Government IT Contractors (2008) Online at http://washingtontechnology.com/toplists/top-100-lists/2008.aspx (accessed October 6, 2010).

Turse, N. (2008) *The Complex: How The Military Invades Our Everyday Lives*. Metropolitan Books, New York.

U.S. Defense Advanced Research Projects Agency (2008) Broad Agency Announcement National Cyber Range. DARPA-BAA-08-43. 5 May.

U.S. Defense Information Systems Agency (2008) Strategic Planning Office (SPO). Online at http://www.disa.mil/dso/spo/index.html (accessed October 25, 2008).

U.S. Department of Defense (2007) Base Structure Report Fiscal Year 2007 Baseline. Online at http://www.defense.gov/pubs/bsr_2007_baseline.pdf (accessed October 6, 2010).

U.S. Government Accountability Office (2003) *Telecommunications: Comprehensive Review Of U.S. Spectrum Management With Broad Stakeholder Involvement Is Needed*. GAO-03-277.

U.S. Government Accountability Office (2004) *Defense Acquisitions: The Global Information Grid and Challenges Facing Its Implementation*. GAO-04-858.

U.S. Government Accountability Office (2005) *Critical Infrastructure Protection: Department of Homeland Security Faces Challenges in Fulfilling Cybersecurity Responsibilities*. GAO-05- 434.

U.S. Government Accountability Office (2006) *DOD Management Approach and Processes Not Well-Suited to Support Development of Global Information Grid*. GAO-06-211.

U.S. Government Accountability Office (2008) *Critical Infrastructure Protection: DHS Needs to Fully Address Lessons Learned from Its First Cyber Storm Exercise*. GAO-08-825.

U.S. House of Representatives, Armed Services Committee (2007a) Subcommittee Chair Ellen Tauscher Strategic Forces Subcommittee FY08 Posture Hearing for U.S. Strategic Command. March 8. Online at http://armedservices.house.gov/apps/list/speech/armedsvc_dem/tauscher_opening030807.shtml (accessed October 25, 2010).

U.S. House of Representatives, Armed Services Committee (2007b) Statement of General James E. Cartwright Commander United States Strategic Command Before The Strategic Forces Subcommittee On United States Strategic Command. March 8. Online at http://www.armedservices.house.gov/pdfs/Strat030807/Cartwright_Testimony030807.pdf (accessed October 25, 2008].

U.S. Office of Management and Budget (2007) Department of Defense. Online at www.ombwatch.org/files/budget/defense.pdf (accessed October 10, 2010).

Wallerstein, I. (2006) The curve of American power. *New Left Review* 40, July/August, 77–94.

Wilford, H. (2008) *The Mighty Wurlitzer: How The CIA Played America*. Harvard University Press, Cambridge, MA.

Williams, W. A. (1980) *Empire as a Way of Life*. Oxford University Press, New York.

13

Journalism Regulation
State Power and Professional Autonomy

Helena Sousa and Joaquim Fidalgo

It is widely accepted that journalism plays a relevant role in forming the concepts, images, and belief systems used to interpret the world. There is a robust dispute, however, as to the best approach to ensure the positive functions of this performative role and to reduce the negative social consequences of journalists' actions and omissions. Though in different ways, media regulation is expected to raise journalistic standards and therefore to contribute to the expansion of public and private media social responsibilities.[1]

Quite frequently, the opposition between journalistic duties and obligations, on the one hand, and media freedom, on the other hand, has been dichotomized as if both dimensions were not constitutive of democratic societies. Commercial media companies tend to argue for more autonomy in order to pursue their business objectives, suggesting that the market is the most adequate regulatory mechanism. Other social actors have been defending a progressive sophistication of regulation, particularly state-centered, as a last resort to ensure fundamental values in an increasingly commercially driven environment. Though the balance of power between state-centered regulatory bodies and professionally based mechanisms differ quite considerably from country to country, the overall regulatory construct is designed to bring about change in the name of the "public interest" and it is the ongoing result of different (often conflicting) views regarding the role of the state in society.

Because we believe that the national level of analysis is central to any in-depth examination of the relationship between media systems and democratic processes, this chapter focuses on the intricate regulatory mechanisms of the journalistic profession in a specific Western European country – Portugal. It presents the main traits of the legal apparatus relevant to journalistic activity, the state media

The Handbook of Political Economy of Communications, First Edition.
Edited by Janet Wasko, Graham Murdock, and Helena Sousa.
© 2014 John Wiley & Sons, Ltd. Published 2014 by John Wiley & Sons, Ltd.

regulatory body (*ERC- Entidade Reguladora para a Comunicação Social*), and the diverse journalistic self-regulatory instruments, namely newsroom councils, internal codes, newsroom stylebooks, the journalistic ethical code, the ethical council, ombudsmen, and media criticism. We shall provide detailed empirical evidence of the "hard" and "soft" power structures that are supposed to promote the quality of the media discourses and therefore the overall quality of democratic institutions.

Analyzing the journalistic regulatory apparatus and its historical development within a national framework (despite noteworthy international links and influences), this chapter argues that general interest values cannot be guaranteed by a single regulatory body, legal setting, or individual action. Indeed, the Portuguese case shows that, despite the prominence of state media regulation, the efficiency of the system depends on the systemic functioning of the entire regulatory construct. Professional self-regulation and citizens' participation are perceived as indispensable constituents in the development of a responsible and accountable media culture. The basic assumptions of this chapter are in line with the central characteristics of political economy as examined by Golding and Murdock (1991) and Mosco (1996): social change and history, social totality, moral philosophy, and practice.

Regulation for What?

Media regulation is often perceived as uniquely (or mostly) a state-centered activity, developed according to the "command-and-control" model (Black 2002), and primarily focused on the economic welfare of consumers in an open market society. This view has been increasingly challenged over recent years. Regulation should be regarded not only in a "negative" way (to prevent any area of activity, institution, or company, from causing harm to the basic rights and needs of people in a community), but also in a "positive" mode (to enhance and actively stimulate an area of activity, institution, or company, to fulfill those basic needs and expectations, under the supposition that in a community there is such a thing as the "public interest" which deserves to be protected).

Regulation should also be perceived as a much wider set of rules, prescriptions, directions, and mechanisms than those put in practice by the state, in a top-down, unilateral approach. Actually, as Black (2002) puts it, power and control are nowadays exercised throughout society in a variety of ways, and so the regulatory systems existing within social spheres can be seen "as equally, if not more, important to social ordering as the formal ordering of the state" (Black 2002, 3–4). Regulation "occurs in many locations, in many *fora*" (Black 2004, 4), and so a "decentered" perspective is more suitable if we want to understand its complexity in contemporary societies.

Furthermore, regulation should not be restricted to the correction of market failures or abuses, that is to say, to the goal of welfare economics. If it was traditionally regarded (and dealt with) as such, regulatory concerns have recently expanded to other areas of social life. This means that instead of treating people basically as "consumers" (or even as "customers"), we must perceive them as "citizens." And this opposition of terms – "citizens" versus "consumers" – runs in parallel with other oppositions that usually structure regulatory discourse: "needs versus wants, society versus individual, language of rights versus language of choice, and regulation *for* the public interest versus regulation *against* consumer detriment" (Livingstone et al. 2007, 65, emphasis added). This broader perspective is particularly relevant in what concerns media regulation, even if we assume that "the citizen interest is, by contrast to the consumer interest, difficult to define clearly and unambiguously" (Livingstone et al. 2007, 73). The fact is that regulation of the free "marketplace of ideas" can't be regarded (like the marketplace of goods) just in terms of economic theory – and of its accordance to the supply-and-demand rules – but also in terms of political, democratic theory, taking into consideration its importance for the creation of well-informed, self-governing citizens (Napoli 1999).

Lastly, regulation should not be treated as a technical activity, but also as a kind of moral activity (Silverstone 2004). The right question to be asked by regulatory discourses must be "regulation for what, and for whom?" as Silverstone puts it (2004, 446). This means that, in the sensitive domain of mass media, regulation must be concerned not only with their production and content, but with their real contribution to a "critical literacy" of mediated communication, as well as to the development of a "civic sense" that stresses the responsibilities each one of us should feel for the other. And this concern with "media civics" is, again in Silverstone's words (2004, 448), something "crucial to citizenship in the 21st century."

Since there was a wide consensus that the media in general, and journalism in particular, play a significant role in society, regulatory mechanisms have been put in place in almost all advanced democracies. Significantly, as Reinard and Ortiz (2005, 603) point out, "scholars with an interest in international development have found the study of mass communication regulation a valuable index of national development." Briefly, we shall put forward some reasons for this correlation.

First of all, the particular nature of the service (provision of discursive products) provided by the media to society should be considered. The relevance of both entertainment and informative content to community life makes it impossible to think about these narratives as mere commodities, freely traded in the marketplace and subject to no law other than supply and demand. Notwithstanding different views regarding such a thing as "common good," it can be generally agreed that the media "make a necessary contribution to the working of a modern social system," including here "many basic and sensitive social and political processes" (McQuail 2005, 238).[2] And "necessity, if nothing else, brings with it an obligation" (2005, 238), particularly in an area where important consequences, both for individuals and the society as a whole, can arise from its concrete way of doing things. So it is the simple idea of a pluralistic, democratic functioning of a society (where a free flow of information runs together with the supply of all the information and opinion necessary for citizens to actively participate in the common life) that seems to require media responsibility and some kind of accountability, either to prevent any harm to basic rights, or to foster their positive contributions to the community.[3]

The correct articulation of the two (sometimes conflicting) ideals of freedom and responsibility implied in media activity has been discussed for decades, especially in the context of the "social responsibility theory." This theory was first systematized in 1956 by Siebert, Peterson, and Schramm in *Four Theories of the Press* (1963), but its roots can be found either in the work of the Hutchins Commission (1947) in the USA – with its well-known final report, *A Free and Responsible Press* – or in a variety of measures taken in European countries during the first half of the twentieth century, for example, those that led to the establishment of a public broadcasting service.[4] Common to these reflections and efforts was, after all, the "need in democratic societies to develop a workable philosophy of and policies for the press" (Christians and Nordenstreng 2004, 4), under the supposition that media have a duty to serve society, and that the liberal/libertarian model, with its emphasis only on the individual freedom as a "natural" and "non-negotiable" right, cannot apparently fulfill that duty in proper terms.

The Hutchins Report clearly stressed the idea that the *right of the press* to be free is inseparable from the *right of the people* to have a free press and, going a step further, the supplementary right of the people to have *"an adequate press"* (Nerone 1995, 97). So the shift somehow turns from the rights of the press to the rights of the people. Even the individual right to free expression (which is not exactly the same thing as the right to a free press) should be regarded, in this context, not as a *natural* right, but as a *moral* right. And a moral right, as it was put by Siebert et al. (1963, 96), evoking the Hutchins Report's background, is "a value which I am not free to relinquish, as I am free to relinquish a personal interest." Besides, this moral right to free speech is inseparable from a complementary duty, a duty toward one's consciousness and toward others; that is why, according to social responsibility theory, one's right to free expression "must be balanced against the private rights of others and against vital social interests" (Nerone et al. 1995, 97).

The importance granted to the people's *right to free expression* as the cornerstone and "founding myth" of journalism (Giroux 1991, 129) should be balanced, in this context, with another similarly fundamental societal bedrock: the people's *right to information* – complete, comprehensive, pluralistic, true and fair information, and essential to civic participation in a democratic society. And free competition in a free market place does not mechanically guarantee this basic right.

The rationale for "a free and responsible press," in the terms in which it has been developed over the last decades, stresses the importance of a "negative" freedom (or *"freedom from"*) as well as of a "positive" freedom (or *"freedom for"*). Removing obstacles to the free functioning of the press (as the liberal tradition insists) is only part of the story. The other half derives from the obligation for the press to actively fulfill its duties toward citizens and society as a whole, giving a positive / constructive content to a free environment. Freedom cannot be dissociated from the conditions of its effective exercise.

In their critical review of the work *Four Theories of the Press*, Nerone and his coauthors (1995, 84) argued that this "positive freedom" is "the conceptual axis around which social responsibility [theory] revolves." In this sense, freedom (of expression, of the press) is not an "unconditional" right, but instead something that "involves the necessity of assuming and performing duties beyond self-interest," because, in this perspective, "the self, community, and universal human-ness are interdependent and consubstantial" (Nerone 1995, 86–87). Thus for someone to be free means "to have the use of one's powers of action (i) without restraint or control from outside, and (ii) with whatever means or equipment the action requires" (Nerone 1995, 94). Likewise, for the press to be free means being *"free from"* any restraints or pressures to its functioning, but also being *"free for"* the search and attainment of the purposes defined by its unavoidable ethical sense and by the basic social needs it is supposed to serve. What the press does wrong is something that must be criticized (and regulated); similarly, what the press does not do at all, but should do, is similarly a matter for concern (and for regulation) on behalf of the public interest.

If the basis of most arguments regarding the need for media and journalistic regulation is the "public interest," how could it possibly be defined? Despite some conceptual confusion, this vague notion is central to democratic societies. It is so because it represents "the values of any particular society" (Morrison and Svennevig 2007, 45). Therefore, every society should work on its understanding of "public interest" in order to foster its pursuit and to prevent abuses under its name. It is well known that "it is difficult at times to separate what the public is interested in from that which is in the public interest" (Morrison and Svennevig 2007, 50), even when some issues covered by the media are justified by the professional use of traditional "news values." Recently, Morrison and Svennevig suggested that the alternative concept of "social importance" would be preferable to the one of "public interest." And they explain it in the context of their research about acceptable or unacceptable intrusions, by the media, into someone's privacy: "For intrusion to be justified it had to expose something that had importance for a collective – it could not be justified on grounds of personal interest, or even the interests of many if the knowledge provided did not impact in some collective manner" (Morrison and Svennevig 2007, 59).

The alternative term of "social importance" could, in their opinion, not only "get rid of the troublesome referent, *the public*, and the cognitively bothersome word, *interest*" (Morrison and Svennevig 2007, 61, original emphasis), but also introduce a notion of proportion that could be useful for practical decisions:

> The term "the public interest" has a gravitas attached that makes it too severe a test for intrusion of privacy – it has little sensitivity. Social importance can be scaled from

very high social importance to very low social importance. Once the level of social importance is understood, it then follows that the degree of intrusion considered to be appropriate is dependent upon that importance; it is almost arithmetic. (Morrison and Svennevig 2007, 61)

This concept of "social importance" (linked to an idea of social solidarity, of some social cohesion based on commonly shared values) could then, according to these authors, be used as some kind of test of the public interest in any particular situation, helping to give it a more concrete meaning. Besides, this perspective of the "public interest" would help to place it in the field of political and social issues, which seems to be specially relevant in a time when an "economic-led approach, operationalised in terms of market research, is emerging as dominant" (Lunt and Livingstone 2007, 5) to define the "public interest."

Moving Regulation Forward

Regulation takes place because the media have responsibilities toward society.[5] The general consensus regarding media responsibilities has led societies to develop some sort of media regulation. What is highly disputed, however, is "the degree and kind of obligation that might be involved" in those responsibilities, and "how [they] should be promoted" (McQuail 2005, 249). Reducing media responsibility to a word or to a couple of good intentions, without any practical follow-up, would not serve society. That is why, after defining proper conduct – which is the task of responsibility – one must move toward the real obligation to execute it – which is the task of accountability. As Hodges (1990) puts it, someone is responsible *"for"* something (for an obligation, for a need), and the next step implies that someone is also accountable *"to"* (in the case of the media, to the people, to the citizens, to society). Accountability, to use McQuail's words (1997, 515), "refers to the processes by which media are called to account for meeting their obligations." Responsibility without accountability would risk being an empty concept; likewise, accountability must be put in practice through different instruments and mechanisms that allow the several actors of the communication process to actually ask for media's accounts and to get some answers from them.[6] And this leads us to regulation in its multiple forms.

To understand regulation in a "positive" sense requires that we go beyond the state–media / market–media relationship. In addition to these fundamental dimensions, another component must be added: citizens themselves: "Discussions of democracy and the media, however the relationship may be formulated, miss the point if they concentrate on the sterile debate between state and the media" (Colin Sparks, quoted in Josephi 2005, 579). Reducing regulatory concerns to the market–media relationship – under the supposition that it is the best way of preserving both media freedom and consumers' freedom to choose – leads us to forget that "there is no such thing as a naturally and neutrally regulating media marketplace" (Wahl-Jorgensen and Galperin 2000, 31). Instead, to leave things dependent only on the unrestrained functioning of the marketplace means to be taken by "the subtle and not-so-subtle ways in which it imposes its own regulatory logic" (Wahl-Jorgensen and Galperin 2000, 31). Furthermore, to reduce freedom to the possibility of buying one or another newspaper, or of switching this or that TV channel, hoping that (according to the old libertarian traditions) some kind of "self-righting process" will select the best and eliminate the worst, seems to be little to expect for a participatory citizenship in a democratic society. Once again, it's the consumer-centered perspective taking over the citizen-centered perspective: "When access to the public forum is structured around the possession of money and power, of stock and professional position rather than the level to which the individual is affected, a significant step on the road toward the complete deterioration of rational public debate, or communicative action, has been taken" (Wahl-Jorgensen and Galperin 2000, 33–4). Moving citizens from the sidelines of the communication process (or just from the "audience," as they are commonly regarded) to the public arena where they really belong (Nordenstreng 1997) means a new understanding of freedom of expression and of the right to communicate. This right, actually, is a right "for all citizens rather than [for] the media and its professionals" (Nordenstreng 1997, 14). And, if it is so, citizens must also play a part in media regulation – together with the state, the market, and the media themselves.

A citizen-centered perspective of these issues, instead of a media-centered one, tries to change a situation where, in general terms, "the people have become the *target* of influence" of the mass media, while, according to the general theory of democracy (the sovereignty of the people), "they should have been the *source* of influence" (Nordenstreng 1997, 16–17, emphasis added). And if people are to be a central partner in media regulation processes, it is because the media must be accountable in the first place to the people they work for – and in whose name they claim to work.

Meeting these same concerns, Bardoel and d'Haenens suggest that "the 'switch' to a citizen-based perspective [of the media] will have to be made more often," particularly in the present (and evolving) conditions induced by new media:

> Where formerly the government and the market fought for priority, today we are more likely to hear the slogan: "Citizens first, then the market, and the government last." Along with this, we see in this sector that with the variety of what is on offer and the arrival of new media, power has in fact shifted from the sender to the receiver. (Bardoel and d'Haenens 2004, 172)

This reinforces the idea that, as far as media regulation is concerned, "the traditional legal and market-oriented accountability mechanisms alone are no longer sufficient," and so it seems advisable "to bring back the citizen in the media and media policy debate" (Bardoel and d'Haenens 2004, 172). In fact, if citizens are to play an effective role in the regulatory processes, one assumption must be definitely challenged: that freedom (freedom of expression, freedom of the press) is necessarily inconsistent with accountability. As McQuail puts it:

> Normative media theory has allowed the debate to be narrowed down to a choice between freedom of the media market on the one hand and control or censorship by the state in one form or another on the other, as if greater accountability can only be achieved by sacrificing more freedom. This ignores the complexities of what freedom means in media publication, the inevitability of constraint in public communication and the diversity of means by which the interests of "society," as variously manifested, can be identified, expressed and achieved, without violating the essence of freedom of expression. It also ignores the many responsibilities that are actually and properly entailed in the exercise of freedom by public media. (McQuail 2005, 237)

So the core of this challenge is not the simple refusal of any regulatory mechanisms or instruments, but the need to find "effective *means* of accountability that would be consistent with the notion of responsibility ... and also with essential principles of free expression" (McQuail 2005, 242, original emphasis). Moreover, the whole task of media regulation would be best achieved – either in terms of efficiency or in terms of, so-to-speak, civic and democratic pedagogy – if responsibilities are dispersed among various actors: the state, the market, media companies, media professionals, and the public. In an attempt to systematize the different levels in which the regulatory effort may take place, we can follow the outline designed by McQuail (1997, 2005):

- the *frame of law and formal regulation* – the level of political accountability, comprising regulatory documents concerning what media may and may not do. The main issues here relate mostly to prevention of alleged harm to individuals;
- the *market frame* – the level of accountability linked to the processes of demand and supply in a free and competitive marketplace, which should, at least in theory, encourage "good" and discourage "bad" performance;
- the *frame of public responsibility* – the level of public accountability referring to the assumption that media organizations are economic companies, but are also social institutions that fulfill certain important tasks, subsumed under the definition of the "public interest";
- the *frame of professional responsibility* – the level of professional accountability, the one that "arises out of the self-respect and ethical development of professionals working in the media ... who set their own standards of good performance" (McQuail 2005, 247).

If the first frame relates typically to the "*assigned*" responsibilities of the media – and calls, therefore, for some formal, "centered" regulation – the last two frames relate more to the *"contracted"* and the *"self-imposed"* responsibilities (see note 5), thus asking for self-regulatory (or co-regulatory) instruments and mechanisms. Nevertheless, the entire regulatory structure for the media should pay attention to all these layers at a time, because that seems the only way to search for an adequate balance of power between the state, the market, and society. This attempt means, after all, an ongoing struggle for a balanced relationship between *individual* and *collective*, between *people-as-consumers* and *people-as-citizens*, between *freedom* and *responsibility*.

Journalism Regulation and the Pervasive State

Though it has been argued that regulation should not be seen as a process tied exclusively or even predominantly to the state, the Portuguese state plays an all-encompassing role in the regulation of journalistic activity. First of all, there is a wide legal framework which is developed by state institutions, predominantly by the government and approved by Parliament. The Constitution is by far the most critical legal construct and it has a number of prerogatives that directly concern the journalistic profession. It deals with fundamental rights and duties (articles 16, 17, 18, 19, 25, 26), with freedom of expression and freedom of information (article 37), with freedom of the media (article 38), with the media regulatory body (article 39), and with right to reply and political broadcasts (article 40).

The core of the constitutional protection of the journalistic activity *per se* is in article 38. This article clearly demonstrates the relevance given by the constitutional legislator to journalism as a pillar of the democratic regime. Fundamental journalistic rights are inscribed here, namely freedom of expression and freedom of creation, the right to participate in the editorial position of the medium, the right to access to news sources, the right to independence and to professional secrecy (including the protection of news sources). But article 38 goes beyond the protection of journalistic activity in the strict sense. It contemplates a number of media companies' principles which are perceived as indispensable for an adequate journalistic performance. These are the principles of transparency of financing and property, the principle of nonconcentration, the principle of nondiscrimination, and the principle of independence from economic and political power.

In addition to the Constitution, there is a vast range of laws and legal documents that outline the regulatory construct in which Portuguese journalists operate (see, e.g., Carvalho et al. 2005). The sectoral laws (Press Law, Television Law, and Radio Law) are pivotal in this context. The Press Law (*Lei de Imprensa*) is a detailed document discussing journalists and citizens' rights and duties in terms of public information. The public interest of the press is underlined and the conditions for access to the market are set out. This law also considers the specific responsibilities of journalistic companies, publishers, editors, and journalists. Both the Television Law (*Lei da Televisão*) and the Radio Law (*Lei da Rádio*) aim to regulate access to television / radio activity and its use within the national territory. These are meticulous documents covering a wide array of issues from fundamental freedoms and rights up to technical aspects and programming strategies and content (pluralism, diversity, prohibited material, etc.). The specific nature of public television and radio is also covered. Furthermore, other general laws such as the Penal Code (*Código Penal*), Penal Process Code (*Código do Processo Penal*), and the Civil Code (*Código Civil*) also have a number of articles directly linked with journalistic performance.

As a legislator, the state goes far beyond the production of legal tools specifically related to the journalistic profession. Media companies are part of a wider economic apparatus which is under the scope of national laws and is supervised by economic regulatory bodies such as the Competition Authority (*Autoridade da Concorrência*). It is also up to the state to define the main rules for the development of technological infrastructures (access to the infrastructure and services markets, spectrum allocation, etc.). It is up to the Communications Authority (ICP-*ANACOM – Autoridade Nacional das Comunicações*) to ensure the regular functioning of the "technical" aspect (despite the economic interests involved) of media and communications.

As an external regulator of the journalistic activity, the state is not merely a *legislator*. The state plays a fundamental role also as *owner* and as a *subsidizing body* of media companies. Like most European countries, the Portuguese state owns a public television and radio company. The state-owned company, *Rádio e Televisão de Portugal* (RTP), runs the following eight television channels: RTP 1 (generalist), RTP 2 (generalist), RTP Açores (regional), RTP Madeira (regional), RTP Internacional (international), RTP África (international), RTP N (news) and RTP Memória (classic entertainment programs), and seven radio channels: Antena 1 (generalist / talk radio), Antena 2 (classical music), Antena 3 (adult contemporary / urban), RDP África (international), RDP Madeira (Ant 1) (regional), RDP Madeira (Ant. 3) (regional) and RDP Açores (regional). Furthermore, the state has a strong position in the national news agency, LUSA.

The overt rationale for the state's intervention as proprietor of media companies relates to the exceptional value of public service radio and television, and of the national news agency. Being the owner (either totally or partially, as in the case of LUSA) of such socially relevant tools, the state aims to guarantee that citizens are served at the highest possible level (both in terms of programming and information) and, at the same time, the public service media are expected to act as a system regulator, stimulating the quality of the entire media system. Whether this has ever materialized or not is not the main focus of this chapter (for more on the relationship between public service media and political power in Portugal, see Sousa and Santos 2003, Sousa 1996). What seems nevertheless quite evident is that owning the media and defining the basic rules of their action, namely through concession contracts, the state outlines its vision regarding what public service media should be and how they should behave. The constitutional guarantee of public service media independence from the political and economic power is ensured (or attempted) by the existence of a media regulatory body, *Entidade Reguladora da Comunicação Social* (ERC).

Indeed, as an external regulator, the state also has a say in the system as a media financing entity. Once again the underlying principle of the state's financial support of the media system relates to the exceptional value of media in a democratic society. Helping the media companies financially, the state hopes to regulate the market and to ensure diversity and pluralism. Public service broadcasting and the regional press are the main beneficiaries of the state's financial support. RTP is financed annually, while the regional press has to apply for subsidies and is strongly supported on delivery costs. The end result of the state's support of the regional press is not yet fully understood, but authors such as Ferreira (2005) argue that consequences of this support are disastrous. Poor quality regional press is said to be maintained merely due to subsidies and the editorial independence of newspapers and radio stations is undermined.

As we have seen, the legal framework defines the basis of the state's understanding about societal expectations regarding media performance in general and journalistic activity in particular. But if a legal system is to be more than a dead letter, it needs implementation mechanisms. The ERC is the newly created body designed to implement the law and to ensure that journalists behave according to certain standards. The Portuguese Constitution has one article (no. 39) dedicated to this media regulatory institution. The Constitution states that, in addition to the courts, the media should be regulated by an external independent body. It is up to the ERC to ensure:

- the right to information and to press freedom
- nonconcentration of the media
- independence of the media from political and economic power
- respect for personal rights, freedoms, and guarantees
- respect for the professional rules of the media professions
- the possibility of expression and discussion of divergent opinions
- the exercise of political broadcasts and the right to reply.

According to the basic law, the board of the media regulatory body is to be designated by Parliament. Both the Constitution and Law no. 53 of November 8, 2005, which established the ERC (it started operating in 2006), reflect the legislator's preoccupation with the independence of the regulator. Despite the infancy of the ERC, Portugal has a 30-year tradition of media regulation, although up to 1989 the regulator merely covered the public sector media. The ERC is the successor of the High Council for the Media (*Alta Autoridade para a Comunicação Social*), the first regulatory body to have the responsibility for both private and public media. From the High Council, the ERC inherits a legacy of public distrust in its efficiency and independence. In this context, the ERC's Law attempts to reinforce its human, technical, and financial resources, as well as its independence from the political power of the day and from media companies.

The "pure" state-regulatory model, in which no social actors are represented (apart from an advisory council with no effective powers), was strongly criticized by the national journalist's union (*Sindicato dos Jornalistas*) and by the Confederation of the Media Companies (*Confederação de Meios da Comunicação Social*). The minister responsible for the media, Augusto Santos Silva (2007), has strongly defended the model, arguing that it is necessary to avoid the "capture of the regulator" by private/corporatist interests. The minister argues that the ERC is one pillar of the regulatory construct and this one, in particular, is exclusively concerned with the defense of the public interest (in the press). It is nevertheless one of the ERC's functions to promote other forms of co-regulation, but this is still in its infancy.

The absence of interest representation and the notorious reinforcement of the ERC's powers (ranging from recommendation to the withdrawal of operating licenses) has been cause for much concern in the journalistic profession. Indeed, the ERC has to ensure that the journalistic codes of conduct are followed, but – despite the constitutional guarantees of independence from the political and economic power – there is deep suspicion regarding the ERC's capability and fairness. The ERC's ability to defend citizens from the media's negative consequences and to positively influence programming and journalistic output has yet to be proven.

The Blurred Domain of Self-Regulation

Through legal and administrative mechanisms, the Portuguese state has the capability to define the main traits of the conditions under which the journalistic profession is practiced. The state's ability to legislate penetrates what is frequently perceived as self-regulatory mechanisms (e.g., journalists' professional legislation, public service broadcasting ombudsman). But if the state regulates self-regulation, can we talk about self-regulation? If that is the case, what sets self-regulation apart from the state regulation? In Moreira's perspective (1997), three main aspects characterize self-regulation. First, it is a *particular form* of regulation, not absence of regulation. Secondly, it is *collective* regulation, as there is no individual self-regulation; self-discipline or self-restraint are not forms of self-regulation. Self-regulation implies a collective organization which establishes and imposes rules and a specific discipline to its members. Lastly, it is a *nonstate* regulation, independent from its private or public legal nature (Moreira 1997, 52–3).

Contrary to state regulation, self-regulation is a private domain process, even if its consequences are felt in the public realm (Aznar 2005). Hoping to qualify its professional performance and to strengthen its social contract with the public, Portuguese journalists have set up (or have contributed to) a number of self-regulatory mechanisms, though often as an integral part of the legal sphere. Despite the intertwined nature of self-regulation, we shall briefly cover some institutions which are perceived as mechanisms of journalists' autonomous regulation.

The Journalist's Statute (*Estatuto do Jornalista*) is law (no. 1/99 of January 13, 1999). In addition to the detailed clarification of what it is to be a journalist, the Journalist's Statute defines the professionals' rights and duties. It pays a great deal of attention to access to official sources and to public places, professional secrecy, participation rights, and specific duties regarding rigor, impartiality, nondiscrimination, privacy, and other aspects of accuracy and the preservation of human dignity. This document reflects what society expects from journalists and it makes clear the particular rights they can benefit from in their professional activities. The Journalist's Statute can also be seen as a basic definer of journalists' identity as it states both what it is to be a journalist and how journalists are supposed to behave. Still, if the Journalist's Statute is approved by a parliamentary majority, even if against the views of the journalists' representatives, can it be seen as a self-regulatory tool? As it stands, it does not necessarily represent the journalists' perception of their own nature, rights, and social responsibilities.

As opposed to the Journalist's Statute, the Ethical Code (*Código Deontológico dos Jornalistas Portugueses*) is the product of professionals' ethical concerns, as they were discussed and approved by the professional group itself. The present-day code was approved in 1993, following a consultation process.[7]

The code sets the standards for journalists' professional behavior. It mentions, among many other aspects, rigor, honest interpretation of the facts, the attention that should be given to different sides in a given conflict, plagiarism, sensationalism, identification of news sources, the use of adequate means to obtain information, the safeguard of citizens' rights and human dignity, independence and professional integrity.

It is up to the Ethical Council of the Journalists' Union (*Conselho Deontológico do Sindicato dos Jornalistas*) to guarantee that the code is respected. Therefore, it might be argued that both the Ethical Code and the union's council are typically self-regulatory institutions, as journalists themselves set the rules and developed a monitoring system and an implementation mechanism to enforce those rules among the union's members. Scrutinizing, issuing statements and recommendations, the council expects to ensure that ethical values are preserved and that therefore the dignity of journalists is enhanced.

There is, however, an unsolved difficulty with the present-day model. The ethical code was approved within the journalists' union framework and the ethical council is a structure of the very same union. Nevertheless, to become a journalist it is not necessary to belong to the journalists' union (or to any union for that matter). One could therefore argue that neither the ethical code or the council express the standards set by the entire class, but simply reflect the understanding of the professionals in the journalists' union.

Clearly, professional self-regulation goes beyond the rules of the corporation and has its own mechanisms within particular newsrooms. In Portugal, newsroom councils (*Conselhos de Redacção*) are probably the best known of these institutions. Newsroom councils are committees elected by all journalists working in newsrooms with more than five professionals. In smaller news companies all journalists are part of the *Conselho de Redacção*. The institution of newsroom councils draws from the constitutional prerogative of journalists' participation in the editorial position of the news media they work in (article 38). The establishment and the functioning of these particular councils are inscribed in both the Journalist's Statute (*Estatuto do Jornalista*, see article 13) and in sectoral laws. The Press Law, for example, details (article 23) the role of the newsroom council. Indeed, it covers considerable ground: it has a say in the nomination of the newsroom management and in the editorial regulations of the medium, and plays a role in judging ethical and disciplinary issues. The newsroom council represents the views of the professional body of journalists regarding fundamental labor and ethical questions. It implies that the management of a newspaper, radio, or TV station cannot decide by itself in crucial issues such as editorial stance or disciplinary matters.

The Constitution and the media laws were intended to guarantee power distribution in the newsrooms. This preoccupation dates back to the mid-1970s revolutionary period when the first Press Law established the institution of press councils in all newsrooms with much wider powers than today. At the time, newsroom councils had binding powers in matters such as the appointment of directors or editorial options. Today, the relevance of newsroom councils varies considerably among newsrooms, as most of its functions are merely advisory. However, in general terms, Portuguese journalists strongly value this institution (see Fidalgo 2002).

Another institution imposed by law within the framework of the particular setting of each medium is the Editorial Statute (*Estatuto Editorial*). The Press Law asserts (article 17) that all news media should adopt an editorial statute stating clearly its position, objectives, and respect for professional ethics and the public's good faith. The Editorial Statute is signed by the medium's director after consultation with the newsroom council and ratified by the medium's owner. The statute should be public and sent to the media regulatory body. The Editorial Statute is a social contract between the news media and their employees and with the public.

The Editorial Statute is linked to the newsroom stylebooks. Though not all Portuguese news media have adopted stylebooks, they became important tools for newsroom internal functioning, and not just for technical reasons (Fidalgo 2006). In fact, as in most countries, the first generation of stylebooks could be seen as essentially writing manuals. Today, several newsrooms have adopted far more sophisticated newsroom tools. In addition to crucial aspects regarding news writing and content, a second generation of stylebooks incorporates detailed aspects regarding editorial stance and ethical issues. The publication of such stylebooks is also an empowering instrument for readers, listeners, and viewers, as they have access to newsroom rules and guidelines. The social contract with the public is therefore strengthened.

Looking for an (Im)possible Balance

When looking at the journalistic regulatory structures in Portugal, it is clear that it has changed considerably over recent years: legal instruments have been developed and the links between different social actors have become more complex. Despite the efforts of journalists themselves, the state appears to be the most relevant actor in the sphere of media and journalistic regulation in Portugal. The state – as a legislator, as a media owner, and as a financing body of the system – is at the center of the most visible "sustained and focused attempt to alter the behaviour of others" (Black 2002, 20). Analyzing the overt dimension of media regulation in Portugal, it could be argued that the state is still the most powerful actor, probably because other regulatory mechanisms are still incipient. Co-regulation is embryonic and journalists themselves are still struggling to go beyond very fragile modes of professional self-regulation. The traceable reinforcement of state regulation might be perceived as a consequence of the professional failure to ensure self-regulation.

If it seems noticeable that the state has extended its regulatory arm in the journalistic field, legislating inclusively about professional ethics, one could question the efficiency of such an accomplishment. Indeed, it is highly doubtful that more legal tools and a new state media regulatory body *per se*, even if necessary, have a significant impact in the overall quality of journalistic output. The "invisible" daily commercial pressures might have a more significant impact on the daily choices journalists are expected to make. Due to the increasing fragmentation of audiences and the concomitant reduction of advertising revenues, media companies are under increasing pressure and most journalists perform in commercial contexts.

If the defense of public interest depends on the overall functioning of the entire media regulatory construct, state and professional media regulation is far from sufficient. Indeed, citizens' participation – at different stages and levels – is an indispensable dimension in the continuous attempt to develop a responsible and accountable media culture. In Portugal, various mechanisms were put in place in order to make way for citizens' contributions. All newsrooms receive on a daily basis correspondence from their readers, listeners, and viewers by highly differentiated means (phone calls, letters, email, etc.). Frequently, the media dedicate time and space to put forward views and opinions expressed by citizens, both in terms of journalistic coverage and programming. More recently, another institution has emerged in order to represent/express people's opinions in the media companies – the ombudsman. In the daily press, these mediation experiences started in 1997 and the initiative was taken by the newspapers themselves (three daily newspapers, up to now). In the broadcasting arena, the first mediation experiences started in 2006, but only in public service radio and television. The broadcasting company RTP acted according to the Ombudsman Law, approved by the Parliament.

Although the media give some time and space to the public, either directly or with the support of ombudsman mediation, citizens should also play a more active role in the relationship with the media. If media are to be accountable to citizens,

citizens must take at least some responsibility for the media they have (and especially for the media they want). As Daniel Cornu has underlined, together with the social responsibility of the media, there is such as thing as the "mediatic responsibility of the society" (Cornu 1999, 436). That is the point to which Silverstone (2004, 440) called our attention when he argued for our need to develop "a responsible and accountable media culture" – more than just "responsible and accountable media." And he explained that this particular culture "depends on a critical and literate citizenry, and a citizenry, above all, which is critical with respect to, and literate in the ways of, mass mediation and media representation" (Silverstone 2004, 440).

The importance of deep and extended media literacy – regarded as "a critical activity" and "a civic activity" required for all citizens – is thus stressed by Silverstone (2004) as an alternative way to approach the media regulation issues in a long-term perspective. And media education plays an important role here. He argued for:

> a shift away from regulation as narrowly conceived in minds and practices of parliaments and councils, towards a more ethically oriented education, and towards a critical social and cultural practice which recognizes the particular characteristics of our mediated world. We once upon a time taught something called civics. It is perhaps time to think through what civics might be in our present intensely mediated century. (Silverstone 2004, 446)

Regulation, after all, is not just a matter of *production*. Media *consumption*, Cees Hamelink suggested, "should be viewed, like professional media performance, as a social practice which implies moral choices and the assumption of accountability for these choices" (quoted in Silverstone 2004, 448). So citizens themselves must also be accountable for their use of the media, because, as the "ecological" perspectives argue, it is everybody's responsibility to take care of our *cultural* environment (where production and distribution of information play an increasingly central part), just as it is everybody's responsibility to take care of our *natural* environment. After all, what the media do or do not is, partly, the result of their interaction with the public. So "if one accepts the interactive character of the professional–client relationship, it follows that media ethics cannot be limited to the rights and wrongs of the producers only and should also be ethics for media users" (Hamelink 1995, 500).

Contemporary regulatory practice should be more and more open to "policy tools that include both direct interventions and also indirect attempts to shape the market partly by engaging the public in various ways," as Lunt and Livingstone put it:

> In the communications sector … technological developments, such as digital switchover, broadband spectrum and convergence, are driving a shift from state regulation, strongly influenced by a public service ethos, to the complex delivery of diverse contents and services across multiple platforms to a media-literate public. (Lunt and Livingstone 2007, 3)

As for self-regulation, it poses important challenges to the media industry as a whole and to their professionals in particular. Notwithstanding, it will be more or less expanded and efficient according also to the stronger or weaker capacity of citizens to demand it, and to involve themselves in some kind of co-regulatory mechanisms where they can have a voice, too. After all, the various media account-ability systems (MAS) publicized and recommended by Claude-Jean Bertrand – and including a vast array of self-regulatory and co-regulatory instruments – are very accurately defined as an "arsenal for democracy" (Bertrand 1999), thus encouraging citizens to do their share in order to improve media quality and to enhance their own opportunities for civic participation. Within a political econ-omy perspective, one would argue that today it is no longer sufficient to ask "whether, on balance, the media system serves to promote or undermine demo-cratic institutions and practices," as McChesney puts it (2008, 12). In a time of traditional media erosion and unprecedented cultural environmental challenges, one should also question whether, on balance, citizens/consumers serve to pro-mote or undermine democratic institutions and practices.

The Portuguese situation regarding journalism regulation, briefly presented and discussed in this chapter, cannot be dissociated from the country's political and social specific context – a country that became a democracy only in the mid-1970s, after a long period of dictatorship and total absence of press freedom. It is a case study worth considering either for its own merits or as a contribution for further comparative studies with countries where different media systems have been trying different answers for (often) similar problems.

Notes

This chapter is based on a paper delivered at the International Conference "Comparing Media Systems, West Meets East," Kliczków Castle, Wroclaw, Poland, April 23–25, 2007.

1   For the purposes of this chapter, we will use Black's definition of regulation: "the sus-tained and focused attempt to alter the behaviour of others according to defined stand-ards or purposes with the intention of producing a broadly identified outcome or outcomes, which may involve mechanisms of standard-setting, information-gathering and behaviour-modification" (Black 2002, 20). For more on the concept of regulation, see, inter alia, Hans-Bredow Institute for Media Research at the University of Hamburg (2006), McGonagle (2003), Palzer (2003).
2   Wahl-Jorgensen and Galperin (2000, 38) argue that far from being a simple commodity like "cans of fruit and bars of soap," the mass media should actually be viewed as "the sole site for political agency in late modernity" – this meaning that they are "the place where we may get together to justify the norms on which we act, and build the solidar-ity we need to live together."
3   Even more than two sides of a coin, or two extremes in a constant fight with each other, "rights" and "responsibilities" (rights to free speech and to free press,

responsibilities for its adequate use) should be regarded as intimately bound together, like two strings that make a rope, to use Vernon Jensen's metaphor (according to Johannesen 2001, 2008). This author even suggests the use of a new term, "rightsabilities," to stress how both concepts depend on each other, and how the first one can never be understood without the second.

4 Recalling the "Protocol on Public Service Broadcasting" adopted by the European Union (EU) in 1997, in Amsterdam, Christians and Nordenstreng (2004, 7–8) underline the "vital point" that "public broadcasting (vs. commercial broadcasting) should be understood in the EU as part of the cultural and social sphere based in national priorities, instead of the economic sphere based on free competition within the broader European scale. Accordingly, public service broadcasting is defined at the constitutional level as an exception to the principle of a free European market." This helps the authors to assert that "the Social Responsibility theory prevails in the deep structures of political economy and media policy," and, therefore, "one is entitled to say that the spirit of Hutchins [Report] is very much alive in Europe today."

5 These responsibilities are diverse, according to their source and to the degree of compulsion involved – and, therefore, they stress differently the kind of regulatory mechanisms that should be most adequate in each case. The three main types of media responsibility, following Hodges (1990) and McQuail (1997), are the *"assigned"* responsibilities (mostly covered by law and serving to balance media freedom with the rights of other members of society and the public interest), *"contracted"* responsibilities (arising because of some implied covenant between press and society, maintained by convention and mutual agreement), and *"self-imposed"* responsibilities (referring to voluntary professional commitments to observe certain ethical standards and to serve public purposes). And "a full consideration of media accountability" has to take account of all the categories (McQuail 1997, 516).

6 As McQuail (1997, 517) suggests, media accountability can assume different modes, according to the degree of coercion involved and to the main purpose intended: in one model, the mode of *"liability,"* characterized by "an adversarial relationship," deals mostly with issues of harm caused by the media and with material sanctions that can punish that behavior; in the other model, the mode of *"answerability,"* more concerned with improving mass media quality, and specially open to voluntary negotiations and interactions in order to achieve the resolution of differences. However, "there is a range of possibilities in between these alternative models," adds McQuail (1997, 517). And the preference for one or other of these models (the first more suitable for public regulation, the second closer to self-regulation mechanisms) somehow depends on the choice for a particular perspective of political organization of the media system.

7 See http://www.jornalistas.online.pt (accessed April 4, 2007).

References

Aznar, H. (2005) *Comunicación Responsable – Deontología y Autorregulación de los Medios*, 2nd edn. Ariel Comunicación, Barcelona.

Bardoel, J. and d'Haenens, L. (2004) Media meet the citizen: Beyond market mechanisms and government regulations. *European Journal of Communication*, 19(2), 165–94.

Bertrand, C.-J. (1999) *L'Arsenal de la Démocratie – Médias Déontologie et M***A***R***S**. Economica, Paris.

Black, J. (2002) *Critical Reflections on Regulation*. Centre for Analysis of Risk and Regulation at the London School of Economics and Political Science, London.

Carvalho, A., Cardoso, A., and Figueiredo, J. (2005) *Legislação Anotada da Comunicação Social*. Casa das Letras, Lisbon.

Christians, C. and Nordenstreng, K. (2004) Social responsibility worldwide. *Journal of Mass Media Ethics*, 19(1), 3–28.

Cornu, D. (1999) *Jornalismo e Verdade – Para uma Ética da Informação*. Instituto Piaget, Lisbon.

Ferreira, P. (2005) O custo das não-decisões na imprensa local e regional em Portugal. *Comunicação e Sociedade*, 7, 153–80.

Fidalgo, J. (2002) The ombudsman's role in the eyes of the newsroom: Results of a survey among Portuguese journalists. *Proceedings of the 23th Conference of the International Association for Media and Communication Research (IAMCR)*. Barcelona.

Fidalgo, J. (2006) O lugar da ética e da auto-regulação na identidade profissional dos jornalistas. PhD dissertation, Universidade do Minho, Braga. Online at http://hdl.handle.net/1822/6011 (accessed October 7, 2010).

Giroux, G. (1991) La déontologie professionnelle dans le champ du journalisme: Portée et limites. *Communication*, 12(2), 117–38.

Golding, P. and Murdock, G. (1991) Culture, communication, and political economy. In: Curran, J. and Gurevitch, M. (eds) *Mass Media and Society*. Edward Arnold, London, pp. 15–32.

Hamelink, C. (1995) Ethics for media users. *European Journal of Communication*, 10(4), 497–512.

Hans-Bredow Institute for Media Research at the University of Hamburg (2006) *Final Report Study on Co-regulation Measures in the Media Sector*. Study for the European Commission, Directorate Information Society and Media, Unit A1 Audiovisual and Media Policies, Tender DG EAC 03/04, Contract n° 2004-5091/001-001 DAV BST. Online at http://ec.europa.eu/avpolicy/docs/library/studies/coregul/final_rep_en.pdf (accessed October 7, 2010).

Hodges, L. W. (1990) Definindo a responsabilidade da imprensa: Uma abordagem funcional. In: Elliot, D. (ed.), *Jornalismo versus Privacidade*. Nórdica, Rio de Janeiro, pp. 15–34.

Johannesen, R. (2001) Communication ethics: Centrality, trends and controversies. In: Gudykunst, W. (ed.), *Communication Yearbook 25*. International Communication Association (ICA), New York, pp. 201–35.

Josephi, B. (2005) Journalism in the global age. *Gazette*, 67(6), 575–90.

Livingstone, S., Lunt, P., and Miller, L. (2007) Citizens, consumers and the citizen-consumer: Articulating the citizen interest in media and communications regulation. *Discourse and Communication*, 1(1), 63–89.

Lunt, P. and Livingstone, S. (2007) Regulation in the public interest. *Consumer Policy Review*, 17(2), 2–7.

McChesney, R. W. (2008) *The Political Economy of Media: Enduring Issues, Emerging Dilemmas*. Monthly Review Press, New York.

McGonagle, T. (2003) Co-regulation of the media in Europe: The potential for practice of an intangible idea. In: *IRIS plus - Legal Observations of the European Audiovisual Observatory* European Audiovisual Observatory, Strasbourg.

McQuail, D. (1997) Accountability of media to society – Principles and means. *European Journal of Communication*, 12(4), 511–29.

McQuail, D. (2005) Publication in a free society: The problem of accountability. *Comunicação e Sociedade* 7, 235–52.

Moreira, V. (1997) *Auto-regulação Profissional e Administração Pública*. Almedina, Coimbra, Portugal.

Morrison, D., and Svennevig, M. (2007) The defence of public interest and the intrusion of privacy. *Journalism*, 8(1), 44–65.

Mosco, V. (1996) *The Political Economy of Communication: Rethinking and Renewal*. Sage, London.

Napoli, P. (1999) The marketplace of ideas metaphor in communication regulation. *Journal of Communication*, 49(4), 151–69.

Nerone, J. C. (ed.) (1995) *Last Rights – Revisiting Four Theories of the Press*. University of Illinois Press, Chicago.

Nordenstreng, K. (1997) The citizen moves from the audience to the arena. *Nordicom Review*, 18(2), 13–20.

Palzer, C. (2003) Co-regulation of the media in Europe: European provisions for the establishment of co-regulation frameworks. In: *Iris Plus, Legal Observations of the European Audiovisual Observatory* European Audiovisual Observatory, Strasbourg.

Reinard, J. and Ortiz, S. (2005) Communication law and policy: The state of research and theory. *Journal of Communication*, 55(3), 594–631.

Siebert, F., Peterson, T., and Schramm, W. (1963) *Four Theories of the Press*. University of Illinois Press, Chicago.

Silva, A. S. (2007) A hetero-regulação dos meios de comunicação social. *Comunicação e Sociedade*, 11, 15–27.

Silverstone, R. (2004) Regulation, media literacy and media civics. *Media Culture and Society*, 26(3), 440–49.

Sousa, H. (1996) Communications Policy in Portugal and its Links with the European Union – An Analysis of the Telecommunications and Television Broadcasting Sectors from the mid-1980s up until the mid-1990's. PhD dissertation, School of Social Sciences, City University, London.

Sousa, H. and Santos, L. A. (2003) A RTP e o Serviço Público: Um percurso de inultrapassável dependência e contradição. In: Pinto, M. et al. (2003) *Televisão e Cidadania*. Universidade do Minho, Braga, Portugal, pp. 61–80.

Wahl-Jorgensen, K. and Galperin, H. (2000) Discourse ethics and the regulation of media: The case of the U.S. newspaper. *Journal of Communication Inquiry*, 24(1), 19–40.

Suggestions for Further Reading

Feintuck, M. and Varney, M. (2006) *Media Regulation, Public Interest and the Law*, 2nd edn. Edinburgh University Press, Edinburgh.

Frost, C. (2007) *Journalism Ethics and Regulation*, 2nd edn. Pearson, Harlow, UK.

McQuail, D. (2003) *Media Accountability and Freedom of Publication*. Oxford University Press, New York.

Schulz, W. and Held, T. (2004) *Regulated Self-Regulation as a Form of Modern Government: A Comparative Analysis with Case Studies from Media and Telecommunications Law.* University of Luton Press, Luton, UK.

Von Krogh, T. (ed.) (2008) *Media Accountability Today... and Tomorrow – Updating the Concept in Theory and Practice.* Nordicom, Gothenburg.

Part III

Conditions of Creativity
Industries, Production, Labor

14

The Death of Hollywood
Exaggeration or Reality?

Janet Wasko

Once again, the Hollywood film industry is being challenged by a wide array of sources – everything from new technologies to other film industries to copyright infringers. Some of these challenges are not new, although one might think so by reading discussions in the popular press, entertainment blogs, or film industry trade papers, where, once again, the end of Hollywood, and even the end of film, has been predicted. Some examples:

- "Hollywood as a business model is … facing deep and fundamental challenges" (Florida 2009).
- "The business model that formed the motion picture business … is changing profoundly before our eyes" (Disney CEO, Bob Iger, cited in Sandoval 2009).
- "As almost (or, truly, virtually) every aspect of making and viewing movies is replaced by digital technologies, even the notion of 'watching a film' is fast becoming an anachronism" (publicity material for Rodowick 2007).
- "… in case you've missed this decade altogether, it's no secret that the entire Hollywood movie industry is dying" (Edelman 2007).
- "… cinema as we know it is falling apart" (Francis Ford Coppola cited in Sandoval 2009).

Certainly, there can be little doubt that the media in general are undergoing significant changes, primarily because of digital technologies but for other reasons as well. Indeed, this period has been called "the largest, most fundamental transformation in the history of the media since the advent of typeface, the moving image, and terrestrial broadcast transmission" (Levin 2009, 258). While it may be too soon to agree with this sweeping statement, there is no shortage of commentary about

The Handbook of Political Economy of Communications, First Edition.
Edited by Janet Wasko, Graham Murdock, and Helena Sousa.
© 2014 John Wiley & Sons, Ltd. Published 2014 by John Wiley & Sons, Ltd.

this transformation and no overall agreement about the consequences. As Cunningham and colleagues have noted:

> the problem is that most debate … about industry structure and change is based on an exaggerated opposition between enthusiastic optimism versus determined skepticism over the potential of new technologies. There are assertions of "fundamental crisis" in the strategies of the media and communications industries versus counter assertions of "plus ça change, plus la même chose" – that the present is a minor blip in the march of hegemonic capital. (Cunningham et al. 2009)

It is not surprising that the US film industry is experiencing change nor that there are differing opinions regarding this process. But what is actually changing? This chapter explores some of the challenges and changes confronting the film industry that have been cited in recent discussions of Hollywood's death. The chapter also considers some of the features that are not changing, or in other words: what continues to characterize Hollywood? The discussion draws on a political economic analysis of film, which seeks to understand Hollywood specifically as an industry that produces and distributes commodities within a capitalist system, as well as the political, social, and cultural implications of that process (see Wasko 2003, Pendakur 1990). The chapter also relies on various accounts from industry insiders and the trade press in an attempt to get a sense of the reactions to various changes actually taking place in the industry.

What's Changing About Hollywood?

This section will consider some of the major claims that have been made in the declarations of Hollywood's death, as well as other ongoing changes that the industry is experiencing.

Changes in film financing

Financing is fundamental for the production of any kind of film, but increasingly for Hollywood films that cost, on the average, well over $100 million (not including marketing costs). Banks and other financial institutions, as well as outside investors, have been involved with the industry in various ways since the early years of the twentieth century. However, the type of loans and the amount of financial institutions' involvement in Hollywood companies have consistently changed over the years (see Wasko 1982).

In the not too distant past (during the last decade), investment funds for major motion pictures seemed plentiful and cheap. An example was Legendary Pictures, a production company that was funded by important Wall Street private equity and hedge fund investors, including ABRY Partners, AIG Direct Investments, Bank of America Capital Investors, Columbia Capital, Falcon Investment Advisors, and M/C Venture Partners. Legendary arranged a five-year, 25-picture agreement to coproduce and cofinance with Warner Bros. in 2005, and released several successful blockbusters, including *Batman Begins*, *Superman Returns*, and *The Dark Knight*.

However, with the recent economic meltdown, most of these types of funds have disappeared (Clarke 2009). Florida (2009) reports that "Some [Wall Street investment houses and hedge funds] have closed their L.A. offices and are reportedly peddling their ownership interests in upcoming movies at discounts of 30 to 70 percent." Meanwhile, major Hollywood companies have had difficulty raising funds for films and thus the number of films produced is declining. So here we have the first challenge to the most important film companies – finding new funding sources (hopefully, "other people's money") for the very pricey films that Hollywood tends to produce.

Changes in film production

Other recent challenges have been associated with the transition from film to digital production. Many Hollywood players welcome the new digital technology; as actor/producer Ethan Hawke once exclaimed: "Digital video is the single greatest thing to happen to film since Marlon Brando," arguing that digital means more power for writers and actors (Bing and Oppelaar 2000). However, production crews, laboratories, and other production personnel have struggled with the digital transition. While these adjustments are significant, the industry has dealt with this kind of change in the past, and for the most part, the Hollywood production community accepts digital filmmaking.

But not only have production technologies changed, digital filmmaking equipment is available to those outside the major Hollywood studios. Thus one of the challenges to Hollywood's control over the cinematic world is the development of these new production technologies that enable truly independent film production.[1] As Edelman (2007) notes: "Films that once required a film lab, a team of special effects gurus, and a roomful of dedicated Silicon Graphics workstations are becoming the province of some dude with a $500 camcorder and a Mac."

Of course, it's not the first time that technology has been available for independent filmmaking. For instance, in the 1980s, director Francis Ford Coppola commented in an interview in the documentary film *Heart of Darkness*:

> To me the great hope is that now these little 8 mm video recorders and stuff have come out, some people who normally wouldn't make movies are going to be making them … Suddenly one day some little fat girl in Ohio is going to be the new Mozart … and make a beautiful film with her father's little camera-corder, and for once this whole professionalism about movies will be destroyed forever and it will become an art form.

The current claims of Hollywood's death also proclaim the democratization of filmmaking. For instance: "inexpensive digital cameras, cheap (or free) editing software, and newly-accessible avenues of distribution (like digital cinemas and the Internet) are democratizing the art of cinema" (Kirsner 2008, 198). And filmmakers, such as George Lucas, are arguing that inexpensive production equipment will lead to more freedom from the Hollywood studios in terms of what kind of films can be produced (Kirsner 2008, 199). There is no doubt that digital filmmaking technology is available at relatively low costs (compared to professional filmmaking equipment of the past). However, it remains to be seen whether independent filmmakers can actually challenge the Hollywood hierarchy, which has remained in place despite previous technological developments.

Changes in film marketing/promotion

Promotion and marketing have become key components for Hollywood films, with expenditures equaling or going considerably beyond production costs. *Variety* reports that during the first two quarters of 2009, around $1.7 billion was spent on promotion of theatrical releases (McClintock 2009a). And new media technologies are increasingly used in studios' promotion campaigns.

For many years now, studios have integrated websites into most films' promotional campaigns. These sites include a wide variety of features, including games, photos, trailers, and tie-ins with other products. More recently, new forms of promotion have developed with the popularity of social networks, such as Facebook and MySpace, as well as emails, blogs, podcasts, Twitter, widgets, and so forth. It's claimed that social media promotion incorporates a strategy that directly involves the audience and aims to create "viral word of mouth" for a film. While Hollywood has attempted to build fan support in the past in various ways, including fan magazines, contests, and personal appearances, the tools being used these days are different. Several recent examples include low budget films that became box office successes using "innovative, viral marketing campaigns" (*Paranormal Activity*, *District 9*, and *The Hangover*) – prompting some to claim that new marketing techniques have taken over. As one observer says: "Good-bye, massive Burger King promotions – hello MySpace guerrilla marketing" (Edelman 2007).

It's not clear, however, that the traditional forms of marketing are disappearing so quickly. By late 2009, various forms of digital marketing represented only 8–12 percent of a film's promotional budget. While traditional marketing strategies, such as newspaper, broadcast, and outdoor advertising, and theatrical trailers, declined somewhat, they still represented the dominant forms of promotion. As one studio marketer commented: "The landscape is shifting … While everyone is clearly focusing on the Internet, we're just not at a place yet where we can do less television. That's why it's such a confusing, interesting and scary time." (McClintock 2009a).

Some Hollywood marketers even wonder whether the new forms of promotion are actually that effective. Twitter, for instance, may be "just pitching it out into the void," as one studio executive observed (McDonald 2009). In addition, these social media tools can actually work against a film. A few examples of well-promoted, big films that collapsed during their opening weekends have been blamed on Twitter and other social networking sites "that can blast instant raves – or pans – to hundreds of people just minutes after the credits roll" (McClintock 2009a).

An obvious example of these sentiments is represented by the marketing campaign for *Avatar*. As Hampp (2010) notes, "With all the talk of the 'Twitter effect' and social media making or breaking Hollywood releases, Fox took a decidedly big-picture approach to go to market with the most expensive film ever made," using many traditional forms of promotion (television advertising, tie-ins, etc.). Thus it seems clear that digital promotion definitely has not taken over from traditional Hollywood marketing strategies – at least, not yet.

Changes in film distribution

We move next to the distribution sector, traditionally the most powerful component of the film industry, and the site of some of most significant challenges to the status quo. Hollywood films are typically distributed to a number of outlets or platforms, including theaters, home video, cable and broadcast television, as well as a number of smaller markets (hotels, airplanes, military bases, etc.). While these "old" distribution outlets are still attracting customers, much attention is being directed at a few new outlets, as well as some future platforms.

Online distribution   Much of the hoopla over Hollywood's demise is connected to the Internet and its potential for distributing films outside of Hollywood's control. The major companies have been reluctant to offer their films online for a variety of reasons, including the lack of adequate technology (video compression and hardware), the problems associated with piracy, and a workable business model (see Cunningham et al. 2009).

As the technology has improved, the ongoing challenge has been to figure out a workable business model that also prevents the rampant piracy that the music industry experienced in the 1990s; in other words, how to make money from distributing movies online without losing control of the product. While several sites have come and gone over the last decade, a snapshot of current online distribution services reveals primarily three different models: advertising-supported (e.g., YouTube, Hulu, Crackle, Veoh); rentals and/or sell-through (e.g., Amazon, Apple iTunes, Blockbuster); and subscription (e.g., Netflix). Note that some of these sites have changed models, or, in some instances, are combining them (see Table 14.1). Interestingly, a few of the most important online distribution sites are owned by non-Hollywood players: iTunes (Apple), YouTube (Google), and Amazon. While the major studios sell their films to these sites, pricing and timing continue to be thorny issues.

Table 14.1   Types of online film distribution

	Advertising-supported	Rent	Purchase	Streaming content	Monthly membership fee	Individual rental/ purchase
YouTube	X					
Hulu	X					
Crackle	X					
Veoh	X					
CinemaNow		X	X		X	X
Amazon		X	X			X
Vongo		X			X	
Apple iTunes		X	X			X
Netflix		X			X	
EzTakes			X			X
MovieFlix			X		X	
TotalVid		X	X		X	
Blockbuster		X	X			X
Superpass				X	X	

Sources include Movie Downland Review. *TopTenReviews.* Online at http://movie-download-review.toptenreviews.com/

The studios have developed their own services (Hulu, Crackle, and Veoh), which obviously offer more control, yet represent another form of vertical integration and sometimes, concentration, for the industry. For instance, Hulu was founded in March 2007 by NBC Universal, News Corp., and Providence Equity Partners. The Disney Company joined the partnership in April 2009. Hulu offers films online (although currently it offers mostly television programming) and provides an example of integration, as well as another example of collaboration rather than competition.

Other new distribution outlets   In addition to the Internet, other new technologies offer distribution outlets that are especially useful in reaching the technologically savvy youth markets. A recent study found that "kids spend most of their leisure time watching or interacting with entertainment, with 34 hours each week spent playing videogames, listening to music or watching movies" (Graser 2009a).

It's not surprising, then, that films have found their way onto videogame consoles, with Sony and Xbox offering digital downloads of films and television programs through deals with the major Hollywood companies. Meanwhile, films are available in various ways on mobile phones. For instance, mobile customers can access film clips on the mobile version of YouTube and movie rentals from the iTunes store. Verizon Wireless offers V Cast, which features sports, news, and comedy clips. Undoubtedly, more access to movies on mobile phones will be forthcoming.

Future distribution developments   In 2008, a consortium of studios, retailers, and electronics manufacturers formed the Digital Entertainment Content Ecosystem (DECE), which is working on a system called Buy Once, Play Everywhere. The service involves a digital storage system using "cloud computing" to store films in a "digital locker" on a remote server, which can be accessed from any device (TV, computer, phone). The consortium agreed on a format in January 2010, with the first devices and services using the format to be available in early 2011.

This type of technology offers several advantages to the Hollywood studios. One standard file format would offer significant savings for distributors, as just one file will be needed. (Currently, multiple files are required for various formats.) In addition, pricing would be in the hands of the studios, not the retailers.

Not all of the players are involved with the DECE's system, however. Apple hasn't joined the DECE project, which, many argue, is crucial in light of iTunes, iPods, iPhones, and iPads (see below). In addition, Disney is working on its own system called KeyChest, which is expected by the end of 2010.

Meanwhile, Apple's acclaimed iPad offers yet another potential distribution outlet for Hollywood films. *Variety*'s reaction to the announcement of the device in January 2010 may be indicative of the industry's attitude: "At a time when a growing number of people are accessing entertainment on the go, the iPad provides studios and networks with yet another attractive platform on which they can digitally distribute movies, TV shows, music, games and other content – and put more coin in their coffers" (Graser 2010). Disney's Bob Iger echoed these sentiments, stating that the iPad "could be a game changer in terms of enabling us to essentially create new forms of content" (quoted in Wilkerson 2010). Clearly, the film industry looks forward to yet another means of collecting revenue from their products.

Changes in independent film distribution

The challenge of the Internet and other new distribution outlets for Hollywood is not only to find a business model that works, but the "threat" of independently produced, inexpensive, Internet-distributed films that will compete with and, some would argue, ultimately undermine the entire Hollywood system. As new techniques of generating revenue from Internet distribution develop, filmmakers may realize "they don't need Hollywood anymore. And then ... and then the movies will be a whole new ballgame" (Johanson 2008).

A wide range of individuals and companies offer opportunities for independent filmmakers to circulate their films. Some sites offer resources for promoting and distributing independent work, while others represent sites where independent films can be accessed.

New models of distribution are emerging for independent producers, incorporating new media outlets and new ways of maintaining distribution control. For example, independent film consultant Peter Broderick encourages "hybrid distribution," which combines direct sales by filmmakers with distribution by third parties (e.g., DVD distributors, TV channels, VOD companies, educational distributors) (Broderick 2009).

While many of these outlets have been available for some time, the "revolution" for independents is often assumed to be with the Internet, where near unlimited capacity allows some sites to offer millions of film/video clips. In early 2010, YouTube launched a rental service featuring independent films, inaugurated with five films from the Sundance Film Festival. The move prompted one film instructor to conclude:

> new avenues for distributing and consuming full-length independent films will now give anyone with the talent and drive to make movies, a viable and well-trafficked platform for getting their work in front of huge audiences and more importantly – sold. ... Indeed, the day when nearly everyone has made an independent film, in the same way that most people today have both an e-mail address and a Facebook page (and perhaps a blog and a Twitter account), may not be far off. (Martin 2010)

YouTube is only one new site where independent films may find audiences, but it may become one of the most important. It claims one of the largest audiences on the Web, boasting more than 70 million unique visitors each month in the US alone (see Vonderau and Snickars 2010). YouTube is owned by Google, the mammoth Internet search engine company that has expanded rapidly into a variety of digital/online businesses, and earns revenue by selling advertising, as well as dealing with many of the major Hollywood companies. One of the problems for independent filmmakers might be the vastness of YouTube. The company has amassed a collection of more than 100 million video clips, so a film can possibly become lost on the site.

Another example of online distribution for independents is Vimeo, an advertising-supported site that calls itself "a respectful community of creative people who are passionate about sharing the videos they make." The site claims to have amassed 14.7 million videos and 28 million members since its inception in November 2004. It is also owned by a larger company – IAC, a publicly traded corporation that owns more than 50 other sites/brands, including Ask.com, Match.com, and Citysearch.

One way to summarize the changing world of film distribution and the advantages for independent filmmakers is captured by Broderick in his summary of the Old World and New World Distribution (see Table 14.2). Broderick and others are clearly enthusiastic about the shifting landscape that provides more outlets for displaying independent films, and more control for independent filmmakers (see Dargis 2010, Irvine 2009). Yet, with continuing issues of finding financing and effective distribution, it remains to be seen whether increasing numbers of independents can survive, much less challenge the Hollywood system.

Table 14.2 Old world and new world film distribution

Old world distribution	New world distribution
Distributor in control	Filmmaker in control
Overall deal	Hybrid approach
Fixed release plans	Flexible release strategies
Mass audience	Core and crossover audiences
Rising costs	Lower costs
Viewers reached through distributor	Direct access to viewers
Third party sales	Direct and third party sales
Territory by territory distribution	Global distribution
Cross-collateralized revenues	Separate revenue streams
Anonymous consumers	True fans

Source: http://www.peterbroderick.com

Changes in film exhibition

And what about movie theaters? Will they become extinct in the new world of distribution? For years, many people have bemoaned the decline of the movie-going experience, especially in light of the availability of movies in other venues that increasingly compete with the traditional movie theater (see Clark 2009). Although Hollywood films are still most often released first in theaters, the exhibition business faces numerous challenges. But again, this isn't the first time. As one observer points out: "we're talking about an industry that not only survived, but ended up thriving amid the arrival of television in the 1950s, videotapes in the 1980s, and DVDs in the '90s. The reason? An ability to continually remake themselves and find new ways to generate revenue, by introducing everything from the multiplex and more elaborate concessions to lengthy pre-show advertising" (Irvine 2009).

Recent changes in theatrical exhibition that will be discussed below involve technological innovations (some of which have been around for awhile), as well as new features added to the traditional theater setting.

Digital cinemas, 3D, IMAX As one industry report concluded: "Every phase of the way that movies are made and shown is undergoing a total transformation from analog to digital. We believe that there are no islands in the digital world" (Digital Cinema Report 2010). Digital cinema involves films distributed on hard drives, optical disks, or by satellite and projected on digital projectors. The advantages include lower distribution costs, alternative content for exhibitors, and more protection of content. However, the cost of converting theaters (as much as $150,000 per screen), as well as the higher obsolescence of digital systems compared to film projectors, have been stumbling blocks for theater owners. Other problems relate to storing digital material.

For years, US exhibitors and distributors debated who would pay for the switch to digital projectors. That dispute was resolved when a consortium of exhibitors and studios agreed on a plan for conversion of nearly 20,000 theater screens with financial assistance from JPMorgan Chase & Co. The process slowed down considerably when credit markets froze, making it difficult to finance the conversions (Verrier 2009). Meanwhile, in other countries, a variety of financing options (including public subsidies) have funded the digital conversion of cinemas (Hanson and McDonald 2009). By 2008, there were around 8,600 digital screens worldwide, with 65 percent of all digital screens in the US (a total of over 5,400) (MPAA 2009b). Digital cinemas seem inevitable and will probably dominate theatrical exhibition eventually, especially when major distributors only produce digital versions of their films, as is likely some time in the future.

Another new development in theatrical exhibition is not new at all. 3D is a system of presenting film images so that they appear to the viewer to be three-dimensional. The earliest 3D films were available in the 1920s, followed by several "waves" of 3D film distribution. In the 1950s, 3D was offered by some theaters to compete with television; however, the process has been considered mostly as a novelty. More recently, 3D has gone digital, with various systems available and the number of 3D screens and 3D films increasing.

While there have been a number of companies offering 3D technology (Dolby Laboratories, Master Image, and XpanD), a relatively small firm called RealD has become the leading provider of digital 3D and claims to have "revolutionized the cinema industry." The company currently dominates the market, with 90 percent of the US 3D screens and 4,800 screens installed in 48 countries with 300 exhibitors. At the end of March 2009, only about 2,000 of 40,000 screens in North America were 3D ready (Verrier 2009).

The tremendous success of *Avatar* brought increased attention to 3D, with more than 70 percent of the film's box office revenue from 3D versions (Cieply and Barnes 2010). However, *Avatar*'s success has also led to a "3D bottleneck" – there aren't enough 3D screens to accommodate the increasing number of 3D films. For instance, *Avatar* was to be replaced in many theaters in early March 2010 by Disney's new *Alice in Wonderland*. However, theaters were reluctant to let go of the *Avatar* goldmine for the unknown Disney remake. By the end of 2010, there may be around 5,100 3D screens in the US and 60 films set for 3D release over the next three years (Cieply and Barnes 2010).

Another advanced system is IMAX, which uses frames 10 times the size of 35 mm film, thus enhancing the quality of the image. IMAX theaters use oversized screens as well as special projectors. The IMAX Corporation was founded in 1967 in Canada and has enjoyed some limited success with a few films since then. As of September 2009, there were more than 400 IMAX theaters operating in 44 countries. IMAX introduced a digital system in July 2008, with more than 120 digital projection systems in operation early in 2010. The majority of IMAX theaters are equipped with IMAX 3D technology, while the company claims that nearly a billion people have enjoyed the "IMAX experience."

Filmmakers are relying on these technological innovations to attract audiences away from their computers and home systems. "That's why more theaters are focusing on movies with monster special effects that don't show well on a computer screen or in-home theater ... and why major filmmakers such as Jeffrey Katzenberg and James Cameron are banking on 3D and IMAX technology as the future of cinema" (Irvine 2009).

Enhanced theatrical environment   Theater owners are also employing other strategies to lure audiences to their establishments, such as more comfortable seating, even lounge chairs and bean bags, as well as seeking additional revenue through midnight movie premieres and opening-night parties. Thanks to digital systems, some theaters are able to broadcast live events, operas, and symphony performances, as well as hosting in-theater video game competitions on their screens. Some theater owners in the US are adding restaurants and bars, similar to cinemas in other countries. Meanwhile, in Europe, cinemas are taking it a step farther by remaking themselves as entertainment destinations – with bowling alleys, karaoke bars, comedy clubs, and children's play areas.

New home exhibition technology   But while theater owners attempt to lure audiences back to their cinemas, cable companies offer cheaper video-on-demand or pay-per-view options and the electronics industry continues to develop new television technologies to keep audiences at home. Home television systems featuring high definition, flat panel technology and improved sound systems present higher-quality movie viewing experiences that obviously compete with movie theaters. Furthermore, 3D is expected by many to revolutionize the television medium, as well as the cinema. During 2010, electronics manufacturers began offering 3D TVs and 3D-ready Blu-ray players, while 3D programming was introduced on a wide range of channels and services.

The threat of piracy

Another major issue that continues to haunt Hollywood is piracy, a problem that not only hasn't gone away, but is becoming even more urgent. For some observers, it is at the heart of the "end of Hollywood" scenario. As one independent production company head exclaimed, "We have to stop it today. We can't wait until tomorrow, or it's the end of the film business" (Hiltzik 2010). Others have suggested that Hollywood has an "unreasonable obsession with piracy," which is linked to the industry's fear of new technologies (Edelman 2007).

The costs of movie piracy to the film industry are difficult, if not impossible, to measure accurately, although the Motion Picture Association of America (MPAA) continues to announce specific amounts. In 2005, the organization claimed that the direct loss to its member companies was $6 billion and the total loss to the global industry was $18 billon, or about 5 percent of all revenue. Around the same time, a Washington think tank placed the cost in lost or forgone US jobs and tax revenue at nearly $27 billion (Hiltzik 2010). Moreover, in a 2009 study of piracy's links to organized crime, the RAND Corp. warned that all estimates "should be taken with caution," yet concluded that, whatever the real figure, it was increasing dramatically (see Yar 2005).

Hollywood has been fighting piracy for several decades, utilizing a variety of strategies to prevent copyright infringement. These efforts are co-ordinated by the MPAA, which recently overhauled its operations, changing the name of the "antipiracy" unit to "content protection." The organization has been working with government agencies, such as U.S. Immigration and Customs Enforcement (ICE) and the National Intellectual Property Rights Coordination Center (IPR Center). In addition to agents at the IPR Center and around the country, ICE uses 61 Attaché Offices located in 44 countries to combat counterfeiting and piracy. The IPR Center partners include the Federal Bureau of Investigation and U.S. Customs and Border Protection (U.S. ICE 2010).

While there are a number of different types of copyright piracy, the two most obvious examples involve DVDs and digital downloading or file sharing. While imports of pirated discs have plagued creative industries for years, the traditional sale of knock-off DVDs has become more sophisticated, imitating packaging, marketing, and even the product codes from "legal" discs. According to the 2009 RAND Corp. study, many of the same groups that illegally trade in pirated copies of films are also involved in everything from human smuggling and document fraud to contract killing and the drug trade, all crime areas under ICE's jurisdiction. The RAND study also found that busting DVD counterfeiting rings remains a low priority for police in most countries, which only adds to piracy's appeal. In addition, the penalties for movie piracy are relatively minor, the product is easy to sell, and the profit margin is often better than for heroin or cocaine (Hiltzik 2010).

Numerous Internet sites also stream movies and TV shows without permission from copyright holders. In addition, indexing sites serve as search engines for "torrents" files – links to TV, film, and music files on other users' computers. Peer-to-peer (p2p) software connects users to one another and shares files (Sandoval 2009). While large-scale p2p services such as BitTorrent may be a promising distribution option for independent companies, they are seen as potential competitors and a real threat to major distributors.

The MPAA and the film industry have tried various techniques to combat these activities, including hiring security firms, such as MediaDefender and MediaSentry, which promised to discourage file sharers by blocking or slowing the sharing process. Some of these tactics have proven problematic. For instance, Comcast, which owns cable channels as well as a cable service and (soon) NBC Universal, was caught blocking subscribers' access to BitTorrent and other file-sharing services in 2007. Recently, it settled a lawsuit for that action at an expense of $16 million (Hiltzik 2010).

Legal proceedings have also been employed with some success. In February 2006, the MPAA launched legal proceedings against isoHunt, TorrentBox, TorrentSpy, ed2k-it, and several other BitTorrent indexing or tracker sites, alleging that these sites facilitate copyright infringement. As a result, for instance, TorrentSpy was fined $111 million in damages in 2008 and Gary Fung of Isohunt was found guilty of copyright infringement in December 2009.

In another case, the owners of Pirate Bay were found guilty of breaking copyright law and sentenced to one year in jail and fines of $4.5 million in April 2009. One of the defendants explained: "We still don't think we have done anything illegal under Swedish law. We don't share any files; we just link to material. We don't say what people should or should not download. .... It's open platform, an open technology, for people to find and share content. There's no difference between us and Google" (Waters 2009). Following the verdict, the site was sold to a Swedish software firm, Global Gaming Factory, for 60 million kronor.

However, legal actions don't always work. The major Hollywood companies lost a landmark piracy case against a small Internet service provider in Australia. The studios claimed that ISP iiNet infringed their copyright by failing to stop users engaging in illegal file sharing. But the Federal Court of Australia disagreed, finding for iiNet, arguing that the ISP was not responsible for the actions of its users, and "did not have relevant power to prevent infringements occurring."

This issue is especially significant in global markets, where pirated DVDs abound and copyright infringement is common. The major US distributors have been utilizing near simultaneous foreign release dates recently to prevent some forms of piracy. However, the industry also relies on governmental negotiations. Intellectual property relations between the US and most foreign countries are governed by an array of multilateral treaties and conventions as well as bilateral agreements, including the Universal Copyright Convention (UCC) and the Berne Convention. The MPAA and the global Motion Picture Association encourages foreign governments to abide by, and fully implement, important agreements, such as the Trade Related Aspects of Intellectual Property Rights (TRIPS) agreement and the World Intellectual Property Organization (WIPO) treaties.

Despite all of these activities, different types of piracy are growing, especially with the ongoing development of new forms of media technology. Ultimately, they may be impossible to stop.

Changes in global markets

Those who claim that Hollywood is dead or dying often point to developments in global film production and distribution as important contributing factors. While the global market for film is said to have expanded over the last few decades – and Hollywood has certainly benefited from that expansion – other developments are claimed to be challenging Hollywood's global domination.

Resistance to US dominance Historically, there have been various ways in which countries have attempted to resist Hollywood's dominance. To the dismay of the MPAA and the major Hollywood studios, these efforts continue. Forms of resistance include tariffs, licensing, screen and television quotas, local ownership requirements, and frozen earnings.

US domination is also challenged though support of indigenous film production. Subsidies for domestic film industries sometimes are funded through taxation of foreign film revenues or taxes added to theater tickets. Licensing fees, tax rebates, loans, and grants are other ways in which nations fund film subsidies.

Hollywood's anti-competitive tendencies also have been challenged in some markets, specifically by the European Union and Korea. The more dominant the major transnational entertainment corporations become, the more attention they bring to their market power. And it is possible that more countries will actually enforce antitrust laws in the future.

These various forms of resistance have been aimed at US film in markets around the world for many, many years. Even though some have been successful over the years, Hollywood's overall domination has continued. It remains to be seen whether or not this kind of resistance, combined with other developments, can more seriously challenge Hollywood in the future.

Foreign production Ironically, some of the forms of resistance mentioned above have actually benefited Hollywood (or at least, some parts of the US film industry). Film incentives in many countries around the world are prompting Hollywood producers to look outside the US for reasons other than locations. Film production outside the US contributes to building indigenous film infrastructures and enhances the local talent pool (although Hollywood has successfully raided such pools for many years).

As film incentives and cheaper labor costs in foreign countries (as well as many states in the US other than California), claims of "runaway production" have been growing among Hollywood film workers. The issue of runaway production is of paramount importance to Hollywood film workers, whereas producers may be less concerned, as they are the ones who are taking advantage of incentives in other locations (see Miller et al. 2001, McDonald 2010). Many have argued that incentives are now driving decisions on where films are shot. For instance, a study by the Center for Entertainment Industry Data and Research (CEIDR) reported in 2006: "The analysis reveals that, while there are certainly general economic factors at play, such as relative labor and exchange rates, the data over the past several years strongly suggests that proliferation of production subsidies around the globe has been one of the most significant factors affecting the choice of production venues for a significant volume of production" (CEIDR 2006).

New formations and competition Other new forms of competition also threaten to undermine Hollywood's global strength, as an increasing number of films are being produced by other countries and many of the "death of Hollywood" proponents strongly emphasize this point. For instance: "Foreign language films, too, are chipping away at the assumed finality of the Hollywood hegemony as more and more moviegoers around the world discover the beauty of the dream-making available on their own shores" (Clarke 2009).

Even though American movies continue to dominate most European markets, European films have had some domestic and international success in recent years. European Union funding of coproductions and distribution, plus box-office-driven policies for awarding subsidies, have given European filmmakers more opportunities to compete with Hollywood's products. Growing competition in the television industry, channel proliferation, digital television, and continuing deregulation of broadcasting markets also have tended to increase coproduction activity (see, for instance, Kim 2003).

Meanwhile, in other parts of the world, film industries that have been relatively provincial in the past are beginning to pay attention to global film marketing. For instance, in addition to the prolific Bollywood – the Hindi-language film industry based in Mumbai – India has several other film industries. The Tamil, Telegu, Malayalam, Kannada, and Bengali language industries are significant, even though Bollywood, as the largest, receives much more attention from the rest of the world.

Although the Indian market is limited by the number of cinemas in the country (12 cinemas per million people in India compared to 116 per million in the US), Indian films are distributed in other venues, as well as, increasingly, around the world. India's government is encouraging the industry through improving access to bank finance and reforming taxation laws to encourage exports.

In addition to Bollywood, other national film industries (such as China or Korea) may also threaten to put chinks in Hollywood's global armor (see Ryoo 2008). As geographer Allen J. Scott, pointed out a few years ago: "If the history of other formerly triumphant industrial juggernauts – from Manchester to Detroit – is any guide, however, the continued leadership of Hollywood is by no means automatically assured. In spite of Hollywood's acquired competitive advantages, it cannot be ultimately free from economic threats emanating from elsewhere" (Scott 2002).

What's Not Changing: Hollywood and Continuity

Again, this is not the first time that Hollywood or film itself has been threatened or declared dead. As one commentator recently noted: "there is something strangely cyclical about reports of cinema's demise" (Clarke 2009). Despite the many changes and ongoing challenges, there is still a good deal of continuity about the Hollywood film industry. Only a few of these characteristics will be briefly discussed here. (For more extensive discussion see Wasko 2003, McDonald and Wasko 2009.)

Hollywood and profit

Motion pictures developed in the US primarily as an industry and have continued
to operate in this mode for over a century. Above all, the primary driving force and
guiding principle for the industry is profit, and capital is used in different ways to
achieve that goal. The industry is cyclical – constantly changing to maximize profits, to survive. Inevitably, individuals and companies come and go as companies
move from one project to another, to other businesses, to new or more profitable
technologies. Nothing is "sacred" – not even film. As Thomas Guback pointed out
many years ago, "the ultimate product of the motion picture business is profit;
motion pictures are but a means to that end" (quoted in Wasko 2003, 3).
A Hollywood executive explained it this way: "Studios exist to make money. If they
don't make a lot of money producing movies, there's no reason for them to exist,
because they don't offer anything else. They offer entertainment, but you don't
need studios to make entertainment. You don't need studios to make movies. The
reason they exist is to make money" (Taylor 1999, 59).

People in the industry typically take it for granted that film is a business and
sometimes find it surprising that there might be any discussion of this characteristic. In this sense, they may be similar to film scholars and others who pay little
attention to the commercial nature of Hollywood. Yet the profit motive and the
commodity nature of the Hollywood model have implications for the kind of films
that are produced (and not produced), who makes them, how they are distributed,
and where / when they are viewed. While many who study film, and some within
the industry, consider film an art form, it still seems important to point out that
Hollywood films cannot be understood outside of the context in which they are
actually produced and distributed, that is, within an industrial, capitalist structure.

Film as commodity

The industry continues to produce films as commodities that are distributed in
many outlets or markets (theaters, television, home video, online, etc.), in addition
to inspiring additional commodities (video games, music, merchandise, etc.). For
instance, merchandise can be particularly lucrative, as the retail sales of products
featuring entertainment characters came to about $9.88 billion in 2008.

Since the 1980s, changes in governmental and corporate policies have fostered
the organization of media conglomerates around expanding markets for intellectual properties. This form of marketization encouraged conglomerates to integrate and co-ordinate their operations across multiple media industries so that a
single property – or franchise – could feed multiple markets using strategies of
corporate synergy (see Meehan 2005, Wasko 2003).

The production and distribution of additional commodities contributes additional revenues for the copyright holder (which is often overlooked in assessing the

Table 14.3   2009 US film revenues

Market	2009 Revenues	Increase from 2008
Theatrical	$10.7 billion	9.8%
DVD and Blu-ray rentals	$8.15 billion	0.5%
DVD and Blu-ray purchases	$8.73 billion	− 13.3%
VOD rentals (cable/satellite/telco)	$1.27 billion	16.3%
Online purchases	$250 million	72.8%
Online rentals	$111 million	60.1%
Total	$28.4 billion	

Source: Magiera, 2010

revenues associated with a franchise), as well as helping to publicize the film (especially in the case of tie-ins). The continuous production of additional merchandise based on the film concept and characters also prolongs the life of the franchise. In addition, these activities often connect to other parts of the media conglomerates that typically own successful film franchises, thus creating various forms of corporate synergy. Thus, while blockbuster films aim to reap profits from box-office circulation, as well as release (and rerelease) in home video and television formats, what makes a film franchise especially attractive to Hollywood companies these days are these supplementary products and activities.

As film critic Leonard Maltin notes, "There's no such thing as a surefire hit in Hollywood. But a franchise is as close to surefire as it gets" (quoted in Hoffman and Rose 2005). As for quality: "The studios and the movie chains start falling back on 'sure bets' – sequels, popular franchises, formulaic comedies with bankable stars. Quality (which was never all that high to begin with) dips precipitously" (Edelman 2007).

Big pictures/big box office

Despite the predictions of Hollywood's death, the industry continues to attract sizable revenues. In 2009, the US film industry reported the largest box office gross in history, in addition to an increase in attendance. By one company's calculations, Americans spent $28.4 billion on all movie transactions in 2009, including theatrical, DVD rentals and purchases, video-on-demand rentals, and online rentals and purchases (Magiera 2010). The specific amounts for these markets are listed in Table 14.3. It should be noted that these figures do not include other markets where feature films are also sold (television, cable, airplanes, hotels, etc.), nor does it account for revenues from merchandising and tie-ins for many films.

It is likely that Hollywood will continue to produce big blockbuster films, in addition to taking advantage of cheaper films that "go big." A recent study found that films with budgets of more than $100 million generated higher returns (an average of $247 million in net profits per release), than mid-range pictures. The study looked at films from 2004–8. The conclusion? "Mid-range" films with around $50 million budgets are riskier. However, the study did not include marketing expenses and thus ignores the fact that "big" films may be marketed more aggressively than mid-range or smaller films (Graser 2009b). Interestingly, a record of 30 films grossed more than $100 million in 2009. (See Cucco 2009, for more discussions of blockbusters.)

So big films like *Avatar* will likely continue, but the studios also will continue to be on the lookout for "miracle" films, such as *Paranormal Activity*, which was produced for $154,000, picked up by Paramount, and has so far grossed over $178 million worldwide. As one Hollywood columnist observes:

> Whether or not "Avatar" and "Paranormal" ever appear on a double bill, the two films dramatize the polarization of the Hollywood agenda. Studios are trying to nurture either very pricey franchise films or very inexpensive projects, often to the neglect of the "tweeners" that have racked up surprising numbers this past year. … [for instance], a $460 million blockbuster like "The Hangover," a movie without star-casting or special effects or even an entirely coherent plot. It's a vivid reminder to the conglomerates that Hollywood has always defied efforts to come up with a business plan. Hits happen at any budget. (Bart 2009)

The attention that *Avatar* has received is significant, as many Hollywood players have praised its release as "a revolutionary moment in the history of cinema," and a "game-changer." DreamWorks Animation head Jeffery Katzenberg exclaimed: "I think the day after Jim Cameron's movie comes out, it's a new world" (quoted in Acland 2010).

Charles Acland neatly ties this attention into the issue of technological change in his examination of *Avatar* as a "technological tentpole":

> So, while extraordinarily conventional in story and characterization, *Avatar* is celebrated and promoted to stand out as a flagship work beckoning the next wave of industrial and consumer technologies and entertainments. … *Avatar* is a technological tentpole under which we find not only other movies and appended commodities, but media formats and processes that slide into our lives as supposedly essential. … In this way, an individual audio-visual commodity like *Avatar*, while working to entrench the dominance of key corporate participants, effectively continues a primary mode of investment in changing media materials and processes. The seizing of milestone moments is one way in which the very notion of technological change is made a comprehensible and vital part of our attention. At one level, even with all the local instances of innovation – and yes, to be sure, parts of the entertainment business are shifting dramatically – the language of "game changing" is another way to talk about business as usual. (Acland 2010)

Corporate Hollywood

One of the ongoing issues related specifically to Hollywood is the continuing oligopoly that dominates the US film business. It is indisputable that the Hollywood major studios maintain a stranglehold over film distribution and thus ultimately determine what feature films actually reach cinemas and other media outlets. Furthermore, these companies are able to dictate how box office receipts are distributed, using their oligopolistic power to enforce production and distribution policies that many feel are not competitive or even ethical. As a former film executive concluded at the end of the 1990s: "the pervasive market power of the major studio/distributors in the US has been gained and is maintained by engaging in numerous questionable, unethical, unfair, unconscionable, anti-competitive, predatory and/or illegal business practices" (Cones 1997, 1).

Many argue that since the major film companies have become part of large entertainment conglomerates, they have become profit-driven and commercially oriented. For instance, these thoughts on contemporary Hollywood were by Scott Foundas in a recent issue of *DGA Quarterly*: "So what happened? There are various official histories, all true to an extent: the studios were taken over by corporations that cared more about commerce than art; the audience's taste shifted, away from reality and toward blockbuster escapism; the budgets got too big, emblemized by the waterloo of Michael Cimino's *Heaven's Gate*" (Foundas 2010). While this is certainly the case, it should be noted that Hollywood companies have always been driven by profit and mostly interested in the bottom line rather than artistic creation. The companies' ownership by diversified conglomerates often means that there is increased interest in building blockbusters and franchises that continue to attract revenues, often in conjunction with other business owned by the parent corporation.

It's interesting that despite an economic downturn and dire predictions of the end of Hollywood, the major Hollywood companies seem to be doing fairly well. In 2009, Warner Bros. led the major studios with $4 billion in worldwide ticket sales, a first for any studio. That included $2.13 billion in domestic receipts, and $1.87 billion overseas. Fox reached at least $4.04 billion in global ticket sales, with an estimated $1.74 billion in domestic receipts and a record-breaking (for any studio) $2.45 billion overseas (McClintock 2009b). (Again, these are only box office receipts.) And the "good news" will likely continue, at least for some of the major studios, as indicated in *Variety*, in early February 2010: "News Corp. topper Rupert Murdoch was jubilant Tuesday amid signs a brutal economic slump that's hammered the media business for the better part of two years may be coming to an end. 'Avatar's' $2 billion in worldwide B.O. to date and the nine Oscar noms the pic collected Tuesday didn't hurt the mood among News Corp.'s top brass, either" (Goldsmith 2010).

Hollywood and the world

Finally, the international box office also seems to be growing, and US films still dominate most film markets around the world. For instance, the Australian box office reached a record high in 2009 ($A1.09 billion, or $1 billion), with US films accounting for 83 percent of the total. The Italian box office grew 5 percent to $868 million in 2009 with admissions stable at 99 million and 3D pictures, which have a higher ticket price, accounting for the slightly higher intake. The Hollywood market share rose to 63 percent last year from 60 percent in 2008 and 55 percent in 2007.

This is not a new phenomenon and has been perpetuated for a number of reasons – not just the popularity of Hollywood films (see Silver and McDonnell 2009). Hollywood employs a wide range of strategies to protect its products and business interests in global markets. These efforts include a strong trade association and ongoing efforts to enlist the state in supporting the industry. The MPAA does not only become involved in piracy, but actively lobbies for favorable policies that clear the path and open markets for the US entertainment industry's products. To give just one example: in December 2009, the World Trade Organization confirmed a decision that China was to provide greater access to its market for US films and DVDs. The decision prompted the head of the MPAA, Dan Glickman, to observe: "At this time of economy difficulty, gaining access to the Chinese market is of the utmost importance to the working men and women of this country" (MPAA 2009a).

However, MPAA members are not only distributing "American" films, but producing films for specific markets, in those markets. Often taking advantage of lucrative incentives and subsidies, foreign production continues to provide Hollywood with additional products to further dominate global film markets.

The Future?

Although Hollywood is experiencing significant change, it is still premature to celebrate or bemoan its death. As we have pointed out, some Hollywood observers see these changes as positive and are optimistic about Hollywood's future. For instance:

> The entertainment biz has a long history of technophobia. And yet new technologies inevitably bring opportunities and create new markets. Music publishers tried to sue player-piano makers out of existence, fearing that no one would ever buy sheet music again. Fifty years later, in 1984, Motion Picture Association of America President Jack Valenti uttered what's undoubtedly the most infamous comment in the history of technophobia: "The VCR is to the American film industry what the

Boston strangler is to a woman alone." Today, video rentals account for more than 40% of studio revenues. The same will be true of digital filmmaking and distribution, digital asset-management systems and yes, even P2P software. It will take time. But in the future, as in the past, technology will ultimately deliver a happy Hollywood ending. (Black 2002)

Meanwhile, others are less sure that Hollywood will survive, at least in its current configuration, and are far more critical of Hollywood's attitude. For instance:

The world will always need entertainment, and Southern California is the odds-on favorite to produce it. It has the history, the people, the infrastructure and the creative energy. But as Detroit automakers and New York's financiers have learned, these natural advantages can disappear when an arrogant and insular industry comes to view its dominance as inevitable and its outsized compensation as an entitlement. (Florida 2009)

It is folly to predict the future without an adequate grasp of the past. Even then, it is a dicey business. While this short chapter has not allowed the opportunity to fully explore the history of Hollywood's various encounters with changing economic, technological, and social developments, the discussion has hopefully made clear that the current challenges are numerous and complex. And while Hollywood today may be "confusing, interesting and scary," it is inevitable that if there is a happy ending, as predicted above, it certainly would not be celebrated by everyone.

Note

1   The reference to "independent film" is not related to those companies that work closely with or are owned by the Hollywood major studios (for instance, New Line, Fox Searchlight). Genuine independent production can be defined as one in which "the filmmaker has full creative and distribution control, investors have no involvement with the film outside of providing financing, and the filmmaker undergoes substantial risk to produce and distribute the film" (Erickson 2010).

References

Acland, C. R. (2010) Avatar as technology tentpole. *FlowTV*, vol. 11. Online at http://flowtv. org/?p=4724 (accessed October 8, 2010).

Bart, P. (2009) Hollywood busts the plan: Show business rarely adheres to rules. *Variety*, December 18. Online at http://www.variety.com/index.asp?layout=print_story&arti cleid=VR1118012940&categoryid=1 (accessed October 8, 2010).

Bing, J. and Oppelaar, J. (2000) Confab explores digital trends. *Variety*, September 28. Online at http://www.variety.com/article/VR1117787068.html?categoryid=17&cs=1&quer y=digital+filmmaking+laboratories (accessed October 8, 2010).

Black, J. (2002) Hollywood's digital love/hate story. *Business Week*, December 10. Online at http://www.businessweek.com/technology/content/dec2002/tc20021210_0483.htm (accessed October 8, 2010).

Broderick, P. (2009) Declaration of independence: The ten principles of hybrid distribution. Online at http://www.peterbroderick.com/writing/writing/declarationofindependence.html (accessed October 8, 2010).

CEIDR (Center for Entertainment Industry Data and Research) (2006) The global success of production tax incentives and the migration of feature film production from the U.S. to the world. Online at http://www.ceidr.org/form_ok.asp (accessed October 8, 2010).

Cieply, M. and Barnes, B. (2010) Avatar faces traffic jam at 3D screens. *New York Times*, January 30, p. C1.

Clark, D. (2009) 10 reasons for death of cinema. *Donald Clark Plan B*. Online at http://donaldclarkplanb.blogspot.com/2009/04/10-reasons-for-death-of-cinema.html (accessed October 8, 2010).

Clarke, N. (2009) The death of Hollywood? *t5m Collective*, October 23. Online at http://www.t5m.com/nick-clarke/the-death-of-hollywood.html (accessed October 8, 2010).

Cones, J. W. (1997). *The Feature Films Distribution Deal*. Carbondale, Southern Illinois University Press.

Cucco, M. (2009) The promise is great: The blockbuster and the Hollywood economy. *Media, Culture & Society*, 31, 215–30.

Cunningham, S., Silver, J., and McDonnell, J. (2009) Rates of change: Online distribution as disruptive technology in the film industry. Paper presented at What is Film? conference, Portland, Oregon, November 6.

Dargis, M. (2010) Declaration of indies: Just sell it yourself. *New York Times*, January 17, p. AR1.

Digital Cinema Report (2010) About us: What we believe. Online at http://www.digitalcinemareport.com/about-us (accessed October 8, 2010).

Edelman, D. L. (2007) The end of Hollywood. February 26. Online at http://www.davidlouisedelman.com/film/end-of-hollywood/ (accessed October 8, 2010).

Erickson, M. (2010) The independent brand: Corporate partnerships and independent film. Paper presented at the Society for Cinema and Media Studies Conference, March, Los Angeles, CA.

Florida, R. (2009) The end of Hollywood. *Creative Class*. Online at http://www.creativeclass.com/creative_class/2009/03/29/the-end-of-hollywood/ (accessed October 8, 2010).

Foundas, S. (2010) The New Wave is Dead, Long Live the New Wave. DGA Quarterly, Winter. Online at http://www.dgaquarterly.org/BACKISSUES/Winter2010/CriticsCornerScottFoundas.aspx (accessed October 8, 2010).

Goldsmith, J. (2010) News Corp. reports $254 million profit. *Variety*, February 2. Online at http://www.variety.com/article/VR1118014596.html?categoryid=18&cs=1 (accessed October 8, 2010).

Graser, M. (2009a) Study: devices distract kids: kids tuned in to even more gizmos. *Variety*, June 9. Online at http://www.variety.com/index.asp?layout=print_story&articleid=VR1118004746&categoryid=1009 (accessed October 8, 2010).

Graser, M. (2009b) Study: big budget, big profit. *Variety*, October 22, p. 2.

Graser, M. (2010) Shiny new Apple: will the tablet change the game?" *Variety*, January 27. Online at http://www.variety.com/article/VR1118014385.html?categoryid=10&cs=1 (accessed October 8, 2010).

Hampp, A. (2010) "Avatar" soars on fat ad spending, mass marketing. *Advertising Age*, January 4. Online at http://adage.com/madisonandvine/article?article_id=141262 (accessed October 8, 2010).

Hanson, S. and McDonald, P. (2010) D-cinema in Britain: The UK Film Council and the Digital Screen Network. Paper presented at What is Film? Conference, Portland, Oregon, November 7.

Hiltzik, M. (2010) Casual purchase of counterfeit DVD shines light on piracy. *Los Angeles Times*, January 4. Online at articles.latimes.com/2010/jan/04/business/la-fi-hiltzik4-2010jan04 (accessed October 8, 2010).

Hoffman, L. and Rose, L. (2005) Most lucrative movie franchises. *Forbes*, June 15. Online at http://www.forbes.com/2005/06/15/batman-movies-franchises-cx_lh_lr_0615 batman.html (accessed October 8, 2010).

Irvine, M. (2009) Big screen vs small: Cinemas get a remake to compete for growing ranks of online video fans. *Entertainment Daily*, August 28. Online at http://blog.taragana.com/e/2009/08/28/big-screen-vs-small-cinemas-get-a-remake-to-compete-for-growing-ranks-of-online-video-fans-28646/ (accessed October 8, 2010).

Johanson, M. (2008) Will 2009 be the beginning of the end of Hollywood? *Film.com*, January 24. Online at http://www.film.com/features/story/2009-beginning-of-end-hollywood/18071225 (accessed October 8, 2010).

Kim, J.(2003) The funding and distribution structure of the British film industry in the 1990s: Localization and commercialization of British cinema towards a global audience. *Media, Culture & Society* 25, 405–13.

Kirsner, S. (2008) *Inventing the Movies: Hollywood's Epic Battle Between Innovation and the Status Quo, from Thomas Edison to Steve Jobs*. CreateSpace.

Levin, J. (2009) An industry perspective: Calibrating the velocity of change. In: Holt, J. and Perren, A. (eds) *Media Industries: History, Theory and Method*. Wiley-Blackwell, Malden, MA, pp. 256–63.

Magiera, M. (2010) Movie tickets tops in '09. *Variety*, January 3. Online at http://www.variety.com/article/VR1118013242.html?categoryid=3284&cs=1&utm_source=feedburner&utm_medium=feed&utm_campaign=Feed%3A+variety%2Fnews%2Ftechnology+%28Variety+-+Technology+News%29&query=video+on+demand+revenues+2009 (accessed October 8, 2010).

Martin, R. (2010) Can the Internet save independent film? *YouTube Biz Blog*. February 4. Online at http://ytbizblog.blogspot.com/2010/02/can-internet-save-independent-film-nyu.html (accessed October 8, 2010).

McClintock, P. (2009a) New focus for film marketing. *Variety*, December 30. Online at http://www.variety.com/index.asp?layout=print_story&articleid=VR1118013209&categoryid=13 (accessed October 8, 2010).

McClintock, P. (2009b) WB, Paramount top summer Universal's market share drops. *Variety*, September 7. Online at http://www.variety.com/article/VR1118008222.html?categoryid=13&cs=1&nid=2562 (accessed October 8, 2010).

McDonald, A. (2010) Runaway production research. Online at www.stop-runaway-production.com (accessed October 8, 2010).

McDonald, K. A. (2009) Oscar hopefuls launch viral campaigns. *Variety*, October 28. Online at http://www.variety.com/article/VR1118010512 (accessed October 8, 2010).

McDonald, P. and Wasko, J. (eds) (2008) *The Contemporary Hollywood Film Industry*. Blackwell, Malden, MA.

Meehan, E. (2005) *Why Television is Not Our Fault: Television Programming, Viewers and Who's Really in Control*. Roman & Littlefield, Lanham, MD.

Miller, T., Govil, N., McMurria, J., and Maxwell, R. (2001) *Global Hollywood*. British Film Institute, London.

MPAA (2009a) MPAA hails WTO ruling. Press Release, December 21. Online at http://www.mpaa.org/resources/ce952425-86fd-485a-a371-db59ac867b17.pdf (accessed October 8, 2010).

MPAA (2009b) Theatrical market statistics 2009. Online at http://wwwmpaa.org/policy/industry/091af5d6-4f58-9a8e-405466c1c5e5.pdf (accessed October 8, 2010).

Pendakur, M. (1990) *Canadian Dreams and American Control: The Political Economy of the Canadian Film Industry*. Wayne State University Press, Detroit, MI.

Rodowick, D. N. (2007) *The Virtual Life of Film*. Harvard University Press, Boston, MA.

Ryoo, W. (2008) The political economy of the global mediascape: The case of the South Korean film industry. *Media, Culture & Society*, 30, 873–89.

Sandoval, G. (2009) End of the world as Hollywood knows it. *cnet.com*. October 20. Online at http://news.cnet.com/8301-31001_3-10378654-261.html?part=rss&subj=news&tag=2547-1_3-0-20 (accessed October 8, 2010).

Scott, A. J. (2002) Hollywood in the era of globalization. Online at http://yaleglobal.yale.edu/content/hollywood-era-globalization (accessed October 8, 2010).

Silver, J. and McDonnell, J. (2009) Hollywood dominance: Will it continue? Paper presented at What is Film? conference, Portland, Oregon, November 7.

Taylor, T. (1999) *The Big Deal: Hollywood's Million-Dollar Spec Script Market*. HarperPerennial, New York.

U.S. Immigration and Customs Enforcement (ICE) (2010) ICE hosts motion picture industry summit on fighting film piracy. News Release, January 26. Online at http://www.ice.gov/pi/nr/1001/100126washingtondc.htm (accessed October 8, 2010).

Verrier, R. (2009) 3D technology firm RealD has starring role at movie theaters. *Los Angeles Times*, March 26.

Vonderau, P. and Snickars, P. (eds) (2010) *The YouTube Reader*. National Library of Sweden, Stockholm.

Wasko, J. (1982) *Movies and Money: Financing the American Film Industry*. Ablex Publishing, Norwood, NJ.

Wasko, J. (2003) *How Hollywood Works*. Sage Publications, London.

Waters, D. (2009) Countdown to Pirate Bay verdict. Online at http://news.bbc.co.uk/1/hi/technology/8002171.stm (accessed October 8, 2010).

Wilkerson, D. B. (2010) Disney CEO: iPad could be a game changer. *MarketWatch*, February 9. Online at http://www.marketwatch.com/story/disney-ceo-ipad-could-be-a-game-changer-2010-02-09 (accessed October 8, 2010).

Yar, M. (2005) The global "epidemic" of movie "piracy": Crime-wave or social construction? *Media, Culture & Society*, 27, 677–96.

15

The Political Economy of the Recorded Music Industry
Redefinitions and New Trajectories in the Digital Age

André Sirois and Janet Wasko

The fact of the matter is that popular music is one of the industries of the country. It's all completely tied up with capitalism. It's stupid to separate it.

Paul Simon

Introduction

Media and communication scholars often overlook the study of recorded music, so it may not be surprising that those who study the political economy of communications may neglect it as well. Yet recorded music is a significant component of the culture industry, providing entertainment and leisure activities for audiences and contributing to other media and cultural production. We need to understand how this cultural form has developed as a commodity and an industry. This chapter suggests a political economic approach to studying the recorded music industry that emphasizes history and technology. A review of various approaches to studying recorded music is presented, followed by an overview of the history of the recorded music industry. The current industry is briefly outlined, with possible future business models considered.

Of course, music has not always been a commodity. Before musical labor was incorporated into a tangible thing – what Attali has called an "immaterial pleasure turned commodity" (1985, 2) – it was consumed as representation without a

The Handbook of Political Economy of Communications, First Edition.
Edited by Janet Wasko, Graham Murdock, and Helena Sousa.
© 2014 John Wiley & Sons, Ltd. Published 2014 by John Wiley & Sons, Ltd.

distinct form. Marx (1863) thought that musical performance was an instance where labor did not result in a tangible commodity for sale, observing that: "the service a singer performs for me satisfies my aesthetic needs, but what I enjoy exists only in an action inseparable from the singer himself, and once his work, singing, has come to an end, my enjoyment is also at an end; I enjoy the activity itself – its reverberation in my ear."

With the introduction of recording technologies, however, music did become commodified and the recorded music industry grew to become a formidable component of the cultural industries. This history will be summarized later in this chapter. But it is important here to emphasize that a political economy of culture framework is appropriate for understanding this cultural form. According to Golding and Murdock (2000, 70), this form of analysis "sets out to show how different ways of financing and organizing cultural production have traceable consequences for the range of discourse and representations in the public domain and for audiences' access to them." As Hesmondhalgh (2007, 12) notes, the "music industries" are one of the core cultural industries that "deal primarily with the industrial production and circulation of texts." And while many studies of cultural industries have focused on commodified texts, it is important to remember that recorded music is both text and commodity. The focus here is on the commodity that is produced by the recorded music industry, not necessarily the text or the musical content itself.

The study of the political economy of recorded music draws on the theoretical foundations of political economy and its application to media and culture. The study of political economy is about how societies are organized and controlled, and thus involves the analysis of power. The study of political economy of the media is about the production, distribution, and consumption of media. Importantly, the approach is interested in how the media are organized and controlled within the larger political economy. In other words, it is concerned with who has power to make decisions about the media, and who benefits from these decisions. It is about understanding how power relations actually work within and around the media. More specifically, the study of political economy of the media entails the historical analysis of media commodities, industries, and institutions, including but not limited to corporations. The roles of labor and the state are fundamental components of political economic analysis, as well as issues relating to globalization.

Thus the study of the political economy of recorded music is concerned with the production, distribution, consumption, and reproduction of various forms of recorded music. While the "music industry" is composed of many related industries, the focus here is on recorded forms of music, which means a special interest in recording and distribution technologies. We suggest that the political economy of recorded music should be understood through its historical development as a commodity and the evolution of an industry through all its stages of production to consumption to reproduction. We also stress the technologies involved in the recorded music industry, arguing that recorded music has been more about technology and less about art/music from its inception. In other words, historically, technology has made music into a commodity.

The Study of the Recorded Music Industry

"Music is spiritual. The music business is not"
Van Morrison

When analyzing the industry that produces music as a commodity, few studies have *explicitly* linked critical political economy with recorded music. The brief review of literature that follows will hopefully provide a framework for how the recording industry has been studied, focusing especially on the ways that political economic analyses have been applied.

Many scholars agree that there is a dearth of serious writing about this industry (e.g., Gronow 1983, Chanan 1995) and that academic research in general has "shown little systematic interest in popular music" (Burnett 1996, 3). McQuail (2005, 36) notes that "little attention has been given to music as a mass medium in theory and research." Malm and Wallis (1992, 15) also point out that until the late 1970s "remarkably few studies of the socio-economic aspects of the industrial processing of music" have come from communication scholars. Nevertheless, there still is a body of work that examines music and the recorded music industry, and may contribute to an understanding of the political economy of recorded music.

Classic studies of music

In his historical treatment of western classical music, Attali traces music's transformation from a social experience as representation to its repetitive function as commodity. For Attali, music "became an industry, and *its consumption ceased to be collective*" (1985, 88, original italics) as people began the individualized act of stockpiling music commodities. The historical development of recording, which was a means of social control, pushed music into background noise as "a factor in centralization, cultural normalization, and the disappearance of distinctive cultures" (1985, 111).

Weber (1958) suggested that western music itself was the product of capitalist institutions, highlighting how seemingly "irrational" cultural production could become rationalized. However, Frith (1988, 12) later warned that industrialization doesn't happen *to* music – a problematic argument "which fuses (and confuses) capital, technical, and musical arguments" – but instead, recorded music is the final product of that process.

Benjamin (1969/1936) considered the potential emancipatory effects of mechanical production on artworks, arguing that this historical development democratized access to, and critical thinking toward, cultural objects and destroyed the social control ("aura" and "authenticity") of works of art that existed in a specific time and place. On the other hand, Horkheimer and Adorno (2001/1947, 95) argued that a monolithic "culture industry" logic existed which then transmuted art into "a species of commodity," while earlier work by Adorno (1990/1941) tackled the standardized production/consumption of popular music. Adorno wasn't concerned with industry structure, but how popular music applied an ideological "mechanical schemata" to its production, which promoted an audience who passively listened with rhythmic obedience as the commoditized and reified music maximized economic dividends.

Critical theory and Marxist approaches

In an argument reminiscent of Benjamin, Théberge (1997, 185) contends that, with the advent of the mechanical production/reproduction of sound, a "new relationship between technology, musical practice, and the capitalist organization of production began to evolve." Breen (1995, 501) points out that the record business is just another element of corporate structure, and therefore, "Institutional economics is a valuable tool in describing the historical development of popular music within corporate society."

Chapple and Garofalo (1977) apply an economic analysis to rock and roll, highlighting how capitalist corporations who control the means of production determine the actual music (as commodity and content) that consumers get. However, Garofalo (1986, 83), in some ways, rejects his initial assertion with Chapple, arguing that "there is no point-to-point correlation between controlling the marketplace economically and controlling the form, content, and meaning of music."

More recent Marxist works on recorded music include Callahan (2005, 58), who believes the industry feeds consumers corporately controlled and homogenous "anti-music" produced by "the labor of the musician." In a business concerned only with "money derived from the exploitation of musicians and copyright" (228), the industry "lords it" over musicians: "Within the capitalist market system, the productivity of [the musician's] labor is not in the artistic creation, per se, but in the profit it generates for the record company or publisher through mass production, promotion and sales" (199). Eisenberg makes a Marxist argument that the music commodity transforms both the musician and consumer into a fetishist: "The musician need never see the working man behind the money; the listener need never see the working musician behind the vinyl" (2005, 20).

Studies of music genres

Other political economic analyses of specific genres within the recording industry include Hobart's essay, "The Political Economy of Bop" (1981), which examines the contradictions of musical idiom between bop's origins in the black ghettos and as a symbol of intellectualism. While George's (1988) polemic explores how the white music industry transformed black culture into an exploitable commodity, Kelley (2005), in his poignant edited volume, explores how white-owned entertainment conglomerates have profited from a "structure of stealing" from the black community. Another important contribution includes Kofsky's (1998) political economic analysis of how jazz musicians work and are exploited under capitalism.

Sociological studies of music

There has also been a considerable amount of sociological research on the industry with foci on the production, content, and reception of recorded music. For example, Frith (1981) makes an argument (similar to Benjamin) that corporations don't necessarily co-opt popular culture as they tend to follow, rather than lead, in trends; therefore, the record industry has developed strategies for market control simply because they do not control the market. According to Dowd (2003) these genre-based markets are in fact manufactured by the industry itself to maintain as much control as possible (of the music and its consumption).

Keith Negus (1992, 1996, 1999) has made similar arguments about corporate control within the industry and of its market. Negus suggests that there is a corporate "machine" but also that we should consider the "human beings who inhabit the machine" (1996, 36) – those who make creative decisions and not just financial ones throughout the entire corporate structure. This idea is elaborated upon when Negus looks at the sometimes awkward interplay between economics and culture in the record business – a concept where *"an industry produces culture and culture produces an industry"* (1999, 14, italics in original). Swiss et al. (1998) refer to Negus's concept as a "production-text-consumption" model where the industry affects musicians, marketing and genres, technology, and broadcasting, as well as musical aesthetics and meaning. Similarly, music commodities have a symbolic significance and thus two parallel economies are operating in the recorded music business: "the economy of use and the economy of exchange" (Storey 1996, 98).

Other sociologically grounded studies have looked at the tension between major and independent companies, which Negus (1999) suggests is based on distribution and not production. For instance, Hesmondhalgh (1998a) looks at the underground British dance music industry as one that, while pursuing profit and sometimes conforming to the capitalist system in order to reach a wider audience, may truly offer alternative messages/lifestyles. Other work by Hesmondhalgh (1998b, 1999) uses specific case studies of independent companies and genres (mainly punk) to demonstrate the tensions between the institutional politics of the recording industry and oppositional cultural forms. And, finally, Lee (1995), using Wax Trax! Records as a case study, examines "independent" as an industry concept.

Other sociological perspectives focus on the "empirical" relationship between market concentration and diversity (Peterson and Berger 1971, 1975, Peterson 1976, Lopes 1992, Dowd 2004) and organizational structure (Scott 1999, Huygens et al. 2001). These studies suggest that market concentration corresponds to homogeneity while competitive markets lead to diversity; however, Lopes (1992) contends that diversity and innovation depends more on the operations of companies and market structure than merely levels of concentration.

Legal studies of the music industry

Many scholars argue that, in order to properly understand the recording industry as a capitalist enterprise that exploits commodified labor, a political economic analysis of this industry should emphasize copyright (e.g., Fabbri 1993, Cvetkovski 2007, Hesmondhalgh 2007). Fabbri believes that researchers must explore copyright because a "considerable part of the overall turnover of the music industry is based on the exchange of immaterial items" (1993, 159).

Sanjek (1998) argues that music is no more than a "rights package" and thus we should examine the recording industry on two interrelated levels: (1) the "corporate regime" of mergers and influence in production and consumption; and (2) the "legal-legislative regime" of ownership deregulation and the increased scope and duration of intellectual property rights. According to Cvetkovski (2007, 27), "Copyright should be considered as the common thread that binds the entire industry ... without it, there is no music business."

While Lessig (2005, 2008) and Bollier (2005) argue that copyright's scope and duration have deviated from its constitutional framing in favor of corporate interests, other discussions by McLeod (2001, 2005) and Vaidhyanathan (2001) demonstrate how the music industry, as part of the "copyright cartel," privatizes culture and chills creativity. Other interesting research has looked at how the recording industry has relied on copyright law to curtail digital sampling, as well as addressing the cultural and economic tensions surrounding this issue (e.g., Demers 2006, Hesmondhalgh 2006, Toynbee 2006). Frith's edited volume, *Music and Copyright* (1993), contains studies from international perspectives and serves as a strong point of departure from analyses of the American copyright system.

International studies of music

While many of the previously mentioned studies of the recording industry have focused on the US market, there are sources that focus on other markets (e.g., Gronow 1983, Manuel 1993, Taylor 1997), as well as how the hegemony of

American industrialized music has affected music produced outside of the US (e.g., Robinson et al. 1991). Burnett (1996, 6) looks at how the Internet is helping the record business create a globalized cultural economy, suggesting that "the music industry, like others, constantly tries to develop new ways to control both supply and demand. ..." Looking at the interaction between music in the mass media and the larger musical activities in society – specifically in the context of the Caribbean, Africa, and Europe – Malm and Wallis claim that the record industry has been at the forefront of the "global standardization of cultural products" (1992, 7).

Studies of digital music

There is also a growing body of research examining the music business and its challenges in the era of digital capitalism and technology (e.g., McCourt and Burkart 2003, Katz 2004). Alexander (2002) offers a helpful exploration of the relationship between market structure and digital distribution, as well as how the recording oligopoly's dominance is fading along with its long-established distribution stronghold. In Burkart and McCourt's (2006) historically grounded analysis, the authors document how the Internet has untied the industry's physical business model in an age of the "celestial jukebox" where music commodities are instantly available.

Although the current economic outlook for the recording industry may be precarious, some authors have suggested future models for market capitalization (e.g., Fox 2004, Kusek and Leonard 2005). Interestingly, while the record industry has essentially criminalized its own market, Kusek and Leonhard (2005, x) suggest that the industry may have to accept a model "where access to music becomes a kind of 'utility.' Not for free, per se, but certainly for what feels like free."

Popular sources for studying the music industry

While most of this literature is academic, more popular publications also provide important sources for understanding the recorded music industry. For instance, both Dannen's *Hitmen* (1990) and Elliot's *Rockonomics* (1993) are excellent accounts of the relationship between money and power within the industry during the 1970s and 1980s. Furthermore, since the music business itself is bound by legality – on both creative and financial ends – then who better to learn from than the entertainment lawyers who are involved in these processes? Therefore, "how-to" books (e.g., Passman 1997, Lathrop 2003, Rudsenske and Denk 2005) provide interesting insider accounts of how the recording industry operates, not only legally, but also through its stages of production and distribution.

The History of the Recorded Music Industry

We find that, as in other fields, capitalism has created the most magnificent appara-
tus for the production, distribution and consumption of music that the world has ever
seen: yet this apparatus is so riddled with contradictions basically economic in origin
that it negates its own potentialities and is rapidly becoming unable to function.
              Composer, Elie Siegmeister, Worker's Music Association, 1938

By reviewing the technological history of the recorded music industry, we find, much like Marx, that the present condition can be illuminated by examining the past. While historically new recording technologies, companies, and artists have come and gone, the prevalent logic of this industry and the music commodity itself has remained – capital. The history also reveals an ongoing battle between playback formats and the companies that produce them, the inevitable movement toward consolidation and conglomeration, and the tensions between recording companies and the consumers who have demanded cheap or free music. Technology has been a major historical contradiction within the industry as it has both helped to propel the music commodity to the far reaches of the globe, while simultaneously seeking to destroy it from its material core.

In other words, while the development of recorded music has been "completely carried out within the capitalist structure" (Chapple and Garofalo 1977, 300), the history of the recorded music industry is fundamentally about technology, as recorded music is very much the product of science. Millard writes, "This is a story primarily of change, for the industry built on the phonograph was driven by the constant disruption of innovation … one invention after another arrived to upset the fragile balance between the great companies and change the relationships of the old power with the new" (2005, 5–6).

In one of the most detailed technological histories of recorded sound and business, *The Fabulous Phonograph*, Gelatt (1977, 11) writes that a "history of the pho-nograph is at once the history of an invention, an industry, and a musical instru-ment." Kenney (1999, 44) argues that a critical-cultural history of the phonograph "demonstrates the important ways in which economic and cultural forces have shaped technological inventions." To analyze the record business through its his-tory, Frith (1988, 13) suggests three specific issues: (1) the effects of technological change; (2) the economics of popular music; and (3) a new musical culture as technol-ogy transforms musical experiences, thus leading to "the rise of new sorts of musical consumption and use." As these three scholars suggest, any historical analysis of the recorded music industry should consider the relationship between technologies, culture, and economics, as well as evolving modes of production and consumption.

Thus the history of the recorded music industry presented here is divided into four eras marked by different methods of recording and playback: the acoustic era (1877–1923), the electrical era (1924–1960s), the cassette era (1970–82), and the tangible digital era (roughly 1983–2000). This historical account will ultimately lead us to the present age of digital capitalism and its crowning format – the MP3.

The acoustic era

Shortly after Thomas Edison patented his phonograph in 1878, a device that used a vertical method for cutting sound onto a cylinder, the "talking machine" business was born and thus "music began to become a thing" (Eisenberg 2005, 13). At first, there was a proliferation of companies interested in recorded sound. However, by the turn of the twentieth century – a time marked by competition for hardware development and sales – three dominant companies emerged in the US: Edison's National Phonograph Company, the Columbia Phonograph Company, and the Victor Talking Machine Company. These "Big Three" companies dominated the early industry because they were large enough to manufacture and market their products on a large scale, support research laboratories, and control almost every important patent for talking machines and records (Chanan 1995, Morton 2000, Coleman 2003, Millard 2005).

While Columbia was the first to release prerecorded music, initially all cylinder recordings were "original," as no method for mass duplication existed until Berliner's lateral gramophone discs were released in 1894. This is when the recording process became separate from the reproduction stage (Day 2000) as eventually discs would be reproduced using a gold master disc to stamp copies.

The disc was also important because, unlike Edison's or Columbia's devices that allowed consumers to record sound on cylinders, the gramophone was playback only, thus allowing for a one-way flow of musical content. While the earlier technologies were intended as dictation devices, Berliner's disc recordings "would be made solely by manufacturers, not by consumers" (Morton 2000, 32). The mass production of discs ultimately lowered production costs and allowed for mass consumption; thus Berliner's invention ultimately set the stage for the recorded music industry as we now know it.

The introduction of the disc also initiated the perpetual format war in the recording industry and the struggle for industry standardization. The disc forced Edison and Columbia to adapt in order to compete in the market, but because of the lack of industry standardization the disc initially confused consumers (Steffen 2005, 33). According to Millard (2005, 213), "standardization of recorded sound products is an invisible technology" – it can only be heard. Throughout the twentieth century, many sound delivery technologies would be released, but the successful ones were those that would achieve industry-wide standardization.

In 1897, 500,000 records were sold; two years later, that number increased to 2.8 million. Sometime between 1901 and 1903, Berliner sold his interests in the gramophone to Eldridge Johnson, a skilled inventor and an exceptional businessman, and the Victor Talking Machine Company was born.

By 1902 Victor was valued at $2.7 million, and through reinvestment into research and development, the company's value increased to $12 million in 1905. This jump in value may have been due to the 1903 patent pool between Victor and Columbia. Because Victor developed the use of wax recordings and Columbia implemented the disc format (both clearly infringed on each other's patent rights), this cross-licensing agreement virtually left Edison's company and the cylinder in the dust.

Johnson realized that the phonographs of the early 1900s were, like most developments of modernity, aesthetically industrial. Thus by 1906 the Victor gramophone had become the Victrola, the first mass-market record player. This new playback device acted as "Victorian camouflage for the industrial machine" (Kenney 1999, 51) as it hid the mechanics within a wooden cabinet. By Johnson advertising the device as "a standard musical instrument," the Victrola fostered the industry ideology that "phonographs should look as little like phonographs as possible" (Gelatt 1977, 192). While early recordings were used to sell playback hardware by displaying its technical virtues and the inventor's genius, by 1907 the inventor had been replaced by the opera star as the selling point of the record (Millard 2005, 61) – the "moment at which one might pinpoint the reification of music" (Eisenberg 2005, 13). Because of the highbrow tastes of the men owning the Big Three, the music produced by their record companies reflected such values (Morton 2000, 29) – signaling that even in the early days of the record business, those in control of material production also had an influence on the ideological production of the era.

Before the prominence of musical recordings, the act of producing and consuming music relied on the sale of composers' sheet music by publishers, as well as live performances of those compositions. In the same year that music "reified," American composer and conductor John Philip Sousa wrote his famed essay, "The Menace of Mechanical Music" (1906), decrying the talking machine business and its "canned music." Sousa's piece demonstrated the tensions between different levels of musical production as he criticized the phonograph for victimizing the "moral rights" of composers' musical works, as well as for encouraging a passive relationship to the world of music by transferring the human quality of music to a soulless machine.

By 1910 a mass market for recorded music was flourishing as Victor sold 94,557 machines (compared to 7,570 in 1901). Edison realized that grooved discs were the way of the future, and in 1913 released Edison Diamond Discs – a blatant rip-off of the Victrola – which faired poorly in the market. In 1914, the same year that ASCAP (American Society of Composers, Authors, and Publishers) formed to protect the publishing copyrights of Tin Pan Alley's composers used in mechanical recordings, the Big Three controlled a market in which 18 recorded sound companies brought in a total of $27 million in profits. While Victor's value grew to $33 million in 1917, most of the basic patents for the phonograph and gramophone expired that same year, thus opening the market in 1918, when 166 recorded sound companies made $158 million in profit (a 500% profit increase in just four years).

"The economics of record production during this period are easy to comprehend. The low cost of entry into the business stimulated new labels, catering to relatively small markets, thus a distinction appeared between independent companies and the majors" (Chanan 1995, 54).

With a surge in postwar consumption, Edison's company experienced its best year in 1920 with $22 million in profits. However, this success would be short-lived as the sales of radio sets in the US nearly doubled from 1921–2, which cut into the record industry's sales – a mere $106 million during that same period. Hit by falling sales and overproduction, as well as the new radio technology that provided music to consumers for free, the 1920s was a decade in which the recording industry felt its first real economic hardship.

The electrical era

The electrical era, represented by the shellac 78rpm disc and eventually transistor technology, is characterized by technological innovation, as well as increased industry concentration brought on by the Great Depression in the US. It is important to note that the dominant firms in the music business in the early twentieth century were not vertically integrated and the industry as a whole was quite fragmented. Hobart (1981) observes that four distinct forms of capital existed in the early twentieth century, each exerting its own pressures and priorities upon the character of music, its production and reproduction: publishing, touring, broadcasting, and sound recording. During this period, these discrete activities became controlled within vertically integrated recording companies.

By 1924 Western Electric had patented its electric sound recording microphones; before this recording development, sound was collected acoustically by a horn and piped to a diaphragm which vibrated the cutting stylus. This "acoustic process of recording therefore limited what music could be attempted, it affected how the musicians performed in various ways, and it seriously distorted the sounds they actually made" (Day 2000, 11). The new electric recording process (then known as Orthophonic recording) was able to capture the musical energy lost through the inefficient acoustic process.

In 1925 Victor was still trying to sell its stock of acoustic machines, but announced that November 2, 1925, would be "Victor Day" – the day they would release the first consumer phonograph, the Orthophonic Victrola, that would play electrically recorded discs. A week after "Victor Day," there was more than $20 million in orders for Orthophonic Victrolas.

Throughout the late 1920s, profits for the industry remained steady at around $70 million yearly, but radio was cutting into the business and the record industry had to compete with broadcasting or join it. Finding a market for the sale of records when consumers could get the music free from radio proved to be a challenge. Victor had reached an agreement with RCA to incorporate Radiolas into

Victrolas by 1925, and, a year later, with many profitable years behind him, Johnson sold his company for over $28 million to two New York banking houses. Johnson's Victor Talking Machine Company had also successfully "reinforced the upper and middle levels of an American musical hierarchy in recorded music" (Kenney 1999, 64). In 1927 Columbia invested in United Independent Broadcasters to get airtime to promote its records, which signaled a convergence between industries and technologies. By 1929, RCA had completed its buyout of Victor to create the RCA-Victor subsidiary, had taken over Victor's Camden, New Jersey, factory, and stopped manufacturing talking machines in order to start mass pro-ducing radios. RCA not only eliminated a major competitor from outside the burgeoning radio industry by absorbing all of Victor's assets, but gained "an extensive plant and a well-organized system of distributors and dealers" for its radios (Gelatt 1977, 247).

Although the Depression affected the radio industry, it "decimated the record business" (Kenney 1999, 158) as record sales dropped from $75 million in 1929 to $16.9 million two years later. The early 1930s, then, marked the most "doleful phase" for the recording industry as both the sales of discs and phonographs plum-meted (Gelatt 1977, 255). During the decade, new strategies developed between the radio and recording industries as the various mergers and acquisitions reflected a shift in power from record companies to large entertainment corporations. "They were now empires of sound," writes Millard, "huge, integrated business organiza-tions based on the reproduction and transmission of sound" (2005, 175). In this phase of recorded music's history, the importance of the inventor was eclipsed by the business-oriented CEOs of these new sonic empires.

By 1931, UK Columbia merged with the Gramophone Company to create Electrical and Musical Instruments (EMI) – a deal that gave EMI licensing rights to the popular HMV record label in Europe – thus making it the largest record com-pany in the world. After purchasing American Columbia in 1932 and selling six million units, the American Record Company (ARC) was the largest record com-pany in the US and was the leader in the inexpensive record market. In 1936, two years after the incorporation of American Decca (another producer of cheap records) by Jack Kapp, more than 50 percent of the records being produced were destined for jukeboxes across America. Indeed, the 13 million discs used yearly by jukeboxes actually saved the music industry. American Decca was not only the first record company to create economies of scale through aggressive marketing schemes and jukebox sales, but they also introduced the star system within the recording industry (Sanjek and Sanjek 1991).

By the end of the 1930s, recorded music was no longer a distinct business, but was part of the integrated entertainment industry as a new Big Three had emerged: RCA-Victor, Decca, and Columbia. At this point, radio was king, and, in an effort to promote regional music ("hillbilly" and "race" records) while serving the local stations that ASCAP had largely ignored, radio broadcasters formed a rival per-formance rights organization in 1939, Broadcast Music, Incorporated (BMI).

While only 100 million discs sold in the US prior to entering World War II, military research and the US forces' capture of Radio Luxembourg's magnetic taping technology on September 11, 1944, as well as postwar consumerism, fueled the sale of 350 million records in 1946. However, as industry sales rose to $89 million and recording companies began shifting their focus toward instant successes in the form of the pop record, the lion's share went to Columbia, Decca, RCA-Victor, and Capitol (85% or 300 million records).

In 1948 the music industry met another foe, television. But instead of succumbing to the new technology, as it had done with radio, the music industry fought back with a weapon of its own: the long-playing microgroove record (LP). Invented by Dr Peter Goldmark at CBS, the LP extended recording time to a half hour, and in its first year on the market the format topped $3 million in sales. RCA-Victor would not be outdone, so in 1949, after a $5 million marketing campaign, they debuted the 7inch 45rpm single disc – a four-minute format that was perfect for the pop single. Because CBS didn't want to delay the release of the LP until it had a player, and perhaps learning from the past failures of delivery technologies that were introduced into the marketplace without industry-wide standardization, they developed an adapter that would play LPs on existing phonographs.

By the early 1950s, however, RCA-Victor began producing LPs and CBS 45s, once again proving that industry standardization between hardware and software was key to financial success. It is interesting to note that the industry move to the LP also encouraged record manufacturers to buy new pressing machines. In turn, the old machines were bought by people who used them to make bootleg copies of records produced by the industry. In 1952, the RIAA (Recording Industry Association of America) formed to set a technical standard for recording and playback on vinyl records and to lobby in Washington on behalf of its members in the recording industry, but also partly in response to the new rash of LP piracy (Morton 2000).

Moving into the 1950s, the recording industry again experienced a flurry of independents (similar to the indie proliferation in 1918). With magnetic tape dramatically lowering recording costs, and LPs and 45s being relatively cheap to press, the barrier to entering the market decreased rapidly. However, the major players solidified their dominance through full vertical integration. The major companies "owned their own manufacturing plants and directly controlled their distribution outlets in addition to simply producing records" (Chapple and Garofalo 1977, 15) and were designated as "majors" because they did their own nationwide distribution (Dannen 1990, 112). Previously, market control had come from technological innovation and musical production, but, by the end of the 1950s, market domination was firmly in control of those firms with distribution power. Thus controlling the means of production was no longer enough; instead, the most profitable companies controlled distribution – the means by which a recording made its way to retailers and ultimately into the hands of the consumer.

From 1955 to 1959 record sales nearly doubled to $511 million, largely due to the rise of big-box store retailers such as Sam Goody, as well as the new "one-stop" distributors who would buy from the major distributors and sell to small independent stores. Undoubtedly, records were finding their place in a national market and were not limited to regional distribution. While the Big Four had a 75 percent share of the $277 million US market in 1955, by 1959 this share dwindled to a mere 34 percent of the booming $603 million market. The indies were producing most of the popular and profitable music and were marketing their records through radio disc jockeys. However, independent retailers and distributors began disappearing as the major companies controlled most distribution outlets and started their own record clubs for direct sale, and the big-box stores expanded. In addition, people who rented space in department stores to sell popular records, known as rack-jobbers, grew to become more important, accounting for more than half of US record sales at this time (Gelatt 1977).

During this era of consolidation, sales jumped from $600 million in 1960 to $1.2 billion by the decade's end. Record companies were looking like enormous cash cows, ready for conglomerate slaying. The independents were introducing new popular music through radio, but in order to sell those records they relied on the major companies who had complete control over the channels of distribution. Instead of taking over the independents, the major companies made arrangements to invest in them and handle their distribution, but it wasn't a big step to fully take over, as the majors "squashed the entrepreneurialism by putting it in the structure of a conglomerate" (Callahan 2005, 9). By 1967, the market was controlled by CBS Records, RCA-Victor, and Capitol, each with a 12–13 percent share of the US market. Behind the "independent" labels were a small number of integrated entertainment corporations; thus the multitude of independents was merely an "illusion" (Millard 2005, 333). By the end of the 1960s, the American market had attracted foreign companies, such as EMI, which took over Capitol, and the PolyGram group, which bought MGM, Verve, and the United Artists distribution system. Competition for the acquisition of independent record labels also began to heat up between the major companies. And, as these companies became further horizontally integrated, "label federations" developed. What we now refer to as "music groups" involved loosely affiliated labels that set up divisions (usually genre-based) within major conglomerates. This strategy offered the major companies a way to cope with market uncertainty by spreading their risks, and to reap synergistic benefits by creating company-wide manufacturing in order to exploit economies of scale.

Overall, these new highly diversified corporations became adept at promoting and distributing products. Equipped with music publishing arms and vertically integrated labels, the Big Six (CBS, Warner Bros, RCA, Capitol-EMI, PolyGram, and MCA), as well as a half dozen smaller companies, dominated the market. In the 1970s and into the 1980s, these media conglomerates grew even bigger, making independent production and distribution a thing of the past. In addition, many observers have argued that the logic of the corporation took over the creative logic of music-making (Chapple and Garofalo 1977, Chanan 1995, Morton 2000, Coleman 2003). According to Chapple and Garofalo, the merger movement of the 1960s was:

> a "natural" process of centralization in which the successful companies joined to save expenses, to control prices and the market more effectively, and to amalgamate companies specializing in different types of music into one corporation that provided greater financing and simpler, central distribution. ... Because the music business had become so profitable and because as part of the entertainment industry it was a high growth field, outside conglomerates looking for new acquisitions found music corporations attractive. (1977, 82)

The cassette era

While radio popularized the notion of free music in the 1920s, the cassette took this consumer empowerment to a whole new level. Philips, a Dutch electronics company, began the manufacture and sale of compact cassette tapes in 1963 (selling them under the Norelco brand in the US), and, by 1965 polls showed that 40 percent of the people buying tapes were doing so to make copies of LPs. This implied that record labels were coming up short and "did not satisfy the demands of consumers" (Morton 2000, 137). Nevertheless, cassette tapes did not produce major consumer waves until the oil crisis of the 1970s caused a shortage in the vinyl used to manufacture LPs. As Japanese manufacturers (Sony and Matsushita) began incorporating cassette players into home stereos that could rival the reel-to-reel format, the sale of blank cassette tapes soared to 125 million in 1970. After complaints of piracy by the RIAA and its representatives, Congress enacted the Sound Recording Act of 1971 to finally give mechanical recordings federal copyright protection.

With the growth of cassette piracy, music was for the first time circulated en masse outside of its market. Although Dr Peter Goldmark predicted, "The disc and tape will exist side by side" (quoted in Coleman 2003, 62), Americans spent $861 million on tape players and only $577 million on record players in 1973. The recording industry still raked in $2 billion as "Records were sold like toothpaste" (Gelatt 1977, 336), despite an estimated $200 million in losses from the sale of bootlegs. With the Big Six controlling more than 80 percent of the US market, sales of recorded music grew to $4.1 billion through 1978. 1978 was also the year that PolyGram had over $1.2 billion in sales – the first recording company to top the $1 billion mark. The constant market growth made the major record companies an attractive investment to large multinationals, an interest signaled when in 1979 Thorn Electrical Industries, a highly diversified British conglomerate, merged with EMI to form Thorn EMI. (This merger eventually allowed Thorn EMI to make a number of acquisitions – most notably the eventual high-profile purchase of Richard Branson's Virgin Records in 1992.)

Nevertheless, 1979 proved to be problematic for the recording industry, with an 11 percent decrease in sales from the previous year – the first such decline since World War II (Dannen 1990). The major companies were forced to restructure, including cutting back on marketing and promotions, as well as the development of new talent. In the early 1980s tape sales were almost equal to LPs, but by 1986 the sale of prerecorded cassettes surpassed records and most home stereos came equipped with two cassette decks. Thus a CBS study claimed $700–800 million in losses to piracy, while the RIAA declared billions. Though radio and film had been the main conduit for music promotion for nearly 60 years, the introduction of MTV and the music video format in 1981 proved a far more effective marketing tool, reaching over 56 million homes by the end of the decade. As one observer noted, the major companies had become "too big for their own good, they never know where and when the next trend is going to emerge because they are not really in touch with the audience" (Chanan 1995, 156). It was at this point that the economic downturn really began to hit the music industry.

The recording industry, however, would not go down without a fight over piracy. Although Philips and Sony had released the compact disc (CD) as early as 1978, the industry didn't begin to support the new digital format until 1982. Not only would the record industry see this new format as a way to curb piracy, but the CD encouraged market growth as consumers started to replace their LP and cassette collections with CDs. The introduction of the CD also led to an industry revelation: exploiting copyrights attached to old recordings could be very profitable. Because of this epiphany, the large entertainment conglomerates realized the inherent value of owning large back catalogs of music. Thus many of the mergers that took place in the 1980s were partly motivated by the profitable promise of acquiring extensive copyright catalogs. Not only did major companies become interested in owning the rights to sound recordings, they also began to purchase publishing companies so that they could fully exploit music through television, radio, and film, as well as license those rights to their competitors. According to Callahan (2005, 228), the record business became interested in "money derived from the exploitation of musicians and copyright."

The tangible digital era

While the CD was slow to find a market, the recording industry went to great lengths to make sure that the format would succeed by quickly phasing out LPs and later cassettes (LP sales fell 80% in the 1980s). In addition, the CD signaled a return to a familiar format, as Steffen (2005, 30) argues: "The shape of recorded music that we are still most familiar with is the disc … the stamped record has been a mainstay delivery system of recorded music." The CD's similarity to Berliner's disc may have contributed to the format's consumer appeal; however, the "superior" sound quality of the CD and digital recording contributed to its success as well. During the same year that cassettes eclipsed LPs in sales (1986), the CD had its first big year with 50 million sold. While CBS and RCA battled over formats in the late 1940s, Philips and Sony were able to use piracy as the motivation for the Big Six recording companies to swiftly make the digital move – one that would give an industry lead to the two non-US-based consumer electronics companies.

While the 1980s was a decade marked by technological innovation, it was also an era filled with a series of mergers and acquisitions fueled by easy money and lax regulation. In 1988, Sony bought CBS Records for $2 billion, an acquisition that gave the electronics company a roster of artists and a back catalog. Three years earlier, GE had purchased the RCA Corporation, then sold its 50 percent interest in RCA Records and its subsidiaries to Bertelsmann (soon renamed BMG Music). Thus three of the six leading major record companies in the US were owned by international media conglomerates.

According to Frith (1988) and Dannen (1990), the increased consolidation of the 1980s had its effect on musical diversity as fewer titles were being released into the market (in the 1970s, 4,000–5,000 titles were released yearly, while in the 1980s that number dropped to about 2,000). Gronow (1983) observed that the industry's corporate structure and mode of operations in the early 1980s were similar to that of the early 1900s. These large sound empires had spent the better part of the century swallowing up smaller competitors, and the 1990s would be no different as "this feeding continued at a faster pace in the digital era" (Millard 2005, 367).

With an increasing number of new releases available only on CD or cassette, record stores dropped LPs and 45s from the shelves. In 1989, vinyl sales dropped to 6 percent of the recorded music market, while CD sales rose to 200 million and cassettes to 450 million. By 1991, vinyl records had vanished from most stores. The CD had cut manufacturing and distribution costs dramatically, but as those costs decreased the retail price of CDs remained much the same through the early 2000s.

With 20 million CD players in use by 1990, the industry experienced a steep rise in sales of prerecorded CDs – an increase that happened to coincide with the rapid sale of blank cassettes. While the cassette had, in some ways, liberated consumers from the structure of the LP, the CD suggested a return to the "one-way, monopolistic, homogenizing tendencies" of the LP format (Manuel 1993, 15). With the flurry of formats and speeds introduced in a relatively short period of time, it is no wonder that consumers experienced confusion as technological innovation continued to change how consumers experienced music (Frith 1988).

In 1990, the Japanese electronics manufacturer Matsushita paid $6.13 billion in cash for MCA Inc. Thus by 1995 Sony, Matsushita, and Philips were the modern equivalent to the original Big Three as these companies developed hardware, software, and talent. However, in 1998 Seagram, in what was then the largest merger in the industry's history, bought PolyGram for $10 billion. Two years later, Vivendi bought Seagram's entertainment assets for $34 billion, and the PolyGram and MCA family of labels eventually became the Universal Music Group.

As the new millennium approached, the US recording industry was worth $13.7 billion, while the global market was valued at $38.1 billion. In early 2000, the Big Six of the 80s had morphed into the Big Five (UMG, BMG, EMI, WMG, and Sony), an oligopoly accounting for about 95 percent of all records sold globally in 2000. Consumers paid roughly $16 per CD for the format's first two decades, but once they were able to buy blank CD-Rs and duplication hardware and see how cheap it was to produce music CDs, it became obvious how the industry had taken advantage of the market. The digital CD's advantage of eliminating piracy disappeared as consumers gained access to duplication media and again music circulated outside the commercial market. While consumers used blank CDs for perfect replication of prerecorded discs, the industry was becoming involved in another format battle – actually, this time a war. The struggle would not occur between any of the major players as it had in the past – this time war was waged by the industry on its consumers and *their* new format: the MP3.

The contemporary recorded music industry

The music business is a cruel and shallow money trench, a long plastic hallway where thieves and pimps run free, and good men die like dogs. There's also a negative side
Hunter S. Thompson

For the first 110 years of recorded music, the primary commodities produced by the industry were physical objects, which allowed the major companies to maintain control over the material production and distribution of records. By 2009, the recorded music industry was in disarray – the CD format dying and the physical distribution model crumbling, forcing the major recording companies to restructure and try to adapt to consumer demands. More than ever, the industry was being forced to follow trends rather than set them.

A review of MP3 technology illustrates some of the dilemmas facing the recorded music industry. It might be argued that the MP3 has been at the heart of the industry's woes. The format was originally designed to compress video files in the early 1990s, and has been spreading on the web since 1994. Unlike many of its predecessors – from the phonogram to the CD – MP3 technologies were not introduced by the recording industry itself. Rather, the software and hardware used in the playback of digital music were developed and marketed by huge computer technology corporations (e.g., Apple and Microsoft) – companies with little interest in the production or marketing of recorded music.

The MP3 and music piracy became part of popular discourse because of the extensive media coverage surrounding the 2001 *A&M Records, Inc. v. Napster, Inc.* case, which pitted a successful recording company against the first popular peer-to-peer (p2p) file-sharing network. Napster enabled people to make copies and distribute MP3s, allowing music to circulate outside the market, which, of course, drew accusations of copyright infringement from the recording industry. The Napster company was decried and then sued by the RIAA, its members, and several mega-recording stars for direct and contributory copyright infringement. The recording industry won the suit, thus forcing Napster to shut down its operations and move into bankruptcy. However, the company was resurrected two years later as Napster 2.0, an à la carte and subscription service, which was then purchased by Best Buy Co.

With the recording industry emerging as victors, the Napster case set a precedent for future suits against p2p services (e.g., *MGM v. Grokster* in 2005). But despite the concern over lost revenues and various legal measures taken, the recording industry remained blind to evolving distribution platforms, customer demands, and supporting technologies in the early 2000s. The industry won several court battles, thousands of legal settlements, and the right to preserve its "properties" through an economy of scale production model and physical distribution infrastructure. In the process, however, it lost its grip on an increasingly volatile market. While the major recording companies fought illegal file-sharing, they failed to develop and implement digital distribution into their repertoire; therefore, many musicians and labels (independent or otherwise) successfully filled the void. Digital technology reduced both production and distribution costs, and, according to Fox (2004, 205), diminished the industry's control over music production and "the major labels' historical hegemony over traditional distribution methods."

Finally, in 2009, the recording industry began to capitalize on digital distribution – another obvious example of how major record companies follow trends rather than set them. While physical distribution was giving way to new digital models, Roberts (2005, 38) notes that the recording industry is still "dominated by entities that control distribution and are less focused on production," thus distribution should be understood as the key to generating profit and market power in the digital age.

Typically, recording artists work for specific record labels, which are owned mostly by major entertainment corporations. Corporate labels are able to draw on extensive capital resources to market and promote new albums, as well as to front large advances to recording artists, who must pay back these advances from the royalties they receive from album sales. In other words, an artist must pay all of the expenses associated with the production of the album (from sound engineers to licensing), as well as expenses involved in producing music videos, and so forth. Thus the label's only risk in producing an album is fronting the money for marketing and promotion, which is typically recouped from sales.

After an album is recorded, the label arranges for manufacture and then focuses on distributing it through the company's own distribution network. Distribution is not only the key to the success of the company's labels, but also attracts products from independent labels that employ these distribution networks. A strong distribution network will ensure that an album will end up at retailers and then finally in consumers' hands. Therefore, control over distribution leads to control of the market and the industry. Thus the major companies are currently trying to find ways to dominate channels of digital distribution.

In the industry, a record label is considered independent if it self-distributes or goes through an "independent" distributor (e.g., ADA, RED, Caroline, or E1 Entertainment Distribution). Therefore, a label owned by the Big Four may utilize independent distribution and thus claim to be independent (e.g., Zomba). It is interesting to note that both EMI and WMG are no longer owned by transnational entertainment conglomerates. WMG was bought from Time Warner in 2004 by an investment group (led by Edgar Bronfman Jr. of Seagram fame) for $2.6 billion, and, after an appalling financial year in 2006, the private equity firm Terra Firma Capital Partners bought EMI for £3.2 billion.

Since 2000, when the overall market in the US was $14.3 billion ($36.9 billion globally), revenues to $8.3 billion in 2008, an 18 percent decrease from 2007. Trade associations around the world blame illegal downloading for the loss in revenues. The International Federation of the Phonographic Industry (IFPI) estimates a 20 to 1 ratio of illegally to legally downloaded music files, which is supported by a recent study by the Institute for Policy Innovation estimating that global piracy took a $12.5 billion slice out of the US economy, displaced 71,000 jobs and $2 billion in wages. These figures, however, have been created by the recording industry to paint itself as the victims and derive its estimates by equating illegal downloads of CDs to physical theft from a retailer. It is relevant to point out, though, that MP3 files are nonrivalrous goods, meaning that the consumption of an MP3 by one does not prohibit its consumption by others (nor does its theft).

While revenues have shrunk significantly according to RIAA data, the sale of product has increased dramatically: in 2008, 1.85 billion units were shipped, which is 730 million more than in 1999, one of the best years for industry sales. While the physical distribution model yielded more profit, digital distribution sold more product with less payoff – what NBC Universal's CEO Jeff Zucker has referred to as "trading analog dollars for digital pennies" (quoted in Arango 2008).

The lion's share of the US music market is controlled by Universal Music Group (30.2%), Sony Music Entertainment (28.58%), Warner Music Group (20.55%), and the EMI Group (9.2%), while the rest of the market goes to "indie" labels (11.47%) (Nielsen SoundScan 2009). These figures represent the production sector of the recorded music industry. In terms of distribution, the Big Four control approximately 95 percent of the music being shipped to physical and digital retailers.

The industry is finally restructuring itself to meet the consumer demand for cheap, and now even free, instant, and intangible recorded music, and has started to monetize legal digital distribution. Record companies are now exploiting new music through digital sales, including satellite radio and webcasting, ringtones and ringbacks, iTunes sales and subscription services. But they are also recycling old content sold as MP3s. Back catalogs can make up more than 40 percent of sales and 70 percent of profits for a typical major label (Singh 2001, 4). With new digital platforms, labels are looking at more than album sales as the barometer of success. Rio Caraeff, an executive at UMG, said, "We look at the total consolidated revenue from dozens of revenue lines behind a given artist or project, which include digital sales, the physical business, mobile sales and licensing income" (quoted in Sisario 2008).

In 2008, 32 percent of overall US sales were digital (compared to just 9% in 2005), while digital sales accounted for over 20 percent of the world market. Total physical units shipped were down 26 percent in 2008 in the US market (12% globally). With such a decrease in physical sales, big-box stores such as Wal-Mart and Best Buy (the second and third largest music retailers behind iTunes), which have typically accounted for 65 percent of all retail purchases, have sharply reduced the floor space allotted to recorded music (although Best Buy is now trying to sell vinyl records at some of its stores). However, in 2008 one physical format did exceptionally well: the EP/LP, which saw a 124 percent increase in units shipped from 2007. Conversely, while over one billion singles were downloaded in 2008, in the same year a mere 400,000 12 inch vinyl singles were shipped (down from 5.4 million in 1999).

The industry has started to embrace and capitalize on new digital distribution models, from à la carte MP3 stores (e.g., iTunes, where singles/albums are sold) to subscription services (e.g., Napster 2.0, where monthly fees are paid for unlimited downloads) to advertising-based sites (e.g., MySpace Music and YouTube, where "free" music is supplemented by advertising sales). However, many signs within the industry are pointing toward a model where music is "free" for consumers as they pay for recorded music indirectly, which is a model gaining momentum in Europe. Mark Mulligan, an analyst at Forrester Research, explains that the industry is shifting to its "Plan B": "The record companies have realized that the only way they can fight free is with free itself" (quoted in Pfanner 2009).

The goal of these "free" models is to find new ways to connect music to consumers. One model, called "Comes With Music," involves electronic devices, such as cellular phones, that include musical content. "Music can become an important element that enhances the value of consumer electronics devices, providing consumers with a very complete and satisfying experience," said Thomas Hesse, an executive at Sony Music (IFPI 2009, 8). Record companies are also trying to find ways to connect their music with advertisers and specific campaigns, essentially branding a band and a product simultaneously.

In addition, the industry is increasingly exploring licensing deals with video games, as well as developing other models such as the "multiple rights" or "360" contracts. These deals focus less on the sale of recorded music and the need to quickly recoup label investments in advances and promotion, and more on how record companies can capitalize on a recording artist as a whole – from concert tickets and merchandise to fragrance and clothing lines. While 360 deals may allow (or force) labels to develop not only talent, but a coinciding fan-base, artists' ancillary income also could potentially offset future declines in album sales. "We don't sell records any more, we act wherever people experience music," said Elio Leoni-Sceti, an executive at EMI, "Our role is not to put physical discs on the shelf but to reach consumers wherever they are" (IFPI 2009, 5). In other words, the major recording companies are scrambling to monetize the music they produce by further exploiting artists and copyrights in a desperate attempt to maintain their market hegemony.

Conclusion

Music is everybody's possession. It's only publishers who think that people own it.
John Lennon

This chapter has looked at the historical relationship between technology and music, a somewhat antagonistic connection that has created the contemporary recorded music industry. Through critical historical analysis, we have noted the cyclical nature of this industry, as well as how such an analytical framework may help to explore contemporary market conditions.

For nearly a century, as this chapter reveals, the major players in the recorded music industry have profited by creating artificial scarcity of the commodities they produced, using an economies of scale model, as well as by controlling physical distribution networks. While the industry struggled to standardize and control its playback formats and hardware, current problems facing it are not only because recorded music is circulating outside its market, but because the industry has lost much of its control over hardware production to companies in other industries. The MP3 format has in many ways destroyed the recorded music industry's production and distribution models as very little is physically produced and thus made scarce.

However, the industry is increasingly realizing that it can make even intangible commodities such as MP3s scarce, and thus valuable, through the continued exploitation of the copyrights attached to music. It could be argued that the MP3 in reality merely represents, and in fact is, a copyright for which consumers pay (or do not pay). Indeed, recorded music itself is actually becoming a secondary commodity; that is, much as in the early 1900s, recorded music is being used to sell hardware and other commodities. This is evident, for example, in the licensing of its music for video games and ringtones, for use in branding other commodities, or to be included with hardware. In other words, we suggest that the industry will stay afloat by licensing its copyrighted music to other cultural industries or other corporations, based on nothing more than a legal process. In other words, copyrights may end up being the industry's only valuable commodities.

It is interesting to note several signs indicating that the industry's woes may possibly lead to a more "profitable" state of music as an art form. First, with digitization, more music is being produced, distributed, and consumed, but at a significantly lower rate of profit. Music is recorded, produced, and distributed much easier in the digital age and may free musicians from the control of major labels. This may be good for the art of music, but clearly not as beneficial to the business of music. Second, other indicators of musical experiences have been observed. For instance, Callahan (2005) notes that the sale of musical instruments recently has increased exponentially.

Meanwhile, recent figures show an increase in the sale of concerts tickets in North America (accompanied by consolidation in the live music performance business).

The future of recorded music is indeed in a precarious state. As the market for digital music continues to grow, the industry is likely to respond with both promises and threats in attempts to monetize its assets and regain control of the market. While we can't predict the future of this volatile industry, we can certainly look to the past to understand and possibly even predict how the recorded music business may adapt to new technologies. We suggest issues relating to this industry should be explored further through critical political economic analysis – issues which could be, as Smythe (1960) suggested, addressed in dissertations and other academic publications for decades to come.

References

Adorno, T. W. (1990/1941) On popular music. Simpson, G. (trans.). In: Frith, S. and Goodwin, A. (eds), *On Record: Rock, Pop, and the Written Word*. Routledge, New York, pp. 301–14.

Alexander, P. J. (2002) Peer-to-peer file sharing: The case of the music recording industry. *Review of Industrial Organization*, 20, 151–61.

Arango, T. (2008) Digital sales surpass CDs at Atlantic. *The New York Times,* November 25. Online at http://www.nytimes.com/2008/11/26/business/media/26music.html (accessed April 14, 2009).

Attali, J. (1985) *Noise: The Political Economy of Music*. Massumi, B (trans.). University of Minnesota Press, Minneapolis.

Benjamin, W. (1969/1936) The work of art in the age of mechanical reproduction. In: Benjamin, W., *Illuminations: Essays and Reflections*. Arendt, H. (ed.). Schocken, New York, pp. 217–51.

Bollier, D. (2005) *Brand Name Bullies: The Quest to Own and Control Culture*. John Wiley & Sons, Inc., Hoboken, NJ.

Breen, M. (1995) The end of the world as we know it: Popular music's cultural mobility. *Cultural Studies*, 9(3), 486–504.

Burkart, P. and McCourt, T. (2006) *Digital Music Wars: Ownership and Control of the Celestial Jukebox*. Rowman & Littlefield, Lanham, MD.

Burnett, R. (1996) *The Global Jukebox: The International Music Industry*. Routledge, New York.

Callahan, M. (2005) *The Trouble with Music*. AK Press, Oakland, CA.

Chanan, M. (1995) *Repeated Takes: A Short History of Recording and its Effects on Music*. Verso, London.

Chapple, S. and Garofalo, R. (1977) *Rock 'n' Roll is Here to Pay: The History and Politics of the Music Industry*. Nelson Hall, Chicago.

Coleman, M. (2003) *Playback: From the Victrola to MP3, 100 Years of Music, Machines, and Money*. Da Capo Press, Cambridge, MA.

Cvetkovski, T. (2007) *The Political Economy of the Music Industry: Technological Change, Consumer Disorientation and Market Disorganisation in Popular Music*. VDM Verlag Dr. Müller, Saarbrücken, Germany.

Dannen, F. (1990) *Hitmen: Power Brokers and Fast Money Inside the Music Business*. Times Books, New York.

Day, T. (2000) *A Century of Recorded Music: Listening to Musical History*. Yale University Press, New Haven, CT.

Demers, J. (2006) *Steal This Music: How Intellectual Property Law Affects Musical Creativity*. University of Georgia Press, Athens.

Dowd, T. J. (2003) Structural power and the construction of markets: The case of rhythm and blues. *Comparative Social Research*, 21, 147–201.

Dowd, T. J. (2004) Concentration and diversity revisited: Production logics and the U.S. mainstream recording market, 1940–1990. *Social Forces*, 82(4), 1411–55.

Eisenberg, E. (2005) *The Recording Angel: Music, Records and Culture from Aristotle to Zappa*, 2nd edn. Yale University Press, New Haven, CT.

Elliot, M. (1993) *Rockonomics: The Money Behind the Music*. Carol Publishing Corporation, Secaucus, NJ.

Fabbri, F. (1993) Copyright: The dark side of the music business. In: Frith, S. (ed.), *Music and Copyright*. Edinburgh University Press, Edinburgh, pp. 159–63.

Fox, M. (2004) E-commerce business models for the music industry. *Popular Music and Society*, 27(2), 201–20.

Frith, S. (1981) *Sound Effects: Youth, Leisure, and the Politics of Rock 'n' Roll*. Pantheon, New York.

Frith, S. (1988) *Music for Pleasure: Essays in the Sociology of Pop*. Routledge, New York.

Frith, S. (ed.) (1993) *Music and Copyright*. Edinburgh University Press, Edinburgh.

Garofalo, R. (1986) How autonomous is relative: Popular music, the social formation, and cultural struggle. *Popular Music*, 6(1), 77–92.

Gelatt, R. (1977) *The Fabulous Phonograph: 1877–1977*, 2nd edn. Macmillan Publishing, New York.

George, N. (1988) *The Death of Rhythm & Blues*. Pantheon, New York.

Golding, P. and Murdock, G. (2000) Culture, communication and political economy. In: Curran, J. and Gurevitch, M. (eds), *Mass Media and Society*, 3rd edn. Edward Arnold, London, pp. 70–92.

Gronow, P. (1983) The record industry: The growth of a mass medium. *Popular Music*, 3, 53–75.

Hesmondhalgh, D. (1998a) The British dance music industry: A case study of independent cultural production. *The British Journal of Sociology*, 49(2), 234–51.

Hesmondhalgh, D. (1998b) Post-punk's attempt to democratise the music industry: The success and failure of rough trade. *Popular Music*, 16, 255–74.

Hesmondhalgh, D. (1999) Indie: The institutional politics and aesthetics of a popular music genre. *Cultural Studies*, 13, 34–61.

Hesmondhalgh, D. (2006) Digital sampling and cultural inequality. *Social & Legal Studies*, 15(1), 53–75.

Hesmondhalgh, D. (2007) *The Cultural Industries*, 2nd edn. Sage Publications, London.

Hobart, M. (1981) The political economy of bop. *Media, Culture, and Society*, 3(3), 261–79.

Horkheimer, M. and Adorno, T. W. (2001/1947) The culture industry: Enlightenment as mass deception. In: Durham, M. G. and Kellner, D. M. (eds), *Media and Cultural Studies: Key Works*. Blackwell, Malden, MA, pp. 71–101.

Huygens, M., Baden-Fuller, C., Van Den Bosch, F. A. J., and Volberda, H. W. (2001) Co-evolution of firm capabilities and industry competition: Investigating the music industry, 1877–1977. *Organizational Studies*, 22(6), 971–1011.

IFPI (2009) Digital music report 2009. Online at http://www.ifpi.org/content/library/dmr2009.pdf (accessed May 24, 2009).

Katz, M. (2004) *Capturing Sound: How Technology Has Changed Music*. University of California Press, Berkeley.

Kelley, N. (ed.) (2005) *R&B, Rhythm and Business: The Political Economy of Black Music*. Akashic Books, New York.

Kenney, W. H. (1999) *Recorded Music in American Life: The Phonograph and Popular Memory, 1890–1945*. Oxford University Press, New York.

Kofsky, F. (1998) *Black Music, White Business: Illuminating the History and Political Economy of Jazz*. Pathfinder Press, New York.

Kusek, D. and Leonhard, G. (2005) *The Future of Music: Manifesto for the Digital Music Revolution*. Berklee Press, Boston, MA.

Lathrop, T. (2003) *The Business of Music Marketing and Promotion,* revised and updated edn. Billboard Books, New York.

Lessig, L. (2005) *Free Culture: The Nature and Future of Creativity*. Penguin, New York.

Lessig, L. (2008) *Remix: Making Art and Commerce Thrive in the Hybrid Economy*. The Penguin Press, New York.

Lee, S. (1995) Re-examining the concept of the "independent" record company: The case of Wax Trax! Records. *Popular Music*, 14, 13–31.

Lopes, P. D. (1992) Innovation and diversity in the popular music industry, 1969–1990. *American Sociological Review*, 57(1), 56–71.

Malm, K. and Wallis, R. (1992) *Media Policy and Music Activity*. Routledge, London.

Manuel, P. (1993) *Cassette Culture: Popular Music and Technology in North India*. University of Chicago Press, Chicago.

Marx, K. (1863) Productivity of capital. Productive and unproductive labour. B. Fowkes (trans.). *MECW* 34, 121–146. Online at http://www.marxists.org/archive/marx/works/1861/economic/ch38.htm (accessed March 10. 2009).

McCourt, T., and Burkhart, P. (2003) When creators, corporations, and consumers collide: Napster and the development of on-line music distribution. *Media, Culture & Society*, 25, 335–50.

McLeod, K. (2001) *Owning Culture: Authorship, Ownership & Intellectual Property Law*. Peter Lang Publishing, New York.

McLeod, K. (2005) *Freedom of Expression: Overzealous Copyright Bozos and Other Enemies of Creativity*. Doubleday, New York.

McQuail, D. (2005) *McQuail's Mass Communication Theory*, 5th edn. Sage Publications, London.

Millard, A. (2005) *America on Record: A History of Recorded Sound*, 2nd edn. Cambridge University Press, New York.

Morton, D. (2000) *Off the Record: The Technology and Culture of Sound Recording in America*. Rutgers University Press, New Brunswick, NJ.

Negus, K. (1992) *Producing Pop: Culture and Conflict in the Popular Music Industry*. Edward Arnold, London.

Negus, K. (1996) *Popular Music in Theory: An Introduction*. Wesleyan University Press, Hanover, NH.

Negus, K. (1999) *Music Genres and Corporate Cultures*. Routledge, London.

Nielsen SoundScan. (2010) 2009 U.S. music purchases up 2.1% over 2008; Music sales exceed 1.5 billion for second consecutive year. *Business Wire*, January 6. Online at http://www.businesswire.com/news/home/20100106007077/en/2009-U.S.-Music-Purchases- 2.1-2008-Music (accessed October 11, 2010).

Passman, D. S. (1997) *All You Need to Know about the Music Business*. Simon & Schuster, New York.

Peterson, R. A. (1976) The production of culture: A prolegomenon. *American Behavioral Scientist*, 19(6), 669–84.

Peterson, R. A. and Berger, D.G. (1971) Entrepreneurship in organizations: Evidence from the popular music industry. *Administrative Science Quarterly*, 10(1), 97–107.

Peterson, R. A. and Berger, D. G. (1975) Cycles in symbol production: The case of popular music. *American Sociological Review*, 40(2), 158–73.

Pfanner, E. (2009) Global music sales fell 7% in '08 as CDs lost flavor. *The New York Times*, January 16. Online at http://www.nytimes.com/2009/01/17/business/media/17music.html?_r=1 (accessed May 20, 2009).

Roberts, M. (2005) Papa's got a brand-new bag: Big music's post-Fordist regime and the role of independent music labels. In: Kelley, N. (ed.), *R&B, Rhythm and Business: The Political Economy of Black Music*. Akashic Books, New York, pp. 24–44.

Robinson, D.C., Buck, E. B., and Cuthbert, M. (1991) *Music at the Margins: Popular Music and Global Cultural Diversity*. Sage, London.

Rudsenske, J. S. and Denk, J. P. (2005) *Music Business Made Simple: Start an Independent Record Label*. Schirmer Trade Books, New York.

Sanjek, D. (1998) Popular music and the synergy of corporate culture. In: Swiss, T., Sloop, J., and Herman, A. (eds), *Mapping the Beat: Popular Music and Contemporary Theory*. Blackwell Publishers, Malden, MA, pp. 171–86.

Sanjek, R. and Sanjek, D. (1991) *American Popular Music Business in the 20th Century*. Oxford University Press, New York.

Scott, A. J. (1999) The US recorded music industry: On the relations between organization, location, and creativity in the cultural economy. *Environment and Planning, A* 31(11), 1965–84.

Singh, A. (2001) *Cutting Through the Digital Fog: Music Industry's Rare Chance to Reposition for Greater Profit*. Bain & Company, Inc., Boston.

Sisario, B. (2008) Music sales fell in 2008, but climbed on the web. *New York Times*, December 31. Online at http://www.nytimes.com/2009/01/01/arts/music/01indu.html (accessed October 11, 2010).

Smythe, D. (1960) On the political economy of communication. *Journalism Quarterly*, Autumn, 563–72.

Sousa, J. P. (1906) The menace of mechanical music. *Appleton's Magazine* 8. Online at http://explorepahistory.com/odocument.php?docId=418 (Accessed April 12, 2009).

Steffen, D. J. (2005) *From Edison to Marconi: The First Thirty Years of Recorded Music*. McFarland & Company, Jefferson, NC.

Storey, J. (1996) *Cultural Studies and the Study of Popular Culture: Theories and Methods*. University of Georgia Press, Athens.

Swiss, T., Sloop, J., and Herman, A. (1998) *Mapping the Beat: Popular Music and Contemporary Theory*. Blackwell Publishers, Malden, MA.

Taylor, T. D. (1997) *Global Pop: World Music, World Markets*. Routledge, New York.

Théberge, P. (1997) *Any Sound You Can Imagine: Making Music/Consuming Technology*. Wesleyan University Press, Hanover, NH.

Toynbee, J. (2006) Copyright, the work and phonographic orality in music. *Social & Legal Studies*, 15(1), 77–99.

Vaidhyanathan, S. (2001) *Copyrights and Copywrongs: The Rise of Intellectual Property and How it Threatens Creativity*. New York University Press, New York.

Weber, M. (1958) *The Rational and Social Foundations of Music*. Martindale, D., Riedel, J., and Neuwirth, G. (ed. and trans.). Southern University Illinois Press, Carbondale.

16

The Political Economy of Labor

Vincent Mosco

The Labor Blind Spot

Scholarship in the political economy of communication has tended to cluster around the exploration of three intertwined topics: media, messages, and audiences. Those who focus on media tend to look at questions of power and control, including media ownership and the social, political, and economic relations that are at play in the construction of messages and of audiences. Studies concentrating on messages tend to look at the content of the messages themselves, ranging from news to propaganda to advertising, and at the discursive and technological forms these messages take. Those concentrating on audiences tend to look at the way individuals or groups receive, make sense of, understand, act on, ignore, or incorporate messages into their daily lives. Although the field has produced rich and varied work, one aspect has received too little attention: labor.

Intellective and physical labor are required to produce messages and the technologies used to disseminate them. Receiving and acting on messages also requires labor. Yet communications scholars, including those working in the political economy tradition, insufficiently address the various forms of laboring. In addition, the organizations that represent media and information workers, and the presentation of labor in the media, also receive relatively little attention. As this chapter documents, some researchers are now working in this area. But it is probably accurate to conclude that if, as Dallas Smythe (1977) famously remarked, communication is the blind spot of western Marxism, then labor remains a blind spot of western communication studies, including the political economy tradition.

The Handbook of Political Economy of Communications, First Edition.
Edited by Janet Wasko, Graham Murdock, and Helena Sousa.
© 2014 John Wiley & Sons, Ltd. Published 2014 by John Wiley & Sons, Ltd.

Harry Braverman's (1974) work gave rise to an intellectual drive to address the significance of labor by directly confronting the transformation of the labor process in capitalism. According to him, labor is constituted out of the unity of *conception*, or the power to envision, imagine, and design work, and *execution*, or the power to carry it out. In the process of commodification, capital acts to *separate* conception from execution, skill from the raw ability to carry out a task. It also *concentrates* conceptual power in a managerial class that is either a part of capital or represents its interests. Finally, capital *reconstitutes* the labor process to correspond to this new distribution of skills and power at the point of production. In the extreme, this was accomplished through the application of scientific management practices, pioneered by Frederick Winslow Taylor. These amounted to the precise measurement of the time and the amount of labor it takes to accomplish tasks most efficiently, that is, to permit the maximum return on investment. In the process, management became the scientific brains of an enterprise and workers, who once possessed the craft skill to control the labor process, were turned into appendages of the machinery. Braverman documented the process of labor transformation in the rise of large-scale industry, but he is particularly recognized for producing one of the first sustained examinations demonstrating the extension of this process into the service and information sectors. Braverman's work gave rise to an enormous body of empirical examination and theoretical debate, the latter focusing principally on the need to address the contested nature of the process and the active agency of workers and of the labor union movement (Burawoy 1979, Edwards 1979). Much of this work constituted what the philosopher Thomas Kuhn (1970) would call "normal science," that is, working through and expanding upon the wide range of problems and implications contained in Braverman's contribution. This included mapping the contested terrain at the point of production, documenting its history, and demonstrating how the transformation of the labor process was experienced differently by industry, occupation, class, gender, and race. Recent work, including scholarly assessments and business press accounts, has tended to incorporate an interest in how the means of communication, sharpened by steady improvements in technological proficiency, have enhanced the commodification of the general labor process (Baldoz et al. 2001, Huws 2003, Mosco and McKercher 2008).

Despite a strong political economy tradition and a broad interest among economists and policy makers in the cultural industries, communication studies has tended to situate its object within the sphere of consumption, and this has contributed to a focus on the relationship of audiences to texts more than on the media labor process. Political economists of communication have paid considerable attention to institutional control over media production and to the impact of this control on audiences, including the concept of audience labor. Although this is changing, arguably more attention has been directed to the labor of audiences than to the traditionally understood labor process in the media industries. Moreover, media industry labor carries strong craft, professional, and artisan traditions that continue, even as the labor process is transformed (Deuze 2007). The image of the crusading professional journalist or the high-tech entrepreneur overwhelms the less romantic reality of a media and high-tech world most of whose workers toil under conditions that industrial workers of the past would recognize. There is an understandable tendency to emphasize the individual creative dimensions of media production that distinguish this sector from the many occupational sectors that share the characteristics of industrial production. Authors write books, some directors are the *auteurs* of film, stars make movies and television programs, and so forth. There are substantial grounds for this view, principally based on the relatively high level of conceptual thought that this industry requires. This is the chief reason why print workers and their labor unions have historically occupied a privileged position in the workforce. But the emphasis on individual creativity only obscures a complex process of production, one that, however unevenly, has come to look more like the labor process in the general economy.

Organizational Communication and Labor

Organizational communication and sociology have provided some of the better insights into the bureaucratic structure and production processes in the media industries. The work of Tuchman (1978), Fishman (1980), Gans (1979), and more recently Deuze (2007) among others, has examined the system of bureaucratic controls that manage the complex process of, principally, news production. Their work highlights those simplifying routines such as beat reporting, a detailed division of labor, and regularized features that establish a template for what is potentially an open-ended production process. This body of research demonstrates that a substantial amount of organizational planning and preprocessing are used to gather, package, and distribute news and information on a routine basis. This line of research is important for a political economy that addresses the labor process because it describes in rich empirical detail the sociotechnical processes that help to constitute the work of producing media even as it turns labor into a marketable commodity. Nevertheless, although this work gestures to political and economic influences, these are left untheorized in favor of a framework based on theories of bureaucracy and organization that foreground abstract administrative needs and functions. Notwithstanding nods to power and profit, this approach concentrates on how the structural pressures of bureaucracy, following on a literature originating in the work of sociological and political theorists like Max Weber and Robert Michels, rationalize production in the cultural industries, just as they do throughout an economy managed by complex bureaucracies.

From a political economic perspective, the organizational literature contributes rich empirical detail but rests on an idealist foundation that substitutes an administrative essentialism for what it perceives to be the economic essentialism of the market. It places, as Weber suggested, the determining influence of the *means of administration* over that of the means of production. The challenge that the organizational literature poses to political economy is to develop a position that examines the process of production foregrounding political and economic power, specifically the commodification of labor. This would constitute an important link between institutional and textual analysis that retains the materialist strength of a political economic approach. The point is not to reclaim ground lost to one essentialism by restoring another, but to theorize the commodification of labor in the process of media production. The political economy literature has taken some steps in this direction but considerable work remains to be done (Huws 2003, Wasko 2003, Martin 2004, McKercher and Mosco 2006, 2007, Kumar 2007, Mosco and McKercher 2008).

The Laboring of Culture

It is useful to begin the process of reinserting labor into the political economy of communication by describing Michael Denning's conception of the laboring of culture (1996, xvi–xvii). Denning's masterful cultural history of the United States in the middle years of the twentieth century, *The Cultural Front* (1996), uses the phrase to sum up a number of interrelated themes, all of which put labor at the forefront of the cultural struggles of the era. The period from the Great Depression to the 1950s saw the word "labor" join "work," "industry," and "toil" as key words in the vocabulary of cultural workers. As a result, the language itself was "labored." Those years also saw the increased influence on – and participation of – working-class Americans in the arts and culture. This was largely the result of a rapid expansion of mass education and mass entertainment, as the children of immigrants and working-class families grew up to become artists and employees of the cultural industries and as American workers became the primary audience for those industries. Denning also uses "the laboring of culture" to refer to the new visibility of the labor that went into cultural production. He contends that one of the central narratives of the era was the organization of cultural workers into labor unions, including teachers, newspaper reporters, motion picture actors, and radio stars, as well as the workers whose technical expertise ensured that people could watch the movies, listen to the music, and communicate with each other about how to consume the products of the cultural front. The phrase is also a reminder that culturally and politically, the middle years of the last century were characterized by working people embracing social democracy, not simply

New Deal liberalism. Finally, Denning contends that the laboring of culture connotes one of the earliest conceptions of labor: the work that leads to a birth. The laboring of culture, therefore, entailed work and toil, and it had its successes and failures: "To labor is to plod, to be hampered, to pitch and roll in a storm. In all these senses, the cultural front was a laboring, an incomplete and unfinished struggle to rework American culture, with hesitations, pauses, defeats, and failures" (Denning 1996, xvii).

A political economy sensitive to the laboring of communication would bring into the field of communication studies a clearer sense of the work that goes into communication and culture, and of the workers who perform it. Rather than remaining on the fringes of the discipline where it may be treated instrumentally or, more frequently, ignored or dismissed, labor and those who perform it become part of the common vocabulary of communications scholarship. This is especially important given the growth of employment in the communication and related knowledge industries. The laboring of communication also takes up the question of worker organizing, ranging from the creation of social movement unions that attempt to represent the unorganizable to the efforts of conventional unions to organize new groups of cultural workers, recapture lost work (and lost workers), rebalance the relationship between employers and employees, and not only survive but thrive in a globalizing economy. Unions and worker movements are cultural and political organizations as well as economic ones and it is important to ask what that means for their members and for the larger society. The laboring of communication also raises policy questions, ranging from whether and how to regulate mass media and mass messages to how to deal with skilled, creative workers who produce ideas, rather than goods. Finally, the phrase recognizes that the laboring of communication is a difficult and painstaking phenomenon, full of victories and failures. To paraphrase Denning, it is a difficult, imperfect, and unfinished struggle, but an important one for scholars to explore.

Labor Enters the Political Economy of Communication

In the 1980s and 1990s political economy literature took some steps toward labor, particularly by examining the introduction of new communication and information technologies into the workplace (Mosco and Wasko 1983). Research started to address the transformation of work, including patterns of employment and the changing nature of labor in the media and telecommunications industry. Decrying the absence of a labor perspective in journalism history, Hardt (1990) connected what is primarily a political economic perspective with a cultural history of the newsroom that focuses on the introduction of new technologies deployed to carry out work. This extended the pioneering research of political economists working outside communication studies who have examined the labor process in the newsroom (Zimbalist 1979). Following a useful overview that situates current conflicts over electronic news production technologies in the context of over one hundred years of struggle in which "newsrooms, like factory floors, have been a laboratory for technological innovations and a battleground of economic and social interests," Hardt offers a political economic perspective to explain the neglect of labor: "under prevailing historical conditions that privilege dominant visions of the press, press histories ignored working-class issues and questions of labor practices (reflecting the anti-labor attitudes of publishers)" (Hardt 1990, 355).

Repeatedly, research addressed the application of new technologies to reduce employment in the industry and to restructure the work of editors by implementing electronic page layout and by transforming reporters' jobs with electronic news gathering (Russial 1989). These provided specific applications of the labor process view that points to the use of communication and information technologies to shift the balance of power in conceptual activity from professional newsworkers, with some control over their means of communication, to managerially controlled technological systems. Similar work began to address the transformation of the labor process in film (Nielsen 1990), broadcasting (Wasko 1983), telecommunications (Mosco and Zureik 1987), and the information industries (Kraft and Dubnoff 1986).

During this time, a start was also made on political economic work that addressed the international division of labor and labor internationalism. The former resulted from the pressures to rationalize production and the opportunities that technologies, particularly in computers and telecommunication, provided to overcome space and time constraints that once set limits on business. This research began to probe the formation of global labor markets which enabled business to take advantage of differential wages, skills, and other important characteristics on an international scale. Much of the early political economic work in this area concentrated on the spread of the hardware (Southeast Asia) and data entry (the Caribbean) businesses into the developing world where companies were attracted by low wages and authoritarian rule (Sussman 1984). The growth of the international division of labor in communication sparked an interest in labor internationalism. Specifically, this involved making use of the means of communication, including new technologies, to forge close links among working class and labor union interests across borders (Waterman 1990, 2001).

The History of Communication from a Political Economy Perspective

Contemporary communication historians are building on this research. Radio was a central instrument for Denning's cultural front, and communication scholars writing history today from a political economic perspective are explicitly and implicitly telling the detailed story of the media's role in the cultural front. Some have continued to enrich the story of radio. For example, Nathan Godfried (1997) examines the history of a Chicago radio station, WCFL, that was established and run by a labor federation representing unions in that city (Chicago Federation of Labor). Providing a voice for labor in a sea of commercial broadcasting was no easy task, particularly since many of the unions, whose members were also big fans of commercial stations, struggled to define a labor alternative. In the face of enormous commercial and business pressures, WCFL was able to retain its unique character through the 1940s, providing both news and entertainment from a labor standpoint. Returning to WCFL, Elizabeth Fones-Wolf (2006) describes the broader role of radio in the effort to build a democratic Left in twentieth-century America. She not only tells the story of several alternatives to commercial radio, but also describes the political battles that pitted labor and its allies against business in some of the central policy debates of the time. These included decisions about granting and renewing broadcast licenses, determining the limits of station ownership, setting rules about acceptable content, and deciding precisely what should be the requirements to air diverse perspectives (see also Fones-Wolf and Fones-Wolf 2007).

Political economy has also addressed the historical labor trajectories of other media, especially print journalism. For example, Tracy (2006) has written about the crucial role of the International Typographical Workers Union in battles to control the labor process and the introduction of new technologies in the printing industry. They culminated in a 1964 strike that shut down the newspaper business in New York City for four months. Drawing on interviews with the leader of the labor action, Tracy documents labor's once powerful voice in the media industry and assesses its strengths and also its weaknesses, such as hanging on to a narrow craft ideology that ultimately contributed to muting that voice. As political economists who study media concentration have demonstrated, one of the ways business was able to defeat those calling for more democratic communication and press for a singular commercial form of media was through cross-ownership or the purchase of multiple media located in a single community or region. But that also met with strong opposition from coalitions of citizen and labor organizations (Fones-Wolf and Fones-Wolf 2007). The battle for control over Hearst-dominated media in San Francisco provides a stunning example of a company that refused to tolerate the slightest deviation from a conservative viewpoint in either print or broadcast media. One can also find major recent examples that document the history of resistance in the telecommunications and computer industries. Countering the traditional great inventor, technicist, and procorporate readings of AT&T's story, Venus Green (2001) examines the significant interplay of race, gender, and class in the company's history. Dan Schiller (2007b) recounts the struggles in the workplace and in policy-making circles that challenged business efforts to control the postal and telephone system. Pellow and Park (2002) take the analysis into Silicon Valley by telling the story of the struggles first of indigenous people, then of agricultural workers, and now those of immigrant women who do the dirty hardware work and of more privileged but often exploited young software workers. My research with Catherine McKercher extends this view by telling the story of the battles between craft and class among communication workers throughout the history of American media (see also Mosco and McKercher 2008). The remainder of this chapter concentrates on what this research has contributed to the political economy of communication labor.

Labor Union Convergence

In an era characterized by declining labor union penetration, increasing corporate concentration, and the rise of global conglomerates that feed into – and are fed by – the spread of new communication and information technology, knowledge workers have begun to explore new ways to increase labor's power. This is especially the case in the communication sector, which provides the equipment that makes globalization possible, and the production and distribution of the ideas that make it work (Mosco and McKercher 2008). One approach is to pursue labor union mergers, designed strategically to restructure labor unions along much the same lines as the corporations that employ their members. There is considerable research on the value of merger or convergence among labor unions, including in the communication and information industries (Batstone 1984, Katz 1997, Stone 2004). Convergent unions like the Communications Workers of America (CWA) or the Communications, Energy and Paperworkers Union of Canada (CEP) bring together workers in what were once independent industries – newspapers, telecommunications, sound recording, broadcasting – but are now part of cross-media conglomerates. These unions also recognize that it is not just the boundaries between employers that have become blurred; the boundaries between what were once distinct forms of work have also been obscured through the spread of digital technology. Labor convergence, therefore, is seen as an appropriate response to technological and corporate convergence (McKercher 2002, Swift 2003, Bahr 1998). A second approach is to create nontraditional worker organizations, which draw into the labor movement people who cannot or will not join a traditional labor union. Such groups provide a range of services and support for workers, their families, and their communities but do not engage in collective bargaining. In North America, they are particularly prominent in the high-technology area (Kline et al. 2003, Stone 2004, van Jaarsveld 2004).

It is understandably difficult to take seriously the suggestions that political economists should focus on labor resistance, especially in North America, because these are not the best of times for organized labor. In 2007, 12.1 percent of wage and salary workers in the US were represented by labor unions. The good news, from the unions' perspective, was that this was up 0.1 percent from the year before. The increase was the first in the US in a quarter-century, and it occurred despite continuing declines in manufacturing jobs (Greenhouse 2008). But however you look at it, an increase of 0.1 percent is a very slight change. And it followed several years of steady decline, from 12.9 percent in 2003 to 12.7 percent in 2004, 12.5 percent in 2005, and 12.0 percent in 2006. In 1983, the first year for which comparable data are available, the rate was 20.1 percent (U.S. Bureau of Labor Statistics 2008, 2007). The situation is somewhat better in Canada, where 29.7 percent of workers were union members in 2007. But in Canada, too, this is significantly lower than the 1981 rate of 38 percent. Canadian labor union membership dropped steadily between 1989 and 1998, but has stabilized at about 30 percent since then (Statistics Canada 2007, 2005). In both countries, there is a significant gap between union membership rates in the private sector, which formed the backbone of the American Federation of Labor and Congress of Industrial Organizations (AFL-CIO) and its Canadian counterparts for much of the twentieth century, and the public sector. In 2007, the private-sector union membership rate stood at 7.5 percent in the US and at 17 percent in Canada. The public-sector rate, by contrast, was 35.9 percent in the U.S. and 71.7 percent in Canada (U.S. Bureau of Labor Statistics 2008, Statistics Canada 2007).

Admittedly, we need to place these numbers in their historical context because union density rates were at these low levels in the 1920s only to bounce up to highs in the 1930s that were maintained into the early 1950s. As late as 1932, an eminent American labor economist, speaking to a meeting of the American Economics Association, reflected on the American Federation of Labor's loss of 40 percent of its members and pronounced that technological change made it nearly impossible for the union movement to regain its earlier strength (Clawson 2003). Furthermore, although union density is declining, the absolute number of union members is growing, with an overall expansion of the workforce in both the United States and Canada. While it is the case that the United States and Canada have more unionized workers than ever before, density rates continue to decline and there is general agreement among scholars and labor unionists themselves that workers in the knowledge economy face serious problems. Two strategies stand out for doing something to rectify the problem: labor union convergence and social movement-based labor organizations. Established labor unions in the United States and Canada have adopted a merger strategy to better mobilize and concentrate resources. This has especially been the case in the knowledge and communication sectors. In order to understand this strategy, as it applies to the knowledge and media sector, it is useful to consider the concept of convergence.

Convergence is an important concept to describe central developments taking place across the media, telecommunications, and information sectors of the communications industry. Generally speaking, it refers to the integration of technologies, arenas, and institutions in these industries and more specifically to the integration of the devices that these industries use and to the information they process, distribute, and exchange over and through these devices (McKercher 2002,

Mosco and McKercher 2008). By integrating computers and telecommunications, the Internet is now an iconic example of technological convergence. This form of convergence is linked to, and partly responsible for, the convergence of once separate industries into a common arena providing electronic information and communication services. Differences in the social relations of technology, including corporate and regulatory arrangements negotiated in the nineteenth and twentieth centuries that divided up the media into fields of mutually exclusive dominance, once erected thick walls between print media, electronic media, telecommunications, and information services and between labor processes and labor union structures in those industries. Now, owing largely to the power of private communication companies, the weakening enthusiasm of governments for supporting public service communication, and the decline in social movements committed to public service communication, the walls are breaking down, eliminating many of the distinctive features that divided these separate industries and creating one large electronic information and communication services arena.

Convergence has enabled the interconnection of technologies to create new systems of hardware and new levels of service, such as wireless networking in Wi-Fi and Wi-Max systems. Hardware convergence has been greatly advanced with the development of a common digital language that does not distinguish among audio, video, or data transmission, reducing all communication to one language that provides a manifold increase in the quantity and quality of electronic communication. Digitization has the technological advantage of providing enormous gains in transmission speed and flexibility over earlier forms of electronic communication, which were largely reliant on analogue techniques (Longstaff 2002). But digitization takes place in the context of, and greatly expands, the process of commodification, or the transformation of what amounts to a resource into a marketable product or service. On the one hand, the expansion of the commodity form provides the context for who leads the process of digitization and for how it is applied. On the other hand, digitization is used to expand the commodification of information and entertainment, specifically to enlarge markets for communication products, deepen the commodification of labor involved in the production, distribution, and exchange of communication, and expand markets in the audiences that receive and make use of electronic communication (Mosco 2009).

Companies are taking advantage of technological convergence by creating corporate or institutional convergence. This is embodied in the scope of merger and acquisition activity that is most prominent within the knowledge and media industry, though not limited to this sector (McChesney 2007, Schiller 2007a). Convergence is bringing together communication firms that want to take advantage of opportunities to integrate products and services, to cross-promote and cross-market in previously separate spheres like entertainment and news, and to cross-produce content for a range of media. Corporate convergence does not, in and of itself, guarantee success. In the short run, it sometimes does not produce the synergies that companies anticipate, such as integrating the cultures of the print newsroom and the broadcasting station. It also sometimes results in content that cannot attract audiences. These facts help to explain the difficulties experienced by convergent media firms like AT&T, Bell Canada Enterprises, and AOL Time Warner. Indeed, according to the *Wall Street Journal*, in 2006 Time Warner executives were no longer talk about "synergies" but about "adjacencies" (Karnitschnig 2006). Moreover, digitization itself is not a flawless process and technical problems do slow its development. Another stumbling block in the process of technological and institutional convergence is the state of government regulation. Technological and institutional convergence has raised fundamental problems for regulatory policies that were established for discrete industries based on discrete technologies. But these may be short-term problems, which can result in cyclical declines over the course of a secular trend, rather than evidence that convergence has failed. Large units enable businesses to better control their environments, limiting competitive pressures even as they benefit by developing internal market competition among divisions.

Convergence is not just a technological, political, and organizational process. It is also a myth or a story about how computer communication is revolutionizing technology, politics, and society. As such it is part of a sublime vision that, in its strongest form, envisions the technology creating the conditions for the end of history, the end of geography, and the end of politics (Mosco 2004). Convergence is therefore more than just a term to describe an ostensible change in technology and organization. It is part of a utopian discourse that aims to lead us from the coarse materiality of, in Nicholas Negroponte's terms, "the world of atoms" (1996, 69) so that we can learn to be digital. This affirmative vision is used to rationalize deepening social inequalities, tightening surveillance practices, especially in the workplace, and the growing control of a handful of companies over the production and distribution of communication and information. To say that convergence is a myth is not to imply that it is false. Rather, myths take a basic empirical reality and enlarge it by attributing transformative social and cultural consequences that are not currently justified by empirical evidence. Convergence, as both a political and cultural process, creates considerable pessimism among those who support public service communication; diversity in the form and content of knowledge, information, and entertainment; and universal and equitable access to media (Artz and Kamalipour 2003). But the growth of labor union convergence is creating some grounds for optimism.

In the United States, a range of media unions – the International Typographical Workers Union (ITU), the Newspaper Guild, and the National Association of Broadcast Employees and Technicians (NABET) – have joined the Communications Workers of America (CWA). The model of a convergent union (or, as the CWA likes to call itself, "a trade union for the information age"), the CWA represents workers employed in telecommunications, broadcasting, cable TV, newspaper and wire service journalism, publishing, electronics, and general manufacturing, as well as airline customer service, government service, health care, education, and other fields. Among the major employers of CWA members are AT&T, Verizon, the NBC and ABC television networks, the Canadian Broadcasting Corporation (CBC), and major newspapers such as the *New York Times, Wall Street Journal*, and the *Washington Post*. In Canada, the Communications, Energy and Paperworkers Union (CEP) has pursued a similar pattern. It has merged with many of the Canadian units from the ITU, Canadian units from the Newspaper Guild, and Canadian NABET. Its members work in pulp and paper mills, telephone companies, newspapers, radio, and television. They are also employed as graphic artists, hotel workers, computer programmers, truck drivers, and nurses. Furthermore, the Telecommunications Workers Union (TWU), which historically represented telephone workers in British Columbia, was able to extend its jurisdiction over telecommunications workers in other parts of the country because Canada's labor regulatory body determined that technological and industry convergence was best represented by one converged union.

To a degree, the unions see these actions as defensive, or as ways of protecting their members. But, significantly, they also see labor convergence as an attempt to take advantage of synergies brought about by growing convergence in the nature of their work (Bahr 1998). Since these unions represent workers who are increasingly involved in producing for a converging electronic information services arena, they see improved opportunities for organizing and bargaining. In essence, converging technologies and converging companies have led workers to come together across the knowledge industry (Mosco and McKercher 2008).

This strategy has not always been successful. For example, one of the keys to mobilizing against the increasingly integrated video and film industries, encompassing mainly television and Hollywood, is to merge unions representing both sectors, just as companies like Disney and Fox have used their merged power to control their respective workers. For example, without a unified workforce, these companies can dictate the terms of contracts on how revenues from multiple uses of the same television program or film are to be divided. Specifically, labor union convergence in this sector would mean bringing together AFTRA, the American Federation of Television and Radio Artists, and SAG, the Screen Actors Guild. But attempts to accomplish this have failed, most recently in 1999 and 2003, in very close votes (Mosco and McKercher 2008). In Canada, attempts to build closer ties among its major telecommunications unions have also not been particularly successful. Setting up the National Association of Communication Unions created formal federation links between the CEP and the Telecommunications Workers Union. But perhaps because the latter has a history of radicalism (it once took over the telephone exchanges of Vancouver during a strike action in 1981) and because the TWU has eschewed the convergent union idea, the two unions have not worked closely together (Mosco and McKercher 2008).

Convergence also creates cross-border challenges, as workers at the CBC experienced when, to facilitate bargaining, CBC management convinced the Canadian government to order its unions to merge. Prior to this time, CBC journalists had been members of the CWA (which won the right of representation when it merged with the Newspaper Guild) and its technicians were part of the CEP. This meant that some employees of Canada's national broadcaster were members of an American union while others were members of a Canadian union. In the ensuing vote, members decided to join the larger CWA, making all the employees at Canada's national public broadcaster part of an American union. Nevertheless, this form of cross-border convergence has proven to be very useful, contributing significantly to the surprising success of CBC workers against a management which locked them out in August 2005. This case demonstrated the ability of different types of knowledge workers, in this case journalists and technicians, to work together and maintain solidarity with the help of a strong union, even though that union is based in another country. Unions like the CWA have demonstrated that convergence can sometimes "bite back" at the very companies that support it (Mosco and McKercher 2008).

In 2005, the union convergence issue heated up in the United States when, in the wake of the big Republican victory in the 2004 general election and continued decline in union density rates, one of the major unions in the AFL-CIO threatened to pull out unless the federation permitted significant new mergers and other organizational changes. Specifically, the fastest growing major union in the United States, the Service Employees International Union (SEIU), demanded that the federation consolidate several of its member unions and shift funding from its own research and political activity to grass roots organizing. Holding out the threat of withdrawal, the SEIU was backed by the powerful Teamsters Union. The AFL-CIO proposed a compromise but was not successful and several unions left the federation to form their own "Change to Win" coalition comprising 5.4 million members committed to stepped-up union organizing. Partly in response to this major defection, the AFL-CIO set up an industry co-ordinating committee made up of 10 unions covering the arts, entertainment, media, and telecommunications industries. The committee's goal is to build labor power in the industries that have been rocked by corporate concentration and technological change. Convergence, therefore, may also take place in response to the failure of an organization to maintain its membership.

It is uncertain just how far the urge to merge or the convergence movement will take labor unions in the communication, knowledge, and cultural industries. Will it bring back the idea of One Big Union, once popular a century ago with the Knights of Labor and Industrial Workers of the World? Can it expand democracy and citizen engagement by empowering a segment of society that has declined over the past three decades? Is it a genuine new start for labor or a last gasp? It is too early to answer these questions. But it is useful to consider different perspectives on the significance of this development.

On the one hand, labor union convergence increases the centralization of power and of bureaucracy, thereby making it less likely that union leadership can maintain close contact with the rank-and-file membership. Indeed, the evidence from outside North America is not encouraging. For example, in the 1990s the Australian labor movement succeeded in halving the number of its unions, but this did not stop the erosion of union density. Does labor union convergence mean sacrificing union democracy for various forms of cartel unionism?

On the other hand, convergence does give unions greater clout in collective bargaining, thereby diminishing the power that has been concentrated in big companies over the past three decades. To support this view one can point to the CWA's success in organizing wireless telecommunication workers and in defending technical and on-air staff at the CBC. Moreover, mergers allow unions to be more involved in social and political activities. For example, Swift (2003) cites Canada's CEP as a case in point of a converged communication union that has been more deeply involved in major policy issues since it expanded across the converged information industries, including the struggle to limit media concentration in Canada, as well as in the fight against lifting restrictions on foreign ownership of Canadian media. The CEP has been in the forefront of lobbying to maintain public telecommunications in the province of Saskatchewan and public electrical power in Ontario. Moreover, one of the advantages of a converged union is its ability to rise above the narrow interests of some of its members. So, for instance, even though the CEP represents energy workers, it is fully behind the Kyoto Accords to limit the expansion of greenhouse gases. Furthermore, it was able to stand up for its paper workers against a powerful wood products company because convergence permitted the CEP to draw from the strike funds of its energy and communication industry members. It also has the resources to create a Quebec Solidarity Fund that permitted it to invest in declining Quebec paper mills and keep them from closing. Furthermore, the CEP has been extensively involved in the antiglobalization movement and in supporting unionization in Mexico and throughout Latin America with the help of the CEP Humanity Fund. Additionally, research conducted by Kiss and Mosco (2005) on what unions are doing about surveillance in the workplace has demonstrated that knowledge worker unions, especially convergent unions like the CEP, provide the best protection for workers in their collective agreements. Finally, convergence allows unions to work co-operatively as never before, as in the AFL-CIO's industry co-ordinating committee which brings together labor organizations in the arts, entertainment, media, and telecommunications industries to build labor power in industries that have been shaken by corporate concentration and technological change.

Nevertheless, it is not entirely clear whether converged unions are genuinely bringing together different kinds of workers in the knowledge, information, and communication sectors, such as newsworkers and telephone operators, or merely becoming federations of what are, in effect, dissimilar employees.

Social Movement Worker Organizations

A second response to the crisis in organized labor is the formation of worker associations or worker movements that provide benefits to workers without formally negotiating collective agreements. These have been especially prominent in the high-tech sector where union organizing has been especially difficult. Worker associations are particularly prominent among part-time permanent workers who are difficult to organize by traditional unions because they typically work for an employment agency, not the high-tech company itself. Such is the case in California's Silicon Valley where fully 40 percent of workers are employed in non-standard ways and in Microsoft's territory in the Pacific Northwest, which gave rise to the term "permatemp" or permanent temporary worker, so named because they work full time but on hourly contracts that contain practically no benefits or overtime pay. Among the goals of these associations are portable benefits for a highly mobile workforce, lifelong training, job placement, providing assistance to individual workers, dissemination of information to workers, and offering health care plans to workers who are not eligible for employer-paid benefits.

Two types of such associations feature significantly in the knowledge sector, those that represent technology-intensive workers and those that primarily pro-duce content, including cultural workers. Perhaps the leading example and model of the former is WashTech, an offshoot of the CWA in the Seattle high-tech indus-try formed, by disgruntled Microsoft permatemps who were successful in a legal action against the company for salary and benefits denied them because they were placed in the temporary worker category (Rodino-Colocino 2007). One of the big-gest difficulties workers face in the high-tech industry is that many of them do not formally work for the high-tech company itself but for companies like Manpower which provide high-tech firms with workers. Nevertheless, what helped forge WashTech was Microsoft's use of its political power to create the permatemps category, thereby denying a large group of otherwise full-time employees the sal-ary and benefits that would go to recognized full-time workers. The lawsuit and the assistance of the CWA helped to galvanize a sufficient number of Microsoft workers to form WashTech.

WashTech includes programmers, editors, web designers, systems analysts, proof-ers, testers, and engineers, who aim to win higher pay, health benefits, vacation, access to retirement plans, discounted stock options, and workplace training. In addi-tion to taking successful legal action against Microsoft, WashTech members have used their technical skills to unearth a secret Microsoft database on employee per-formance and distribute it to members. WashTech also found contract documents dating back to 2001 cementing deals to outsource high-end software architecture to Indian firms that the company hoped to keep secret. WashTech has been successful at Microsoft, helped by its association with research advocacy groups such as the Center for a Changing Workforce and its online site Techsunite.org, which provides information and online organizing for high-tech workers. But it has at best enjoyed mixed success in expanding to other knowledge sector workers. It failed to organize disgruntled workers at the online bookseller Amazon.com, but did succeed in organ-izing workers at Cingular wireless. Today, WashTech is especially involved in fighting the outsourcing of tech jobs to places like India and China and has been successful in convincing some state legislators to stop outsourcing government tech work.

Alliance@IBM was also formed by the CWA and, like WashTech, fought to win benefits that were initially denied to workers in the loosely defined temporary category from its employer, in this case, IBM. The company has been notorious for the concerns about toxic chemicals in the workplace and Alliance has been particularly active in fighting occupational safety and health cases before the courts. It has also been successful in winning some formal representation for workers at both Manpower and IBM.

It is unusual to think of engineers and the labor movement in the same sentence, but the Society of Professional Engineering Employees in Aerospace (SPEEA) has made it necessary for the management at Boeing to do so because in 2000 the Society led the largest white-collar strike in US history against the giant manufacturer. Indeed, what makes the SPEEA particularly interesting to those who believe that knowledge work offers the potential for new forms of organizing is that much of their success was achieved by the use of email and the web. For example, the union managed to collect home email addresses while building a communications network for their strike against Boeing in 2000. In perhaps the most effective use of its database, SPEEA was able to generate a picket line of 500 people in six hours by email alone, to disrupt an unannounced meeting of the Boeing board of directors in a local hotel. There are other noteworthy high-tech worker associations organizing efforts as well. Systems Administrators Guilds have been set up in the US (and in the UK and Australia) to organize computer workers and intervene in policy debates.

Worker associations are also increasingly prominent among content producers. The Freelancers Union, a national nonprofit organization, grew out of the group Working Today, which was founded in 1995 to provide benefits to people working in the New York City electronics district known as Silicon Alley. Membership is free of charge and open to all freelancers, consultants, independent contractors, temps, part-timers, and the self-employed, but members pay fees for the services they choose. Today, the group is able to offer group health insurance for members and their families in 30 states. By 2006, 13,000 of its members had purchased health care insurance and the union had grown to 37,000 members with annual revenues of $38 million and $4 million in funds for advocacy (*Economist* 2006). By the end of 2007, the union passed the 40,000 member mark and received national attention when freelancers walked off the job at the music video channel MTV after its parent, the media giant Viacom, approved a cut in benefits. Assisted by the Freelancers Union, picketing workers won a restoration of benefits and called attention to the plight of so-called permalancers who, like the permatemps at Microsoft, perform near full-time work for part-time wages and minimal benefits (Stelter 2007). The Graphic Artists Guild – representing people who work in illustration, graphic design, photography, cartooning, web design, multimedia, and other forms of design – combines elements of a professional association with labor unionism. It offers workshops that improve members' skills, but it also runs a legal defense fund and acts as an advocate for artists, particularly on the issues surrounding copyright. The National Writers Union, which participated in the early meetings that founded WashTech, gives members advice on freelance contracts and on asserting or protecting copyright. It also runs a job hotline and a campaign to get employers to hire a union writer.

In Canada, the Communications, Energy and Paperworkers union has organized a freelance writers' local, working in co-operation with a professional association, the Professional Writers Association of Canada. In December 2006, the fledging unit announced that it would urge freelancers to "just say no" to a new freelance contract being handed out to writers at Sun Media, a subsidiary of the Quebecor newspaper chain. It has also tried to fight for higher freelance rates, protection of intellectual property, and better benefits for freelancers. By early 2007, it had roughly 350 members and had launched a recruiting drive in Toronto, Winnipeg, Ottawa, London, ON, Edmonton, Calgary, and Montreal. Plans for 2008 included a job board, described in the union's newsletter as a "hiring hall" for freelancers, and a survey of writers to find out who really pays what for freelance work (Canadian Freelance Union 2007).

Finally, building on the freelance writers' movement and demonstrating that practically every form of new media, from the telegraph to the Internet, has given rise to labor agitation, in August 2007 an annual convention of bloggers hosted a panel on "A Union for Bloggers: It's Time to Organize." The panel featured speakers who are members of a national coalition aiming to develop a labor organization for bloggers. Organizers hope a labor group will not only showcase the growing professionalism of web-based writers, but also the importance of their roles in candidates' campaigns. Blogging has become increasingly popular in the US, where roughly 8 percent of Internet users have created their own blogs or online journals. A union or worker association might help bloggers receive health insurance, carry out collective bargaining, and set professional standards. "It would raise the professionalism," said Leslie Robinson, a writer at Colorado Confidential. com. "Maybe we could get more jobs, bona fide jobs" (Heher 2007). It is difficult to say whether these social movement worker organizations will be able to sustain their ability to help communication workers in the long run. This will depend on the ability of technology and content workers to join together in a convergence across a major barrier in the communication industry. It will also depend on their ability to build bridges across international divides.

Even those labor organizations that have successfully achieved a measure of national or even, as in the case of the CWA, binational convergence, are limited in what they can accomplish because they lack a strong international scope. For example, when the worker association WashTech, which has received strong CWA support, successfully defended information technology workers, Microsoft fought back by outsourcing the work to India and elsewhere (Brophy 2006). Examples like this make it imperative to broaden the study of labor convergence to include the international arena. In doing so, it responds to calls in the scholarly literature to rethink international labor federations in light of a changing global political economy (Jakobsen 2002). But it is important to do so with research that is grounded in the complexities of a changing international division of labor that is not easily reducible to simple conclusions. Consider the issue of outsourcing labor. Labor union organizations invariably consider it negatively, while most businesses conclude that it is an unalloyed gain for economic growth. Basing policy, including the strategies of international labor organizations, on these simple responses is dangerous because outsourcing is not without its contradictions. A large share of outsourcing in the knowledge and communication sectors is contained within the developed world where, for example, Canada has become Hollywood North and Ireland continues to benefit from its skilled workforce and wage premium. Moreover, although India is a major source of low-wage knowledge labor, its major companies such as ICICI, Tata, Infosys, and Wipro are taking a leading role in the outsourcing industry. Their movement into key markets in the developed world suggests that place still matters and that culture continues to count. Finally, resistance is growing from labor organizations and that is one reason why the expansion of convergent unions and worker associations in the knowledge and communication sectors is particularly important. (Mosco and McKercher 2008; see also Elmer and Gasher 2005). Political economy research that assesses the strategies and prospects of international labor organizations needs to be grounded in a recognition that the dynamics of the international division of labor, particularly in the knowledge and communication sectors, is complex and not easily reduced to singularities, however attractive as political slogans or mythic symbols.

Toward a Global Labor Movement: Will Communication Workers of the World Unite?

Specifically, sensitive to these complexities, the political economy of communication needs to examine the state of international labor organizations in the communication and information sectors and the relationships among them, and assess the extent to which they enable workers to meet the challenges of informational capitalism. This research needs to be situated in a political economy perspective that concentrates on power relationships at the institutional level and at the point of production, and addresses the extent and effectiveness of labor convergence at the international level.

Specifically, Catherine McKercher and I are currently in the process of producing a global map of labor convergence by describing four primary types of international labor organization. These comprise international federations that remain rooted in one of the major forms of communication and information, global federations of unions that span the communication and information industries, government or public federations that represent the interests of workers, and worker associations that may be rooted in one nation but which are testing new forms of organizing and partnering with unions and federations outside the nation. We are interested in identifying the major organizations in each category, describing their successes and failures, and the relationships among them. In essence, it is intended to produce an assessment of the state of global labor convergence and the prospects for building international solidarity among workers and their organizations. This provides the groundwork for detailed case studies that examine organizations facing a range of convergence related challenges, including the challenge of making use of converging technologies to meet the needs of workers and their labor organizations.

Our first case deals with the International Federation of Journalists (IFJ), an example of convergence that continues to focus on one sector of the media industry. The IFJ is the world's largest journalism organization, representing 500,000 journalism professionals who comprise its 161 member unions from 117 countries. One of the arguments made in defense of union convergence is the ability to take on broad policy issues that smaller unions cannot afford to address. We are investigating the extent to which the IFJ succeeds on four of the issues to which it gives prominence: media concentration, women's rights in the media, authors' rights to control their work, and institutional attacks on press freedom. The IFJ also claims to bring together journalists from both rich and poor nations. This practice is particularly important because companies like Reuters have begun to outsource journalism work from wealthy nations like the UK to low-wage nations like India. Has convergence enabled the IFJ to address this practice? Finally, as technological and corporate convergence challenges traditional definitions of journalism and as some of its member unions, like the CEP in Canada, enlist workers across both the content and technical segments of the knowledge industries, can the IFJ continue to succeed by focusing on one media sector?

Our second case considers the Union Network International (UNI), a global federation that spans all sectors of the converging electronic services arena. Unlike the IFJ, UNI fully embraces convergence. Calling itself "a new international for a new millennium," it was founded in 2000 and by 2008 brought together 15.5 million workers from 900 unions in 140 countries. It primarily spans the newly converged electronic information and communication sectors including workers in the postal, media, entertainment, telecommunications, and culture sectors. A driving force behind its creation was the growth of companies that span these sectors by taking advantage of converging electronic technologies. Although it is new, UNI has been in the forefront of global labor issues like outsourcing and prominent in applying pressure to global companies and international organizations like the World Trade Organization. It has pioneered the use of global framework agreements with multinational corporations to protect basic labor standards worldwide and has produced the first global charter of rights for call center workers (Mosco and McKercher 2008). How effective is the strategy of creating a labor network of networks that is not confined to one sector? How successful has it been in bridging major divides in the knowledge sector, such as those separating technical from content producers, and news workers from entertainment and other cultural workers? Finally, we are examining how UNI has fared in one of its major goals, building connections between first and third world workers on the vital issue of outsourcing knowledge work.

Next, we consider the International Labour Organization (ILO) to consider how labor convergence works in a UN agency. The ILO differs from both the IFJ and UNI in that it is an arm of the United Nations and was chartered in 1919 to promote justice and human rights for workers. Formally, it produces conventions and recommendations that establish minimum standards for labor rights including freedom of association, the right to organize, collective bargaining, abolition of forced labor, and equality of opportunity and treatment. It also provides technical assistance to workers and labor organizations. This case enables us to consider the state of an international public institution charged with protecting workers and their unions. How does convergence affect the ILO's operation? Specifically, how has it dealt with the shift from industrial work, the main form of labor throughout most of its history, to the increasingly important category of knowledge and communication work, as well as with the differing regional balances of those two forms of labor? We are also assessing the extent to which the ILO has or has not been a force in building networks between first and third world information workers, between those occupying different positions on outsourcing and the changing international division of knowledge work.

Our final case takes up two labor federations in India, the New Trade Union Initiative, which brings together 300 labor unions representing over 500,000 Indian workers, and the Union for IT Enabled Services (UNITES), which organizes workers across the information and communication technology sectors including completing successful contract drives with a major outsourcing firm as well as an international call center located in Hyderabad. We are concentrating on these organizations because they represent new efforts to transcend traditional political party-oriented labor unionism in India, because they each respond in different ways to convergence in the knowledge and communications sectors (NTUI is broad-based, while UNITES focuses on information technology), and because each has relationships with the organizations in the first three case studies, particularly in attempts to build global labor networks to meet the challenge of outsourced communication and knowledge labor. Our project is examining this new burst of labor union activity in India, and is assessing how it is facing the challenges of convergence. Specifically, how effectively are these new organizations mobilizing knowledge and communication workers in India and how successful are they in building ties to labor federations based in the developed world?

In sum, political economists of communication have correctly reminded communication scholars that they should not simply focus on the "the next new thing": new technology, new programming concept, new audience. Now we need to assert the importance of a question that developments in labor insist we ask: will communication workers of the world unite?

References

Artz, L. and Kamalipour, Y. R. (eds) (2003) *The Globalization of Corporate Media Hegemony*. State University of New York Press, Albany.

Bahr, M. (1998) *From the Telegraph to the Internet*. National Press Books, Washington, DC.

Baldoz, R., Koeber, C., and Kraft, P. (eds) (2001) *The Critical Study of Work*. Temple University Press, Philadelphia.

Batstone, E. (1984) *Working Order*. Blackwell, Oxford.

Braverman, H. (1974) *Labor and Monopoly Capital*. Monthly Review, New York.

Brophy, E. (2006) System error: Labour precarity and collective organizing at Microsoft. *Canadian Journal of Communication*, 31(3), 619–38.

Burawoy, M. (1979) *Manufacturing Consent*. University of Chicago Press, Chicago.

Canadian Freelance Union (2007) *CFU Newsletter*. Spring (1).

Clawson, D. (2003) *The Next Upsurge: Labor and the New Social Movements*. ILR Press, Ithaca, NY.

Denning, M. (1996) *The Cultural Front*. Verso, London.

Deuze, M. (2007) *Media Work*. Polity Press, Cambridge, UK.

The Economist (2006) Freelancers of the world, unite! November 9. Online at http://www.economist.com/node/8135077?story_id=8135077 (accessed October 13, 2010).

Edwards, R. (1979) *Contested Terrain*. Basic, New York.

Elmer, G. and Gasher, M. (eds) (2005) *Contracting Out Hollywood*. Rowman & Littlefield, Lanham, MD.

Fishman, M. (1980) *Manufacturing the News*. University of Texas Press, Austin.

Fones-Wolf, C. and Fones-Wolf, E. (2007) Labor off the air: The Hearst corporation, cross-ownership and the union struggle for media access in San Francisco. In: McKercher and Mosco (eds), *Knowledge Workers in the Information Society*. Lexington Books, Lanham, MD, pp. 1–18.

Fones-Wolf, E. (2006) *Waves of Opposition*. University of Illinois Press, Urbana.

Gans, H. (1979) *Deciding What's News*. Pantheon, New York.

Godfried, N. (1997) *WCFL, Chicago's Voice of Labor, 1926–78*. University of Illinois Press, Urbana.

Green, V. (2001) *Race on the Line*. Duke University Press, Durham, NC.

Greenhouse, S. (2008) Union membership sees biggest rise since '83. *The New York Times*, January 26. Online at http://www.nytimes.com/2008/01/26/us/26labor.html?scp=1&sq=greenhouse&st=nyt (accessed January 26, 2008).

Hardt, H. (1990) Newsworkers, technology, and journalism history. *Critical Studies in Mass Communication*, 7, 346–65.

Heher, A. (2007) Bloggers consider forming labour union. *Globe and Mail*, August 7. Online at http://www.theglobeandmail.com/news/technology/article774102.ece (accessed October 12, 2010).

Huws, U. (2003) *The Making of a Cybertariat*. Monthly Review, New York.

Jakobsen, K. A. (2002) Rethinking the international confederation of free trade unions and its interamerican regional organization. *Antipode*, 33(3), 363–83.

Karnitschnig, M. (2006). Time Warner stops pushing synergy. *Wall Street Journal*, June 2. Reprinted in the *Pittsburgh Post-Gazette.com*. Online at www.post-gazette.com (accessed October 12, 2010).

Katz, H. C. (1997) Introduction and comparative overview. In: Katz, H. C. (ed.), *Telecommunications: Restructuring Work and Employment Relations Worldwide.* Cornell University Press, Ithaca, NY, pp. 2–28.

Kiss, S. and Mosco, V. (2005) Negotiating electronic surveillance in the workplace: a study of collective agreements in Canada. *Canadian Journal of Communication,* 30(4), 549–64.

Kline, S., Dyer-Witheford, N., and de Peuter, G. (2003) *Digital Play.* McGill-Queen's University Press, Montreal.

Kraft, P. and Dubnoff, S. (1986) Job content, fragmentation and control in computer software work. *Industrial Relations,* 25, 84–196.

Kuhn, T. (1970) *The Structure of Scientific Revolutions,* 2nd edn. University of Chicago Press, Chicago.

Kumar, D. (2007) *Outside the Box.* University of Illinois Press, Urbana.

Longstaff, P. (2002) *The Communications Toolkit.* MIT Press, Cambridge, MA.

Martin, C. (2004) *Framed!* ILR Press, Ithaca, NY.

McChesney, R.W. (2007) *Communication Revolution.* Free Press, New York.

McKercher, C. (2002) *Newsworkers Unite.* Rowman & Littlefield, Lanham, MD.

McKercher, C. and Mosco, V. (eds) (2006) The labouring of communication. *Canadian Journal of Communication,* 31(3), special issue.

McKercher, C. and Mosco, V. (eds) (2007) *Knowledge Workers in the Information Society.* Lexington Books, Lanham, MD.

Mosco, V. (2004) *The Digital Sublime.* MIT Press, Cambridge, MA.

Mosco, V. (2009) *The Political Economy of Communication,* 2nd edn. Sage, London.

Mosco, V. and McKercher, C. (2008) *The Laboring of Communication.* Lexington Books, Lanham, MD.

Mosco, V. and Wasko, J. (eds) (1983) *Labor, The Working Class, and the Media.* Ablex, Norwood, NJ.

Mosco, V. and Zureik, E. (1987) *Computers in the Workplace: Technological Change in the Telephone Industry.* Government of Canada, Department of Labor, Ottawa.

Negroponte, N. (1996) *Being Digital.* MIT Press, Cambridge, MA.

Nielsen, M. (1990) Labor's stake in the electronic cinema revolution. *Jump Cut,* 35, 78–84.

Pellow, D. N. and Park, L. S. (2002) *The Silicon Valley of Dreams.* New York University Press, New York.

Rodino-Colocino, M. (2007) High-tech workers of the world, unionize! A case study of WashTech's "new model of unionism." In: McKercher, C. and Mosco, V. (eds), *Knowledge Workers in the Information Society.* Lexington Books, Lanham, MD, pp. 209–27.

Russial, J. T. (1989) Pagination and the newsroom. Doctoral dissertation. Temple University, Philadelphia.

Schiller, D. (2007a) *How to Think About Information.* University of Illinois Press, Urbana.

Schiller, D. (2007b) The hidden history of US public service telecommunications, 1919–1956. *Info,* 9, 17–28.

Smythe, D. W. (1977) Communications: Blindspot of Western Marxism. *Canadian Journal of Political and Social Theory,* 1(3), 1–27.

Statistics Canada (2005) Study: Diverging trends in unionization. *The Daily,* April 22. Online at http://www.statcan.ca/Daily/English/050422/d050422c.htm (accessed May 15, 2007).

Statistics Canada (2007) Unionization rates in the first half of 2006 and 2007. *Perspectives on Labor and Income*, August. Online at http://www.statcan.ca/start.html (accessed January 26, 2008).

Stelter, B. (2007) Freelancers walk out at MTV networks. *The New York Times*, December 11.

Stone, K. V. W. (2004) *From Widgets to Digits*. Cambridge University Press, Cambridge, UK.

Sussman, G. (1984) Global telecommunications in the third world: Theoretical considerations. *Media, Culture and Society*, 6, 289–300.

Swift, J. (2003) *Walking the Union Walk*. Communications, Energy and Paperworkers Union of Canada, Ottawa.

Tracy, J. F. (2006) "Labor's monkey wrench": Newsweekly coverage of the 1962–63 New York newspaper strike. *Canadian Journal of Communication*, 31(3), 541–60.

Tuchman, G. (1978) *Making News*. The Free Press, New York.

U.S. Bureau of Labor Statistics (2007) Union members summary, January. USDL 07-0113. Department of Labor, Washington, DC.

U.S. Bureau of Labor Statistics (2008) Union members in 2007, January 25. USDL 08-0092. Department of Labor, Washington, DC.

Van Jaarsveld, D. D. (2004) Collective representation among high-tech workers at Microsoft and beyond: Lessons from WashTech/CWA. *Industrial Relations*, 43(2), 364–85.

Wasko, J. (1983) Trade unions and broadcasting: A case study of the National Association of Broadcast Employees and Technicians. In Mosco, V. and Wasko, J. (eds), *Labor, The Working Class, and the Media*. Ablex, Norwood, NJ, pp. 85–113.

Wasko, J. (2003) *How Hollywood Works*. Sage, London.

Waterman, P. (1990) Communicating labor internationalism: A review of relevant literature and resources. *The European Journal of Communication*, 15, 85–103.

Waterman, P. (2001) *Global Social Movements and the New Internationalisms*. Mansell, London.

Zimbalist, A. (1979) Technology and the labor process in the printing industry. In: Zimbalist, A. (ed.), *Case Studies in the Labor Process*. Monthly Review, New York, pp. 103–26.

17

Toward a Political Economy of Labor in the Media Industries

David Hesmondhalgh and Sarah Baker

Political economy once had a near monopoly on the critical analysis of media production in relation to questions of power and social justice. Now a host of new entrants compete over the same territory, threatening to swallow political economy whole. A field of "media production studies" that draws on cultural studies theory is now thriving (Mayer et al. 2009, Holt and Perren 2009). Political economists' interventions have been largely marginal in major critical studies of the Internet and new media (e.g., Benkler 2006). Although political economy has had a major impact on studies of media, cultural, and communications policy, an increasing number of publications on these issues (for example, on the "creative industries") contain barely a reference to core political economic research and concepts. Important and useful work undoubtedly continues to be published from within a set of approaches identifiable as "political economy." But even the impact of the best work has for some time seemed rather muted. In general, political economy has been in decline since its 1970s and 1980s heyday.

This situation may reflect a failure on the part of those who define themselves principally or in large part as political economists to keep track of changing empirical realities and theoretical developments. Political economy, for example, has had very little to say about the rise of creative industries policies in many parts of the world (though see Shorthose and Strange 2004, Miller 2009); or about the fundamental importance of copyright to media and cultural production and consumption. And, rather stunningly, given the importance of Marxian theory to political economy, and given that labor was fundamental to Marx's conception of history and emancipation, there has been a remarkable lack of attention to the labor that underpins contemporary media and communication (some of the honorable

The Handbook of Political Economy of Communications, First Edition.
Edited by Janet Wasko, Graham Murdock, and Helena Sousa.
© 2014 John Wiley & Sons, Ltd. Published 2014 by John Wiley & Sons, Ltd.

exceptions are discussed below). By contrast, scholars influenced by cultural studies – traditionally considered, with some reason, to be the principal adversaries of
political economy on the academic cultural Left – have paid serious attention to
labor in recent years. To do so, they have drawn on developments in social theory
that seem to have been of remarkably little interest to political economy, such as
governmentality theory (Rose 1999) and the work of writers such as Hardt and
Negri (2000) or Boltanski and Chiapello (2005).

In the spirit of intellectual and political renewal, this chapter examines political
economy, cultural studies, and other resources to consider what we refer to as
"creative labor." While all work, at least potentially, has cultural and creative aspects,
we use this term to refer to those forms of labor with an especially strong element
of aesthetic, expressive, and informational symbol making. This covers work in the
media and cultural industries, which, in line with political economy, is our central
concern here, but also artistic work, often in publicly subsidized sectors.[1]

We provide an overview of two main bodies of research and thought in order to
illuminate the resources that political economy might draw upon in investigating
creative labor. In the first section, we trace modern conceptions of work, and of
work organizations, in three separate but sometimes overlapping traditions: those
of Marxists, management analysts, and sociologists. We discuss how creative labor
has been conceived in these traditions of analysis, pointing to its increasing importance and centrality. We then turn to the second main body of research, on cultural production itself. There is now a formidable literature on this topic, from a
variety of normative and theoretical standpoints, and we introduce some of them.
We then look at the surprisingly rare cases where such studies have examined creative labor specifically. We show that political economy of culture is just one available perspective here – an important and useful one, but nevertheless not as
significant as some political economists would appear to believe. Our argument is
that research on creative labor needs to provide analysis that combines understanding of power, institutions, and subjectivity, but has not yet succeeded in doing so.
In order to lay the foundations for such analysis, we here introduce a number of
concepts that we believe need to play a critical role in analysis of creative labor as
a specific form of labor in modern societies and to clarify some of the ways in
which these have been conceived. These include exploitation, alienation, autonomy, tensions between creativity and commerce, normativity, agency, and ethics.

Thinking About Work and Organizations

Marx and the Marxists

C. Wright Mills (1951) once traced a number of competing meanings that have
been attributed to labor. For the Greeks, work was drudgery, but for Lutheran
Protestantism, it was a path to salvation. A famous essay by Max Weber analyzed

how the Calvinist ethic – that everyone should work hard but the fruits of that labor were not for idle enjoyment in this life – served as the basis of a "spirit of capitalism." For Enlightenment philosopher John Locke, labor was the source of all value, and this was codified as the basis of neoclassical economics and liberal society by Adam Smith. Mills detected a countertrend to this cold-blooded utilitarianism, going back to the Renaissance, which emphasized the value of creative and craft labor (for example, in the writings of Leonardo da Vinci). When, in the nineteenth century, intellectuals and workers reacted against the appalling conditions faced by industrial workers, many of them drew on this countertrend. It included Ruskin's ideal of a society of artisans, in which craft labor was understood as more free than other forms of labor. It also included a conception of art, and therefore of artistic labor, as expressive and autonomous, a view fostered by the Romantic movement's celebration of the new individualism made possible by modernity and secularism, but according to many nineteenth- and twentieth-century commentators, one that was under threat from industrialization.

It was in this context that the most lasting and influential critical view of labor under capitalism was developed, by Karl Marx, who drew a sharp contrast between the labor of artisans, craftsmen and so on, and the factory-based manufacturing work that supplanted it. As Cohen (1982) shows, Marx's views on this historical transition are complex. The development of capitalism allows workers to become detached and relatively independent of their work in a way that signals the birth of a new freedom and of new forms of collectivism (for example, feelings of class unity with other workers in the same propertyless position, the same factory). But Marx sees losses, too, not only in that workers who were previously artisans become propertyless, but also in terms of their subjective experience of work. The central concept that Marx used to register this subjective dimension was *alienation* – a state in which people and societies become estranged from the products of their labor, from the process of production, and from their own nature as humans. This was so because instead of making their lives the object of their will and consciousness (a capacity that in Marx's view distinguished humans from other creatures), capitalist relations turned work into a means only for existence. Such ideas led to accusations in the late twentieth century that Marx was "essentializing" humans. But it can hardly be denied that work has historically been a necessary feature of most human societies, and that humans have a greater degree of self-consciousness than animals. The deeper problem, from the point of view of an analysis that seeks to take into account both the subjective and objective dimensions of work (as does ours), is whether alienation acts adequately as a normative notion to capture the subjective problems of "bad work." There can be no denying the misery of clock-watching, and of wasting years of life making or selling products and services that are meaningless to the worker. The problem though, as we shall see, is that caring about our work – being emotionally invested in it – might actually have consequences just as challenging for human well-being as alienation. Being so invested in work that one feels addicted to it, resulting in forms of "self-exploitation" – long working hours, high levels of stress and anxiety, and so on – is seemingly a condition of much modern working life. And this is arguably a particular problem with creative labor, with its historical residues of premodern craft and artisanal work, involving a relatively close relationship with the product (see Miège 1989, Ryan 1992). We return to this vital issue in due course.

Even if Marx's concept of alienation is only partially helpful for understanding creative labor, nevertheless he points to an important fact. In modern capitalist societies, we are surrounded by commodities that are produced by distant others, but the human experience of that production is usually forgotten or concealed. Marx attempted to illuminate this problem through his concept of commodity fetishism. A fetish is an object that is believed to have magical properties. Marx's idea is simply that things that are bought and sold in capitalist societies come to be invested with such magical powers. For Marx, the advent of an economy based on money as opposed to barter dissolves the bonds and relations that make up traditional communities and "money becomes the real community" (Harvey 1989, 100). Money ends up masking the social relationships between the things in our world. As a result, the conditions of labor and life, "the sense of joy, anger, or frustration that lie behind the production of commodities, the states of mind of the producers, are all hidden to us as we change one object (money) for another (the commodity)" (Harvey 1989, 100). Production becomes what Marx calls "a hidden abode." We are, in other words, dependent in capitalism on the work of others but for nearly all of the time we are not aware of this fact. Marx was making a kind of serious joke: capitalism fancies itself as modern, but in fact commodities are like "primitive" fetishes. It's as if they've magically appeared from nowhere.

Marx, then, provides a foundation for appreciating one of the main reasons why work matters. He forefronts the fact that there are huge fissures in modern societies; unpleasant and underpaid work by entire groups of people is the basis of the relative comfort of others – the problem of class inequality and *exploitation*. What's more, he draws attention to some important subjective features of this system. Most of the time we forget – or are only very hazily aware – of how our own lives are interlinked with those of others, and, arguably, this is all the more true of the very groups who most stand to gain from such divisions. This implies the ethical importance of raising awareness of that suffering, and of collective action to alleviate it.

There are many workers who are more exploited than those in the cultural and media industries. Few would deny that the people discussed in Barbara Ehrenreich's remarkable and damning exposé of low-paid work in the USA, *Nickel and Dimed* (2001), should be a greater cause for moral concern and political action than should pretty much everyone who works in television. But the apparent privilege of cultural and media workers, the sense that they work in relatively desirable jobs, should not lead us to neglect entirely some of the difficult conditions they face. What's more, the very *desirability* of these jobs makes it interesting to scrutinize what conditions workers face, for creative labor can be seen as something of a test case of whether capitalism can provide rewarding and meaningful work. And this desirability, and lack of alienation, may lead to the dynamics of self-exploitation we mentioned earlier, where people invest themselves emotionally and physically in their work to a damaging degree. Marxism, then, provides a crucial critical vocabulary for a political economy of labor, involving exploitation and alienation, but it needs some modification for the specificity of creative labor. A further feature of Marxism should be noted too: that until the 1970s (with the publication of Harry Braverman's influential book in 1974), Marxism paid little attention to the organization and institutions of work. Elsewhere, however, a massive body of research has developed, which examines organizations and institutions, but often in highly problematic ways.

Management and organizational studies

By the 1950s, a crisis in work was raging in the capitalist world (contemporary treatments include Bell 1956 and Whyte 1956). In the emerging business schools, this crisis helped to fuel an increasing interest in "postbureaucratic" forms of organization, including "craft" forms. It was at this point that the term "creativity" emerged as a major part of the management lexicon, as part of a growing advocacy of the individual responsibility and autonomy of workers. Bureaucracy was portrayed by critics of capitalism as stifling of adaptability, enterprise, individuality, and creativity. The celebration of these qualities by managers and academics was a powerful way of countering the critique and crisis of capitalist work.

For many Marxists, however, the crisis in work was a product of the exploitation of labor, and so organizational forms and management techniques were therefore of little interest. This was changed by Harry Braverman's Marxian analysis (1974), which launched a whole new generation of labor process studies by condemning management's separation of mental and manual labor, and the degradation or deskilling of working-class jobs. But Braverman paid little attention to subjective understanding or experience of work, whether in the form of surveys of job satisfaction and the like, or theorization of the role of subjectivity in the workplace. One strand of the new generation of critical workplace studies began to fill this gap by analyzing worker experiences and subjectivities via ethnography or observation, sometimes within a Gramscian framework (Burawoy 1979, Cockburn 1983).

Another strand, however, less inclined to Marxism and more toward poststructuralism, found such studies guilty of setting up simplistic dualisms of structure and agency, control and resistance (e.g., Wilmott and Knights 1989). These poststructuralist studies suggested, following the work of Foucault and others, ways in which particular "technologies of the self" underpinned modern capitalism and contemporary forms of work. Individual entrepreneurship and self-realization were presented as superficially desirable but potentially problematical aspects of modern labor (Rose 1999). The poststructuralists were supported by other more ethnographically oriented analysts, who emphasized the way that employees might "internalize" organizational goals and values. For example, Gideon Kunda's

1992 study of an engineering company found that productive work there was "the result of a combination of self-direction, initiative, and emotional attachment, and ultimately combines the organizational interest in productivity with the employees' personal interest in growth and maturity" (Kunda 1992, 10).

The result of this two way split, as a writer from a different tradition put it, was that "in the labour process literature the person tends to be either depicted as a passive reflection of social structure, or as an active autonomous subject resisting the influence of oppressive social forces" (Ezzy 1997, 428). The attention to the politics of subjectivity in the post-Braverman literature on work and organizations is potentially valuable, yet it has been largely ignored by political economy writers, who have been suspicious of the theoretical underpinnings of such studies. With good reason, too: such studies usually leave difficult problems of normativity (what is good work?) and agency (what can workers, unions, managers, and policy makers do to make work better?) out of the picture. However, the high degree of personal investment that many workers in the cultural and media industries invest in their work, an investment that may derive from the residues of artistic, craft, and artisanal labor to be found there, mean that these studies of "internalization" offer a resource for critical studies of creative labor. We suggest below that the more appropriate and constructive response from political economy is to engage with the best elements of such research, rather than pretend that it does not exist, and to develop it in directions that pay greater attention to normativity and agency.

Sociologists

Along with the Marxists and management analysts, sociologists, too, have paid attention to work and organizations, and in particular to the question of *transformation*. A number of wide-ranging sociological accounts have analyzed the rise of flexible knowledge work as part of a broader analysis of transformations in western society. Zygmunt Bauman, for example, sees work as a key form of what he calls "liquid modernity" (Bauman 2000) embodying new uncertainties, whereas in "solid" modernity it gave shape to the future and replaced chaos and control with order. For Ulrich Beck (2000), "individualization" compels people to make themselves the center of their own planning of their life, and work is especially important in this. Manuel Castells (1996) wrote of the displacement of manufacturing work by information and knowledge work as the basis of a new epoch in capitalist modernity. Richard Sennett (1998) has registered, in essayistic but powerful fashion, the hidden costs of "flexible capitalism."

At best, these accounts are stimulating, and capture something vital about contemporary change; at worst, they can appear speculative and overgeneralized. At times, there is an exasperating tendency to simplify the nature of the historical period that has supposedly been transcended. But, whatever the accuracy or otherwise of all these claims about transformations in work, such sociologists have drawn attention to ways in which work has been reconfigured and restructured – partly to deal with the postwar crisis of work noted above. Moreover, their emphasis on information or knowledge production potentially makes creative labor of central interest in contemporary social theory. In Andrew Ross's words,

> the traditional profile of the artist as unattached and adaptable to circumstance is surely now coming into its own as the ideal definition of the knowledge worker: comfortable in an ever-changing environment that demands creative shifts in communication with different kinds of clients and partners; attitudinally geared towards production that requires long, and often unsocial hours; and accustomed, in the sundry exercise of their mental labor, to a contingent rather than a fixed, routine of self-application. (Ross 2000, 11)

Pierre-Michel Menger, the leading sociologist of artistic labor markets, has taken a similar view with regard to how artistic workers fit with the growing emphasis on creativity in modern approaches to work, for example, the way in which economic theory of endogenous growth assigns a central role to idea generation, creativity, and knowledge, and sees human creativity as the "ultimate inexhaustible source of growth" (Menger 2006, 801). According to myth, says Menger, "artists supply the golden legend of creation, that of a subversive, anti-conformist, inspired behavior, rebelling against social conventions and commercial utilitarianism" (801). In fact, Menger goes on to point out, surveying considerable evidence, that artistic work is characterized by conditions highly compliant with the demands of modern capitalism: "extreme flexibility, autonomy, tolerance of inequality, innovative forms of teamwork." One of the major works of social theory of recent times, Boltanski and Chiapello's *The New Spirit of Capitalism*, portrays an increasing focus on autonomy and creativity in work and management as an *appropriation* by capital and managers of the critique of capitalism (2005). They lay special emphasis on the *political* importance of artistic creativity in changes in the world of work, and in the organization and legitimation of capitalism.

It seems then that changes in the world of work have meant a new centrality for creative labor. There is still some controversy about whether such work has objectively become of greater economic significance in modern economies, and if so, to what extent. Putting aside the many difficulties of classification and measurement, the size of the cultural industries, which is the sector where creative labor as we define it here mainly takes place, appears to be steadily but slowly increasing as a proportion of economic activity (Hesmondhalgh 2007, 177–84). What is clear from the above discussion though is that creative labor is certainly of rapidly increasing importance in terms of how contemporary societies *conceptualize* economic life. This discussion also suggests some of the questions that research into creative cultural labor might fruitfully explore. To what extent is such labor marked by the exploitation and alienation that Marxists believe is fundamental to other forms of labor under capitalism? Is it really less alienated than other types of labor? To what extent might it be possible to achieve greater levels of meaningful autonomy within creative cultural workplaces? Critical management studies, of the kind discussed above, raise the important possibility that autonomy and creativity might be used as techniques for control, by making insecurity bearable and even (on balance) desirable for workers. Our survey of these different traditions of work analysis has also suggested that an adequate answer to such questions will require not only the appreciation of systemic structural power that the Marxists emphasize, but also of institutional and subjective dimensions more often found in other modes of research. This triumvirate of power, institutions, and subjectivity, in our view, needs to be the basis of a political economy of labor in the media and cultural industries.

Studies of Cultural Production

Given that creative cultural labor is essentially, as we define it here, centered on cultural production, what light can studies of such production throw on our analysis? For the purposes of clarity, our overview of studies of cultural production divides the research into four divergent traditions or approaches.

The first approach is the political economy of culture (PEC) itself, the main subject of this book. At its best, this focuses, in Murdock and Golding's well-known definition, on "the interplay between the symbolic and the economic dimensions of public communications," and aims to show how "different ways of financing and organizing cultural production have traceable consequences for the range of discourse, representations and communicative resources" available to different publics "and for the organization of audience access and use" (Murdock and Golding 2005, 60). For our purposes, it represents a superior alternative to media and cultural economics (such as Caves 2000). Political economists have carried out some sociological studies of workplaces, but more often focus on conceptual analysis based on overviews of contemporary developments drawing on secondary data. The dual emphasis in PEC on the commercial and symbolic aspects of the media and popular culture, in relation to questions of power and social justice, needs to be a crucial element in any analysis of creative labor.

The second tradition, which we will call organizational sociology of culture (OSC), has been less directly concerned with normative questions of power and social justice than has PEC. But as the name we've given it suggests, it offers a greater sensitivity to the specifically organizational dimensions of cultural production, including routines, rituals, and values (Hirsch 1972, DiMaggio 1977, Tuchman 1978, Gans 1980). The better studies within this tradition see cultural-industry organizations as themselves the products of social and historical forces. It emerged in US sociology departments in the 1970s, and an important strand has been the "production of culture approach" (Peterson and Anand 2004), but it has been developed in the burgeoning fields of management, business, and organizational studies. Encouraged by the rhetoric of creative industries policies, many analysts began to see the cultural or creative industries as a potential route for understanding innovation and imagination in workplaces and this fueled new studies (such as Davis and Scase 2000). Like a certain strand of PEC ("the cultural industries approach" associated especially with Miège 1989 and Garnham 1990), OSC takes into account the specificity of cultural production as opposed to other forms of production. So this tradition permits analysis of the specific ways in which creative labor is organized and managed, including how this varies across particular cultural industries. At the same time it needs to be recognized that creative labor is often organized beyond the boundary of formal organizations (and certainly beyond traditional workplaces) in entities that might in some cases be better thought of as networks (Saundry et al. 2007).

A third tradition of production analysis has identified itself closely with the intellectual practice known as cultural studies, which sought to take popular culture seriously and to understand its imbrication with sociohistorical forces. In so doing, it was reacting against approaches in the arts and humanities that had tended towards formalism, aestheticism, or the treatment of history as mere "context." Against reductionist forms of Marxism and positivist and functionalist social science, some cultural studies, drawing on poststructuralist social theory, turned its attention to questions of meaning, subjectivity, and power in relation to culture. In the early years of cultural studies, however, many of its key researchers seemed to view analyses of production as *per se* very closely linked to reductionist or "economistic" forms of Marxism. A later generation of researchers sought to fill the resulting gap by invoking cultural studies theory to claim that "processes of production are (themselves) cultural phenomena ... that construct certain ways for people to conceive of and conduct themselves" (du Gay 1997, 4) and they examined the "cultures of production" of culture-making organizations. Others emphasized "broader culture formations and practices that are within neither the control nor the understanding of the company" (Negus 1999: 19). The interest in "cultures of production" has involved considerable convergence with organizational and management studies, or with sociological and anthropological studies of meaning and ritual in production contexts (see Caldwell 2008). The stress on meaning, power, and subjectivity to be found in some cultural studies of media production is valuable, but it brings with it some problems, which we discuss below.

A fourth tradition is field theory (FT), especially Pierre Bourdieu's analysis of the fields of literary and artistic production (1993, 1996, see also Benson and Neveu 2005). Elsewhere, one of us has discussed some limitations of Bourdieu's analysis of cultural production, in particular its failure to analyze – to use Bourdieu's terms – large-scale cultural production as opposed to restricted production (which is akin to "independent" production), and its failure to theorize relations between production and consumption (Hesmondhalgh 2006). Nevertheless, Bourdieu in key respects offers a superior alternative to one strand of PEC (the "Schiller–McChesney tradition," see Hesmondhalgh 2007, 5–8) in that he strongly recognizes differentiation in cultural production, and to the OSC (for example, DiMaggio 1977, Davis and Scase 2000), in that it provides a more adequate theoretical and normative analysis of power, structure, and agency in culture, based on Bourdieu's triumvirate of field, habitus, and capital. Especially important is the way that Bourdieu makes the concept of autonomy – the capacity to act as the author of one's actions – central to his conception of cultural production. Bourdieu provided a highly critical historical account of the forms that autonomy has taken, while holding on strongly to its positive dimensions. His claim was that in the neoliberal, postmodern conjuncture of the 1980s onwards, "there is a threat to the most precious collective achievements of intellectuals, starting with the critical dispositions which were simultaneously the product and the guarantee of their autonomy" (Bourdieu 1996, 339). Elsewhere (see Hesmondhalgh and Baker 2010), we discuss constraints on autonomy, and its limitations as a normative concept, arguing that a reconstructed notion of autonomy is indispensable to a political evaluation of contemporary labor, including creative labor. For aspirations to autonomy in creative labor, whether workers are conscious of it or not, have a close historical connection to modern quests for freedom from the demands of commerce, the state, and religion.

Labor in the Political Economy of Culture

These, then, are four major approaches to cultural production. As is always the case with analytical traditions, a number of separate subfields and approaches are subsumed within broad categories such as these. Many of the best studies of production combine interests from these different approaches, or transcend the divisions altogether (for example, Todd Gitlin's 1983 study of the production of US prime-time television or Georgina Born's 2004 anthropological study of the BBC). And there has been some synthesis. Bill Ryan (1992) partially fills the gap between PEC and OSC through his combination of political economy and historical sociology. Nevertheless, this rough way of dividing the field can serve for now as a heuristic device to make sense of the research debates and conflicts which we seek to intervene in and draw upon, in analyzing creative labor.

There is a problem though. Until recently, only a very small proportion of these studies focused on such labor. A number of reasons might be offered for this: the commodity fetishism we discussed earlier; the way in which much discourse about culture emphasizes individual inputs and downplays the complex division of labor; an emphasis on consumption rather than production in much media sociology. More recently, the devaluation of work in communication and cultural research has taken a new form, as digitalization has led to a proliferation of new forms of amateur and semiprofessional production, celebrated by some as the basis of a new era of cultural production (for example, Bruns 2008). However, as Andrew Ross notes with reference to open source software, it is not clear how such new technologies might act as a model for sustainable employment (Ross 2009, 168–9).

More surprising, given its Marxian heritage, has been the general neglect of labor in political economy of culture (noted by Mosco 1996, 158, among others). Among the important exceptions[2] has been Vincent Mosco, who, in his 1996 book on *The Political Economy of Communication*, commented on a challenge posed to political economy by organizational sociology, "to develop a position that examines the process of production foregrounding political and economic power, specifically the commodification of labor." Acknowledging Bernard Miège's work as a rare attempt to provide the basis of such a theory, Mosco criticized Miège for making too broad a distinction between cultural production involving "artistic input" and that which does not. Mosco also suggested that Miège underestimated the way that concentration and rationalization were leading to the reduction of capital/labor contradictions associated with this artistic input. Mosco has returned to the question of labor more recently in an edited collection with Catherine McKercher (McKercher and Mosco 2007a). Here rather than labor in the media industries, the focus is on the broader category of knowledge work and, significantly, in their introductory chapter, McKercher and Mosco operate the broadest possible definition of this term, to encompass all those who handle and distribute information (McKercher and Mosco 2007b). They argue against a definition restricted to creative labor, in the sense of work involving the direct manipulation of symbols (which is roughly what is meant by Miège's translated term "artistic input"). Instead, they want to broaden the term to include workers such as postal transportation workers and librarians. They give two main reasons for wanting to do so. First, "an increasing amount of the work involves making use of information to efficiently and effectively deliver an information product. The line between what is and what is not creative labor in the knowledge field is fuzzy" (McKercher and Mosco 2007b, x) and workers who appear to be more marginal to production nevertheless add tangible value. Second, "the meaning of knowledge labor is not measured simply by external criteria but by how it is subjectively experienced by workers themselves" (2007b, x).

We agree with these statements in and of themselves. And let us be absolutely clear that we consider the working lives of librarians and transportation workers to be of no less (or more) intrinsic interest or worth than those of workers involved more directly with symbol making. But as assumptions underlying research on work in the cultural and media industries, these considerations may well, in the name of inclusiveness, lead to the exclusion of certain key issues. One exclusion relates to a principal reason why political economy has tended to be interested in cultural producers in the first place. This is the potential power cultural producers have to make texts (artifacts that are primarily symbolic, aesthetic, and informational in nature, intended to inform, edify, and/or please audiences), which are then circulated, to greater or lesser effect, in society. Political economy is often interested in cultural production, not entirely but to a pretty large degree, because of a concern with the specific nature of cultural products, with their ability to shape and influence societies, be they films, songs, news bulletins, documentaries, reality TV shows, pornography, or sports magazines. It is perfectly valid to study all knowledge workers. But it is also valid to study creative cultural labor specifically.

Indeed, there are good reasons for being more specific. For another potential exclusion is an issue to which Mosco (1996) makes only passing reference (as part of his discussion of Miège) and which Mosco and McKercher (2007) seem to ignore entirely, concerning the importance of "artistic input" or symbol making in the cultural industries. This raises the even more fundamental question of contradictions between creativity and commerce, an understanding of which is necessary (though not sufficient) for a sociological analysis of creative labor. In fact, although it has gone uncited by many of the leading names in political economy (Murdock 2003 is an exception), there is an important account of this contradiction by Bill Ryan (1992), which combines political economy insights with those of organizational sociology. In particular, Ryan, building on the work of Raymond Williams and Nicholas Garnham but also on that of organizational sociologists such as Hirsch and diMaggio, constructs a Marxian-Weberian explanation of the specific nature of the creative cultural labor process.

To summarize briefly, Ryan's view is that, in spite of their overwhelming motivation to produce profit (to accumulate capital), capitalist businesses cannot make artistic input completely subservient to the drive for accumulation. This is because cultural production is generally understood, in most modern societies, as deriving from the expressive individual artist. In reality, of course, as we have already observed, artistic-cultural production is based on a complex division of labor; Ryan's point concerns how the value of artistic-cultural production is widely *perceived*. This attachment of artistic value to the expressive artist leads to a tendency for artistic objects to appear as the product of recognizable persons, and this means that in cultural production, unlike most other forms of work, the concrete and named labor of "the artist" – a particular and relatively privileged form of cultural worker – is paramount and tends to be preserved. This causes a constant problem for capitalist businesses, and of course many of them overcome it, and make a very nice profit out of cultural goods. For Ryan, they are able to do so by *rationalizing* cultural production, both at the creative stage and the circulation stage. Indeed, most of Ryan's book is framed as an examination of the extent to which capital has succeeded in achieving such rationalization. This is achieved at the creative stage through "formatting," especially via the use of genre-based series of production and by attaching productions to the names of star performers. At the circulation or distribution stage, the central organizational move is the institutionalization of marketing within corporate production, in order to produce a more controllable sequence of stars and genres. But such rationalization is always struggling against the relative autonomy given to creative workers, especially for "star" creators. This further fuels the irrationality, or at least the arationality, of the creative process.

As a result, for capitalists, artists represent an investment in variable capital in a way that consistently threatens to undermine profitability. We analyze some contemporary manifestations of this tug between autonomy, creativity, and commercial imperatives elsewhere (Hesmondhalgh and Baker, 2010). Here, however, our point is a more limited one: whether or not one agrees with all aspects of Ryan's account, it points to the *specificity* of creative cultural labor as fundamental to an understanding of cultural production. In this respect, it builds on the work of PEC approaches that emphasize the specificity of cultural industries as opposed to other forms of capital accumulation (cf Miège 1989, Garnham 1990).

Cultural Studies Approaches to Creative Cultural Labor

Although we strongly believe that a political economy of creative labor needs to retain this emphasis on creativity/commerce relations, we want to raise some problems concerning Ryan's approach, and one he shares with the Marxian labor process theory that he drew some inspiration from. This is the lack of attention to the questions of subjectivity and experience, which, as we saw above, have been of interest to critical management studies and sociologists of work. Creative labor has come to be seen as a special case of some emergent features of contemporary capitalism, and so has a neighboring set of labor practices, in new media. A series of studies of these forms of labor have added to a growing sense of "a turn to cultural work." Much of the impetus driving this turn has come from researchers who have been influenced by cultural studies (e.g., McRobbie 2002a, 2002b, Banks 2007, Ross 2009). Like political economy's general neglect of creative labor, this is perhaps surprising, given the hostility that cultural studies showed toward studies of production, and its almost complete neglect of questions of creative labor in earlier times. These cultural studies writers are not alone; there have also been significant contributions from other disciplines.[3] But it is cultural studies writers who have particularly served to spark debate about creative cultural labor in recent years.

A large part of the motivation of this strand of cultural studies research has been to counter some of the complacency surrounding creative and new media labor on the part of policy makers (especially "creative industries" policy) and some of their academic cheerleaders who extol the benefits of creativity and entrepreneurship. These cultural studies writers have drawn, to varying degrees, on sociology and social theory concerning work and organizations, for their examinations of new media and cultural labor. Gillian Ursell's research on television workers, for example, applied Foucauldian insights to work in the creative or cultural industries, showing how "pleasure, self-expression, self-enterprise and self-actualisation ... seem to be at the heart of explanations of why people want to work in the media" (Ursell 2006, 161, see also Ursell 2000). She was followed by others who have shown a similar interest in how self-actualization or self-realization might serve as a mechanism for control and even exploitation in creative cultural work, without necessarily being fully paid-up Foucauldians. Angela McRobbie (2002a, 517) argued that creative work was increasingly characterized by neoliberal values of "entrepreneurialism, individualization and reliance on commercial sponsorship." She pointed to the way in which aspirations to autonomy and personal freedom in fashion and music-related cultural industries often led to disappointment and self-exploitation. Notions of workplace rights were sidelined in favor of fluidity and speed. However, she acknowledged that hers was a "preliminary and thus provisional account" (2002a, 517). Andrew Ross followed with a very thorough ethnography of two New York City new media workplaces in the dot.com era, working environments that offered "oodles of autonomy along with warm collegiality" but which ended up enlisting "employees' freest thoughts and impulses in the service of salaried time" (Ross 2003, 17). Also writing about new media work, Andreas Wittel (2001) saw there a paradigmatic case of an emergent form of community that he calls "network sociality," one which appears to be individualistic and instrumental, involving an assimilation of work and play, while Tiziana Terranova (2000), from an autonomist Marxist perspective, provided an early analysis of the unpaid labor underlying the emergent digital economy, countering the optimistic visions of Marxian utopians who hoped that gift economies might undermine capitalism from within. Ros Gill, in a study of European freelance new media workers (2002), found evidence that features of the work that seemed superficially attractive, such as its informality and high levels of autonomy, were in fact particularly problematic for women because of the lack of clear criteria for evaluating work and especially because of the difficulties such informality caused when seeking new contracts.

All this amounts to a bleak picture of these forms of labor, often represented as glamorous, autonomous, and flexible.[4] Many of the findings from our own research (see Hesmondhalgh and Baker 2008, 2010) confirm aspects of the picture of creative labor that emerges from these studies. A question raised, sometimes explicitly, by these accounts is an important normative one in the study of culture. To what extent is it possible to do "good work" in the cultural (or media, or creative) industries? Is it really as difficult as this body of research suggests? In the most sustained and valuable contribution to analysis of labor in the media and cultural industries in recent years, Mark Banks (2007) has endorsed the pessimism of many of these accounts, but has also partly qualified it, drawing on his own empirical work and on a range of social theorists. Firstly, drawing on the work of writers such as Williams (1980) and Wolff (1993), Banks claims that in contemporary capitalism a practical belief persists in the ability of the aesthetic realm to provide resources and inspiration to a range of actors. This has ambivalent consequences, opening up new realms for commodification, but at the same time keeping alive the desires of cultural producers to "live a life of one's own" (Banks 2007, 105, citing Lloyd's 2006 rich study of "neo-bohemia"). Secondly, and related to this, he finds evidence that creative workers continue to be oriented toward forms of production that can generate "internal rewards" (those that can only be specified and recognized in relation to the particular activity under question – see MacIntyre 1981 and Keat 2000) rather than "external rewards" such as wealth, fame, and power. Finally, Banks also points to the way that moral systems of trust, honesty, obligation, and fairness remain present in contemporary capitalism, and he provides examples of the resilience of social and cultural values among the creative cultural workers he had interviewed in previous research.

Concluding Comments: Toward an Adequate Normative Conception of Creative Labor

This perspective is valuable, and we believe that researchers of creative labor would benefit by taking on Banks's challenge to complicate and enrich the normative language by which we understand work. There are other resources that we might draw upon to undertake such enrichment of our understanding of "good" and "bad" creative labor – including debates in political theory about justice in relation to work (Muirhead 2006), about the psychological characteristics and benefits of professional work (Gardner et al. 2001), and a considerable literature on meaningful work (Schwartz 1982) and "dignity" in work (Hodson 2000). There is much of value in such research (we assess them in greater detail in Hesmondhalgh and Baker 2010), but the problem that keeps returning is the *specificity* of creative cultural labor. These more general discussions of work inevitably downplay a fundamental aspect of the political economy of culture: that the cultural and media industries are oriented toward the production of texts, or communicative artifacts. In the cultural industries approach to the political economy of culture, this fundamental aspect is seen as generating a set of dynamics distinctive (though, of course, not unique) to the cultural and media industries (Miège 1989, Garnham 1990, and see Hesmondhalgh 2007, 17–25). Indeed, a large proportion of the importance of cultural industries as a social phenomenon can be said to derive from this cultural function. A huge amount of social discourse concerns the quality of these products, not only among critics and academics, but in everyday discussions between work colleagues, family members, and friends. In all industries, "good work" and "bad work" have double meanings: they can refer to the process and experience of work; and they can also refer to the products or outcomes, to good or bad texts.

While a properly normative assessment of creative labor is still in its infancy, the situation with regard to discussion of how producers conceive of the quality of their products is somewhat complex. A number of sociological studies have included some reflections of producers on their outputs, including classics such as Cantor (1971) and Gitlin (1983). Yet surprisingly little research has focused in a sustained way, empirically and theoretically, on how cultural workers themselves conceive of the quality of their own output, and what this might mean for our understanding of cultural production in general. A major exception to this lack can be found in the work of Georgina Born. In an essay on the way in which aesthetic value has been treated in television studies, Born (2000) trenchantly critiques debates about quality in television for their relativist unwillingness to adjudicate between producer and audience discourses of quality, and she argues for the importance of analyzing the discourses of media professionals. In particular, Born suggests that researchers should attend to "a category of specifically media intellectuals whose task is to mediate the generic dynamics that bridge the past, present and future of media output. Their skill is in the art of judging how to progress a set of generic possibilities in given conditions, and how to balance the enhancement of the entertainment, pleasure and education of the audience" (Born 2000, 406). Crucially, this puts emphasis on the *positive possibilities* of cultural production, by asking when its powers might be used "responsibly, creatively, inventively in given conditions, and when not" (406). It also suggests the importance of theorizing agency, reflexivity, and value. In later work, based on her own ethnographic research, Born analyzed the "situated ethics and aesthetics" of BBC television producers in documentary, drama, and current affairs (Born 2004, 84–7). Born does not claim that reflexivity always results in better television; rather, she argues that a key analytical task is to consider how the reflexivity, intentionality, and agency of cultural producers conditions the creativity and innovation possible within a given medium. This task in turn she locates within the context of genre theory, stressing the difference between various attitudes to generic change: "nostalgic repetition, the rich mining of the familiar, which may itself be achieved in more and less inventive ways"; "a self-conscious exceeding of the previous horizons of expectation"; and the production of generic stasis, involving the entrenching of given codes (Born 2000, 421). Born's point is that this issue of aesthetic or informational quality and innovation represents a significant component of the *ethics* of cultural work.

Our claim then is that social analysis needs empirically informed research that contributes to a normative conception of creative labor, paying attention to this dual aspect of work, as both process and the making of products, and to the key concepts elaborated here, and paying attention to questions of power, institutions, and subjectivity (we attempt to provide such research in Hesmondhalgh and Baker 2010). By focusing on the crucial question of the labor that goes into media and cultural products, we hope that such research may serve to revive the credibility of the political economy of media, culture and communication, which has been marginalized for too long in cultural analysis.

Notes

1 We recognize, of course, that there is a division of labor in cultural production, involving primary creative personnel, craft and technical workers, creative managers, executives, and unskilled labor (see Hesmondhalgh 2007, 64–5). "Creative cultural labor"
refers to the work of all these groups, even though the extent to which their input into
"creative" outputs clearly varies. See also Banks (2007, 3, 189) on "creative cultural
labour."

2 Others include various contributions by Janet Wasko (e.g., 1994), Sussman and Lent's
1998 collection, and reflections by Toby Miller on the "New International Division of
Cultural Labour" (e.g., Miller et al. 2005).

3 These include geography (Pratt 2000, Christopherson and van Jaarsveld 2005,
Christopherson 2008) and sociology (Neff et al. 2005, Huws 2006–7). Film studies was
particularly ahead of its time in addressing questions of cultural labor (Wasko's work,
mentioned above, and also the British Film Institute's important and somewhat
neglected studies of television workers conducted in the 1990s, see for example
Paterson, 2001; see also Gray and Seeber's 1996 collection). There is no space to discuss
these other contributions in detail here; see Hesmondhalgh and Baker (2010) for further details.

4 See Stahl 2006 and 2008 for a rigorous and thoughtful discussion of how creative labor,
especially musical labor, is articulated and framed in contemporary regimes of
representation.

References

Banks, M. (2007) *The Politics of Cultural Work*. Palgrave Macmillan, Basingstoke, UK.

Bauman, Z. (2000) *Liquid Modernity*. Polity Press, Cambridge, UK.

Beck, U. (2000) *The Brave New World of Work*. Polity Press, Cambridge, UK.

Bell, D. (1956) *Work and its Discontents*. Beacon Press, Boston.

Benkler, Y. (2006) *The Wealth of Networks: How Social Production Transforms Markets and
Freedom*. Yale University Press, New Haven, CT.

Benson, R. and Neveu, E. (eds) (2005) *Bourdieu and the Journalistic Field*. Polity Press,
Cambridge, UK.

Boltanksi, L. and Chiapello, E. (2005) *The New Spirit of Capitalism*. Verso, London.

Born, G. (2000) Inside television: Television research and the sociology of culture. *Screen*,
41, 68–96.

Born, G. (2004) *Uncertain Vision: Birt, Dyke and the Reinvention of the BBC*. Vintage,
London.

Bourdieu, P. (1993) *The Field of Cultural Production*. Polity Press, Cambridge, UK.

Bourdieu, P. (1996) *The Rules of Art*. Polity Press, Cambridge, UK.

Braverman, H. (1974) *Labor and Monopoly Capital: The Degradation of Work in the Twentieth
Century*. Monthly Review Press, New York.

Bruns, A. (2008) *Blogs, Wikipedia, Second Life and Beyond*. Peter Lang, New York.

Burawoy, M. (1979) *Manufacturing Consent*. University of Chicago Press, Chicago.

Caldwell, J. (2008) *Production Culture: Industrial Reflexivity and Critical Practice in Film/Television*. Duke University Press, Durham, NC.

Cantor, M. (1971) *The Hollywood Television Producer*. Basic Books, New York.

Castells, M. (1996) *The Rise of the Network Society*. Blackwell, Oxford.

Caves, R. E. (2000) *Creative Industries*. Harvard University Press, Cambridge, MA.

Christopherson, S. (2008) Beyond the self-expressive creative worker: An industry perspective on entertainment media. *Theory, Culture & Society*, 25, 73–95.

Christopherson, S. and van Jaarsveld, D. (2005) New media after the dot.com bust. *International Journal of Cultural Policy*, 11, 77–93.

Cockburn, C. (1983) *Brothers: Male Dominance and Technological Change*. Pluto, London.

Cohen, G. (1982) *History, Labour and Freedom*. Clarendon Press, Oxford.

Davis, H. and Scase, R. (2000) *Managing Creativity*. Open University Press, Buckingham, UK.

DiMaggio, P. (1977) Market structure, the creative process and popular culture: Towards an organizational reinterpretation of mass-culture theory. *Journal of Popular Culture*, 11, 436–52.

Du Gay, P. (1997) Introduction. In: du Gay, P. (ed.), *Production of Culture/Cultures of Production*. Sage, London, pp. 1–10.

Ehrenreich, B. (2001) *Nickel and Dimed: On (Not) Getting By in America*. Owl Books, New York.

Ezzy, D. (1997) Subjectivity and the labour process: Conceptualising "good work." *Sociology*, 31, 427–44.

Gans, H. (1980) *Deciding What's News*. Vintage Press, New York.

Gardner, H., Csikszentmihalyi, M., and Damon, W. (2001) *Good Work. When Excellence and Ethics Meet*. Basic Books, New York.

Garnham, N. (1990) *Capitalism and Communication*. Sage, London.

Gill, R. (2002) Cool, creative and egalitarian? Exploring gender in project-based new media work in Europe. *Information, Communication and Society*, 5, 70–89.

Gitlin, T. (1983) *Inside Prime Time*. Basic Books, New York.

Gray, L. S. and Seeber, R. L. (eds) (1996) *Under the Stars: Essays on Labor Relations in Arts and Entertainment*. ILR Press, Ithaca, NY.

Hardt, M. and Negri, A. (2000) *Empire*. Harvard University Press, Cambridge, MA.

Harvey, D. (1989) *The Condition of Postmodernity*. Blackwell, Oxford.

Hesmondhalgh, D. (2006) Bourdieu, the media and cultural production. *Media, Culture and Society*, 28, 211–32.

Hesmondhalgh, D. (2007) *The Cultural Industries*, 2nd edn. Sage, London.

Hesmondhalgh, D. and Baker, S. (2008) Creative work and emotional labour in the television industry. *Theory, Culture & Society*, 25, 97–118.

Hesmondhalgh, D. and Baker S. (2010) *Creative Labour: Media Work in Three Cultural Industries*. Routledge, Abingdon, UK.

Hirsch, P. M. (1972) Processing fads and fashions: An organization-set analysis of cultural industry systems. *American Journal of Sociology*, 77, 639–59.

Hodson, R. (2000) *Dignity at Work*. Cambridge University Press, Cambridge, UK.

Holt, J. and Perren, A. (2009) *Media Industries: History, Theory and Method*. Wiley Blackwell, Malden, MA.

Huws, U. (2006–7) The spark in the engine: Creative workers in a global economy. *Work Organisation, Labour & Globalisation*, 1, 1–12.

Keat, R. (2000) *Cultural Goods and the Limits of the Market*. Routledge, New York.

Kunda, G. (1992) *Engineering Culture: Control and Commitment in a High-Tech Corporation*. Temple University Press, Philadelphia.

Lloyd, R. (2006) *Neo-Bohemia: Art and Commerce in the Post-Industrial City*. Routledge, New York.

MacIntyre, A. (1981) *After Virtue: A Study in Moral Theory*. Duckworth, London.

Mayer, V., Banks, M. J., and Caldwell, J. (eds) (2009) *Production Studies: Cultural Studies of Media Industries*. Routledge, Abingdon, UK.

McKercher, C. and Mosco, V. (eds) (2007a) *Knowledge Workers in the Information Society*. Lexington Books, Lanham, MD.

McKercher, C. and Mosco, V. (2007b) Introduction: Theorizing Knowledge Labor and the Information Society. In: McKercher, C. and Mosco, V. (eds), *Knowledge Workers in the Information Society*. Lexington Books, Lanham, MD, pp. vii–xxiv.

McRobbie, A. (2002a) Clubs to companies: Notes on the decline of political culture in speeded up creative worlds. *Cultural Studies*, 16, 516–31.

McRobbie, A. (2002b) From Holloway to Hollywood: Happiness at work in the new cultural economy? In: du Gay, P. and Pryke, M. (eds), *Cultural Economy*. Sage, London, pp. 97–114.

Menger, P. M. (2006) Artistic labor markets: Contingent work, excess supply and occupational risk management. In: Ginsburgh, V.A. and Throsby, D. (eds), *Handbook of the Economics of Art and Culture*. Elsevier, Amsterdam, pp. 765–811.

Miège, B. (1989) *The Capitalization of Cultural Production*. International General, New York.

Miller, T. (2009) Can natural Luddites make things explode or travel faster? The new humanities, cultural policy studies, and creative industries. In: Holt, J. and Perren, A. (eds), *Media Industries: History, Theory and Method*. Wiley Blackwell, Malden, MA, pp. 184–98.

Miller, T., Govil, N., McMurria, J., et al. (2005) *Global Hollywood 2*. British Film Institute, London.

Mills, C. W. (1951) *White Collar: The American Middle Classes*. Oxford University Press, Oxford.

Mosco, V. (1996) *The Political Economy of Communication*. Sage, London.

Muirhead, R. (2006) *Just Work*. Harvard University Press, Cambridge, MA.

Murdock, G. (2003) Back to work: Cultural labor in altered times. In: Beck, A. (ed.), *Cultural Work: Understanding the Cultural Industries*. Routledge, London, pp. 15–36.

Murdock, G. and Golding, P. (2005) Culture, communications and political economy. In: Curran, J. and Gurevitch, M. (eds), *Mass Media and Society*, 4th edn. Arnold, London, pp. 60–83.

Neff, G., Wissinger, E., and Zukin, S. (2005) Entrepreneurial labor among cultural producers: "Cool" jobs in "hot" industries. *Social Semiotics*, 15, 307–34.

Negus, K. (1999) *Music Genres and Corporate Cultures*. Routledge, New York.

Paterson, R. (2001) Work histories in television. *Media, Culture & Society*, 23, 495–520.

Peterson, R. A. and Anand, N. (2004) The production of culture perspective. *Annual Review of Sociology*, 30, 311–34.

Pratt, A. C. (2000) The cultural industries: A cross national comparison of employment in Great Britain and Japan. In: Kawasaki, K. (ed.), *Cultural Globalisation and the Cultural Industries: Experiences in the UK and Japan*. Ministry of Education, Science and Culture, Tokyo.

Rose, N. (1999) *Powers of Freedom: Reframing Political Thought.* Cambridge University Press, Cambridge, UK.

Ross, A. (2000) The mental labor problem. *Social Text*, 18, 1–32.

Ross, A. (2003) *No-Collar: The Humane Workplace and its Hidden Costs.* Basic Books, New York.

Ross, A. (2009) *Nice Work If You Can Get It: Life and Labor in Precarious Times.* NYU Press, New York.

Ryan, B. (1992) *Making Capital from Culture.* Walter de Gruyter, Berlin.

Saundry, R., Stuart, M., and Antcliff, V. (2007) Broadcasting discontent – freelancers, trade unions and the Internet. *New Technology, Work & Employment*, 22, 178–91.

Schwartz, A. (1982) Meaningful work. *Ethics*, 92, 634–46.

Sennett, R. (1998) *The Corrosion of Character: The Personal Consequences of Work in the New Capitalism.* Norton, New York.

Shorthose, J. and Strange, G. (2004) A more critical view of the creative industries: Production, consumption and resistance. *Capital and Class*, 84, 1–7.

Stahl, M. (2006) Reinventing certainties. PhD thesis, University of California, San Diego.

Stahl, M. (2008) Sex and drugs and bait and switch: Rockumentary and the new model worker. In: Hesmondhalgh, D. and Toynbee, J. (eds), *The Media and Social Theory.* Routledge, Abingdon, pp. 231–47.

Sussman, G. and Lent, J. (eds) (1998) *Global Productions: Labor in the Making of the "Information Society."* Hampton, Cresskill, NJ.

Terranova, T. (2000) Free labor: Producing culture for the digital economy. *Social Text*, 63, 33–50.

Tuchman, G. (1978) *Making News.* Free Press, New York.

Ursell, G. (2000) Television production: Issues of exploitation, commodification and subjectivity in UK television labour markets. *Media, Culture & Society*, 22, 805–25.

Ursell, G. (2006) Working in the media. In: Hesmondhalgh, D. (ed.), *Media Production.* Open University Press/The Open University, Maidenhead, UK, pp. 133–72.

Wasko, J. (1994) *Hollywood in the Information Age.* Polity Press, Cambridge, UK.

Whyte, W. (1956) *The Organization Man.* Simon and Schuster, New York.

Williams, R. (1980) *Culture.* Fontana, London.

Willmott, H. and Knights, D. (1989) Power and subjectivity at work: From degradation to subjugation in social relations. *Sociology*, 23, 535–58.

Wittel, A. (2001) Toward a network sociality. *Theory, Culture and Society*, 18, 51–76.

Wolff, J. (1993) *The Social Production of Art*, 2nd edn. Macmillan, Basingstoke, UK.

Part IV

Dynamics
of Consumption
Choice, Mobilization, Control

18

From the "Work of Consumption" to the "Work of Prosumers"
New Scenarios, Problems, and Risks

Giovanni Cesareo

As the MacBride Report emphasized in 1980, "readers, listeners, and viewers have generally been treated as passive receivers of information." It is still the case today that many people who are concerned with information and communication technologies (ICT) take for granted that the "consumer" is somebody who passively receives what is offered to him or her in the universe of information/ communication.

But this is not true. Information is manifold. It is a product, but also a source. It is a material that, when consumed, offers the possibility of producing new material, and so on and on. However, it also must be constantly processed to produce significance, and therefore to be used. That is why we can say that the consumption of information always requires specific work, which is what I call the "work of consumption." This implies that the output is deeply influenced by the quantity and quality of this work and therefore by the user's competence, skill, and purpose. Moreover, the "work of consumption" producing significance brings about new information material: so it is also a "work of production." That is why we can say that consumption is always productive, even if at different levels.

It must be considered also that when information is "consumed," it is not destroyed. It can be transferred to others and still remains in our possession and may be consumed again and again. So the consumption of information is always a "work in progress" and may deliver different outputs at different levels – outputs that can be employed again, selected and manipulated to produce new items,

The Handbook of Political Economy of Communications, First Edition.
Edited by Janet Wasko, Graham Murdock, and Helena Sousa.
© 2014 John Wiley & Sons, Ltd. Published 2014 by John Wiley & Sons, Ltd.

new images, new symbols. Finally, it is correct to take into account also a different kind of information that consumers systematically produce every time they carry out their "work of consumption." While searching and consuming information through the Internet, everybody produces a lot of data about his or her life and social being – data which are very much appreciated by national and multinational conglomerates.

What Does "Consumer" Mean?

If we start from here, the true significance of the term "consumer" may become questionable. Semiologists and psychologists have gone deeply into the mental and emotional process that every consumer is obliged to perform, at different levels, in order to make use of information of any kind. And when we talk about "passivity"– for instance, the "passivity" of a television audience – we know that this process must be nevertheless carried out, more or less, also by "passive consumers." Even when there is mostly an emotional response, even when the receiver-consumers are solicited to simply enjoy themselves, this process must be considered.

It is a process that puts to work and blends direct life experience, simulated experience – offered by symbolic materials – and the global imagery that newspapers, cinema, television, books, posters, and more recently the Internet, have placed and stored within every consumer. It is said that today direct life experience is declining. But is it possible that it is the longing for a broader, more diversified, intense experience – a desire induced over the years by the increasing circulation of signs and images and fantasies – that makes actual daily experience increasingly poorer in ordinary people's feelings?

We could say that these mental and emotional processes are spontaneous and almost automatic. But when we consider information in a strict sense, the process of consumption demands and implies a voluntary and deliberate work, know-how, and competence, at least at a basic level – a kind of work that every consumer of information was also obliged to carry out in the past, of course. Nowadays, though, the new media and new technologies are enormously increasing and partially changing this "work of consumption."

In the past, information pursued people through different media and we might say that it sought out consumers. Today, this kind of search is still going on and is becoming quite obsessive. But the "explosion of information" has contradictory characteristics. Information is glorified, it is said to be indispensable at any time and in any circumstance, but at the same time it is fragmented and partial and, very often, it is difficult to interpret. Information is offered by countless sources, but the sources that are strongest, most attractive, or easiest to find may not be the most trustworthy. Information is delivered through messages and symbols that aim to be plain and easily "consumed," but for this very reason it may be insufficient and disappointing (that is why it is often stated that it has lost most of its significance).

Information is globally homogenized but, at the same time, is more and more targeted. This means that each consumer must find his or her "personalized" information, testing different channels and media and, nowadays, endlessly surfing the Internet. The quantity of information available makes it more difficult to verify and compare sources in any case. Consumers can find basic data, but that data's assurance must be controlled and this requires difficult work and specific experience to achieve one's purpose. On the other hand, even the most trustworthy data are just approximations that make sense only if they are used to develop new information. "For citizens to make sense of the information they receive, they need skills. In particular, they need skills to discriminate between authoritative information and information whose provenance is detached from its originator" (Mansell 2002, 410).

The "work of consumption," then, today involves more and more searching, selecting, assembling, cleaning up, critical valuing, digging out, and connecting information items. And it therefore involves more time and commitment, greater know-how, and a greater competence in order to fulfill the needs of consumers, leaving aside professional operators. Even entertainment products, for instance, videogames, require more and more "work of consumption." In this case, we may ask whether the work is pleasure or is neurotically performed just because it is the only way to reach some sort of satisfaction.

The Different Levels of the "Work of Consumption"

Obviously, the "work of consumption" may be carried out at different levels, but the level is seldom determined by free choice only. It also depends on economic and educational factors. The trouble is that the level at which the "work of consumption" is carried out directly affects the cognitive process and, of course, the relative outputs. In the first place, the hardware and software used makes a great difference, and here the economic assets of the consumer are certainly determining. This is the first factor in what is called the "digital divide." It is true that nowadays there are increasingly more new technologies that may substitute for or at least integrate those already in use and which are simpler and also less expensive. For instance, cellular phones are substituting for computers at certain levels (mail and some Internet surfing, for example) and are much easier to use and less expensive. In Kenya, just to cite one example out of many, one adult out of three has a cellular phone. And it is also important to remember that cellular phones make it possible to send images as well as words.

But we must also acknowledge that in many cases the machines, even the most sophisticated, do not satisfy the user's needs and aspirations. It is possible that an information technology that is very helpful and quite liberating in a professional environment turns out to be frustrating and alienating when it is put to work by a user at home. In the second place, know-how and competence are a crucial factor: this is a commonsensical certainty. Here we find a strong public and private commitment – throughout the western world, it must be stressed – to improve training among children, adolescents, and adults. But it must be emphasized that know-how and competence in this field rapidly decline and go out of use if the user does not continue to engage in the "work of consumption."

Then we have the problem of time. The "work of consumption" requires time, of course, and – as I stressed above, in discussing sources – we must not take it for granted that the time employed is directly related to the quality of the output in this domain. However, time is another conditioning factor: this is one of the reasons why statistics always place young people at the top when considering the home consumption of information – or at least the use of information technologies.

We cannot take it for granted that people will always be inclined to carry out the "work of consumption." The European Union research group FAST (Forecasting and Assessment in Science and Technology), stated in one of its reports that the use of information technologies is conditioned by three factors: economic resources, know-how and competence, and willingness (FAST 1985). It must be pointed out, though, that the last factor is, of course, subjective, but not definitely beyond social and cultural influence. We can see that even gender has an impact on the use of information and its purposes, and therefore on the willingness to carry out the "work of consumption." Some social researchers have found that the difference between women and men when they use computers is their attitude: women use computers just to satisfy their practical needs; men use them hoping to satisfy their desire for domineering.

Nevertheless, the practical utility of the information acquired through the "work of consumption" can nurture willingness, for instance, and this is why online services and markets are increasingly successful with clients. But we must also consider what we may call the "social productivity" of information in general, which involves some other weighty questions.

The Productivity of the "Work of Consumption"

Since, as we have seen, the "work of consumption" is carried out at different levels, there are different levels of final outputs. But it is not so easy to assess the content of the different outputs, their intensity and meaningfulness. For instance, an information output that is perhaps weightier, including more items than another, may still be less meaningful because it does not include the core, the specific information items, which are indispensable to penetrate and evaluate the significance of the others. The trouble is that the core information items are often not available. Secrecy still exists even on the Internet, which we will discuss when we tackle the problem of access.

It is important, in any case, to try to measure the productivity of the "work of consumption" and we must start by comparing, at least, the time employed by the consumer and the level of output reached. For instance, how helpful is research done using Google when the quantity of links found is almost unlimited?

The "work of consumption" may be very complex, so consumers often tend to obtain "easy" technologies and use them at their lowest level. This means that the "work of consumption" in the end becomes not a way to explore the information universe, or to reach and increase knowledge, but only a way to practice standards. And this is exactly what the software producers and corporate management want: to sell the most profitable technologies.

It is no coincidence that, because there is a ceaseless glorification of speed, faster and faster machines and "intelligent" software are marketed. The trouble is that this hardware and software may lighten the "work of consumption" by accelerating the computer's operations, and making the search and selection of information items easier, but at the same time they inevitably incur the risk of impoverishing the final output. For instance, there is more and more new "intelligent" software organized to speed up the selection of websites and their related information items. But, as may easily be understood, however flexible and "intelligent" they may be, they have a prescribed logic and so may leave out some items which the searcher might be interested in.

The truth is that speed may be increased with a remarkable advantage in the diffusion of information or in the passage from one text or image to another inside a hypertext or from one online site to another. But the "work of consumption" in the information domain implies a lot more than this and it is not in any case comparable to the work involved in material production. In the latter, it is a common practice to increase productivity by cutting down the time worked because the technical innovation and the concentration of the physical energy expended in the production process – unfortunately, we must say, because here we find the root of the exploitation of workers – can provide the same amount of products with the same quality as before. But when nonmaterial production is at stake – and this implies mental work, or the selection, reflection, and penetration of any symbolic items – the time to work out the process may not be reduced without damaging the final output, or at least oversimplifying and leaving out a fair amount of significance. So we should be very careful when taking into consideration the information universe when we try to discuss the productivity of the "work of consumption."

The Problems of Access

"Information is power" is a trite commonplace. But we can easily agree that information surely brings more power to people who already have power. For the ordinary consumer, it certainly can be a source of knowledge and self-awareness, but, paradoxically, it can also be a cause of frustration. And here we come to the possible social productivity of information. Being informed about social processes, getting more and more detailed information about a situation that is conditioning our personal life, is not sufficient to give us the means and the power to change things. We know what we should do but lack the necessary economic or social means to do it. And so information may increase our frustration and, possibly, our desire for vengeance.

However, out of this paradoxical teaching, it would be a fatal mistake to infer from the difference between being informed and having the concrete possibility of changing one's social and personal situation that the circulation of information is socially unproductive. Democracy, to consider a general theme, certainly works better when citizens are better informed. And nowadays the circulation and exchange of information is definitely enforcing popular movements all over the world. But to penetrate the possible social productivity of information, we must look into the "work of consumption," analyze the significance of the different kinds of information which are stored or circulated through different channels, distinguish between social factors of change, and bear in mind the difference between knowledge and social action. The "Information Society" theories seem to have answers, in general, to all the questions that may arise from the different levels of analysis, or they may ignore them. And this is one of the reasons why they are "inadequate and unconvincing" (Garnham 2001, 164). As Garnham writes, "no theory of totality can be assumed" today (2001, 164).

In analyzing the "work of consumption," we also meet the problems of access. There is a tendency to consider the quantity and the quality of a consumer's access depending only on the development of the media system and, in particular, on the network and ICT diffusion. It is one of the multiform effects of the "telematic squint" based on technological determinism. It should be clear, instead, that this connection is not mechanical: the development of the media system and the diffusion of new technologies and networks are the prerequisite for an increase in the access level, of course, but the conditions and even the possibilities of fully accessing information depend on many different factors. "The degree of access to information ranges from zero to infinity and depends on knowledge, inclinations, technologies, economic availability, social status and environmental conditions," wrote Bragg and colleagues many years ago, refusing an easy view of the information universe (Bragg et al. 1993).

As we have seen, to find the sources and the information items that each consumer is interested in depends on the "work of consumption," but not only on this. There is also what we might call a "visibility logic." There are sources on the Internet, for instance, that come directly to consumers, interfering in their work and trying to attract them. This presents the very alarming problem of privacy and of its defense. In fact, these interferences are made possible by the marketing of consumers' lists and the acquisition of consumers' profiles. This is the basis of the strategy of control that has been at last publicly acknowledged. But paradoxically, these violations of privacy also give rise to an opposite practice: the strategy of secrecy. We can contact a myriad of sources and find millions of different information items, but the result may be a nebula of details that lack the core that could give them true significance. Many relevant data, many information items of great importance and of public interest – because they are referable to the social and political driving forces of the most powerful nations or to events which will deeply affect the daily life of consumers – are strictly concealed at many levels. The demonstrations of break-ins by hackers to lighten the darkness have proved by now how precious a secret, or at least concealed, information item can be. And not by chance, these hackers' political actions are systematically prosecuted as criminal offenses. "Information Guerrilla" and other similar groups in many countries have denounced concealed information and have revealed many secrets and still do so, providing at the same time a great deal of information about grassroot movements. But they constantly meet many difficulties in fulfilling their tasks.

Finally, there is the tendency to appropriate information and extend the market logic throughout the information universe. From this perspective, as well as in the ongoing discussion about intellectual property rights and copyright, even a basic truth such as "knowledge production is highest with free exchange" is still far from being generally applied. "Now that PCs and the Internet have become mainstream tools, there's rising pressure to turn them into the appliances they've defeated: to close them, in some case forbidding outside tinkering altogether, and in others allowing them only under closely monitored and controlled circumstances" (Zittrain 2008).

The "work of consumption" becomes much weightier and more difficult in this context at the economic and symbolic level. So consumers are pushed toward simplistic and, once again, fast practices. But information and communication always begin from listening. If it is more difficult to find appropriate sources, the information process practically comes to an end. Is this the "culture" that the "Information Society" brings about?

The Fallacy of Technological Determinism

The questions raised by the "work of consumption" demonstrate the fallacy of the determinism that sees technologies as an independent variable mechanically triggering a series of radical changes and begetting the new era of the "Information

Society." We must consider, by the way, that these myths and prophecies are not all optimistic. A catastrophic determinism also exists, though it is obviously much less popular than the supportive version.

Technologies have an influence on social development, to be sure, but it must always be taken into account that they are the output of research and the research is increasingly financed, at every level, by private capital. So the research is expected to find solutions to some specific problems and must meet some specific needs just to make technologies more profitable in the market. Once a retired researcher previously working for a big software company confessed that the management invited researchers to leave aside certain problems to solve them later, or even to leave aside some solutions they may have already found, just to give the company the possibility of marketing the software over and over again as "new."

Some social experimentations carried out in different communities adopting the "creative/participatory" method have proved that new technologies often do not meet the specific needs of different groups of consumers. For instance, experiments carried out in Italy with groups of old people found that the software at their disposal was too difficult or did not satisfy the requests of the involved participants. So the experts modified the software to make it meet the specific needs of those groups. The experts' intervention was based, of course, precisely on a detailed analysis of the "work of consumption" carried out by the old people involved in the experiment.

Leaving aside technological determinism and the myths of the Information Society may help us fight what may be called "the obligation to adjust." In the deterministic perspective, in fact, ordinary people – and above all young people – are invited to face the inevitability of future developments, trying to reach the pole position and adopt the right attitude to adjust to the demands of the predicted social change.

So people should from the start reject the "culture of choice" and the alternative potential that the information universe might develop. And, after all, this would be, from the ordinary people's point of view, a real waste. It would entail the loss of possibly favorable social effects that might be brought about, instead, if the available technological potential were fully developed and used in the general interest. In the first place, as we have seen, there is the possibility of enlarging social relations at a distance – which does not in any way substitute for face-to-face confrontation but enriches it enormously – and creating movements aimed at achieving better life conditions and social changes.

Therefore, in studying the "work of consumption," we must clear away the fallacies of some of the misleading theories and probe the manifold questions which are still facing us. Given that we are in a world full of uncertainties, we may find help only by adopting a systematic critical approach, and asking at all times, "why?" and "how?" as Bertolt Brecht wrote in his poem "In Praise of Doubt." This offers us the best way to look at the present and also at the future.

From "Consumer" to "Prosumer"?

The problem of access does not only concern the right to be informed. It concerns also, and sometimes more, the right to produce information and to put it into circulation.

As we have seen, the output of the "work of consumption" is the result of a process that requires a specific know-how, we could say even a skill, that is obtained through training and doing. Since consumers are obliged to tackle and perform this process to find, work out, and use information, they may feel at last that they can also be "producers" wishing to exchange the information they have received/ obtained or to produce radically new material.

We can say from experience that this happens with individual consumers and more often when the "work of consumption" has been carried out by groups. It happens especially with young people, with those who are born with the new information technologies and have grown up with the development of the Internet – the ones today called the "Net Generation." So the "work of consumption" generates the "work of production" and the "consumers" become "prosumers" (producers-consumers). Some of them immediately aspire to spread the information they produce, while others aim to become a source by opening blogs, for instance.

Is this a reaction to the dominating individualism or is it a consequence of it? Does it suggest that there is still a strong need for social relations or is it only a new way of exhibiting oneself? Or is it aimed at striving toward cultural and social changes? It is difficult to generalize. In any case, "prosumers" work to produce specific information and to put it into circulation. First of all, then, they try to become sources in the media system. It is still difficult to access the traditional media: at most, papers publish letters from readers, or radio and television programs may solicit phone interventions (but only to ask something or, less often, to answer questions from the radio/television performer). However, setting aside the question of censorship, traditional media tend to select the items which concur with their positions and accept or even solicit only the "voices" that enforce their strategy of communication.

The boundless space of the Internet looks different and, as a matter of fact, is different. As Rosen writes, the means of production in the editorial field have been distributed to the population at large (Rosen 2006). But even here, things are not so favorable. As Annalee Newitz (2008) writes, examining the corporate control of the Internet, "sure you can write almost anything you want. But will you be able to publish it? Will you be able to get a high enough ranking on Google to be findable when people search your topic? Probably not. So your speech is free, but nobody can hear it." However, the skill acquired through the "work of consumption," the ongoing improvement of ICTs, the free availability of the Internet (but for how long?) have created the best conditions for the development of "participatory information": information produced and circulated from the bottom up by ordinary people or by journalists in collaboration with nonprofessional people. This trend has been expedited by the decreasing production of journalistic enquiries. These days, professional journalists tend to hold on to the editorial office, rarely trying to delve into social processes. At the same time, there are people who explore their communities and produce information just to call attention to the local environment or to fight for human rights, to help people living in developing countries, to defend the eco-environment, to offset the strategy of surveillance, to reveal institutional black holes, or to promote democracy. For instance, in Spain and in Latin America, there is what is called *Periodismo Ciudadano* (citizens' journalism), which is a very rich information grassroots universe which is followed by Spanish-speaking people living all over the world.

So we have bloggers and citizen journalists, producing what is called UGC (user-generated content), some putting information in their blogs and offering it to other bloggers, others producing information for some website reserved for nonprofessional operators or collaborating with professional journalists. Style and content are appropriate for this kind of information: short items, even when they deal with complex social processes; news circulated as a story or event is developing; and little care about objectivity or impartiality.

The blogs are a sort of conversation place, destined above all to build relations. Sometimes a blog publishes something that may interest many other bloggers – it has happened that within 24 hours, a blog has been visited by more than one hundred thousand visitors. Blogs may contain photos, sounds, and links to connect visitors to other blogs or other network sites. There are sites that allow people who participate in an international event to exchange their experiences through blogs while the event is still going on. Nowadays famous people, MPs, party leaders, and other members of institutional systems have also opened their blogs to be in touch with ordinary people.

There are also initiatives called "citizens' journalism" that aim at giving volunteers the possibility of producing and circulating information in collaboration with professional authors and journalists. For instance, Global Voices Online is a leading participatory media news room for voices from the developing world. Started in 2005 as a simple blog at Harvard University, Global Voices has grown into a vibrant global community of more than 150 active volunteer authors and translators and more than 20 freelance part-time regional and language editors. It bases its coverage on the words, images, and videos of ordinary people across the globe who use the Internet to communicate and broadcast their thoughts, analysis, and observations.

These initiatives run many risks, though. Amateurism can prevail and invalidate the information that is produced by this kind of collaboration. Volunteers may use the collaboration with professionals just to be introduced into a world where they aim to become professionals themselves (volunteers often pretend to be paid after awhile). Above all, it is difficult to verify information produced by citizens' journalism and because of this, it is very often controlled through the "regular" methods. Thus it loses its specific value and ends up obeying the logic of the main-stream media.

Before considering citizens' journalism, we can define "information workers" as those who extend the "work of consumption" into the "work of production" and try to circulate – with or without collaboration with professionals – their informa-tion items, this not being their main or gainful jobs. How does this affect the market logic? And what kind of rules would be necessary to really guarantee the "right to inform" and the consequent possible contracting between professionals and nonprofessionals, between consumers who also produce information to be circulated and the apparatuses, old and new, in a media system increasingly domi-nated by global conglomerates? More research and reflections are needed to answer these basic questions.

However, many researchers and media professionals have claimed that citizens' journalism is very weak or almost dying. Others claim that it is vital and that it is a fundamental shift in the way information necessary to a democracy is transmitted. The trouble is that there are many and continuous attempts to control and domi-nate it by the mainstream media conglomerates.

It is true that citizens' journalism may greatly help the development of democ-racy, which is currently at a very critical point. It may develop through participa-tion and bottom-up information, but, on the contrary, it may give new space to authoritarianism. Because of this, the new information technologies and their use by the masses may be decisive. A great number of studies and researchers tell us that, in spite of the Information Society worshipers, if we are not affected by the "telematic squint," we can see that the path to change is still long and hard. But it is absolutely true that once again we find here the ambiguity of the social reality we are living in: we may be at the dawn of a new mode of production or in the middle of a huge, treacherous deception. However, the debate about these kind of ideas is waning nowadays, and this may be a significant sign, too.

References

Bragg, C., Le Baron, Nelson, and O'Donnel (1993) Harness the power of technology: Developing minds in an information age. In: Didsbury, H. F. (ed.), *The Years Ahead: Perils, Problems, and Promises*. World Future Society, Bethesda, MD.

FAST (1985). *Europa 1995 – Trasformazioni tecnologiche e sfide sociali, Bruxelles: CECA, CEE, CEEA* – Forecasting and Assessment in Science and Technology, Programme of the European Union, Brussels.

Garnham, N. (2001) Information society theory as ideology: A critique. *Studies in Communication Sciences*, 1(1), 129–66.

Mansell, R. (2002) From digital divides to digital entitlements in knowledge societies. *Current Sociology*, 50(3), 407–26.

Newitz, A. (2008) How do we fight corporate control of the Internet? AlterNet, May 22. Online at http://www.alternet.org/story/86205/how_do_we_fight_corporate_con trol_of_the_internet/(accessed October 14, 2010).

Rosen, J. (2006) *Fans, Bloggers and Gamers*. New York University Press, New York.

Zittrain, J. (2008) The Internet is closing. *Newsweek,* December 8. Online at http://www. newsweek.com/2008/11/28/the-internet-is-closing.html# (accessed October 14, 2010).

Suggestions for Further Reading

Castells, M. (1998) *The Rise of the Network Society*. Blackwell, Malden, MA.

Cesareo, G. (1981) *Fa notizia, fonti, processi tecnologie e soggetti nella macchina dell'informazione*. Editori Riuniti, Rome.

Cesareo, G. (1992) Privacy and secrecy: Social control and prospects for democracy in the information system. In: Wasko, J. and Mosco, V. (eds), *Democratic Communications in the Information Age*. Garamond Press, Toronto, pp. 87–97.

Cesareo, G. (1995) Lo strabismo telematico: Tra previsioni e profezie: trent'anni di pronostici sul futuro della comunicazione. In: Di Spirito, F, Ortoleva, P., and Ottaviano, C. (eds), *Lo Strabismo Telematico*. UTET Libreria-Telecom, Turin, Italy, pp. 3–42.

Cesareo, G. (2004) ICT and social change: Fate or choice, and who makes the choice? *Javnost-The Public*, 11(3), 105–14.

Cesareo, G. and Rodi, P. (1996) *Il mercato dei sogni*. Bruno Mondadori, Milan.

Garnham, N. (1990) *Capitalism and Communication*. Sage, London.

Israel, G. (2001) Pour des technologies à dimension humaine. *Le Monde Interactif,* October 24.

MacBride, S. and International Commission for the Study of Communication Problems (1980) *Many Voices, One World*. Unesco, Paris.

Mattelart, A. (2001) *Histoire de la Société de l'Information*. Editions La Découverte, Paris.

Webster F. (1995) *Theories of the Information Society*. Routledge, London.

19

The Political Economy of Audiences

Daniel Biltereyst and Philippe Meers

... the audience remains a problem for media research, as indeed it must. It [is] a potentially crucial pivot for the understanding of a whole range of social and cultural processes that bear on the central questions of public communication.

Silverstone 1990, 173

Introduction

If there is one truism in media and communications research then it is the one about how people rely on the cultural industries for the images, words, and voices with which they interpret and interact with their social environment. The degree to which people depend upon or use products and technologies from those industries is probably the key question along which various research traditions and perspectives develop and compete. Research on the audience, the public, or whatever other instance referring to the receiver's or user's end, draws on what Sonia Livingstone (2005a, 17) has called, a "long and distinguished intellectual history" which has proved to be "creative, even provocative, in its analysis of processes of mediation, participation and influence." Although political economy perspectives are often described as "holistic" in their approach, "seeing the economy as interrelated within political, social and cultural life" (Hesmondhalgh 2002, 33; Golding and Murdock 1991, 18), we seldom find references to these perspectives in mainstream overviews of audience research (though in some cases there are smaller references, such as the one to Dallas Smythe in McQuail 1997, 14). The clichés on political economy approaches are widespread. They are

The Handbook of Political Economy of Communications, First Edition.
Edited by Janet Wasko, Graham Murdock, and Helena Sousa.
© 2014 John Wiley & Sons, Ltd. Published 2014 by John Wiley & Sons, Ltd.

still often considered narrow and deterministic, limited to structural analysis, thereby focusing primarily on the economic or production sides of the communication process.

This chapter tries to indicate how political economy perspectives can play an important role in understanding various key issues in relation to media audiences. It wants to set the record straight by showing how and why a political economy of audiences could help clarify core questions on media, power, and society. A crucial idea in this chapter is, as Silverstone (1990, 175) continued to stress, that "the audience is not a discrete phenomenon," that it is "both ephemeral and partial," that one cannot escape the "plurality of the audience." The audience is no stable entity, as another established audience researcher argued, "which we can isolate and identify" and which is "unproblematically 'there' for us to observe and analyse" (Moores 1993, 1–2). Beside media or technological differences (referring to readers, viewers, listeners, internet users, up to producers), audiences can be distinguished in terms of geography, time, race, identity, income, or social and cultural capital. Inspired by this idea on the plurality of the audience, we think that people are (possibly and at the same time) citizens as well as consumers, concrete and unique as well as proto-, quasi- or pseudo-audiences (Livingstone 2005a), rational and sovereign as well as irrational, emotional, and dependent, active and autonomous as well as driven and created by corporate strategies, selective as well as segmented by the industry.

As critical audience researchers trained in the tradition of ethnographic and reception studies (Bitereyst 1991, Meers 2004, Bitereyst and Meers 2006, Bitereyst et al. 2011), we think that political economy approaches are extremely important for investigating questions on media power, more precisely in exploring the conditions and the limits of cultural production, control, and governmentality. In its engagement with questions of "justice, equity and the public good," critical political economy, as Golding and Murdock (1991, 18–19) have forcefully argued, is much more than the study of structures and economic dynamics behind (the range of) cultural production and texts, but it also incorporates questions on cultural consumption, access, and cultural competence. Political economy insights are important not only to deliver the necessary contextual data for audience studies, or to tackle the continued importance of the commodification of audiences (in terms of finance, time, geography, desire, fantasy). The integration of these insights makes it possible, we think, to fully understand the broader production and circulation of meaning. Warning against the opposition between production and consumption "as binary opposites," Calabrese (2004, 10) convincingly underlined that if we want to understand "substantive questions about determination, the autonomy of culture, and human agency, or about the relationships among class, race, gender, and other bases of inequality," we need "to avoid seeing the audience as being on the 'other side' of production."

In critical research, the debate on media audiences in essence dealt with questions about the crisis in people's social engagement as a result of the increasing commercialization and mediation of society, whereby cultural studies and political economy approaches were often presented as opposing factions. This chapter aims at revisiting these 1990s debates, which are crucial to a political economy of audiences since the main arguments between political economy and cultural studies scholars were voiced precisely around the conceptualization and the study of audiences. In this highly polemical debate, where the audience even became "the site for accusations of collusion with the enemy" (McLaughlin 1999, 337), both positions were respectively linked to ideas about, on the one hand, passive consumers determined by media structure and the industrial-commercial logic, and on the other hand, active, selective, and interpretative audiences. After a discussion of these debates, we continue by reviewing how the media/communications audience has been conceptualized and studied by scholars associated with the political economy perspective. This includes the seminal work done by Dallas W. Smythe on audience commodity, as well as the debates and various research approaches to audiences following up on this, thereby indicating how other scholars sometimes not associated with the approach contributed to a critical political economy of media audiences.

Revisiting the Debates: Schisms, Collaboration, Interconnectedness

Although the 1990s debate between cultural studies and political economy scholars has been considered "sterile" (Curran and Morley 2006, 6), "futile" (Kellner 1997, 120), or "an excellent example of ritualized combat masquerading as reasoned debate" (Meehan 1999, 151), we think it is important enough to locate some epistemological differences, misunderstandings, and schisms within critical research on audiences. Starting off with the debates, though, should not obscure waves of rapprochement or initiatives, which were taken in order to come to a broader view upon the circulation of meaning and the role of audiences in it. Some of these proposals and paths for collaboration remain highly valuable when writing about media audiences.

The impetus for the critical debate on audiences went back to the 1980s and the early 1990s, when a whole wave of qualitative audience or reception studies emerged under the cultural studies flag. Stressing the ordinary, everyday life experience, pleasure, and subjectivity of (popular) media culture, many of these studies argued for a more complex view of influence and cultural domination, seen "from below" (audience, community, agency) rather than "from above" (industry, state, structure). "New" audience studies covered various forms of qualitative research, whereby notions of overall effects were rejected and replaced by a more "limited" model. Inspired by Stuart Hall's encoding/decoding-model, researchers dealt with the complexities of the meaningful text, the inscription of meaning to it (encoding) and the variations in the modes of viewing and using or the process of making sense of it (decoding). A first wave of reception studies was soon followed by more ethnographical work on the conditions and identities of media users, often put in their domestic relations and practices. For an overview, see Alasuutari (1999).

A case in point in the discussions were some "new" audience studies dealing with questions in relation to the experience of media globalization and media imperialism, in particular the dominance and the worldwide influence of the western (US) cultural industry – a topic with a strong political economy research tradition. Following Morley's (1991, 1) argument that "any analysis of these macro-processes which is not grounded in an adequately understanding of the complexities of the process of (principally domestic) consumption" runs the risk "of being so over-schematic," various studies were conducted on the everyday reception of US popular culture (for an overview of the debate, see Biltereyst 2003 and Sinclair 2007). A key study in this respect was *The Export of Meaning* (1990), in which Liebes and Katz reported about the everyday engagement and cross-cultural reception of the blockbuster soap *Dallas*, often seen as the symbol of American cultural imperialism. Stressing the polysemic value and openness of US television fare, Liebes and Katz underlined the active process of negotiation between the text and the receivers.

The new audience perspective soon started a virulent debate about methodology, ideology, and epistemology in relation to the effects and power in the international cultural economy. Scholars working within the political economy perspective in particular acted strongly against this type of relativist accounts on the societal distribution of power, criticizing the failure to deal with the deep structural changes in national and global media systems. Reception studies and other forms of new audience research were accused of overstressing the dispersion of power, of replacing structural by audience power, of romanticizing audience activity and resistance, while celebrating consumer choice and the complexities of popular culture, thereby undermining any acknowledgment of economic or structural determination. (The key reference is Fiske 1987.)

Critics argued that the new audience studies to a great extent coincided with the rhetoric of consumer choice and sovereignty, which had been the main guideline in liberal communications policies under Reagan, Thatcher, and many other conservative governments in the USA, Europe and elsewhere. New audience studies also came along when those governments strengthened their policy to break media monopolies (e.g., public broadcasters in most European countries) and oligopolies (networks in the USA), leading to more competition, commercialization, and a greater availability of content. This rhetoric on audience power and consumer choice was strengthened by new communication technologies and products which facilitated individuation, interactivity, and selectivity, including the idea of the "productive" user and spatial and temporal autonomy (VCRs in the 1980s, Internet and the digital media in the 1990s).

In his sharp "new revisionism" article, Curran (1990) argued that new audience studies seemed to be unaware of the fact that many of their research methods (e.g., lengthy individual interviews) and key concepts (e.g., the active and creative role of the audiences, the multiple meanings generated by texts, relative audience autonomy) were only miming specific lines of inquiry within the traditional effects research tradition. Herbert Schiller, a key figure in the political economy perspective, claimed that this audience-centered approach was a primary effort "to minimize or discredit the idea of cultural domination" (1991, 13), while Roach (1990, 296) talked about an "essentially political agenda: to undermine the very idea of ideology and its connection to capitalist expansion."

The debate between scholars representing political economy and cultural studies reached its momentum in the mid-1990s with the publication of a series of articles on the issue in *Critical Studies in Mass Communication* (1995), where both positions were clearly opposed. In his contribution, Garnham (1995, 71), one of the main political economy contenders, argued that "the antagonism (was) based on a profound misunderstanding of political economy." Questioning how it was "possible to ignore in any study of culture and its political potential, the development of global cultural markets and the technological and regulatory processes and capital flows that are the conditions of possibility of such markets?" Garnham recognized the usefulness of studying the audience, mainly in relation to the concept of false consciousness as the basis for empowerment. Furthermore, Garnham contended that modern forms of racial and gender domination were founded on economic domination, putting class again in the middle of the analysis. Garnham's provocative stance was rejected by Grossberg (1995, 72), who responded that cultural studies and political economy were always divided "over the terms of an adequate theory of culture and power." Grossberg (1995, 78) proposed to integrate research on production, consumption politics and ideology, while for the argument of class and economics' primacy over race and gender, he argued that "the appropriate ways of accounting for, or struggling against, structures of domination organized around race and gender" could be connected to, but are not determined by economics.

The debate, though, was not always as confrontational. In fact, it turned out to be quite productive, not only leading to internal critique within both positions, but also to collaboration and integration, as well as to more conceptual work and reflection upon the audience and audience research. One move to overcome the divide has been to separate "critical" or "cultural materialist" from "celebratory," "poststructuralist," or "postmodern" cultural studies (Babe 2008, 4, Meehan 1999, 150). Several scholars from within the political economy perspective combined – or at least approached – both worlds. Authors such as Meehan (e.g., 2000, on the creation of fans) and Wasko (e.g. Wasko et al. 2001, on the global Disney project) have combined political economy with other approaches such as textual and audience studies. This went hand in hand with a rethinking of political economy (Mosco 1996). In this reworking, there is room for internal critique. In their introduction to a collaborative book project, *Consuming Audiences* (2000b), Hagen and Wasko (2000a, 22), for instance, wrote that while the primary focus in political economy was "most often on macro structures" and that it wanted to make the "argument that there are implications for consumption," they admitted that "these points have not been explored empirically." On the other hand, qualitative audience studies "focused on the micro levels on the consumption side, without always relating them to larger cultural and political frameworks that set the premises for both media institutions and for consuming audiences."

One of the first to come up with a firm plea for integration, or at least an empirical examination of consumption as part of a *critical political economy* of cultural production, is Graham Murdock. In an article with Golding (1991, 15), he located its focus "on the interplay between the symbolic and economic dimensions of public communications," with three core tasks or priorities. Beside the examination of the production of cultural goods, critical political economy studies the interplay between the material and symbolic in relation to media texts and cultural consumption. Claiming that a critical political economy is a necessary starting point for a critical analysis of contemporary culture, Murdock (1995) argued that "it can specify the dynamics that shape the fields on which cultural activities are played out." Rejecting audience determination, Murdock (1995) equally recognized that specific acts of production or consumption cannot be "unproblematically deduced or read off from economic dynamics." Arguing for the complementarity of political economy and cultural (audience) studies, Murdock recognized the "repertoire of choices" for audiences. Also in his contribution to *Consuming Audiences*, Murdock (2000) rejected the separation between economy and meaning because "modern communications is self-evidently both a symbolic and an economic system, its analysis has to be a matter of both/and rather than either/or." Therefore, "a political economy that helps to explain how the material, social and symbolic resources for everyday action are assembled and allocated and how patterns of access are shifting as a result of the recomposition of contemporary capitalism and commodity culture, is essential to any attempt to explain patterns of creative consumptions." This political economy should go hand in hand with "ethnographies that detail how these altering conditions are encountered, worked through, and challenged 'on the ground'" (Murdock 2000, 59, 65).

An interesting figure, who illustrated the shift in recognizing the importance of empirical audience study as part of an integration and combination of approaches and methodologies, is Armand Mattelart, one of the main protagonists of the cultural imperialism and Americanization thesis in the 1970s and 1980s. While in 1987 he still referred to Katz and Liebes as an example of neoliberal research to denounce international dominance and promote the free flow doctrine (Mattelart and Mattelart 1987), he later on acknowledged the importance of forms of interpretive audience resistance. One decade later, he recognized the necessity to expand the critical analytical toolkit with concepts which illustrate the new ambiguities of the contemporary global media context (creolization, hybridity). This, though, doesn't mean that concepts of dependency and cultural imperialism are useless, because they "could still be used to apprehend the imbalance in worldwide flows of information and communication" (Mattelart and Mattelart 1998, 138). A good example, in this respect, of a critical combination and integration is the work done by Miller et al. (2001) in their analysis of "global Hollywood" with its focus on "the imbrication of power and signification at all points on the cultural continuum" (2001, 2). Both areas have come to realize the importance of a "radical historiciza-tion of context" (13), in order that the analysis of text and audience can now be supplemented by "an account of occasionality that details the conditions under which a text is made, circulated, received, interpreted and criticised" (Miller et al. 2001, 13).

The fact that political economy scholars showed an interest in audience studies did not mean that they were not met with skepticism. Meehan (2001, 208), for instance, did not spare her critique for one-sided cultural studies analyses, espe-cially when cultural scholars "define culture as a whole way of life and then opera-tionalise the study of culture as the analysis of texts." Arguing that this is a blunt reduction obscuring experiential differences, Meehan (2001, 213) claimed that "the discourse of cultural studies is so dominated by 'text' and 'reading' that the meta-phoric nature of these terms seems to be lost." Schiller (2000, 119), whose highly skeptical stance against audience studies was well known, argued that the empha-sis on audience resistance undermined "any effort to tangibly resist corporate cul-tural domination." Arguing for an alternative path for audience research to be a fruitful area to study, Schiller maintained that it should take a politicized stance, motivated by "a desire to do battle with the controlling corporate cultural forces of the day" (2000, 119).

On the other side of the debate, scholars equally argue for a critical re-examination of cultural studies-inspired audience research, whereby some – more or less explicitly – referred to a need for linking or complementing it with political econ-omy. A crucial figure is Douglas Kellner, who combines reviving and rethinking the Frankfurt School (2002) with a keen interest in audiences and consumption. After the big debates, Kellner (1997, 102) suggested a "multiperspectival cultural studies" arguing that "the construction of media texts and their reception by audi-ences is deeply influenced by the system of production and distribution within which media products circulate and are received" (104). Kellner (1997, 2002) set an ambitious research agenda for an all encompassing cultural studies: "Thus, a cul-tural studies that is critical and multiperspectival provides comprehensive approaches to culture that can be applied to a wide variety of artifacts. ... Its com-prehensive perspectives encompass political economy, textual analysis, and audi-ence research, and provide critical and political perspectives that enable individuals to dissect the meanings, messages and effects of dominant cultural forms" (Kellner 1997, 120).

It is interesting to note that several of the early "new" audience pioneers criti-cally looked back at some of the key foundations of the young research tradition. David Morley, for instance, who had published in 1980 his groundbreaking *The "Nationwide" Audience* inspired by Hall's encoding/decoding model, later harshly criticized celebratory audience studies for neglecting the structural contexts and offering "an improperly romanticized image of the media consumer, which tends to ignore institutional questions of cultural power" (Morley 1997, 121). Reacting against the textualization of cultural studies, whereby cultural phenomena drift entirely free from their social and material foundations, Morley (1997, 122, 127) argued for critical cultural studies based on "a combination of sociological materialism, epistemological realism and methodological pragmatism." Thereby "our objective must not be to substitute one (micro or macro) level of analysis for the other, but rather to attempt to integrate the analysis of the broader questions of ideology, power and politics (... the vertical dimension of communication) with the analysis of the consumption, uses and functions of television in everyday life (the horizontal dimension ...)" (Morley 1997, 127).

Another heavyweight of the early reception studies tradition, Janice Radway, who had published in 1984 a highly influential study on the meanings of romance novels from a reader-response perspective (Radway 1984), also recently reflected upon her own research practices and their context (i.e. literary reception studies). Thereby she firmly argued for the complementarity with political economy approaches. Radway (2008, 340–1) claimed that "it might now be far riskier to tolerate the conceptual occlusions that accompany the reception paradigm and the methodological practices that follow from it than it was when reception analysis first appeared." Her anxiety stemmed from the fact that the majority of the cultural material distributed and consumed around the world comes from four or five international media conglomerates. Strangely enough, Radway (2008, 340–1) now argued for a reconsidering of the cultural imperialism thesis, given the dominance of primarily US media products, "crowding out indigenous, alternative, even avant-garde creation." Radway (2008) strikingly worried about an "ever more pervasive ideological domination, leading to the production of desiring, fluid and mobile subjects doubly functional for capital as consuming subjects."

In the work done by Ien Ang, clear signs of rapprochement can also be observed. Although her *Watching Dallas* (1985) is mostly seen as a landmark study in early reception studies, some of Ang's later work contained clear references to political economy sensitivities. *Desperately Seeking the Audience* (1991), for instance, looked at the political economy of television audience measurement as a knowledge-producing element, dealing with the institutional need to know or control their audiences behaviors, thought, and feelings. In *Living Room Wars* (1996), she more explicitly responded to the debates and to the criticism that in audiences studies not much attention had been paid to "the relation between the cultural and the economic." She (1996, 10, 12–13) suggested to "go beyond the view that attention to the 'active audience' is necessarily antagonistic to a consideration of media power," adding that the concept of the active audience is nothing less than "a condensed image of the 'disorder of things' in a post-modern world." In a postmodern consumer culture, which is based on individuation, pleasure, and consumer's sovereignty, the "discourse of choice has expanded exponentially – it is a discourse in which the rhetoric of the liberatory benefits of personal autonomy and individual self-determination has become hegemonic" (Ang 1996). Coming to another issue, which political economists take at heart, Ang (1996) concludes that in this imposed discourse on lifestyle, there seems to be no longer "restrictions to class, gender and race," while "life is defined as the ability to make an ever-increasing number of choices."

A final crucial author of the new audience research, which recently came to give more space to issues of political economy perspectives in her concept of audience, is Sonia Livingstone. Coming from a social psychology background and having worked on social and family contexts and uses of ICT, she had already recognized that "the link to political economy is crucial if ... we are to understand the differing significance of active audiences in democratic and totalitarian regimes" (Livingstone 1998, 201). In more recent work, mainly on children, young people, and the Internet, she openly criticizes the "huge, commercialized, globalised leisure industry, devoted in its sophisticated targeting of youth as the new consumer opportunity; canny in its cross-promotion of non-media consumer goods within the media domain; ever more global in its reach; keen to evade or counter hitherto-dominant ethical norms that had regarded childhood as off-limits ('private')" (Livingstone 2005b). Recognizing that "individualization is itself promoted by sophisticated marketing," she warns against the privatization of online contents and services, where these "contain difficult-to-avoid advertising," where "behind the scenes, they collect personal data on the user's every click, search and download," where "ever-younger children are drawn into a commercialised repackaging of peer, or youth, culture," and where "fandom becomes an increasingly dominant mode of engaging with popular (and even high) culture" (Livingstone 2005b). In these recent pages which could have come from a critical political economy handbook, Livingstone (2005b) puts issues such as (the practices and the imposed rhetoric of) individualization, privatization, fragmentation, commercialization, and consumer culture high on the agenda of audience research, thereby tackling the "rhetoric of the Internet as a democratic and open space of links and connections, freedom and choice." In her concept of the audience, Livingstone (2005b, 173–5) implicitly links up to the idea of plurality, where she argues that audiences have to be interpreted as consisting of four interconnected spaces, where from a critical communications perspective people should be seen in their relation to the state (as "citizens," "public," the audience as object of media education), the public sphere (audiences as active, engaged, informed, possibly resistant), the personal or intimate sphere (audiences as selective, interpretative, pleasure-seeking, creative in doing identity work), as well as the economy (audiences as commodity or market, characterized through ratings, market shares, consumerism). Critical audience study, then, should look at the intersections of these spaces.

Taking into account projects of collaboration, integration, and the acceptance of the plurality or interconnectedness of audiences, one might argue that the tension between critical parts of political economy and cultural studies research seem to have eased. Whether they have been empirically thoroughly dealt with or not, is another question, but it is clear that issues which are central to political economy approaches have clearly come on the agenda of cultural studies inspired audience researchers, and vice versa. In this context, Curran and Morley (2006, 1) recently argued that "nowadays, some of the debates that characterised this field in the 1990s … such as that between political economy and reception studies … do (happily) seem to have worn themselves out," and that the recognition of the "insights produced by these different perspectives" might be "a sign of increasing maturity – but we hope not sclerosis – in the field."

Audiences from a Political Economy Perspective

Although in the debate it was argued that political economists often forget to deal with the audience, we now examine how there has been a greater interest in the last few decades, mainly in the directions of audiences as commodity, as objects of surveillance, segmentation, and exclusion. When talking about how the media/ communications audience has been conceptualized and studied by scholars in this perspective, the point of departure and reference is the pioneering work done by Smythe (1977, 2001) and the debates following up on this. Launching a fascinating debate on the "audience as commodity," Smythe (2001) argued that the most important commodity produced by the media industry is the audience itself, which is constructed and then sold to advertisers:

> The answer to the question, what is the principal product of the commercial mass media in monopoly capitalism was simple: audience power. *This* is the concrete product which is used to accomplish the economic and political tasks which are the reason for the existence of the commercial mass media. … Because audience power is produced, purchased and consumed, it commands a price and it is a commodity. Like other "labor power" it involves "work." (Smythe 2001, 233)

Although the production of audiences is obviously far less precise than the production of manufactured goods such as automobiles and shoes, the underlying logic is essentially the same (Gandy 2002). Smythe (2001, 234) argued that advertisers buy the services of "audiences with predictable specifications which will pay attention in predictable numbers and at particular times to particular means of communication … in particular markets." The work which audience members perform for the advertiser, to whom they have been sold, is learning to buy goods and to spend their income accordingly. This is not a comfortable position from the standpoint of the audience, because it bears much heavier costs for audience members than for the advertisers: "working without pay as audience members, marketing consumers goods and services to themselves" (Smythe 2001, 239). This new perspective indicated that the primary focus no longer was on cultural meanings or on what mass media put into audiences (messages), but rather on what they take out of them (value). Media content becomes secondary, a free lunch at best. Media industries were neither dream factories nor consciousness industries: they became "hunter-gatherers of the audience" (Meehan 2002, 211).

Smythe's view initiated a debate among political economists, drawing attention to the role of the audiences. The invitation to debate was taken up by several scholars including Murdock (quoted in Meehan 2007), who replied that this analysis would only count for advertisers-supported media as opposed to public service media. Sut Jhally (1987) made an extension of Smythe's initial representation of the television audience as labor producing surplus value for capital. When the audience watches commercial television it is working for the media, producing both value and surplus value. "This is not meant as an analogy," Jhally (1987, 83) wrote, "indeed watching is an extension of factory labour, not a metaphor." The act of viewing commercials is identified as the work performed by audiences in exchange for entertainment. Writing the history of commercial television in the UK, Seaton (2003) made a quite similar analysis, stating that British commercial broadcasting produces audiences, not programs: "Advertisers, in purchasing a few seconds of television time, are actually buying viewers by the thousand. The price they pay is determined by the number of people who can be expected to be watching when their advert is shown. Hence advertisers regard programmes merely as the means by which audiences are delivered to them" (Seaton 2003, 179). Seaton (2003) illustrated this point within the context of the regional basis for commercial television, where habits and tastes of the various regional audiences became an essential feature of sales campaigns. Similar to the situation in the US, the real purpose of producing audiences for advertisers deeply affects the apparent purpose of producing programs for audience consumption (and the kinds of programs being made). When advertising promotes minority programming, it tends to be in a form that produces marketable viewers (e.g., audiences for cars and cooking). A greater choice of channels offers advertisers more refined groups of audience interests. Seaton argued that audiences with less material interests in common have been, and will continue to be, less favored.

The next logical step is segmenting the audience along demographic and psychological characteristics, the most important criterion being economic, more specifically income. Market segmentation or the practice of grouping the audience, refers to how media audiences are created, addressed, or constructed along income, gender, race, age, and other lines of segmentation and segregation. Working on the issue of commodity audience in the context of race and class segmentation, in particular segregation and discrimination in US media, Gandy (2007, 116–17) has argued "media that are targeted to African Americans are likely to be characterized by lower quality editorial content and an oversupply of advertisements for potentially harmful commodities." A common practice among advertisers is to demand a "minority discount" for accepting "lower-quality" audiences. Gandy's (2002) empirical work on ethnicity, race, and class, has far-reaching consequences. Consumer segmentation being one of the most important strategies used by commercial media and communication firms "in an effort to exercise more effective and efficient control" over the audience, Gandy (2007) forcefully maintained that the media normalized and reinforced patterns of racial and ethnic segregation.

Meehan (2005) expanded this political economy analysis of audiences in various ways, including longitudinal work on US television ratings, whereby she distinguished three interlinked markets: ratings, audiences, and programs. Turning around the classical liberal view on audiences (television gives the audience what it wants), Meehan (2005) argued that the "cybernetic audience" only exists in ratings. The three markets are mainly organized around satisfying advertisers' demands, whereby quantitatively defined ratings are taken as the measure of satisfaction. Television business is driven by the dynamics between advertisers, networks, and the ratings companies, whereby national ratings are crucial in defining the commodity audience and guiding networks and cable channels in their strategies and the decisions about the prices they charge. Ratings also lead advertisers' decisions regarding the purchase of audiences and their exposure to commercials (Meehan 2007). Not everybody, though, is part of the commodity audience. Besides the importance of income, class, and/or financial capital, leading to segmentation and segregation, Meehan (2002) also proposed to deal with the commodity audience from a feminist political economy point of view. Claiming that (US) television is structured "to discriminate against anyone outside the commodity audience of white, 18- to 34-year-old heterosexual English-speaking upscale men," Meehan (2002, 220) underlines how the "overvaluing of a male audience reflects the sexism of patriarchy."

It is only a small step from ratings and measuring audiences to ideas about monitoring, control, and consumer surveillance. We have already referred to Livingstone's arguments about children and the Internet, but political economists have developed this line of thinking often in more provocative or crude terms (Mosco 1996, Maxwell 2007). Maxwell (2000, 107), for instance, used the metaphor of a "second cold war of culture" whereby market research puts people into categories of audiences and consumers in order to extend corporate control over the infrastructure of consumption. Some even go as far as to include academic research on audiences, as a practice of "conducting surveillance for the purpose of classifying people into audiences" (Maxwell 2000, 98). In their analysis of political economy of audiences for global Hollywood, Miller et al. (2001) stressed the crucial role of marketing. Arguing that "audiences are an untamed labour force that must be domesticated for consumption," Miller et al. (2001, 182) referred to the role of film marketing as a tool for an "ever deepening surveillance of people's feelings, opinions, loves and hates in a much more intense, even righteous, quest for knowledge of the film-going experience." Miller et al. (2001) give the quite worrying example of *MovieFone*, an operation owned by AOL-Time Warner that is disguised as a phone service offering movie times, locations, and bookings, but in fact does nothing less than spying on filmgoers. The system generates personal information which the company then transforms into proprietary market research. Inspired by Smythe, Miller et al. (2001, 210) called for "a labour theory of consumption," whereby the "labour of audiences owned by market research and protected by IP laws deny the research subjects access to the very speech acts that constitute the labour of reception," and where "consumers *themselves* become the product."

Much of this analysis on film audiences is driven by a combination of methodologies, including those related to political economy (structural analysis, economic and distribution strategies), as well as textual and reception analysis. This type of research has not only been conducted on questions dealing with contemporary power relations, but also historical research has been done, often inspired by Guback's (1969) pioneering work (Wasko 2003). Although mostly not explicitly linked to political economy, film studies saw the growth of a distinctive tradition on historical film audiences in recent years. This type of critical historical work has been labeled in different directions, from historical reception studies to research on the social practice of cinemagoing and the film experience (Meers et al. 2008). One particular line of thought on film reception is linked to Staiger's (1992) work on historical materialist reception research. Using textual analysis, audience testimonies, and other sources referring to the reception of movies (e.g., film reviews), it tried to reconstruct the public discourse and reception surrounding a movie, a genre, cycle, or film author. Using this "context-activated" approach, which is clearly distinguished from "text-activated" models in film studies and "reader-activated theories" in television studies, Staiger (1992) tries to understand the historical reception and social meaning(s) of a movie, genre, or author. This includes the struggle around those meanings, negotiated by the industry, the press, censorship, religious and other interest groups. Ultimately, her research deals with the way ideologies and dominant discourses in a given historical context influence and limit the discursive horizon for the reception of a media product. Another line of critical historical reception research is associated with Jackie Stacey (1994), who investigated lived Hollywood film culture in the UK in the 1950s. In her work, Stacey distinguished how female audiences negotiated with the explicit consumer culture represented in Hollywood movies. Although the movie fans were successfully constructed as consumers, Stacey argued that they were not simply victims, as they used the products and the stars in a variety of ways. For Stacey (1994, 185), they were "subjects as well as objects of cultural exchange, in ways that are not entirely reducible to subjection."

A very particular segment of the audience, one that is probably the most exploited and continuously attached to particular media products or symbols, is the fan audience. Meehan (2000) showed how a nuanced political economy of fan audiences is a feasible enterprise, where the collaboration of fan ethnography (emphasizing viewer autonomy, pleasure, creativity) and political economy (focus on ownership, relations of production and institutional structures) can be very productive in terms of understanding the specific processes around fan media. Using the concept of leisure time to bridge the two positions, Meehan (2000) demonstrated how leisure time is a construction of dominant ideology and a cultural and economic category developed in the context of American capitalism. This contextualized account puts fandom in the ideological mainstream as opposed to descriptions of subcultural resistance from within cultural studies. Using Smythe's frame, leisure time spent working with media then becomes a necessary element of contemporary capitalism. The key example Meehan uses is Paramount's *Star Trek*. She observes how oligopolized and integrated US media markets provoke the strange effect that as long as trekkers routinely buy the product line, they can be taken for granted. Fans are used by media conglomerates as tools to recycle content across internal markets. Fans guarantee revenues across all recycling operations. In order to understand the political economy of fans, the researcher needs analytical distance. But besides this research on how subcultures relate to dominant ideology and how subcultures operate in terms of the entertainment/information sector of a capitalist economy, one also needs a closer (emic) look to understand the vision of the subculture and to see how fandom works as subcultures: "By integrating emic ethnography, etic ethnography and political economy, we will better address the actual phenomenon that we experience daily: cultural expressions packaged as media products designed to earn profits – yet capable of exciting the imaginations and of motivating individual "consumers" to create subcultural communities" (Meehan 2000, 89).

Following up on this point, it might be interesting to study more closely the discourses produced by the industry around fandom in order to lure the audience. An interesting author, who is not associated with political economy perspectives, is Hills (2002), one of the key references in fan studies. In his work, Hills has shown how marketing discourses and fan discourses work together to give cult status to a media product. In an account that rejects the romanticization of cult media and fans and speaks of a "dialectic of value," cult fandom doesn't merely "escape" or "resist" the processes of commodification. Hills underlines how these discourses also intensify – and are increasingly caught up in – these same processes. In general, political economy-inspired approaches might invest more in the analysis of corporate discursive strategies. A key issue in understanding this production of discourses deals with how concepts of consumer choice and autonomy are promoted, thus strengthening the hegemony of marketization as a central force in the media and communications landscape. The exploitation of public discourse for corporate interests is a rather undeveloped line of possible research, which also touches key questions on the public sphere and public debate. An example here is how media industries try to exploit public debate, thereby creating public events and controversies, leading sometimes to moral panic – all with the purpose of maximizing audiences and increasing sales and profits. Some reality television formats heavily invest in controversy and panic as a tool for maximizing public attention (Biltereyst 2004), but the creation of media events is, one might say, a standard practice. In our study (2006) on *The Lord of the Rings*, for instance, we tried to understand the blockbuster series as a constructed event. Distinguishing several dimensions in it, we saw the event around the blockbuster as a key connection between the product, marketing, and audiences. Public discourse management strategies had different audience-oriented purposes such as the (discursive) creation of a horizon of expectation, the promise of pleasure, spectacle, and imagination, as well as an attempt to mediate audience's movie experiences, public reception and discourses. Using empirical audience research, an analysis of distribution strategies, and of the public debate on *The Lord of the Rings*, we came to the conclusion that the blockbuster series became both a marketing event (traditional marketing initiatives) and a media event (successful attempts to get attention from and control discourses produced by the media), as well as succeeding in growing into a societal event, inspiring wider public discourses in society about the movie. A political economy-inspired perspective should then take into account the constructed character of these events, that is, the corporate strategies in terms of orchestrating an event around their media products, thereby guiding audience's expectations, imagination, and reception.

This raises the question of the concept of audience resistance and freedom, or the question of how audiences freely exert and organize resistance to institutional media power. Does this concept have a place within a political economy of audiences? Political economy perspectives have often been associated with audience's sheer rejection or at least questions about how audiences can develop negotiation or even an oppositional decoding of media content. One example of a study combining political economic contextualization and audience research, is the large-scale *Global Disney Audiences* project, led by Wasko et al. (2001). Covering 18 countries, the study combines reception analysis (questionnaires and interviews) with individual national profiles outlining Disney's marketing activities and the specific context for reception. One of the main conclusions of the project was that although a certain amount of negotiation takes place, it always happens "within the intersection of the political economy of the mediated text, the national context within which that text plays economic as well as cultural roles, the cultural practices of a society and its social units (like families) and finally individual consciousness" (Wasko and Meehan 2001, 336).

A key issue in a political economy perspective, though, remains audience access, exclusion, or the material and cultural barriers to access (Golding and Murdock 1991). A case in point is the Internet and the digital media. Although much work has been done on digital divide, cyber democracy and other ideas on building a digital commons, Murdock and Golding (2004, 245) firmly rejected "one dimensional thinking definitions," by which they mean the simplistic view on (universal) access to a computer and network. Access to the Internet, for instance, "remains highly stratified by income, age and education with substantial numbers of poorer households, elderly people and educational drop-outs facing the prospect of permanent exclusion" (Murdock 2004). Digital exclusion calls for an intensified study of hierarchies of access and differences in use, whereby Bourdieu (1984) and its critical concepts of economic, social, and cultural capitals can still be highly useful.

Conclusion

Although political economy is mostly not associated with audience research, this chapter indicated how a political economy perspective can play an important role in understanding various key issues in relation to media audiences. We considered political economy capable of delivering the necessary contextual analysis for audience studies but equally as a specific approach for analyzing audiences. We also indicated how in the 1990s sharp confrontations between "new" audience studies within cultural studies and political economy slowly turned into self-reflection, internal critique, and a refinement of the (plurality of the) audience concept. Recognizing that collaboration and integration of research approaches might be extremely useful for investigating questions on media, audiences, and power, an interesting dialogue emerged, which is essential "if we are to fully appreciate the complex phenomena collapsed into the term *media*" (Meehan 1999, 161). This intellectual cross-fertilization and interdisciplinary work among scholars who specialize in different methodologies is interesting (McChesney 2004), precisely because power is located at different levels, in ownership structures, hierarchies and political alliances of media corporations, as well as in access and reception.

This overview is most probably not exhaustive, while a great deal of work still needs to be done, both theoretically and empirically. In a broader context, more has to be done on the impact of the commercialization, marketization, privatization, and individualization of the audience, both in material and symbolic terms. One might think here of more systematic work on barriers to access and real choice, to the importance and interconnectedness of class, gender, ethnicity, or age-group. In general, more research can be done on the different registers by which audiences, consumers, or citizens are created and defined, segmented and segregated, counted, monitored, and controlled by media industries. The critical study of audiences is then, finally, about "our ability to achieve critical consciousness," which is "rooted in the intersection between the political economy in which we live, the collectivities with whom we live, the sense that we make of lived contradictions and the agency that we exercise together" (Meehan 2007, 168).

References

Alasuutari, P. (ed.) (1999) *Rethinking the Media Audience: The New Agenda*. Sage, London.
Ang, I. (1985) *Watching Dallas: Soap Opera and the Melodramatic Imagination*. Methuen, London.

Ang, I. (1991) *Desperately Seeking the Audience*. Routledge, London.

Ang, I. (1996) *Living Room Wars: Rethinking Media Audiences for a Postmodern World*. Routledge, London.

Babe, R. E. (2008) *Cultural Studies and Political Economy: Toward a New Integration*. Lexington Books, Lanham, MD.

Biltereyst, D. (1991) Resisting American hegemony: A comparative analysis of the reception of domestic and U.S. fiction. *European Journal of Communication*, 6(4), 469–97.

Biltereyst, D. (2003) Globalisation, Americanisation and politicisation of media research: Learning from a long tradition of research on the cross-cultural influences of U.S. media. *Northern Lights. Film and Television Studies Yearbook*, 3, 55–89.

Biltereyst, D. (2004) Reality TV, troublesome pictures and panics: Reappraising the public controversy around reality TV in Europe. In: Holmes, S. and Jermyn, D. (eds), *Understanding Reality Television*. Routledge, London, pp. 91–110.

Biltereyst, D. and Meers, P. (2006) Blockbusters and/as events: Distributing and launching *The Lord of the Rings*. In: Mathijs, E. (ed.), *The Lord of the Rings: Popular Culture in Global Context*. Wallflower Press, London, pp. 71–87.

Biltereyst, D., Meers, P., and Van de Vijver, L. (2011) Researching cinemas in Flanders: Combining databases and oral history accounts. In: Maltby, R., Biltereyst D., and Meers, P. (eds), *The New Cinema History: Approaches and Case Studies*. Wiley-Blackwell, Oxford.

Bourdieu, P. (1984) *Distinction: A Social Critique of the Judgement of Taste*. Routledge, London.

Calabrese, A. (2004) Toward a political economy of culture. In: Calabrese, A. and Sparks, C. (eds), *Toward a Political Economy of Culture: Capitalism and Communication in the Twenty-First Century*. Rowman & Littlefield Publishers, Boulder, CO, pp. 1–12.

Curran, J. (1990) The new revisionism in mass communication research. *European Journal of Communication*, 5(2–3), 135–64.

Curran, J. and Morley, D. (2006) Editors' introduction. In: Curran, J. and Morley, D. (eds), *Media and Cultural Theory*. Routledge, London, pp. 1–13.

Fiske, J. (1987) *Television Culture*. Methuen, London.

Gandy, O. H. (2002) The real digital divide: Citizens versus consumers. In: Lievrouw, L. and Livingstone, S. (eds), *Handbook of New Media: Social Shaping and Consequences of ICTs*. Sage, London, pp. 448–60.

Gandy, O. H. (2007) Privatization and identity: The formation of a racial class. In: Murdock, G. and Wasko, J. (eds), *Media in the Age of Marketization*. Hampton Press, Creskill, NJ, pp. 109–28.

Garnham, N. (1995) Political economy and cultural studies: Reconciliation or divorce? *Critical Studies in Mass Communication*, 12(1), 62–71.

Golding, P. and Murdock, G. (1991) Culture, communications, and political economy. In: Curran, J. and Gurevitch, M. (eds), *Mass Media and Society*. Edward Arnold, London, pp. 15–32.

Grossberg, L. (1995) Cultural studies vs. political economy: Is anybody else bored with this debate? *Critical Studies in Mass Communication*, 12(1), 72–81.

Guback, T. (1969) *The International Film Industry*. Indiana University Press, Bloomington.

Hagen, I. and Wasko, J. (2000a) Introduction: Consuming audiences? In: Hagen, I. and Wasko, J. (eds), *Consuming Audiences? Production and Reception in Media Research*. Hampton Press, Cresskill, NJ, pp. 3–28.

Hagen, I. and Wasko, J. (eds) (2000b) *Consuming Audiences? Production and Reception in Media Research*. Hampton Press, Cresskill, NJ.

Hesmondhalgh, D. (2002) *The Cultural Industries*. Sage, London.

Hills, M. (2002) *Fan Cultures*. Routledge, London.

Jhally, S. (1987) *The Codes of Advertising: Fetishism and the Political Economy of Meaning in the Consumer Society*. Routledge, London.

Kellner, D. (1997) Overcoming the divide: Cultural studies and political economy. In: Ferguson, M. and Golding, P. (eds), *Cultural Studies in Question*. Sage, London, pp. 102–19.

Kellner, D. (2002) The Frankfurt school and British cultural studies: The missed articulation. In: Nealon, J. T and Irr, C. (eds), *Rethinking the Frankfurt Legacy*. SUNY Press, New York, pp. 31–58.

Liebes, T. and Katz, E. (1990) *The Export of Meaning: Cross-cultural Readings of Dallas*. Oxford University Press, New York.

Livingstone, S. (1998) Audience research at the crossroads: The "implied audience" in media and cultural theory. *European Journal of Cultural Studies*, 1(2), 193–217.

Livingstone, S. (2005a) On the relation between audiences and publics. In: Livingstone, S. (ed.), *Audiences and Publics: When Cultural Engagement Matters for the Public Sphere*. Intellect, Bristol, pp. 17–41.

Livingstone, S. (2005b) In defense of privacy: Mediating the public/private boundary at home. In: Livingstone, S. (ed.), *Audiences and Publics: When Cultural Engagement Matters for the Public Sphere*. Intellect, Bristol, pp. 163–85.

Mattelart, M. and Mattelart, A. (1987) *Le Carnaval des Images*. Editions Anthropos, Paris.

Mattelart, M. and Mattelart, A. (1998) *Theories of Communication*. Sage, London.

Maxwell, R. (2000) Surveillance and other consuming encounters in the informational marketplace. In: Hagen, I. and Wasko, J. (eds), *Consuming Audiences? Production and Reception in Media Research*. Hampton Press, Cresskill, NJ, pp. 95–110.

Maxwell, R. (2007) Imperious measures: A Schillerian approach to global marketing research. In: Murdock, G. and Wasko, J. (eds), *Media in the Age of Marketization*. Hampton Press, Cresskill, NJ, pp. 33–48.

McChesney, R. (2004) Making a molehill out of a mountain: The sad state of political economy in U.S. media studies. In: Calabrese, A. and Sparks, C. (eds), *Toward a Political Economy of Culture: Capitalism and Communication in the Twenty-First Century*. Rowman & Littlefield Publishers, Boulder, CO, pp. 41–64.

McLaughlin, L. (1999) Beyond "separate spheres": Feminism and the cultural studies/political economy debate. *Journal of Communication Inquiry*, 23(4), 327–54.

McQuail, D. (1997) *Audience Analysis*. Sage, London.

Meehan, E. R. (1999) Commodity, culture, common sense: Media research and paradigm dialogue. *Journal of Media Economics*, 12(2), 149–63.

Meehan, E. R. (2000) Leisure or labor: Fan ethnography and political economy. In: Hagen, I. and Wasko, J. (eds), *Consuming Audiences? Production and Reception in Media Research*. Hampton Press, Cresskill, NJ, pp. 71–92.

Meehan, E. R. (2001) Culture: Text or artifact or action? *Journal of Communication Inquiry*, 25(3), 208–17.

Meehan, E. R. (2002) Gendering the commodity audience: Critical media research, feminism and political economy. In: Meehan, E. and Riordan, E. (eds), *Sex and Money:*

Feminism and Political Economy in the Media. University of Minnesota Press, Minneapolis, pp. 209–22.

Meehan, E. R. (2005) Watching television: A political economic approach. In: Wasko, J. (ed.), *A Companion to Television*. Blackwell, Malden, MA, pp. 238–55.

Meehan, E. R. (2007) Understanding how the popular becomes popular: The role of political economy in the study of popular communication. *Popular Communication*, 5(3), 161–70.

Meers, P. (2004) It's the language of film! Young audiences on Hollywood and Europe. In: Stokes, M. and Maltby, R. (eds), *Hollywood Abroad: Audiences and Cultural Relations*. British Film Institute, London, pp. 158–75.

Meers, P., Biltereyst, D., and Van de Vijver, L. (2008) Lived experiences of the "Enlightened City" (1925–1975): A large scale oral history project on cinema-going in Flanders (Belgium). *Iluminace. Journal of Film Theory, History and Aesthetics*, 20(1), 208–14.

Miller, T, Govil, N., McMurria, J., and Maxwell, R. (2001) *Global Hollywood*. British Film Institute, London.

Moores, S. (1993) *Interpreting Audiences*. Sage, London.

Morley, D. (1980) *The "Nationwide" Audience: Structure and Decoding*. British Film Institute, London.

Morley, D. (1991) Where the global meets the local: Notes from the sitting room. *Screen*, 32(1), 1–15.

Morley, D. (1997) Theoretical orthodoxies: Textualism, constructivism and the "new ethnography" in cultural studies. In: Ferguson, M. and Golding, P. (eds), *Cultural Studies in Question*. Sage, London, pp. 121–37.

Mosco, V. (1996) *The Political Economy of Communication: Rethinking and Renewal*. Sage, London.

Murdock, G. (1995) Across the great divide: Cultural analysis and the condition of democracy. *Critical Studies in Mass Communication*, 12(1), 89–94.

Murdock, G. (2000) Peculiar commodities: Audiences at large in the world of goods. In: Hagen, I. and Wasko, J. (eds), *Consuming Audiences? Production and Reception in Media Research*. Hampton Press, Cresskill, NJ, pp. 47–70.

Murdock, G. (2004) Building the digital commons. The 2004 Spry Memorial Lecture, Vancouver/Montreal, Nov. 18 and 22. Online at www.com.umontreal.ca/spry/spry-gm-lec.htm (accessed October 15, 2010).

Murdock, G. and Golding, P. (2004) Rethinking the dynamics of participation and exclusion. In: Calabrese, A. and Sparks, C. (eds), *Toward a Political Economy of Culture: Capitalism and Communication in the Twenty-First Century*. Rowman & Littlefield Publishers, Boulder, CO, pp. 244–60.

Radway, J. (1984) *Reading the Romance*. The University of North Carolina Press, Chapel Hill.

Radway, J. (2008) What's the matter with reception study? Some thoughts on the disciplinary origins, conceptual constraints, and persistent viability of a paradigm. In: Goldstein, P. and Machor, J. L. (eds), *New Directions in American Reception Studies*. Oxford University Press, Oxford, pp. 327–52.

Roach, C. (1990) The movement for a new world information and communication order: A second wave? *Media, Culture & Society*, 12, 283–307.

Schiller, H. (1991) Not yet the post-imperialist era. *Critical Studies in Mass Communication Research*, 8, 13–28.

Schiller, H. (2000) Social context of research and theory. In: Hagen, I. and Wasko, J. (eds), *Consuming Audiences? Production and Reception in Media Research*. Hampton Press, Cresskill, NJ, pp. 111–22.

Seaton, J. (2003) Broadcasting history. In: Curran, J. and Seaton, J. (eds), *Power without Responsibility: The Press and Broadcasting in Britain*. Routledge, London, pp. 109–236.

Silverstone, R. (1990) Television and everyday life: Towards an anthropology of the television audience. In: Ferguson, M. (ed.), *Public Communication: The New Imperatives*. Sage, London, pp. 173–89.

Sinclair, J. (2007) Cultural globalization and American empire. In: Murdock, G. and Wasko, J. (eds), *Media in the Age of Marketization*. Hampton Press, Creskill, NJ, pp. 131–150.

Smythe, D. W. (1977) Communications: Blindspot of western Marxism. *Canadian Journal of Political and Social Theory*, 1(3), 1–27.

Smythe, D. W. (2001 / 1981) On the audience commodity and its work. In: Durham, M. G. and Kellner, D. (eds), *Media and Cultural Studies: Key Works*. Blackwell, Malden, pp. 253–79.

Staiger, J. (1992) *Interpreting Films: Studies in the Historical Reception of American Cinema*. Princeton University Press, Princeton, NJ.

Stacey, J. (1994) *Star Gazing: Hollywood Cinema and Female Spectatorship*. Routledge, London.

Wasko, J. (2003) *How Hollywood Works*. Sage, London.

Wasko, J. and Meehan E. R. (2001) Dazzled by Disney? Ambiguity in ubiquity. In: Wasko, J., Phillips, M., and Meehan, E. R. (eds), *Dazzled by Disney? The Global Disney Audiences Project*. Leicester University Press, London, pp. 329–43.

Wasko, J., Phillips, M., and Meehan, E. R. (eds) (2001) *Dazzled by Disney? The Global Disney Audiences Project*. Leicester University Press, London.

Suggestions for Further Reading

Calabrese, A. and Sparks, C. (eds) (2004) *Toward a Political Economy of Culture: Capitalism and Communication in the Twenty-First Century*. Rowman & Littlefield Publishers, Boulder, CO.

Ferguson, M. and Golding, P. (eds) (1997) *Cultural Studies in Question*. Sage, London.

Gandy, O. H. (2003) The political economy approach: A critical challenge. In: Miller, T. (ed.), *Television: Critical Concepts in Media and Cultural Studies*. Routledge, London/ New York, pp. 1–19.

Gandy, O. H. (2004) Audiences on demand. In: Calabrese, A. and Sparks, C. (eds), *Toward a Political Economy of Culture: Capitalism and Communication in the Twenty-First Century*. Rowman & Littlefield Publishers, Boulder, CO, pp. 327–41.

Garnham, N. (1997) Political economy and the practice of cultural studies. In: Ferguson, M. and Golding, P. (eds), *Cultural Studies in Question*. Sage, London, pp. 56–73.

Gibson, T. (2000) Beyond cultural populism: Notes toward the critical ethnography of media audiences. *Journal of Communication Inquiry*, 24(3), 253–73.

Liebes, T. and Katz, E. (1986) Patterns of involvement in television fiction: A comparative analysis. *European Journal of Communication*, 1(2), 151–71.

Livingstone, S. (2004) The challenge of changing audiences: Or, what is the audience researcher to do in the age of the Internet? *European Journal of Communication*, 19(1), 75–86.

Mansell, R. (2004) Political economy, power and new media. *New Media and Society*, 6(1), 96–105.

Morley, D. (1999) "To boldly go ...": The "third generation" of reception studies. In: Alasuutari, P. (ed.), *Rethinking the Media Audience: The New Agenda*. Sage, London, pp. 195–204.

Morley, D. (2006) Globalisation and cultural imperialism reconsidered: Old questions in new guises. In: Curran, J. and Morley, D. (eds), *Media and Cultural Theory*. Routledge, London, pp. 30–43.

Mosco, V. and Kaye, L. (2000) Questioning the concept of the audience. In: Hagen, I. and Wasko, J. (eds), *Consuming Audiences? Production and Reception in Media Research*. Hampton Press, Cresskill, NJ, pp. 31–46.

Murdock, G. (2004) Past the posts: Rethinking change, retrieving critique. *European Journal of Communication*, 19(1) 19–38.

Peck, J. (2006) Why we shouldn't be bored with the political economy versus cultural studies debate. *Cultural Critique*, 64, 92–126.

Schiller, H. (1989) *Culture Inc.* Oxford University Press, New York.

Wasko, J. (2004) The political economy of communications. In: Downing, J. (ed.), *The Sage Handbook of Media Studies*. Sage, London, pp. 309–30.

20

The Political Economy of Personal Information

Oscar H. Gandy, Jr.

Introduction

Developing a political economy of personal information is a troubled project right from the start. Because its disciplinary origins are materialist, examining its character is immediately challenged by the fact that the product at its core is immaterial. Information is not tangible in its essence; it is only made tangible through a process of abstraction and symbolic representation. Information must be distinguished from the material forms in which words, images, and even more abstract formulas and mathematical expressions of its essence may be impressed and made concrete. More critically, the closer its symbolic representation gets to its essence, the closer the costs of its reproduction come to zero.

Because of information's intangibility, it is also extremely difficult to manage, control, or limit the access that others may have to it. Indeed, unlike other commodities that may be sold, or exchanged within markets, information, in its essential form, is not consumed as it is used. In general, we assume that the total stock of information available for use may actually expand each time it is used. Obviously, these characteristics make information an extremely troublesome commodity (Landes and Posner 2004).

These troubles begin with efforts to determine information's value, and to set appropriate prices. Problems in establishing value have their roots in the fact that information, at least in its essential form, has no commonly agreed upon units. It is impossible to determine, by any uniform measure, just how much information has been produced, supplied, or consumed. Although we "make do" with measures based on its symbolic representation in characters, words, paragraphs, pages, or

The Handbook of Political Economy of Communications, First Edition.
Edited by Janet Wasko, Graham Murdock, and Helena Sousa.
© 2014 John Wiley & Sons, Ltd. Published 2014 by John Wiley & Sons, Ltd.

even bits, we know that these are rather arbitrary approximations. We can easily find examples to demonstrate that more words do not necessarily convey information, or insight more completely, or effectively than fewer words. Our assessment of the ability of particular words to convey the idea, or the essence, of some facts about the world is part of the justification for establishing rights in particular expressions, but not in the facts or ideas that they make available to some of us.

This chapter is concerned with a particular kind of information: information about individuals. We refer to it as personal information (PI) because of its role in the identification, classification, and evaluation of individuals (Gandy 1993). It is used to distinguish one person from another; it is also used to compare individuals with others and to assign them to groups on the basis of attributes shared in common. As David Phillips (2004) reminds us, it is also used to enable actors with power to reach out and "touch" a specific individual. As we will see, conflicts over the legal status of this particular kind of information have earned it a special place within the political economy of information.

Theories of Value

Dominant theories of value rise and fall in response to changes in the fundamental characteristics of the economy. Understandably, a theoretical perspective that was focused on productive labor and the production of use values was important for subsistence, and later, trade-based economies. A production-oriented theory of value (Marx 1971) remained appropriate even in the context of an expanded role for trade in commodities, except that attention to the nature of the exchange values associated with markets for tangible goods became relatively more important than consideration of use values. And, as the economies of the world became increasingly shaped by the activities of service providers, it became important for economic thinkers to develop approaches to the valuation of service functions, including those associated with the production and distribution of information and knowledge (Beniger 1986, Garnham 1990, Mosco 1996, Preston 2001). This emerging emphasis on service functions helped to transform our thinking about the nature of labor power and the ways in which it might be differentiated in terms of the knowledge and skill that establish the comparative worth of information workers.

However, in the development of theory appropriate to changes in the structure of the economy, debates about the nature of productive forces failed to resolve some critical issues about resources used in the promotion of sales. Following Marx and classical economists, Paul Baran and Paul Sweezy (1966) characterized marketing and other activities that were necessary for the "realization" of surplus value as nonproductive because they did not actually contribute, or add value, to that which had been generated by industrial labor. They sought to distinguish the work of those in marketing from the work of "a menial servant" who, according to Adam Smith (1937, 314–15), "adds to the value of nothing." Indeed, in Smith's view "A man grows rich by employing a multitude of manufacturers; he grows poor, by maintaining a multitude of menial servants." Smith suggested that there were many other kinds of workers in society that should also be seen as unproductive. He noted that despite the usefulness, and even necessity of their labors, they "produce nothing for which an equal quantity of service can afterwards be procured."

It is not that Baran and Sweezy (1966, 112–41) sought to minimize the role of the "sales effort"; indeed, it was quite the opposite that they set out to establish. Unfortunately, as they noted, it was becoming increasingly difficult to distinguish between costs attributable to selling, and those attributable to the design and manufacture of commodities (Galbraith 1967). Perhaps in the wake of that realization, it seemed to make little sense for political economists to maintain the distinction between productive, and nonproductive labor (Webster 2002, 44–51). Nevertheless, some theorists continue to argue that the distinctions between the two forms of labor helped to inform us about the changing nature of capitalism (Resnick and Wolff 1987, 132–41). Even some observers from positions deep within the financial infrastructure of the US economy still hold on to the classical notion that the costs of providing financial services represents a drain, or a diversion, and ultimately a loss in profit or surplus for many investors (Bogle 2009).

Even greater complications have emerged as the transformation of capitalist economies into information or service economies has meant that the ratio of so-called unproductive to productive workers had actually exceeded 1:1 (Schiller 1988, Castells 2000). One analytic solution was to treat the labor of workers engaged in the circulation of capital (marketing and finance, etc.) as commodities that could be considered part of production. However, some active participants in the ongoing debates about the nature of the emergent post-Fordist "new economies" questioned whether the pursuit of measurement along these lines was something of a fool's mission. Nevertheless, discussions continue to surround efforts to aid the development of social and cultural capital, especially with regard to the role that public and private investment should be allowed to play. As policy discussions, these debates necessarily invite considerations of efficiency and effectiveness, and at some level, such a determination requires some kind of measurement.

Part of what remains especially challenging for this kind of policy planning and analysis is the fact that the production of a great deal of our social and cultural capital takes place in the home. The household is also the place where the reproduction of labor power is thought to occur. Unfortunately, careful analysis of investment and productivity in the household has traditionally been marginalized as being outside the scope of mainstream economic analysis. However, to the extent that the reproduction and training of consumers and citizens also takes place in the household, it seems to be even more important for us to include some analysis of this aspect of the production of value.

Unpaid Labor

Criticism of classical economic theory, especially that offered by feminists, has focused on the tendency of the mainstream to exclude consideration of labor that was unpaid, or was paid for indirectly through taxation.

There are other relationships in which unpaid labor plays an important role that should be included in any analysis of personal information. For example, marketing theorists have become increasingly explicit in their discussion of the relationship between vendors and consumers in terms of an exchange of value. The primary exchange that we are most familiar with is the one in which goods and services are exchanged against tokens of value – some monetary equivalent. We are told, however, that there is also a "second exchange," wherein consumers provide personal information as a "nonmonetary" resource in exchange for better quality goods and services, or in the expectation of some discounts on future purchases (Culnan and Bies 2003). The fact that consumers tend not to be aware of the terms of trade governing this "exchange" makes this relationship substantially different from the labor contract through which workers exchange labor power against wages.

Without question, much of the transaction-generated information (TGI) being captured regarding the citizen-consumer should be treated not only as uncompensated labor, but perhaps, even petty larceny, since it is something of value that it taken without notice or compensation. This is not to deny that there is a substantial amount of valuable information about the citizen-consumer that is freely provided to the organizations of business and government. This information is often simply volunteered in response to surveys. The underlying assumption governing this widespread form of volunteerism is a belief that by responding, the consumer is assisting in the development of better quality goods and services, including those provided by government.

On the other hand, the rather spectacular increase in the number of individuals who have refused to participate in surveys because they believe that the surveys are actually marketing scams, or simply annoyances, might lead us to underestimate the numbers of people who believe that they are acting in the public interest when they respond to these surveys. Indeed, research suggests that even without regard to what they actually might say in response to a survey, their mere participation in a survey tends to generate a positive orientation and subsequent behavior toward the firm or product identified in the questionnaire item (Sprott et al. 2006).

We might assume that marketers and others seeking to gather information from the public would be willing to offer explicit compensation to respondents for their time and energy. However, the evidence suggests that token monetary incentives do not dramatically improve the response rates. In addition, some respondents believe that is inappropriate, or unfair for researchers to pay people who initially declined to participate in order to include their responses in the shrinking pool of data. It is ironic, even if understandable, that it is the people who are the poorest, and therefore least likely to be of long-term value to marketers or political actors, who are the most likely to require a monetary incentive before they will partici-pate in a survey. In addition, because researchers often limit their offer of financial rewards to people they assume to be poor, there is good reason to think of these payments as being coercive, rather than compensatory.

It is also important to understand the special status of survey information gath-ered from a "representative sample." This is not solely, or even primarily, informa-tion about individuals. The individuals who respond to surveys are in fact surrogates or unelected representatives for the thousands of people "like them" who have not been surveyed, for one reason or another. In one sense, these unsurveyed millions are being "sensed" without their consent, and possibly against their will.

Because the Federal Trade Commission's (FTC) "Do Not Call Registry" does not limit noncommercial survey calls (Link et al. 2006), such as those by legitimate public opinion pollsters, there is still a significant amount of volunteer labor that should be included in any estimate of the cost of producing PI. That is, while there continues to be a substantial rate of decline in the willingness of individuals to participate in telephone surveys, there is still a segment of the population that is quite willing to volunteer their time and respond to a broad range of questions about knowledge, attitudes, and behavior.

Volunteering is an important source of value generation. In the United States, upwards of 28 percent of the available population over 16 donated some of their time and energy in 2001. Like unpaid household labor, the value of which may exceed 50 percent of the value of the gross domestic product (GDP) in the US, volunteer labor is not included in the calculation of GDP because it is not traded in the market-place. The Independent Sector (2008), a representative of the nonprofit sector, pro-vided estimates of the value of the time donated to nonprofit organizations at $19.51 per hour in 2007. There are, however, estimates of the economic value of this labor that range from 1.9 to 5 percent of GDP. Conservative estimates thus placed the value of this work in the US somewhere between $116 and $153 billion in 2005 (Pho 2008).

We understand that volunteers are motivated in part by a sense of community, such that they make a contribution to the commons without consideration of the maximization of personal/private interests that neoclassical economists place at the core of all rational action. As we will discuss later, many consumers of popular culture are also identified with the writers, producers, and talent whom they see as working on their behalf. As a result, many of them voluntarily contribute to the production of this content (Andrejevic 2007).

The Labor of Consumption

There is important scholarly and theoretical work being generated that has been focused on understanding the contribution being made to the market value of commodities by the consumers who try to incorporate them into their lives. This is work that extends the insights developed by Dallas Smythe regarding the work for capital that we do when watching television (Smythe 1977), or in consuming other cultural materials (Arvidsson 2004, Bermejo 2007). Contemporary research and theory has moved beyond Smythe's initial focus on making sense of commercials and representations of consumption to examine the value in commercial brands that is created jointly by marketers and the consumers they target (Foster 2007, Zwick et al. 2008).

Paying attention to consumers in order to capture and make sense of the TGI being generated as they make their way through environments filled with sensors has become a growth industry. In the new economy, "the integration of advertising, marketing research, point-of-sale devices, and just-in-time inventory control makes the monitoring of the consumer as integral to the production cycle as that of the worker. Work, school, and domesticity are re-formed into a single, integrated constellation" (Dyer-Witheford 1999, 81).

Ironically, many consumers reportedly pay higher prices for the commodities that they have been most actively involved in developing for the market. Their assistance in enabling a commodity to become distinguished as a unique and valuable brand allows its providers to charge a higher price to reflect its separation from the commonplace (Arvidsson 2005). Because of this work, we are coming to understand the "brand" as a representation of an aspect of a product or commodity that is associated with a kind of transformation. Because this transformation is informational, it is immaterial in its essence. Adam Arvidsson (2005, 237) has referred to the kind of premium that consumers pay for identification with a product that has been distinguished in this way as an "ethical surplus." A ready example can be seen in the elevated prices that consumers of Apple-branded products seem quite willing to pay.

Unfortunately, estimates of the value of brands depend upon highly unreliable forecasts of future income streams based on competitive advantages that branded commodities expect to realize in the market. These future streams are not truly predictable as the next competitor is always just around the corner. There is also no direct way of estimating the present value that brands represent to the average consumer, or more critically, their cumulated value across local markets.

There is also considerable theoretical difficulty involved in clarifying just how the collapsing of the production, distribution, circulation, and realization stages of the circuits of capital actually take place in the context of a rapidly changing global economic system. While these difficulties have been noted in earlier debates about the nature of the "information economy," they have not been resolved in the context of what we have been encountering in a much-transformed financial sector (Stiglitz 2009).

Information about consumers is essential for the operation of the high velocity markets enabled by the Internet. Marketers would like to be aware of the continually changing relationship of their customers to their products, as well as to the products of their competitors. They are also interested in knowing how their customers behave as they navigate the Internet environment. Behavioral tracking allows sophisticated marketers to segment, target, and dynamically "tailor" content, special offers, and "bargain" prices for consumers in cyberspace "on the fly." Firms engaged in e-commerce also desire to be informed about changes in their customers' financial, social, and emotional status. This kind of "total information awareness" is thought to be necessary in order to know not only what to say, but when to say it to a potential customer. The dynamic nature of Internet commerce allows marketers at least conceptually, to move beyond gross segmentation by demographic group toward more individualized marketing (Turow 2006).

The Valuation and Pricing of Intangibles

Marxian contributions to our thinking about the value of information commodities have not been impressive. This is due in part to the circularity of the labor theory of value, wherein the value of a commodity is determined by the amount of socially necessary labor used up in its production (Caffentzis 2005). Because in its reproduction, and later in its distribution, information is nearly costless, the determination of its value in a continually expanding global market is nothing short of impossible. Neoclassical efforts have not done much better (Hausman 1992, Reder 1999). We are told that we are being myopic when we treat the price, or the exchange value of a commodity, as its true value (Angelis 2005). The reasons are complex, and especially so with regard to information goods and services.

Information is an economic good, but as with other intangible goods, it is difficult to determine its value, in part because its market price bears no necessary relationship to its cost of production. This is due, in part, to the fact that more often than not the price being paid is for the packaging, rather than the product. As we noted earlier, the information is not the same as the symbolic resource used to convey or express it. It is certainly not the same as the material resource that makes it relatively permanent, suitable for storage and transport. The information at issue is distinct from the tangible markers, such as the books, discs, or even digital databases that are used to store, transmit, or otherwise provide access to users.

In addition to its intangible nature, the ease with which information can be copied, reproduced, and shared with others makes its market value quite unstable. Copyright and other forms of "intellectual property" law, which includes the somewhat draconian attempt to impose criminal liability on sophisticates who might attempt to "circumvent" technical safeguards against unauthorized copying, still appear to be incapable of controlling this troublesome feature of the information commodity (National Research Council 2000). The fact that the Internet facilitates the redistribution of unauthorized copies across the globe with a single click further disrupts any meaningful relationship between market price and value for information.

The difficulty of barring nonpayers from gaining access to information is not the only challenge to the market's role in associating a commodity's value with its price. The production and consumption of information goods are marked by substantial externalities, or impacts on individuals not party to these transactions. Externalities, depending upon whether they are positive or negative, mean that the market price will always depart from the true social value or cost, because producers won't pay for value they can't capture. For a somewhat different reason, producers understand that they can't be held responsible for harm that is caused to others with whom they had no financial relationship (Baker 2002). What this means is that information goods that would generate substantial positive externalities or social benefits are undersupplied; and those that generate negative externalities, like global warming or pollution, are produced and consumed in excess. Examples of cultural pollution are easily identified or imagined.

Again, this doesn't mean that intangibles like information are so troublesome that they are simply not produced for the market. Nothing could be further from the truth. In the view of some, intangible assets have replaced traditional fixed assets as the basis for determining a firm's competitive status and market value. These intangibles are not considered to be a distinct factor of production in the same way that land, machinery, and labor are, yet there is no doubt that they are a necessary component of the realization of profit or surplus value. Although most of the intangibles that contribute to profitability and competitive advantage are generated within the organization, it is also possible to acquire these resources in the market as products and services.

However, once again, despite the presumed importance of intangibles, such as information, knowledge, and reputation, there is little agreement over how best to define, measure, and assign value to these assets. It is not at all clear that a return on investments in accumulating this form of capital can be easily identified, although it is quite common for firms to assign and make claims regarding the economic value of these assets when the value of a firm is determined in part by its value in the stock market (Cummins 2004).

Three approaches are commonly taken in the valuation of intangibles like databases that are owned or controlled by corporations. A traditional cost-accounting approach links a resource's value to the resources expended in developing or producing it. However, as we have already noted with regard to markets in knowledge and information, the costs of production have no necessary relationship to the value of the resource in the marketplace. Alternatively, the value of the resource can be estimated in relation to the income that it is expected to generate over its lifetime of use. Of course, the accuracy of future income projections is not very impressive. The most common approach to the valuation of corporate intangibles is one that bases estimates of value on the prices or values established for similar resources in the market. Of course, here too, the absence of appropriate comparisons and reliable data generate problems in the establishment of comparable worth. Although the crisis in the mortgage markets that emerged in 2007 certainly raised questions about the reliability of estimates of "fair market value," this method tends to be treated as an "objective" means of valuation.

Among the attributes of intangible assets that generate the most difficulty for firms and their accountants is the expectation that a particular asset has a legal status that includes ownership and the ability to transfer that ownership to a third party. The ownership of personal information about their customers or marketing targets is among the most difficult ownership claims for a company to make.

The Valuation of Personal Information

Estimating the value of PI is difficult for the same reasons that estimating the value of information goods in general is troublesome. However, unlike books, records, and films that can be marketed in units that can be individually priced, there are no standard units of PI that are uniform, or have reliably predictable prices. However, there are different categories of information about individuals that have been associated with prices or bulk rates, based on the perceived value to users.

The problems that consumers face in assigning appropriate value to PI is that its value is generally not reflected in each "unit" of information. The value of PI as an adjunct to marketplace discrimination is realized primarily in combination with other information. By itself, no single bit or unit of PI is necessarily important. Of course, there may be an accumulation in value as each additional bit completes the picture or profile of a consumer in a way that makes the identification, and classification of the individual possible. What matters most, however, is the bit of information that is the key, or the missing link that provides the clue that solves the puzzle of identification in a way that conveys short-term competitive advantage. In one sense, the additional value of each additional bit of TGI is akin to the notion of cumulation within the concept of marginal productivity, or marginal returns to scale. The contribution from each bit may be quite near, if not precisely zero. However, because of the nature of the complex systems in which increments in information play a role, there is likely to be a dramatic change of state, marking the take-off point from which there would be a rapid advance toward a solution, or a decision.

It is highly unlikely that any individual would know which bit of PI is the most valuable in this regard, because the individual citizen-consumer has no knowledge of the complex analytics that will generate the profile or the decision (Elmer 2004). It is not the total or outcome that is produced by cumulation, or even compounding, but by rather dramatic increases in "knowledge" about the consumer that is generated over time. Indeed, in terms of most analytical systems, it is likely to be information about numerous other individuals whose profiles actually contribute to any marked improvements in the models used to identify and evaluate individuals or market segments. Assigning value to individual bits of information in this kind of environment seems hopeless.

Customer or prospect lists acquired in the database market have prices assigned, and those prices reflect both scarcity and expected value of the PI (Novek et al. 1990). The value is not associated with specific information about an individual, although there are vendors within the market with price lists for information such as "mother's maiden name," or social security number, because of the special value of this information as marks of distinction. Most of the PI is sold on the basis of information that facilitates the characterization of an individual as a member of a valued segment.

Users of presegmented lists are interested in being able to reach people who are Democrats, or who are immigrants, or who are regular voters, or who frequently donate to charities. Consumers are able to request the development of a list of people, with their contact information, who fit a number of specified categories: a list of all the people in the following zip codes, with household incomes above $125,000, who have contributed at least $250 to the Republican party, and have voted in the past three elections. While they may pay a little more to exclude African Americans from that list, such a list wouldn't have that many in the first place.

Firms acquire and develop analytical techniques to help them determine the relative value of the customers already in their own databases (Danna and Gandy 2002, Banasiewicz 2004). These are important determinations because of the fact that investments in the acquisition of new customers often does not return as much to the bottom line as investments in identifying the individuals within a database already determined to represent the segment with the highest long-term value. This long-term value tends to be associated with commitment to the brand, as well as to a category of goods and services. Analytic resources are routinely applied to the segmentation of consumers into value groups based on the extent to which high brand loyalty is combined with a propensity to consume that can be achieved at minimum marketing cost.

Ideally, marketers seek to identify a particular "type" of consumer to pursue, while ignoring, or even "firing" the others. Loyalty programs are just one of the many ways in which marketers provide rewards for good behavior to the consumers they would like to retain (Yi and Jeon 2003). Loyalty programs are designed to decrease the length of time in which a strong, reliable relationship between consumers and the providers of branded goods and services could be expected to develop. Research evidence suggests that loyalty programs lead their members to perceive that they are receiving a higher level of service than they actually might for the prices they face (Bolton et al. 2000). This is akin to the tendency of community members, and members of groups with which they identify, to give individuals and institutions within that community the "benefit of the doubt" when questions about performance arise.

Understanding the nature of these markets requires identifying the variety of users and uses to which PI will be of value. Researchers use surveys and experiments in an effort to estimate the value that people put on information about them. Recent efforts have focused on the difficulty firms face in estimating the value that people place on keeping their locations private. This is of particular importance for firms offering location-aware services. Although the market for information about the location of individuals in motion has yet to reach its take-off point, considerable progress has already been made in transforming information about more permanent residential location for use in geodemographic segmentation and targeting (Burrows and Gane 2006).

Estimating the Value of PI at its Origin

The markets for personal information do not provide accurate information about the value that consumers place on their TGI, or their desire to preserve or control its distribution. The reason we have inaccurate estimates of the value that people place on their ability to control access to and use of PI is that the markets for PI are like the markets for lemons, or faulty products, where consumers are ill-informed, and predators are unregulated. Eventually, the lemons tend to push legitimate quality products and vendors out of the market.

The problems of assessing the value of PI are substantial, but because the costs associated with a loss of control are difficult to assess, and are assumed to be small, people therefore tend to conclude that it is not worth the costs of taking legal action to address wrongful use. People seem to be more concerned about the disclosure of PI to the extent that they believe they are "different" from the "average person." Being different increases the risk of discrimination. It is not clear, however, whether public resistance to price discrimination is primarily personal, or is generalized through a sense of unfairness. Because price discrimination functions in part on the basis of accumulated TGI, consumers who are able to make purchases behind a screen of anonymity or pseudonymity may be able to avoid or at least minimize this risk.

People will expend resources to limit the distribution of information about them to the extent that the information could readily support actions harmful to them. Mainstream economic theory suggests that we can assign value to that information on the basis of the value of the resources they will expend to limit or control access to that information. It is frequently suggested that consumers must obviously place little value on their PI because they tend not to invest very much in the way of time or money to protect it through the use of privacy-enhancing technologies (PETs) or commercial services designed to protect them against aligned threats.

We are reminded that consumers will invest in other "self-defense" systems, such as locks and passwords. It is true that nearly all of the commercial firms that have attempted to serve this particular consumer market have failed. This apparent reluctance on the part of consumers to invest in limiting access to PI is especially difficult to understand in the context of rising costs associated with identity theft (Cole and Pontell 2006). Estimates from 2006 place the total losses for some 8.4 million US consumers at around $49 billion, averaging nearly $6,000 per victim of identity theft (Schreft 2007). Of course, because it is so easy to gather the kind of PI that makes identity theft possible, and because it is so difficult to prevent it, there are few attractive options in the market at this time (Camp 2006). Most of the services provide assistance to victims only after the fact. And while there is a market for insurance that might cover losses due to identity theft, the coverage is quite limited, especially with regard to losses due to fraud. Once again, it appears that consumers tend to "discount" or minimize their estimates of the consequences of failing to protect the privacy of their PI.

Because part of the cost or value that consumers should associate with TGI is based on the risks they face if the information is disclosed to others, it seems likely that consumers underestimate these risks (Solove 2004). This is due to more than the fact that most of us are not equipped to estimate probabilities or evaluate risk very well. In large part, it is because we are largely ignorant about the hazards associated with the use of TGI. It is extremely difficult for individuals to discover how, and with what consequences, their PI has been used to their disadvantage.

Consumers are also limited in their ability to imagine how any bit of information about them might be used in the future in ways that might harm or disadvantage them. As Daniel Solove (2004, 88) suggests:

> a person who signs up for a discount supermarket shopper card may have some vague knowledge that her personal information will be collected. In the abstract, this knowledge may not be all that disconcerting. But what if the person were told that information about the contraceptives and over-the-counter medications she buys would be made available to her employer? …Without being informed about how the information will be used, the individual lacks the necessary knowledge to assess the implications of surrendering her personal data.

Consider the case of genetic information. Because of concerns about the ways in which genetic information can be used to support discrimination by employers and insurance companies, the US government finally passed a bill to bar some forms of genetic discrimination (Harmon 2008a). Yet fear among some members of the public remains palpable. Because they believe that progress in genetic research is being held back by this fear, a group of volunteers have lent their support to a Personal Genome Project, a Harvard University project designed to challenge the view that genetic information should be kept secret. But even here, appreciation of the high-risk nature of a decision to release one's genetic map to the general public is reflected in a determination by the project that only individuals with the "equivalent of a masters degree in genetics" will be allowed to participate (Harmon 2008b). That seems like a pretty high platform upon which to build a consumer market based on trust.

It's not that consumers don't care about the capture and strategic misuse of their PI. Consider new services that rely on locational information. A person's location, captured by the cell phone or GPS device, will be of value to restaurants and service establishments that would offer services, perhaps with discounts, when appropriately identified individuals enter their zone. In addition to not wanting to be marketed to, some individuals may not want to generate an accessible record of their location, especially if they want to claim that they have been in the library all evening studying, rather than in a part of town known for its offer of "life in the fast lane."

People do tend to respond negatively when they read about some business that has engaged in price discrimination on the basis of captured TGI or other PI, but they fail to associate this kind of capture with the risks they face in their own trans-actions, including their online searching behavior. For this reason, it is quite rare that consumers can identify a personal experience with price discrimination or other privacy-related losses. If they do, they are rarely able to associate that loss with any particular transaction or search.

Consumer awareness of the role that TGI plays in support of price, service, and quality discrimination is low, in part because much of the PI used within the ana-lytical software has been acquired from, or combined with information sold by brokers and consolidators that package information from public sources.

Negative Value, or Consumer Sensitivity

While market prices can be used to infer something about the value that firms place on gathering information about consumers, there is no comparable way to estimate the value that consumers place on keeping information about themselves private, or at least, not readily available to the organizations with which they do business. This is a concern about the ways in which firms use PI as an aid to price discrimination.

People seem not to be so concerned that other people may know or learn some-thing about them. They are far more concerned about the extent to which people can use what they know in ways that will harm or disadvantage them. A high pro-portion of Internet-savvy consumers think that it should be against the law for e-commerce sites to collect and use information about their search and purchase behavior. They also think that price discrimination should be against the law. For these reasons, anxiety about the amount of TGI that information service providers like Google have accumulated has increased. There are additional concerns about how easily that information can be accessed by government or corporate investigators.

Personal information supports price discrimination in ways that enhance profit. Because of the near zero marginal cost of reproduction for information goods, there is an especially strong pressure for firms in these markets to engage in price discrimination in an effort to maximize the capture of surplus in the short term. Information about consumers helps marketers establish prices that are as near as possible to the consumers' reservation prices (Chan and Yuan 2007). Consumers would prefer to avoid that kind of discrimination. Technology that facilitates the collection and processing of this kind of information, especially when the information is gathered without the knowledge of the data subject, is more highly valued than technology that might warn a potential consumer about the dangers of price discrimination.

Orthodox economic theory would suggest that markets, the perfectly competitive kind that none of us have ever seen, would ensure that the maximally efficient amount of personal information would always circulate freely. Presumably, this market would distinguish between types of information and its value to consumers, as well as its value to the persons being identified who might wish that it not be disclosed or shared.

Willingness to Pay as a Source of Valuation

For such a market to operate efficiently, the economics of personal information would have to identify and price the various "identities" that individuals maintain. There are distinctions between the identities that people seek to maintain when they are at work, and those that they bring into play at home, in the neighborhood, and in their political lives. These distinctions also include those that people seek to maintain between their online and offline identities or personae. This is a problem that has been addressed to some degree by means of surveys designed to enable "contingent valuation" (Hanemann 1994). While people are usually asked what is the most they would pay to have some resource, we also need to consider whether this is the same as asking what people would pay not to lose something they have, such as control over their personal information.

Although mainstream economists suggest that the value of personal information to the individual it refers to would be captured entirely by the value of what they will sell or exchange it for, critics suggest that individuals would tend to underestimate its true value. Consumers cannot reliably estimate the "expected negative utility" or costs they might face if the vendor/agent mishandles the information, doesn't secure it, trades it or sells it, or uses it to their disadvantage. This kind of "moral hazard" is real, and we should assume that its scope is extensive.

An especially central aspect of the economics of personal information has to do with the nature of one's reputation. Lior Strahilevitz (2007) suggests that there is an emergent "reputation revolution" occasioned by the ready availability of information about individuals. This is referred to as the "reputation market." Observers of this market have noted the importance of seller ratings in the online auction market eBay (Josang et al. 2007). Researchers find a not surprising result: prices charged are positively associated with the reputation of the vendor. The value of reputations is shaped not only by the actions of the agent, but also by the responses of those with whom the agent interacts. In some reputation systems, such as that reflected in Google Page Ranks, there is a bias toward agents who are popular with other popular agents. The high quality, but unknown, information sources earn very poor ratings within this kind of system, and there is very little that they can do about it.

Credit scores are also part of this market, and arguably, the existence of this form of PI has enabled the expansion of a variety of markets that depend upon the extension of credit (Mester 1997, Foust and Pressman 2008). Of course, the recent global credit crisis suggests that not all participants in the real estate market were really as concerned about the "creditworthiness" of individuals in search of financing as they were before the market value of homes escalated at historic rates. Consumers who might be willing to have these "scores" used to determine whether they would be a good candidate for a loan, might not be as willing to have the same score used as a filter in determining whether they could acquire automobile insurance, rent an apartment, or compete for a job, but there has been a historic tendency for such measures to become normalized as an index of "trustworthiness" (Marron 2007).

The Capture of PI

Part of the difficulty in establishing markets in personal information is based on the difficulty that entities face in establishing and enforcing property rights in intangible goods like information. And part of the difficulty in assigning ownership rights to PI is to be seen in the fact that individuals generate information about themselves through behaviors rarely thought of as labor, and certainly not under any contract or agreement. Most of the PI that is routinely and automatically gathered each day is accumulated without attracting the attention, notice, or consent of the individual. Property rights in PI are of little value to consumers in that corporate actors have many ways to compel disclosure of that information. Even more troublesome, monopoly firms can compel disclosure at no cost to them. They are also able to gain access to information that has been collected by the government – this is information that individuals can rarely refuse to supply, and they have almost no ability to limit its disclosure.

Users of information systems generate all sorts of transaction-generated information (TGI) simply through their use of a search engine like Google (Andrejevic 2007). The fact that Google continues to increase the number and variety of systems that capture PI only adds to the use value that the accumulated data represent (Zimmer 2008). The point is made by Gregory Conti (2006), a military computer security specialist, who reminds us that Internet services are not free, they are financed by micropayments in the form of PI that is captured with each transaction or query. The widespread use of "spyware" is another example of the limitations on the ability of most individuals to avoid the capture and use of PI.

Consumers value their privacy, and are concerned about the capture and sale of TGI by business. It is important to understand that the capture and sale of TGI generates harm by supporting discrimination in markets in ways that capture consumer surplus.

Unfortunately, consumers' assignment of value to their own information has to be tempered in light of the tendency of the courts to deny any reasonable expectation of privacy or control over information that they have "voluntarily" shared with some third party (Solove and Hoofnagle 2006). The fact that it is nearly impossible to engage in electronically mediated transactions without relying on third-party intermediaries is simply not taken into account by the authorities.

Markets in Personal Information

Because the value of PI to the data subject is so difficult to establish, the best alternative is to estimate its value for the organizations that gather and process PI for the market. An early study of this market noted that prices varied with the social status and wealth of the names within a list, or "package" of names (Novek et al. 1990). In the midst of the most dramatic financial crisis in recent memory, predatory lenders could acquire a list of subprime borrowers who were behind in their payments for around $5 a name (Stone 2008).

The data brokerage industry has expanded rapidly since the mid-1990s. Its growth has been enabled in part by the development of a commercially accessible telecommunications network, as well as more efficient techniques for searching multiple databases. Following the terrorist attacks in 2001, law enforcement agencies added to the demand for PI from public and private sources. The data brokerage industry grew rapidly in response to this elevated demand.

Government and private corporations have come to depend upon a thriving network of data brokers who supply detailed dossiers on virtually every adult in the United States (O'Harrow 2005). While the government services market is a relatively small share of the billions in annual revenue derived from the sales of identification and classification services, this business has increased substantially following the terrorist attacks in 2001. One of the leaders in this industry is Acxiom, a corporate name largely invisible to the average person who has been identified, classified, and evaluated by the firm (Behar 2004).

The most infamous of these brokers is ChoicePoint, a rapidly evolving conglomerate that became the subject of public attention because of a massive security breach exposing private financial information about some 163,000 consumers. This breach was so serious that the Federal Trade Commission (FTC) assessed the largest civil penalty ($10 million) in the agency's history, and demanded substantial improvement in the firm's efforts to protect consumer privacy. Somewhat less publicity was generated when a ChoicePoint subsidiary was identified as being responsible for errors in its database that resulted in hundreds of voters, primarily African Americans, being identified as convicted felons, and thereby denied the right to vote in the 2000 presidential election in Florida (O'Harrow 2005).

The providers of these consumer intelligence services suggest that they have developed a highly reliable set of "triggers" or indicators of changes in consumer status that help them to predict the kinds of options an individual is more likely to respond to. For example, Equifax, one of three major credit bureaus in the US, offered a cross-selling resource that would routinely notify its customers of opportunities for selling new financial products to existing customers on the basis of 30 event and predictive triggers. One such trigger promised to identify individuals who were likely to consolidate a student loan within the next 90 days (Equifax 2008). TransUnion, an Equifax competitor, uses consumer event triggers and predictive modeling to assist debt collectors in determining when the possibility of collection is highest, and adds value to those predictions by noting where the debtor is likely to be found (Business Wire 2006).

We readily understand the concern about the costs generated by false information being distributed by data brokers and service agencies. There is less consideration about the social and economic costs that flow from the distribution of correct, but incomplete or readily misinterpreted, information. This includes information that supports discriminatory exclusions from markets and opportunities.

On the basis of revenue reported for 2005, ChoicePoint earned in excess of $400 million for information provided to insurance companies, another $380 million to business service organizations, somewhat less to government agencies ($140 million), and a still respectable base among marketing services earning $91 million. Their earnings reportedly exceeded $982 million in 2007. Information vendor Reed Elsevier acquired the company for $4.1 billion in 2008 (Reed Elsevier 2008). Although it is believed to be quite substantial, the size of the market in PI is nearly impossible to estimate, in part because such a large part of the market is illegal, and therefore not reported in routine economic surveys (Wall 2007).

The same techniques that have been applied to the segmentation and targeting of consumers on behalf of commercial marketers has been brought to bear in the market for voters and campaign contributors. In the context of the new media, and the updated and automated old media of targeted telephone calls, we find the list vendors supplying resources that enable "narrowcasting" with great precision. Voter profiling with the aid of readily accessed voter lists that are then enhanced with additional data from public and private sources has become something of a cottage industry. Some 22 states allow unrestricted access to voter lists, and there are almost no limitations on their use for political purposes. There are few barriers, and many database marketers allow subscribers to acquire tailor-made voters lists online. In comparison with the prices charged for consumer lists, voter lists are relatively inexpensive. This is explained in part by the fact that voter lists are public records, whereas enhanced lists that include information about donations, magazine subscriptions, and past purchases are proprietary. The prices reflect the relative scarcity of the information.

Within the political arena, just as in traditional marketing for consumer goods, narrowcasting is designed to take advantage of more highly detailed information about individuals in order to create and deliver specially tailored appeals. These communications efforts tend to be focused on those determined to be most likely to act appropriately, although strategic manipulation of the attitudes of those identified as undecided or malleable is also enhanced by the use of newer databases. Of particular concern is the tendency for targeted communications to avoid or bypass those citizens most in need of mobilization.

Tomorrow's Market

Mark Andrejevik (2007) includes Google among the leading firms acting to realize a form of digital enclosure in which constant surveillance will enable the increasingly efficient incorporation of citizen-consumers as active participants in the design and continual adjustment of the environments into which they move. It is Google's single-minded determination to know, indeed to anticipate, what information each and every one of us might need, even if we don't know it at the time, that represents the most serious challenge we face in trying to understand the political economy of personal information (Battelle 2005). Google and its competitors intend to disrupt, and perhaps destroy forever, any expectation of ownership and control over information – any information. Its business plan is certain to change in order to accommodate the global supply of information and deliver it upon demand without marginal, and perhaps even without subliminal or embedded, advertising. The secondary exchange of our TGI may be enough to meet Google's needs.

Yet, despite the promise of providing affordable access to whatever information each of us thinks we need, I still fully expect that the vast amount of information about us will enable those with the interest and the capacity to do so to actually limit the opportunities available to us to become the kinds of people we've admired. Google's success will make it especially difficult to become the kind of person who believes that there is value in having private moments in thought and in communication with others in whom we have placed our trust.

References

Andrejevic, M. (2007) *iSpy: Surveillance and Power in the Interactive Era*. University Press of Kansas, Lawrence.

Angelis, M. D. (2005) Value(s), measure(s) and disciplinary markets. *The Commoner*, 10, 66–86.

Arvidsson, A. (2004) On the "pre-history of the panoptic sort," mobility in market research. *Surveillance & Society*, 1(4), 456–74.

Arvidsson, A. (2005) Brands: A critical perspective. *Journal of Consumer Culture*, 5(2), 235–58.

Baker, C. E. (2002) *Media, Markets and Democracy*. Cambridge University Press, New York.

Banasiewicz, A. (2004) Acquiring high value, retainable customers. *Journal of Database Marketing & Customer Strategy Management*, 12(1), 21–31.

Baran, P. and Sweezy, P. (1966). *Monopoly Capital: An Essay on the American Economic and Social Order*. Monthly Review Press, New York.

Battelle, J. (2005) *The Search: How Google and its Rivals Rewrote the Rules of Business and Transformed Our Culture*. Penguin Portfolio, New York.

Behar, R. (2004) Never heard of Acxiom? Chances are it's heard of you. How a little known Little Rock company – the largest processor of consumer data – found itself at the center of a very big national security debate. *Fortune*, February 23. Online at money.cnn.com/magazines/fortune/fortune_archive/2004/02/23/362182/index.htm (accessed October 15, 2010).

Beniger, J. (1986) *The Control Revolution: Technological and Economic Origins of the Information Society*. Harvard University Press, Cambridge, MA.

Bermejo, F. (2007) *The Internet Audience: Constitution and Measurement*. Peter Lang, New York.

Bogle, J. C. (2007) Enough. Commencement Address, Georgetown University. Washington, DC. Online at www.scribd.com/doc/201226/Enough-Commencement-Address-John-C-Bogle-Founder-Vanguard-Group (accessed October 15, 2010).

Bolton, R., Kannan, P., and Bramlett, M. (2000) Implications of loyalty program membership and service experiences for customer retention and value. *Journal of the Academy of Marketing Science*, 28(1), 95–108.

Burrows, R. and Gane, N. (2006) Geodemographics, software and class. *Sociology*, 40(5), 793–812.

Business Wire (2006) TransUnion showcases how a triggers platform can deliver results in the collections arena. Online at www.tmcnet.com/usubmit/-transunion-showcases-how-triggers-platform-deliver-results-the-/2006/03/16/1465311.htm (accessed October 15, 2010).

Caffentzis, G. (2005) Immeasurable value? An essay on Marx's legacy. *The Commoner*, 10, 87–114.

Camp, L. J. (2006) The state of economics of information security. *I/S: A Journal of Law and Policy*, 2(2), 189–205.

Castells, M. (2000) *The Rise of the Network Society*. Blackwell, Malden, MA.

Chan, W. and Yuan, S.T. (2007). An overview of information goods pricing. *International Journal of Electronic Business*, 5(3), 294–314.

Cole, S. and Pontell, H. (2006) "Don't be low hanging fruit": Identity theft as moral panic. In: T. Monahan (ed.), *Surveillance and Security: Technological Politics and Power in Everyday Life*. Routledge, New York, pp. 125–47.

Conti, G. (2006). Googling considered harmful. *New Security Paradigms Workshop*. Schloss Dagstuhl, Germany. Online at www.rumint.org/gregconti/publications/20061101_NSPW_Googling_Conti_Final.pdf (accessed October 15, 2010).

Culnan, M. and Bies, R. (2003) Consumer privacy: Balancing economic and justice considerations. *Journal of Social Issues*, 59(2), 323–42.

Cummins, J. (2004) A new approach to the valuation of intangible capital. Board of Governors of the Federal Reserve System. Abstract online at papers.ssrn.com/sol3/papers.cfm?abstract_id=559461 (accessed October 15, 2010).

Danna, A. and Gandy, O. (2002) All that glitters is not gold: Digging beneath the surface of data mining. *Journal of Business Ethics*, 40, 373–86.

Dyer-Witheford, N. (1999) *Cyber-Marx: Circles and Circuits of Struggle in High-Technology Capitalism*. University of Illinois Press, Urbana.

Elmer, G. (2004) *Profiling Machines*. The MIT Press, Cambridge, MA.

Equifax Corporation (2008) TargetPoint Cross-Sell: Service description. Online at http://www.equifaxmarketingservices.com/pdfs/TargetPoint-Cross-Sell-F06.pdf (accessed October 15, 2010).

Foster, R. J. (2007) The work of the new economy: Consumers, brands, and value creation. *Cultural Anthropology*, 22(4), 707–31.

Foust, D. and Pressman, A. (2008) Credit score: Not-so-magic numbers. *Business Week*. Online at http://www.businessweek.com/magazine/content/08_07/b4071038384407.htm (accessed October 15, 2010).

Galbraith, J. K. (1967) *The New Industrial State*. New American Library, New York.

Gandy, O. H. (1993) *The Panoptic Sort: A Political Economy of Personal Information*. Westview, Boulder, CO.

Garnham, N. (1990) *Capitalism and Communication: Global Culture and the Economics of Information*. Sage, London.

Hanemann, W. M. (1994) Valuing the environment through contingent valuation. *The Journal of Economic Perspectives*, 8(4), 19–43.

Harmon, A. (2008a). Congress passes bill to bar bias based on genes. *The New York Times*. Online at http://www.nytimes.com/2008/05/02/health/policy/02gene.html? (accessed October 15, 2010).

Harmon, A. (2008b) Taking a peek at the experts' genetic secrets. *The New York Times*. Online at http://www.nytimes.com/2008/10/20/us/20gene.html? (accessed October 15, 2010).

Hausman, D. (1992) *The Inexact and Separate Science of Economics*. Cambridge University Press, New York.

Independent Sector (2008) Value of volunteer time. Online at: http://www.independentsector.org/programs/research/volunteer_time.html#value (accessed October 15, 2010).

Josang, A., Ismail, R., and Boyd, C. (2007) A survey of trust and reputation systems for online service provision. *Decision Support Systems*, 43(2), 618–44.

Landes, W. and Posner, R. (2004) *The Political Economy of Intellectual Property Law*. The AEI Press, Washington, DC.

Link, M., Ali, M., Kulp, D., and Hyton, A. (2006) Has the National Do Not Call Registry helped or hurt state-level response rates? A time series analysis. *Public Opinion Quarterly*, 70(5), 794–809.

Marron, D. (2007) "Lending by numbers," credit scoring and the constitution of risk within American consumer credit. *Economy and Society*, 36(1), 103–33.

Marx, K. (1971) *Value, Price and Profit*. International Publishers, New York.

Mester, L. (1997) What's the point of credit scoring? *Business Review* (September/October), 3–16.

Mosco, V. (1996) *The Political Economy of Communication*. Sage, London.

National Research Council (2000) *The Digital Dilemma: Intellectual Property in the Information Age*. National Academy Press, Washington, DC.

Novek, E., Sinha, N., and Gandy, O. (1990) The value of your name. *Media, Culture and Society*, 12, 525–43.

O'Harrow, R. (2005) *No Place to Hide*. Free Press, New York.

Phillips, D. J. (2004) Privacy policy and PETS: The influence of policy regimes on the development and social implications of privacy enhancing technologies. *New Media & Society*, 6(6), 691–706.

Pho, Y. H. (2008) The value of volunteer labor and the factors influencing participation: Evidence for the United States from 2002 through 2005. *Review of Income and Wealth*, 54(2), 220–36.

Preston, P. (2001) *Reshaping Communications*. Sage, London.

Reder, M. (1999) *Economics: The Culture of a Controversial Science*. University of Chicago Press, Chicago.

Reed Elsevier (2008) Reed Elsevier to acquire ChoicePoint, Inc. *Press Release*. Online at http://www.reedelsevier.com/MEDIACENTRE/PRESSRELEASES/2008/Pages/ReedElseviertoacquireChoicePoint,Inc.aspx (accessed October 15, 2010).

Resnick, S. and Wolff, R. D. (1987) *Knowledge and Class: A Marxian Critique of Political Economy*. University of Chicago Press, Chicago.

Schiller, D. (1988) How to think about information. In: Mosco, V. and Wasko, J. (eds), *The Political Economy of Information*. University of Wisconsin Press, Madison, pp. 27–43.

Schreft, S. (2007) Risks of identity theft: Can the market protect the payment system? *Economic Review, Federal Reserve Bank of Kansas City* (Fourth Quarter), 5–40.

Smith, A. (1937) *An Inquiry into the Nature and Causes of the Wealth of Nations*. Random House, New York.

Smythe, D. W. (1977) Communications: Blindspot of western Marxism. *Canadian Journal of Political and Social Theory*, 1(3), 1–27.

Solove, D. (2004) *The Digital Person: Technology and Privacy in the Information Age*. New York University Press, New York.

Solove, D. and Hoofnagle, C. J. (2006) A model regime of privacy protection. *University of Illinois Law Review*, 2006, 357–403.

Sprott, D., Spangenberg, E., Block, L., Fitzsimons, G., Morwitz, V., and Williams, P. (2006) The question-behavior effect: What we know and where we go from here. *Social Influence*, 1(2), 128–37.

Stiglitz, J. E. (2009) Capitalist fools. *Vanity Fair*. Online at www.vanityfair.com/magazine/2009/01/stiglitz200901 (accessed October 15, 2010).

Stone, B. (2008) U.S. banks mine data and pitch to troubled borrowers. *The New York Times*. Online at http://www.nytimes.com/2008/10/22/business/worldbusiness/22iht-22-target.17157595.html? (accessed October 15, 2010).

Strahilevitz, L. (2007) Reputation nation: Law in an era of ubiquitous personal information. Public Law and Legal Theory Working Paper Series, Chicago. Online at http://ssrn.com/abstract_id=1028875 (accessed October 18, 2010).

Turow, J. (2006) *Niche Envy: Marketing Discrimination in the Digital Age*. The MIT Press, Cambridge, MA.

Wall, D. (2007) *Cybercrime. The Transformation of Crime in the Information Age*. Polity Press, Malden, MA.

Webster, F. (2002) *Theories of the Information Society*. Routledge, New York.

Yi, Y. and Jeon, H. (2003) Effects of loyalty programs on value perception, program loyalty, and brand loyalty. *Journal of the Academy of Marketing Science*, 31(3), 229–40.

Zimmer, M. (2008) The gaze of the perfect search engine: Google as an infrastructure of dataveillance. In: Spink, A. and Zimmer, M. (eds), *Web Search*. Springer-Verlag, Berlin, pp. 77–99.

Zwick, D., Bonsu, S., and Darmody, A. (2008) Putting consumers to work. "Co-creation" and new marketing govern-mentality. *Journal of Consumer Culture*, 8(2), 163–96.

Suggestions for Further Reading

Arvidsson, A. (2006) *Brands: Meaning and Value in Media Culture*. Routledge, New York.

Napoli, P. (2003) *Audience Economics: Media Institutions and the Audience Marketplace*. Columbia University Press, New York.

21

The Political Economy of Political Ignorance

Sophia Kaitatzi-Whitlock

Introduction

In this study I focus on the phenomenon of "political ignorance," which is on the increase even though we ostensibly live in "knowledge societies" and in an age of momentous scientific advances. I claim that ignorance will continue to grow, since its production is inherent in the prevailing political economy, notably, that of symbolic goods. Indeed, this is a media-induced affliction, since commercial channels, notably television, compete fiercely for the control and exploitation of the human commodity in leisure time-bound economies. The problem is that political knowledge is constitutive for democratic regimes and, as such, ought self-evidently to be guaranteed in democracies. Given this status, political ignorance should be extinct. I argue that this situation cannot be reversed under the premises of a capitalism that commodifies not only contents, communication processes, and systems, but also citizens themselves, that is, a system which makes the acquisition of *sine qua non* knowledge conditional to competition between market forces, which inescapably results in what I would term "market censorship." My aim, therefore, is to analyze prevalent economic and power relations that result in the phenomenon of civic ignorance. I start by conceptualizing the notions of knowledge and ignorance and, subsequently, by exposing instances of political ignorance and its growth – in Europe – over the last decades. Findings regarding increasing political ignorance are examined and compared to corresponding content analysis research, linking deficits of political information in mainstream media with ignorance.

In my main analysis of political economy, I explore the whys and wherefores of ignorance and its galloping trends by interrogating economic structures, motives,

The Handbook of Political Economy of Communications, First Edition.
Edited by Janet Wasko, Graham Murdock, and Helena Sousa.
© 2014 John Wiley & Sons, Ltd. Published 2014 by John Wiley & Sons, Ltd.

and economically driven role transmutations. My aim is to identify the mechanisms through which political ignorance is produced by the media and associated systems, by confronting the nexus of political ignorance and economic structures that have transformed not only communicative functions, but also human roles, beyond recognition. But if political ignorance is increasing as a consequence of media transmutation, could not citizens circumvent this trend and rid themselves of this influence by turning to the Internet for political knowledge? In order to address this issue, albeit briefly, I focus on the role of political economy in regard to key aspects of search engines and their impact on active efforts to acquire knowledge.

Civic Knowledge and Ignorance

Even though it is seemingly a clear-cut notion, ignorance is rather difficult to conceptualize, mainly because it signifies a default entity – a black hole.[1] Normally, we conceive of ignorance simply as the opposite of knowledge. Lasswell (1948, 224) defines it as "the absence, at a given point in the process of communication, of knowledge which is available elsewhere in society. Lacking proper training, the personnel engaged in gathering and disseminating intelligence is continually misconstruing or overlooking the facts, if we define the facts as what the objective, trained observer could find." He moreover deems that "sheer ignorance is a pervasive factor whose consequences have never been adequately assessed" (1948, 224).

Human societies have treated knowledge as a strategic resource, since it has always been vital to community survival (Morin 1986). Political consciousness and awareness in particular are the building blocks of modernity and the foundations of human emancipation. Knowledge is *power*, just as ignorance stands for *powerlessness*. Particularly when it is profound, ignorance may induce personality disorders, underpinning syndromes of cultural impoverishment. Uncertainty, confusion, indecisiveness, gullibility, insecurity, and feelings of resignation or being at a loss are familiar symptoms related to ignorance. Most crucial are symptoms manifesting lack of strategic knowledge about how to face challenges (Morin 1986). The worst manifestations of this phenomenon are being unaware of one's ignorance or unable to distinguish opinion or abusive propaganda from fact. Such disabilities result in political marginalization and, indeed, *depoliticization*.

Political ignorance

Political ignorance, which concerns me, is the opposite of a supreme civic value: awareness. Citizenship is a condition which requires essential information (Kellner 1990, 65, Dahl 2000); conversely, political ignorance annuls citizenship and alienates citizens by undermining civic roles or concealing rights. Acquired political knowledge is, therefore, indispensable for any civic identity or action (Dagger 1997) and for democratic co-operation. Identifying its existence or absence as well as its trajectories is therefore crucial.

As a mental and psychological invalidity syndrome, political ignorance hinders citizens' appreciation of established power relations. But if people ignore which power institutions govern the polity, they cannot grasp how, to what purpose or interests, political institutions operate. Neither can citizens influence policies, even in matters concerning them directly.[2] Political ignorance limits citizens' ability to judge, decide, or calculate action on politically induced outcomes, a situation which amounts to depoliticization. In effect, political ignorance renders citizens incapable of living their civic lives or benefiting from rights, let alone participating in "self-government." Ignorance, so conceived, is a complex affliction.[3]

The media were originally legitimated as providers of social knowledge, even as guarantors of continued political socialization. In this conception, their hypothetical abolition would bring democratic breakdown. My analysis suggests that the media have themselves largely abandoned that political role and renounced corresponding responsibility by effectively vacating their political mission. Instead, they have turned to serving the profit-making machineries of capitalism. Thus civic ignorance acts itself as a testimony to this abandonment.

Rather than the term "ignorance" some authors adopt approximations such as "information gaps," "knowledge gaps," "information poverty," or "information divides" (Watson and Hill 2002, Meyer 2002).[4] My conception of ignorance as invalidity points to intricate, yet lasting or chronic, afflictions, entailing loss of personal control and undermining trust in social institutions and community organizations. Such invalidity significantly corrodes self-confidence, thereby feeding suspicion, itself a fertile ground for anomie and the politics of intimidation. Ignorance fosters gullibility, disarming people even in the face of abusive propaganda. Xenophobia, racism, and sexism breed in ignorance, generating habitats sustained by commercial media "cultures" intent to infotain or entertain us to death (Postman 1986).

Knowledge still a civic prerequisite

Schattschneider raises the symbiotic link between democracy and knowledge: "An amazingly large number of people do not seem to know very much about what is going on. The significance of this kind of popular ignorance depends on what we think democracy is" (1960, 128–9). What is provocatively underestimated is that citizenship requires knowledge (Keane 1991, 140). Indeed, political knowledge as a civic fortification of the public interest is *essential* for democracy.

Two modalities leading toward ignorance

We can distinguish two main modalities resulting in ignorance. The first stems from lack or underprovision of knowledge, while the second, which has alarmingly risen recently, emanates from inundating people's minds with redundant material. Either form in itself is harmful, but their combination, as advanced currently, is crushing. Structural attacks against knowledge-producing institutions are manifest in pressures to commercialize university systems or when privileging marketable research and intensifying its exploitation. These trends suggest a near total commodifying assault on knowledge, which thereby results in the radical transformation of its purpose, nature, supply, and its relation to individuals. Knowledge is sold by those who possess it as a commodity exclusively to those who can afford it. Fundamental principles, such as universal access to knowledge as a public good, are thus subverted along with the consensus about knowledge as a prerequisite for citizenship. Rather than a politically empowering factor, knowledge mutates into a key economic asset by which competitive advantages are pursued in zero sum games.

Profound ignorance results in the inability to distinguish between valuable knowledge and useless or harmful information. Yet power relations are determined by that very capacity. In addition, the exponential growth in communication systems and contents overloads individuals with masses of redundant information, which undermines cognitive capacities as vital control tools. It is therefore critical to appreciate strategic knowledge in terms of "real interests" as opposed to "perceived" or "subjective" interests (Gramsci 1971, Lukes 2004).

Today, individuals are supposed to empower themselves through knowledge, not only in sociopolitical matters, but as economic agents – consumers, polyvalent employees, competitive entrepreneurs – to whom knowledge is paramount. However, elementary knowledge gaps in public affairs, notably about prevailing power relations, generate powerlessness and frustration, thereby debilitating individuals within the very technoeconomic paradigm that celebrates knowledge-intensive capital. Not surprisingly, corruption thrives in conditions of ignorance and lack of transparency by constraining understanding of intricate economic processes (Strange 1986).

Political Ignorance in the EU

To most of its citizens the European Union (EU) is a distant political entity, but political ignorance alienates it still further. Once in a while, this acknowledged malaise fuels concern, particularly when linked to the notorious "democracy deficit." Indeed, civic ignorance has even been blamed for stalling the Union's process of integration (Wallström 2006, Kaitatzi-Whitlock 2008, Golding 2006, Peel 2004).[5]

EU citizens are monitored by rolling surveys, measuring awareness over longer periods (several years to decades), thus providing sources for further research on ignorance. Eurostat charts respondents' perception of information about EU institutions and policies. Such horizontal social history or opinion depictions, cumulatively form a valuable corpus conducive to a longitudinal, comparative analysis. By reading such surveys longitudinally, we gain historical depth, but also a systematic comparison of fluctuations in perceptions.[6] The originality of this material lies in the fact that it synthesizes an *interface* between reception and content analyses, yielding valuable, albeit pessimistic, findings.[7] This approach reveals growing trends of political ignorance while linking this outcome with corresponding default media outputs. Matching the two processes over time unravels the origins of ignorance. When additionally supplementing the results of two ad hoc investigations regarding citizens' knowledge of Europolitics, we obtain a mutually reinforcing research result. Hence we can indisputably identify the structures and processes that produce ignorance.

Awareness about EU institutions   To chart perception of mediated contents concerning the European Parliament (EP) since its establishment,[8] citizens were asked whether they had: "recently seen or heard, in the papers, on the radio, or on television, anything about the European Parliament?" (Eurobarometer). In the examined period (25 years), respondents who learned about the EP in the news were few, while the statistical picture presents significant changes over time. In 1977, nearly 50 percent of respondents, on a cross-country average, confirmed learning about the EP from the press. Conversely, those answering negatively were 42 percent. Ten years later, in November of 1987, these rates were reversed. Citizens perceiving news about the EP in the press constituted only 42 percent, whereas those unaware of such news rose to 50 percent. This inversion is most intriguing. First of all, there is the anticipated learning curve regarding Europolitics. Secondly, throughout the 1980s, the EP was remarkably active. Thirdly, it underwent a significant strengthening of its role within the intra-EU policy-making constellation, acquiring joint decision-making powers. Fourthly, EP forces launched controversial projects promulgating a political rather than economic approach to European integration, thereby gaining distinctive momentum. The combination of these elements should have raised the EP's visibility enormously. Yet the opposite occurred. A decade later (November 1998), the picture had deteriorated still further. Only 40 percent of Eurostat respondents confirmed perceiving news about the EP, resulting in negative answers exceeding positive ones, by a full 10 percent.[9] Interviewees also responded to similar questionnaires about the EU's "executive," the Commission. Again, negative answers steadily exceeded positive ones over the nine-year period examined on cross national average. A majority of 60 percent of respondents did not recall news about the Commission or its policies, an outcome suggesting a sharp drop in corresponding political information supplies.

In summary, perception of news was decreasing steadily, while eventually only four in ten Europeans perceived something about their directly elected institution. The overall number of citizens perceiving information about the EP from the media decreased by a full 10 percent over the period surveyed. Given the fact that concurrently the number of media outlets proliferated exponentially and that media exposure increased explosively, such findings demonstrate that Europeans were informationally starved, gradually getting less and less political information, thereby generating high levels of ignorance about their crucial affairs.

The revenge of the ignorant   Interest in EU affairs had already started to be monitored in 1973, at a time when the EC consisted of 12 member-states. Interviewees were asked: "And as far as European politics are concerned, that is matters related to the European Community, to what extent would you say that you are interested in them? The "not much interested" column prevailed throughout. Respondents bracketed in the "not at all interested" option were the second largest group. By contrast, those interested in Europolitics "a great deal," formed the smallest group.[10] Meanwhile, over the years, interest in Europolitics decreased, although it was already tiny at the start.[11] These trends, taken in combination with the fact that decision-making power was conceded from the national to the supranational level, are most troubling. Although the scope of political prerogatives transferred to the EU kept growing precisely while politics immigrated to "Europe,"[12] a steep drop in political interest was manifest.

Ad hoc studies

Growing civic ignorance is confirmed variously, but at least two related studies deserve particular attention. The first was conducted in the early 1990s and the second in 2001. Cross-comparing the findings of my longitudinal reading of Eurostat surveys with these ad hoc studies[13] is interesting, not least because all are concerned with citizens' political knowledge about Europolitics and the sources of it. They also link knowledge deficits with citizens' disaffection with Europolitics, while attributing manifest gaps of knowledge and rising political ignorance to information deficits.

Communication deficits, political ignorance, and disaffection
Reactions against the Maastricht Treaty (1992), expressed in the disapproving referendum in Denmark, alarmed EU politicians, who blamed such a popular verdict on ignorance. So an independent committee of experts was appointed to study and face this crisis of legitimacy. Its mandate was threefold: to establish the truth concerning political knowledge, to assess causes for the communication deficit, and to submit policy recommendations to remedy the problem. Indeed, the De Clercq Report diagnosed ignorance,[14] linking this condition outright with communication deficits,[15] while stressing that "there is great dissatisfaction with current Community processes everywhere" (Clercq 1993, 5). "The contents and aims of the Maastricht Treaty are not at all well known, even in those countries where a debate took place before a referendum" (1993, 184), this being a "perfect example of the phenomenon of confusion" (185). Many citizens "deplored the lack, inadequacy, and inappropriateness of the information available to them" (205).

Indeed, the report highlighted that citizens are "open and welcoming to information about Europe" (205). The report recommended a political communication that would promulgate interactive relations between media, politics, and citizens, thereby advocating nothing less than a recasting of the democratic system. Ignorance was attributed to default media practices and deficits in political communication.[16] Overall, the De Clercq findings were shockingly revealing, but most shocking of all were its recommendations that urged imperative democratization of communication frameworks and processes. Not surprisingly, these were rebuffed vehemently and tacitly buried by the ultra-neoliberal establishment of Brussels.[17]

"Abysmal ignorance" in perceptions of the EU   The Debony study corroborated facts about entrenched ignorance, as well as its continuation into the new millennium. The most striking of its findings was the observed divides in knowledge between member states. Political knowledge was greater "in the pro-European countries of the 'South' (Greece, Portugal and Spain, including Ireland), where even people in the middle to low socio-economic categories can name many of its spheres of public activity" (Debony 2001, 8), but also among candidate countries (Sweden, Finland, Austria), irrespective of "whether or not they are inclined to view the EU as a good thing" (2001, 8).[18] Political knowledge was poor in the large, most populous states, notably Germany and the UK, where "there is the greatest lack of knowledge" (ibid).[19] These results concur with corresponding Eurobarometer data, as German and British respondents hardly ever passed the 50 percent threshold in awareness counts. In addition, a 2004 Eurostat survey confirmed "still an awful lot of ignorance about the EU – and often more in the old member states than in the new" (Peel 2004). Since these were the educationally richest Europeans, such findings are as shocking as they are embarrassing. Debony highlights this in stinging language.[20]

> There is a considerable, sometimes abysmal, lack of knowledge, in the other countries, where ignorance, confusion or very rough approximations are a general phenomenon. The Commission and the Parliament are often known only by name; the two are sometimes confused; knowledge of their roles and responsibilities is very vague; there is often almost total ignorance of the institutional mechanisms; it all seems extremely remote. (Debony 2001, 9)

Debony corroborates the prevalence of ignorance through a different methodology, elaborating, moreover, on the "abysmal gaps of knowledge" and their implications for civic readiness.

Matching knowledge gaps with content deficits

Over the last decades, content analysis studies have explored political information and press coverage of Europolitics.[21] They show that the media, including some of the most prestigious ones, deselect or severely cut down news and current affairs on Europolitics, treating them as unnewsworthy. Mainstream media downplayed Europolitics as of negligible importance. Intriguingly, such treatment applied even to crucial milestones of EU integration, such as the Maastricht Treaty, the adoption of the common currency – the Euro – or the Constitutional Convention of 2004.[22] Their news coverage was assessed as minimal and never rising to a net positive balance. Given that such milestones mark quite substantial power transformations in the EU process of integration and decision making, such "media snobbery" is preposterous (Media Tenor 2005a, 2005b, Ludes 2004, Kaitatzi-Whitlock 2005). Content analyses show, moreover, that among the three most important EU institutions, the Commission is given the most media coverage, while the EP, the only institution elected by popular vote across the Union, is given the least. The EP being treated as the least newsworthy institution of all, it was effectively liquidated from current affairs programs (Media Tenor 2005a, 2005b).[23] Given such remarkable deficits in supplies of regular political information, a correlation between the two interlinked phenomena – first, the rising levels of political ignorance among citizens, and secondly, the corresponding lack of coverage by the media – is imperative, since no one can acquire unavailable contents. Ignorance is thus attributed to deficits in political content supplies by the mainstream media. Analysis thus far explains how ignorance is produced by refusing to provide knowledge. In the following section, I explore the second modality by which ignorance is produced, that is, by seizing the minds and occupying the attention of people.

Intensified Production Modes of Political Ignorance

Having established the growth of political ignorance and its relation with content deficits, it is important now to question why it evolves and how it is determined by the political economy of contemporary capitalism. I attribute default, yet indispensable, civic knowledge to economy and media functions. Therefore, I need to disentangle the nexus which implicates the human commodity in its various functions.

Economic structures, actors and roles

The economy at large comprises the *sui generis*, supplementary domain of media markets which constitutes its motive force. As highlighted by Dallas Smythe (1977), commercial media sell the commodity of audiences to advertised industries for funding in the form of advertising revenue. In the inverse transactional cycle, commodities are sold to individuals, as customers who thus pay first for products' use value, but secondly also for their advertising costs, which remunerates advertisers and the media, which will then resell viewer packages all over again. This "vicious economic circle" involves an array of subsidiary, parasitic transactions and actors developing around the basic market equation. Although channels produce the commodity, audience time, together with viewers, the fundamental economic role played out by viewers is one about which they are mainly unaware. Obviously this ignorance is essential, because if the media enlightened citizens about this relation, they would inevitably betray their abuse of viewers as exploitable commodities. What is socially dangerous is the maintenance of ignorance for strategic and competitive purposes. And this condition applies here. Implicit in this approach are the links between ignorance and corruption, the incidents of which are innumerable during the ongoing global economic crisis. Nonetheless, free market economics is predicated on full awareness of parties involved in the market as sellers or buyers. Even though market imperfections are conceded, due to faulty knowledge, non-profit agencies that would "reduce knowledge imperfections" (Hill 1997, 15) are missing.

Charting a rough map of actors and functions in play here apart from entrepreneurs, products, and media owners, that is, the controlling players of the economy, we can see that actors and assets of the media-centered domain include the following: individuals in their respective capacity as audiences (commodity) and product buyers (agency); journalists, content creators; politicians and politics; political and cultural programming (content); airtime on screens, especially prime time; commercial propaganda messages and suppliers; advertised products on sale; viewer ratings companies, quantifying program competitiveness; opinion pollsters. All these thrive around the profit machine of the now genetically diverted communications media. In these cycles, individual viewers combine a number of economic roles with corresponding exploitations.

Intense structural control is exerted on all roles, as during daily market operations, (1) airtime is "sold" by channels to advertisers; (2) conversely, aggregates of viewers are sold to advertisers and, subsequently, to advertised industries having first produced audience time; (3) advertisements are sold by advertisers/advertised industries; (4) news, entertainment, or hybrid programming is supplied, ostensibly free of charge, to viewers; (5) channel performance ratings are sold to both advertisers and channels, thereby determining newsworthiness and program priorities, whereas (6) media-commissioned opinion polls usually vet popularity fluctuations and competitiveness of political personnel, which overtly serve as staple, publishable news but are also useful covertly.

Central mutual exploitation engages the media and the advertisers. They exchange viewers jointly and exploit them interchangeably, first as *commodity* and subsequently as *consumer*. Yet the capital that changes hands between these two controlling agencies is paid by consumers. This process produces the public as the ignorant financier of the media. Consequently, the most exploited but also the most deceived factor of all in this political economy are individuals, in their multiple roles as: (1) freely choosing viewers, (2) captive audiences of commercial messages, and (3) consumers of advertised products.

In order for this syndrome of lucrative economic roles to obtain, the synergetic commodity of viewing time is a prerequisite. Audiences and networks "produce the commodity audiences' watching time" (Jhally 1990, 75) jointly in a tacit accord entered whenever individuals become viewers. Yet as soon as they do so, and by inadvertently conceding to become captive audiences of commercial propaganda in tandem with watching their chosen programs, viewers simultaneously become trapped. They constitute a uniquely precious commodity, since it is in this way that they are manipulated toward consumerism. Commercial channels strive frantically to screen attractive programs in their competition to capture the largest audience segments. During these processes all political actors are commodified and intensely commercialized. Such crucial transmutations initiate not only the genesis of the human commodity, but also that of the commodified politician.

The symbolic mediated domain

Focusing on the mediated subdomain and its specificities for viewers as citizens, we ascertain that, once individuals join mediated flows, various economic roles emerge. The first evolves when viewers watch programs of their own choosing and the second when they are coerced to watch commercials in intervals during programs. Viewers must enact both of these roles in order to be readily salable to advertisers. During the course of the first, broadcasters strive both to capture viewers' attention amid tough competition for audiences and to keep viewers hooked. What viewers watch while hooked is economically paramount to broadcasters, firstly, because this condition is their pass to achieving the sale of viewer packages. People are thus unwittingly "cast" in economic roles, which prepare the way for the key economic role of the consumerist society: when the commodity viewer emerges as paying customer. For all targeted exploitation to happen in such a complex setting, it is imperative to occupy and colonize the minds of such a multiply exploitable asset. This colonization can only be guaranteed by supplying attractive rather than taxing shows, that is, contents emptied of political or educative significance. To this end, both competition and deregulation are crucial structural premises, dictating and concurrently underpinning redundant information supplies. The importance of such functions is crucial, as they inherently prioritize lowest common denominator programming, which pertains rather to entertainment, at the expense of knowledge-supplying genres. In the face of intense competitive pressures, programming not conforming to lowest common denominator features is threatened with extinction. Hence, such competitive market modalities foster the massive growth of ignorance.

Nonetheless, citizens expect to receive political information from the media. Indeed, the press is the only institution accredited with such a remit. Television was "the main, though largely unacknowledged, educator in the country" (Schiller 1989, 320). This is not the case any more. Television could fulfill such a politically pivotal role only if it were, primarily or exclusively, dedicated to an education system mission as proposed by Schiller (1989), Garnham (1990), and Bourdieu (1996). Such a mission has now been relinquished, either *de jure* or *de facto*. The role of public service broadcasting, in raising civic awareness and forming democratic agoras for dialogue, is largely submerged, while it is deplored by commercial media. Hence, commercialization of television marks the most decisive turn toward the transmutation of the fundamental role of the media and inherently of the political.

The human commodity and the cycles of its exchange

Commercial media orchestrate several processes of exploitation: consecutive, cyclical, or concurrent. The fact that commercialization and competition are now relentless has diminished the options for beneficial media contents enormously, in terms of citizens' real interests. By the same token, viewers' choices have shrunk dramatically, since most knowledge-enhancing programs are filtered out, just as hooked viewers get trapped in media habitats that aggressively recycle empty signifiers (see Patrick 2009).[24] Media attention is ostensibly a leisure time engagement but, as has been aptly stressed, since viewers create surplus value for the exploiting agencies, attention constitutes labor.

People's available leisure time is limited as it is occupied predominantly by television viewing.[25] The number of individual hours spent watching, multiplied by the number of programs and advertising messages exposed, multiplied by advertised products sold, are key links in the chain of this lucrative economy. Statistics regarding informative contents show that political programming is declining sharply, a trend evident also in journalistic and production job losses (Hobsbawm 2006). The emerging disequilibrium consists of more hours of TV exposure with more redundant information. Competition pits programming genres against each other: entertainment versus political communication and civic education. The former are in demand and promoted aggressively, while the latter are sidelined. Battles end with quantitative decreases and qualitative distortions to the detriment of knowledge.

Political communication is waning in a process where the "attention of the reader, listener or viewer has to be grabbed quickly if one media firm is to take custom from another" (Crouch 2004, 46–7). Competition "prioritizes simplicity and sensationalism, thereby degrading the quality of political discussion and reducing citizens' competence" (Crouch 2004, 47). But what is politics if knowledge about it is, conditionally, locked out of the domain of public visibility, dissemination, and communication? The sector with the utmost political significance, in its genetically diverted shape, has become the playmaker of several other, ulterior market games. This attention and time economy thus serves to disempower viewers.

Electronic public spaces were largely free from the constraints of market control and the corrosive effects of commercialism. However, following the neoliberal onslaught on electronic public spaces since the 1980s, democratic politics has lost out to the market in the domain of communications. By far the most underestimated consequence of the Transfrontier Television Directive (Council of European Communities 1989)[26] is the absolute subjection of public spaces to competition and deregulation. The once inherently political public space is now dominated by the market, exclusively for profit objectives and the consequence of the market imposed as the exclusive censor of media content.

Modes of market censorship: qualitative transmutation and distortions

In such a high-intensity market setting (Leiss 1976), commercial propaganda holds three pivotal roles: first, as monetary broker; secondly, as human commodity broker; and, thirdly, as content censor. The most important element, in relation to ignorance-producing processes, is that the former two functions could not succeed without tightly controlling the third. As a result, while advertising supplies audiences to advertisers and revenues to media simultaneously, it censors all "counterproductive" knowledge contents. Herein then lies the crucial nexus of this media-induced ignorance: concepts such as political judgment, political will formation, citizens' demands, and policy rationales have turned into odd terms of a bygone age. A regression of this magnitude generates long-lasting damage to political knowledge, the fundamental premise of democracy. This then is the political economy of political monopoly control.[27]

Decisive battles occur in the interface between markets of material and of symbolic goods, where the former prevail and control outcomes for the latter. This is why viewers set off to marketplaces of ideas – seeking, let us say, knowledge on current affairs – but instead end up buying packages of blurred clichés, having meanwhile paid the advertising industry on top of it. The clash is between an anticipated, responsible "civic trustee" role of the media, as political agency, versus the harshly economic role of the media as the "pimp" of viewers.

Since they are unaware of their commodification, and of transactions operating on their back, viewers participate in power games beyond their control. The deception consists in viewers turning to broadcast media for information, which the media do not deliver because they deal in quite different markets. Viewers become frustrated regarding their civic-cognitive expectations, because the alliance between advertisers and media supplies menus – subject only to profitability criteria – censoring out content beyond such objectives. Hence, the en bloc imposition of genres "that sell" favoring outright light entertainment over current affairs, a situation which causes civic ignorance.

But even within political programming zones, similar competition strategies displace the more serious programs in favor of infotainment, which superficially features political material, though it is essentially devoid of its essence.[28] The market strategy then pits two major categories against each other and, in doing so, condemns the category of political information either to displacement or to genetic diversion. Since the historical legitimation of the media derives from their civic trustee role, they cannot abolish political communication altogether. So they vacate it, maintaining simply the external form of that legacy in the hybrid caricature of infotainment. Knowledge deficits in current affairs are thus masked under that form.

Due to their multifaceted and pivotal economic role, viewers evidently constitute the most sought-after resource. They are the object of desire in fierce competition battles. Coveted viewers must be enticed ingeniously. Within cut-throat competition settings, knowledge-conferring programs seem heavy, boring, or plain indigestible. According to market logic, they must be supplanted by attractive, popular shows. Novel program concepts and recipes are frantically sought only to engage viewers' attention. Enticing contents become the tempting bait for viewers, who subsequently become the bait for the advertiser. The market censor rejects any programming not serving such compulsive purposes. Within such a harsh framework, quality is dispensable as unfit for economies of scale, and so are citizens' needs for political knowledge. Clichés justifying cuts in politically informative material indicate that "viewers reject it" or "it does not sell."[29] Consequently, a totally *sui generis* division of values is imposed.

By simply juxtaposing attractive with demanding programs, we can observe that the mere comparison favors the former. After having impoverished program menus and cultivated superficial entertainment approaches so that the discontinuity of information has made hard data seem even harder or knowledge contents off-putting, the media blame people for finding it indigestible. Consequently, news and current affairs programs are marginalized; along with other cultural forms they are filtered out from screen visibility.

In such a high-intensity market, ratings meters become central. They calculate channel performance, ranking their competitiveness in catching larger segments, thereby being instrumental in allocating advertising revenue and in censoring contents. Current affairs programs or documentaries are reduced, while, conversely, reality shows proliferate. A wave of populism is sweeping television screens, subverting previous hierarchies of programming and imposing the criteria of market viability. Journalists, too, are afflicted, as jobs are lost, casualized, or bureaucratized.[30] Journalists can avoid clashing with the market censor through self-censorship, conforming to bias or to nondescript output, or adapting their work to suit the infotainment mask (Hobsbawm 2006, Meyer 2002, Thussu 2007, Rosen 1992). Overall, such market conduct censors politics out, while keeping citizens politically numb and nicely suppressed.[31] This market, then, liquidates citizenship, while elected politicians look on.

From lowest common denominator to highest rating

As already indicated, the battle between commercial channels is about assembling larger audiences for aggressively marketed products, thereby securing economies of scale. Two mutually reinforcing mechanisms operate in this process. The first involves projection of mass appeal, eye-catching shows, constructed around the objective of mass satisfaction, accruing either from standardized recipes of sex, scandals, violence, and private life gossip or from bland, homogenized, yet viewable shows. The rise in scandal-specific contents in current affairs zones (Tumber and Waisbord 2004, Thompson 2005) cannot be explained simply by improved investigating methods. Intense interchannel competition grants comparative advantage to scandal and that matters in incessant races for highest ratings. Since all mainstream media compete basically for the same audience, standard recipes for success prevail and kill diversity. Competition-driven processes simplify and trivialize complex or sophisticated political programs as simplicity gains over complexity. Generally, the "what sells" concern prevails as the iron rule, effecting utter trivialization. Responsibility to inform clashes with the need to attract. The implicit business logic is to magnetize and capture attention, either by simplifying or scandalizing. The second mechanism occurs in synergy with viewers, just when they coproduce the commodity of audience time.

Selection of programs accrues in what media economists call "lowest-common-denominator programming" (Cave 1989). In multichannel markets, viewers gauge available options in search of preferred programs. When not finding their preferred programs, but wanting to retain the option of watching television – it being a cheap form of entertainment – they negotiate viewing second-best programs. In lowering their expectations, either in terms of quality or genre (e.g., art documentary versus soap), eventually they end up watching their second, third, or other choice. But each time a viewer condescends to a least-bad type of show he or she is obliged to watch only a partly satisfactory program. Nonetheless, precisely via such discounting viewers aggregate into large groups, notably granting that critical distinguishing mass that turns shows to scale economies. So the total sum of those watching their second, third, or other choice cumulatively builds up the much-coveted top rank position.[32] Paradoxical though it seems, those choosing a rather nondescript program X, as their last option, contribute to elevating X into a mass-appeal show conferring to it that extra, critical mass in this covert race. Thus, lowest-common- denominator programs gain dominant rank status.[33]

Poor informational quality is nothing compared to such a market prize. Redundant programs prevail precisely because they grant economies of scale, and push consumers to triumph over citizens (Crouch 2004). Conversely, even though high quality programs gratify significant segments of first-choice viewers, over time both are penalized. Notwithstanding high quality, when programs fall to the bottom of the ratings' lists, they are eclipsed as the market censor operates on numerical control and quantitative criteria. The impact of such sacrifices on citizens' knowledge is crushing. The supreme market censor thus determines collective ignorance and its corollary: depoliticization.

Thus citizens sustain such ignorance-inducing censorship indirectly, thereby debilitating their own position. Since availability of programs is conditioned on viewers compromising to watch minimally satisfying programs, viewers collude with the market censor's dictates. In addition, in entertainment, criteria of pluralism, diversity, or quality are questionable, since we trespass on subjective terrain where *de gustibus non est disputandum* (there is no disputing about tastes). Knowledge of facts, however, is quite distinct from aesthetic preferences, as it is a civic requirement that cannot be relinquished "for fun."

Citizens' ignorance and collateral damage

As numerous aggressive approaches to viewers betray, the medium of television has refined methodologies of entrapping people's senses. This happens, firstly, by colonizing audience time and by attracting their attention, thereby "walling people's awareness" (Mander 1978, 53). Secondly, it disorients minds ideologically, for example, via cult fetishisms, identity manipulation, or agenda setting. Thirdly, through the effect of confusion as stressed in both the ad hoc studies described above (see the section on Political Ignorance in the EU); such high intensity market setting "works to make individuals increasingly confused as to the nature of their needs" (Jhally 1990, 19). By the same token, such overloading systems confuse people about their real interests and the priorities in their needs (Lukes 2004, Kaitatzi-Whitlock 2007). Fourthly, it suspends critical ability, implicit in the moving image, yet accentuated by staging or shooting techniques. Fifthly, it cultivates infantilization or even brutalization, implicit in the worst reality shows. Furthermore, belonging to a captive audience itself incurs vulnerability. Adverts bombard viewers at moments of susceptibility and dispositional weakness, during relaxation, when critical ability tends to be suspended.

Seventy percent of EU citizens turn to television for (political) information (Wallström 2006, Vissol 2006). An equally high rate (71%) admit being "little or not at all informed" (Peel 2004).[34] Is this coincidence accidental? The analysis in this section, which focuses on the reasons for the depletion of essential information from channels, but also the modalities by which people's minds are possessed with redundant content, suggests that such exorbitant knowledge gaps are due to the commitment of commercial channels to profiteering and to transmitting torrents of homogenized, redundant contents. That is a system of disorienting and confusing citizens, rather than enlightening them.

The Political Economy of Active
Knowledge Seeking

One of the key problems of the web is its indiscretion in terms of genres and kinds of information. Unlike journalism, a key professional task of which is the clear distinction between the categories of facts and opinion, on the web, where anybody can upload symbolic goods, contents are entirely mixed and blurred. Inherently, no generic search engine (SE) will deliver such categorizations. This situation is highly problematic in itself, because of mingling and confusing diverse kinds. As such, it is detrimental as both knowledge and significant information are central categories for learning, and therefore, need to be treated systematically. SE data-mining processes on the web fail to do so. Moreover, overall, knowledge or significant information makes up only a fraction of sources retrievable on the web. But the economics of web information supplies is the factor that hinders properly cognitive processes.

The only way to avoid bias and abuse in allocating information and knowledge sources is to exclude all parasitic exploiting functions and agencies. This general rule applies also on the web. The only way then would be to constitute retrieval functions as public utility services, that is, universally accessible, but publicly accountable and transparently operated facilities. This entails avoiding commercialization of such web services at any cost. However, given the near total commercialization of cyberspace, alternatives exist only within commercialization, basically involving direct or indirect exploitation. Put differently, for SEs to run viable businesses, their services can either operate direct business-to-customer transactions or mediated ones with the intervention of a parasitic third partner, advertising.

Experience shows that the markets for goods that are not indispensable are not fit for business-to-customer transactions. The devise of a tandem exploitation scheme, just like the one undertaken by mass media, therefore becomes unavoidable. This scheme consists of the supply of the commodity of web user to advertised companies. In short, while SEs provide requested information, concurrently and conversely, they push users to advertisements or sites of preselected, best-paying companies, as in the case of Google. Here, then, the brokerage function revisits the public, causing its tacit collusion. By assuming the insidious ostensibly free-rider role, users concede concurrently to the function of advertiser exploitation. Just as in the mass media, SEs coproduce together with seekers the commodity of seeking time during which advertising slips in.

Focusing on this nexus of relations from the perspective of SE, in order for them to draw revenue, they must undertake the classical double brokerage role. The service they deliver is directed to individual users looking for some order in the chaos. By developing catalogue files and filtering data, on the basis of devised algorithms, SEs guide seekers to relevant sites. So the actors engaging in SE-orchestrated processes comprise: (1) information seekers, (2) search engines, and (3) companies advertised (either through ad banners or pay-per-click). But whereas (2) and (3) negotiate directly at a profit, (1) functions, unwittingly, as "bait" toward the mutual exploitation objectives of (2) and (3). Hence commercial media, notably television and SEs, exploit viewers and web users respectively in very comparable ways.

In the young market of SEs operating in the vast domain of the web, Google has rapidly become the most popular search companion. Its popularity hinges on an irresistible business concept which turned it into the indisputable market leader, that is, PageRank: its method of using web link structures, rather than just elementary co-ordinates of sites or documents (O'Reilly 2005). Google distinguished itself also thanks to an innovating business approach (Vise and Malseed 2005). Apart from PageRank, Google launched its "Ad Sense" policy, thereby converting users into business allies in enabling advertising against remuneration, in a virtual kind of outsourcing. However, such comparative-advantage-generating strategies effectively overshadow the considerable shortcomings of this SE.

Users are not aware of the fact that PageRank[35]disregards considerable amounts of useful sources. It is estimated that Google will furnish only about 60–70 percent of all public entries on the web, that is, of technically retrievable information, on any single demand. Thus sites not considered for selection belong to PageRank information rejects. Yet this is only the first stage of Google's information-censoring practice. The second stage occurs within the bulk of scanned retrievable material, via processes of arbitrary prioritizing. Google marginalizes "less worthwhile sources" simply by ordering them at the tail ends of huge lists of items. Conversely, it prioritizes sources with the most optimizer links attached to them. So linking becomes strategic once somebody sets up shop on the Internet. This is of course a modified replica of the lowest common denominator process operated by the mass media. Consequently, this system furnishes only a small fraction of significant information, along with prioritizing it, to the effective detriment of web-searchers. Because selection criteria – determined by commercial considerations – operate inherently in the algorithm of PageRank, constant and systematic bias accrues. PageRank prioritizes popular or "most visited," rather than most appropriate or, critically, most significant sites on specific entries and requests. This procedure amounts to a perfectly populist business strategy. Nonetheless, what cognitively appears as a shortcoming, makes perfect business sense. Site visitors click on flashing links; however, for each click on artificially optimized and paying links, that advertised customer of Google remunerates it, automatically, with a handsome prenegotiated price. This action locks together two willing partners and one transient, unsuspecting commodity partner.

The financial mechanism that is based on pay-per-click is conducive to satisfying implicated actors, that is, individual seekers, SE business funding, and ad promoting. So although a fair amount of valuable information is left out by PageRank, this method is cost-effective commercially. The unprecedented amounts of Google traffic testify to this but also to the superiority of the pay-per-click system when compared to ad banners. Interestingly, the comparative advantage of this dominant market player consists of prioritizing – and thus rewarding – sites which are already maximally linked up, thereby granting further popularity to "haves" and channeling preference to already recognizable brands. This practice explains why the absolute majority of web users gravitate towards the 100 best known information brands worldwide, many of which are already famous offline brands. Although SE traffic covers only a part of Internet traffic such bias tarnishes its heralded equality and diversity.

The second equally crucial relation is between SEs and offline and online competitor media. The breakthrough of Google's pay-per-click application impacts dramatically not only on web markets and the entire system of symbolic goods' markets, but also the economy at large. Notably, financial resources emigrate from offline to online media where the share of SEs is growing exponentially. Market research demonstrates that SEs lead with the highest percentage of the overall online advertising expenditure.[36] Long-term effects in the allocation of information, knowledge, opinion, public discussion, evaluation, and critique can be gleaned as a consequence of such remarkable web market trends. Firstly, advertising revenue is rapidly migrating from offline to online media, with dire anticipated repercussions on the former's sustainability. Secondly, in online applications, advertising revenue seems to be migrating to SEs and particularly so to Google. This rising movement converts network economies and the SEs, in particular, into crucial brokers not only of online knowledge, but also determinants of the sustainability of other sources of knowledge.

Google leads, then, a remarkable concentration trend in market power and control. Trends in online advertising funding are very much determined by its overwhelming success. Consequently, the responsibility of Google in furthering and entrenching concentration in symbolic goods' markets is paramount. By the same token, its traffic occurs at considerable risk for systematic and accurate knowledge and significant information. In other words, although active seekers head for knowledge, the virtual system systematically imposes its own biasing criteria. Hence, web-bound processes determine allocation of power in terms of knowledge, apparent knowledge, and ignorance.

Concluding Remarks

Political ignorance about substantive power relations within the EU, as analyzed in this study, constitutes a political embarrassment for a region comprising, arguably, the best-educated populations worldwide. In the face of such regressive conditions and related legitimacy backlashes, the Commission of the EU launched its *Plan-D* for *Democracy, Dialogue and Debate* to "reinvigorate European democracy," thereby aiming to create a "public sphere, where citizens are given the information and the tools to actively participate in the decision-making process and gain ownership of the European project"[37] (Commission 2005, 2–3) and promising to initiate long-term consultations on the principles behind its communications policy. Although rhetorical, this policy pronouncement is doubly significant: firstly, because EU elites acknowledge the severity of the problem, and, secondly, because they confess that communications media constitute our fundamental collective means for political knowledge and democratic discussion. Conversely, increasing political ignorance undoubtedly constitutes major regression, since people's ignorance results in abuse of power. The twin trends of rapidly diminishing civic awareness and of concurrently decreasing political interest effect the dire condition of depoliticization, which entails a terminal democracy deficit.

Media markets under regimes of deregulated competition are positively harmful for civic knowledge. The causal links between these phenomena indicates that democracy deficit will only be remedied when political knowledge and communication are rectified. Citizens' understanding of power relations and politics can only be fostered by transparency about political institutions, power relations, and decisions. The failure of contemporary capitalism lies in bartering its own ultra-profitability with an ignorance-producing media regime and hence with the essential demise of democracy. It is a capitalism which dictates the commodification and the marginalization of both citizens and politicians, by making knowledge and democracy deficits structurally prerequisite for its own predomination.

Notes

1   *"Ignorance"* is absent in communication dictionaries. See Lilleker (2006), Watson and Hill (1997), O'Sullivan et al. (1992).
2   This conception derives from Steven Lukes's three-dimensional concept of power (2004).
3   Indeed, even factual bits of knowledge, if irrelevant or oversegmented, may contribute to effective ignorance.
4   The "'knowledge gap' research has revealed that the spread of television consumption to more people involving larger segments of their time does not equalize the stock of politically relevant knowledge among subgroups of society, but instead widens such gaps between them" (Meyer 2002: ix).
5   The most striking case being the "You Do Not Know, Vote No" campaign in the 2008 Irish referendum (www.indymedia.ie/article/87345).
6   This is not identical to knowledge. Yet it is an essential source for political knowledge. "Perceived knowledge" is a gray, often imperceptibly counterproductive, mental condition.
7   Eurobarometer publishes regular Eurostat surveys twice a year. Surveys regarding the European Parliament started in 1977 and lasted until 2001; surveys regarding the

Commission started in 1987. The first Eurostat survey in 1973 addressed "interest" in EU affairs. Some surveys still continue, while others have been discontinued.

8 The EP was established in 1977 and was first elected in 1979. By far the lengthiest survey is on awareness about the EP.

9 Pan-European EP election years present exceptions to this pattern.

10 An upturn surged in 1986, yet raised interest in Europolitics was short-lived. 1986 marked a turning point in the power battles between the market and "the political."

11 Weak interest in politics is corroborated by De Clercq: "*La majorité des Européens (55%) ne s' intéressent pas beaucoup ou pas du tout a la politique*" (1993: 28).

12 Notwithstanding such "denationalization," the media continued to focus on national arenas, thereby breeding a peculiar depoliticization.

13 Both were commissioned by the EU in 1993 and 2001 respectively.

14 Hjarvard (1993, 90) highlights "cleavages between capital growth and administrative development in the EU, without commensurate 'public knowledge'."

15 "*Les débats occasionnés par la ratification du Traité de Maastricht dans nos Etats membres ainsi que le résultat de diverses consultations populaires ou parlementaires auxquelles ils donnent lieu révèlent un manque préoccupant de connaissance de la construction européenne et une perception parfois déforme de sa réalité. Le déficit est d' autant plus accusé que sont grandes les espérances et les inquiétudes du grand public sur ce sujet*" (De Clercq 1993, 5).

16 The "absence or weakness of channels of European information is worrying – while at the same time the need for sources close at hand is manifest" (De Clercq 1993, 208).

17 Fierce attacks against it were targeted by British media, leading to its burial. For the Report's fate and its recommendations, see also Tumber (1995). For propaganda against it, see Booker and North (1993). The fact that it is unavailable in official EU libraries, even for research purposes, is an indication of its "burial."

18 Given the referenda of 2005 on the Constitutional Convention, the issue of whether citizens knowingly dismissed it is crucial. See Introduction to Kaitatzi-Whitlock and Baltzis (2006).

19 Leys confirms such findings with British statistics concurring with Debony's qualification about "abysmal ignorance": "One voter in five was functionally illiterate. Knowledge of modern history was confined to a tiny minority … Images, music and other non-verbal signifiers increasingly displaced words" (Leys 2001, 52–3). Besides, "two thirds of teenagers had little or no interest in politics and scant political knowledge (2001, 20). See also Lloyd and Mitchinson (2006) on "general ignorance" and the "comprehensive and humiliating catalogue of all misconceptions, mistakes and misunderstandings in 'common knowledge'" (2006, xv).

20 There exists "gross ignorance in the UK and in Germany" (Debony 2001, 9). Discrepancies in ignorance between countries need to be further investigated in conjunction with the role of hegemonic and ethnocentric media and elites in respective countries. A positive correlation between better knowledge and pro-European stances is observable. This is a valuable insight per se. Besides, one might speculate that anti-Europeans might have used it strategically. In smaller, better informed countries "a fairly high amount of interviewees could at least identify the Commission and the Parliament and had an approximate idea of their respective composition and role, [and] institutional mechanisms" (Debony 2001, 9).

21   Such studies examine political information output in key media, notably, journals and channels in major EU countries such as Germany and the UK.

22   Poor media coverage, even of historical milestones such as the adoption of the common currency, is commented on by Ludes (2004).

23   Surveys suggest that the EP is the most recognizable among EU institutions. Counterbalancing coverage among local and regional press and the fact that 500 Euro-Parliamentarians communicate interpersonally, dialoguing with citizens in local constituencies, offsets such mainstream media effacing.

24   For the concept of "empty signifiers," see Laclau (1996).

25   Seventy percent of Europeans turn to TV for their information (Wallström 2006, Vissol 2006).

26   In 1989 the EC and the CoE subjugated electronic public spaces to the control of global market forces, through their transfrontier television policies.

27   "Media bias becomes the only real knowledge owned by the public sphere" (Lilleker, 2006, 119). See also Crouch (2004, 48).

28   "Infotainment, incorporating talk shows and reality based programming has been the most forceful growth trend in the five major European markets in recent years" states Dahlgren (1995, 49), invoking data by the Geneva- based media analyst, Paolo Baldi (1994).

29   Both research evidence and political campaigns demonstrate citizens' urge for knowledge. See the section on Political Ignorance in the EU above.

30   The 2005 film *Good Night, and Good Luck* features journalism fighting successfully, though at considerable cost, against political censors and McCarthyist intimidation, though failing to beat the market censor.

31   This fits Marshall's description of "the 'war' of the capitalist class system against citizenship" (1995,103).

32   This is described as Hotelling's principle (Cave, 1989).

33   Exceptions to the rule exist. Programs of high quality may genuinely attract massive audience as viewers' first choice.

34   The equivalent figure 30 years back, in 1973, were 63 percent (Peel 2004).

35   There are "over 200 Search Engine Optimization (SEO) factors" that Google uses to rank pages in the Google search results (SERPs). Anyone wishing to pursue artificial optimization for high ranking can find it on confirmed Google SEO Rules on the web.

36   Market research conducted by Price Waterhouse Coopers (2007) (IAB).

37   The Commission's "Plan-D" policy was its stillborn project against a crushing civic defiance expressed in the referenda on the Constitutional Convention (in France and the Netherlands, May 2005).

References

Baldi, P. (1994) New trends in European programming, *Diffusion*, Summer, EBU, Geneva.
Booker, C. and North, R. (2003) *The Great Deception: The Secret History of the EU*. Continuum, London.
Bourdieu, P. (1996) *Sur la Télévision*. Liber-Raisons d'Agir, Paris.

Cave, M. (1989) An introduction to television economics: Regulating a partly-deregulated broadcasting system. In: Hughes, G. and Vines, D. (eds), *Deregulation and the Future of Commercial Television*. Aberdeen University Press, Aberdeen, pp. 9–39.

Commission of the European Union (2005) *Plan D for Democracy, Dialogue and Debate,* COM(2005)494 final 13.10.2005. Brussels.

Council of European Communities (1989) *Television Without Frontiers Directive,* EEC/552/89. Brussels.

Crouch, C. (2004) *Post-Democracy*. Polity Press, Cambridge, UK.

Dagger, R. (1997) *Civic Virtues: Rights, Citizenship and Republican Liberalism*. Oxford University Press, New York.

Dahl, R. A. (2000) *On Democracy*. Yale University Press, New Haven, CT.

Dahlgren P. (1995) *Television and the Public Sphere*. Sage, London.

Debony D. (2001) Perceptions of the European Union: A qualitative study of the public's attitude to and expectations of the EU in the 15 M-S and in 9 candidate countries, Summary Results. European Commission, June, Brussels.

De Clercq, W. (1993) *Reflection on the Information and Communication Policy of the European Community*. Commission of the European Union, Brussels.

Eurobarometer electronic editions. Online at http://ec.europa.eu/public_opinion/cf/sub-question_en.cfm (accessed October 19, 2010).

Garnham N. (1990) *Capitalism and Communication: Global Culture and the Economics of Information*. Sage, London.

Golding, P. (2006) Eurocrats, technocrats and democrats: Conflicting ideologies in European information society. In: Kaitatzi-Whitlock, S. and Baltzis, A. (eds), *Innovations and Challenges in the European Media*. University Studio Press, Thessaloniki, pp. 3–24.

Gramsci, A. (1971) *Selections from the Prison Notebooks of Antonio Gramsci*, Hoare, Q. and Smith, G. (eds). Lawrence and Wishhart, London.

Hill, M. (1997) *The Policy Process in the Modern State*. Prentice Hall / Harvester Wheatsheaf, London.

Hjarvard S. (1993) PanEuropean television news. Towards a European political public sphere? In: Drummond, P., Paterson R., and Willis, J. *National Identity and Europe*, London, British Film Institute, pp. 71–94.

Hobsbawm J. (ed.) (2006) *Where the Truth Lies: Trust and Morality in PR and Journalism*. Atlantic Books, London.

Jhally, S. (1990) *The Codes of Advertising: Fetishism and the Political Economy of Meaning in the Consumer Society*. Routledge, New York.

Kaitatzi-Whitlock, S. (2005) *Europe's Political Communication Deficit*. Arima, Bury St Edmunds, UK.

Kaitatzi-Whitlock, S. (2007) Subjection and the power of ignorance. In: Kaitatzi-Whitlock, S. (ed. and trans.), *Introduction to S. Lukes: Power: a Radical View*. Savalas, Athens, pp. 9–66.

Kaitatzi-Whitlock, S. (2008) Why the political economy of the media is at the root of the European democracy deficit. In: Bondebjerg, P. and Madsen, P. (eds), *Media Democracy and European Culture*. Intellect, Bristol, pp. 25–47.

Kaitatzi-Whitlock, S. and Baltzis, A. (eds) (2006) *Innovations and Challenges in the the European Media*. University Studio Press, Thessaloniki.

Keane, J. (1991) *Media and Democracy*. Polity Press, Cambridge, UK.

Kellner, D. (1990) *Television and the Crisis of Democracy*. Westview Press, Boulder, CO.

Laclau, E. (1996) Why do empty signifiers matter to politics? In: *Emancipation(s)*. Verso, London, pp 36–46.

Lasswell, H. D. (1948) The structure and function of communication in society. In: Lyman, B. (ed.), *The Communication of Ideas*. Institute of Religious and Social Studies, New York, pp. 37–51.

Leiss, W. (1976) *The Limits to Satisfaction*. Marion Boyars, London.

Leys, C. (2001) *Market Driven Politics: Neo-liberal Democracy and the Public Interest*. Verso, London.

Lilleker, D. (2006) *Key Concepts in Political Communication*. Sage, London.

Lloyd, J. and Mitchinson, J. (2006) *The Book of General Ignorance*. Faber, London.

Ludes, P. (2004) Eurovisions? Monetary union and communication puzzles. In: Bondebjerg, I. and Golding, P. (eds), *European Culture and the Media*. Intellect Books, Bristol, pp. 213–31.

Lukes, S. (2004) *Power: A Radical View*. Palgrave, New York.

Mander, J. (1978) *Four Arguments for the Elimination of Television*. William Morrow, New York.

Marshall, T. H. and Bottomore T. (1992) *Citizenship and Social Class*. Pluto Press, London.

Media Tenor (2005a) Business as usual: The media image of the EU in Germany and abroad, 2003–2005. April, pp. 84–7.

Media Tenor (2005b) Europe – a quantité négligeable. Long-term study: Europe in the media. January, pp. 30–5.

Meyer, T. (2002) *Media Democracy: How the Media Colonize Politics*. Polity Press, Cambridge, UK.

Morin, E. (1986) *La Méthode: 3. La Connaissance de la Connaissance*. Seuil, Paris.

O'Reilly, T. (2005) What Is Web 2.0? Online at www.oreillynet.com/pub/a/oreilly/tim/news/2005/09/30/what-is-web-20.html (accessed October 19, 2010).

O'Sullivan, T. et al. (1992) *Key Concepts in Communication*. Routledge, London.

Patrick, A. O. (2009) Relaxation of TV restraints urged. *Wall Street Journal*, January 22. Online at http://www.jstic.com/Newsgroup/WSJE/2009/WSJEWJ_January_22nd.pdf (accessed October 18, 2010).

Peel, Q. (2004) A summer of heated haggling for Barroso. *Financial Times*, July 29, p. 13.

Postman, N. (1986) *Amusing Ourselves to Death: Public Discourse in the Age of Show Business*. Penguin, New York.

Rosen, J. (1992) Politics, vision, and the press: Toward a public agenda for journalism. In: Rosen, J. and Taylor, P. (eds), *The New News vs. the Old News: The Press and Politics in the 1990s*. Twentieth Century Fund, New York, pp. 3–33.

Schattschneider, E. E. (1960) *The Semi-Sovereign People: A Realist View of Democracy in America*. Dryden Press, Hinsdale, IL.

Schiller, H. (1989) The privatization of culture. In: Angus, I. and Jhally, S. (eds), *Cultural Politics in Contemporary America*. Routledge, New York, pp. 317–32.

Smythe, D. W. (1997) Communications: Blindspot of western Marxism. *Canadian Journal of Communications*, 1(3), 1–27.

Strange, S. (1986) *Casino Capitalism*. Blackwell, Oxford.

Thompson, J. B. (2005) *Political Scandal: Power and Visibility in the Media Age*. Polity Press, Cambridge, UK.

Thussu, K. D. (2007) *News as Entertainment: The Rise of Global Infotainment*. Sage, London.

Tumber, H. (1995) Marketing Maastricht: The EU and news management. *Media, Culture and Society*, 17, 511–19.

Tumber. H. and Waisbord, S. (2004) *Political Scandals and Media Across Democracies*. Sage, London.

Vise, D. A. and Malseed, M. (2005) *The Google Story*. Bantam Dell, New York.

Vissol, T. (2006) Is there a case for an EU information television station? Office for Official Publications of the European Communities, Luxembourg.

Wallström, M. (2006) Preface. In: Kaitatzi-Whitlock, S. and Baltzis, A. (eds), *Innovation and Challenges in the European Media*. University Studio Press, Thessaloniki, pp. xiii–xv.

Watson, J. and Hill, A. (1997) *A Dictionary of Communication and Media Studies*. Arnold, London.

Part V

Emerging Issues and Directions

22

Media and Communication Studies Going Global

Jan Ekecrantz

Introduction

How is media research to be conducted in a globalized world? Are new paradigms and methodologies needed when the nation state is no longer an unproblematic measure of everything, or a presupposed conceptual frame, in a world where global interdependencies and transborder exchanges are supposedly more significant than structures and processes contained within national borders?

The geopolitical and geocultural consequences of the collapse of the Soviet Union in conjunction with the information and communications technology revolution have changed the terms of everything "international" and caused academic concerns about "space" in general. Not only media systems, but also political and economic systems generally, are in flux in the new millennium. There is an often-noted new instability in the world after the fall of the Berlin Wall and the crackdown in Beijing in 1989 and, not least, after 9/11 in 2001.

Media studies shares with sociology and political science difficulties in coming to grips with the realities of a transnationalized and transforming world. One explanation is a certain, lingering "methodological nationalism" (Beck 2002), implying that the nation state still provides the presupposed and mostly implicit conceptual frame – also when the focus is on phenomena beyond the nation state. Considerable thinking is called for and much is also going on, not least in the field of globalization studies, with its notorious problematization of all kinds of borders, including disciplinary ones.

For many decades, media and communication studies have contributed substantially to our general knowledge of international conditions and processes. There

The Handbook of Political Economy of Communications, First Edition.
Edited by Janet Wasko, Graham Murdock, and Helena Sousa.
© 2014 John Wiley & Sons, Ltd. Published 2014 by John Wiley & Sons, Ltd.

may be a problem with the older disciplines, from which communication research originated, in that they have not incorporated this body of knowledge into their own thinking, modern media and modern media studies now often being a blind spot (in sociology, political science, literary theory, etc.). This may also explain what seems to be a diminishing inflow into media studies from its "founding" disciplines. It should be remembered that a series of original, path-breaking thinkers in our field came from outside media and communication studies: Max Horkheimer, Theodor Adorno, Jürgen Habermas, Raymond Williams, and many others. On the other side of the North Atlantic, we find many other scholars coming from the "outside" and producing modern classics in our field – from Robert Park and Paul Lazarsfeld to Herbert Schiller.[1]

It seems to be the case that media and communication studies, now a discipline in its own right, has lost touch with these other disciplines, which, in turn, have now largely eliminated media from their research agendas and curricula. As a consequence, they often regard media as epiphenomena, or neglect them altogether.[2] This is the classical problem of an increasing division of intellectual labor at a time when integrated and truly interdisciplinary approaches and transnational theorizing are needed more than ever, owing to the increasing complexity of, and interdependencies in, a globalized world.

Media studies (and forerunners) originated as a cross-disciplinary or interdisciplinary undertaking. Now it is, in most places, a discipline in its own right with regard to academic institutionalization. With this come academic prestige, professorships, and research funding. But there are also problems and costs associated with being a specialized discipline. In the field of media and communications, an increased division of intellectual labor runs counter to developments in the late-modern world, where the "system of the media is losing its specificity and becoming an integral part of the economic, cultural and political system" (Martín-Barbero 1993, 215). This is just one dimension of globalization that impacts on national systems. Globalization means increased complexity (change and heterogeneity) and this is the new raison d'être for cross-disciplinarity.

Media studies have always been international, long before the term "globalization" was popularized in the early 1990s by Roland Robertson (1992), sociologist of religion. There have been a number of approaches in internationally oriented media and communication studies, from international news and propaganda to *Four Theories of the Press* (Siebert et al. 1956), and media and development (Lerner 1958, Lerner and Schramm 1967, Pye 1963). Later came the cultural imperialism critique (Schiller 1969, 1976) and the New World Information and Communication Order process (see Carlsson 2005), then media globalization and new media studies. Much of this is covered by international communication (Thussu 2006), a field that has bordered on and sometimes been interfolded with international politics, international sociology, translocal anthropology, and other fields. Media studies has also taken on board, in innovative ways, theory complexes such as world system theory (McPhail 2006), modernity theory (Thompson 1995), media and migration (Appadurai 1996), the network society (Castells 1996), diaspora studies (e.g., Tsagarousianou 2004), and research on the new (informatized) wars (Kaldor 1999). Most recently, studies of new global social movements and media have proved to be fertile ground for cross-breeding between several fields, as in research on civil society media (e.g., Atton 2002, Couldry and Curran 2003).

I will continue on this track and argue for (1) more dialogue with "nonwestern" theory and research perspectives, (2) more basic cross-disciplinarity, and (3) a stronger focus on global inequalities and social transformation. These research concerns are interrelated and mutually reinforcing. Globalization forces us not only to focus more on transnational phenomena in general, but also to highlight social change and difference, which are almost unprecedented in pace and scope and directly and indirectly caused by globalization processes. Stability and equality do not characterize contemporary societies. Further, as increasingly central institutions around the world, the media are deeply ingrained in most societal processes. This calls for broad and integrated approaches in media studies, for cross-disciplinarity in a very basic sense: as theorizing and empirical research across both disciplinary and sociocultural borders. Such transnational theory-building would seem necessary to take care of some of the new complexities in the contemporary world and its media-driven modernities. What they have in common are the facts of change and difference, and the centrality of the media as institutions. Theorizing media and social change in a globalized world implies questioning some received categories and distinctions based on assumptions that no longer hold.

These arguments will be developed below. Far from proposing a new theory of media and globalization, I will try to show how media studies can and need to be opened up to experiences and realities outside the center of the world system. I will first wind back half a century, when media and social development were frequently on the agenda of development research, then reflect on the contemporary scene, which is largely characterized by global divides and their concomitant media phenomena. Following this will be a brief section on the meanings of "dewesternization" and the decreased relevance of some firmly rooted disciplinary distinctions. This theme will then be concretized using Russian, Brazilian, and Chinese examples.

Media and the Development of Underdevelopment

A brief history of internationally oriented studies of media and social change could start with the Schramm, Lerner, and Pye era in mass communication research. In the 1950s and 1960s, there was a strong reliance on the purportedly universal correlation between growth in media consumption and political democratization and social development in general (see e.g., Lerner 1958, Pye 1963, and Lerner and Schramm 1967). It was assumed, by Daniel Lerner and others, that the media created a psychic mobility among people living in the countryside in traditional (i.e., premodern) societies, in turn resulting in a geographic and then social mobility, owing to people's longing for a modern life and salaried employment in the cities. The media served as "mobility multipliers," thus contributing to the "passing of traditional society," to refer to the title of Lerner's famous book.[3] This was before the decolonization of several countries in Africa and the democratization of Latin American countries, processes that had nothing to do with the rise of public media, at least not in the former colonies. This was also before the cultural imperialism thesis, associated above all with Herbert I. Schiller, who stated that the content of media worldwide was strongly dominated by imperial, that is, US, military, economic, political, and ideological interests (Schiller 1969, 1976). And the world had not yet seen the "barrios," "favelas," and "banlieus" surrounding the megacities of Asia, Africa, and South America, which housed millions of unemployed and destitute. This is where Lerner's mobile hordes ended up, once they got moving – for reasons other than media consumption.

At the time, the given fact was that the statistical correlation between the number of radio and TV receivers per capita, on the one hand, and participation in elections and a number of welfare indicators, on the other, tended to be quite strong (around +0.40 across all countries). It should also be underlined that an important component of the theoretical setup was developmentalism, a belief in unilinear development.[4] Socioeconomic differences between countries were translated into a time scale – there were underdeveloped, developing, and developed countries – assuming a considerable time-lag, separating the former from the latter.[5] Difference related to dominance and exploitation in the contemporary world was not yet on the media research agenda, but was to be focused on by dependency theory in the 1970s.

The correlation was mostly a spurious one. If one bothered to look at partial correlations, one could easily see that it did not hold for most of the countries in the world – not for the "underdeveloped" or the most "developed." In the poorest and richest countries, respectively, more media meant more market, but not more democracy – media development being above all a consequence and indicator of economic growth. For the 10 richest countries, there was even a strong negative correlation between the number of TV sets and political participation. There were also some significant clusters. One group of countries stood out as relatively media-saturated, but this had no relationship whatsoever to socioeconomic or political development: More media did not mean that these countries were better off in other respects. To this group belonged most of the Latin American countries, many of them then with authoritarian military regimes and a heavy influx of commercial US television, the developmental potential of which was questioned early on by Latin American intellectuals.[6]

The manifold lessons from these statistical exercises are still valid. These studies largely overlooked:

1 Socioeconomic differences within countries (Sklair 1995, 1997).
2 Global power relationships – center–periphery relations.
3 The relation between the two – norths and souths reproducing themselves on national and local levels (Lash 2002), thus producing a globalization of poverty (Nederveen Pieterse 2003, 2004).
4 Further, authoritarianism is perfectly compatible with free market commercialism. This historical fact creates problems for attempts at homogenizing categorizations of national media systems (cf post-Soviet Russia and China, below).
5 Media functions cannot be universally ascertained. In particular, socioeconomic level and position in the world system determine uses and political effects of the media system on social, cultural, and political life and processes.

A generation later, the difficulties in finding easily applicable classificatory principles for the purposes of comparative media research are reflected in attempts to sort countries in terms of their media systems, one reason being that these systems are reflections of complex and differentiated socioeconomic orders. Curran and Park, in their groundbreaking *De-Westernizing Media Studies* (2000), introduced the following two major dimensions as a way of sorting the media systems in today's world: *democratic* vs. *authoritarian* and *neoliberal* vs. *regulated*. However, these authors had to include an extra, fifth category for *"transitional or mixed societies,"* including China, Eastern Europe, Russia, South America, and the Middle East. This category, particularly interesting from the point of view of theorizing media and social change, comprises the most dynamic regions, the new media modernities. It is obvious that we need to introduce other dimensions as well. It is even reasonable to ask whether there exist any nontransitional or non-mixed societies. At least it seems as if most countries are moving along both these dimensions – and others.

I will return to this comparative model, but already here we can use it to speculate about the directions in which these countries might be moving – given the axes of the model. In which of the four possible directions are China, Russia, and the rest of the "transitional and mixed" nations moving? And how far have they advanced since the publication of Curran and Park's book? One thing we know for sure is that the direction of change, given the alternatives defined by this model, depends greatly on interdependent economic and political developments globally *and* nationally. We also know that things move fast in the globalized world and that that in itself creates social and political tensions that have to be taken into consideration when theorizing media and social change.

Postmodern Poverty

Fifty years after the "media and development" paradigm (and the Bandung conference) and 25 years after the cultural imperialism critique, the geopolitical structure of the first, second, and third worlds and one of the two superstates has evaporated with the Cold War. Some 50 new countries have seen the light of day and television and the Internet have turned into dominant media worldwide. Internet access is restricted, but nevertheless a significant factor in Third World countries. Television, however, has a strong presence even in poor countries. I will reflect on this fact below. During the same period, socioeconomic divides within as well as between countries have increased. This also runs parallel to the introduction of parliamentary democracy in Africa, Latin America, and most recently in the post-Soviet world. This "misfit" between economy and politics needs to be taken into account in any analysis of national or local media systems and cultures.[7]

The World Bank's development reports show how the Gini index has developed in a select number of countries over the past 50 years.[8] These are within-country measures, and there is a general long-term increase in economic inequality. Three groups of countries emerge from these statistics:

1   *Extreme inequality*: many Latin American countries (the situation in the Sub-Saharan region is even worse according to other data); Gini exceeds 0.50.
2   *Strong and steadily increasing inequality*: USA, UK, China, Russia, India; Gini within the 0.3–0.40 range.
3   *Moderate inequality* (as everything is relative): continental and northern Europe; Gini below 0.35.

This is about differences *between* countries with respect to differences *within* countries. How does this correlate with media systems and media cultures? The first group, with extreme inequality, is with few exceptions composed of democratic, capitalistic countries with colonial and authoritarian pasts (including apartheid) under military regimes. The media systems are advanced and strictly commercial, especially when it comes to broadcast media (e.g., the Globo and Televisa media empires). The second group is a mixed bag of old and new capitalistic economies, including some old empires, some of the largest parliamentary democracies, but also China (though according to other estimates, China belongs to the first group). The media systems vary considerably, but things in common include strong central (federal) governments and big, more or less globalized media corporations with large nationwide audiences. The third group includes a number of European countries (EU members or not), many of them, especially in the north, (post)welfare societies with public service media as one component of the media structure. Were we to use the above categories, these European systems would be deemed "democratic and regulated" (Curran and Park 2000), or "democratic corporatist/polarized pluralist," to use the typology suggested by Hallin and Mancini (2004).

Inequalities based on economic factors, gender, ethnicity, and so forth, and class divides are the causes of many other conditions, such as crime, violence, corruption, trafficking, and HIV/AIDS (Marmot 2005, Wilkinson 2006). If equality is taken to be an aspect of democracy (for instance as equality of life chances), one has to conclude that economic growth and marketization have little, if anything, to do with democratization. This goes against the grain of liberal political science but, nevertheless, the empirical foundations for this conclusion are overwhelming.

In a study of 14 countries, picked to represent the three groups above, I plotted economic equality (global ranking based on Gini values) against press freedom (global ranking based on interviews and official data) and then dichotomized these variables (high and low positions in the world ranking). The overall correlation is almost nonexistent, meaning that the degree of equality is not linked to the level of press freedom. For instance, in Egypt there are restrictions on press freedom, but the country has relatively high equality. In South Africa, as in Brazil, the situation is the opposite: enormous divides and booming, noncensored commercial media. This is the static picture. In order to capture the dynamics of media and economic growth, I plotted economic growth between 1990 and 2004 (change in global ranking) against press freedom.

The important finding here is that the most expansive new capitalist economies have the poorest record when it comes to press freedoms, parliamentary democracies or not, but with old or neoauthoritarian traits. We are beginning to discern a pattern in which a number of fast-moving capitalist economies (Russia and China being two of them) are also moving in the direction of neoliberalism *and* neoauthoritarianism. This is happening not with the help of old-fashioned, state-driven propaganda machineries, but in media environments seemingly based more on the pleasure principle – which is supportive of both nationalism and patriotism – than on the reality principle, to put it in Freudian terms (Stallybrass 1996). This is not to say that reception is predictable, just that hundreds of millions of people are continuously exposed to the production of consensus from above.

More sophisticated indicators and statistical analyses could probably take us a little further along this path of enquiry, but in order to better understand media in a globalized world, we have to think through some concepts in media and communication studies, developed mostly within the European/Anglo-American orbit. What does it mean, for a start, to move beyond the national confines?

Dewesternizing as Dedisciplining

With the globalization rhetoric that came to the fore in the 1990s, a number of concepts have become problematic and there are many suggestions as to how to get "beyond" or "deconstruct" this and that. What follows is my own contribution to this particular genre.

First, the urge for "internationalization," within academia and elsewhere, leads us to a number of related, but more far-reaching, concepts:

Internationalizing (for instance, media studies): In a strict sense, this refers to relations between or comparisons across nations or nation states. In international politics, a political science subdiscipline, this is often unproblematic. It is simply about interstate relations and activities, or nation-based comparisons. To the extent that the nation as such is problematized, however, "international" dissolves into something "foreign" or, for that matter, "global."[9] In a much broader sense, as pointed out in the Introduction, it may include both comparative approaches and global and transnational processes (Thussu 2006).

Transnationalizing, on the one hand, reflects the conceptual change from "multinational" (no center) to "transnational" corporations (operating from core centers in the world economy). On the other, it is an expression of an ambition to move beyond methodological nationalism and "transnationalize" theory, which I interpret as a way out of locally produced universalizations (wherever they are produced). A third meaning would be a focus on cross-border or translocal processes, mostly reflecting the "deterritorialization" of communication practices.

Dewesternizing (to pick up on Curran and Park's book title) expresses an ambition to make room in media studies for perspectives in the east and south. It also implies that we, at the end of the day, give up our western canons in favor of African, Asian, and Latin American ones. Before that, it would be a great step forward to have these different canons productively confront each other in truly globalized media studies.

This agenda of caveats (or "de-" catchwords) for the global age is far from exhaustive. I have already pinpointed methodological nationalism, which would entail a *denationalizing* of media studies, a giving up of concepts firmly rooted in the figure of thought (or mental container) of the nation-state and its inherited institutions and national myths. A *decolonizing* of media and communication studies, originating in core imperial and colonial nation states, takes a great deal of imagination, a "planetary" perspective (Dussel 1998) or "thinking from the border," from outside European and north-American modernities (Mignolo 2000).

All this adds up to a *dedisciplining* of media and communication studies. I started out with a call for more dialogue with "nonwestern" theory and research perspectives, more cross-disciplinarity, and a return to historical, disciplinary roots, reinserting media in the social and the cultural. From this follows, among other things, a questioning of basic categories and a deconstruction of disciplinary dichotomies such as *politics/culture*,[10] *symbolic/material*, *public/private*, *real/unreal*, *fact/fiction*, *time/space*,[11] *production/consumption*, *word/image*, *text/reader*, *self/other*, *we/them*.[12] This is not the place to discuss these further, beyond the selective endnote explications. Instead, we shall see how the criticism applies to the situation in some concrete societies. Even cursory studies of some "nonwestern" worlds confirm that globalized media studies would benefit considerably from a further dissolution of these binary opposites or, as the case may be, from further inquiries into the inherent dialectics that come into play in actually existing societies. The deconstruction of some such dichotomies does not constitute philosophical word play, but something that is already affected by the media in their mediation, in its broadest sense, not least between institutions.

Difference and Change in Media Modernities

In recent years, I have studied media developments and media cultures in "postau-thoritarian" and "neoauthoritarian" systems, "new democracies," and whatever other labels have been used (Curran and Park's fifth category). These societies, for instance Brazil, China, and Russia, have served as laboratories for natural experiments in media and social change (Ekecrantz et al. 2003).

They have many things in common, distinguishing them from most other countries: size; rapid immersion into the world capitalist system (ratified by WTO or Nafta membership);[13]economic growth; democratic deficits by the exclusion of large groups in terms of class, gender, and ethnicity from public spheres; economic and social divides; and political, cultural, and regional divisions, thus problematizing the notion of the nation as a homogenous and meaningful unit. Divides are not only between countries in the north and south, respectively, but very much within nation-states, the poor and the rich often living quite close together.[14]

What they also have in common is that they are *media modernities*, or media-driven modernities. How do media mediate between the social classes and between other groupings, producing a mediated visibility with repercussions for social relations and struggles? National, urban bourgeoisies are certainly visible in news, entertainment, and advertising, and this applies to Brazil, Russia, and China (cf Lerner's model).[15]

The media modernities of these huge polities are thus based on differentiations that are political, social, regional, and temporal, but also ideological and cultural. All of these are heightened by the rapid transformations. The different Chinas, for example (Zhao 2003), are bound to produce diverging discourses, impossible to harmonize in a unified hegemonic order, even when history is sometimes effectively suppressed – or when foreign news and the Internet are censored (Lagerkvist 2006).[16]

In post-Soviet Russia, the relationship between politics and economy, with media as mediator, defies most known models. The first years of the 1990s were characterized by independent media that operated as a "fourth power" (1991–5). Then entered a highly politicized media system that operated in a society turned into a spectacle (1996–2000). This fragmented "media-political system" (termed the "media-political complex" by Curran and Park 2000, 14) operates in a full-fledged commercial environment. However, the fluidity of the "Russian" media system[17] has its spatial counterparts. In 87 out of 89 regions in Russia, one finds seven different "media models."[18] This raises doubts as to whether there exists a "Russian," or for that matter, a "Brazilian" or "Chinese" media system.

Before Putin's presidency (starting in 2000), Brian McNair saw the implications of the Russian system in terms of a new and unique form of capitalism that seriously threatens the democratic transition: "In this respect Russia, for all its robber-baron primitivism, may turn out to be a pioneer of the media-driven capitalism of the twenty-first century, in which the controller of information in all its commodity forms – journalism, entertainment, computer software, data services – are established as the key sub-sector of the capitalist owning class as a whole" (McNair 2000, 89). What could now best be described as media-driven state capitalism, a system yielding both financial and political profits, defies most known media models. Outside academia, however, it has been subjected to both intellectual criticism and literary satire.[19] This appeals not least to the younger generations, who are turning away from television. These Russian generations today seem totally alienated from official politics, as enacted on national TV channels, today directly or indirectly controlled by the Kremlin.[20] It tends to "adapt to any conditions and turn to private lives as spheres of self-realization while almost completely ignoring the virtual community of the nation state" (Zassoursky,2009). To the extent that this is a valid description of today's Russian youth, it has gone a long way since the attempted coup in August 1991, when various groups of young people were active on the barricades, embodying a politics of pleasure, which challenged the dominant meaning of politics (Pilkington 1994, 303 ff), or since young protesters spread red paint on the White House in Moscow as a demonstration against the first war in Chechnya.

One may not agree with all of these analyses, but they have served here to concretize my thesis that some prevailing disciplinary dichotomies (politics/economy/culture) – and western institutional models – do not hold. A lack of institutional stability and national homogeneity undermines methodological nationalism. Political communication forms in northern and southern mainland China, closer to westernized Hong Kong, are almost as different as popular cultural forms in different parts of Brazil, from Afro-Brazilian capoeira in the northeast to favela hip hop in Rio, to gaucho cowboy culture in the south.

The spatial structures of modernity have a temporal side. The timing and speed of entry into the world capitalist system and the rate at which a society has been transformed in the recent past ("keeping pace with time" in today's official Chinese rhetoric) seem to be significant factors for at least two reasons. First, there exists a collective experience of change in society and in everyday life for a large portion of the population. Zhen describes how this is related to "a larger cultural anxiety about temporality … the rapid transition from socialism to a market economy … different temporalities – old and new, socialist and capitalist, global and local – have collided … the perils of speed have made anxiety a central feature of public discourse" (Zhen 2001, 132). This quote certainly apostrophizes the collapse of some received dichotomies as far as rapidly transforming societies are concerned.

Conclusion

The emerging global system of social classes and power structures is the most significant trait pertaining to "globality," which means that there are winners and losers and all kinds of widening gaps and divisions. The rise to power of global elites is mirrored at the other end of the socioeconomic scale in the masses of forced national and international migrants and hundreds of millions of unemployed owing to economic globalization – read capitalist expansion – into new world regions led by globalized elites with their feet in transnational corporations and neoliberal governments.[21] Comparative cross-disciplinary case studies can take us a long way if we are interested in getting to know what all this means in actually existing media modernities. Let me conclude by returning to the introductory arguments for basic cross-disciplinarity in media studies and point at some such efforts under way.

A new *macrosociology of media* would focus on the intersection of global and national class systems and the ways in which they shape the media, media cultures, and mediated conflicts. Other cross-disciplinary encounters have already made an imprint in global media studies. *Anthropology*, for instance, is a relative newcomer in media studies, but it could contribute substantially to our understanding of translocality and "transmodernity," based on a deterritorialized notion of culture that privileges *routes* instead of *roots* (Clifford 1997).

Comparative literature could show us experiences of media modernities outside the North Atlantic orbit. Latin America and Asia, for instance, provide us with a wealth of literary reflections on what it means to live in media-saturated urban environments (if read in that way) far away from the core areas of the modern world system – as did many of the classical modernist authors in Europe.[22] *Comparative media history* is needed to unravel the deep historical structures of today's global communications, such as the circuits of commerce that produced western and other modernities in the first place ("globalization" being the cause, not the consequence of modernity – in this perspective). I have already mentioned the field of *new global social movements*.

Globalizing media and communication studies thus implies more than an aggrandizement of the research object and more than adding countries to the bag of comparisons. For one thing, it is about the inclusion of other kinds of media users, cultural producers, and political animals, than those typified or implicated in much research – those who happen to live in rich countries, who are targeted as consumers or even citizens with entertainment or information, while sitting comfortably in their homes after work. This was the type codified within the paradigm of affluence out of which mass communication research sprung in the postwar period.[23] As we all know, however, there are masses of nonrich people "out there" (also in the rich part of the world) and they are not consumers, do not think of themselves as citizens of a polity and they do not come home after work, because they have no work and hence no leisure time and no place to spend it anyway. But they also have in common that they inhabit and are dependent on what goes on in heavily media-saturated societies. This is a historically new equation or paradox, calling for new alliances in media studies, both between and beyond disciplines and their national habitats.

Notes

A version of this chapter was previously published in *Nordicom Review*, Jubilee Issue 2007, pp. 169–81. It draws on three papers presented, respectively, at the IAMCR conference in Cairo, July 24–28, 2006, the conference "Internationalising Media Studies: Imperatives and Impediments," University of Westminster, London, September 15–16, 2006, and the Russia in Flux Research Programme Seminar, Academy of Finland, Helsinki, October 27, 2006.

1 Zelizer (2004) has reviewed a broad range of contributions to journalism studies from many different disciplines. A similar treatment of media studies, as a broader field, would require a book series.
2 See, for instance, Downing's (1996) criticism of political science for its neglect of media and communication aspects, also when it is concerned with political influence.
3 See also Thompson's retrospective discussion and contextualization of Lerner's book, 40 years after the publication of *The Passing of Traditional Society* (Thompson 1995, 188–97).
4 See McPhail (2006) for brief overviews of models at the time, including the economic growth model. Rostow's theory of stages is now, after 1989, being reintroduced in a new shape in much "transition" research. Updates of the debate on developmentalism are found in Hemer and Tufte (2005).
5 This was a form of "denial of coevalness": people in "backward" parts of the world are not really our contemporaries (Fabian 1983).
6 For data on the phenomenal, continued growth of media around the world, Latin America included, between the 1970s and the late 1990s, see Carlsson (2005, 209).
7 In the following, I have used secondary data and done some simple calculations myself. My IAMCR paper, Cairo 2006, gives the more complete picture.
8 Roughly speaking, the Gini index measures the ratio between the income of the richest and that of the poorest. It ranges from 1 (maximum inequality: one person has all the income) to 0 (no one has more than any other).
9 In Swedish academia, an "international publication" may be a text (1) in an "international" journal (in one of the so-called world languages), or a text either (2) published in English, anywhere, for instance by Nordicom in Gothenburg, or (3) published abroad, in any language.
10 See Brooksbank Jones (2000, 1) on "the progressive 'enculturing' of politics in response to deepening social divisions," "the political significance of cultural practices in extra-institutional politics," and "the imbrication of culture and politics (as analytic

categories and as practices)." See also Sassen (2006) on how cultural events become political, e.g., street activities, and about the increasing importance of the nonformal forms and places of politics: real political processes that cannot be contained within the formal political system. I have tried to systematize this thematic in Ekecrantz (2006).

11 See Bakhtin (1981/1934–5) on the study of chronotopes (timespaces) as determining, together, the capacities of fictional genres; Wallerstein (1997) shows how the temporal and the spatial are interlinked in sociological and historical forms of knowledge.

12 There is a risk that the ubiquitous criticism of this figure of thought just reproduces Orientalism by producing a similarly universalist (meta)discourse. Sardar voices a concern over representations of the "Other" in history, anthropology, and politics: "Postmodernism's obsession with representation of the Other in fiction is designed to project this representation back as reality and hence shape and reshape the Other according to its own desires" (Sardar 1998, 176). We/them is an often taken-for-granted distinction, sometimes downplaying similarities and mystifying difference (not least when the "east–west" dyad is evoked).

13 In Brazil and China, half of their gigantic populations are younger than 25–27, which means that in China this group amounts to some 650 million people.

14 The richest person in Brazil, the owner of the Globo empire, has his well-guarded mansion on a slope in Rio de Janeiro, with favelas uphill.

15 A Russian reality soap showing the everyday life of the immensely rich in a secluded block on the edge of the Moscow River attracted a huge audience.

16 Chin-Chuan Lee catches this well: "In China the media have been battling a confluence of ideological currents and moulding a hybrid ideology ridden with conflicting identities, images, and subjectivities. In this sense, the media have been a site of ideological contestation and accommodation, derived from the ambiguities and contradictions between the revolutionary rhetoric of Communism and the practical discourses of marketization" (in Lee 2003, 17).

17 This is based on Zassoursky (2004), but there are other such short-term periodizations.

18 The market model; the transitional to market model; the conflict model; the modernized Soviet model; the paternalistic Soviet model; the authoritarian Soviet model; the depressed model (Koltsova 2006, 166).

19 As in the works of Viktor Pelevin, for instance *Generation P*, and the not yet translated *Vampyre*. Among other critical analysts, Irina Petrovskaya and Alexij Pankin should be mentioned.

20 Through state channels or large holdings in companies such as Gazprom, in its turn owner of major media since the ousting of media moguls and oligarchs such as Berezovskij and Guzinski.

21 The transnational capitalist class as conceived of by Leslie Sklair is composed of four groups or fractions: (1) transnational corporation executives and their local affiliates, (2) globalizing state bureaucrats, (3) globalizing politicians and professionals, and (4) consumerist elites (merchants, media) (Sklair 1998, 299 ff).

22 Like Josef Conrad and James Joyce, see Donovan (2001).

23 From Paddy Scannell's presentation at the "Internationalising Media Studies: Imperatives and Impediments" conference, University of Westminster, London, September 15–16, 2006.

References

Appadurai, A. (1996) *Modernity at Large: Cultural Dimensions of Globalization*. University of Minnesota Press, Minneapolis, MN.

Atton, C. (2002) *Alternative Media*. Sage, London.

Bakhtin, M. (1981/1934–5) *The Dialogic Imagination*. University of Texas Press, Austin.

Beck, U. (2002) The cosmopolitan society and its enemies. *Theory, Culture & Society*, special issue on Cosmopolis, 19(1–2), 17–44.

Brooksbank Jones, A. (2000) Cultural politics in a Latin American frame. In: Brooksbank Jones, A. and Munck, R. (eds), *Cultural Politics in Latin America*. Macmillan, Basingstoke, UK, pp. 1–26.

Carlsson, U. (2005) From NWICO to global governance of the information society. In: Hemer, O. and Tufte, T. (eds), *Media and Glocal Change*. Gothenburg. *Rethinking Communication for Development*. Clacso/Nordicom, Buenos Aires, pp. 216–46.

Castells, M. (1996) *The Information Age, Vol. I: The Rise of the Network Society*. Blackwell, Oxford.

Clifford, J. (1997) *Routes: Travel and Translation in the Late Twentieth Century*. Harvard University Press, Cambridge, MA.

Couldry, N. and Curran, J. (eds) (2003) *Contesting Media Power: Alternative Media in a Networked World*. Rowman & Littlefield Publishers, Lanham, MD.

Curran, J. and Park, M.-J. (eds) (2000) *De-Westernizing Media Studies*. Routledge, New York.

Donovan, S. (2001) Literary modernism and the press, 1870–1922. Dissertation, Göteborg University.

Downing, J. D. H. (1996) *Internationalizing Media Theory: Transition, Power, Culture*. Sage, London.

Dussel, E. (1998) Beyond eurocentrism, the world-system and the limits of modernity. In: Jameson, F. and Miyoshi, M. (eds), *The Cultures of Globalization*, Duke University Press, Durham, NC, pp. 3–31.

Ekecrantz, J. (2006) Espetáculos midiazados e comunicações democráticas, entre a hegemonia global e a ação cívica. In: Maia, R. and Castro, M. C. (eds), *Mídia, Esfera Pública e Identidades Coletivas*. Editora UFMG, Belo Horizonte, pp. 93–116.

Ekecrantz, J., Maia, R., and Castro, M. C. (2003) Media and modernities, the cases of Brazil and Russia. *Stockholm Media Studies I*. JMK, Stockholm.

Fabian, J. (1983) *Time and the Other: How Anthropology Makes its Object*. Columbia University Press, New York.

Hallin, D. and Mancini, P. (2004) *Comparing Media Systems: Three Models of Media and Politics*. Cambridge University Press, Cambridge, UK.

Hemer, O. and Tufte, T. (eds) (2005) *Media and Glocal Change: Rethinking Communication for Development*. Clacso/Nordicom, Buenos Aires.

Kaldor, M. (1999) *New and Old Wars: Organized Violence in a Global Era*. Polity Press, Cambridge, UK.

Koltsova, E. (2006) *News Production and Power in Post-Soviet Russia*. Routledge, New York.

Lagerkvist, J. (2006) *The Internet in China: Unlocking and Containing the Public Sphere*. Department of East Asian Languages, Lund University, Sweden.

Lash, S. (2002) *Critique of Information*. London: Sage Publications.

Lee, C. C. (ed.) (2003) *Chinese Media, Global Context*. Routledge, New York.

Lerner, D. (1958) *The Passing of Traditional Society*. The Free Press, Glencoe, IL.

Lerner, D. and Schramm, W. (eds) (1967) *Communication and Change in the Developing Countries*. East-West Center, Honolulu.

Marmot M. (2005) *Status Syndrome: How Your Social Standing Directly Affects Your Health*. Bloomsbury, London.

Martín-Barbero, J. (1993) *Communication, Culture, Hegemony*. Sage, London.

McNair, B. (2000) Power, profit, corruption, and lies, the Russian media in the 1990s. In: Curran, J. and Park, M. J. (eds), *De-Westernizing Media Studies*. Routledge, New York, pp. 79–94.

McPhail, T. L. (2006) *Global Communication: Theories, Stakeholders, and Trends*. Blackwell, Oxford.

Mignolo, W. D. (2000) *Local Histories/Global Designs: Coloniality, Subaltern Knowledges and Border Thinking*. Princeton University Press, Princeton, NJ.

Nederveen Pieterse, J. (2003) *Globalization and Culture: Global Mélange*. Rowman & Littlefield, New York.

Nederveen Pieterse, J. (2004) *Globalization or Empire?* Routledge, New York.

Pilkington, H. (1994) *Russia's Youth and its Culture: A Nation's Constructors and Constructed*. Routledge, New York.

Pye, L. (ed.) (1963) *Communications and Political Development*. Princeton University Press, Princeton, NJ.

Robertson, R. (1992) *Globalization: Social Theory and Global Culture*. Sage, London.

Sardar, Z. (1998) *Postmodernism and the Other: The New Imperialism of Western Culture*. Pluto Press, London.

Sassen, S. (2006) *Territory, Authority, Rights: From Medieval to Global Assemblages*. Princeton University Press, Princeton, NJ.

Schiller, H. I (1969) *Mass Communication and American Empire*. Beacon Press, Boston, MA.

Schiller, H. I (1976) *Communication and Cultural Domination*. M. E. Sharp, New York.

Siebert, F. S., Peterson, T., and Schramm, W. (1956) *Four Theories of the Press: The Authoritarian, Libertarian, Social Responsibility and Soviet Communist Concepts of What the Press Should Be and Do*. University of Illinois Press, Urbana, IL.

Sklair, L. (1995) *Sociology of the Global System*. Harvester, London.

Sklair, L. (1997) Classifying the global system. In: Sreberny-Mohammadi, A., Winseck, D., McKenna, J., and Boyd-Barret, O. (eds), *Media in Global Context: A Reader*. Arnold, London, pp. 41–7.

Sklair, L. (1998) Globalization and the corporations: The case of the California *Fortune* Global 500. *International Journal of Urban and Regional Research*, 22(2), 195–215.

Stallybrass, J. (1996) *Gargantua: Manufactured Mass Culture*. Verso, New York.

Thompson, J. B. (1995) *The Media and Modernity: A Social Theory of the Media*. Polity Press, Cambridge, UK.

Thussu, D. K. (2006) *International Communication: Continuity and Change*, 2nd edn. Hodder Education, London.

Tsagarousianou, R. (2004) Rethinking the concept of diaspora, mobility, connectivity and communication in a globalized world. *Westminster Papers in Communication and Culture*, 1(1), 52–66.

Wallerstein, I. (1997) SpaceTime as the basis of knowledge. Online at http://fbc.binghamton.edu/iwsptm.htm (accessed October 20, 2010).

Wilkinson, R. G. (2006) *The Impact of Inequality: How to Make Sick Societies Healthier.* Routledge, London.

Zassoursky, I. (2004) *Media and Power in Post-Soviet Russia.* M. E. Sharpe, London.

Zassoursky, I. (2009) Media and politics in Russia in the nineties. Online at http://www.oocities.com/zassoursky/paper.htm (accessed October 20, 2010).

Zelizer, B. (2004) *Taking Journalism Seriously: News and the Academy.* Sage, London.

Zhao, Y. (2003) "Enter the world": Neo-liberalism globalization, the dream for a strong nation, and Chinese press discourses on the WTO. In: Lee, C. (ed.), *Chinese Media, Global Context.* Routledge, New York, pp. 32–56.

Zhen, Z. (2001) The "rice bowl of youth" in fin de siècle urban China. In: Appadurai, A. (ed.), *Globalization.* Duke University Press, Durham, NC, pp. 131–54.

23

New International Debates on Culture, Information, and Communication

Armand Mattelart (translation by Liz Libbrecht)

One of the main changes in recent years in the fields of culture, information, and communication has been in the topography of the places in which their status is negotiated, in relation to their increasing appropriation by private or corporate interests. UNESCO, the World Trade Organization (WTO), the International Tele-communications Union (ITU), and the World Intellectual Property Organization (WIPO) have all been involved in setting this international agenda. Notwithstanding the division of tasks assigned to them in the United Nations system, a guiding principle runs through the themes that each organization deals with: cultural diversity, liberalization of services and audiovisual flows, the information society, intellectual property.

The topography of the agents has also changed. A new configuration of socio-political and professional players has emerged and is making itself heard in these institutions: industry trade associations and lobbies exerting pressure to break down public regulations in the name of freedom of trade and self-regulation, as well as the multiple components of civil society. For example, the international coalition of professional organizations promoting culture for cultural diversity, relayed by a network of national collectives; the collective of networks against neoliberal globalization, CRIS (Communication Rights in Information Society), participating in debate on the architecture of information and communication networks and Internet governance; the collectives against the intrusive technologies of mass surveillance and registration; and the world network of cities and local authorities committed to participating in the struggle against "digital exclusion." This new motley configuration of actors from organized civil society has

The Handbook of Political Economy of Communications, First Edition.
Edited by Janet Wasko, Graham Murdock, and Helena Sousa.
© 2014 John Wiley & Sons, Ltd. Published 2014 by John Wiley & Sons, Ltd.

moreover given itself new agoras: the world social forums of Porto Alegre, Brazil, since 2001, are one example among many. Finally, there has also been the creation, by collectives of citizens, of permanent critical watchdogs known as "observatories" of the cultural industries and the media.

To fully grasp the changes that have occurred concerning the place of the culture –information–communication triad in the debates of international institutions, the first part of this chapter considers the process that culminated in UNESCO's adoption, in October 2005, of the Convention on the Protection and Promotion of the Diversity of Cultural Expressions. The idea is not to analyze it in detail, but to point out some elements of its genealogy, and to highlight its strengths as well as revealing its blind spots. More so than the others, this case affords the opportunity to put things into perspective. Why? Because this convention was the first major political battle waged by UNESCO since the 1980s. It took place more than 20 years after the achievements of the particularly fecund debates on cultural and communication policies, held within this institution, had been shelved – 20 years that coincided with the unfolding of the international process of dismantling public regulations, started with Ronald Reagan's United States and Margaret Thatcher's Britain walking out of the institution in 1984–85. In the second part of the chapter, I examine the philosophy guiding the new sociopolitical actors in their intervention in all these places where the status of the triad is debated and decided.

The UNESCO Convention on Diversity of Cultural Expressions

Who controls the concepts?

The projection of culture, information, and communication into the debate on the new architecture of the world order has highlighted contrasts between social projects and between value systems. Increased jamming of the semantic field of these key concepts attests to the significance of the battle over the meaning of words. To be sure, this is nothing new. In 1974 Michel de Certeau noted, in *La Culture au pluriel*, that: "Any talk about cultural problems advances on the ground of unstable words; it is impossible to determine a conceptual definition of these terms: their meanings depend on their functioning in ideologies and disparate systems" (Certeau 1974, 189). But the phenomenon of impoverishment of language has intensified with the tendency of the market of words to be reduced to the words of the market. In this respect the notion of information, spawned by communication engineering, has been a Trojan horse. And it seems that the spirit of commerce has done the rest: not the one of Immanuel Kant who thought that trade was a factor of peace between people, the base of a world community, but one of the distant disciples of classical political economics. By severing itself from culture, as a production of meaning and memory, the notion of information has short-circuited all the other terms of the triad. Hence, there is nothing surprising about a technical organization like the ITU being promoted host of a summit on the future of "society," via the intermediary of information. And what could be more natural than the WTO classifying "culture" under "services" and demanding prerogatives concerning it!

It cannot be stressed enough that the "ground of unstable words" carries with it mental and institutional tools that shape the norms, classifications, nomenclatures, and schemas of perception and interpretation on which action models, strategies, and policies are aligned. This instability also paves the way for amnesic neologisms destined to be converted into logotype concepts; closed concepts that produce "effects of reality," precisely through the action models that they frame and legitimize as the only possibilities. An eloquent example is the role played by the black box of "globalization." Put into circulation in the first half of the 1980s – the heyday of challenging the public sphere, with the deregulation of finance networks, telecommunications, and big advertising groups – it contributed to producing a vision of a world reorganized on the basis of fatality. The multisecular movement aimed at world unification found itself stripped of its history and its conflictual geopolitics. Reduced to a phenomenon that was no older than two or three decades, it was proof that erasing traces of the production of words is concomitant not only with forgetting history, but also with historical revisionism.

The "quarrel with the short-term" launched by Fernand Braudel in the 1950s against anthropologists and sociologists seduced by the mathematical model of linear causality, is no less relevant today. The social sciences, noted the historian, have got into the habit of "putting themselves at the service of the present" and confining themselves to "only those actors who make themselves heard." But the social is a "game with a different kind of cunning" (Braudel 1958, 35). The historian of the *Annales* school encouraged a revival of the plurality of social time and the "dialectic of duration" by turning the hourglass both ways: from the structure to the event; from freedom to belonging, with the constraints that any construction of identity entails; from the universe to the place and diversity (Braudel 1958). This need to escape the race for the present, for "presentism," guides my genealogical approach.

Institutionalization of the "culture industries" concept

From the early 1970s two concepts were established at UNESCO that were to prove pivotal in guiding the debates, proposals, measures, and strategies that worked towards legitimizing the idea of public policy on communication and culture: the "right to communication" and the "culture industries."

The idea of the "right to communication" was put forward publicly in 1969 by Jean d'Arcy, pioneer of French television and then director of the radio and visual services division at the UN Information Service in New York. At the time, the debate on civil rights in the information field was taking shape at UNESCO. In an article in the journal of the European Broadcasting Union (EBU) he wrote: "The time will come when the Universal Declaration of Human Rights will have to encompass a more extensive right than the right to information, first laid down twenty-one years ago in Article 19. This is the human right to communicate" (d'Arcy 1969, 14).

Throughout the next decade, in the numerous panel discussions and controversies, the idea of the validity of the vertical model with a one-way information flow simply spewing out content started to crack. A representation started to emerge of communication as a dialogical and reciprocal process, where access and participation became essential. Experts in one of the first panel discussions on communication policies and planning, organized in 1972 by UNESCO, asserted their refusal of the idea of communication from the elite to the masses, from the center to the periphery, or from the information-rich to the information-poor, for example. From these meetings between legal experts emerged the principle of difference, with no distinction on the grounds of nationality, race, language, religion, or gender.

The concept of "cultural industries," introduced in the second half of the 1970s, was designed to change the prevailing perception of "culture." An expert committee, convened by UNESCO in co-operation with the Canadian National Commission for UNESCO, met in Montreal in June 1980. The following are some excerpts from the founding texts.

> The increasing place given to cultural industries in UNESCO's programme is linked to a process of reappraisal that has been going on for a number of years in thinking about culture.
>
> [...]
>
> Thinking during the past decade has had the merit of seeking to implant the cultural debate in the material context of its subject, particularly when it has deliberately focused on the problems of cultural production (how cultural products are thought up, selected, designed, manufactured, distributed, promoted and consumed), even though some authorities still refuse to grant the due importance of the "industries of imagination." (UNESCO 1980, 1, 6)

With this new perspective, "the trend towards the economic and financial concentration and internationalization of cultural industries" was seen as a fundamental issue from the outset.

> Economic analyses should remain central to a programme of reflection which aims to be exhaustive. They should also study in greater detail the general problems and the sectoral aspects of the cultural industries. It is also quite clearly on the basis of such analyses that the public sectors will set up or develop national cultural industries. (UNESCO 1980, 14)

The outcome was a general philosophy on development, articulated in the conclusions of this meeting in Montreal:

In any case, what is at stake is the establishment or resumption of a dialogue between cultures, which would no longer take place only between producers and consumers but would foster conditions for collective and truly diversified creative effort in which the receiver would become a transmitter in his turn, while guaranteeing that the transmitter, even when institutionalized, would learn to become a receiver once again. What is at stake is harmonious development in diversity and mutual respect. (UNESCO 1982a, 236)

The themes "dialogue of cultures" and "harmonious development in diversity and mutual respect" were already prevalent. At the time, they inspired the work of the International Commission for the Study of Communication Problems, appointed by the then Director General of UNESCO, Senegalese Mohtar M'Bow, and presided over by Sean MacBride, Nobel Peace Prize laureate from Ireland. The MacBride Report, the first document on the inequality of cultural and information exchange to be issued by an international institution, endorsed by the UNESCO general conference in 1980 in Belgrade and published under the symbolic title *Many Voices, One World*, explained the urgency of considering the right to communication as an expression of new social rights: the right to know, the right to transmit, the right to discuss, the right to a private life. Most importantly, from the right to communication it inferred the necessity for a new world order and for public policy on culture and communication (MacBride and International Commission for the Study of Communication Problems 1980).

Rehabilitation of cultures

Entry into the postcolonial era overturned the north/south balance of power throughout the United Nations system. At the time, the challenge to the cultural and communication world order was in phase with the crisis of the diffusionist development/modernization paradigm, an offshoot of the ideology of linear and infinite progress. The way of seeing the world that had prevailed in UNESCO's strategies since the 1950s and had consecrated the ideology of communication as a solution, backed by functionalist sociology, was being eroded. The counterpoint of this discontinuity was the recognition of the singularity of cultures as a source of identity, meaning, dignity, and social innovation. As the linear view of the transmission of values collapsed, diversity was established as a prerequisite in the quest for a way out of so-called underdevelopment. It was seen as an alternative to the therapies guided by the ideology of calculation (the GNP) and technical determinism. The rehabilitation of the creativity of cultures was combined with the emphasis on solidarity at local, national, and global level, the celebration of the "spirit of place," the categorical imperative of citizen's participation, and the concern for biodiversity. This new philosophy of growth made it possible to unearth a buried historical memory, kindled by the thinkers of the unity–diversity duo in the Third

World, from Mahatma Gandhi to Brazilian educator Paulo Freire. It was also a warning against misuse of the quest for cultural diversity: shirking shared global responsibility; chaotic fragmentation without due regard for the numerous inequities based on systems of privilege rooted in cast, race, class, gender, and nation (Galtung et al. 1980). The plea of the Movement of Non-Aligned Countries for a new world order in the field of culture and communication paralleled the efforts deployed by the Group of 77 to change the terms of commercial trade through a "new economic world order."

The challenging of the existing cultural and communicational order was also in phase with the change of paradigm in a sector of academic research. It was the period in which the project of a political economy of communication and culture – or, more broadly, as Raymond Williams put it, an approach inspired by "cultural materialism" – was being established, primarily in Europe and Latin America, always within specific contexts. The intellectual challenge was to avoid the two pitfalls of economic reductionism and idealist autonomization of culture, and to articulate its various levels and dimensions: imagination and infrastructure; international, national, and local; public policies and grass roots.

In 1982 the World Conference on Cultural Policies (Mondiacult) in Mexico City crowned a process initiated 12 years earlier at the Venice Conference on the same subject, punctuated by regional conferences on both cultural and communication policies (Mattelart et al. 1984). Mondiacult emphasized the link between economy and culture, economic development and cultural development. It outlined the principle of a cultural policy based on the recognition of diversity, aimed at enhancing individual and collective creativity way beyond the arts, in other forms of invention. The main contribution of this conference was above all the establishment of the anthropological definition of culture in institutional references: "The set of distinctive spiritual, material, intellectual, and emotional features of society or a social group. In addition to art and literature, it encompasses lifestyles, basic human rights, value systems, traditions, and beliefs" (UNESCO 1982b). This broad and all-encompassing view of the role of culture articulated the universal idea of fundamental rights, to the particular features of lifestyle through which members of a group experienced their bond with others. Another contribution of Mondiacult was to build bridges between the concepts of cultural policy and communication policy, two themes that had developed on the different continents in the 1970s, sometimes in parallel, sometimes in synergy through numerous regional conferences. The rehabilitation of the anthropological definition of culture, which had been given a rough handling since UNESCO's foundation, was a way of breaking free of the ascendancy of the instrumental conception of communication and information severed from peoples' history and memory. This conception had governed the crafting of diffusionist development strategies by social planners throughout the 1960s. It was, however, the anthropological definition of culture that made the notions of cultural diversity, cultural identity, and intercultural relations meaningful.

For a number of reasons, the debate at UNESCO on questions of communication and culture, and particularly on a new world order, turned into a dialogue of the deaf: the intolerance of Reagan's United States, clinging to its doctrine of free flow of information, which managed to narrow the focus down to freedom of journalism and journalists only, especially around issues of societies of professional journalists and the international code of ethics; the opportunism of the Soviet Union, taking advantage of the Third World's demands to better justify the closure of its own communication system to "foreign intervention"; the contradictions in the Movement of Non-Aligned Countries, in which certain governments grasped this international tribune as an opportunity to single out scapegoats and overlook their own violations of their journalists' and creators' freedom of expression (in addition to the extreme heterogeneity of the technological equipment of the nonaligned countries); finally, the incapacity to bridge the gap between the concerns of nonaligned countries and those of countries of the European Community, as the latter started to fear the threats to their public services and cultural democratization policies, spawned by the internationalization of the cultural industries.

As regards the nonstate protagonists in the debate on the new order, we could say that while, on the one hand, media and advertising trade associations rapidly became aware of the necessity for a united front to counter the demands of the Third World, there was, on the other hand, an absence of structured action by organized civil society. At the time, the prevailing approach to communication among the nongovernmental organizations (NGOs), labor unions, and political parties was still strongly influenced by an instrumental view of communication devices. This was all the more paradoxical in that NGOs in many fields had invented the slogan "think global, act local." They had mobilized via new forms of networked action around issues such as the environment, human rights, and the excesses of transnational companies (e.g., in the pharmaceuticals or agrifood sectors). It was only in 1983 that one of the first networks, the World Association of the Community Radio Broadcasters (AMARC), was structured, in Montreal. Unsurprisingly, the third general assembly of this network was held in Managua, five years later, in a revolutionary Nicaragua where communication and popular education experiences were flourishing, radio occupied a predominant place, and Paulo Freire's *Pedagogy of the Oppressed* inspired adult literacy campaigns (Mattelart 1986).

The cultural exception

From the second half of the 1980s, the commonly accepted belief of deregulation and privatization established itself as the guiding principle of globalization on an international scale. It contributed to freezing public policy debate on culture and communication within the UN system.

Only in debate on the role of the communication space in the construction of large trade zones was the principle that "products of the mind" were not merchandise like any other still questioned in the 1990s. This was the case of the European Union, the first experience of macroregional integration. The tug-of-war between the EU and the US in 1994 within the General Agreement on Tariffs and Trade (GATT), during the so-called Uruguay Round – just before the GATT became the WTO – ended with recognition of the "cultural exception" clause that legitimized public policies on broadcasting and films at both national and regional level. The experience of debate on cultural exception in the European Union was a test case. On this occasion, the first mobilization of culture professionals around the citizen's right to communication and against culture as a commodity appeared, notably through the organization in 1987, in France, of the *"Etats généraux de la culture,"* a grand Assembly which rallied people of culture and arts not only in France but throughout the EU (Ralite 1987).

The legitimization of the rule of exception represented the third failure of the US's strategy to liberalize the sector. In 1989 it had suffered its first setback when it tried to suspend application of the EU directive "television without borders" on the policy of quotas for European programs on TV channels in the Union. During negotiations in the same year on the free trade agreement between the US and Canada, the latter had secured a "cultural exemption" clause that it was to renew five years later at the signing of the North American Free Trade Agreement (NAFTA). This enabled it to continue or to adopt policies favorable to public television, tax credits for the development of television, a national fund for cable and satellite TV, and measures concerning publishing and cinema. In 1994 the Mexican government nevertheless refused to include in the NAFTA agreement a clause similar to the one secured by Canada.

Canada and France (supported by the Francophone countries) were the two states that had distinguished themselves in the construction of this philosophy, which reserved a special status for culture. It was therefore no coincidence that in 2001 they found themselves as leaders in the promotion of the project for an International Convention on the Protection and Promotion of the Diversity of Cultural Expressions. This was evidence that in the new configurations of institutional and citizen players, the idea of the necessity of cultural and communication policies designed at a global level was also the fruit of historical processes anchored in singular cultures. In these two countries, there was a close connection between the clause of contemporary cultural exception, the philosophy underlying the establishment of their public audiovisual services, and the cinematographic policies of quotas on Hollywood films from the 1920s and 1930s.

All these antecedents of culture and communication policies served as a background to debate, from 2001 to 2005, on the adoption of the convention on diversity.

Cultural diversity: a conflictual and contradictory paradigm

At the 33rd general conference of UNESCO in October 2005, the member states almost unanimously approved the Convention on the Protection and Promotion of the Diversity of Cultural Expressions. The United States and Israel were among the very few countries to abstain. The US's hostility was proportional to the importance of the document. After the vote at least 30 countries had to have ratified the Convention for it to come into force, a condition that was not met until March 2007. Washington therefore took advantage of that interval to maintain its demands on bilateral trade partners to open their film and audiovisual markets in exchange for commercial compensation in other sectors. An emblematic case was South Korea, a country that had distinguished itself since 1985 for the independence of its film policy, which had enabled it to nurture a high-quality, internationally recognized film industry. Yet in bilateral trade negotiations, it bowed to pressure by agreeing to halve the quota of locally produced films shown in the country.

The Convention has unquestionably been a symbolic step. By making cultural diversity part of humanity's common heritage, it opposes "inward-looking fundamentalism" and "humanized globalisation," as the Director General of UNESCO put it (Koïchiro 2001, 3). Its key principle of diversity in dialogue is deliberately contrary to Samuel Huntington's claim that a clash between cultures and civilizations is inevitable (Huntington 1996). Moreover, by recognizing the specific nature of cultural activities, goods, and services, the convention has laid the foundations of a supranational law that runs counter to the project of unbridled liberalization. It has established rules for the rights and obligations of states: "The parties reaffirm their sovereign right to formulate and implement their cultural policies and to adopt measures to protect and promote the diversity of cultural expressions and to strengthen international cooperation to achieve the purposes of this convention" (Article 5).[1] Unlike the principles of cultural exception and exemption, its field of application stretches beyond the preserve of the audiovisual and cultural industries, spreading "to the manifold ways in which the cultures of groups and societies find expression. These expressions are passed on within and among groups and societies" (Article 4). The "manifold ways" include not only language policies but also the promotion of native peoples' knowledge systems.

The kingpin of the legal structure is the principle of sovereignty: a state can recover its right to make its own cultural policies, even if it previously relinquished that right in bilateral trade agreements. For the convention to be legally binding, the definition of its relationship with the other international instruments determining states' rights and obligations is crucial. That is the importance of Article 20. It confirms that the convention's relations with the other treaties have to be guided by the idea of "mutual supportiveness, complementarity and non-subordination." "When interpreting and applying the other treaties to which they are parties or when entering into other international obligations, parties shall take into account the relevant provisions of this convention."

In terms of Article 21, dialogue and coordination "with other international forums" (unspecified) is one of the premises of the application of Article 20. The "other forums" in question are those in which the fate of cultural diversity is also decided: the WTO, and especially the General Agreement on Trade in Services (GATS), where audiovisual and cultural services are on the liberalization agenda, as well as the World Intellectual Property Organization (WIPO), attached to the UN system in 1974. The WIPO's function, through its treaties, is to define the standards regulating the production, distribution, and use of knowledge and know-how. All these authorities participate in the definition of norms as the baseline of international trade and the driver of the so-called postindustrial technical system. In every field the advocates of a shared elaboration of international standards, based on the universal competence of the law as decreed by the state or interstate organizations, clash with those who support a globalization of sectoral and minimal norms, defined primarily by the only operators in the market.

It took three sessions of intergovernmental meetings to finalize the document submitted in October 2005 to the member states of the UNESCO general conference. As the host at UNESCO was its Division of Cultural Policies and Intercultural Dialogue, the authors tried to compromise between two positions: on the one hand, the majority, including the European Union, which defended the principle of international legislation ratifying special treatment for cultural goods and services as "vehicles of identity, values and meaning"; on the other, a minority led by governments such as the US, Australia, and Japan, inclined to see this document as yet another form of "protectionism" in a sector where, as in other services, free trade should prevail. Between the two lay a variety of standpoints, including those of states that expressed their fear of seeing their national cohesion undermined by contamination of the principle of diversity. From this point of view, the document was also an intercultural production.

The drafting of the convention was a tortuous process punctuated by battles over concepts, words, and tenses, and even over ideas that had long since been ratified by UNESCO. This was the case for instance with the furtively mentioned notion of "cultural industries." The wording in the title of the convention was changed from "cultural diversity" to "the diversity of cultural content and artistic expressions" and finally to "the diversity of cultural expressions." The word "protection" was objected to for its protectionist connotations. Its use was consequently justified by referring to its recurrent appearance in many international conventions ratified by the UN, on the protection of vulnerable categories or victims of discrimination. This was the case with children's rights, for example. The anthropological definition of culture, despite being enshrined in the "Universal declaration on cultural diversity," unanimously adopted in the wake of September 11, 2001, and present in the first round of intergovernmental negotiations, paid the price of many compromises. These impacted on the formulation of strategic articles, leaving them open to contradictory interpretations. For instance, whereas French diplomacy celebrated Article 20 as a victory over the mercantile view of culture, the British government failed to see it as signifying the possibility of extracting cultural goods and services from the WTO's jurisdiction.

Culture and communication: the dissociation

The fuzziness of concepts was, however, far from being conjunctural. Nor was it the fruit of compromise between distinctly different positions. In 1998 Tony Bennett and Colin Mercer, two researchers from the Australian Key Center for Cultural and Media Policy participating at UNESCO's intergovernmental conference on cultural policies for development, in Stockholm, deplored "the absence of conceptual clarity in the cultural policy field." They ascribed this to a combination of factors including: the relative immaturity of cultural policies as an interdisciplinary field of study and research; the low priority granted to research funding by the institutions responsible for defining and implementing these policies; the private or privatized nature of many studies; the scarcity of relations between universities and cultural sectors; the lack of resources for systematic research funding by civil society institutions and organizations; the excessive focus on national research capacity and the inequality of its international distribution. Finally, the delegates pointed out the fact that: "The sensitivity of many questions of cultural policy – around questions of censorship, for example – means that key policy decisions are often made on political grounds in ways which minimise the value of research findings." To illustrate this, these specialists in cultural and media policies noted that "crucial cultural policy issues – the distribution of media ownership, for example – are strongly affected by the lobbying power of influential constituencies" (Bennett and Mercer 1997, 4–5). Nearly 20 years after the introduction of the notion of "cultural industries" in the institution's references, they urged UNESCO to engage in "knowledge of the cultural industries."

Cultural policy making can hardly be considered without taking into account the question of communication policies. Yet the Convention and even, more fundamentally, the philosophy guiding UNESCO's action in matters of cultural diversity, tend not only to dissociate the two issues but even to disregard the second one. The Convention contains two references to "diversity of media." One is in Point 12 of the preamble which stipulates that "freedom of thought, expression and information, as well as the diversity of media, enable cultural expressions to flourish within societies." The second, Article 6, includes at the bottom of the list of recommended measures (point h): "measures aimed at enhancing diversity of the media including public service broadcasting among forms of intervention." What exactly such "diversity of media" might be is not clarified. The word "concentration," for example, is absent; the concept is too disturbing. Proposals from organized civil society to include a reference to this subject were all refused.[2] The two world summits on the information society, organized by the ITU – in Geneva in 2003 and Tunis in 2005 – likewise overlooked the general phenomenon of concentration hindering citizens' appropriation of the communication space and widening the gap between those who broadcast and those who receive, those who know and those who supposedly do not.

Was this for fear of scaring off the United States, which contributed more than 20 percent of UNESCO's budget and had finally returned to the fold in 2003, after walking out in 1984 to mark its refusal of the Movement of Non-Aligned Countries' demands for more balanced information flows through a New World Information and Communication Order (NWICO)? Certainly. Was it a compartmentalization of tasks between the divisions of a big international bureaucratic machine like UNESCO? Yes again. But there was more to it. This international institution created its own dark legend about the 1970s, when the cultural policies debate was conceived of only in relation to the debate on communication policies, and vice versa. This taboo precluded the possibility, within the institution, of critically assessing the past and its contradictions. The cultural focus became increasingly autonomous as, outside the institution, strategic reflection of political science, the political economy of communication and culture, and cultural studies, in their critical form, turned toward communication policies defined as: a set of principles, constitutional measures, laws, rules, and state, public and private institutions comprising the normative framework of television, cinema, radio, Internet, advertising, editorial production, the record industry, the arts and show business. During the period of stalemate in the debate, between 1985 and the turn of the century, the series of questions on cultural diversity raised within UNESCO was dealt with – one could say exclusively, with time – on the one hand, by the anthropological approach and, on the other, by the discourse on the alliance between biodiversity and cultural diversity. Even though we can but celebrate this reconciliation with the anthropological approach, since the early twentieth-century controversies between anthropologist Marcel Mauss and some of his colleagues, we have been aware that there is a risk in the autonomization of the cultural field: it could make ethnographic study on the social uses of cultural goods and products say what it would otherwise be unable to express from a macrosociological point of view. As for the discursive reunion between biodiversity and cultural diversity, we know how much, in the history of communicational thinking, biomorphic metaphorization has proved to be a source of numerous misunderstandings and oversights. The analogy is in any case made at the expense of a sociopolitical approach to the mechanisms of production, circulation, and consumption of communication and culture. The actual effect of these two biases means that the issue of concentration, in the context of internationalization that reigned when the "cultural industries" issue was on the agenda in the 1970s, has become a blind spot in the discourse on cultural policies at UNESCO. Actually, the communicational approach has been dismissed by a perspective that Michel de Certeau would probably have branded as "culturalist."

The official documents that UNESCO chose in 2005 to illustrate the unfolding of the cultural diversity issue in its strategies, from its inception in 1946, contain no traces of any intellectual accumulation by the institution on the cultural industries, nor on communication policies and measures (Stenou 2003). The same tendency is found again with regard to the MacBride Report in 2005, 25 years after its approval by the General Conference of Belgrade. This institutional silence contrasts with the many initiatives taken that year throughout the world by researchers who studied the document, reassessed it, and compared it to the new questions raised by the challenges of the construction of a knowledge society for all (Institut de la comunicacio 2005). It likewise contrasts sharply with the equally recurrent abundance of references to the figures of a hegemonic stream of thought in the Anglo-Saxon countries, spawned by anthropology and Cultural Studies in documents that have marked out the debate on culture since the late 1990s. Examples include Anthony Giddens's contribution on "globalization, culture and inequalities," along with that of Indian anthropologist Arjun Appadurai, in collaboration with Katerina Stenou, head of the Division of Cultural Policy and Intercultural Dialogue on "Sustainable Development and the Future of Belonging," in the *World Culture Report, 2000*, subtitled "Cultural diversity, conflict and pluralism" (UNESCO 2000). Paradoxically, UNESCO's engagement in reflection on the role of states in the promotion and protection of cultural diversity is based on the "postnational" concept. This is a rather fuzzy notion that excludes all reflection on the changes and redefinitions of the forms taken on by the state and nation state confronted with the global space. Its theoreticians even announce their disappearance, leaving the newly sovereign community of consumers face to face with transnational flows. In the conclusion to an archaeology of theories put into circulation by these theoreticians of cultural globalization, Mattelart and Neveu wrote:

> Faced with a world whose complexity is not simply a convenient slogan, they have taken up the challenge by an excessive use of meta-discourse, instead of endeavouring to theorize this complexity. Following Norbert Elias, we wish to point out that the label theory is warranted only by conceptual constructions that make it possible to solve problems, to renew the intelligibility of objects. From now on conceptual sophistication conceals a thinking steeped in conformisms, ill at ease with the complexity of new inter-cultural balances of power in the context of generalization of technical and productive systems. (Mattelart and Neveu 1996, 42)

The bursting of the financial bubble in October 2008 belied the myth of the senescence of nation-states, repeatedly used to legitimize processes of unbridled deregulation of all systems of social solidarity.

The New Sociopolitical Actors' Philosophy
of Life and Action

Can we expect more today from the leading international organizations, to advance the debate? Probably not. Moreover, that is not where the problem lies. It resides in the way in which the various public and private sector agents appropriate the regulatory principles forged in protracted intergovernmental negotiations, not only to implement them but also to push back their limits. Article 11 of the Agreement invites them to do so: "Parties acknowledge the fundamental role of civil society in protecting and promoting the diversity of cultural expressions. Parties shall encourage the active participation of civil society in their efforts to achieve the objectives of this Convention." Actually, during the process of drafting the Convention, and before that, in the process of approval of the very idea of a legal tool, in many places throughout the world these actors' awareness often preceded that of the public authorities, whom they urged to take a stand. Major lessons in the intense mobilization at national and international level consist in the fact that the debates on cultural diversity at UNESCO, and on networking, held at the information society summits, have included the social movement and the national collectives of professional cultural organizations.

What is the philosophy behind the interventions of the new sociopolitical players in this changing topography of places where the private appropriation of culture, the media, information, and knowledge is negotiated? It can be defined as two principles.

The first pertains to the exercise of "communication rights" as new social rights. Although the intuition that fueled the initial phase of the debate on "the right to communication" in the 1970s was endorsed, its range was widened. Reference to the right to plurality signifies the desire to concretize existing communication rights, to put them into practice and not to wait for a new legal instrument guaranteed by international law. As noted in the *Assessing Communication Rights Handbook* designed by the CRIS network: "'Communication rights' is a useful term that relates immediately to a set of existing human rights denied to many people, and whose full meaning can only be realised when they are considered together, as an inter-related group. The whole is greater than the parts" (World Association for Christian Communication 2005, 20).

These "existing rights" are defined in the three main human rights documents: the Universal Declaration of 1948, the Pact on Civil and Political Rights, and the Pact on Economic, Cultural and Social Rights (1966). Communication rights encompass not only communication in the public sphere (freedom of expression and the press, access to public and governmental information, diversity and plurality of the media and their content); they also cover the production and sharing of knowledge, civil rights such as privacy, and cultural rights such as linguistic diversity. In contrast to the restrictive conception, which reduces diversity to the offer that is supposedly self-regulated by the market, diversity in its full sense is assumed to be impossible without diversity of the protagonists, of the sources of creation and the content of knowledge, and of cultural and media expression.

This human rights philosophy formalized by a new generation of public law specialists entails a critique of the essentialist view of human rights. The right to communication is indissoluble from civil and social rights. It is possible only if there is a guarantee of the political and economic, social and cultural conditions enabling human beings to exercise what Spinoza called the *conatus*, the power of transformation and change that enable them to pursue their struggle for recognition of the human dignity of each individual. The idea is to create the conditions for the deployment of human potential. The recognition of these rights, including the right to communication, means recognition of the right of all to participate in the transformation of society (Herrera Flores 2005). This reading of the Universal Declaration of Human Rights is particularly relevant in today's global geopolitical context, where countries tend to have double standards when it comes to human rights. Transformed into a catechism, the Universal Declaration serves both to denounce human rights abuses in foreign lands, and to hide countries' own violations of those same rights.

The second principle that makes a desacralized approach to human rights meaningful is found in the philosophy of common public goods – admittedly still in its infancy – opposed to the privatization or "patenting" of the world and human beings. The category "common public goods" encompasses all the areas that ought to be exceptions to the law of free trade, because they are a common heritage that should be shared in conditions of equity and liberty. This principle motivates citizen mobilization around not only communication and knowledge but also health, life forms, the environment, water, software, and the radio spectrum. All these domains should be governed by the rules of public service.

Very recently, under the effect of the crisis triggered by the subprimes and excessive financial speculation, critical economists put forward the idea that financial networks and channels should also be considered as "common public goods" and governed by an international law guaranteed by multiple authorities. A handful of traders would thus be unable to play with the circulation of financial flows, to the detriment of entire societies. Such a radical about turn, away from the logic of neoliberal globalization, implies the need to put the primacy of politics, the sovereignty of the people, and the meaning of public intervention and of the state's economic role back onto the agenda. It also implies a qualitative leap forward in citizens' participation in knowledge and in the management of the main issues preoccupying society today.

From alternative communication to public service: widening the horizon of democratization

These two principles – communication rights and philosophy of common public goods – inspire various modes of intervention and speech. I will illustrate this in two significant fields of action.

The first pertains to the broadening of reflection and action concerning the democratization of communication. The new sociopolitical players have amplified their strategic perspectives. Not only do they struggle for the legalization and sustainability of citizen media (community, associative, free, and independent); they have also become a force to be reckoned with as they strive to structurally change the organization of the entire media system and to legitimize the notion of regulation by rehabilitating the public concept. The aim is: (1) to perpetuate a third sector of communication; (2) to reform, consolidate, or create, when it does not exist, a public service that is not simply a mouthpiece for the state; and (3) to demand that the private-commercial sector be consistent with the authorization granted to it to use a public good: the range of frequencies. Evidence of this process of "citizenization" at work in the communication field is the proliferation of debates and mobilizations in favor of the change of broadcasting laws in countries such as Mexico, Argentina, and Brazil, all of which have media monopolies or duopolies. Echoing this position of critique in action are the continental campaigns, again in Latin America, for communication rights and against concentration, on the initiative of popular communication networks and the alterglobalist movement. Their agenda for action, research, and work gives some idea of the maturity of their collective pleas for a change of the communication system. The topics of debate proposed are: legislation and regulation of communication; digital technology and social change; media concentration; and public broadcasting and community communication. Strategies include: construction of public control of the means of communication; enabling society and citizens to gain knowledge and the capacity to act in the communications field; and developing a national culture policy.

Through ebbs and flows, steps forward and steps backwards, all these actions and the debates animating them attest to the slow and arduous social appropriation of this field of questioning on the public sphere, in its relationship with media. As noted above, the public authorities are loath to acknowledge the existence of these new citizen actors in the field of information and communication technologies, whether they are old or new; just as they are reluctant to recognize the role of public mediators, "intermediate corps" between the state and the market, that they are destined to fulfill in reality. One of the essential contributions of these new collective sociopolitical subjects lies in their capacity to shift the horizon of the political stakes of democratization of the communication space, and their ability to seek and to build new strategic alliances.

The diversity of subjects composing the social movement is a guarantee of its richness. Possible limits are those stemming from the very nature of polyphony: the spaces and processes in which organizations and networks with multiple objectives are involved. Conceptualizing life in a democracy from diverse standpoints supposes agreement that even though democracy and truth are mutually dependent, they are also mutually threatening. This is a paradox that Foucault summed up neatly in a lecture on the "government of self and others": "There is no true discourse without democracy. But true discourse introduces differences into democracy. There is no democracy without true discourse. But democracy threatens the existence of true discourse" (Foucault 2008, 168).

Towards a new social contract around the question of knowledge/power

The second illustration of the reshaping of thinking and critical action concerns the changes that have occurred in the forms of collective organization of reflection and intervention on hegemonic media.

As we know, the 1980s witnessed the rediscovery of the activity of receivers, the nonpassivity of audiences. It was a rediscovery that nevertheless suffered from ambiguities, for all too often it was made at the expense of critical questions on the radical transformation of media and cultural industries in the context of increasing deregulation and privatization. The excesses and neopopulist aspects of the belief in audiences' free will, enabling them to "resist" by "resemantizing" media discourses, are ample evidence of that shortcoming.

The contribution of the citizen movement since the beginning of the new millennium contradicts that ironic view of the active status of audiences. It is based on the assumption that media users' freedom is constructed through citizen counterbalances and therefore cannot be taken for granted. The recent phenomenon of proliferating critical monitoring and research organizations known as "observatories" – observers of information, communication, and culture – bear witness to that. In Latin America, for example, there were about 55 such organizations of culture, cultural policies, and the media in 2007, and the number of new ones is constantly growing (Albornoz and Herschmann 2007). This new form of organization of critique and intervention in the cultural and communication sphere attests to a state of social consciousness of the necessity and urgency for citizens to participate in setting public agendas and, more generally, in promoting the democratization of those spaces. Of course, we know how difficult it is to bridge the divide between awareness of a phenomenon and the sustained engagement that "observation of the media" implies. The short experience of these citizen observatories has shown that their modes of organization and functioning depend heavily on local conditions, even if they necessarily have a common philosophy. They are created and develop in widely diverse situations of social and financial sustainability: diversity of approaches, themes, funding mechanisms, working methodologies, thrusts of action and modes of integration with other components of the citizen movement. It is only by looking at these specific characteristics that we can compare them, identify what they have in common, and draw conclusions on their different experiences. Each one of them endeavors to invent a new ecology of communication, grouping together diverse actors.

The media observatory approach, that I have personally been involved in at national and international level, was inaugurated by the World Social Forum of Porto Alegre in 2003 with the launching of the Global Media Watch (Mattelart 2007). This type of observatory groups together three categories: journalists, academic researchers, and media users. Being an observer means deciphering the information content and analyzing the structural causes of silences, censorship, and distortions. It means investigating, alerting, proposing, and studying the modes of production of information that impact on journalists' rights and duties. It means solidarity with those who are exposed to pressure by their private or public sector employers, and those who work in firms that refuse independent information. It means supporting media projects based on the diversity of content and voices. Finally, it means being attentive to the type of training dispensed for communication professions in higher education institutions. The advantage of this tripartite mode of organization is that it promotes contact, exchanges, and debate between people and organizations usually kept apart by their respective professional experiences. Interaction between journalists and researchers, for example, implies the necessity to transcend corporatist isolation. It questions the practices on both sides, and this leads – or should lead – to questions posed together, in co-operation with civil society, on the way in which their analyses are conducted and transmitted in accordance with society's noncommercial needs.

To investigate the relationship that producers of information and knowledge have with society, we have to put the upsurge of new approaches to the communication–democracy nexus back into the context of challenges created in democracies by a real sharing of knowledge. It is in this sense that struggles for the collective appropriation of the "media question" have indeed become ideal observation posts. They make it possible to measure the road that is still left before a knowledge society different to the one promised us over the past two decades by the technodeterminist mirage of general-interest connection can effectively be achieved. What the struggles for the democratization of communication teach us is that there cannot be diversified knowledge societies without calling into question relations between knowledge and power, and therefore the status in that system of all producers of knowledge. The main challenge is to conceive of new alliances, a new social contract between these categories of intellectuals and the new sociopolitical subjects. Only the sciences that defy elitism and the academic ivory towers, while at the same time avoiding the game of populism, can serve as a counterbalance to the myth of a global information society conveyed by the cognitive monopolies and their short-term logic. This myth simply recycles the old diffusionist paradigm of information and knowledge delivery from those who know to those who are supposed not to know.

In my opinion, this radical approach is necessary if the right to communication is to be fully deployed in the invention of new democratic uses of both old and new information and communication technologies. That is the only condition on which the new utopia of knowledge sharing can help us to construct democracies conceived of not only in terms of multiple identities but also in light of the categorical imperative of equality and social justice.

Notes

1   For the text of the Convention, see http://unesdoc.unesco.org/images/0014/001429/142919e.pdf
2   See, for example, the proposals of the world network CRIS (Communication Rights in the Information Society), http://mail.kein.org/pipermail/incom-l/2005-October/000908.html and www.crisinfo.org, November 11, 2004.

References

Albornoz, L. A. and Herschmann, M. (2007) Balance de un proceso iberoamericano: Los observatorios iberoamericanos de información y cultura. *Telos*, 72.

Bennett, T. and Mercer, C. (1997) *Improving Research and International Cooperation for Cultural Policy. Intergovernmental Conference on Cultural Policies for Development* (CLT-98/Conf.210/Ref.6). UNESCO, Paris.

Braudel, F. (1958) Histoire et sciences sociales: La longue durée. *Annales. Economies, Sociétés, Civilisations*, 13(4), 725–53.

Certeau, M. de (1974) *La Culture au pluriel*. Christian Bourgois, Paris.

D'Arcy, J. (1969) Direct broadcast satellites and the right to communicate. *EBU Review*, 118, 14–18.

Foucault, M. (2008) *Le Gouvernement de soi et des autres: Cours du Collège de France, 1982–1983*, Ewald, F. and Fontana, A. (eds). Seuil/Gallimard, Paris.

Galtung, J., O'Brien, P., and Preiswerk, R. (eds) (1980) *Self-reliance: A Strategy for Development*. IUED/ Bogle-L'Ouverture, London.

Herrera Flores, J. (2005) *Los derechos humanos como productos culturales: critica del humanismo abstracto*. Ediciones Catarata, Madrid.

Huntington, S. (1996) *The Clash of Civilizations and the Remaking of World Order*. Simon and Schuster, New York.

Institut de la comunicacio (2005) XXV aniversario del informe MacBride: Comunicación internacional y politicas de comunicación. *Quaderns del consell de l'audiovisual de Catalunya*, 21.

Koïchiro, M. (2001) Introduction. *Universal Declaration on Cultural Diversity*. UNESCO, Paris, pp. 16–21.

MacBride, S. and International Commission for the Study of Communication Problems (1980) *Many Voices, One World*. UNESCO, Paris.

Mattelart, A. (2007) Quarante ans de critique des médias. *Contretemps*, 18 (February), 62–73.

Mattelart, A. (ed.) (1986) *Communicating in Popular Nicaragua*, D. Buxton (trans.). International General Editions, New York.

Mattelart, A., Delcourt, X., and Mattelart M. (1984) *International Image Markets: In Search of an Alternative Perspective*, D. Buxton (trans.). Comedia/Methuen, London.

Mattelart, A. and Neveu, E. (1996) "Cultural studies" stories: La domestication d'une pensée sauvage? *Réseaux*, 80, 11–58.

Ralite, J. (ed.) (1987) *La Culture française se porte bien pourvu qu'on la sauve*. Messidor/Editions Sociales, Paris.

Stenou, K. (2003) *UNESCO and the Issue of Cultural Diversity: Review and Strategy, 1946–2003*. UNESCO, Paris.

UNESCO (1980) *Meeting on the Place and Role of Cultural Industries in the Cultural Development of Societies. Reports and Studies of the Division of Cultural Development* (CC80/CONF.629/COL.10). UNESCO, Paris.

UNESCO (1982a) *Cultural Industries: A Challenge for the Future of Culture*. UNESCO, Paris.

UNESCO (1982b) *Final report, World Conference on Cultural Policies* (Mondiacult). UNESCO, Paris.

UNESCO (2000) *World Culture Report: Cultural Diversity, Conflict and Pluralism*. UNESCO, Paris.

World Association for Christian Communication (WACC) (2005) *CRIS Campaign, Assessing Communication Rights: A Handbook*. WACC, London.

24

Global Capitalism, Temporality, and the Political Economy of Communication

Wayne Hope

Over the last two decades, a concatenation of world-historical developments have produced a world of temporal acceleration in which time itself conforms to the technological imperatives of instantaneity and simultaneity. Corporations, financial enterprises, and media systems are constituted by real time networks of communication. But the impacts are contradictory. Technologized representations of instantaneity and simultaneity may reify the global present and occlude the historicity of powerful global institutions. Conversely, real time technologies and networks may be used to depict and challenge global configurations of power. Added to which, temporal acceleration and real time cannot erase the counter temporalities of duration, sequentiality, and historicity. With these thoughts in mind, I shall critique the accelerative tendencies of global capitalism and identify the conflicting temporalities of globally mediated communication.

Time, Space, and Globalization

My approach to these developments and tensions stands against epistemological accounts of space which overlook concomitant epistemologies of time. Richard Ek's article, "Media Studies, Geographical Imaginations and Relational Space," is a case in point. He argues that contemporary information and communication technologies produce symbolic worlds which generate feelings of placelessness

The Handbook of Political Economy of Communications, First Edition.
Edited by Janet Wasko, Graham Murdock, and Helena Sousa.
© 2014 John Wiley & Sons, Ltd. Published 2014 by John Wiley & Sons, Ltd.

and that unfolding actualizations of the virtual erase the distinction between mediation and spatialization. Thus, "space IS media and media and communication technologies ARE space" (Ek 2006, 56, capitalization in original). Equally, however, one could make the observation that mediation is synonymous with the constitution of time and temporality. In this view, experiences of placelessness have an inbuilt temporal aspect. If one's geographic sense of here and there weakens, local feelings of history and prospectivity will diminish.

The idea that temporality and spatiality are mutually constituting needs to inform our understanding of globalization. As David Harvey has argued in his discussion of "time-space compression," the apparent shrinkage of space "to a 'global village' of telecommunications and a 'spaceship earth' of economic and ecological interdependencies" also shortens time horizons "to the point where the present is all there is" (Harvey 1990, 240). The mutual constitution of time and space is not a unilinear process. As Doreen Massey notes, globalist teleologies of technological advance, market expansion, and/or developmental progress erase the multiplicities of spatial experience. Adjacent countries in the so-called developing world, for example, do not necessarily share the same developmental aspirations. Equally, globalist teleologies preclude openness toward the future (Massey 2005, 82). Massey's nuanced appreciation of time–space mutuality is evident in her discussion of "contemporaneous geographic differences" and "power geometries within the contemporaneity of *today's* form of globalization" (italics in original). For me, these formulations raise fundamental questions about historical change. How should one conceptualize and periodize global contemporaneity? My answer here draws upon Aril Dirlik's notion of global modernity, an emergent category designed to decenter an older Eurocentric conception of modernity associated with western Imperialism, colonialism, and the presumption of civilizational progress. Today, against the backdrop of decolonization and the demise of cold war spatialities, a plurality of cultural modernities intermingle (Dirlik 2007, 94–7). Confucian, Arabic, Islamic, African, Japanese, western, Hindu, and other cultures, each internally differentiated, share the global stage. Across different scales and within virtual spaces, global modernity is facilitated by the density of transport, information, and communication networks. These networks underpin everyday socioeconomic connections within and between diasporic communities. Their fluidity and contingency is highlighted by French social theorist Jean Francois Bayart who notes that Moroccan small traders out of Marseilles "work hand in hand with Turks from Brussels and Frankfurt, Pakistanis and Indians from London, Senegalese, Italians, Catalan and Andalusian gypsies and Tunisians, who open up new doors to them that enable them to make other connections with Libyans, Lebanese or sub-Saharans" (Bayart 2007, 120–1).

Let us now consider the temporal features of contemporary globalization. What are these features and how did they emerge? These questions have been addressed by social theorist Barbara Adam. She notes that within late medieval

Europe, the calendric system and the mechanical clock enabled precise, standard measurements of sequential time. These innovations became the template for commercial enterprises, trading networks, and the early-modern state. Increasingly, standardized measures of sequential time defined the routines of private and public life at the expense of seasonal and biological time. The growth of industrial capitalism after 1850 positioned clock time as the absolute indicator of productivity, costs, and profit. Disciplined workers and their families were expected to internalize these principles of time use. Bankers, accountants, and retailers instinctively equated clock time and monetary value. The standard demarcations of clock time were exported worldwide through the establishment of railway and steamship networks (Adam 2004, 111–17, see also Thompson 1967). In 1884 the inaugural International Meridian Conference agreed to stand-ardize time zones across the globe (Adam 2004, 112). Crucially, however, this ascendant temporal regime had to absorb the arrivals of wireless telegraphy, telephony, and radio broadcasting. With these innovations, speed of transmission transcended the durational and sequential properties of clock time. Subsequent technological advances such as satellite television and networked computers ush-ered in a new form of time standardization and reordered the global-temporal environment.

Like global modernity and global manifestations of real time, global capitalism is a contemporary phenomenon. It was presaged by the collapse of national and Third World liberation movements, Soviet Communism, and national Keynesianism. The concomitant spread of neoliberalism helped to globalize finan-cial flows and production networks and marketing strategies. According to politi-cal economist William Robinson, macroeconomic activity, broadly conceived, is dominated by transnational corporations (firms with headquarters in more than three countries). He draws from various World Investment Reports published by the United Nations Conference on Trade and Development (UNCTAD) and from privately commissioned financial reports to outline the growth of such corpora-tions (7,000 in 1970, 60,000 in 2000) alongside the growth in cross-border mergers/acquisitions (14 in 1980, 9,655 in 1999) (Robinson 2004, 55, 58). The latter trend is especially telling: for the largest corporations, the distinction between home and host country has weakened. Between 2000 and 2007 inclusive, cross-border merger and acquisition deals in excess of US $1billion totaled 1,335 (compared to 479 from 1992 to 1999) (UNCTAD 2008, 5–6). Each World Investment Report indexes the overall transnationality of a corporation against a composite of three ratios: for-eign assets to total assets, foreign sales to total sales, and foreign employment to total employment. From 1993 to 2006, average transnationality values for the top 100 transnational corporations rose by 40 percent (29). The internal and external operations of transnational corporations are driven by the demands of temporal acceleration. The following section will explicate the logic and fragility of these developments.

Global Capitalism, ICTs, and Temporal Acceleration

Information and communication technologies (ICTs) drive the temporal accelerations of global capitalism. To understand this process one must first appreciate that ICTs constitute a new and substantial sector of global capital accumulation. In 2001, historian Jerry Harris identified four emergent subsectors. Established hardware corporations such as Cisco, Hewlett Packard, Sun Microsystems, and Compaq produced chips, boards, boxes, servers, routers, and other infrastructural components. The next wave of corporations wrote software applications, developed operational systems, and installed network architectures. Intuit, Microsoft, Oracle, and Novell quickly became the dominant players. Subsequently, Internet and dot.com companies attracted speculative and longer term investment. Resilient innovators such as AOL, Amazon, EBay, Google, and Yahoo developed expanding services and popular profiles. Meanwhile, landline-based telecommunication corporations such as AT & T, Cable and Wireless, Deutshe Telecom, and Nippon T&T developed or purchased Internet services, cable and broadband connections, satellite hook-ups, and wireless communication services. Industrially based electronic corporations invested in the manufacture of semiconductors, fiber optics, software wireless phones, and other ICT-related products. Such corporations included Motorola, Nokia, Samsung, and Toshiba (Harris 2001, 36–7). By 2003, 18 of the top 100 nonfinancial corporations came from the ICT sector (UNCTAD 2005, 267–9). Between 1995 and 2000 the global telecom equipment market alone grew from US $62.5 billion to US $141.7 billion. Similarly, worldwide revenues from various telecom service markets increased from US $300 billion in 1990 to US $925 billion in 2000 (Yin 2005, 291–2). Over the same period the telecommunications industry ranked second in the global mergers and acquisitions market behind commercial banking (Yin 2005, 295). In the United States the proliferation of telecom infrastructures and Internet applications encouraged aggressive lending from banks and speculative investment from equity traders and fund managers. Throughout the ICT sector, new stock offerings drove up share prices and increased trading volumes. Exaggerated projections of increased demand for network capacity attracted more lending and speculation until share prices fell. The subsequent collapse and/or contraction of debt-laden corporations led to further transnationalization of the ICT sector. Critical communications analyst Dan Schiller outlines this process. During 2004 Telefonica from Spain purchased South and Central Americas wireless networks from Bell South. Telenet from Mexico acquired wireline networks from MCI in Brazil and AT&T in Argentina, Brazil, Chile, Columbia, and Peru. China Netcom gained a major regional affiliate from the bankrupt Global Crossing, and a subsidiary of India's Tata group purchased a transnational cable network from Tyco International. Schiller describes these appropriations of telecom properties by transnationals from the global south as a "historic sea change" (Schiller 2007, 99).

Within global capitalism, the emergent ICT sector has intermeshed with a media-entertainment system transformed by convergences of technology, content, and cultural consumption. Advances in Internet applications, digital television, and, more recently, mobile telephony have blurred traditional separations between broadcasting, computing, telecommunications, and consumer electronics. Such is evident in the evolving structures and strategies of corporate ownership. From about 1980, media conglomerates with lucrative holdings across key media markets took over stand-alone businesses. Major players such as Time-Warner, Bertelsmann, Viacom, Disney, NBC Universal, and News Corporation subsequently acquired worldwide cross-media portfolios. During the 1990s, a broader picture took shape. A global oligopoly of media-entertainment corporations effectively established a dominating presence across core areas of cultural production and leisure activity (film, television, recorded music, print media, hotels, resorts, theme parks). Each corporation sought to control the production and distribution of cultural content through vertical integration. In film and television, for example, News Corporation conjoined Twentieth Century Fox with the Fox Network (1985), Disney acquired the ABC network (1995), CBS merged with Viacom (1999), and Universal appropriated NBC (2004) (Winseck 2008, 38). Media-entertainment corporations have also integrated new media acquisitions with established holdings. Thus Viacom bought NeoPets, a major children's website in the United States, for US $160 million in 2004. Similarly, in 2005 News Corporation purchased the social networking site MySpace for US $500 million, a gaming and entertainment site IGN.com for US $620 million, and America's largest sports site, Scout Media, for US $60 million (Winseck 2008, 42).

Concurrently, ICT corporations have become involved with the media-entertainment sector. In 1988–89 consumer electronics company Sony purchased CBS records for US $2 billion and Columbia Pictures Entertainment for US $3.4 billion. Further acquisitions over the next 15 years positioned Sony as a major media-entertainment conglomerate. In 1998 telecom corporate AT&T acquired cable conglomerate TCI along with Liberty Media Group for US $148 billion. Two years later, Internet service provider AOL merged with Time-Warner to produce a combined valuation of US $125 billion (Hesmondhalgh 2007, 160–2). From the late 1990s, Microsoft's growing involvement in digital media and electronic games gave it a top tier ranking as a media-entertainment corporate. On a larger scale, General Electric assumed a triple profile in diversified industrial products, ICTs, and media-entertainment (Flew 2007, 71). In 2006 Google, with over 50 percent of the search engine market, purchased video-sharing site YouTube for US $1.65 billion. This transaction was preceded by technology, traffic, and advertising revenue arrangements with NBC-Universal, Time-Warner, Viacom, and News Corporation. Media political economist Dwayne Winseck notes that

Google has become a "powerful nexus in the unfolding relationship between the 'old' and 'new' media" (Winseck 2008, 42–3).

As ICT-media corporations became transnational profit generators, ICT-media infrastructures precipitated the acceleration of financial transactions, production cycles, and consumption patterns on a global scale. Real-time communication networks allowed investors and corporate executives to speed up profit rates, cross-tabulate profit ratios, and contract the temporal parameters of profit measurement. Once government control over exchange rates and capital movements became unsustainable, private financial institutions were able to independently generate credit and currency units. In this context, the Eurodollar market that emerged in the 1970s eventually became part of a vast stateless system of financial transactions. Major banks and financial institutions offered syndicated loans, international securities, currency trades, forward exchange contracts, and derivative options from various branches in cities worldwide. Meanwhile, the opening of national stock exchanges to foreign institutions generated a massive global equities market. Within this market, institutional investors and speculative traders fueled the growth of transnational mergers and acquisitions. The globalization of finance capital depended upon microchip computers and associated advances in telecommunications. Satellite, optical fiber, and cellular networks expanded and accelerated information transfer between computer terminals. All of these developments created an unprecedented economic environment; multiple currency units and complex financial assets worth trillions of dollars were traded globally in real time (Castells 1996, 2000, Held et al. 1999, Singh 2000).

The proliferation of ICT infrastructures has also globalized networks of management, production, and distribution. Corporates allow affiliates greater autonomy and encourage channels of two-way communication (e.g., via email, e-commerce, intranets, video conferencing, mobile telephony, and interenterprise computer networking). Such arrangements underpin the management of complex, technologically innovative production chains in response to changing market conditions. Transnational corporations use information and communication systems to decentralize and subcontract operations and to centralize financial control. This pattern is common to otherwise separate sectors of production, such as textiles, garments, automobiles, and semiconductors (Dicken 2003, 317–436). At the same time, major firms in the same industry co-operate through joint ventures, subcontracting, franchising, and research projects that will design specific products for identifiable markets. For Manuel Castells, these innovations were indicators of the network enterprise. Within this organizational model, firms remain the primary unit of capital accumulation, property rights, and strategic management, while routine business practices are performed by flexible ad hoc networks (Castells 1996, 2001, 67–78). High-speed interactive communication within and between businesses has transformed the temporal environments of corporate management. Ida Sabelis, a leading researcher in this field, points out that almost all of the executives included in her various research projects identified "acceleration and speed" as the "core organizational challenge" that had emerged over the previous 20 years (Sabelis 2007, 261). She quotes a female manager of an ICT corporation who was said to schedule teleconferences "during the day and after hours in order to synchronize with Asian and American partners in *real time*" (Sabelis 2007, 262, italics in original).

The spread of ICT-media infrastructures, products, and services has also accelerated everyday practices of consumption. The idea of convenient, ready-made solutions had always been inherent to modern consumer culture. However, recent devices such as MP3 players, digital cameras, Internet search engines, handheld remotes, and multifunctional cell phones have opened up new time-saving opportunities. Personal media technologies are easy to operate, ready to hand, and offer instant access to an emporium of purchasable commodities. Online shopping exemplifies the widespread assumption that the delivery of consumer goods should be rapid and continuous. For cultural theorist, John Tomlinson, the character of consumption practices has shifted from "an emphasis on steady accumulation and the enjoyment of continued possession" to that of "the immediate and repeated appropriation of new goods" (Tomlinson 2007, 137). Quickening rhythms of consumption are intimately associated with technological mediations of experience. In this regard, global communication infrastructures combined with personal media technologies allow cultural industries spanning film, music, fashion, sport, celebrity promotion, tourism, and related leisure activities to normalize immediate gratification and the "nowness" of consumer lifestyles. At the same time, the globalization of fast-paced consumer lifestyles remains tempered by socioeconomic inequalities and cultural traditions. In a major exploration of these themes, Edward Comor points out that the growing middle classes of India and China remain demographic minorities with the majority of rural and urban dwellers within each country still lacking sufficient income for repeat, aspirational buying (Comor 2008, 117). In China, Comor notes, traditional "from scratch" food preparation has limited the spread of supermarkets and the demand for processed food (Comor 2008, 125–6). Nevertheless, over the long term there is little doubt that capitalist consumption "'frees' modernizing cultures by elaborating more mediated, commodified and abstracted forms into everyday life," installing rapidly circulating brands and lifestyles as taken-for-granted indicators of socioeconomic development.

Global capitalism's drive toward internetworked instantaneity has polarized the human condition. Wealthy global elites enjoy the personal and material advantages of extraterritorial mobility, while the poor are consigned to the secondary experience of locality (as slum dwellers, rural laborers, refugees, office, factory, or domestic workers). From a temporal perspective, those who benefit most from the rapid circulations of money, imagery, information, and knowledge routinely position the poor as "out of time." From within lifeworlds of impoverishment, time is experienced variously as loss, insecurity, exhaustion, boredom, or fate. Beyond the squalor, institutions of academic accreditation and technical-managerial expertise produce mobile knowledge workers in the form of marketing experts, computer consultants, lawyers, accountants, financiers, and managerial specialists (Hoogvelt 2001, 138).

Meanwhile, intracorporate and intercorporate infrastructures globally inter-connect downtown metropoles, technology parks, and gated suburban enclaves in a process of insularity that requires the constant surveillance of public spaces and the expulsion of surplus humanity into densely packed or sprawling slum areas (Davis 2006). Although rich and poor may, in given circumstances, live far apart, these bifurcations are as much a temporal as a spatial phenomenon. Wealthy elites inhabit time-worlds of business, travel, consumption, and leisure activity which are phenomenologically distanced from the poor. The real-time networks of global capitalism stratify temporal experience within and across urban-suburban environments. The real time tendencies of global capitalism are, however, self-undermining as well as being socially divisive. In the absence of countervailing temporalities, the drive toward internetworked instantaneity magnifies instability and uncertainty. Within global finance derivatives and futures trading via compu-terized funds, transfer systems accelerate high-risk speculative activity that impli-cates and destabilizes the surrounding economy (Soros 1998). The 1997 Asian currency crisis, the 1998 Long Term Capital Management collapse, and the Wall Street financial crisis beginning in 2008 have, successively, provoked calls for trans-parent, international standards of accounting, auditing, insurance payment bank-ruptcy resolution, and interbank settlement (Rude 2005, Krugman 2008, 165–91).

The prevailing temporal precepts of global finance strongly influence the priori-ties of nonfinancial corporations. Institutional equity investors and investment analysts in the capitalist west measure corporate performance against short-term profit imperatives. In the United States during the 1980s, for example, specialist takeover firms broke up old, diversified conglomerates. Profit and share price pro-jections rather than yearly/half yearly results, have become the standard perform-ance criteria (Zorn and Dobbin 2005, 269–89). In contrast, corporations from East Asia have fostered long-term business-to-business relationships based upon mutual obligations. Bilateral arrangements are embedded within a broader ensemble of interrelated companies, and diversified industrial groups are often centered around a core bank (Dicken 2003, 225–35). Ongoing global rivalry between these discrep-ant temporal priorities of corporate activity will determine the future organiza-tional culture of transnational corporations.

The accelerative, short-termist tendencies of global capitalism also clash with the national-temporal precepts of state authority. The worldwide consequences of neoliberal privatization illustrates this point. In a state-facilitated national economy, energy transport infrastructures operate over long periods of time in response to long-range socioeconomic needs. Under private corporate owner-ship, these infrastructures are reorganized to fit short-term measures of commer-cial profit and shareholder value. Nation-states thereby lose the fiscal and temporal capacity to shape macroeconomic futures. In these circumstances, national-temporal rhythms of judicial process, electoral democracy, and representative assembly are circumvented.

Global Mediations of Real Time: Reification and Critique

Discussion thus far has proceeded to the following position. The technological capacity for instantaneous and simultaneous communication underpins both the pluralistic expressions of global modernity and the routine practices of global capitalism. International conference delegates, diasporic bloggers and street traders, transnational political activists, foreign exchange dealers, corporate middle managers, and International Monetary Fund (IMF) officials all make use of the Internet, mobile telephony, and electronic mass media. These observations pose a major question for critical theorists of communication. How does one distinguish between progressive and pejorative manifestations of instantaneity-simultaneity? This is not just a matter of infrastructural usage or application; real-time capacities are also symbolically displayed throughout traditional and emergent media domains (i.e., in the form of language, imagery, textual and technological formats). Such displays can be positioned as an ideological expression of global capitalism *or* as a resource for alternative communication practices. My understanding of this dual perspective builds upon John Thompson's insight that although symbolic constructs serve, ideologically, to reproduce prevailing relations of power, they are not always employed for this purpose (Thompson 1994, 56). The ideological technique of reification is especially relevant to the present argument. Here, Thompson remarks that: "relations of domination may be established and sustained by representing a transitory, historical state of affairs as if it were permanent, natural, outside of time. Processes are portrayed as things or as events of a quasi-natural kind, in such a way that their social and historical character is eclipsed" (Thompson 1994, 65). From this standpoint, ideological representations of real time obscure the sociohistorical circumstances of its own emergence as the functional basis of global capitalism. Examples include the unfolding immediacy of global television formats; multimedia advertising and corporate branding; the illusion of disembodied presence within the cyberworlds of electronic gaming and immersive virtual reality; and the built kinetics of theme parks, expos, shopping malls, and moving billboards. The scale, intricacy, and pervasiveness of such developments presents a formidable challenge to critical communication researchers. The ideology of real time appears to be everywhere at once and nowhere in particular. My own investigations will, nevertheless, start with a critique of satellite-driven television news. There are sound reasons for this selection.

Firstly, satellite television is a long-recognized, worldwide manifestation of real time. According to television historian Lisa Parks, the first truly global satellite spectacular was the 1967 two-hour program, *Our World*, co-ordinated by the European Broadcasting Union, edited from BBC studios in London, and transmitted to approximately 500 million viewers in 24 countries. The significance of this accomplishment was clearly understood at the time. As Parks points out, "*Our World*'s producers fully exploited what they understood to be the unique properties of live satellite television: its capacity to craft a global now" (Parks 2005, 22).

Secondly, the subsequent routinization of live satellite television and global "nowness" invites examination. Global television news began with CNN World Report in October 1987, launched as a complement to CNN's already established domestic network and world headline service (Medina 2003, 86). Over the next decade, CNN established numerous bureaux outside of the United States and signed joint ventures with media companies in different national markets. By 2003 CNN International had been regionalized into six scheduled channels: North America, Europe, Middle East/Africa, Asia/Pacific, South Asia, and Latin America (Chalaby 2003, 467). As CNN expanded, BBC television developed its own global strategy. A worldwide news channel was formed in 1991 and the BBC World brand was launched in 1995 to capitalize on the Corporation's international profile and spread its news-gathering costs over more services. Satellites with global reach were complemented by those with pan-regional, national, and subnational footprints, further increasing the availability of live 24/7 news coverage. A 2007 survey identified over 100 24/7 news channels worldwide. Four were entirely global (CNN and CNNI, BBC World, CNBC, and Bloomberg TV) and one was almost global (Fox News). Another 27 could be classified as pan-regional, of which Al Jazeera (Arabic) and Al Jazeera (English) had major international reach (Rai and Cottle 2007, 54–7).

Thirdly, global satellite television is worth examining because it meshes with other technologies of real time. From the late 1990s wireless infrastructures decoupled computers and communications from fixed locations, further multiplying the locales from which live sound and images could be constructed and received. Laptops could be linked to satellite phones. Images from digital cameras could be edited onto a laptop and transmitted via the Internet, from the site of a breaking story, back to the reporter's central office. Miniature video cameras enabled freelancers to obtain vivid footage from disaster sites and conflict zones. Together, these news-gathering innovations have normalized the rolling, 24/7 news cycle (Jukes 2002, 15). Information and communication technologies have also multiplied the sites of news reception and reshaped the experience of news consumption. Major, real-time news events are streamed throughout the Internet via specialist news sites and rolling headlines. In May 2005, TV Media, a consortium of South Korean companies, launched Digital Multimedia Broadcasting (DMB), allowing cell phone and laptop users to access television content from 24/7 news channels. Telecom and ICT corporations worldwide are developing similar services as the global market for mobile television expands (Lee 2005, 59). Ongoing remediations of television reception allows the real-time world of global television news to merge with the everyday routines of work, leisure, and domesticity.

Fourthly, global television news requires examination because of its relationship with other real-time formulations. As I will show, financial, political, military, and televisual networks of communication overlap to the point where global mediations of real time eclipse the historical character of unfolding events.

Real-time feedback loops

In the mid-1990s, in a prescient analysis of global media events, McKenzie Wark noted that the technological vectors of satellite television were integrally connected with the technological vectors of financial, diplomatic, and military communication. Consequently, everyone and everything was, potentially, the "object and/or subject of a mediated relation, realized instantly" (Wark 1994, 15). Because these vectors implicated the entire globe, there was no synoptic vantage point from which to represent global events. In these circumstances, the constitution and development of major events could not be easily separated from their mass mediation, and mass-mediated, globally transmitted information about an event became inexorably drawn into other, media- and event-related vectors of communication (e.g., global finance, international diplomacy, military networks). This in turn activated a process whereby the representations of a momentous event made by journalists, camera teams, editors, and interested parties fed back into the event itself via a global loop encompassing television, radio, telephone, and fax technologies (Wark 1994, 22).

Since Wark's initial observations, the proliferation of satellite channels, computer-mediated communication, and mobile telephony has continuously generated intersecting global vectors and feedback loops. Digitalized foreign exchange markets, for example, adhere to time practices corresponding with those of global television news. Traders worldwide watch and participate in the market continuously and simultaneously while market transactions and associated information arrives continuously on networked computer screens. As Karin Knorr Cetina observes, in this environment, information is not verified against any external reality. Instead, "the material on screen can only disclose itself as information in as far as it is new compared to earlier material." Consequently, "the new is presented as-things-happen and vanishes from the screens as newer things come to pass" (Cetina 2005, 43).

It is clear from this account that the reified time-world of foreign exchange trades and other related financial transactions parallels the world constructed by television news. These worlds are conjoined by the routine activities of major business-financial news brokers such as Reuters and Bloomberg, who offer multiple streams of news and information worldwide to the financial press, business magazines, daily newspapers, radio stations, television channels (including their websites), and specialist clients (traders, analysts, and investors). Simultaneously, global television news programs present unfolding information about currencies, equities, bonds, and futures. Within equities markets, for example, analysts collate, condense, and interpret business-related information for major corporates. The relevant information includes announcements from central banks, ratings agencies, and government-appointed monetary authorities, along with earnings reports from listed companies. At the same time, analyst assessments enable financial-business news journalists, specialist news channels, and news brokers to compile summary accounts of stock market activity. These accounts are combined and re-presented continuously on 24/7 satellite channels (global, pan-regional, national).

Real-time communication networks then, conjoin the activities of financial-business journalists, market traders and market analysts. Interlinked major players from all of these groups respond to financial-information flows which are endogenously generated. Market participants routinely make buy-and-sell decisions based on expectations of future prices which are partly shaped by incoming analyst reports and by updated financial news content across all media. The real time feedback loops that proliferate are inherently volatile and globally infectious (Thompson 2003, 34–7, 2004, 14–18).

The real-time news flows of global television also interact with the decision-making practices of government foreign policy and international diplomacy. The immediacy of high profile political events may exert an accelerating influence upon the course of those events and shorten the time available for policy making. Failure to act swiftly may create a media image of political indecision or dissension (Gilboa 2003, 99). In some cases, the very intensity of live news coverage may influence a foreign policy decision. According to Piers Robinson, this occurred in February 1994 when the mortar bombing of a Sarajevo market place provided instant CNN footage of human carnage, which impelled the Clinton administration to issue an ultimatum to Bosnian Serb nationalists: namely, that if the shelling of Sarajevo continued, air strikes would ensue (Robinson 2002, 86–7).

This turn of events is not automatically generalizable, however. Global television news coverage will not alter a predetermined policy position. From a macroperspective, however, global television news flows and international political communication are integrally and continually connected. Thus televised images of an unfolding atrocity or catastrophe accelerate diplomatic exchanges whatever the policy outcome. To this extent, global television has partly replaced ambassadors and policy experts as a source of critical information about major international events.

Of course, similar observations could be made about the international impact of the telegraph, the telephone, or radio transmission. Nevertheless, it can be argued that a qualitative shift in the nature of international diplomacy has recently occurred. In this respect, Eyton Gilboa makes the following observation: "Before the global communication revolution a leader could have sent one message through local media to his people and another through foreign media to other peoples. Today this distinction has disappeared and a policy statement reaches at the same time both local and foreign audiences including enemies and allies" (Gilboa 2003, 107). This scenario typically occurs in the period before a war or military intervention. If the imminent conflict is of maximum news value then feedback loops occur whereby statements and actions from major protagonists generate multiple responses worldwide. This in turn provides journalists from every television news network and other media outlets with ever-replenishing sources for breaking news stories.

Real-time flows of global television news also interact with military communication networks and the prosecution of military campaigns. The 1991 Gulf War offers an obvious starting point. For the first time, a major military intervention unfolded televisually for audiences worldwide. Amid the US bombing of Baghdad, reporters often provided traumatic pieces to camera by focusing on their own location in relation to surrounding events (Hoskins 2004, 50–1). Behind the scenes, global television and military networks relied upon the same technologies. Night vision lenses developed for night combat enabled 24-hour reportage from combat locations. Satellite communication itself enabled global telecasting and military mapping of the globe. The installation of missile tip cameras fused global media communication with the exercise of military power: the vision of a target became connected in real time to its destination (Wark 1994, 42–4). The critical point, for my purposes, was that these interactions between military and media communication networks were reflexively reinforcing. On certain occasions journalistic interventions and news judgments directly affected military statements and decisions, which in turn generated further news stories. After 1991, the reflexive interaction between media and military communication intensified, reflecting the rapid proliferation of 24/7 satellite channels in combination with the digital remediation of television news gathering and news reception. During the US invasion of Iraq in March 2003, events on the ground were intensively and rapidly circulated outward into global, pan-regional, and national mediascapes. These multiple mediations influenced the tactics and communication strategies of military commanders. At the same time, regional and international circuits of political communication reflexively overlapped with the real-time force field of media–military events.

There are, of course, many other networked organizations involved in the global mediation of real time. Examples include nonfinancial corporations and business organizations, millenarian terrorists, and armed resistance groups in conflict zones. Empirically, the reflexive repercussions of these multiple interconnections play out across different communicational domains (i.e., global, international, transnational, national, local). The extensity and the density of real-time feedback loops across scales depends, however, on the location (as well as the magnitude) of the event and events in question. A financial collapse, military alert, or political assassination within a global city will have multiscalar repercussions. In a more peripheral location, such events will unfold less extensively and less prominently.

The detemporalized present versus temporal contemporaneity

As I have indicated, instantaneous and simultaneous media communication constructs an ever-present world of immediacy. In a similar vein, social theorist Carmen
Leccardi identifies a present which has become detemporalized. This is not a
present that progresses, conventionally, from the past toward the future. Rather, it
is a self-defining present disconnected from any sense of past or future. Drawing
from Agnes Heller, Leccardi argues that the present has become "all there is"
(Heller 1999, 7, cited in Leccardi 2007, 30). Under such conditions, historical time
and prospective futures cannot be subjects of open debate. Yet, as I have also argued,
we inhabit a world of temporal contemporaneity in which real-time information-
communication networks facilitate a plurality of cultural modernities. This is
exemplified by the contraflows that shape the ecology of satellite television news,
such that various diasporas draw upon particular channels to reaffirm linguistic and
cultural ties. Middle Eastern networks, for example, cater to audiences in North
Africa, Central Asia, Europe, and North America (Rai and Cottle 2007, 63).

It is in this context that one can appreciate the global and temporal significance
of Qatar's Al Jazeera. Formed in 1996, it soon established a studio infrastructure,
24-hour coverage, a field correspondent team, regional bureaux, website services,
and an expanding global presence that attracted diasporic Arab audiences in
Europe and North America (El-Nawawy and Gher 2003). When the United States
subsequently decided to invade Iraq, Al Jazeera confronted an enormous real-time
orchestration of power and propaganda organized around spectacular narrative
forms that were "fully integrated into military and corporate public relations campaigns" and which furnished "hog fuel for 24 hour news channels and websites"
(Compton 2004, 3). In response, Al Jazeera replaced its usual live and recorded
program schedule with 24-hour rolling news providing on-the-spot stories and
footage from Baghdad, Mosul, Basra, and the Kurdish zone. Once Iraqi hostilities
began, the term "Al Jazeera" became a major searched-for web topic and Aljazeera.
net became the world's most popular Arabic site (Allan 2004, 353–4). Against the
US narrative of "Shock and Awe," Al Jazeera footage was captioned "War on Iraq."
Initial news bulletins ended with the anchor saying "we leave you now with live
pictures from Baghdad." Silent panoramic camera shots of the flame-lit city carried the byline "Baghdad is burning" (Miles 2005, 241–2). Over subsequent days,
rolling news footage revealed bombed houses, distraught families, children and
adults with missing limbs, overrun hospitals, and bloodstained corpses. Such coverage sparked a wave of protests around the Middle East and Al Jazeera gave these
substantial prominence. This had political and diplomatic repercussions worldwide (Miles 2005, 242).

Al Jazeera's countercoverage, and precipitation of, globally televised news events
associated with the invasions of Afghanistan and Iraq are of historic importance.

BBC World and CNNI no longer monopolized real-time reportage of international events involving the Middle East. Temporal contemporaneity had successfully challenged the detemporalized present. There are, however, inbuilt limits to such challenges. The major global networks continuously disseminate real-time versions of globality which obscure structural configurations of economic power. Other satellite channels do not have the operational scale or global reach to confront this symbolic world.

Depicting Global Capitalism: Coevality and Critique

Global mediations of real time obscure the historicity and geosocial totality of global capitalism. At the same time, global news, remediated by digital technologies, also vividly illuminates the social worlds of wealth and poverty. This contrasts sharply with the sinecured metropolitan worlds of late nineteenth-century capitalist imperialism. The occupants of these worlds do not "want to know about their colonies or about the violence and exploitation on which their own prosperity is founded, nor do they wish to be forced into any recognition of the multitudinous others hidden away beneath the language and stereotypes, the subhuman categories of colonial racism" (Jameson 2003, 700)

The crucial issue here is not that these metropolitan citizens lacked knowledge about imperial and world capitalist expansion; but that the knowledge available was not constructed by marginalized populations themselves. Their particular experiences of capitalist imperialism could not be communicated between colonial outposts and had no public voice within the metropole. In his historical critique of western anthropological research, Johannes Fabian argues that anthropology constructed its object in ways that erased the historical and temporal perspectives of the cultures under investigation, a process he calls "the denial of coevality" (Fabian 1983, 30–1). While *synchronous* events occur within the same physical process of time and *contemporary* events occur within the same qualitatively termed period of time, *coevality* refers to the sharing of time. It involves reorganizing historical time in a way that gives identity to the other (in relation to oneself), openness to the possibility of cotemporal understanding (with regard to otherwise disparate ways of life), and an appreciation that cotemporal relations are embedded within broader social totalities and relations of power (Fabian 1983, 31–2). Conversely, its denial occurs when marginalized peoples and colonized subjects are positioned as "other" to the assumed centrality of "our" time (as backward, traditional, premodern, tribal, rural, peasant) or when a univocal discourse of historical time overrules or silences the specificity of their experiences.

Global modernity, temporal contemporaneity, and real-time communication networks presuppose cosmopolitan social worlds shaped by transnational, global-local, and translocal interactions. Such interactions constitute a vast mosaic of interpersonal, diasporic, intercultural, and ecumenical activity. It appears, therefore, that Fabian's argument has been overtaken by events. The Eurocentrist preconditions for the denial of coevality no longer hold. However, as I have argued, the electronic networks and temporal accelerations of global capitalism continue to insulate the rich and excommunicate the poor. In light of these developments, Fabian's argument can be recast: global mediations of real time reify the suppression of coevality between the lifeworlds of wealth and poverty. In one sense, this is a paradoxical statement. Compared to colonial times, contemporary mediations of wealth and poverty are all-enveloping. Images of opulence pervade Hollywood and Bollywood film and high-end advertising for cars, electronic goods, exclusive real estate, and luxury travel. Global, pan-regional, regional, and national flows of remediated, 24/7 television news highlight the celebrity lifestyles of world leaders, corporate CEOs, royalty, film stars, writers, artists, musicians, and athletes. Associated breaking news stories filter into radio reports, daily and weekly newspapers, and celebrity gossip magazines. Summit gatherings of global elites in Genoa, Quebec City, Sydney, Prague, Davos, and Washington DC receive prominent coverage. League tables of the rich and powerful are regularly published worldwide. Meanwhile, the poor and destitute are kept in the limelight by aid agencies and news media as the victims of floods, earthquakes, famines, disease outbreaks, and insurgencies. With the Internet, portable cameras, and mobile telephony depictions of poverty, crime, and violence freely proliferate. Additionally, news stories often feature critical juxtapositions of wealth and poverty. Press coverage of the 2008 G8 summit in Tokyo disdainfully listed the conference dinner menu and wine list alongside discussion of the world food crisis. Headlines worldwide in July 2008 included "Food for thought" and "Eat as we say, not as we do – a rich answer to hunger."

In a mediated world of unfolding immediacy, however, the structural and temporal relationships between wealth and poverty are denied representation. This obfuscatory process is built into global disseminations of banal, cosmopolitan outlooks. Openness toward peoples, places, and experiences from different cultures and nations is superficially celebrated through branded products and advertising with images of fashion, food, music, wine, sport, and celebrity figures constituting a "ready-at-hand" global world of "exceptional co-presence" (Urry 2000, 6). This consumerist cosmopolitanism is continuously reproduced through personal computers, the Internet, cell phones, modems, planes, billboards, neon signs, and television (Urry 2000, 6). The ubiquity of television generates a world of "imaginative travel" where "sensations of other places especially facilitated through channel-hopping and programmes that simulate channel-hopping" can "create an awareness of cosmopolitan interdependence" (Urry 2000, 8). In this context, media researcher Dayan Thussu notes that "symbiotic relationships between the news and new forms of current affairs and factual entertainment genres such as reality TV have developed, blurring the boundaries between news, documentary and entertainment" (Thussu 2007, 69).

Although the global news and entertainment media systematically denies the structural and temporal relationalities between wealth and poverty, powerful countertendencies are at work. In an economically interdependent world, driven by instant transfers of knowledge and information, the whereness of one's felt life can, potentially, be positioned in relation to other lived places. The televisual and ICT infrastructures that project the ontological givenness of global business activity also enables workers, feminists, Greens, human rights activists, and indigenous peoples to mobilize against global capitalist organizations. Examples include multiscalar campaigns against corporations (Shell, Nike, Exxon), supranational institutions (IMF, WTO, World Economic Forum), and associated summit gatherings. The proliferation of transnational social movements opposed to global capitalism has been synonymous with the formation of real-time alternative news forums such as Indymedia, which force global configurations of power and the coeval disconnections between rich and poor into public view. Film historian Tom Zaniello has compiled and indexed what he calls "the cinema of globalization," noting the recent proliferation of short films on political, investigative, and news websites, and predicting the growing availability of "longer films about globalization made in this new media" (Zaniello 2007, 16).

Detailed investigation of these developments is beyond the scope of this chapter. It is, however, pertinent here to identify the preconditions for oppositional practices of communication which might utilize the real-time capacities of satellite transmission, Internet, broadband, mobile telephony, satellite phones, portable video cameras, and desktop editing. Oppositional forms of political expression must avoid representing the global as a fact or force of nature. For any given film, documentary, or news story, various geographically located perspectives and temporalities must be foregrounded and compared. It is also vital to thematize the capitalist underpinnings of long-term global trends such as climate warming and resource depletion. Global patterns of finance, production, consumption, transportation, and distribution depend on a corporately designed system of fossil energy flows which threaten our biosphere. If this general diagnosis is not publicly explicated, 24/7 satellite channels and associated news flows will endlessly remediate the outward symptoms of a chronic global condition (hurricanes, droughts, famines, floods, squalor, and social breakdown). Countering the superficial immediacy of such coverage also requires a predictive understanding of global trends. Before a major news event appears, activists, journalists, and filmmakers must prepare audiences for the inundation of breaking stories registering popular fears and panic behavior. The likely consequences of an influenza outbreak or a full-scale stock market collapse, for example, could be explored via documentaries drawing upon similar events from the past. Finally, oppositional practices of media communication need to capture the linked simultaneity of a global capitalist network such as an oil company, a consumer goods manufacturer, an agribusiness corporation, or a hedge fund. In each case, the concurrent nodal points of business transactions, profit realization, and human exploitation could be visually portrayed within a coherent narrative. This kind of representation will require multimedia networks of communication with the capacity to counteract global reifications of real time. Contributing to the construction of these networks is one of the most urgent tasks facing a critical political economy of communications that aspires to translate theory into practice.

References

Adam, B. (2004) *Time*. Polity Press, Cambridge, UK.

Allan, S. (2004) Conflicting truths: On-line news and the war in Iraq. In: Paterson, C. and Sreberny, A. (eds), *International News in the 21st Century*. John Libbey, Eastleigh, UK, pp. 285–300.

Bayart, J. F. (2007) *Global Subjects*, A. Brown (trans.). Polity Press, Cambridge, UK.

Castells, M. (1996) *The Rise of Network Society*. Blackwell, Oxford.

Castells, M. (2000) Information technology and global capitalism. In: Hutton, W. and Giddens, A. (eds), *On the Edge: Living with Global Capitalism*. Jonathan Cape, London, pp. 52–75.

Castells, M. (2001) *The Internet Galaxy*. Oxford University Press, Oxford.

Cetina, K. K. (2005) How are global markets global? The architecture of a flow world. In: Cetina, K. K. and Preda, A. (eds), *The Sociology of Financial Markets*. Oxford University Press, Oxford, pp. 38–61.

Chalaby, J. (2003) Television for a new global order: Transnational television networks and the formation of global systems. *Gazette: The International Journal for Communication Studies*, 65(6), 457–62.

Comor, E. (2008) *Consumption and the Globalization Project*. Palgrave, MacMillan, New York.

Compton, J. (2004) Shocked and awed: The convergence of military and media discourse. Paper presented at International Association for Media and Communication Research (IAMCR) Conference, Porto Alegre, Brazil, July.

Davis, M. (2006) *Planet of Slums*. Verso, London.

Dicken, P. (2003) *Global Shift*, 4th edn. Sage, London.

Dirlik, A. (2007) *Global Modernity: Modernity in the Age of Global Capitalism*. Paradigm, Boulder, CO.

Ek, R. (2006) Media studies, geographical imaginations and relational space. In: Falkheimer, J. and Jansson, A. (eds), *Geographies of Communication*. Goteborg University, Nordicom, Sweden, pp. 43–66.

El-Nawawy, M. and Gher, L. (2003) Al Jazeera: Bridging the East-West gap through public discourse and media diplomacy. *Transnational Broadcasting Studies*, 10 (Spring-Summer) Online at http://www.tbsjournal.com/Archives/Spring03/nawawy.html (accessed October 21, 2010).

Fabian, J. (1983) *Time and the Other*. Columbia University Press, New York.

Flew, T. (2007) *Understanding Global Media*. Palgrave, London.

Gilboa, E. (2003) Television news and US foreign policy: Constraints of real-time coverage. *Press/Politics*, 8(4), 97–113.

Harris, J. (2001) Information technology and the global ruling class. *Race and Class*, 42(4), 35–46.

Harvey, D. (1990) *The Condition of Postmodernity*. Blackwell, Oxford.

Held, D., McGrew, A., Goldblatt, D., and Perraton J. (1999) *Global Transformations*. Polity Press, Cambridge, UK.

Heller, A. (1999) *A Theory of Modernity*. Blackwell, Oxford.

Hesmondhalgh, D. (2007) *The Cultural Industries*. Sage, London.

Hoogvelt, A. (2001) *Globalization and the Post Colonial World*, 2nd edn. Palgrave, London.

Hoskins, A. (2004) *Televising War: From Vietnam to Iraq*. Continuum, London.

Jameson, F. (2003) The end of temporality. *Critical Inquiry*, 29(4), 695–718.

Jukes, S. (2002) Real-time responsibility. *Harvard International Review*, 24(2), 14–19.

Krugman, P. (2008) *The Return of Depression Economics and the Crisis of 2008*. Penguin, London.

Leccardi, C. (2007) New temporal perspectives in the high speed society. In: Hassan, R. and Purser, R. (eds), *24/7: Time and Temporality in the Network Society*. Stanford University Press, Palo Alto, CA, pp. 25–36.

Lee, J. (2005) Getting the small picture. *Newsweek*, June 6–13, 59.

Massey, D. (2005) *For Space*. Sage, London.

Medina M. (2003) Time management and CNN strategies 1980–2000. In: Albarran, A. and Arrese, A. (eds), *Time and Media Markets*. Lawrence Erlbaum, Mahwah, NJ, pp. 81–94.

Miles, H. (2005) *Al Jazeera: How Arab Television News Challenged the World*. Abacus, London.

Parks, L. (2005) *Cultures in Orbit*. Duke University Press, Durham, NC.

Rai, M. and Cottle, S. (2007) Global mediations: on the changing ecology of satellite television news. *Global Media and Communication*, 3(1), 51–78.

Robinson, P. (2002) *The CNN Effect*. Routledge, London.

Robinson, W. (2004) *A Theory of Global Capitalism*. John Hopkins University Press, Baltimore.

Rude, C. (2005) The role of financial discipline in imperial strategy. In: Panitch, L. and Leys, C. (eds), *Socialist Register*. Merlin Press, London, pp. 82–107.

Sabelis, I. (2007) The clock-time paradox: Time regimes in the network society. In: Hassan, R. and Purser, R. (eds), *24/7: Time and Temporality in the Network Society*. Stanford University Press, Palo Alto, CA, pp. 255–78.

Schiller, D. (2007) *How to Think About Information*. University of Illinois Press, Urbana.

Singh, K. (2000) *Taming Global Financial Flows*. Zed Books, London.

Soros, G. (1998) *The Crisis of Global Capitalism*. Little Brown, London.

Thompson, E. P. (1967) Time, work-discipline and industrial capitalism. *Past and Present*, 36, 57–97.

Thompson, J. (1994) *Ideology and Modern Culture*. Polity Press, Cambridge, UK.

Thompson, P. (2003) Making the world go round? Communication, information and global trajectories of financial capital. *Southern Review*, 36(3), 20–43.

Thompson, P. (2004) The political economy of information in the global financial markets and their insulation from democratic accountability. Paper delivered at the International Association for Media and Communication Research (IAMCR) Conference, Porto Alegre, Brazil, July.

Thussu, D. (2007) *News as Entertainment*. Sage, London.

Tomlinson, J (2007) *The Culture of Speed*. Sage, London.

United Nations Conference on Trade and Development (UNCTAD) (2005) *World Investment Report*. United Nations, New York and Geneva.

United Nations Conference on Trade and Development (UNCTAD) (2008) *World Investment Report*. United Nations, New York and Geneva.

Urry, J. (2000) The global media and cosmopolitanism. Paper presented at Transnational American Conference, Munich, June. Online at http://www.lancs.ac.uk/fass/sociol ogy/papers/urry-global-media.pdf (accessed October 21, 2010).

Wark, M. (1994) *Virtual Geography*. University of Indiana Press, Indianapolis.

Winseck, D. (2008) The state of media ownership and media markets: Competition or concentration and why should we care. *Sociology Compass*, 2(1), 34–47.

Yin, D. Y. (2005) The telecom crisis and beyond. *Gazette: The International Journal for Communications Studies*, 67(3), 289–304.

Zaniello, T. (2007) *The Cinema of Globalization*. Cornell University Press, Ithaca, NY.

Zorn, D. and Dobbin, F. (2005) Managing investors: How financial markets reshaped the American firm. In: Cetina, K. K. and Preda, A. (eds), *The Sociology of Financial Markets*. Oxford University Press, Oxford, pp. 269–89.

25

Global Media Capital and Local Media Policy

Michael Curtin

Since the early part of the twentieth century, three cities have served as the creative and operational centers of the international media economy. During the 1920s, Hollywood assumed its leadership of the film industry, followed 30 years later by its global prominence in the television trade. Today, its companies remain the leading providers of screen programming for theatrical, satellite, cable, and broadcast media worldwide. Similarly, New York and London have long prevailed as preeminent centers of news, publishing, advertising, and financial information. They furthermore serve as headquarters to the world's wealthiest media conglomerates and while traveling the globe, one commonly encounters their voluminous cultural output, from Batman to Mickey Mouse, from BBC to CNN, and from Nike ads to the *Financial Times*. Consequently, the political economy of international media has tended to focus on the power and influence of media institutions located in New York, London, and Los Angeles.

Yet throughout the history of modern media, other centers have vied for the attention of audiences as well. Shanghai was, for example, a bustling center of Chinese film production in the 1920s, Bombay became home to several successful movie studios during the 1930s, and Cairo served as the leading producer of Arab cinema for much of the twentieth century. The number of movies produced in these cities and the profits they garnered were modest by comparison to Hollywood, but the cultural influence of these locales was nevertheless expansive and profound. Moreover, the diversity and significance of peripheral media centers have grown substantially since the 1980s, encouraged in part by the growing transnational flow of media products via satellite, cable, Internet, and home video. Londoners can now purchase Nigerian videofilms off the Internet, Chicagoans can subscribe to Indian satellite channels, and Angelenos can follow the latest

The Handbook of Political Economy of Communications, First Edition.
Edited by Janet Wasko, Graham Murdock, and Helena Sousa.
© 2014 John Wiley & Sons, Ltd. Published 2014 by John Wiley & Sons, Ltd.

Chinese television and movie premiers. Some scholars refer to this phenomenon as a reverse flow of media from "the rest" to the west, but just as importantly, one also finds Bollywood fans in the African Sahel, telenovela audiences in Southeast Asia, and Turkish TV buffs in Saudi Arabia. Such lateral media flows are testament to increasingly complicated patterns of cultural influence worldwide and they may furthermore be indicative of shifting institutional relations and professional practices in the global media economy.

Consider the following: Before its New York opening on April 30, 2007, *Spider-Man 3* had already premiered in nine countries, including Russia, Brazil, and Japan. So important is the global market for Hollywood blockbusters these days that studios now pay substantial attention to international promotion and distribution. During its theatrical run, *Spider-Man 3* raked in more than $500 million from the overseas box office, a figure far exceeding ticket sales in the United States. Indeed, global box office has become a crucial factor in the conception, financing, and execution of most Hollywood blockbusters. Whereas international distribution used to be to a backend enterprise, it has over the past decade become a central component of big-budget productions. Films such as *Spider-Man 3* often take in close to a billion dollars worldwide during their theatrical run, setting them up for further revenues in video sales, rentals, and merchandising.

What these enormous revenues fail to convey, however, is the relatively modest reach of such blockbusters. Given the premium price of Hollywood movie tickets, the number of people that actually saw *Spider-Man 3* in a movie theater was only 125 million worldwide. Compare this to the Indian super-hero movie, *Krrish*, which premiered only a few months earlier. In India alone, it sold an estimated 110 million tickets. Worldwide figures are hard to come by, since Indian movie companies have far less control of overseas markets, but one can imagine that audiences in Pakistan, Bangladesh, and the Gulf States were similarly enthusiastic, as were audiences in markets where Hollywood film rental fees are beyond the reach of the average exhibitor. Based on this comparison, one might reasonably presume that *Krrish's* cultural impact was equal to and perhaps exceeded that of *Spider-Man 3*. The spatial location of Indian movie audiences may differ (Asia, Africa, and the Mideast vs. Europe, Japan, and Australia), but its transnational footprint is nevertheless substantial. Consequently, one could certainly argue that *Krrish* is something of a global phenomenon in its own right.

Krrish is also a global phenomenon in another sense, for it was conceived and produced by a Mumbai (Bombay) studio with an eye toward world markets. This was not always the case with Indian movies, but since the mid-1990s, overseas viewers with familial attachments to the subcontinent have come to figure prominently in the strategies of so-called Bollywood filmmakers and distributors. According to Yash Raj Films, one of Mumbai's most successful studios, Indian movies now generate more than $100 million per year in US video and soundtrack sales, making it one of the most lucrative growth markets for the Indian movie industry. It's also estimated that the volume of pirated materials is far larger, suggesting substantial future potential as the distribution infrastructure develops. Europe and the Gulf States have likewise become significant territories for Indian film and television distributors. Only 10 years ago, these markets were relatively inconsequential. Today, they represent one of the most important parts of the business and as a result global perspectives have come to influence the conception and execution of many Indian films.

Chinese movies are undergoing a similar transformation. *Crouching Tiger, Hidden Dragon* is a spectacular example of this shift, but just as intriguing are films such as *Kung-fu Hustle*, starring Stephen Chow, which earned more than $100 million in theaters worldwide, and *Hero*, starring Jet Li, which earned $177 million. All three of these films not only captured the attention of global audiences, they were the product of multinational collaboration, drawing upon finance, talent, and creative resources from Chinese societies around the world. Again, box office revenues tell only part of the story, as these films earned much of their income in markets with lower ticket prices than their western counterparts.

Chinese television is also becoming more transnational. In 1991, Hong Kong entrepreneurs launched Star TV with the aim of creating a pan-Asian platform of satellite TV programming. Though its continental strategy ultimately has to be recalibrated to the distinctive contours of various media markets, it nevertheless proved so successful that it helped to spark the deregulation of television industries throughout the region, instigating a lively and broad-ranging competition among an expanding constellation of media services. Today, Asian media companies that used to operate national or local television stations in Hong Kong, Singapore, and Taipei now run services that telecast throughout the region. Confronted with growing competition in their local markets, they have been prodded to expand their geographical reach, not only in Asia but also to cities in Europe and North America where audiences can now access tens of thousands of hours of Chinese programming via cable, satellite, and home video.

Over the past 20 years, market forces, technological innovation, and government deregulation have engendered new conditions for the production and distribution of Chinese commercial television. Even in the People's Republic of China, where state ownership of media is the standard, the number of services and the range of competitors have increased dramatically. As TV institutions have faced dramatic reductions in government subsidies, they have been encouraged to pursue advertising revenues and new entrepreneurial initiatives. This has resulted in joint ventures with commercial partners from Taipei, Tokyo, and New York, and it has furthermore encouraged CCTV – which is the only PRC television service officially authorized to operate abroad – to forge distribution agreements that for the first time give it carriage in Europe and North America.

Indian entrepreneurs based in Mumbai, Chennai, and Hyderabad have likewise launched transnational television networks, such as Zee, Sun, and ETV. Together they provide programming in a variety of Indian languages to viewers around the world. Similarly, Nigerian videofilm producers churn out thousands of stories each year that circulate across sub-Saharan Africa and to migrant audiences in the Americas, Europe, and South Asia. And among Arab media, transnational satellites offer programming to audiences in the Mideast, Europe, and North Africa.

In light of these shifting geographies, this chapter offers a spatial analysis of film and television industries, explaining key principles that have been driving the commercial development of screen media for more than a century. These principles cluster under the concept of *media capital*, invoking the twin connotations of capital as referring both to a geographic center and to an accumulation of resources, talent, and reputation. The three principles of media capital help to explain why some cities rise to prominence as centers of production and furthermore suggest why certain patterns of cultural circulation emerge. In the sections that follow, I explain these principles: logics of accumulation, trajectories of creative migration, and contours of sociocultural variation. After delineating the factors that influence the spatial deployment of media resources, the chapter turns to a concluding discussion of the policy implications of media capital in an era of globalization. It is suggested that states should be realistic in their assessment of commercial media capacity and resolute in their determination to support a range of media resources, both commercial and noncommercial.

The Logic of Accumulation

The logic of accumulation is not unique to media industries, since all capitalist enterprises exhibit innately dynamic and expansionist tendencies. As David Harvey (2001) points out, most firms seek efficiencies through the concentration of productive resources and through the extension of markets in hopes of realizing the greatest possible return on investment in the shortest amount of time. For example, companies reorganize the spatial layout of factories to increase their efficiency or they use new modes of delivery to expand their market reach. These *centripetal* tendencies in the sphere of production and *centrifugal* tendencies in distribution were observed by Karl Marx (1973, 539) more than a century ago when he trenchantly explained that capital must "annihilate space with time" if it is to overcome barriers to accumulation.

As applied to contemporary media, this insight suggests that even though a film or TV company may be founded with the aim of serving a particular national culture or a local market, it must over time redeploy its creative resources and reshape its terrain of operations if it is to survive competition and enhance profitability. Implicit in this logic of accumulation is the contributing influence of the "managerial revolution" that accompanied the rise of industrial capitalism (Chandler 1977). Modern managers have for over a century sought to apply scientific techniques and technologies of surveillance to the refinement of corporate operations. During the twentieth century, capitalism became more than a mode of accumulation; it also became a disposition towards monitoring and adaptation, as it continually reorganized and integrated manufacturing and marketing processes, achieving efficiencies through a concentration of productive resources and through the ongoing enhancement of delivery systems.

The history of the American cinema – the world's most commercial and most intensively studied media industry – provides an instructive example of these core tendencies. During the first decade of the twentieth century, US movie exhibitors depended on small, collaborative filmmaking crews to service demand for filmed entertainment. Yet as theater chains emerged, as distribution grew more sophisticated, and as competition intensified, movie companies began to centralize creative labor in large factory-like studios with an eye toward improving quality, reducing costs, and increasing output. By refiguring the spatial relations of production, managers concentrated the creative labor force in a single location where it could be deployed among a diverse menu of projects under the guidance of each studio's central production office. The major film companies furthermore separated the domains of planning and execution, creating a blueprint (or script) for each film that guided the work of specialized craftspeople in lighting, make-up, and dozens of other departments deployed across the studio lot. As American cinema entered this factory phase during the 1910s, the intensification of production accelerated output and yielded cost efficiencies, providing theater operators around the country with a dependable flow of quality products (Bordwell et al. 1985, Scott 2005, Bowser 1990).

Similar patterns emerged in the Indian commercial film industry with major studios emerging in Bombay and Calcutta by the 1930s. Although the studio system would fall by the wayside for a number of reasons, the concentration of productive resources would intensify, allowing Bombay to emerge as the center of a South Asian film industry that would distribute movies across the subcontinent (Pendakur 2003, Prasad 1998, Rajadhyaksha 2003). In Chinese cinema, transnational cinema circuits were firmly in place by the 1930s, but the mode of production was initially more dispersed for a variety of reasons. During the post-World War II era as prosperity returned to the industry, both Cathay and Shaw Brothers established integrated production operations in Hong Kong that rivaled the scope and productivity of their American counterparts (Bordwell 2000, Curtin, 2007, Fu 2002, 2003). The capital-intensive factory model prevailed with major movie companies around the world, but it is nevertheless important to note that unlike the auto or steel industries, filmmaking employees were creating distinctive *prototypes* rather than redundant batches of products with interchangeable parts. Each commodity was relatively unique, even if production routines grew increasingly standardized and even if the films were intended for mass audiences (Bordwell et al. 1985).

Not only was film production distinctive from other forms of industrialized manufacturing, but so too was film distribution, since movies are what economists refer to as public goods (Kepley 1990, Hesmondhalgh 2002). That is, each feature

film is a commodity that can be consumed without diminishing its availability to
other customers. And given the relatively low cost of reproducing and circulating
a film print when compared to the cost of creating the prototype, it behooves the
manufacturer to circulate each artifact as widely as possible. Unlike other cultural
institutions that needed to be close to live audiences or patrons (e.g., vaudeville
and opera), and unlike industrial manufacturers who incurred substantial ship-
ping costs for their finished products (e.g., automobiles and washing machines),
movie studios could dispatch their feature films expansively and economically.
The key aim of the distribution apparatus was therefore to stimulate audience
demand and insure access to theaters in far-flung locales. They achieved the latter
by establishing theater chains or by collaboration with major exhibitors,
both nationally and internationally (Thompson 1985, Gomery 1986, Balio 1993,
Pendakur 2003, Curtin 2007).

Trajectories of Creative Migration

The second principle of media capital emphasizes trajectories of creative migration, since audiovisual industries are especially reliant on creativity as a core
resource. Recurring demand for new prototypes requires a workforce that is self-
consciously motivated by aesthetic innovation as well as market considerations.
Indeed, attracting and managing talent is one of the most difficult challenges that
screen producers confront. At the level of the firm, this involves offering attractive
compensation and favorable working conditions, but at a broader level it also
requires maintaining access to reservoirs of specialized labor that replenish themselves on a regular basis. This is one of the main reasons why media companies
tend to cluster in particular cities.

Nevertheless, it is rare that such centers of creativity emerge strictly as a response
to market forces, as a longer historical perspective would seem to indicate. During
the premodern era, for example, artists and craftspeople congregated at sites where
sovereigns and clergy erected grand edifices or commissioned vast ensembles of cultural products. Patronage drew artists to specific locales and often kept them in place
for much of their working lives, and they in turn passed their skills along to succeeding generations and to newly arrived migrants. Rather than market forces, one might
imagine that spiritual inspiration and feudal relations of patronage significantly influenced trajectories of creative migration during this period, but it is also important to
acknowledge the tendency of artists to seek out others of their kind. Artists are
drawn to colocate with their peers due to the mutual learning effects engendered by
such proximity. That is, artists improved their skills and enhanced their vision through
their ongoing association with other artists. As the bourgeoisie rose to prominence
in the early modern era, commercial cities became new centers of artistic patronage,
production, and exhibition, even though pre-existing centers retained residual prestige among the cognoscenti (DiMaggio, 1986). Industrialists built performance

venues, established galleries, and subsidized educational institutions, all of which attracted fresh talent to cities such as Berlin, New York, and Shanghai.

Popular culture was layered over this topography of creative labor flows in the fine arts. Outside the major cultural centers, it was difficult for popular artists and performers to subsist in any one locale since they lacked access to a wealth of powerful patrons. Instead, popular performers established circuits of recurring migration, playing to crowds in diverse towns and villages. These circuits were formalized in the nineteenth century by booking agents who rationalized the scheduling of talent across regional chains of performance venues. By concentrating creative laborers into performance troupes and then circulating them around a circuit, vaudeville made it possible for performers to earn a living and to learn new techniques from their fellow artists (Allen 1980, Gilbert 1940, McLean 1965). As vaudeville flourished, it attracted new talent from among the enthusiastic audiences in diverse locales, bringing these budding performers into the circuit of production. During their early years, film industries drew from the talent reservoirs of high culture and popular theater, locating their production facilities close to existing cultural centers. As they flourished, filmmakers relocated to sites where they could build vast factories for the manufacture of celluloid fantasies. Despite their success, reversals in the American (1950s), Indian (1940s), and Chinese (1970s) film industries brought an end to the studio system of production. Artists and laborers found themselves shifting from the security of long-term employment to the uncertainties of the casual labor at a growing number of independent production houses.

Why then did Hollywood, Bombay, and Hong Kong continue to act as magnets for cultural labor? One might suggest that like prior transitions, the residual aura of these cities helped to sustain their status as centers of creative endeavor, but geographers Michael Storper and Susan Christopherson (1987) contend that more importantly, a disintegrated (or flexible or Post-Fordist) mode of production in the movie industry actually encourages and sustains the agglomeration of creative labor due to the fact that constant changes in product output require frequent transactions between contractors, subcontractors, and creative talent. Their study of Hollywood shows that the number of interfirm transactions in the movie business have grown dramatically over the past 50 years at the very same time that the scale of transactions has diminished, indicating that many small subcontractors now provide the studios with crucial services, such as wardrobe, set construction, and lighting, as well as key talent, with many stars now incorporated as independent enterprises rather than as contract labor. Storper and Christopherson contend that although the production system went through a period of disintegration, the spatial concentration of labor persisted due to the demands of institutional and creative collaboration. That is, film producers today subcontract hundreds of tasks with most contracts going to local companies because it is easier for producers to oversee their work and suggest changes as the project progresses. As for the workers, they cluster around Hollywood where studios and subcontracting firms are based, since it helps them "offset the instability of short-term contractual work by remaining close to the largest pool of employment opportunities" (Storper and Christopherson 1987, 110).[1]

Geographer Allen J. Scott extends this principle of talent agglomeration to industries as diverse as jewelry, furniture, and fashion apparel, arguing that manufacturers of *cultural* goods tend to locate where subcontractors and skilled laborers form dense transactional networks. Beside apparent managerial and cost efficiencies, Scott points to the mutual learning effects that stem from a clustering of interrelated producers. Whether through informal learning – such as sharing ideas and techniques while collaborating on a particular project – or via more formal transfers of knowledge – craft schools, trade associations, and awards ceremonies – clustering enhances product quality and fuels innovation. "Place-based communities such as these are not just foci of cultural labor in the narrow sense," observes Scott (2000: 33), "but also are active hubs of social reproduction in which crucial cultural competencies are maintained and circulated."

The centripetal agglomeration of labor encourages path-dependent evolution such that small chance events or innovations may spark the appearance of a culture industry in a particular location, but clustering engenders a growth spiral, as creative labor migrates to the region in search of work, further enhancing its attraction to other talent.[2] Locales that fail to make an early start in such industries are subject to "lock-out," since it is difficult to lure talent away from an existing media capital, even with massive government subsidies. Scott suggests that the only way a new cluster might arise is if its producers offer an appreciably distinctive product line.

In general, we can conclude that cultural production is especially reliant upon mutual learning effects and trajectories of creative migration, and that inevitably particular locations emerge as centers of creativity. These principles have operated throughout history under various regimes of accumulation, but the modern era is distinctive because the centripetal logic of capitalist production has been married to the centripetal trajectories of creative migration, engendering the rise of transnational film production centers. One might imagine that in today's world of increasing commercial flows and diminishing trade barriers, we might be approaching a time when one city would become a dominant global center attracting talent from around the world and producing a majority of the world's popular screen narratives. Yet the complexities of distribution undermine such pretensions to singular dominance, especially when media products rub up against counterparts in distant cultural domains that are often served, even if minimally, by competing media capitals that are centers of creative migration in their own right.

Contours of Sociocultural Variation

Cities such as Hollywood, Mumbai, and Hong Kong lie across significant cultural divides from each other, which helps to explain why producers in these cities have been able to sustain distinctive product lines and survive the onslaught of distant competitors. These media capitals are furthermore supported by intervening factors that modify and complicate the spatial tendencies outlined above. Consequently, the third principle of media capital focuses on forces of sociocultural variation, demonstrating that national and local institutions have been and remain significant actors despite the centripetal biases of production and creative migration and the centrifugal bias of distribution. Indeed, the early years of cinema were exceptional in large part because the logic of media capital unfolded relatively unimpeded by national regulation, but as the popularity of transnational movie narratives increased, many countries established cultural policies to address the growing influence of cinematic imports.

Motion pictures presented governments with a unique policy challenge since they were distributed even more widely than newspapers, magazines, or books, the circulation of which were limited to literate consumers within shared linguistic spheres. By comparison, silent era cinema overcame these barriers and challenged class, gender, and racial boundaries, as well. Hollywood movies enjoyed especially expansive distribution, swelling the size of audiences dramatically and fueling the growth of large-scale studios. According to Kristin Thompson (1985), US movie companies became dominant exporters by the mid-1910s, a trend that contributed to a further concentration of resources and talent in the Los Angeles area. By the 1920s, however, opinion leaders and politicians abroad grew wary and cultural critics began to clamor for regulation. Many countries imposed import quotas and content regulations on Hollywood films and some set up national film boards to subsidize cinema productions with national themes and talent (Crofts 1993, Jarvie 1992, Higson 1989, O'Regan 2002).

Most importantly, however, national governments embraced the new technology of radio broadcasting as a foil against the attractions of foreign movies. In almost every country outside the western hemisphere, radio was established as a public service system intended as a bulwark against cultural invasion from abroad. Britain, which would serve as a model to others, explicitly charged the British Broadcasting Corporation with responsibility to clear a space for the circulation of British values, culture, and information (Scannell 1991, Hilmes 2003). Radio seemed an especially appropriate medium for intervention, since many of its characteristics helped to insulate national systems from foreign competition. Technologically, radio signals traveled only 30 to 60 miles from any given transmitter. As in Britain, one could interconnect a chain of transmitters that would blanket the countryside, but the only way for foreign competitors to reach one's domestic audiences was via shortwave radio, a temperamental technology that was comparatively inaccessible to the masses. Such insulation was furthermore insured by an international regulatory regime that allocated radio frequencies on a national basis, minimizing technical as well as cultural interference between countries. Language provided another bulwark, since radio relied on aural competence in the state's official language, helping to distinguish national radio productions that played in one's parlor from Hollywood "talkies" that played at the cinema. Finally, public service radio systems were bolstered by indigenous cultural resources, since literary and theatrical works were commonly appropriated to the new medium, as were folk tales and music. State ceremonies and eventually sport-ing events also filled the airwaves, as the medium participated in self-conscious efforts to foster a common national culture.

Radio also promoted a shared temporality among audiences. Its predecessor, the national newspaper, pioneered this transformation during the nineteenth cen-tury by directing readers to stories that the editors considered significant and by encouraging them to absorb these stories at a synchronous daily pace (Anderson 1983). Radio extended the daily ritual of newspaper consumption to nonliterate groups, which expanded the horizon of synchronization, such that program sched-ules began to shape daily household routines and create a national calendar of social and cultural events. Radio insinuated itself into the household, interlacing public and private spheres, and situating national culture in the everyday world of its listeners (Hilmes 1997, Morley 2000, Scannell 1991). Even though radio systems were founded under the guiding hand of politicians, educators, and cultural bureaucrats, radio would over time open itself up to audience participation, employing yet another distinctive cultural resource as part of its programming repertoire: the voice of the people. In each of these ways public service radio accentuated national contours of difference in opposition to media capital's desire to operate on a smooth plane of market relations worldwide.

Although the BBC served as a template for public service radio, national radio systems were diverse and their success varied. All India Radio was exceptionally elitist and therefore relatively unpopular. It wasn't until the incursions of foreign satellite competitors that Indian radio and television were forced to compete for the favor of audiences (Jeffery 2006). India was not the only country to experience the negative effects of the state's monopoly of the airwaves. Nigerian broadcasting was rife with political favoritism and censorship until it found itself competing in the 1990s with popular Nigerian video films (Adesanya 2000, Haynes 2000, Haynes and Okome 1998, Larkin 2008, McCall 2004). Despite such problems, regulation of the airwaves provided an effective way for governments to refigure the centripetal and centrifugal tendencies of media capital. It allowed them to staunch the flow of culture from abroad and to cultivate domestic talent and resources. Regulation provided a defensive response to the spatially expansive tendencies of commercial media industries.

Regulation also acted as an influential enabler of commercial media industries in diverse national contexts. Intellectual property (IP) laws are especially compel-ling examples in this regard as are media licensing regimes.[3] The commercial devel-opment of broadcasting in the United States was facilitated by regulations that in effect made it possible to "sell the airwaves" to corporate operators. In so doing, the government created a market-driven system out of an intangible public resource, enabling a national program distribution system that stimulated the growth of national advertising and concentrated creative resources in a handful of urban centers (Streeter 1996). Just as the British system became a model for public service systems around the world, the commercial licensing regime of American broadcasting became the standard for satellite regulation, which in turn pressured governments around the world to adapt to commercial models during the 1990s.

As we can see, the boundaries and contours of markets are subject to political interventions that enable, shape, and attenuate the dynamics of media industries. Concepts such as "free flow" and "market forces" are in fact meaningless without self-conscious state interventions to fashion a terrain for commercial operations. Markets are made, not given. And the logic of accumulation must therefore be interrogated in relation to specific and complex mixtures of sociocultural forces.

Finally, it should also be pointed out that self-conscious state policies are not the only actors that organize and exploit the forces of sociocultural variation. Media industries in Mumbai, Cairo, and Hong Kong have themselves taken advantage of social and cultural differences in their production and distribution practices. Operating across cultural divides from Hollywood and from other powerful exporters, they have employed creative talent and cultural forms that resonate distinctively with their audiences. These industries have furthermore made use of social networks and insider information to secure market advantages, and they invoke cultural and national pride in their promotional campaigns. Forces of sociocultural variation can therefore provide resources for carving out market niches as well as defining a terrain for national public service systems.

Policy Implications

Media capital is a concept that investigates the *spatial* logics of capital, creativity, polity, and culture without privileging one among them. Just as the logic of accumulation provides a fundamental structuring influence, so too do trajectories of creative migration and contours of sociocultural variation shape the diverse contexts in which media artifacts are made and consumed. The analysis of media capital encourages researchers to provide critical accounts that delineate the operations of capital and the migrations of talent, while at the same time directing attention to cultural forces and social contingencies that give shape to discourses, practices, and spatial relations.

Media capital furthermore encourages researchers to challenge the presumption that Anglo-American media are central to the lives of media users worldwide and that they will remain so for the foreseeable future. Evidence suggests on the contrary that Hollywood is at a historical moment that is strikingly reminiscent of 1960s Detroit, when it was difficult for US auto executives to take seriously the prospect of competitive challenges from overseas producers. Yet in less than two decades, the tides shifted in the global auto industry and only a few decades later, the American companies found themselves on the precipice of collapse. Perhaps Hollywood is destined in the short term for a less dramatic fate, but lively competition has already emerged and seems destined to intensify as media enterprises in cities such as Mumbai, Lagos, and Dubai continue to formalize and corporatize their financing and operations. One can certainly applaud the pluck, persistence, and creativity of these producers, for their successes reassure us that audiences will be able to access screen media from a variety of sources for the foreseeable future. Yet a greater appreciation of the diverse competitive landscape of global media is only one benefit of a spatial analysis, for it furthermore offers the opportunity to revisit questions of cultural policy from a new vantage point.

Media policy has long been framed by concerns about foreign intrusions on local and national culture. Such anxieties are likely to grow as the logic of accumulation continues to drive the consolidation of production resources and to encourage expansive transnational distribution strategies among leading commercial media companies. In fact, these core tendencies have already matured substantially since the 1980s under the auspices of neoliberal free trade and structural adjustment policies. Just as importantly, creative talent continues historical patterns of agglomeration and today creative workers move even more swiftly and fluidly among the world's creative centers in search of job opportunities, aesthetic inspiration, and social learning effects. Such patterns of circulation provide enduring advantages for media capitals, making it difficult for new competitors to displace them.

In light of these tendencies, national and metropolitan policy makers have been tempted to compete for talent and resources in hopes of joining the ranks of global media capitals. Those that pursue this course should, however, be judicious about the subsidies and support that they offer, using them primarily to nurture *resident* firms and practitioners that have already proven their transnational potential rather than squandering resources on speculative new start-ups or fleet-footed producers from afar. Many governments have come to regret the subsidies and infrastructural investments they offered to Hollywood producers in an attempt to lure them to their cities. The short-term gains they may have enjoyed soon evaporated when the producers moved on to the next locale that offered even better subsidies and facilities (Goldsmith and O'Regan 2005, Miller et al. 2008, Porter 1998, Tinic 2005). Policy makers should instead make strategic investments in their city's existing productive capacity and creative communities, doing so after a judicious assessment of competing locales with comparable resources. They should consider not only the growth potential of resident producers but also their financial and marketing operations. For media capital tends to flourish where creative endeavor is interwoven with the quotidian facework of deal making and distribution.

Policy makers cannot create new media capitals out of whole cloth, but they can recognize and support locales that seem to be gathering talent and resources. Media policy should intervene selectively to enhance productivity by providing infrastructural, educational, and financial resources that might stimulate further growth and they should facilitate transnational marketing and collaboration. Policy should furthermore promote the enforcement of intellectual property laws, so as to ensure that distribution revenues flow centripetally to producers, allowing further investment and growth. Although the US government is the most vocal proponent of international IP enforcement, piracy is in fact having a far more deleterious effect on media industries in Lagos, Mumbai, and Hong Kong than it is on Hollywood. IP policies should embrace and promote global standards, while reserving the right to shape those standards to local and national circumstances.

As mentioned above, the prospect of nurturing a resident media industry toward capital status is realistic for only a handful of cosmopolitan centers. What about other locales, such as smaller nations that are likely to be eclipsed by larger neighbors and poorer states that are subject to cultural influences from wealthier counterparts? What are the prospects for creative endeavor in Nigeria's neighbor, Benin, or India's neighbor, Nepal? Similarly, what should be done for provinces and cities within large states that find themselves susceptible to cultural influences from distant metropolitan centers, such as Mexico City? And what might be done for metropolitan media that vie with nearby neighbors for cultural and commercial prominence, as is the case in the Pearl River Delta where Hong Kong film and TV prevail over competitors from Guangzhou and Shenzhen? These spatial dynamics are not entirely new. In fact, they have been an enduring feature of modern era ever since the early development of print capitalism during the fifteenth century. Media and markets have long conspired to privilege some places over others and, because of these inequities, modern governments have been anxious to assert their cultural sovereignty and to provide a space for mediated deliberation. So important are these principles that governments have repeatedly intervened in the realm of popular communication so that political capital often counts as much if not more than economic or creative capital. In extreme cases, media became instruments of the state or of an autocratic elite, but at their very best public media institutions have provided the means by which common legacies were maintained, policies debated, and futures imagined.

Media policy should not, however, be invoked in a defensive manner nor should it be used to prop up political parties or national governments. Nor should policy aim to regulate imports, limit access, or censor programs. Such restraints, though relatively effective in the past, are nowadays counterproductive due to the availability of technologies that can circumvent official restrictions. The Chinese government, for example, strictly limits the number of Hollywood movies imported each year, but this has little effect on the actual consumption of American films in China, since they are widely available through black market video distribution channels (Wang 2003). Government sanctions not only fail to limit personal consumption of foreign films, but they paradoxically have a negative impact on Chinese film and TV industries, since they drive audiences out of the formal media economy and encourage resentment and distrust of government institutions. Keeping citizens engaged with the national media agora requires that states acknowledge not only the preferences of users but also their personal capacity to evade official constraints. Given these considerations, the governments should focus on the supply side of the policy equation, looking for ways to sustain and encourage local, national, and regional media that offer distinctive products foreign enterprises are unlikely to provide.

Policy should emphasize the public purposes of modern media, which like parks, libraries, and childcare centers are resources that make places worth living. The analogy to public parks is especially intriguing when one considers the principles of stewardship that inform enlightened policy with respect to natural resources. Commercial enterprises, private interests, and political operators certainly win the attention of environmental planners and policy makers, but so too do other constituencies, such that urban parks make space for multiple uses, arboretums cultivate plant diversity, community gardens expand food sources, and farmers' markets support local agriculture. Each of these spaces is subsidized and sequestered from conventional market forces and although they may contribute to the overall commercial value of a place, they are primarily justified by their ability to offer opportunities the market will not. This ethic extends outside the cities where national forests provide recreational activities, national parks offer public access to the diverse wonders of the natural environment, and wilderness areas shelter species that cannot on their own withstand the pressures of human population growth and commercial avarice. Wilderness areas are particularly intriguing. For public policy supports them knowing that the vast majority of citizens will never venture inside and that access will only be granted to those who are willing to enter on conditions that are specific to the local ecosystem.

These principles of enlightened land management – some would say, stewardship – offer an intriguing new departure point for media policy since they lean towards the active creation and development of public resources at a variety of levels. They presume that markets will provide limited diversity and therefore seek to protect resources and render them productive in ways that the market cannot imagine. These principles judge success as much by the appreciative crowds that gather as by those that don't, knowing that a diversity of uses and pleasures is more important to the overall system than the cold accountability of ticket sales or attendance records. The principles of stewardship are often the subject of intense struggle, but it is nevertheless remarkable that citizens are willing to embrace the principles of land stewardship largely because of a shared presumption that everyone benefits from diversity.

Stewardship principles might have several virtues when applied to media policy outside the world's major production centers. First of all, by presuming that the logic of media capital is spatially expansive and intrusive, they provide a baseline rationale for public intervention to sustain a range of commercial and noncommercial services. Stewardship principles furthermore suggest public media should not be configured as an appendage of the state nor should they promote a singular public sphere. Instead, they should be diverse in their objectives and institutional configurations. They might, on the one hand, blend public and private resources, while on the other, help to sustain microcommunities or oppositional constituencies that have absolutely no commercial potential. Public media should be characterized – like any healthy ecosystem – by tension and antagonism, as well as interdependence and symbiosis. They should be protean institutions that change over time but nevertheless are guided by a long-term ambition to foster a diversity of cultural resources at a variety of spatial scales.

The principles of media capital help to explain the spatial tendencies of commercial film and television, and in so doing they provide a rationale for policy interventions that seek to modify the logic of the market. Historically, media policies established territorial barriers and bolstered the authority of the state, but under current circumstances it seems best to view policy as an enabling influence, helping to nurture and sustain a diversity of voices in a global era. As noted earlier, policy makes markets, but it also helps to make publics. The two can coexist and even complement each other, but only so long as policy is alert to the fundamental tendencies of media capital.

Notes

1   Despite the development of new communication technologies that allow creative collaborations across vast expanses, creative labor still needs to congregate so as to build relationships of trust and familiarity that can enable and sustain long-distance collaborations. Giddens's (1990) discussion of facework and Bourdieu's (1986) notion of social capital both point to the importance of physical proximity.

2   Although it does not address media industries specifically, an extensive literature explores the impact of human capital on the clustering of business firms in particular locations (Florida 2005, Jacobs 1984, Porter 1998).

3   In the United States, court rulings during the 1910s provided movie studios with intellectual property rights so that they – rather than their employees – might claim protection for the films they "authored." Although copyright laws originally aimed to foster creative endeavor by *individuals*, the courts allowed movie factories to claim artistic inspiration as well. Interestingly, they furthermore ruled that waged and salaried laborers at the major studios were neither creators nor authors, but were rather "work for hire." In this way, the American legal system profoundly transformed copyright law, facilitating the industrialization of cinematic production and providing expansive legal protection for movie distributors (Bordwell et al. 1985).

References

Adesanya, A. (2000) From film to video. In: Haynes, J. (ed.), *Nigerian Video Films*. Ohio University Center for International Studies, Athens, OH, pp. 37–50.

Allen, R.C. (1980) *Vaudeville and Film: 1895–1915: A Study in Media Interaction*. Arno Press, New York.

Anderson, B. (1983) *Imagined Communities: Reflections on the Origin and Spread of Nationalism*. Verso, New York.

Balio, T. (1993) *Hollywood as a Modern Business Enterprise, 1930–1939*. Scribners, New York.

Bordwell, D. (2000) *Planet Hong Kong: Popular Cinema and the Art of Entertainment*. Harvard University Press, Cambridge, UK.

Bordwell, D., Staiger, J., and Thompson, K. (1985) *The Classical Hollywood Cinema: Film Style and Mode of Production to 1960*. Routledge & Kegan Paul, London.

Bourdieu, P. (1986) The forms of capital. In: Richardson, J. G. (ed.), *Handbook for Theory and Research for the Sociology of Education*, Greenwood, New York, pp. 241–58.

Bowser, E. (1990) *The Transformation of Cinema: 1907–1915*. Scribner, New York.

Chandler, A. D. (1977) *The Visible Hand: The Managerial Revolution in American Business*. Belknap, Cambridge, MA.

Crofts, S. (1993) Reconceptualizing national cinemas. *Quarterly Review of Film & Video*, 14(3), 49–67.

Curtin, M. (2007) *Playing to the World's Biggest Audience: The Globalization of Chinese Film and TV*. University of California Press, Berkeley, CA.

DiMaggio, P. (1986) *Non-Profit Enterprise in the Arts: Studies in Mission and Constraint*. Oxford University Press, New York.

Florida, R. (2005) *Cities and the Creative Class*. Routledge, New York.

Fu, P. (2002) Hong Kong and Singapore: A history of the Cathay Cinema. In: Wong, A. (ed.), *The Cathay Story*, Hong Kong Film Archive, Hong Kong, pp. 66–70.

Fu, P. (2003) *Between Shanghai and Hong Kong: The Politics of Chinese Cinemas*. Stanford University Press, Palo Alto, CA.

Giddens, A. (1990) *The Consequences of Modernity*. Stanford University Press, Palo Alto, CA.

Gilbert, D. (1940) *American Vaudeville: Its Life and Times*. McGraw-Hill, New York.

Goldsmith, B. and O'Regan, T. (2005) *The Film Studio: Film Production in the Global Economy*. Rowman & Littlefield, Lanham, MD.

Gomery, D. (1986) *The Hollywood Studio System*. St. Martin's Press, New York.

Harvey, D. (2001) *Spaces of Capital: Towards a Critical Geography*. Routledge, New York.

Haynes, J. (ed.) (2000) *Nigerian Video Films*, revised edn. Ohio University Center for International Studies, Athens, OH.

Haynes, J. and Okome, O. (1998) Evolving popular media: Nigerian video films. *Research in African Literatures*, 29(3), 106–28.

Hesmondhalgh, D. (2002) *The Cultural Industries*. Sage, London.

Higson, A. (1989) The concept of national cinema. *Screen*, 30(4), 36–46.

Hilmes, M. (1997) *Radio Voices: American Broadcasting, 1922–1952*. University of Minnesota Press, Minneapolis, MN.

Hilmes, M, (2003) Who we are, who we are not: The battle of global paradigms. In: Parks, L. and Kumar, S. (eds), *Planet TV: A Global Television Reader*, New York University Press, New York, pp. 53–73.

Jacobs, J. (1984) *Cities and the Wealth of Nations*. Random House, New York.

Jarvie, I. C. (1992) *Hollywood's Overseas Campaign: The North Atlantic Movie Trade, 1920–1950*. Cambridge University Press, Cambridge, UK.

Jeffrey, R. (2006) The Mahatma didn't like the movies and why it matters. *Global Media and Communication*, 2(2), 204–24.

Kepley, V. Jr. (1990) From "frontal lobes" to the "Bob-and-Bob" Show: NBC management and programming strategies, 1949–65. In: Balio, T. (ed.), *Hollywood in the Age of Television*, Unwin Hyman, Boston, MA, pp. 41–61.

Larkin, B. (2008) *Signal and Noise: Media, Infrastructure, and Urban Culture in Nigeria.* Duke University Press, Durham, NC.

Marx, K. (1973) *Grundrisse: Foundations of the Critique of Political Economy.* Vintage, New York.

McCall, J. C. (2004) Juju and justice at the movies: Vigilantes in Nigerian popular videos. *African Studies Review,* 47(3), 51–67.

McLean, A. F. (1965) *American Vaudeville as Ritual.* University of Kentucky Press, Lexington, KY.

Miller, T., Govil, N., McMurria, J., Maxwell, R., and Wang, T. (2008) *Global Hollywood 2.* British Film Institute, London.

Morley, D. (2000) *Home Territories: Media, Mobility, and Identity.* Routledge, New York.

O'Regan, T. (2002) A national cinema. In: Turner, G. (ed.), *The Film Cultures Reader,* Routledge, New York, pp. 139–64.

Pendakur, M. (2003) *Indian Popular Cinema: Industry, Ideology, and Consciousness.* Hampton Press, Cresskill, NJ.

Porter, M. E. (1998) Clusters and the new economics of competition. *Harvard Business Review,* November, 77–90.

Prasad, M. (1998) *Ideology of the Hindi Film: A Historical Construction.* Oxford University Press, New York.

Rajadhyaksha, A. (2003) The "Bollywoodization" of the Indian cinema: Cultural nationalism in a global arena. *Inter-Asia Cultural Studies,* 4(1), 25–39.

Scannell, P. (1991) *A Social History of British Broadcasting.* Blackwell, Malden, MA.

Scott, A.J. (2000) *The Cultural Economy of Cities.* Sage, Thousand Oaks, CA.

Scott, A.J. (2005) *On Hollywood: The Place, The Industry.* Princeton University Press, Princeton, NJ.

Storper, M. and Christopherson, S. (1987) Flexible specialization and regional industrial agglomerations: The case of the U.S. motion picture industry. *Annals of the Association of American Geographers,* 77(1), 104–17.

Streeter, T. (1996) *Selling the Air: A Critique of the Policy of Commercial Broadcasting in the United States.* University of Chicago Press, Chicago.

Thompson, K. (1985) *Exporting Entertainment: America in the World Film Market, 1907–34.* BFI Publishing, London.

Tinic, S. (2005) *On Location: Canada's Television Industry in a Global Market.* University of Toronto Press, Toronto.

Wang, S. (2003) *Framing Piracy: Globalization and Film Distribution in Greater China.* Rowman & Littlefield, Lanham, MD.

26

The Challenge of China
Contribution to a Transcultural Political Economy of Communication for the Twenty-First Century

Yuezhi Zhao

Assuming as I do that Mao Zedong correctly predicted the zigs and zags of China's struggles toward socialism, it seems obvious that the fuel is being accumulated which will power a later phase of class struggle taking off from where the Cultural Revolution ended.

Dallas Smythe 1981, 247

I'm not putting bets on any particular outcome in China, but we must have an open mind in terms of seeing where it is going.

Giovanni Arrighi 2009, 84

If the political economy of communication *as an academic field* counts the "blind spot" debate, initiated by Dallas Smythe, as one of the defining moments in its development, political economy of communication as *a praxis* witnessed a historical encounter of an entirely different nature and magnitude, also initiated by Dallas Smythe, in an article entitled "After Bicycles, What?," which was not published during his lifetime, but nevertheless "attained a legendary status" among his peers (Guback 1994, 227). While the "blind spot" debate pitted North American political economists against their British counterparts within western Marxism, this other encounter engaged Smythe with the ideas and political practices of the Chinese Communist Party (CPP) within the international communist movement.

The Handbook of Political Economy of Communications, First Edition.
Edited by Janet Wasko, Graham Murdock, and Helena Sousa.
© 2014 John Wiley & Sons, Ltd. Published 2014 by John Wiley & Sons, Ltd.

Smythe went to China to study ideology and technology between December 1971 and January 1972 on the eve of China's reinsertion into the global capitalist economy, a process that started with the formal breakthrough in diplomatic relations with the US marked by Richard Nixon's visit to China in February 1972 and culminated with post-Mao China's dramatic change in its developmental strategy. Smythe's interviews with officials and academics in various fields led him to conclude that while "proletarian politics" were being put "in command of all cultural life," "our common cultural heritage of capitalist thinking" continued to inhibit Chinese academics from seeing the political nature of techniques and technology (Smythe 1994, 238). Having a "gut feeling" that this could be a problem in the Chinese pursuit of socialism and realizing that this was more than a question of scholarly concern, Smythe submitted his report to the Chinese authorities as a piece of friendly criticism from a concerned "family" member within the international socialist movement (Guback 1994, 229). Although the Chinese authorities never responded directly, the indirect answer to his question "After Bicycles What?" has been a thunderous "Of Course, Cars!," along with all the capitalist social relations that the private automobile embodies. Today, political economists of communication are facing "the challenge of China" produced by this titanic transformation. This chapter explores the theoretical challenges that China's ascending role within the global political economy poses for a political economy of communication and culture in the twenty-first century. Building on an earlier attempt to contribute to a transcultural political economy of communication that aims to transcend the Euro-American biases of the field (Chakravartty and Zhao 2008), I bring the Chinese case to bear upon some of political economy's basic conceptual categories in relation to communication: the nature of the state; the relationships between class, nation, and empire; the problem of history and culture; and finally, by way of conclusion, agencies and alternatives.

The West, the Rest, and the Centrality of the Chinese State

"Like a giant oil tank, the world is turning. New growth poles of the world economy have been emerging in the south and east. Globalization once belonged to the west and now the tables are turning. We have entered the era of the 'rise of the rest'," writes sociologist Jan Neverveen Pieterse (2009, 55). But what makes China's rise stand out? Its demographic weight, continental geographic scale, as well as the dizzying variety of ethnic communities and identities, do not provide an adequate answer – after all, the Indian subcontinent, the other major emerging power center, shares all these features. However, there is one crucial difference: "the modern state of India ... does not carry China's long heritage of political unity or recent experience as a Leninist state" (Cheek 2006, 13).

Despite the mainstream western and Chinese dichotomous portrayal of an economically devastated Mao era versus the economically miraculous reform era, the Mao period laid the essential political, industrial, as well as social foundations for China's spectacular growth in the reform era (Shirk 1993, Meisner 1996). Walden Bello (1999), writing from the Philippines, has gone back further arguing that China's post-Mao economic dynamism "can't be separated from an event that most of us in the South missed out on," that is, "a social revolution in the late forties and early fifties that eliminated the worst inequalities in the distribution of land and income, and prepared the country for economic take-off … in the late 1970s" (Bello 1999).

Bello's observation is especially relevant in the critical area of media and com-munication, where the Chinese state's Leninist and Maoist legacies remain particu-larly strong (Zhao forthcoming). As I have argued (Zhao 2008a), the Chinese state's aggressive promotion of information and communication technologies, along with commodification and state control of both ideology and the "commanding heights" of the media and communication industry, have been key dimensions of the "China rising" story, making the Chinese trajectory of development different from both former communist countries, on the one hand, and other countries in the global south, on the other. In fact, Ann Marie Brady (2008), in a rearticulated Cold War framework, has characterized the post-1989 era Chinese state's incorporation of market mechanisms and western techniques of public relations and mass persua-sion in its propaganda work as an Orwellian case of "marketing dictatorship."

The Chinese state's special position within the current global order, including its veto power in the United Nations Security Council, also place it in "a league of its own" among emerging powers in the global south, with a unique ability to fashion flexible responses to American hegemony. As J. N. Pieterse (2008, 712) has argued, different states have adopted three broad strategies of responses to American hegemony: (1) continued support for reasons such as the appeal of the US market, the role of the dollar, and even "lingering hope in the possibility of American self-correction"; (2) soft balancing, ranging from tactic noncooperation to establishing alternative institutions; and (3) hard balancing, a strategy that "only a few coun-tries can afford" either because they have already been branded as enemies of the US and thus have nothing to lose or "because their bargaining power allows maneu-vering room." The Chinese state has resorted to all three in different spheres. Its position within the postwar capitalist interstate system was not easily assumed. It was a prize the modern Chinese nation-state first earned under a nationalist gov-ernment in a protracted war against Japanese imperialism in Asia. The CCP-led state then fought for it and earned it not only for emerging victorious in the civil war with the Nationalist government, but also for its early commitment to Third World internationalism – as Mao said famously, the People's Republic of China (PRC) was carried into the UN by the brotherhood of Africa's numerous postcolo-nial nation-states, at a time when it was struggling for national autonomy vis-à-vis western capitalism, on the one hand, and Soviet "social imperialism," on the other. Thus, if the PRC owes a historical debt to the aspirations of China's lower social classes, especially the Chinese peasantry, for its domestic political and ideological legitimacy, it also owes a historical debt to the hopes of oppressed peoples in the global south as articulated in a utopian movement, the "Third World" project inaugurated at the Afro-Asia meeting in Bandung in 1955, for its prominent place in the capitalist interstate system (Prashad 2007).

Because China's national history is deeply affected by both its struggle against imperialism and its Communist revolution, "Chinese leaders intend to insert themselves into the global economy as fully respected and integrated members of the transnationalised capitalist class, not as indebted junior partners" (Harris 2005, 9). This raises the question of whether the Chinese leadership can officially shed their communist colors and constitute themselves as members of the transnational capitalist class without losing their political and ideological legitimacy to rule in China. For the political economy of communication, this foregrounds questions regarding the "relative autonomy" of the political and ideological realms vis-à-vis the economic realm. Unfortunately, neither western social theory in general nor the political economy of communication offers the necessary tools for analyzing the Chinese state. Within western social theory, earlier attempts by Marxist political economists to develop a state theory were prematurely buried by the globalization paradigm celebrating the death of the state, on the one hand, and by post-Marxist, poststructuralist, and postmodernist theories displacing the academic focus from "the state and class struggle to the micro-physics of power and the problems of identity formation," on the other (Jessop 1991, 91), resulting in "a remarkable impoverishment of state theory" (Panitch 2002, 93). The theoretical blind spot surrounding the postcolonial nation-state has also been noted, not only in the field of development communication in general, but also within the critical political economy paradigm. Citing Nordenstreng's (2001, 155) acknowledgement that "the state as a concept remains shamefully underanalyzed" among early theorists of the cultural imperialism paradigm, Alhassan (2004, 61) argued that even some of the defining texts on cultural imperialism "were blind on conceptual clarifications on the nation-state, democracy, citizenship, and sovereignty." Sparks (2007, 193, 203–4) has criticized theorists of cultural imperialism for failing to understand the nature of the central conflict of the pre-1991 world between the US and the USSR as "a struggle between different forms of empire," and for remaining silent about the distribution of power inside societies and "defining statist autarchic solutions as an alternative, rather than a complement, to US capitalism."

To be sure, not all the formulations of the cultural imperialism thesis problematically reify the Third World states and their national cultures and pit them mechanically and ahistorically against western capitalist states and transnational capitalist culture. The original critique of cultural imperialism, with its focus on how the "dominating stratum" of postcolonial societies "*is attracted, pressured, forced and sometimes bribed into shaping social institutions to correspond to, or even promote, the values and structures of the dominating center*" of the modern world system (H. Schiller 1976, 9 emphasis in original), "verged upon – though in truth it never fully became – a theory of transnational class struggle" (D. Schiller 1996, 101). This struggle, as Dan Schiller (1996, 101) elaborated, resonated with Franz Fanon's insistence that it is absolutely necessary to oppose vigorously and definitely the birth of a national bourgeoisie and a privileged caste within these societies. It is precisely within this context that one might appreciate Dallas Smythe's fascination with the rhetoric of "proletariat politics" being in command in the PRC and his attempt to grasp not only the nature of "class struggle" between the "capitalist roaders" and "socialist roaders" within the Chinese state, but also to analyze the ideological orientations and knowledge regimes of the officials and academics who were in the leading position to shape China's developmental path. Addressing the challenge that China presents for a contemporary global political economy of communication, then, first and foremost entails an analysis of the nature of the Chinese state in the era of information capitalism. As discussed above, this is a state that began in a social revolution and in Third World internationalism, and has, more recently, in the view of Joshua Cooper Ramo (2004), amassed "asymmetric power" in the global arena. If it is the power of this state that has enabled China to become a pole of growth for global capitalism during the era of neoliberal accumulation, it is the future direction of this state that has rendered "the rise of China" so unsettling for the evolving global capitalist order. The bankruptcy of neoliberalism and the Chinese state's ability to resist wholesale neoliberalization – or, put the other way, China's neoliberal elite's inability to pursue wholesale neoliberalization in the past 30 years due to the Chinese state's communist legacies – has propelled it to the center of the global political economy. However, precisely because its political legitimacy is still based on its socialist pretensions, and because class struggle over its direction is by no means settled despite the ascending power of the bureaucratic, capitalist, and managerial strata, there is the danger that the reforms are reversible, with "the masses" threatening to "seek a restoration of their own unique form of class power" (Harvey 2005, 151), compelling the leadership to rearticulate the state's hegemony in favor of the low social classes to "live up to its revolutionary mandate against foreign capitalists, private interests, and local authorities" (Harvey 2005: 150). As I have demonstrated elsewhere (Zhao 2008a), elite and popular communication politics in China since the early 2000s need to be understood as part of this unfolding struggle over the terms of the CCP's hegemony, and the future direction of China's ongoing transformation.

There is a profound uneasiness and fear on the part of the dominant US elite about the nature and future direction of the Chinese state. Elizabeth Economy and Adam Segal (2009), two analysts at the Council on Foreign Relations, have stated bluntly that the US and China have "mismatched interests, values, and capabilities" and that the US should incorporate "the rest of the world" in its hub-and-spoke China containment strategy. There is a sense of déjà vu here. As Westad has noted: "To elites in the United States, the rise of the Soviet Union as a world power also meant the rise of an alternative form of modernity that America had been combating since 1917" (2007, 25). Although the US won the Cold War with the

Soviet Union, there is widespread fear that the rise of China under CCP rule may actually fulfill the Soviet Union's historical promise of providing "an alternative modernity; a way poor and downtrodden peoples could challenge their conditions *without* replicating the American model" (Westad 2007, 17).

Class, Nation, and Empire: Chinese and Global Dimensions[1]

As the above analysis makes clear, the class character of the Chinese state and its role in the shifting regimes of capitalist accumulation must be taken as an issue of critical importance in any discussion of "the challenge of China." So must the relations between state and "nation." Because much of the debate on cultural imperialism ends up centering on the problem of inequality between nations, the concept of the "nation" has seldom been adequately conceptualized. Recent developments in the field, specifically what Mosco (2009) described as political economy's globalization and the development of feminist and labor "standpoints" of analysis, continue to gloss over questions of interstate struggles, nations, and nationalisms. Furthermore, as Desai (2008, 398) has identified, there is an unproductive scholarly division of labor between a study of nations and nationalisms focused primarily on culture and a political economy of national and international development that foregrounds class. Facing the "challenge of China" – a poor country that has managed to rise up in the global capitalist order while dramatically increasing domestic class inequalities, and a nation with staggering ethnic, gender, urban–rural, and regional divides, as well as a Chinese diaspora that not only has no parallel in its population size and economic power in the world but also perhaps in its economic and cultural linkages with China – necessarily requires a critical examination of the complicated intersections of class, nation, and other marks of status difference both within and beyond Chinese borders.

As Lin Chun (2006) has argued, in China, socialism, nationalism, and developmentalism were closely intertwined historically. The Chinese communists were more nationalists than communists. Because of the Chinese nation's "class" position in an imperialist international system, "the Chinese revolution … was first national and then social, and could not be otherwise" and Chinese communists "held a firm conviction that if social interest conflicted with national interest, the social must yield to the national" (Lin 2006, 40). Nevertheless, to the extent that the PRC was and is still defined constitutionally as a state led by the working class and based on the class alliance of workers and peasants, Chinese nationalism has a strong socialist and international legacy. This is literally embodied in the PRC national flag, which foregrounds the national population's class, rather than ethnocultural, or "nationality" constitution, with four stars representing the workers, peasants, petit bourgeoisie, and national bourgeoisie classes surrounding a larger star representing the CCP.

An international nationalism that differs from European nationalism underpins the PRC's historical self-identification with and participation in the "Third World" project. As Prashad argues, "if European nationalism took as a given that a people (who are perhaps a 'race') need to be organized by a state so that their nation can come into its own," postcolonial nationalists developed an alternative theory of the nation, which "had to be constructed out of two elements: the history of their struggles against colonialism, and their program for the creation of justice" (2007, 12).

The modern Chinese concept of the "nation" was also strongly conditioned by imperial China's long history of political unity and ethnocultural integration. As Wang Hui (2004) has demonstrated, the process of fashioning a modern Chinese nation-state out of imperial China with its long history of integration among different national populations is fundamentally different from the process of nation-state formation in Europe. Earlier Chinese bourgeois nationalists from Zhang Taiyan to Sun Yat-sen initially aimed to build a monocultural Han Chinese state, but quickly realized that this would lead to the disintegration of China. Consequently, the modern Chinese state in its first incarnation, established in 1912, was a multiethnic nation. Similarly, the Communists, influenced by Lenin's European notion of national self-determination, attempted to establish a communist state after the image of the European nation-state. However, they soon discovered through their revolutionary struggles that a Chinese copy of the European nation-state was not tenable. In particular, during the Long March, which brought the mostly Han Chinese revolutionaries into close contact with ethnic minorities in the remote regions of Southwest China, the communists discovered the reality of ethnic integration and realized that although there were ethnic tensions, ethnic conflict was not the "primary contradiction" in the ethnic minority regions. This appreciation for the long history of ethnic integration and the prioritization of class solidarity over ethnocultural identity in the articulation of the CCP's revolutionary hegemony, made the Chinese communist state's solution to the "national question" fundamentally different from those of the Soviet Union and Yugoslavia. While ethnonationalism was an important cause for the disintegration of these other two multinational communist states, China remains unified under a CCP-led state that is ever vigilant not only against western attempts at "xihua" China – that is, imposing western liberal-democratic institutions on China, but also "fenhua" China – that is, disintegrating it by supporting Taiwanese independence or any forms of ethnonationalist independent movement.

The reform period starting in 1978 marked a dramatic rearticulation of class and nation in the political economy of Chinese development, and along with it, a radical reorientation of the class nature of Chinese nationalism and the development of a depoliticized neoliberal cultural politics of class and nation. Information and communication technologies (ICTs) and commercialized media – with TV at its core, but soon followed by computers and cell phones – have played instrumental roles in these processes (Zhao and Schiller 2001, Hong

2008). If Mao had led the communist revolution in the first half of the twentieth century by mobilizing China's lower social classes and championing the cause of anti-imperialism, the CCP under Deng Xiaoping and his successor Jiang Zemin installed China's "digital revolution" from above by relying on the country's technocratic elites and rearticulating China's political economy with transnational capitalism, leading to the de facto formation of a hegemonic power bloc consisting of Chinese state officials, a rising domestic urban middle class, as well as transnational capitalists, foreign state managers and policy makers (Zhao 2003, Schiller 2007). As China became the poster child of the World Bank-promoted strategy of "ICT for development," Chinese society became fragmented, polarized, and deeply divided along class, region, gender, ethnicity, region, and other social and cultural divides. By 1997, the World Bank had reported that China's Gini coefficient index, which measures inequality on a scale of 0.001 to 1 (where 1 reflects absolute equality), had increased from a score of .28 in 1981 to 0.458 (Anagnost 2008: 498), making China, which still claims to be a socialist country, more inequitable than the United States (.408) and one of the most inequitable societies in the world – ranking 90th among 131 countries in a UN assessment in 2005 (Manthorpe 2006). Rather than speaking of "China," it has become more meaningful to think about China in terms of "one country, four worlds": the ultramodern and high-income Beijing, Shanghai, and Shenzhen constitute the first world, the ethnic minority and border areas and extremely low income rural areas the fourth world (Hu et al. 2001,167). ICT's role in constituting China's uneven development was matched by the media's role in rearticulating the neoliberal cultural politics of class and nation.

First, a fortified and modernized media control regime effectively depoliticized development and prohibited open debates about the class orientation of China's "reform and openness" process, debates on the commodification of media, and reflections on the capitalist social relations embedded in commercialized media services. This created the key enabling political condition for cheap labor as China's so-called "comparative advantage" by disenabling the circulation of labor struggles and suppressing the formation of radical working class consciousness (Zhao and Duffy 2007). For better or worse, the most striking fact is this: instead of being able to constitute themselves as an urban working class, members of this massive wage-earning workforce – 225 million by the end of 2008 in the official account, with 140 million as migrant workers (Du 2009) – referred to as "peasant workers" (*nongmin gong*), are not able to reproduce themselves as a "full proletarian" materially and culturally in the cities, with gender, place of origin, as well as a sense of having a piece of land and a rural home to return, playing significant roles in their identities (Ngai 2005, Hong 2008). The 2008–9 economic crisis, for example, has propelled tens of millions of migrant workers back to the countryside. As the other side of the coin of class (dis)formation, as many party members got rich first by becoming capitalists themselves and as the party incorporated the newly constituted capitalists, professional, and comprador elites into its ranks, it continued to frustrate autonomous capitalist class formation by restricting liberal and neoliberal intellectuals from enjoying full press freedom in the mass media, and by prohibiting private capital from entering the core areas of the media and communication system (Zhao 2008a, 2008b).

Second, while still opportunistically mobilizing anti-imperialist rhetoric in its ongoing bargaining with the US for a better deal within the global capitalist order, the party leadership and the mainstream media foreground a pragmatic and cultural form of Chinese nationalism, using it as an instrument for rallying popular support for the state-led project of "the Great Rejuvenation of the Chinese nation." As China attempted to reposition itself "from a Third-World anti-imperialist nation into one of imperialism's 'strategic partners'" (Wang 2006), essentialized Chinese cultural values and symbols, even vernacular beliefs and practices such as the fetish with the "lucky" number of 8, receive the highest level state sanction. The 8.08 p.m. grand opening of the August 8, 2008 Beijing Olympics with the high-tech cultural spectacle directed by Zhang Yimou is the ultimate embodiment of this version of Chinese cultural nationalism in the digitalized neoliberal era.

The concomitant spatial and cultural reconfiguration of Chinese national politics is also profound. On the one hand, the PRC state appeal to a pan-Chinese nationalism, or "modern Chinese transnationalism," both to support its unfinished business of reclaiming sovereignty over all Chinese territories under imperialist and capitalist rule (Hong Kong, Macau, Taiwan) and its coastal-based and exported oriented development strategy, taps into the vast financial and human capital of Chinese nationals living in these territories as well as the "ungrounded empires" of overseas Chinese diaspora (Ong and Nonini 1996, Ong 1999). As Wanning Sun (2002) has demonstrated, reform-era Chinese media, especially Chinese television, has been deeply involved in the cultural politics of migration and the Chinese transnational imagination. On the other hand, this strategy of asymmetric capitalist integration led to a neglect of the social and cultural needs of the ethnic minorities within PRC's hinterlands. As the "special economic zones" established in the coastal provinces in the early 1980s to attract foreign and especially diaspora Chinese capital to jump-start China's economic development assumed a central place in reform-era China's cultural imagination, the ethnic minority "autonomous regions" lost their relative importance. Regional inequalities grew. Class tension, ethnic divides, as well as the ideological void and identity crisis created by the discrediting of the Maoist-era class ideology and its particular articulation of the Chinese socialist nation, have intersected in complicated ways to create heightened social and cultural conflicts. As Yao (2009) has demonstrated, it is precisely within this context that one witnesses the rise of Tibetan ethnonationalism and a profound change in the identity politics of Tibetans, a development that has also been enabled by globalization and modern information technologies and new cultural venues such as online Tibetan literary forums. As Yao goes on to argue, this is a major cultural failure of the reform-era Chinese state and its lopsided economic development process, and one that must not be obscured by the Chinese state's attribution of the creation of the "Tibetan problem" to the Dalai Lama and the interference of western countries. The more dramatic and devastating eruption of ethnic conflicts in Xinjiang in July 2009 further underscored the severity of the problem.

Third, as the media abandoned Mao's discourse of class and class struggle, it embraced the discourse of "social strata" and dedicated themselves to the formation of "the middle class," making its growth "a national project that signifies China's membership in the developed world" (Anagnost 2008, 499). Within this discourse, the middle class – whose size and exact constitution remains fuzzy, ranging between 5 to 15 percent of the population – becomes a prized political and cultural trope, a force for social stability and perhaps even the agents of Chinese democracy. Under this neoliberal mode of citizenship, "citizen-subjects were no longer defined as equal members of a collective political body but by the degree of their individual progress towards middle class status" (Anagnost 2008, 499). Thus one witnessed one of the greatest ironies in the Chinese cultural politics: the discourse of "class struggle" was taken to its essentialist extreme when Chinese society was relatively egalitarian during the Cultural Revolution, and was totally suppressed during a process of rapid class polarization during the reform era.

As the other side of the media's role in its contribution to, and anticipation of, "middle class" formation, workers and peasants, the prized class tropes of the Maoist era and constitutionally still the leading classes of the PRC socialist state, re-emerged as the "vulnerable social groups" in official discourse. Rather than a structural factor and a class-charged political issue, inequality is depoliticized and articulated as "cultural difference in a hierarchy of national belonging" (Anagnost 2008, 497). Rather than the revolutionary and productive backbone of the nation, peasants have become the burden of the nation's march toward its ascendancy in the global capitalist order. At best, they are the ones who need to improve their own individual "qualities," and if they try hard, they can perhaps even become a member of the middle class; at worst, they are doomed to be sacrificed as the "price" for China's "great national destiny" (Zhao 2008a, 318). In perhaps the most ironic, and even cynical, turn in the developmental logic of global capitalism, Chinese peasants, whose basic needs for health care and education have hardly been met and whose unaccounted labor has subsidized the reproductive needs of China's migrant workers (for example, by taking care of the elderly and raising children in the countryside), have since February 2009 been subsidized by the Chinese state and mobilized by the media to overcome global capitalism's crisis of overproduction by purchasing the televisions, refrigerators, washing machines, and other electronic goods that American consumers had no more credit to buy. Through a program called "home electronics go to the countryside," which saw an average monthly growth rate of 74 percent in the amount of subsidies between February and May 2009, with the May 2009 total worth of subsidies standing at 280 million yuan (X. Li 2009), Chinese peasants, once the engine of a Chinese

Communist revolution, are now to serve as the engine for global capitalism's massive industrial machine in China, even potentially saving it by turning them- selves into "consumers of last resort" – a role, until recently, that had been assumed by American consumers.

The Chinese state thus faces the profound challenges of balancing economic growth and social and ecological justice, conflicting class interests and cultural identities. As Lin Chun (2006, 223) put it, the transformation of Chinese social- ism "is yet to strike a balance between market dynamics and private incentives on the one hand, and social cohesion and justice on the other." Recognizing the unsustainable nature of the developmental path in the 1990s, the Hu Jintao leadership, which came to power in 2002, has begun to address these tensions under the slogans of practicing "the scientific concept of development" and building a "harmonious socialist society." Even more interestingly, in an attempt to counter both the west's liberal democratic discourse and Eurocentric notion of nationalism, and a transnationalized Tibetan ethnonationalist move- ment, the Chinese state, while continuing to suppress the language of class, has been compelled to reclaim class-based solidarity with the Tibetan nation. In a highly symbolic move in January 2009, the Tibetan Autonomous Region National People's Congress established March 28 as Tibet's annual "Serf Liberation Day." In the official media discourse, this is to commemorate the Chinese People's Liberation Army's quelling of a March 10, 1959, armed rebel- lion led by "the Dalai Lama and his supporters in the upper ruling class ... with assistance from some western powers," and the subsequent completion of a "democratic reform" leading to "the emancipation of millions of Tibetan serfs and slaves" from the Dalai Lama's "feudal serfdom" and "theocracy" (Xinhua News Agency 2009).

Following Lin (2006), I argue that it remains worthwhile to explore the continu- ing relevance of the Chinese communist revolution's legitimation of "people's sovereignty" and the theory and practices of "people's democracy." As Lin (2006, 136) has pointed out, "whenever the People's Republic failed the people, it turned out not to be because it defied the Western models of government and their colo- nial extension, but because it departed from its own visionary inspiration and promise of democracy." From this perspective, the point that as long as its national government is not chosen through free, fair, and competitive elections, the PRC cannot be a democracy is beside the point. Instead, "It would be more appropriate to not ignore any genuinely democratic components of Chinese socialism and historicize them in such a way that the country is seen as yet to accomplish its own unfinished democratic project" (Lin 2006, 197). Although much attention has been placed on the rising "middle class" as potential agents of Chinese democracy, as Dan Schiller (2008) has reminded us, the making of a gigantic Chinese working class during the reform era and its domestic and global political and cultural implications must command the urgent attention of communica- tion scholars. As I have already alluded to, the nature of this process, partial proletarianization as opposed to full proletarianization, as well as the gender and regional mediation of the Chinese working class, are quite different from the archetypical making of the English working class. Schiller's comparative world-historical framework brings into sharp focus the magnitude of the kind of intellectual challenge that we are discussing:

> In England, propelling the originating movement into capitalism over the centuries between around 1500 and 1800, a few million persons became – made themselves into – what was long taken to be the first wage-earning working class. The world historical significance of this development for politics and culture and social policy registered, and not merely in England, both throughout early modern Europe and into contemporary times. What may we expect from the formation, during a compressed interval of just three decades, of a working class numbering perhaps 200 million wage-earners? (Schiller 2008, 413)

Communication scholars are only now beginning to engage with the multifaceted dimensions of this process (Zhao and Duffy 2007, Zhao 2008a, Hong 2008, Qiu 2009, 2010, Sun 2009). The Chinese state, by following an information technology-based and export-oriented development strategy, has accumulated national wealth on the one hand and intensified a multitude of domestic social conflicts on the other. Minqi Li (2008) has gone so far as to argue that China's economic boom was based on the political defeat of the urban working class and the creation of a massive surplus labor force in the form of rural migrant workers. At the same time, cheap consumer goods, low inflation rates, and the Chinese state's indirect financing of Washington's "war on terror" (by its debt-financing of the US state) allowed the US government to ease the domestic class tensions normally associated with increased income inequality and the massive upward redistribution of wealth. If China's low social classes were suppressed by the Chinese state while bayoneted with a nationalistic discourse of China's triumphant rise in the world, one wonders whether the American working class, whose bargaining power with capital has been undermined by transnational capital's mobilization of China's large reserve army of cheap, healthy, and relatively well-educated labor, has been materially pacified by Wal-Mart and latte consumerisms, while their sense of American political and cultural superiority was reaffirmed by American media stories of Chinese media and Internet censorship, human rights abuses, poor and dangerously made Chinese products, and discourses of "cultural genocide" in Tibet. If the "war on terror" has undermined civil liberties and curtailed the communicative freedoms of the American public – from American journalism's practices of "embedded reporting" to the American state's growing surveillance power over telecommunications and the Internet (Schiller 2007), will the current global financial crisis and a possible readjustment of China's developmental strategy in favor of China's domestic consumption and the welfare of China's lower social classes contribute to intensified class conflicts within the US?

As recent intensified social struggles and environmental conflicts in China and the Hu Jintao leadership's new ideological and policy initiatives have already demonstrated, the "rise of China" cannot sustain itself politically in the long run without the rise of China's lower social classes. As I have demonstrated, by 2004–5, even the Chinese state's fortified regime of media censorship could no longer contain the voices of China's lower social classes and those of their organic intellectuals in the struggle for social justice, environmental sustainability, and a more equitable developmental path (Zhao 2007, 2008a, Zhao and Duffy 2007). It is within this context that Minqi Li (2008, 92) has argued that the creation of a large working class and its rising bargaining power and organizational capacity in China will not only "turn the global balance of power again to the favor of the global working class," but put so much pressure on the capitalist profit rate and accumulation that it will bring about the eventual "demise" of the capitalist world economy as we know it. If the earth's biocapacities cannot accommodate the "rise of China" or the "rise of the rest" as aspiring to current western levels of consumer capitalism, then Smythe's radical insistence in "After Bicycles" on the necessity of transforming capitalist production and consumer relations, and its regime of technological innovation, assumes more urgency today not only for the Chinese, but also for an ecologically sustainable future for humanity as a whole.

This, in turn, raises urgent questions for the political economy of communication: what are the challenges and opportunities for democratic communication at a time when commercialized media systems have become victims of the global economic crisis with the decline of the advertising revenues as their lifeblood? Given that the US corporate media have not only failed to provide any meaningful "check" on the consecutive rise of various economic bubbles, and have more or less blindly endorsed the "war on terror," how far will they go in supporting a "coming conflict" with China, thus once again mobilizing US nationalism to displace domestic class conflict? What kind of media structure, practices, and cultural sensibilities will be necessary for the US to manage its decline in "a non-catastrophic way" (Arrighi 2009, 83)? Will the US media be able to transcend anticommunist and anti-Chinese racist ideologies in representing "China rising" during a period of profound uncertainty in the global order? Can the western media transcend imperialist and orientalist legacies in its coverage of Tibet or other ethnonational independent movements?

Furthermore, if one prong of the Chinese state's strategies in overcoming the crisis of overproduction is to boost domestic consumption by increasing the welfare of China's low social classes, and the other is to export its surplus capital and productive capacities and infrastructure building know-how to less developed countries in the global south, especially Africa, how will such a development contribute to reconfigure class, race, and national politics in Africa? As Franks and Ribet (2009) note, interesting work is already being done in the area of China–Africa media relations. Is Chinese capital creating "a Chinese legend" in African development, and even nurturing "love without borders" there – as the *People's Daily* claims (Yang and Xie 2009), or is it engendering a new form of "neocolonialism"– as the western media claim, or is the situation more complicated? After Africa being rendered the "lost continent" during the era of Euro-American-led neoliberal globalization, will China bring industry to the continent and become "a motor of development which will help transform much of Africa for the better," a process that Edward Friedman (2009, 19) argues is already happening? What kind of media and telecommunications infrastructure development projects are being pursued by Chinese government and industry there, and does the ideological legacy of "Third World internationalism," however compromised, play a role in both the practices and discourses of current Chinese economic and cultural interactions with Africa, and with the Arabic and Latin American countries? A global political economy of communication that reproduces the "hub-and-spoke" power relationship between the US and the rest of the world is clearly no longer adequate, if it ever was, as the new phase of economic and cultural globalization engenders more east–south and south–south financial, technological, and cultural flows.

Finally, in the context of a seismological transformation in the global political economy, and recognizing how growing inequalities have unleashed greater political instability in the global south, an argument has been made that, "it is in the interests of states in the global South to cooperate with each other to change the rules of the game," thus potentially engendering a "new Bandung," and one in which the former "Third World" states have not only the political and moral authority, but also the economic clout to challenge the west (Palat 2008, 721, Arrighi 2007). In this context, the June 16, 2009, inaugural summit meeting among the leaders of the BRIC countries (Brazil, Russia, India, and China) marks a significant development. If the call for a New World Information and Communication Order played such a central role in the previous attempt to build a more just world order, what role will this sector play in either blocking or engendering a possible "new Bandung," or more likely, proliferation of many "mini-Bandungs" along various lines of geopolitical affinity, in the current era of "knowledge economy" and informational capitalism? Will the fact that media and communication industries in the global south are themselves integrated into the transnational circuits of capitalist production and consumption make them complicit in perpetuating the neoliberal capitalist order? Will the "struggle to democratize public communication" in the North Atlantic heartland of global capitalism (Hackett and Carroll 2006) make a difference? What are the potential linkages and points of affinity among media democratization movements in the west, in the global south, and across the globe? How will political economists position themselves in these ongoing struggles? What lies beyond the past's misplaced hope in the Third World states and the current disenchantment with "transnational civil society"?[2]

History, Culture, and Chinese "Soft Power": Between a New "Renaissance" and a Second "Cultural Revolution"?

As Mosco (2009) has argued, one of the central characteristics of political economy is that it prioritizes social change and historical transformation. However, Mosco also recognizes that political economic thought is "mostly building on a metanarrative that sees the discipline rooted firmly within characteristic patterns of Western white male intellectual activity" (2009, 37). Marxist political economy takes as its historical "time zeroes" the rise of capitalism in the west and the beginning of colonization. However, at least two intellectual currents have challenged the adequacy of this temporality and provided useful insights for political economists of communication facing the "challenge of China" today.

The first of these currents has been initiated by world system theorists, in works such as Andre Frank's *Reorient* (1998) and Giovanni Arrighi's *Adam Smith in Beijing* (2007). By analyzing the world economy before the rise of capitalism and turning the east and west and center–periphery relationship upside down and, in Arrighi's case, by detailing the political economy of state and market formation in precolonized China and describing the noncapitalist market economy in East Asia, these theorists have contributed to dereifying capitalism as a "master category" in political economic analysis. In particular, they have made it possible to avoid the conflation between globalization and the spread of capitalism, which has been radical political economists' response to the "globalization paradigm."[3] As Amartya Sen (2006) has argued, globalization is not new, and is a much bigger and immensely greater process than western imperialism. Recognizing this makes it possible to transcend "civilizational confinement" (Sen 2006) and to imagine postcapitalist globalization and a new form of internationalism, or "critical cosmopolitanism," as a more desirable alternative to both capitalist "mobile consumerism" and religious fundamentalism (Murdock 2006) in a post-Cold War era that seems to have effectively put an end to the international communist movement.

By distinguishing between the development of a market economy and capitalist development proper, Arrighi has made it possible to open up the debate on the direction of China's ongoing transformation. According to Arrighi (2007), the capitalist nature of market-based development is not determined by the presence of capitalists but by the subordination of state power to capitalist class interest and the militarization of state power in the pursuit of foreign territories and markets – the latter is what defined the European developmental path as capitalist, and the market-based development in the Ming and early Qing eras as noncapitalist. To be sure, China's current integration with the global capitalist economy has made its contemporary market economy qualitatively different from the market economies of the Ming and Qing eras. But this alone does not rule out the possibility that the territorial logic of power – be it the Chinese state or more likely, a multipolarity of transitional states including China – may manage to subordinate "the capitalist logic of power" – thus ending what Harvey (2003) has characterized as the US-centered "imperialism of the capitalist sort." Although Arrighi claims that "developments in the ideological realm are unreliable indicators of reality" (2007, 17), the fact that the Chinese state continues to prevent private capitalist domination of the ideological and cultural realms and to mobilize the rhetoric of socialism to legitimate itself remain significant factors in considering the future direction of China's ongoing transformation. As I have argued (Zhao 2008a), this discourse of socialism has provided a language for members of China's subordinate social classes and their organic intellectuals to mount their struggles against Chinese versions of "accumulation by dispossession." The "advantage" of this language, as opposed to an anticommunist ideology, for managing the current global economic crisis is also considerable. As Harvey (2009) has noted, in the US, "even the vaguest hint of state direction let alone nationalization creates a political furor." In contrast, although "there may be some vested interests of wealthier party members and an emergent capitalist class to be overcome," there is "absolutely no ideological barrier to redistributing economic largesse to the neediest sectors of society ... The charge that this would amount to 'socialism' or even worse to 'communism' would simply be greeted with amusement in China." Although Colin Sparks (2009, 111) is probably correct in suggesting that the rationale for the Hu Jintao leadership's redistributive policies is to "save capitalism from the capitalists rather than to challenge the system itself," this is more a matter of interpretative framework than an issue of substantive concern. As I have argued (Zhao 2008a, 343), it is "not only the party's official socialist slogans per se, but also their reappropriation by various Chinese social forces and the unfolding societal processes of subordinating both state and market to the social needs of the working people, are what the struggle for socialism in China is about." For the rural girls who were denied school education because of tuition fees, the government's abolishing of school tuition fees is a real gain.

Alongside world system theorists, postcolonial scholars have challenged the temporality of critical political economy from a cultural perspective. As Mahmood Mamdani (2007) has argued, political decolonization won't be complete without an intellectual paradigm shift, or an "intellectual decolonization" that thinks of the present in terms of a past that goes to the colonial period and before:

> One unfortunate tendency of radical political economy was that it tended to reduce the usable past to the colonial period. We should recognize that the various forms of nativism around the post-colonial world – from racialized Black nationalism to ethnicized nationalisms to religious Muslim and Hindu nationalism, what we tend to call "fundamentalisms" these days – have been the first to raise this question. They are the ones who have accused self-declared modernist intellectuals of being nothing

but a pale reflection of their colonial masters. They have emphasized the necessity to link up with the historicity of their respective societies. The only problem is that they rule out the colonial period as an artificial imposition, as a departure from an authentic history ... As a result, they underestimate – or sometimes fail to understand fully – the present by ignoring how the institutional and intellectual legacy of colonialism tends to be reproduced in the present. (Mamdani 2007, 95–6)

While acknowledging the importance of the nativist call for a fuller grasp of historicity, Mamdani also underscores how this project is compromised by its search for authenticity. Consequently, "The point is not just to sidestep the nativist critique but to sublate it, in the manner in which Engels understood sublating Hegel in his critique of Ludwig Feuerbach; to take into consideration that which is relevant, effective, and forceful in the critique but at the same time to break away from its pre-occupation with origins and authenticity" (2007, 96).

Mamdani's argument provides a relevant framework for interpreting the Chinese state's effort to selectively make use of China's nativist cultural traditions without being culturally fundamentalist. On the one hand, as the Marxist heir to the European Enlightenment and the May 4 Chinese modernist tradition, the CCP-led Chinese state has relentlessly promoted a modern market economy and developed modern science and technology. On the other hand, the reform era has witnessed a state- and societal-wide reassertion of Chinese cultural difference from western capitalist modernity, culminating in a cultural politics that lays claim to the transformational power of Chinese culture in sublating western capitalist modernity. To be sure, there are reactionary tendencies in this cultural revivalism. Some versions are highly compatible with the political economy of a globalized capitalism, "which for its own survival depends at once on a valorization of difference, and the convergence of difference into homogeneity through techniques of representation that carefully assign only to those practices that accord with the logic of ongoing capitalist expansion" (Dirlik 2002, 21). No longer content with merely critiquing American cultural imperialism, the Chinese state under the Hu Jintao leadership has embraced Joseph Nye's concept of "soft power" and launched a multifaceted effort to project China abroad through its media and cultural institutions (Sun 2010). The concept, initially discussed in Chinese media and academic circles, was a hot topic at the National People's Congress (NPC) and the Chinese People's Political Consultative Conference (CPPCC) meetings in March 2007. On July 24, 2007, the National Committee of the CPPCC held a seminar to call for advice and contributions on building "soft power" as a means of forging national solidarity and "gaining an upper hand in the international arena" (Xinhua News Agency 2007). By October 15, 2007, Hu Jintao's report to the 17th National Congress of the CCP had made strengthening China's "soft power" an official party policy (Hu 2007). Instead of exporting revolutionary ideology (as in the Mao era), the Chinese state is building Confucian Institutes all over the world, while various branches of the Chinese media industries are trying to expand into overseas markets. The Chinese film industry, for example, after having experienced a major transitional crisis at the time *Titanic* hit China in 1998, has witnessed a market-driven rejuvenation since the early 2000s, buttressed by a systematic state-led effort in overseas market expansion that was institutionalized in 2004, when the China Film Overseas Promotion Corporation was established as a centralized national platform for the promotion of Chinese films abroad.

Within the Chinese news media and the broader cultural realm, reflecting a newly gained cultural confidence, a growing discourse lays claim to the transformational power of Chinese culture in transcending the problems of western capitalist modernity. A signed front page commentary on the May 8, 2009, issue of the overseas edition of the *People's Daily*, by Ye Xiaowen, director of the central government's Bureau for Religious Affairs, is symptomatic of this discourse. Entitled "Greeting the 'Renaissance' of the New Era" and invoking western intellectual and popular cultural sources ranging from Arnold Toynbee to the Hollywood movie *Matrix*, the article offered a dialectical view of the European Renaissance, claiming that its initial liberation of humanity from the darkness of the Medieval age has now degenerated into the "virus" in *Matrix*. It then calls for a "Renaissance of the New Era" which will redeem humanity by drawing on the Chinese state's "double-harmony model" – a harmonious Chinese society and a harmonious world – and its newly articulated "human-centric, all-rounded, coordinated and sustainable scientific developmental outlook" which embodies the "profound wisdom of Chinese culture" (Ye 2009). Whether we consider this as a necessary expression of cultural self-confidence, a strategic discursive retreat from a discredited socialist discourse to win over national and global cultural leaderships, or as a cover for and mystification of Chinese capitalism, this is a new cultural politics that critical political economists must confront in grasping the "challenge of China."

On the other hand, China's official discourse has not entirely buried the revolutionary tradition. The same *People's Daily* column that published the May 8, 2009, call for a new "Renaissance" also published a May 30, 2009, call by Wu Jianmin, a prominent foreign policy expert, for China to seize the ethical-political high ground by anchoring Chinese discourses on global affairs in the spirit of the international communist movement, especially its concern for the "emancipation of humanity as a whole," so that the "rise of China will not only benefit the Chinese people, but also humanity as a whole" (Wu 2009). Even Maoist radical discourses have experienced a revival in China's cyberspace as a dialectical response to the social contradictions of China's capitalistic development.

During his research in China between 1971 and 1972, Smythe tried to explain to his hosts how the western-style TV system is embedded in the authoritarian social relations of consumer capitalism. As an alternative, he suggested that the Chinese design a more democratic "two-way television" system, which he imagined as an "an electronic *tatzupao* system," an updated version of the "big character posters" that had served as such an important means of communication for the kind of "mass democracy" that Mao had envisioned during the Cultural Revolution. As the opening quote for this chapter suggested, Smythe, to the horror of China's post-Mao bureaucratic and intellectual elites who suffered from the Cultural Revolution, even discussed the possibility of a "second great Proletariat Cultural Revolution" to achieve a fundamental transformation of China's reform-era economic policy. Although a more balanced evaluation of the Cultural Revolution remains taboo in Chinese official discourse, and the once constitutionally entrenched right of the Chinese people to post "big character posters" as a means of political communication was soon revoked after Deng came to power in 1979, the legacies of China's experiment with radical democracy have survived in an increasingly dynamic and diverse Chinese communication system. In the aftermath of Hu Jintao's June 2008 visit to the *People's Daily*'s web forum "Strengthen the Nation," and his claim that his leadership heeds online voices, neo-Maoist netizens were quick to frame his visit as a redemption of Mao-style "mass democracy" in the digital age. In this view, at a time when China's established print and broadcast media institutions are dominated by the voices of the "iron triangle" of bureaucratic, business, and intellectual elites, the Internet has opened up spaces for bottom-up popular communication. In particular, online forums and blogs have arguably brought back the "four great freedoms" of the Cultural Revolution era (speak out freely, air views freely, hold great debates, and write big character posters), engendering what one netizen described as "a cultural revolution in new form" (Wujiashangxiaerqiusuo 2008). Another netizen (Su 2008) sees this as a genuinely bottom-up and autonomous initiative that is being carried out "in a more profound and broader way" than before, with the following objectives: to "explore China's developmental path," to "carry out ideological struggles," to "criticize revisionism," to "expose the nature of imperialism," and to "discuss the problem of continuous revolution." Although it is being carried out under the watchful eyes of Internet censors, perhaps Dallas Smythe should feel redeemed in some way.

After Socialist Defeatism, What? Or, Begin from the Beginning?

What's next? Certainly the prospect of China becoming the next hegemon in a capitalist world economy does not appeal to anybody, except perhaps in the private dreams of some of China's transnational capitalist elites and Chinese chauvinists. Nor did Marx provide a clear road map toward the unification of the global working class. But as Zhao Jun, a Guangdong film distributor I encountered in my field research, remarked, the idea of communism won't be obsolete as long as there are injustices in society.[4] This point, made by a "middle-class" Chinese who is not a CCP member, underscores the deeply ingrained impact of the communist idea in China.

Just as communism is both an idea and a movement that reacts to antagonisms in the real world, the political economy of communication is both an academic discipline and an emancipatory praxis. As Slavoj Zizek recently pointed out, there are four antagonisms in capitalism that potentially prevent it from its indefinite reproduction: "the looming threat of ecological catastrophe; the inappropriateness of private property for so-called intellectual property; the social-ethical implications of new techno-scientific developments, especially in biogenetics, and last, but not least, new forms of social apartheid – new walls and slums." In this context, "The new emancipatory politics will no longer be the act of a particular social agent, but an explosive combination of different agents. What unites us is that, in contrast to the classic image of proletarians who have 'nothing to lose but their chains', we are in danger of losing everything." However, Zizek (2009, 53–4) goes on to insist that while the first three antagonisms concern the "commons" of the culture and internal and external nature of humanity, it is the fourth antagonism, "the reference to the excluded, that justifies the term communism."

In China, the CCP-led fight for the inclusion of the Chinese nation in the modern world system on equal terms has generated the very problem that this chapter has attempted to address – the rise of China. This has generated fears, provoked leftist cynicism and even defeatism, although a growing, though small, minority in western scholarly circles has also expressed hope. Arrighi (2007, 389), for one, registered the hope that a reorientation of the Chinese developmental path around " reviving and consolidating China's traditions of self-centered market-based development, accumulation *without* dispossession, mobilization of human rather than non-human resources, and government through mass participation in shaping policies," offers the chance "that China will be in a position to contribute to the emergence of a commonwealth of civilizations truly respectful of cultural differences." On the other hand, if this reorientation fails, Arrighi continued, "China may well turn into a new epicentre of social and political chaos that will facilitate Northern attempts to re-establish a crumbling global dominance or … help humanity burn up in the horrors (or glories) of the escalating violence that has accompanied the liquidation of the Cold War world order" (2007, 389).

As Arrighi also emphasizes (2009, 79), "Chinese peasants and workers have a millennial tradition of unrest that has no parallel anywhere in the world." It was this tradition and the unbearable conditions of Chinese peripheral capitalism that had led to the rise of the CCP and formation of the PRC in the first place. And it is this tradition and the worsening conditions of "socialism with Chinese characteristics" in the reform era that has engendered resistances by all kind of social agents in myriad arenas: tax riots; labor strikes; interethnic clashes; environmental, anticorruption, and gender protests; legal challenges; prodemocracy demonstrations; local electoral disputes; religious rebellions; and even mass suicides (Perry and Selden, 2003). As I have argued, these hydra-headed and interpenetrated struggles have taken many communicative forms – from journalistic struggles for autonomy to workers using blogs to fight against privatization, from farmers circulating a camcorder video to foreign journalists to fight against land seizure to a rural grandmother using a bullhorn to appeal for accountability in a village electoral process (Zhao 1998, 2003, 2007, 2008a, Zhao and Duffy 2007). As Zizek (2009, 55) reminds us, the name for the intrusion of the excluded into sociopolitical space is "democracy." Within China, this started with a long series of revolutions resulting in the establishment of "people's sovereignty" as the foundation of the PRC, and continues in the ongoing struggles over this unfinished democratic project.

As I recounted at the beginning of this chapter, the road to the scholarly consideration of China's political, economic, cultural, and historical specificities within the political economy of communication started with Dallas Smythe. Today, the "challenge of China" has become more far-reaching. The trajectory of the Chinese state's self-proclaimed pursuit for "socialism with Chinese characteristics" and its ongoing reorientation of its developmental path have more profound implications for the evolving global order. Concurrently, the intellectual labor force working on China from a communication perspective has expanded rapidly and their modes of participation have also diversified. Rather than simply reading official documents and interviewing elite intellectuals and government officials through interpreters, as Smythe did admirably more than 40 years ago, political economists studying China today have more resources and opportunities at their disposal. The work has just started. It is an interesting time indeed.

Notes

1 Parts of this section draw upon relevant sections in Zhao (2009a) and Zhao (2010).
2 Much of the academic discussion surrounding the World Summit on the Information Society, which foregrounds a mixed assessment of the role of transnational civil society in challenging a transnational corporatist agenda, for example, betrays a blind spot on the role of the postcolonial state. For a relevant discussion, see Bhuiyan (2010).
3 Colin Sparks's work best exemplifies this tendency when he wrote: "The master category that explains them all [changes in the "past quarter century or so"] is not globalization but capitalism, in its most recent and expansive phase" (2007, 188).
4 For a more detailed description of my encounter with Zhao Jun and his likeminded peers in the production of an independent documentary about China's revolutionary heroes, see Zhao (2009b).

References

Alhassan, A. (2004) Communication and the postcolonial nation-state: A new political economic research agenda. In: Semati. M. (ed.), *New Frontiers in International Communication Theory*. Rowman & Littlefield, Lanham, MD, pp. 55–70.

Anagnost, A. (2008) From "class" to "social strata": Grasping the social totality in reform-era China. *Third World Quarterly*, 29(3), 497–519.

Arrighi, G. (2007) *Adam Smith in Beijing*. Verso, London.

Arrighi, G. (2009) The winding path of capital: Interview by David Harvey. *New Left Review*, 56, 61–94.

Bello, W. (1999) Focus on the global south. Online at http://focusweb.org/publica tions/1999/China at 50-A View from the South.htm (accessed June 28, 2009).

Bhuiyan, A. J. (2010) Postcolonial state and Internet governance: Possibilities of a counter-hegemonic bloc? Doctoral dissertation, School of Communication, Simon Fraser University, Canada.

Brady, A. (2008) *Marketing Dictatorship: Propaganda and Thought Work in Contemporary China*. Rowman & Littlefield, Lanham, MD.

Chakravartty, P. and Zhao, Y. (2008) *Global Communications: Toward a Trancultural Political Economy*. Rowman & Littlefield, Lanham, MD.

Cheek, T. (2006) *Living with Reform: China Since 1989*. Zed Books, London.

Desai, R. (2008) Introduction: Nationalisms and their understandings in historical perspective. *Third World Quarterly*, 29(3), 397–428.

Dirlik, A. (2002) Modernity as history: Post-revolutionary China, globalization and the question of modernity. *Social History*, 27(1), 16–38.

Du, Y. (2009) Quanguo nongmingong zongliang chaoguo 2.25 yi ren [Total national peasant workers surpassed 225 million]. *Renmin ribao [People's Daily, Oversea Edition]*, May 21, p. 5.

Economy, E. and Segal, A. (2009) The G-W mirage. *Foreign Affairs*, May/June, 14–23.

Frank, A. (1998) *Reorient: Global Economy in the Asia Age*. University of California Press, Berkeley, CA.

Franks, S. and Ribet, K. (2009) China-Africa media relations. *Global Media and Communication*, 5(1), 129–36.

Friedman, E. (2009) How economic superpower China could transform Africa. *Journal of Chinese Political Science*, 14, 1–20.

Guback, T. (1994) Editor's note. In: Smythe, D., *Counterclockwise: Perspectives on Communication*. Westview Press, Boulder, CO, pp. 227–30.

Hackett, R. A. and Carroll, W. (2006) *Remaking Media: The Struggle for Democratic Public Communication*. Routledge, London.

Harris, J. (2005) Emerging third world powers: China, India and Brazil. *Race & Class*, 46(3), 7–27.

Harvey, D. (2003) *The New Imperialism*. Oxford University Press, New York.

Harvey, D. (2005) *A Brief History of Neoliberalism*. Oxford University Press, New York.

Harvey, D. (2009) Why the U.S. stimulus package is bound to fail. *Socialist Project/The Bullet No 184*, February 12. Online at http://www.socialistproject.ca/bullet/bullet184.html (accessed March 23, 2009).

Hong, Y. (2008) Class formation in high-tech information and communications as an aspect of China's reintegration with transnational capitalism. PhD dissertation, University of Illinois, Urbana-Champaign.

Hu, A., Zhao, P., and Li, C. B. (2001) 1978–2000: Regional differences in China's economic and social developments. In: Xin, S. T. and Lu, X. R., *2001 China Social Analysis and Forecast*. Shehui kexue wenxian chubanshe, Beijing, pp. 167–84.

Hu, J. (2007) *Hold High the Great Banner of Socialism with Chinese Characteristics and Strive for New Victories in Building a Moderately Prosperous Society in All, October, 15, 2007*. Online at www.china.org.cn/english/congress/229611.htm (accessed June 6, 2009).

Jessop, B (1991) On the originality, legacy, and actuality of Nicos Poulantzas. *Studies in Political Economy*, 34, 75–109.

Li, M. (2008) *The Rise of China and the Demise of the Capitalist World-Economy.* Monthly Review Press, New York.

Li, X. (2009) Jiadian xiaxiang zhengce dailai chanxiao liangwang [Home electronics going to the countryside policy boosts both production and sales]. *Renmin ribao* [*People's Daily, Overseas Edition*], June 8, p. 5.

Lin, C. (2006) *The Transformation of Chinese Socialism.* Duke University Press, Durham, NC.

Mamdani, M. (2007) Postcolonialism and the new imperialism. In: Shaikh, N. (ed.), *The Present as History: Critical Perspectives on Global Power.* Columbia University Press, New York, pp. 94–108.

Manthorpe, J. (2006) Communist party divided on dealing with dissidents. *Vancouver Sun*, January 31, p. E3.

Meisner, M. (1996) *The Deng Xiaoping Era: An Inquiring into the Fate of Chinese Socialism.* Hill & Wang, New York.

Mosco, V. (2009) *The Political Economy of Communication*, 2nd edn. Sage, Thousand Oaks, CA.

Murdock, G. (2006) Cosmopolitans and conquistadors: Empires, nations and networks. In: Boyd-Barrett, O. (ed.), *Communications Media Globalization and Empire.* John Libbey Publishing, Eastleigh, UK, pp. 17–32.

Ngai, P. (2005) *Made in China: Women Factory Workers in a Global Workplace.* Duke University Press, Durham, NC.

Nordenstreng, K. (2001) Epilogue. In: Morris, N. and Waisbord, S. (eds), *Media and Globalization: Why the State Matters.* Rowman & Littlefield, Lanham, MD, pp. 155–60.

Ong, A. (1999) *Flexible Citizenship: The Cultural Logics of Transnationality.* Duke University Press, Durham, NC.

Ong, A. and Nonini, D. (1996) *Ungrounded Empires: The Cultural Politics of Modern Chinese Transnationalism.* Routledge, London.

Palat, R. A. (2008) A new Bandung?: Economic growth vs. distributive justice among emerging powers. *Futures*, 40(8), 721–34.

Panitch, L. (2002) The impoverishment of state theory. In: Aronowitz, S. and Bratsis, P. (eds), *State Theory Reconsidered: Paradigm Lost.* University of Minnesota Press, Minneapolis, pp. 89–104.

Perry, E. J. and Selden, M. (2003) Introduction: Reform and resistance in contemporary China. In: Perry, E. J. and Selden, M. (eds), *Chinese Society: Change, Conflict and Resistance*, 2nd edn. Routledge-Curzon, London, pp. 1–22.

Pieterse, J. N. (2008) Globalization the next round: Sociological perspectives. *Futures*, 40, 707–20.

Pieterse, J. N. (2009) Representing the rise of the rest as threat. *Nordicom Review*, 30(2), 55–68.

Prashad, V. (2007) *The Darker Nations: A People's History of the Third World.* The New Press, New York.

Qiu, J. L. (2009) *Working-Class Network Society.* MIT Press, Cambridge, MA.

Qiu, J. L. (2010) Class, communication and China: A thought piece. *International Journal of Communication*, 4, 531–6.

Ramo, J.C. (2004) *The Beijing Consensus.* Research Report: The Foreign Policy Center, London.

Schiller, D. (1996) *Theorizing Communication: A History.* Oxford University Press, New York.

Schiller, D. (2007) *How to Think About Information.* University of Illinois Press, Urbana, IL.

Schiller, D. (2008) China in the United States. *Communication and Critical/Cultural Studies,* 5(4), 411–15.

Schiller, H. I (1976) *Communication and Cultural Domination.* International Arts and Sciences Press, New York.

Sen, A. (2006) *Identity and Violence.* W.W. Norton & Company, New York.

Shirk, S. (1993) *The Political Logic of Economic Reform in China.* University of California Press, Berkeley, CA.

Smythe, D. (1981) *Dependency Road.* Ablex, Norwood, NJ.

Smythe, D. (1994) After bicycles, what? In: Smythe, D., *Counterclockwise: Perspectives on Communication,* T. Guback (ed.). Westview Press, Boulder, CO, pp. 230–44.

Sparks, C. (2007) *Globalization, Development, and the Mass Media.* Sage, London.

Sparks, C. (2009) Review of "Communication in China: Political economy, power, and conflict" by Yuezhi Zhao. *Chinese Journal of Communication,* 2(1), 109–11.

Su, D. (2008) Wode guancha: Qishi women zhengzhai jingli di'erci wenge [My observation: We are actually experiencing a second Cultural Revolution]. *Utopia.* July 1. Online at http://www.wyzxsx.com/Article/Class17/200807/43930.html (accessed July 4, 2008).

Sun, W. (2002) *Leaving China: Media, Migration, and Transnational Imagination.* Rowman & Littlefield, Lanham, MD.

Sun, W. (2009) *Maid in China: Media, Morality, and the Cultural Politics of Boundaries.* Routledge, London.

Sun, W. (2010), Mission impossible? Soft power, communication capacity and the globalization of Chinese media. *International Journal of Communication,* 4, 54–72.

Wang, H. (2004) *Xiandai Zhongguo sixiang de xingqi* [The *Rise of Modern Chinese Thought*]. Sanlian shudian, Beijing.

Wang, H. (2006) Depoliticized politics, from East to West. *New Left Review,* 41, 29–45.

Wang, H. (2008) Utopia: Wang Hui tan Xizhang [Wang Hui talks about Tibet]. April 27, 2008. Online at http://www.wyzxsx.com/Article/Class17/200804/37585.html (accessed May 27, 2009).

Westad, O.A. (2007) *The Global Cold War.* Cambridge University Press, New York.

Wu, J. (2009) Shijie xiang hechu qu? [Where is the World Heading? *Renmin ribao* [*People's Daily, Overseas Edition*], May 30, p. 1.

Wujiangshangxiaerqiusuo (2008) Wangluo minzhu kaiqi le wenhua gemin xinxingshi (Internet democracy opened up a new form of Cultural Revolution). *Utopia.* July 2. Online at http://www.wyzxsx.com/Article/Class22/200807/43710.html (accessed July 4, 2008).

Xinhua News Agency (2007) China's top advisory body holds seminar on "soft power." July 25. Online at english.peopledaily.com.cn/90001/6223325.html (accessed June 6, 2009).

Xinhua News Agency (2009) *Xinhua Net.* 1 11. Online at http://news.xinhuanet.com/english/2009-01/11/content_10637653.htm (accessed June 5, 2009).

Yang, Y. and Xie, G. (2009) A'er jiliya de Zhongguo chuanqi [Algeria's Chinese legend]. *Renmin ribao* [*People's Daily, Overseas Edition*], May 15, p. 8.

Yao, X. (2009) Shenfen rentong yu han zhang chongtu [Identity and Han-Tibetan conflicts]. *Er'shiyi shiji* [*Twenty-First Century*] 111, 114–22.

Ye, X. (2009) Yingjie xinshidai de "wenyi fuxing" [Creating the "Renaissance" of the new era]. *Renmin ribao* [*People's Daily, Overseas Edition*], May 8, p. 1.

Zhao, Y. (1998) *Media, Market, and Democracy in China: Between the Party Line and the Bottom Line*. University of Illinois Press, Urbana, IL.

Zhao, Y. (2003) Falun Gong, identity, and the struggle over meaning inside and outside China. In: Couldry, N. and Curran, J. (eds), *Contesting Media Power: Alternative Media in a Networked World*. Rowman & Littlefield, Lanham, MD, pp. 209–23.

Zhao, Y. (2007) After mobile phones, what? Re-embedding the social in China's "digital revolution." *International Journal of Communication*, 1, 92–120.

Zhao, Y. (2008a) *Communication in China: Political Economy, Power, and Conflict*. Rowman & Littlefield, Lanham, MD.

Zhao, Y. (2008b) Neoliberal strategies, socialist legacies: Communication and state transformation in China. In: Chakravartty, P. and Zhao, Y. (eds), *Global Communications: Toward a Transcultural Political Economy*. Rowman & Littlefield, Lanham, MD, pp. 23–50.

Zhao, Y. (2009a). Communication, the nexus of class and nation, and global divides: Reflections on China's post-revolutionary experiences. *Nordicom Review* (Jubilee Issue), 91–104.

Zhao, Y. (2009b) Rethinking Chinese media studies: History, political economy and culture. In: Thussu, D. (ed.), *Internationalizing Media Studies*. Routledge, London, pp. 175–95.

Zhao, Y. (2010). For a critical study of communication and China: Challenges and opportunities. *International Journal of Communication*, 4, 544–51.

Zhao, Y. (forthcoming) Back to the future? Sustaining and contesting revolutionary legacies in media and ideology. In: Perry, E. J. and Heilmann, S. (eds), *Chairman Mao's Visible Hand: China's Party-State Resilience in Historical Perspective*. Harvard University Press, Cambridge, MA

Zhao, Y. and Duffy, R. (2007) Short-circuited? The communication of labor struggles in China. In: Mosco, V. and McKercher, K. (eds), *Knowledge Workers in the Information Society*, Lexington Books, Lanham, MD, pp. 229–48.

Zhao, Y. and Schiller, D. (2001) Dances with wolves? China's reintegration with digital capitalism. *Info*, 3(2), 135–51.

Zizek, S. (2009) How to begin from the beginning. *New Left Review*, 57, 43–55.

Name Index

Aaker, D. A. 206, 208
Acland, Charles 324
Adam, Barbara 522–3
Adesanya, A. 550
Adorno, Theodor W. 4, 83, 84, 334, 486
Agnew, J. A. 161
Ahmadinejad, President Mahmoud 235
Alasuutari, P. 418
Albarran, Alan B. 3, 132
Albornoz, Luis 116, 119, 517
Alexander, Allison 3
Alexander, P. J. 337
Alford, M. 153
Alhassan, A. 561
Allan, S. 534
Allen, R. C. 547
Allende, Salvador 142
Almiron, Nuria 94
Alterman, E. 142
Altheide, David L. 278
Ampuero, Jenny 119
Anagnost, A. 565, 567
Anand, N. 389
Andersen, R. 264
Anderson, B. 217, 550
Anderson, C. 29
Andrejevik, Mark 440, 450, 453

Ang, Ien 422–3
Angelis, M. D. 442
Anholt, S. 217
Appadurai, Arjun 210, 212, 487, 513
Arango, T. 350
Aris, A. 132
Arrighi, Giovanni 558, 570, 571, 572, 573, 577
Arrow, K. 55
Artz, L. 368
Arvidsson, Adam 27, 208, 212, 215, 218, 441
Attali, J. 331, 333
Atton, C. 487
Auerswald, P. E. 271
Aufderheide, P. 252
Auletta, K. 36
Azpillaga, Patxi 120

Babe, R. E 419
Bagdikian, Ben 144, 151, 156, 157–9, 236–7
Bahr, M. 365, 369
Baker, C. Edwin 155, 157, 159–61, 443
Baker, M. 182
Baker, S. 390, 393, 394, 395, 396
Baldoz, R. 359
Balio, T. 546

The Handbook of Political Economy of Communications, First Edition.
Edited by Janet Wasko, Graham Murdock, and Helena Sousa.
© 2014 John Wiley & Sons, Ltd. Published 2014 by John Wiley & Sons, Ltd.

Subject Index

The Handbook of Political Economy of Communications, First Edition.
Edited by Janet Wasko, Graham Murdock, and Helena Sousa.
© 2014 John Wiley & Sons, Ltd. Published 2014 by John Wiley & Sons, Ltd.

pay-per-click 474–5
Pear's 211
peer-to-peer sharing 26, 99
pensions 15
Percy 73
perfect competition market 188
Periodismo Ciudadano 412
personal computer (PC) 189, 190
Personal Genome Project 447
personal information
 capture of 450–1
 estimating value of 446–8
 markets in 451–3
Personal Responsibility and Work
  Opportunity Reconciliation Act
  of 1996 252
Philip Morris Tobacco Company 200, 209
Philips 345, 346, 347
phonograph 338–9
photoengraving 191
physiocrats 196
Pirates of the Caribbean 180
Pirates of the Caribbean: Dead Man's Chest
 (2006) 179
Pixar 174
political action committees (PACs) 240
 soft money and 241–2
political economy (PE) 42
political economy of active knowledge
 seeking 473–5
political economy of audiences 415–30
political economy of culture (PEC) 41–2,
 44–6, 51–2, 388
political economy of information 41, 51–2
political economy of labor 358–77, 381–96
political economy of personal
 information 436–53
political economy of political
 ignorance 458–78
political economy of the information
 society (PEIS) 52–4
political ignorance, 458–78
"political liberty" 227
PolyGram group 344, 345, 347
pornography 66
Post Office 265

postindustrial technical system 510
postmodern poverty 490–1
postnational concept 513
poststructuralism 386
potlatch 23–4
print capitalism 218
privacy-enhancing technologies
 (PETs) 446
privatization 2
 of media 230–4
Procter & Gamble 209, 210, 220, 222
production of culture approach 389
production-oriented theory of value 437
Professional Writers Association of
 Canada 374
profit maximization 20, 191
"program media" 135
Progress and Freedom Foundation
 (PFF) 245
progress, mirage of 193–4
Prometheus decision (2003) of the Third
 Court of Appeals 157
promotion of commodity culture 20–1
promotional culture 207'
property rights 227, 450
 in cyberspace 245
prosumers 403–13
prosumption 30
Providence Equity Partners 312
public broadcasting 22, 23
"public goods" 21–2
public interest 283, 285, 287, 288
public reason 227
public service 16
public service broadcasters (PSBs) 232
Public–Private Dichotomy 234–6

QinetiQ 275
Qualcomm 241
Quebec Solidarity Fund 371
Qwest 241, 242

radio
 broadcasting 192–3
 communication, definition 249
 US ratings 70–4